Advanced WebLogic Server A
Administration and Monitoring with I

Oracle In-Focus Series

Martin Heinzl

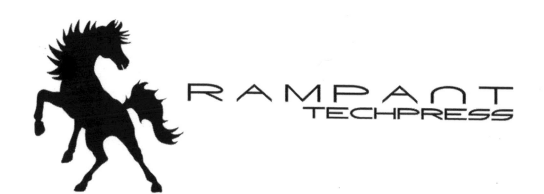

Dedicated to my wonderful wife Lourdes.

Advanced WebLogic Server Automation
Administration and Monitoring with WLST and JMX

By Martin Heinzl

Copyright © 2014 by Rampant TechPress. All rights reserved.

Printed in the United States of America.

Published in Kittrell, North Carolina, USA.

Oracle In-Focus Series: Book #46

Series Editor: Donald K. Burleson

Production Manager: Janet Burleson

Editor: Jennifer Kittleson

Production Editor: Jennifer Kittleson

Cover Design: Janet Burleson

Printing History: May 2014 for First Edition

Oracle, Oracle7, Oracle8, Oracle8i, Oracle9i, Oracle10g, Oracle 11g, and Oracle 12c are trademarks of Oracle Corporation.

Many of the designations used by computer vendors to distinguish their products are claimed as Trademarks. All names known by Rampant TechPress to be trademark names appear in this text as initial caps.

The information provided by the authors of this work is believed to be accurate and reliable. However, because of the possibility of human error by our authors and staff, Rampant TechPress cannot guarantee the accuracy or completeness of any information included in this work and is not responsible for any errors, omissions, or inaccurate results obtained from the use of information or scripts in this work.

ISBN: 0-9916386-1-1

ISBN 13: 978-0-9916386-1-1

Library of Congress Control Number: 2014941276

Table of Contents

PART I - Introduction

PART II - WLST

PART V - Summary and References

Using the Online Code Depot

Purchase of this book provides complete access to the online code depot that contains sample code scripts. Any code depot scripts in this book are located at the following URL in zip format and ready to load and use:

rampant.cc/weblogic.htm

If technical assistance is needed with downloading or accessing the scripts, please contact Rampant TechPress at rtp@rampant.cc.

Conventions Used in this Book

It is critical for any technical publication to follow rigorous standards and employ consistent punctuation conventions to make the text easy to read. However, this is not an easy task. With database terminology there are many types of notation that can confuse a reader. For example, some Oracle utilities such as STATSPACK and TKPROF are always spelled in CAPITAL letters, while Oracle parameters and procedures have varying naming conventions in the database documentation. It is also important to remember that many database commands are case sensitive, are always left in their original executable form and never altered with italics or capitalization. Hence, all Rampant TechPress books follow these conventions:

- **Parameters:** All database parameters will be lowercase italics. Exceptions to this rule are parameter arguments that are commonly capitalized (KEEP pool, TKPROF); these will be left in ALL CAPS.

- **Variables:** All procedural language (e.g. PL/SQL) program variables and arguments will also remain in lowercase italics (*dbms_job*, *dbms_utility*).

- **Tables & dictionary objects:** All data dictionary objects are referenced in lowercase italics (*dba_indexes*, *v$sql*). This includes all *v$* and *x$* views (*x$kcbcbh*, *v$parameter*) and dictionary views (*dba_tables*, *user_indexes*).

- **SQL:** All SQL is formatted for easy use in the code depot, and all SQL displayed in lowercase. The main SQL terms (select, from, where, group by, order by, having) will always appear on a separate line.

- **Programs & Products:** All products and programs that are known to the author are capitalized according to the vendor specifications (CentOS, VMware, Oracle, etc.). All names known by Rampant TechPress to be trademark names appear in this text as initial caps. References to UNIX are always made in uppercase.

Foreword

"Oh no, yaWb!" (yet another WebLogic book), some of you may say at the first glance. But this book is meant to be different.

My name is Martin Heinzl and since 1998 I have been working with Enterprise (Middleware) Systems based on Common Object Request Broker Architecture (CORBA), Java Enterprise Edition (JEE) and other similar technologies. During my assignments in many different companies and various sectors as principal consultant and architect, I have frequently observed administrators busily writing their own shell scripts, tinkering with configuration files, or even using graphical configuration tools to repeatedly alter the same settings across multiple servers in production environments.

In the last few years I have been using WebLogic Scripting Tool (WLST) and Java Management Extensions (JMX) extensively to automate many different aspects of WebLogic, Oracle Enterprise Service Bus (ESB) and other tools like OWSM. The documentation from Oracle was always a good starting point; however, I quickly realized as soon as I wanted to undertake more complicated tasks that the documentation was simply lacking. This is no criticism of Oracle; rather, one can expect vendor documentation to provide reference information covering common tasks but not the more advance scenarios demanded by real life administration of complicated architectures. Besides a number of websites offering blog posts and user forms with incomplete answers to my problems, there was no single authoritative source available that went beyond basic administration techniques using WLST. While the information on the Web is useful to the expert, it is often difficult to find and requires a great deal of effort to piece together in order to form a coherent solution for the difficult, but relatively common, problems administrators face. Often in the case of WebLogic, gaining an understanding required to successfully resolve such problems is time a consuming, time that most administrators simply don't have.

Experienced administrators do not need a tutorial starting from the very beginning. Therefore, I have written this book. This book does not start at the beginning, this book does not explain WebLogic concepts in detail and - very unusual - this book does not (!) use the webconsole of WebLogic. This book is written from real architecture and consultancy assignments and lessons learned during the last years. Its main focus is to teach readers who are already familiar with WebLogic how to use the powerful automation APIs to really operate WebLogic in small to very complex environments. Scripts and automations are essential for every (infrastructure) architect, administrator, deployer, operator, and also developer. Only with automated processes is it possible to create actions that are ideal for auditing, can be reviewed, can run at any time, can run frequently (monitoring!) and can be scheduled with automated scheduler.

Complex environments may consist of hundreds of domains and thousands of Managed-Servers. It is impossible for an administrator group to maintain all those servers with manual tasks or even the web console. The web console is a very useful tool for development and also up to production for human eye checking and verification, but from my experience the web console should never be used in higher integration or even production environments for change tasks of any kind.

This book is all about automation and will discuss the two major ways to automate WebLogic - WLST scripting and Java programming using JMX.

Therefore anyone reading this book must either have a good working knowledge of WebLogic or use an administration handbook to read background information on the different topics discussed in this book.

All efforts have been made to provide as many real life examples and useful production tips and tricks as possible, and all scripts and programs (unless stated otherwise) have been tested for WebLogic 11g and 12c.

So enjoy reading this book. Last but not least I would like to ask all readers to send their feedback. If you have any useful scripts or programs that would be an interesting extension to this book, please send them to me so that it might be considered for a book update.

August 2013
Martin Heinzl
wls_automation@mh-enterpriseconsulting.de

Foreword by Pavan

When I started automating WebLogic Server administration tasks with Jython, there seemed to be a deficit of sources to help complete the necessary tasks quickly. As time passed on, I saw a myriad of resources evolve that led to mixed approaches. Here comes Martin with this great idea of a "WebLogic automation" book, a one-stop solution that helps the reader learn to automate WebLogic administration.

WLST was developed from WebLogic 8.1 onwards, and included enhancements and new features with every released version. WebLogic Jython implementation has a robustness in its scripting capabilities and is much better than other competitor application servers in the JEE market.

This book is divided into 3 parts. Part 1 gives you the intent of each part and includes a quick introduction to get you familiar with the scripting environment. Next, Part 2 takes you into Jython scripting, and includes topics such as WebLogic configurations, deployment, monitoring, and tuning concepts. Here we will see how Oracle developed the strategies to stand in the number one position in the middleware market, with a huge scope on cloud computing in WebLogic 12c suite. Businesses have changed and are now looking for cost-cutting options with private or public clouds. Oracle Fusion Middleware suite come with SOA, BPEL, Developer, and WebCenter suites. Part 3 is all about JMX, and is targeted for those who already know the Java programming. If you are thinking "What if there is a better way for Monitoring?", then this is the part of the book to refer to. I happen to be a JMX newbie, but this part of the book helped me understand the greatness of JMX. It has achieved many of the technical goals that JMX API strives for.

This WebLogic Automation book will be a perfect mentor and guide for both experienced and novice WebLogic users. The book focuses on real-life scenarios that many WebLogic administrators and architects can relate to. This book enables those Administrators to work on automation in order to save their productive hours. I liked Martin's way of explanation, motivation for the reader, and detailed orientation for each scenario. I hope to forever remain shadowed under his exorbitant wisdom. The book touches from the nothing to building blocks for the enterprise architecture with dynamic automations, and with a fine intent to grow or customize further for your technical needs.

As I reviewed the book, I was curious to learn more about JMX. Specifically, I wondered where it covered various security resource configurations, if it had the monitoring capabilities that it does with WLST, and where it requires good knowledge on Java programming and each functionality area of JMX API. This book is a great place to find most of the Jython scripting for effective system administration on

WebLogic suites. It shows us the greater automation power, and is drafted as "Simplicity at its best".

Thank you Martin for being the guiding light, with such a great WebLogic automation book.

August 2013
Pavan Bhavani Shekhar Devarakonda

Foreword by Hussein

From the abacus to the astrolabe, difference engines and vacuum tubes to transistors, organic and quantum computers; if there is one principle, one goal that unites all computers in purpose, it is automation. Computers have increased human productivity in ways that few predicted and have empowered the individual to change society more than any other technological device through their ability to automate simple and complex tasks alike. Yet we still find at the interface of human and computer interaction a huge amount of unnecessary, unproductive, and error prone manual intervention. While the demands of regulatory bodies, compliance boards and security departments may be justified in taxing "four eyes" processes and human intervention, such processes are a tiny fraction of the work demanded in administering and operating enterprise systems today.

Martin's book WebLogic Automation will provide practitioners with all the information they need to liberate themselves from the drudge of administering WebLogic Server. This book is packed full of automation examples graduating in complexity, and is an invaluable guide to systems administrators of both small and large I.T. estates. Important aspects of WebLogic Server administration are addressed in the book with precise demonstrations of automation of administrative tasks for all subsystems. It is my hope that this book will in some measure contribute to raising awareness of the benefits of automation for the enterprise, because ultimately life is too short and precious to waste on repetitive administrative burdens.

August 2013
Hussein Badakhchani
Distinguished Technologist

Preface

Scope of this book

The scope of this book is restricted to Oracle's WebLogic Server version 10.3.5, 10.3.6, 12.1.1, 12.1.2 and above. The scripts and programs are specific to WebLogic and while the principles governing automation are applicable to all JEE application servers, the implementation is targeted to WebLogic Server. The applications detailed in this book may serve as a guide for automation approaches for other JEE servers, however, the reader must understand that adapting the scripts provided in this book to products other than WebLogic is a non-trivial task.

Prerequisites

In order to fully appreciate the contents of the book and all the scripts, a good working knowledge of WebLogic is required. Experience with WebLogic administration will also benefit the reader. The scripts presented within are written in the Jython programming language. A brief introduction to Jython is provided in the first part of the book, but we advise those that are new to Jython to take time to become familiar with this scripting language as Jython offers a powerful access to WebLogic. The third part of this book includes Java source code that makes use of the JMX API, so a good working knowledge of Java and JMX is helpful.

How to read this book

This book is divided into 4 major parts. After an introduction, this book will describe the principle concepts behind WebLogic automation using WLST. JMX is then discussed, and finally a summary with comparisons and recommendations for using these different approaches is provided.

Part 1 is an introduction to the two key technologies used throughout this book (Jython and JMX) and the WebLogic JEE application server. This section is neither meant to be a tutorial nor a complete overview; rather it will give a brief overview of the foundational knowledge needed for understanding the rest of the book. The reader will find a list of resources (links, books) for further reading in this section.

Part 2 introduces WLST as the principle tool for scripted WebLogic administration. It provides many examples of WLST scripts along with corresponding explanations and practical tips for dealing with real-world production tasks facing WebLogic Server administrators. As such, Part 2 is the lengthiest section of the book. For readers not familiar with Jython or WebLogic-WLST, it is advisable to read this part from the beginning without skipping any subsections. Experienced readers may wish to jump to the sections they are interested in. This part will start with creating WebLogic domains, configure and extend domains, and will progress to discuss lifecycle operations for WebLogic Server and deployed components. Finally, we review the various monitoring methods available to through WLST. An important part of this section will talk about security as there are not many references available (especially in the area of OWSM).

Part 3 introduces automation with JMX. Many examples will be similar in the WLST/JMX chapters so that readers can easily compare these two technologies and decide on their own which better fits their needs. The Pros and Cons of each approach will be evaluated wherever applicable. As some automation tasks are not possible with JMX (e.g. complete offline mode) the focus of this part is slightly different. The overall structure of the WLST and JMX part will be as similar as possible so that readers who want to compare those two technologies can easily match the chapters of the different book parts.

Finally, Part 4 will provide a summary with comparisons and recommendations.

Who should read this book?

This book is primarily targeted to administrators, operators, and architects who have identified a need to automate the administration and management of WebLogic Server. Typically such users want to cut costs, improve quality, and develop a higher degree of operational agility through automation. Even if your estate is small enough to be managed manually, automation introduces consistency and ultimately improves your capability to maintain Service Level Agreements (SLAs). Therefore, irrespective of the size or complexity of a WebLogic Server deployment, one should consider automation.

Who should read this book later?

This section is intentionally not headlined "Who should not read this book" as I am convinced that all administrators and other IT people involved with WebLogic will benefit from this book. But this book is neither an introduction to WebLogic nor a WebLogic tutorial. It is also not a book to learn Jython or JMX. For all these topics there are many other excellent books on the market and this book neither can nor wants to emulate those. So for the aforementioned topics, please see the reference list or search the well-known bookstores for appropriate books. After that you should read this book as this one builds upon the knowledge. The first sections of this book will give a very brief summary of Jython, JMX, and WebLogic, which are only meant to be refresher sections.

Source Code and Scripts

Every effort has been taken to provide ready-to-run scripts and examples. Some examples are not printed in full in the book, due to their length; however, you will find the complete code ready for download online. Important note for all code examples: Please always make sure to change path names, server names, file locations, and any other aspects that depend on your local machine prior to testing the scripts. This note applies to all code examples and there won't be a reminder at every code listing.

Whenever possible, efforts have been made to introduce smaller example scripts with more detailed explanations first and then at the end of the chapter/section, provide a more complex and more complete example where the scripts introduced earlier are used (and in most cases improved through better exception handling, useful checks, and/or better flexibility). The rational for this is that scripts and programs used in real (production) systems must be bullet-proof and flexible/configurable. However, explaining concepts/APIs is easier if basic examples are used. Nevertheless, this book is not an academic book but a book written from real project experience for people who need to automate real systems. Therefore I will provide ready-to-use examples wherever possible.

Please note: Due to layout improvements, it is sometimes possible to introduce line breaks and additional formatting that will result in code that can no longer be compiled. If you are in doubt, please see the original sources in the code depot.

WebLogic version: Unless specified otherwise, all code examples have been tested with WebLogic 10.3.5, 103.6, 12.1.1 and 12.1.2. At the time of writing, WebLogic 12.1.2 had just been released. Therefore it is not possible to provide real project experience about 12.1.2. Nevertheless, some automations for WebLogic 12.1.2 have been added to this book.

Acknowledgements

Books are rarely the work of only one person. First of course I would like to say thank you to my wife Lourdes for all her encouragement to continue on this project.

I also would like to thank a number of people who helped me with feedback, review and content submissions. I would like to thank everybody who helped me to create this book.

In particular I would like to thank the following persons:

Pavan Bhavani Shekhar Devarakonda (running the blog site http://wlstbyexamples.blogspot.com), who has offered me the content of many of his blog entries and also reviewed the manuscript. Thanks a lot for all the material he offered to me. His information has provided a lot of added value to the following book sections: WLST/Jython introduction, tips and tricks, JMS, and others.

Attila Demirel has provided a number of scripts that have been added to this book. Especially in the area of monitoring and troubleshooting (like heapdump, threaddump, etc.). He has also provided a number of scripts that show you how to use email notifications out of WLST scripts.

Vinay Shukla, who has offered me the content of his blog at http://enterprisesecurityinjava.blogspot.de, which contains example for OPSS security related information.

Sunil Nagavelli and Hussein Badakhchani, who have helped me in reviewing this book. Thanks a lot for your feedback, ideas and help.

Rampant TechPress for providing me with the opportunity to write this book.

Finally, I would like thank the company Oracle for granting me the permission to quote some listings of the official documentation. This has been added to the book in order to allow reading the book without having to switch too much to the online documentation from Oracle to get a better understanding of certain API usages.

With my sincerest thanks,

Martin Heinzl

Part I

Introduction and Technology Overview

Introduction to Jython

Introduction to Jython

The first section of this chapter provides a very brief introduction to Jython. Jython itself is a complex topic, but it is out of the scope of this book to provide a Jython tutorial. Please see the Jython references in the reference section.

Why are we talking about Jython in a WebLogic book? Well Jython has been chosen by Oracle as the foundation of the WebLogic Scripting Tool (WLST) and therefore it is essential to understand Jython in order to write WLST scripts.

Why Jython?

Python is the basic scripting language, which supports OOP. Python has many of the features such as structure, encapsulation, and modularity, which are mostly required for WLST. It has another excellent feature called customization. It is more like shell scripting but the structure is a well-defined, strongly typed language that cannot be manipulated. Python requires proper indentation of the code otherwise it will reject to interpret the code.

For the Python programmers, it is easy to learn WLST scripting because WLST is based on Jython, and on top of the language it only adds support for the different WebLogic MBeans and the navigation between them. In order to develop Jython scripts, it is important to understand the WebLogic MBeans and their usage.

Jython is an implementation of the Python programming language that is designed to run on the Java Platform. Why are we discussing Jython? As stated earlier, Jython is the foundation of the WebLogic Scripting Toolkit and therefore Jython is the essential administrator tool for WebLogic automations based on WLST.

Jython is complementary to Java and is especially useful for embedded scripting. This means that Java programmers can add the Jython libraries to their application and integrate Jython scripts into their application code and interactive experimentation, providing an interactive interpreter that can be used to interact with Java packages or with running Java applications.

Concepts of Jython

Jython is similar to any OOP language. The Jython script code will be in the following structure:

```
Imports from java/Jython libraries
Imports from python libraries

Global Declaration

Defining class
Defining method
Defining constructor methods
Defining inherited methods

Defining modules

Defining main
```

Jython supports OOP so class and object reference statements can be used for rephrasing. The functions or methods can be defined with sub-programming logic that makes modularity in the script. Object-oriented scripting can be defined and can be reusable with creation of objects.

```
Defining a Class in Jython
class MYCLASS:
    def __init__():         #like C++ constructor
            self.name
            do something initially
    def function1():
            do some task
```

In a class, we can define attributes and we can assign values to them, and we can define functions related to that class that you will make.

So how do we define a function in Jython?

```
def example_function_in_jython (arg1, arg2):

        jython/wlst command

        jython/wlst command

        return expression/variable
```

A function definition starts with the identifier *def*, followed by the function name and a list of arguments. Note that the list of arguments only contains the argument names and not their types. A colon ":" begins the function implementation. The function implementation must be indented. All blocks (function, if/else, loops) must be indented in Jython. Function can return results using the *return* expression. Note that the function definition does not need to define the return type in the *def*-statement.

- **Special class function __init__()**

This function is the same as the C++/Java constructor. It allows us to define a default constructor, where you can set the values for when an object is under construction.

```
class MyClass:
    uname = ""
    def __init__(self, uname="WLST Automation"):
        self.uname = uname
    def greeting(self):
        print "Welcome to Jython Objects, %s" % self.uname
```

The above example will tell you about default constructor when nothing is passed to create the object, and it will take the *uname* value as "WLST Automation". If you pass the arguments to the object instantiation statement, it will overwrite it with the new value for the same *uname*.

- **Using self**

In WLST, *self* is a keyword that refers to the class attributes and methods. We can access the attributes, assign the values to them, and also manipulate them within the class. In the above example, *self.uname* is used to assign the new value to the *uname* attribute. Note that *self* cannot be accessible outside of the class or at the instance variables.

```
The __setter__()
The __getter__()
```

- **Comments in WLST**

To comment the script for one line, the '#' symbol can be used as in shell scripts and Python scripts. Sometimes while testing, a part of code to be commented on is from the code block, so a multi-line comment is required. This can be done with triple single-quote (''') or triple double-quote ("""), at starting and at ending.

```
# This is single line comment
'''
multi
line
commenting
'''
```

- **Jython Variables**

Variables are not used to store the data. In Python, everything is a reference or an object. However, the variables in WLST are neither references nor objects, they are just labels with namespaces that in turn map to objects. In WLST, all variables are Mutable like in Jython.

```
x=10 # now x holds integer object
x='WLST is my automation tool' # now x holds string object
```

- **Scope of WLST variables**

In Jython, three types of variable scopes can be defined, and the same is expected in WLST:

1. **Local**: This is a variable that is defined in the module or in the function, and is valid until it is in the scope of that block. Once the control moves out of the block, it cannot be referred.

2. **Global**: This is a variable that is required in multiple modules or in multiple functions, and therefore can be explicitly declared as global. The changes made in one function can be reflected to another module or function.

3. **Built-in**: This is a variable scope for the main module, which holds all the modules in it.

Jython and WebLogic

The WebLogic Scripting Tool (WLST) is a toolkit that administrators and operators can use to monitor and manage WebLogic domains. It is based on the Java scripting interpreter Jython. WLST does not only offer WebLogic-specific scripting features. As it is based on Jython, it is also possible to use all common features of the Jython language like local variables, conditions, or flow statements. Administrators can extend WLST for their own needs by providing features, functions, and classes based on the Jython language syntax. Three different forms of executions are available: scripting, interactive, and embedded. WLST can be enabled for online and offline connection modes and can act as a JMX client.

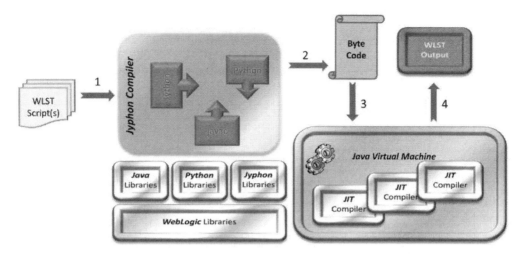

Figure 1.1: *Depiction of the Jython/WebLogic compilation process*

The source code for the WLST script is written in Python script as it is recommended for Jython. The WLST program file must have the extension .py, which is the source code consisting of a set of Jython instructions for WebLogic domain. This source code would use a JVM machine when it is instructed to RUN the script, and its invocation would internally generate Java byte code to interpret with the JVM and produce the desired output.

Summary

Jython is a powerful scripting environment that is hosted on the Java platform and integrated with the virtual machine and also Java. The ability to use Java classes from Jython enables the user to use Java libraries directly from the scripts.

Introduction to JMX

Introduction to JMX

Java Management Extensions, or JMX, is a well-known and established technology for application management in the Java realm. This chapter will only give a short definition and explain the rationale behind using JMX.

What is JMX?

Java Management Extensions is a Java technology that supplies tools for managing and monitoring applications, system objects, devices (e.g. printers) and service-oriented networks. Those resources are represented by objects called MBeans (for Managed Bean). In the API, classes can be dynamically loaded and instantiated. Managing and monitoring applications can be designed and developed using the Java Dynamic Management Kit.[1]

Management is always a difficult topic, especially if we are talking about applications that are not running in standardized container environments. JMX has become a standard for managing Java applications and resources using MBeans. MBeans are basically wrapper objects for any kind of resources-like application, resource, or also external/native resources.

The main component is the hosting environment for all MBeans, called MBean server. All MBeans must be registered with an MBean server, which also offers the different agent services. Connectors for different protocols like RMI, HTTP, IIOP, and T3 can be used for remote applications in order to access the MBean server.

---

[1] © Wikipedia

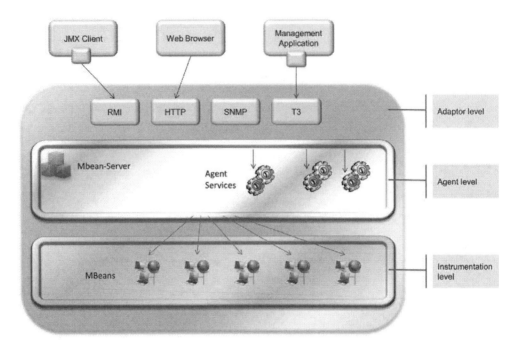

Figure 2.1: *Different levels of JMX*

External applications can interact with the MBeans through the use of JMX connectors and protocol adapters. Connectors are used to connect an agent with a remote JMX-enabled management application. This form of communication involves a connector in the JMX agent and a connector client in the management application. Protocol adapters provide a management view of the JMX agent through a given protocol. Management applications that connect to a protocol adapter are usually specific to the given protocol.[2]

The architecture of JMX consists of three layers that include the instrumentation level, the agent level, and the distributed services level.

Adaptor or Distributed Services Layer

This level provides the interface in order to implement remote JMX clients. It can also be used for integration into management tools like HP-Openview, Nagios, and Geneos. Remote access and security are implemented in this layer. This layer also provides a logical view by collecting and correlating information from the different

---

[2] © Wikipedia

agents. A connector provides full remote access to the MBeanServer API using various communication frameworks (RMI, IIOP, JMS, WS-*), while an adaptor adapts the API to another protocol (SNMP) or to Web-based GUI (HTML/HTTP, WML/HTTP).

Agent layer

The Agent layer provides the management infrastructure. It is composed of an MBean server, a collection of MBeans that can access/control different aspects of your application, agent services, and at least one connector. The core of this layer is the MBean server that hosts all managed MBeans. In addition, this layer provides monitors, timer services, and relation services. This layer can be accessed directly from within the same process or remotely using the connector layer.

Instrumentation Layer

The Instrumentation layer hosts the different managed resources (or MBeans). This layer also contains a notification model and MBean Metadata Classes. MBeans may come in four different implementations: Standard MBeans, Dynamic MBeans, Open MBeans, and Model MBeans.

- **Standard MBeans**

This is the easiest but also most inflexible MBean implementation. It follows naming conventions so that the MBean does not need any meta classes or meta information. This MBean type exposes attributes through getter and setter. Everything that does not match the get/set convention is considered to be an operation. Attributes may be read-only, write-only, or readable and writeable. Only public methods are considered for feature discovery.

- **Dynamic MBeans**

This MBean type requires the implementation of the JMX interface java.management.DynamicMBean because it implements its management interface programmatically. This type is recommended if the managed resources will change frequently as they provide better flexibility.

- **Model MBeans**

This type implements a fully customizable dynamic MBean. The Model MBean (defined: javax.management.modelmbean.RequiredModelMBean) implements the ModelMBean interface that extends other interfaces, including DynamicMBean, PersistentMBean, and ModelMBeanNotificationBroadcaster.

- **Open MBeans**

Open MBeans enable the usage of complex data types without enforcing the management application to have a local copy (class path, class downloading) of the complex type.

- **Notification Model**

The notification model (based on the Java Event Model) allows MBeans to send a notification by implementing the JMX NotificationBroadcaster interface. MBeans can receive notifications by implementing the NotificationListener interface. This enables a management application to move from the inefficient pull mode to a much more efficient push mode, which means that the management application can listen for events and react when those events arrive.

Why JMX?

Almost all modern application servers and more applications adopt JMX as their management interface. It can be used for configuration, state and statistic gathering, and monitoring. JMX is a standard API and different tools already exist that are capable of accessing these MBeans.

JMX and WebLogic

WebLogic makes heavy use of JMX. In fact, everything is organized in a different MBean server and different MBean trees. The WLST (WebLogic scripting environment) is just a Jython interface to the complex MBean structure (beside the other WLST features, of course).

In order to understand the administration and monitoring, it is essential to understand the WLS MBean structures. For example, it is essential to understand the differences between Runtime- and Edit-MBeanServer and the concepts WebLogic is using for their JMX layer.

The first part of this book is talking about WLST, but WLST also in its online mode is only an abstraction layer on top of JMX. The second part of the book will use the JMX API directly in order to talk to WebLogic.

It is advisable for readers to get familiar with the JMX architecture and concepts in order to understand the monitoring concepts better. In the Appendix you will find a list of references that you can use for this purpose.

Summary

JMX is THE management API of Java. WebLogic makes extensive use of JMX and offers different trees of MBeans for administrative purposes. Nearly all management functionality is based on JMX, therefore a thorough understanding of JMX is essential for understanding the WebLogic management capabilities.

Introduction to WebLogic

Introduction to WebLogic

As this book is not a WebLogic tutorial or beginners guide, this chapter only provides a very brief overview of WebLogic concepts. This book will not introduce WebLogic in detail. Please refer to the extensive WebLogic documentation from Oracle, all the various administration books, or the many websites and blogs that are available.

What is WebLogic?

WebLogic is a complex, professional application server environment with a complex and powerful security environment. WebLogic Server at its core implements the J2EE specification stack and its main purpose is to offer a hosting environment for J2EE applications. But WebLogic is much more than that. Like most professional J2EE servers, WebLogic also offers a large number of extended features like very comprehensive management, clustering and failover functionality on different levels, and a number of extended enterprise features not required by J2EE but very useful in the enterprise world and required by many companies.

What is a Domain?

A domain is the basic administration unit for WebLogic. This administration unit consists of one or more server instances and is managed by one of the servers with a special role, the so called Administration Server (=AdminServer). This server hosts the management console and manages zero or more Managed-Servers, which may be hosted local to the AdminServer or remote on different physical machines. Managed-Servers may be grouped into clusters. If Managed-Servers are located on remote machines, separate NodeManager instances can be used for lifecycle operations (start, stop, and monitor). You can define multiple domains based on different system administrators' responsibilities. You may also (although this is definitely not recommended) use a single domain to manage and monitor all WebLogic Server instances. The central configuration file is called config.xml and will play a major role in the further understanding of the scripts and management tasks. This file is stored on the Administration Server together with other files such database configuration files and security files.

Each AdminServer manages exactly ONE domain and all changes or activities will only apply to this domain. All the scripts and source code in this book run against one AdminServer (unless stated otherwise) and therefore targets one domain. For more information on domains, see e.g. the Oracle Documentation

Every domain must contain at least one the Administration Server. For development and testing this might be sufficient as this server can also host applications, but this setup is strongly discouraged in production and production-like systems.

The following diagrams show the most typical WebLogic domain configurations.

Figure 3.1: *Typical development domain*

The typical development domain is the most basic setup. This shows a WebLogic domain with just one server - the Administration Server. This is a typical development setup or setup on a private machine. The Administration Server here also hosts all the application components.

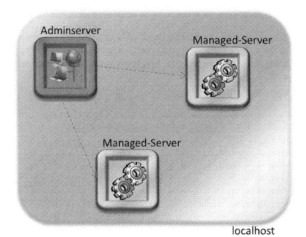

localhost

Figure 3.2: *Local WebLogic domain*

This is a more complex but still local domain. This domain includes an Administration Server for administration tasks and two Managed-Servers that host the application components.

Note that in this setup, the Managed-Server cannot be started by the AdminServer. The Managed-Servers need to be started using the generated start scripts.

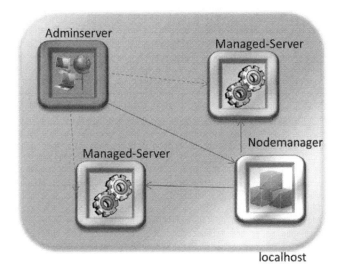

localhost

Figure 3.3: *Domain managed by NodeManager*

Now we are moving to the first complex but fully-managed domain. In this setup we introduce the NodeManager as a local control instance, which is able to start (on the request from the AdminServer) the Managed-Server on its own machine. The AdminServer will request a server to be started and the NodeManager will do the job.

The NodeManager is also responsible to restart a crashed Managed-Server (if configured to do so!)

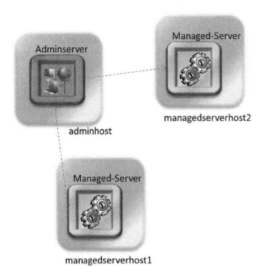

Figure 3.4: *Unmanaged distributed domain*

Now we are moving to a truly distributed domain that spans multiple physical machines. The AdminServer may of course also be collocated with one or many Managed-Servers, but it is advisable to separate it from the Managed-Servers.

In this example, the Managed-Server must be started using the generated scripts. This is a rather rare setup as it involves a number of manual steps on different machines to start/restart a domain.

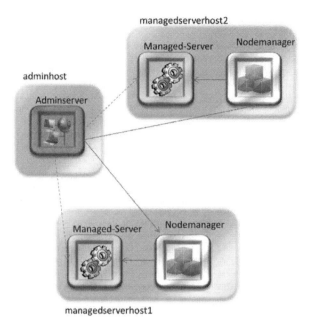

Figure 3.5: *Standard remote domain, managed by NodeManager*

The last example is the most common setup for production and production-like systems. Here we have a fully-managed distributed domain. Each machine must be equipped with its own NodeManager in order to start the Managed-Server on demand. Of course it is necessary to start at the NodeManager during system boot (*init.d* on Linux).

The NodeManager is also responsible to restart a crashed Managed-Server (if configured to do so!).

Deployment, configurations, and monitoring is all done through the NodeManager, which will delegate appropriate actions to the Managed-Servers.

Note: In the above diagrams: dashed lines are AdminServer <-> Managed-Server communications and solid lines are NodeManager communications.

WebLogic Cluster

Every WebLogic domain can be composed of a number of Managed-Servers. Beside the Administration Server, Managed-Servers can be grouped into clusters. Every WebLogic domain can host multiple clusters, but each Managed-Server can only be a member of one cluster (if at all). A cluster hides the complexity of a potential distributed group of servers and offers a single interface to the client, which can be used for communication and deployment. Furthermore, a cluster offers a wide range of features with regards to scalability, load-balancing, replication, failover, and migration.

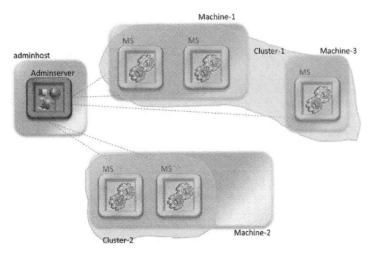

Figure 3.6: *WebLogic domain with multiple clusters*

Every domain can have multiple clusters. Every cluster can (but does not need to) include Managed-Servers hosted on different machines.

From many years working with clusters in different companies and environments, the following rule of thumb has proven to be a good general approach (but this does not mean that it can be applied to all environments!): For development and testing, it has been proven to be beneficial to create domains hosting one cluster only as these domains - including the admin - need to be restarted, reconfigured, and redeployed quite often. Furthermore, those domains are usually under the control of the developers or test teams. Small domains with a small number of Managed-Servers form much better isolated environments and also reduce the start/restart time. Production and production-like systems (like load and performance test, final integration test or similar) have a different character. Those domains are owned by system administrators and are usually stable (besides redeployments during patch or update times). For those domains, it is advisable to create domains hosting many different clusters as this makes the life of system admins much easier. It is a nightmare for all system administrators if they need to do Administration Server hoping all the time. As we will see in this book, automation should be used for most activities but nevertheless the admin console is still a very valuable tool for controlling and error searching. This is frustrating, wastes a lot of time, and makes the monitoring and management much more complex. A good piece of advice is to group applications with similar functionality together, such as all human resource applications, applications for a specific region in the world, or all applications with the same patching/lifecycle requirements. For WebLogic it is often required to group applications with the same security (provider) requirements, as we will see later.

What can be clustered?

A clustered service or component is available on all Managed-Servers of the cluster. For those, failover and load balancing is available.

WebLogic clustering is available for the following: Servlets, JSPs, EJBs, RMI objects, JMS destinations, and JDBC connections. We will see during the upcoming chapters which options are available for the different components.

What cannot be clustered?

The following options cannot be clustered: File services, including file shares, and time services.

Cluster Communication

Since WebLogic 10, a cluster offers two different ways for internal communication: Unicast and Multicast

Prior to WebLogic 10, only multicast was supported. Multicast is based on UDP broadcast for sending announcements to all cluster members who are listening on a specific multicast address and port. There is a defined range for a valid Multicast address (224.0.0.1 to 239.255.255.255). Everyone listening on the given address gets the announcement. Multicast has a number of issues as it must be supported by routers, subnet, firewalls, etc.

Unicast uses a point-to-point UDP protocol to send the packet to a specific member and not everyone. In order to realize cluster communication using unicast, one server in the cluster (not the Administration Server) has the role of the cluster master. In big clusters, WebLogic divides the cluster into different groups with one "group" master for each group. In the case of WebLogic, the oldest Managed-Server in the cluster/group has the role of the cluster master. If this server dies, the next-oldest takes over its role. Unicast is also the preferred option for network administrators. Older environments are sometimes still using Multicast.

A useful tool provided by WebLogic to monitor Multicast traffic is the Multicast-Monitor. This is a command line tool that can be used on the shell. It takes the multicast address, the port, and the domain and cluster information as input:

```
${JAVA_HOME}/bin/java -classpath ${WEBLOGIC_CLASSPATH}
weblogic.cluster.MulticastMonitor <address> <port> <domain-name> c name-of-
cluster>
```

NodeManager

Especially in production systems, almost every WebLogic domain will contain a Managed-Server running on different physical nodes. In order to separate administration from application, it is highly recommended to run the Administration Server on its own physical machines. But who is then in charge of starting/stopping Managed-Servers? The WebLogic AdminServer needs another process that helps the AdminServer to perform lifecycle tasks like start/stop/restart. These are the primary tasks of the NodeManager. The NodeManager is a little process that can communicate, secure or unsecure, with the Administration Server. The Administration Server can issue commands like start/stop/restart/status/etc., to the NodeManager. The communication between Administration Server and NodeManager is pure TCP. It can be secured using a secure SSL protocol. Every machine that hosts Managed-Servers has to have a NodeManager so that the Administration Server can also be used for lifecycle operations of these Managed-Servers. The alternative to the NodeManager is to do it yourself.

Resource

WebLogic is a full J2EE server. One of the main tasks of every J2EE server is to control and coordinate resources and provide them to the applications, normally via JNDI. The developers of a J2EE application should never care about resources. The resources must be provided and maintained by the application environment - the J2EE server.

Many tasks around WebLogic have to be done by the administrators (in an automated way) to configure, maintain, and control resources. The most important resources are:

- **Transactions:** Nearly everything in a J2EE server is based on transactions, so different transaction requirements must be fulfilled depending on the applications. JTA (Java Transaction API) is the top-level API in charge of transactions. Settings include e.g. transaction timeouts, amount of transactions, etc.

- **JDBC based databases:** Can you imagine a modern server based J2EE system without a database? Well there are some but not too many. Databases very often host critical and confidential data, and are therefore critical resources that must be secured and controlled.

- **Java messaging (JMS):** Messaging provides the means for asynchronous communication. JMS (Java Messaging System) is the most common API that must be supported by all J2EE servers.

- **Java mail:** Sending emails as notifications is an often-used feature. JavaMail provides this capability.

- **Threads / Connections:** Threads and connections are very valuable resources and overload protection is key for most server systems, especially if the amount of parallel users vary over time.

- **Any other (proprietary) resources:** WebLogic offers a number of other resources like Tuxedo access, COM access, network access points, etc.

WebLogic Security

Due to its complex nature and the potential usage in many different environments, including DMZ, real-time, high risk financial system, confidential/secret data handling and many other usages, WebLogic has a comprehensive security environment spanning all areas of security. Please refer to the detailed Oracle documentation (including several book dedicated only to security).

Security Stack Overview

WebLogic has a comprehensive security stack that covers all areas of security. Later in this book we will look at different ways to configure the various security aspects using WLST and later JMX. Therefore a brief summary of the different security areas is provided here and will be referenced later.

Security can be divided into a number of areas and technologies/specifications:

Auditing means collecting security-relevant information about operating requests and their results. The collected information is stored and distributed for the purposes of non-repudiation. Auditing is very helpful in critical environments where the company has to make sure that they know and can prove who did what and when. In WebLogic, auditing providers are used to provide auditing services and collect the information. If provided, every call in WLS will go through to the auditing before and after security operations have been performed, when changes to the domain configuration are made, or when management operations on any resources in the domain are invoked.

Authentication means that the systems needs to find out who is the caller and verify that the caller's credentials are valid (e.g. correct password, username is valid, certificate has not yet expired). Authentication providers are used for this purpose and remember, transport, and make identity information available to various components using the JAAS (Java authentication authorization service) subject.

Security Assertion Markup Language (SAML): The SAML standard defines a common XML framework for creating, requesting, and exchanging security assertions between software artifacts.

Authorizations are all actions that have to take place before the real application/resource is called in order to verify if the user credentials, which are provided with the incoming call, have the permission to access the requested resource. An authorization provider or even a chain of providers have to be passed. These providers use security policies or access control lists (ACLs) and answer the question "Who has access to the WebLogic resource?" By default, the XACML Authorization provider is configured in a domain, and security policies are stored in the embedded LDAP server.

Identity and Trust: Establishing trust is a very important aspect of security. Artifacts used and supported in WebLogic are private keys, digital certificates, and trusted CA's (certificate authorities). This is not only needed for establishing trust, but also for verifying identity. The public key is embedded into a digital certificate. A private key and digital certificate provide identity and the trusted CA certificate establishes trust for a certificate. Certificates and certificate chains need to be validated before a trust relationship is established.

Secure Sockets Layer (SSL): WebLogic supports SSL communication, which enables secure communication between applications. SSL can be used for standard client communication with the flavors of SSL over T3 (T3S) or SSL over IIOP (IIOPS). For web applications, WebLogic supports HTTPS.

Security Realms

All security mechanisms for protecting WebLogic resources are grouped into a security realm. WebLogic supports the definition of multiple realms, but unfortunately WebLogic only allows one realm to be active at any given time. The default name of this security realm is *myrealm*. Due to the fact that only one realm can be active, it usually does not make sense to define additional (own) realms. The only reason for defining your own realms might be if you need to exchange default security providers with their own implementations (e.g. if you have special security requirements with their own security backends).

A realm contains a set of configured security providers, users, groups, security roles, and security policies. Users must exist in this realm and be granted the correct rights in order to access WebLogic resources.

The following security provider types currently exist. This does not mean that all of them are always needed or used. The available types are:

- Authentication Providers

- Identity Assertion Providers

- Principal Validation Providers

- Authorization Providers

- Adjudication Providers

- Role Mapping Providers

- Auditing Providers

- Credential Mapping Providers

- Certificate Lookup and Validation Providers

- Keystore Providers

- Realm Adapter Providers

Extended Security Services

RDBMS Security Store: It is possible to setup a WebLogic domain to use an external RDBMS as a datastore, which is beside the user/groups directory used by a different provider to store security information.

OPSS (Oracle Platform Security Services): OPSS is the Oracle implementation of a security framework that provides a standards-based, portable, integrated, enterprise-grade security framework. OPSS is used in many products in the Oracle Fusion Middleware family including WebLogic, ESB, SOA Suite, OWSM ADF and others. This framework provides APIs and an abstraction layer in order to unify and ease security configurations.

OWSM: Oracle Webservice Security Manager is an advanced concept that outsources web service security aspects to an external server. The idea is to have a central repository for web service security policies that can be used by many different servers from (potentially) many different domains. This substantially reduces security configurations for each domain but adds administration, management, and monitoring pain for the administrators. A whole chapter in this book is dedicated to OWSM.

Benefits of WebLogic Automation

WebLogic environments normally grow quickly and I have been working with production environment with hundreds of WebLogic domains with altogether several thousands of Managed-Servers. It is impossible to manage (bigger) WebLogic environments manually. Especially for production and production-like systems, this is close to impossible. For legal and audit guidelines, it is normally always required to use automated environments that will document what has been done, when, where, and from whom.

Therefore, WebLogic offers a comprehensive and powerful automation API that can be used either via WLST (Jython based) or via JMX.

The following is just a list of examples (far from complete) of what can be automated using this API. The rest of this book will explain the different areas of automation with practical examples (mostly coming from real production problems).

Examples for automation that are possible with the WebLogic API:

- Creation of domains

- Using WebLogic templates, extending WebLogic templates, using own WebLogic templates

- Extending domains with cluster, machines, NodeManagers, Managed-Servers

- Configure all kinds of resources

- Configure data sources

- Configure JMS / JNDI resources

- Deploy applications to cluster or individual servers

- Start/stop/restart domains, clusters or Managed-Servers

- Start/stop/restart data sources, deployments

- Settings on-the-fly debug configurations

- Setting log configurations

- Monitor ALL parts of the server, including data sources, JTA pools, thread/connection pools

- Monitor Java heap and other VM settings

- Monitor server/domain/cluster state

- Configuring all aspects of the security layer including SSL, keystores, SSL-NodeManager communications, web service security, security provider, authentication/authorization provider

- Configure user, groups, and user access roles

- Monitor HTTP access counts, EJB access counts, transaction values

- Monitor application state

Production systems should never use the WebLogic GUI console for configurations or administrative tasks. The console is still very useful for control activities but all actions should always be done in a documented and reproducible way. This is not only useful for administrators and saves them time, but is also very often a must have requirement to fulfill audit requirements.

Therefore, WLST and/or JMX are very useful technologies to achieve these goals.

Summary

WebLogic is a comprehensive J2EE hosting environment with a wealth of additional features. The core concept of WebLogic is the WebLogic domain. WebLogic Server instances can have the role of an Administration Server for a domain and/or a Managed-Server for hosting J2EE applications.

Part II

WebLogic Automation using the WLST Scripting Environment

WebLogic Scripting Tool (WLST)

WLST

WLST (WebLogic Scripting Tool) is the main administrative tool provided by Oracle for WebLogic and other Fusion Middleware products. The first (and biggest) part of this book is dedicated to WLST. WLST and all its commands are well documented in the Oracle WebLogic pages and on countless websites, therefore the first section will only give a short overview so that the reader can refresh the basics. Please also see the references section at the end of the book for links for further reading.

Overview of WLST

WLST is the WebLogic Scripting Tool provided for administrating and monitoring WebLogic. The foundation of WLST is the Jython programming language, but WLST is more than that. It provides access to all WebLogic MBeans and it contains many UNIX-like commands (e.g. *ls*, *cd*, *pwd*) for navigation. WLST is like Python and is case sensitive. For convenience, most of the names are defined in the way that Java defines them. The names could be class name, function name, or variable name.

WLST offers an "offline" and "online" mode:

- **WLST Offline**

In offline mode, you do not have to connect to a running Administration Server to do WebLogic administration tasks. This mode is provided primarily for the administration and configuration of domains, e.g. create domains, create/modify templates, extend domains, and modify a non-running domain. In offline mode it is neither possible to view runtime or performance data nor to modify the security data.

- **WLST Online**

WLST can be used to connect to an Administration Server using the *connect* command. This command switches WLST automatically from offline to online mode. Using the online mode you can do administrative tasks and monitor runtime information. It is also possible to issue lifecycle commands like *start*/*stop*/*restart*/*kill*. Typical tasks include deployment of applications, monitoring of MBeans, viewing of JMS and JDBC configurations, security configurations, and monitoring runtime information. The online mode distinguishes between the real runtime view and edit view. The edit view must be used to do changes. After the changes have been done, they need to be activated (hence copied) into the runtime environment.

Modes of Operation

WLST offers 3 modes of operation:

1. **Interactive Mode:** Calling the WLST interpreter using *wlst.sh* and then issuing commands in the interactive shell.

2. **Script Mode:** Calling the WLST interpreter with a readymade script. This allows for automation of complex tasks. In production environments, this will be the most used mode.

3. **Embedded Mode:** Running the WLST interpreter embedded in the Java application.

The following is a list of command categories and is based on the Oracle documentation.

Category	Description	Commands in this category
Browse Commands	Navigate the hierarchy of configuration or runtime beans and control the prompt display.	cd, currentTree, prompt, pwd
Control Commands	Connect to or disconnect from a server. Create and configure a WebLogic domain or domain template. Exit WLST.	connect, disconnect, createDomain, readTemplate, writeDomain, closeTemplate, readDomain, addTemplate, updateDomain, closeDomain, writeTemplate, exit
Customization Commands	Add the command group help and command help that is displayed by the WLST *help()* and *help('commandGroup')* commands.	addHelpCommandGroup, addHelpCommand
Deployment Commands	Deploy, undeploy, and redeploy applications and standalone modules to a WebLogic Server instance. Update an existing deployment plan.	deploy, distributeApplication, getWLDM, listApplications, loadApplication, redeploy, startApplication, stopApplication, undeploy, updateApplication

Category	Description	Commands in this category
	Interrogate the WebLogic Deployment Manager object. Start and stop a deployed application.	
Diagnostics Commands	Export diagnostic data.	exportDiagnosticData, exportDiagnosticDataFromServer
Editing Commands	Interrogate and edit configuration beans.	activate, assign, cancelEdit, create, delete, encrypt, get, getActivationTask, invoke, isRestartRequired, loadDB, loadProperties, save, set, setOption, showChanges, startEdit, stopEdit, unassign, undo, validate
Information Commands	Interrogate domains, servers, and variables, and provide configuration bean, runtime bean, and WLST-related information.	addListener, configToScript, dumpStack, dumpVariables, find, getConfigManager, getMBean, getMBI, getPath, listChildTypes, lookup, ls, man, redirect, removeListener, showListeners, startRecording, state, stopRecording, stopRedirect, storeUserConfig, threadDump, viewMBean, writeIniFile
Life Cycle Commands	Manage the life cycle of a server instance.	migrate, resume, shutdown, start, startServer, suspend
NodeManager Commands	Start, shut down, restart, and monitor WebLogic Server instances using NodeManager.	nm, nmConnect, nmDisconnect, nmEnroll, nmGenBootStartupProps, nmKill, nmLog, nmServerLog, nmServerStatus, nmStart, nmVersion, startNodeManager
Tree Commands	Navigate among MBean hierarchies.	custom, domainConfig, domainCustom, domainRuntime, edit, jndi, serverConfig, serverRuntime

(Source: Oracle Corporation[3])

Table 4.1: List of command categories

WLST Basics

As already mentioned, WLST offers an interactive mode and also a script mode. Let's have a look at the interactive mode first.

---

[3] docs.oracle.com/middleware/1212/wls/WLSTC/reference.htm

WLST is a Jython interpreter that can be extended with plug-ins and scripts. If you have only WebLogic installed, then there is only one version of WLST available. But if you have other products installed, e.g. the Oracle SOA suite (Service Oriented Architecture) or the Oracle ESB (Enterprise Service Bus), then every product may come with its own WLST installation. The issue is that those WLST installations normally have more plug-ins and commands available than the WLST implementations that come with the plain WebLogic Server. This is especially true in the security area. The WLST setup of the SOA suite comes with a number of OWSM (Oracle WebService Manager) commands that are not available in the WebLogic WLST setup. If your script is not running due to unknown commands, then check first if you are using the right WLST setup.

Starting the WLST shell:

```
martin@middlewaretest:$ /opt/weblogic/10.3.6/wlserver_10.3/common/bin/wlst.sh

CLASSPATH=/opt/weblogic/10.3.6/patch_wls1036/...::

Initializing WebLogic Scripting Tool (WLST) ...

Welcome to WebLogic Server Administration Scripting Shell

Type help() for help on available commands

wls:/offline>
```

This will start the WLST shell and by default the shell is in offline mode.

Oracle did a good job in providing online help within WLST. The help command can show you descriptions to all available commands. *help('all')* is a special command as it will list all available WLST commands. *help(<command>)* provides you with specific help information. In order to get a feeling about the commands of the output of *help('all')* and afterwards, the specific help for *connect* is provided in the next listing.

🖫 help_command

```
wls:/offline> help('all')
    help('activate')            Activate the changes.
    help('addListener')         Add a JMX listener to the specified MBean.
    help('addTemplate')         Extend the current domain.
    help('adminHome')           Administration MBeanHome.
    help('assign')              Assign resources to one or more destinations.
    help('assignAll')           (Deprecated) Assign all applications or services.
    help('cancelEdit')          Cancel an edit session.
    help('cd')                  Navigate the hierarchy of beans.
    help('closeDomain')         Close the current domain.
    help('closeTemplate')       Close the current domain template.
    help('closestore')          Closes a store.
    help('cmo')                 Current Management Object.
    help('compactstore')        Compacts and defragments the space occupied by a file store.
    help('config')              (Deprecated) Navigate to the last MBean in configuration hierarchy.
    help('configToScript')      Convert a domain configuration to WLST script.
    help('connect')             Connect WLST to a WebLogic Server instance.
    help('connected')           Variable indicating whether WLST is connected.
    help('create')              Create a configuration bean.
    help('createDomain')        Create a new domain.
    help('currentTree')         Return the current location in the hierarchy.
    help('custom')              Navigate to the root of custom MBeans.
    help('delete')              Delete a configuration bean.
```

```
   help('deploy')           Deploy an application.
   help('disconnect')       Disconnect WLST.
   help('distributeApplication')Copy the deployment bundle to targets.
   help('domainConfig')     Navigate to last domain configuration MBean or root.
   help('domainCustom')     Navigate to the root of domain custom MBeans.
   help('domainName')       Name of the domain to which WLST is connected.
   help('domainRuntime')    Navigate to last domain runtime MBean or root.
   help('domainRuntimeService')DomainRuntimeServiceMBean MBean.
   help('dumpStack')        Display stack trace from the last exception.
   help('dumpVariables')    Display all the variables used by WLST.
   help('dumpstore')        Dumps store contents in human-readable format to an XML file.
   help('edit')             Navigate to last edit configuration MBean or root.

< … list is much longer than printed here … >

wls:/offline> help('connect')

Description:


Connects WLST to a WebLogic Server instance.

You can specify the username and password on the command line, or you
can specify ran encrypted password that is stored locally by specifying the
locations of the user configuration and key files as arguments to the
connect command. For information about creating the user configuration
and key files, see help('storeUserConfig').

If you run the connect command without specifying the username and
<…>

wls:/mydomain/serverConfig>


wls:/offline> username = 'weblogic'
wls:/offline> password = 'weblogic'
wls:/offline> connect(username,password,'t3s://myhost:8001')
Connecting to weblogic server instance running at t3://localhost:8001 as
username weblogic...

Successfully connected to Admin Server 'AdminServer' that belongs to domain
'mydomain'.

wls:/mydomain/serverConfig>


wls:/offline> connect(userConfigFile='c:/myfiles/myuserconfigfile.secure',
userKeyFile='c:/myfiles/myuserkeyfile.secure')
Connecting to weblogic server instance running at t3://localhost:7001
as username ...

Successfully connected to Admin Server 'AdminServer' that belongs to domain 'mydomain'.

wls:/mydomain/serverConfig>


wls:/offline>
```

Offline Mode

The offline mode offers some unique features like working with templates, changing
no-running domains, talking to the NodeManager and more. For all cases it requires
that the WLST interpreter or script is running on the same machine where the actions
should take place. In some occasions it is also sufficient if the WLST environment has
local access to the file system (like NFS, GFS, SAMBA, mount).

💾 offline_mode

```
Offline example:

wls:/offline> readTemplate('/opt/weblogic/10.3.6/wlserver_10.3/common/templates/domains/wls.jar');
wls:/offline/base_domain>pwd()
'/base_domain'
wls:/offline/base_domain>ls()
drw-    Security
drw-    Server

-rw-    Active                                  false
-rw-    AdminServerName                         AdminServer
-rw-    AdministrationMBeanAuditingEnabled      false
-rw-    AdministrationPort                      9002
-rw-    AdministrationPortEnabled               false
-rw-    AdministrationProtocol                  null
-rw-    AutoDeployForSubmodulesEnabled          true
-rw-    ClusterConstraintsEnabled               false
-rw-    ConfigBackupEnabled                     false
-rw-    ConfigurationAuditType                  null
-rw-    ConfigurationVersion                    10.3.6.0
-rw-    ConsoleContextPath                      console
-rw-    ConsoleEnabled                          true
-rw-    ConsoleExtensionDirectory               console-ext
-rw-    DomainVersion                           10.3.6.0
-rw-    ExalogicOptimizationsEnabled            false
-rw-    GuardianEnabled                         false
-rw-    InternalAppsDeployOnDemandEnabled       true
-rw-    LastModificationTime                    0
-rw-    MsgIdPrefixCompatibilityEnabled         true
-rw-    Name                                    base_domain
-rw-    Notes                                   null
-rw-    OcmEnabled                              true
-rw-    ProductionModeEnabled                   false
-rw-    RootDirectory                           null
wls:/offline/base_domain>cd ('Server')
wls:/offline/base_domain/Server>ls()
drw-    AdminServer
wls:/offline/base_domain/Server>cmo
wls:/offline/base_domain/Server>pwd()
'/base_domain/Server'
wls:/offline/base_domain/Server>
```

One characteristic for the offline mode is that "wls:/offline" is always printed on each line. This indicates that WLST is in offline mode. This example reads a template and then navigates IN THE TEMPLATE. See domain creation in the next chapter for concrete usage.

Here is a summary of WLST offline commands:

This command...	Enables you to...
addTemplate	Extend the current domain using an application or service extension template.
assign	Assign resources to one or more destinations.
assignAll	Assign all applications or services to one or more destinations. Note: This command is deprecated as of WebLogic Server 9.0. You should update your scripts to use the assign command.
cd	Navigate the hierarchy of configuration or runtime beans.
closeDomain	Close the current domain.
closeTemplate	Close the current domain template.

configToScript	Convert an existing server configuration (config directory) to an executable WLST script.
connect	Connect WLST to a WebLogic Server instance.
create	Create a configuration bean of the specified type for the current bean.
delete	Delete an instance of a configuration bean of the specified type for the current configuration bean.
dumpStack	Display stack trace from the last exception that occurred while performing a WLST action, and reset the stack trace.
dumpVariables	Display all variables used by WLST, including their name and value.
exit	Exit WLST from the interactive session and close the scripting shell.
get	Return the value of the specified attribute.
loadDB	Load SQL files into a database.
loadProperties	Load property values from a file.
ls	List all child beans and/or attributes for the current configuration or runtime bean.
nmConnect	Connect WLST to NodeManager to establish a session.
prompt	Toggle the display of path information at the prompt.
pwd	Display the current location in the configuration or runtime bean hierarchy.
readDomain	Open an existing domain for updating.
readTemplate	Open an existing domain template for domain creation.
redirect	Redirect WLST output to the specified filename.
set	Set the specified attribute value for the current configuration bean.
setOption	Set options related to a domain creation or update.
startNodeManager	Start NodeManager at default port (5556).
startRecording	Record all user interactions with WLST; useful for capturing commands to replay.
startServer	Start the Administration Server.
stopRecording	Stop recording WLST commands.
stopRedirect	Stop the redirection of WLST output to a file.
threadDump	Display a thread dump for the specified server.
unassign	Unassign applications or services from one or more destinations.
unassignAll	Unassign all applications or services from one or more destinations. Note: This command is deprecated as of WebLogic Server 9.0. You should update your scripts to use the unassign command.
updateDomain	Update and save the current domain.
writeDomain	Write the domain configuration information to the specified directory.
writeIniFile	Convert WLST definitions and method declarations to a Python (.py) file.
writeTemplate	Writes the domain configuration information to the specified domain template.

(Source: Oracle Corporation[4])

Table 4.2: WLST Offline Command Summary

---

[4] docs.oracle.com/middleware/1212/wls/WLSTC/quick_ref.htm

Online Mode

The online mode always means that WLST is connected to a (remote) WebLogic Server. The online mode does not require that the WLST interpreter or script is running on the same box as the WebLogic Server, as long as the script does not contain commands that require local access.

After the *connect* command has returned successfully, WLST changes its appearance in order to signal that it is now in online mode.

🖫 online_mode

```
wls:/offline> connect('weblogic','test1234','t3://localhost:7001')
Connecting to t3://localhost:7001 with userid weblogic ...
Successfully connected to Admin Server 'AdminServer' that belongs to domain 'TestDomain'.

Warning: An insecure protocol was used to connect to the
server. To ensure on-the-wire security, the SSL port or
Admin port should be used instead.

wls:/TestDomain/serverConfig> cd ('Servers')
wls:/TestDomain/serverConfig/Servers> ls()
dr--   AdminServer

wls:/TestDomain/serverConfig/Servers> cd ('AdminServer')
wls:/TestDomain/serverConfig/Servers/AdminServer> pwd()
'serverConfig:/Servers/AdminServer'
wls:/TestDomain/serverConfig/Servers/AdminServer> ls()
dr--   COM
dr--   CandidateMachines
dr--   Cluster
dr--   CoherenceClusterSystemResource
dr--   DataSource
dr--   DefaultFileStore
dr--   ExecuteQueues
dr--   FederationServices
dr--   IIOP
dr--   JTAMigratableTarget
dr--   Log
dr--   Machine
dr--   NetworkAccessPoints
dr--   OverloadProtection
dr--   ReliableDeliveryPolicy
dr--   SSL
dr--   ServerDebug
dr--   ServerDiagnosticConfig
dr--   ServerStart
dr--   SingleSignOnServices
dr--   TransactionLogJDBCStore
dr--   WebServer
dr--   WebService
dr--   XMLEntityCache
dr--   XMLRegistry

-r--   AcceptBacklog                       300
-r--   AddWorkManagerThreadsByCpuCount     false
-r--   AdminReconnectIntervalSeconds       10
-r--   AdministrationPort                  9002
-r--   AdministrationProtocol              t3s
-r--   AutoKillIfFailed                    false
-r--   AutoMigrationEnabled                false
-r--   AutoRestart                         true
-r--   COMEnabled                          false
-r--   ClasspathServletDisabled            false
-r--   ClientCertProxyEnabled              false
-r--   Cluster                             null
-r--   ClusterRuntime                      null
-r--   ClusterWeight                       100
-r--   CoherenceClusterSystemResource      null
```

```
-r--    CompleteCOMMessageTimeout                   -1
-r--    CompleteHTTPMessageTimeout                  -1
-r--    CompleteIIOPMessageTimeout                  -1
-r--    CompleteMessageTimeout                      60
-r--    CompleteT3MessageTimeout                    -1
-r--    ConnectTimeout                              0
-r--    CustomIdentityKeyStoreFileName              null
-r--    CustomIdentityKeyStorePassPhrase            ******
-r--    CustomIdentityKeyStorePassPhraseEncrypted   ******
-r--    CustomIdentityKeyStoreType                  null
-r--    CustomTrustKeyStoreFileName                 null
-r--    CustomTrustKeyStorePassPhrase               ******
-r--    CustomTrustKeyStorePassPhraseEncrypted      ******
-r--    CustomTrustKeyStoreType                     null
-r--    DGCIdlePeriodsUntilTimeout                  5
-r--    DefaultIIOPPassword                         ******
-r--    DefaultIIOPPasswordEncrypted                ******
-r--    DefaultIIOPUser                             null
-r--    DefaultInternalServletsDisabled             false
-r--    DefaultProtocol                             t3
-r--    DefaultSecureProtocol                       t3s
-r--    DefaultTGIOPPassword                        ******
-r--    DefaultTGIOPPasswordEncrypted               ******
-r--    DefaultTGIOPUser                            guest
-r--    ExternalDNSName                             null
-r--    ExtraEjbcOptions                            null
-r--    ExtraRmicOptions                            null
-r--    GatheredWritesEnabled                       false
-r--    GracefulShutdownTimeout                     0
-r--    HealthCheckIntervalSeconds                  180
-r--    HealthCheckStartDelaySeconds                120
-r--    HealthCheckTimeoutSeconds                   60
-r--    HostsMigratableServices                     true
-r--    HttpTraceSupportEnabled                     false
-r--    HttpdEnabled                                true
-r--    IIOPEnabled                                 true
-r--    IIOPTxMechanism                             ots
-r--    IdleConnectionTimeout                       65
-r--    IdleIIOPConnectionTimeout                   -1
-r--    IdlePeriodsUntilTimeout                     4
-r--    IgnoreSessionsDuringShutdown                false
-r--    InstrumentStackTraceEnabled                 true
-r--    InterfaceAddress                            null
-r--    JDBCLLRTableName                            null
-r--    JDBCLoggingEnabled                          false
-r--    JDBCLoginTimeoutSeconds                     0
-r--    JMSDefaultConnectionFactoriesEnabled        true
-r--    JNDITransportableObjectFactoryList          null
-r--    JTAMigratableTarget                         null
-r--    JavaCompiler                                javac
-r--    JavaCompilerPostClassPath                   null
-r--    JavaCompilerPreClassPath                    null
-r--    JavaStandardTrustKeyStorePassPhrase         ******
-r--    JavaStandardTrustKeyStorePassPhraseEncrypted ******
-r--    KeyStores                                   DemoIdentityAndDemoTrust
-r--    ListenAddress                               192.168.56.101
-r--    ListenDelaySecs                             0
-r--    ListenPort                                  47001
-r--    ListenPortEnabled                           true
```

After the *connect* command was executed successfully, WLST switched to the online mode and all commands were issued against the remote WebLogic Server. WLST is by default connected to the runtime environment. The *edit()* command will switch to the edit environment. Typical UNIX commands like *cd()*, *pwd()*, and *ls()* allow navigation in the MBean tree. A special variable *cmo* represents the current MBean (where cmo stands for current managed object).

Here is a summary of WLST online commands:

This command...	Enables you to...
activate	Activate changes saved during the current editing session but not yet deployed.
addListener	Add a JMX listener to the specified MBean.
cancelEdit	Cancel an edit session, release the edit lock, and discard all unsaved changes. This operation can be called by any user with administrator privileges, even if the user did not start the edit session.
cd	Navigate the hierarchy of configuration or runtime beans.
config	Navigate to the last MBean to which you navigated in the configuration MBean hierarchy or to the root of all configuration beans, DomainMBean. Note: This command is deprecated as of WebLogic Server 9.0. You should update your script to use the serverConfig command.
configToScript	Convert an existing server configuration (config directory) to an executable WLST script.
connect	Connect WLST to a WebLogic Server instance.
create	Create a configuration bean of the specified type for the current bean.
currentTree	Return the current tree location.
custom	Navigate to the root of custom MBeans that are registered in the server.
delete	Delete an instance of a configuration bean of the specified type for the current configuration bean.
deploy	Deploy an application to a WebLogic Server instance.
disconnect	Disconnect WLST from a WebLogic Server instance.
distributeApplication	Copy the deployment bundle to the specified targets.
domainConfig	Navigate to the last MBean to which you navigated in the domain configuration hierarchy or to the root of the hierarchy, DomainMBean.
domainRuntime	Navigate to the last MBean to which you navigated in the domain runtime hierarchy or to the root of the hierarchy, DomainRuntimeMBean.
dumpStack	Display stack trace from the last exception that occurred, and reset the trace.
dumpVariables	Display all variables used by WLST, including their name and value.
edit	Navigate to the last MBean to which you navigated in the configuration edit MBean hierarchy or to the root of the hierarchy, DomainMBean.
encrypt	Encrypt the specified string.
exit	Exit WLST from the interactive session and close the scripting shell.
exportDiagnosticDataFromServer	Execute a query on the server side and retrieve the exported WebLogic Diagnostic Framework (WLDF) data.
find	Find MBeans and attributes in the current hierarchy.
get	Return the value of the specified attribute.
getActivationTask	Return the latest ActivationTask MBean on which a user can get status.
getConfigManager	Return the latest ConfigurationManagerBean MBean which manages the change process.
getMBean	Return the MBean by browsing to the specified path.

getMBI	Return the MBeanInfo for the specified MBeanType or the cmo variable.
getPath	Return the MBean path for the specified MBean instance.
getWLDM	Return the WebLogic DeploymentManager object.
invoke	Invoke a management operation on the current configuration bean.
isRestartRequired	Determine whether a server restart is required.
jndi	Navigates to the JNDI tree for the server to which WLST is currently connected.
listApplications	List all applications that are currently deployed in the domain.
listChildTypes	List all the children MBeans that can be created or deleted for the cmo.
loadApplication	Load an application and deployment plan into memory.
loadProperties	Load property values from a file.
lookup	Look up the specified MBean.
ls	List all child beans and/or attributes for the current configuration or runtime bean.
man	Display help from MBeanInfo for the current MBean or its specified attribute.
migrate	Migrate services to a target server within a cluster.
nm	Determine whether WLST is connected to NodeManager.
nmConnect	Connect WLST to NodeManager to establish a session.
nmDisconnect	Disconnect WLST from a NodeManager session.
nmEnroll	Enroll the machine on which WLST is currently running.
nmGenBootStartupProps	Generates the NodeManager property files, boot.properties and startup.properties, for the specified server.
nmKill	Kill the specified server instance that was started with NodeManager.
nmLog	Return the NodeManager log.
nmServerLog	Return the server output log of the server that was started with NodeManager.
nmServerStatus	Return the status of the server that was started with NodeManager.
nmStart	Start a server in the current domain using NodeManager.
nmVersion	Return the NodeManager server version.
prompt	Toggle the display of path information at the prompt.
pwd	Display the current location in the configuration or runtime bean hierarchy.
redeploy	Reload classes and redeploy a previously deployed application.
redirect	Redirect WLST output to the specified filename.
removeListener	Remove a listener that was previously defined.
resume	Resume a server instance that is suspended or in ADMIN state.
runtime	Navigate to the last MBean to which you navigated in the Runtime hierarchy or the root of all runtime objects, DomainRuntimeMBean. Note: This command is deprecated as of WebLogic Server 9.0. You should update your scripts to use the serverRuntime command.
save	Save the edits that have been made but have not yet been saved.
serverConfig	Navigate to the last MBean to which you navigated in the configuration MBean hierarchy or to the root of the hierarchy, DomainMBean.
serverRuntime	Navigate to the last MBean to which you navigated in the runtime

	MBean hierarchy or to the root of the hierarchy, ServerRuntimeMBean.
set	Set the specified attribute value for the current configuration bean.
showChanges	Show the changes made by the current user during the current edit session.
showListeners	Show all listeners that are currently defined.
shutdown	Gracefully shut down a running server instance or cluster.
start	Start a Managed-Server instance or a cluster using NodeManager.
startApplication	Start an application, making it available to users.
startEdit	Start a configuration edit session on behalf of the currently connected user.
startNodeManager	Start NodeManager at default port (5556).
startRecording	Record all user interactions with WLST; useful for capturing commands to replay.
startServer	Start the Administration Server.
state	Returns a map of servers or clusters and their state using NodeManager
stopApplication	Stop an application, making it un available to users.
stopEdit	Stop the current edit session, release the edit lock, and discard unsaved changes.
stopRecording	Stop recording WLST commands.
stopRedirect	Stop the redirection of WLST output to a file.
storeUserConfig	Create a user configuration file and an associated key file.
suspend	Suspend a running server.
threadDump	Display a thread dump for the specified server.
undeploy	Undeploy an application from the specified servers.
undo	Revert all unsaved or unactivated edits.
updateApplication	Update an application configuration using a new deployment plan.
validate	Validate the changes that have been made but have not yet been saved.
viewMBean	Display information about an MBean, such as the attribute names and values, and operations.
writeIniFile	Convert WLST definitions and method declarations to a Python (.py) file.

(Source: Oracle Corporation[5])

Table 4.3: WLST Online Command Summary

WLST Variables

WLST has a number of built-in variables that are quite handy. Some of these variables are only available in the online mode, others available always. The command *dumpVariables()* will show you the actual available variables and their content.

Example:

---

[5] docs.oracle.com/middleware/1212/wls/WLSTC/quick_ref.htm

💾 available_variables

```
wls:/MartinTest_Domain/domainRuntime> dumpVariables()
cmgr
[MBeanServerInvocationHandler]com.bea:Name=ConfigurationManager,Type=weblogic.management.mbeanservers
.edit.ConfigurationManagerMBean
cmo
[MBeanServerInvocationHandler]com.bea:Name=AppRuntimeStateRuntime,Type=AppRuntimeStateRuntime
connected                    true
domainName                   MartinTest_Domain
domainRuntimeService
[MBeanServerInvocationHandler]com.bea:Name=DomainRuntimeService,Type=weblogic.management.mbeanservers
.domainruntime.DomainRuntimeServiceMBean
editService
[MBeanServerInvocationHandler]com.bea:Name=EditService,Type=weblogic.management.mbeanservers.edit.Edi
tServiceMBean
isAdminServer                true
mbs
javax.management.remote.rmi.RMIConnector$RemoteMBeanServerConnection@f55fa6e
recording                    false
runtimeService
[MBeanServerInvocationHandler]com.bea:Name=RuntimeService,Type=weblogic.management.mbeanservers.runti
me.RuntimeServiceMBean
scriptMode                   true
serverName                   AdminServer
typeService
[MBeanServerInvocationHandler]com.bea:Name=MBeanTypeService,Type=weblogic.management.mbeanservers.MBe
anTypeService
username                     weblogic
version                      WebLogic Server 10.3.5.0  Fri Apr 1 20:20:06 PDT 2011 1398638
exitonerror                  true
```

MBean roots

While connected to an AdminServer or a Managed-Server, WebLogic offers different
root MBeans, depending what you want to do. You can switch between those MBean
roots with predefined WLST commands, as shown in the next table.

MBean Root	Description	WLST command	Comment
Server Configuration	This is the root of the actual server configuration.	serverConfig()	Default MBean after connection to a WebLogic Server.
Domain Configuration	This is the root of the complete domain configuration, including all domain services and access to all server configurations.	domainConfig()	Only available on the AdminServer.
Server Runtime	Runtime information for the actual server.	serverRuntime()	Read only runtime information tree.
Domain Runtime	Runtime information for the complete domain, including access to the runtimes of all running servers.	domainRuntime()	Only available on the AdminServer.
Custom MBean tree	MBean tree for custom MBeans.	custom()	No root MBean (cmo) available.
Domain Custom MBean tree	MBean tree for the domain custom MBeans.	customDomain()	No root MBean (cmo) available. Only available on the AdminServer.
Edit MBean tree	Copy of the runtime MBean tree in order to apply modifications.	edit()	Only available on the AdminServer.

Table 4.4: MBean roots

Example:

💾 mbean_roots

```
wls:/MartinTest_Domain/serverConfig>
wls:/MartinTest_Domain/serverConfig> cmo
[MBeanServerInvocationHandler]com.bea:Name=MartinTest_Domain,Type=Domain

wls:/MartinTest_Domain/serverConfig> serverRuntime()
wls:/MartinTest_Domain/serverRuntime> cmo
[MBeanServerInvocationHandler]com.bea:Name=AdminServer,Type=ServerRuntime

wls:/MartinTest_Domain/serverRuntime> domainConfig()
wls:/MartinTest_Domain/domainConfig> cmo
[MBeanServerInvocationHandler]com.bea:Name=MartinTest_Domain,Location=MartinTest_Domain,Type=Domain

wls:/MartinTest_Domain/domainConfig> domainRuntime()
wls:/MartinTest_Domain/domainRuntime> cmo
[MBeanServerInvocationHandler]com.bea:Name=MartinTest_Domain,Type=DomainRuntime

wls:/MartinTest_Domain/domainRuntime> custom()
Location changed to custom tree. This is a writable tree with No root.
For more help, use help(custom)
cmo

wls:/MartinTest_Domain/custom> 'No Stub Available'
wls:/MartinTest_Domain/custom> ls()
drw-    JMImplementation
drw-    com.sun.management
drw-    com.sun.xml.ws.transport.http
drw-    com.sun.xml.ws.util
drw-    dbWLSMonitoring
```

```
drw-    java.lang
drw-    java.util.logging

wls:/MartinTest_Domain/custom> domainCustom()
Location changed to domain custom tree. This is a writable tree with No root.
For more help, use help(domainCustom)
ls()

wls:/MartinTest_Domain/domainCustom> drw-    JMImplementation
drw-    com.sun.management
drw-    com.sun.xml.ws.transport.http
drw-    com.sun.xml.ws.util
drw-    dbWLSMonitoring
drw-    java.lang
drw-    java.util.logging
```

Switching Between MBean-trees

It is often the case to switch between MBean trees. For example, while you are in the edit tree and want to edit something, you might need to get a configuration item from the serverconfig tree or even a runtime value from the server runtime.

The best alternate is using *currentTree()*. This command enables you to store the current location in the hierarchy and easily return to it after browsing:

```
wls:/testdomain/edit> loc=currentTree()
wls:/testdomain/edit> serverRuntime()
... do whatever you want here
wls:/testdomain/serverRuntime> loc()
wls:/testdomain/edit>
```

WLST and the History

WLST offers an interpreter mode where you can enter commands interactively. The frustrating aspect of WLST is that it does not have a history (using the arrow keys like in *UNIX bash history). This means that you always have to retype your commands. I also had the nasty problem that the <delete> key did not always work correctly on all systems, and that I sometimes had to use <shift> <back> instead.

The Java open source community offers an interesting project that can be used to add a history function to WLST. I also experienced much better keyboard support like <del> and arrow keys (left, right). The project is called jLine (jline.sourceforge.net). jLine is an open source Java library for handling console input, and which can be used together with WLST.

After you have downloaded the archive, you need to extract it and add the jar file to the classpath of your WLST *start* command. Instead of starting WLST directly (weblogic.WLST), you will start the jLine console runner and provide the real program - WLST - as an argument.

BE CAREFUL: In my tests, the version 1.0 does not work well with WLST. The problem is that in version 1.0, jLine always jumps to the first character on the left side but WLST is printing its path. The history works well but as soon as you need to delete some characters, in all my tests version 1.0 was a pain to use. I recommend using version 0.9.5, which works fine.

Here is an example Linux shell script to start WLST (DOS batch scripts can be written based on the same concept):

💾 start_wlst

```
#!/bin/sh

MYDIR=`dirname $0`
MYFULLDIR=$(cd $MYDIR && pwd -P)

# set up WL_HOME, the root directory of your WebLogic installation
#
# !!!!!!!!!!!!!!!!!  MUST BE ADAPTED TO INSTALLATION
WL_HOME="/opt/oracle/wls/10.3.6/wlserver_10.3"
JAVA_HOME="/opt/jdks/jdk1.6"

umask 027

# set up common environment
. "${WL_HOME}/server/bin/setWLSEnv.sh"

# all additional libraries like own mbeans, ... so that WLST knows about them.
#WLSTEXTENSIONCLASSPATH=${MYFULLDIR}/../libs/myOwnMBeans.jar
WLSTEXTENSIONCLASSPATH=


CLASSPATH="${MYFULLDIR}/../libs/jline-
0_9_5.jar:${WLSTEXTENSIONCLASSPATH}:${CLASSPATH}${CLASSPATHSEP}${FMWLAUNCH_CLASSPATH}${CLASSPATHSEP}$
{DERBY_CLASSPATH}${CLASSPATHSEP}${DERBY_TOOLS}${CLASSPATHSEP}${POINTBASE_CLASSPATH}${CLASSPATHSEP}${P
OINTBASE_TOOLS}"

#WLST_PROPERTIES="-Dweblogic.wlstHome='.' ${WLST_PROPERTIES}"
#
#export WLST_PROPERTIES


JVM_ARGS="-cp ${CLASSPATH} -Dprod.props.file='${WL_HOME}'/.product.properties ${WLST_PROPERTIES}
${JVM_D64}  -Xms256m -Xmx1024m -XX:PermSize=128m  ${CONFIG_JVM_ARGS}"
eval '"${JAVA_HOME}/bin/java"' ${JVM_ARGS} jline.ConsoleRunner weblogic.WLST -skipWLSModuleScanning
$1 $2 $3 $4 $5 $6 $7 $8
```

(Inspired by the blog schelstraete.dyndns.org/index.php/oracle-weblogic/494-weblogic-wlst-with-bash-alike-history)

EaseSyntax()

WLST uses the "()" notation for all functions. For system administrators, this is often annoying as they are not used to it and they keep forgetting it (happens to me as well). So it would be nice to write "ls" instead of "ls()" or "cd 'Servers'" instead of "cd('Servers')".

WLST offers a limited support for this easier syntax. Use the undocumented command *easeSyntax()* in order to activate this hidden treasure. Note that this only works well in the interactive mode and you should not use it within scripts:

Example:

💾 easeSyntax

```
wls:/offline> connect('weblogic','test1234','t3://localhost:7001')
Connecting to t3://localhost:7001 with userid weblogic ...
Successfully connected to Admin Server 'AdminServer' that belongs to domain 'MartinTest_Domain'.

Warning: An insecure protocol was used to connect to the
server. To ensure on-the-wire security, the SSL port or
Admin port should be used instead.

wls:/MartinTest_Domain/serverConfig> easeSyntax()

You have chosen to ease syntax for some WLST commands.
However, the easy syntax should be strictly used in
interactive mode. Easy syntax will not function properly in
script mode and when used in loops. You can still use the
regular jython syntax although you have opted for easy
syntax.
Use easeSyntax to turn this off.
Use help(easeSyntax) for commands that support easy syntax
wls:/MartinTest_Domain/serverConfig> cd Servers
wls:/MartinTest_Domain/serverConfig/Servers> pwd
'serverConfig:/Servers'
wls:/MartinTest_Domain/serverConfig/Servers> cmo
[MBeanServerInvocationHandler]com.bea:Name=MartinTest_Domain,Type=Domain
wls:/MartinTest_Domain/serverConfig/Servers> help

WLST is a command line scripting tool to configure and administer WebLogic Server. Try:

    help('all')             List all WLST commands available.
    help('browse')          List commands for browsing the hierarchy.
    help('common')          List the most commonly used commands.
    help('control')         List commands for controlling the domain/server.
    help('deployment')      List commands for deploying applications.
    help('diagnostics')     List commands for performing diagnostics.
    help('editing')         List commands for editing the configuration.
    help('information')     List commands for displaying information.
    help('lifecycle')       List commands for managing life cycle.
    help('nodemanager')     List commands for using Node Manager.
    help('offline')         List all offline commands available.
    help('online')          List all online commands available.
    help('storeadmin')      List all store admin commands.
    help('trees')           List commands use to navigate MBean hierarchy.
    help('variables')       List all global variables available.
```

Embedded WLST

WLST scripts can be called from a Java program. It is also possible to call Jython command by command from the embedded WLST interpretation. This is most likely the fastest way to invoke WLST Script, because all class files are already loaded and so all the startup delays of the WLST shell are omitted. A WLSTInterpreter class can be called in the Java program and invoke the WLST script commands or a script file by using *exec()* or *exec file()* methods, respectively.

The *exec()* method will take the string as parameter, which can be a WLST command or set of commands, appended to form a single String object.

Example:

💾 embedded_wlst

```
package wlst;
import java.util.*;
import weblogic.management.scripting.utils.WLSTInterpreter;
import org.python.util.InteractiveInterpreter;

public class EmbeddedWLST2 {
        static InteractiveInterpreter interpreter = null;
        EmbeddedWLST2()
        {
                System.out.println("EmbeddedWLST2...");
                interpreter = new WLSTInterpreter();
        }

        private static void connect()
        {
                interpreter.execfile("MonitorThreads.py");
        }

        public static void main(String[] args)
        {
                System.out.println("main...");
                new EmbeddedWLST2();
                connect();
        }
}
```

Warning: As this is a nice way to call WLST from Java code, it has benefits and drawbacks. One of the benefits of using this approach is that you have all the offline features of WLST - like domain creation and templates - available. But you should also be aware of the drawbacks. From an architectural point of view you are doing the following (in case you are using the command interpreter to issue command by command): You are 1) Developing Java code that creates strings; 2) These strings are provided to a script interpreter embedded in your Java program; 3) This interpreter tries to analyze these strings and can convert it to script code; 4) The interpreter will then compile the script code into Java code; and 5) WLST, in most cases, will result in underlying JMX calls.

This is a nightmare for Java architects and a nightmare for debugging. If you do not need WLST offline functionality or other commands not available to Java or JMX, then this is a valid option. For all other situations, I strongly recommend using JMX (see the end of the book for a technology comparison).

Programming WLST Tips and Tricks

Before going into the development of WebLogic automations, it is important to discuss some basic WLST features and usage information.

Obtaining Environment Variables in WLST

WLST supports the Jython capability of obtaining the environment variables from the System. To do this, we need to import the OS module (operating system) and use the environment dictionary variable:

```
wls:/offline> import os
wls:/offline> os.environ
{'WL_HOME': 'C:\\wls12c\\wlserver', …}
```

You can pull out your required values of environment variables as you access the dictionary variable. For example, you can retrieve WL_HOME or JAVA_HOME values as show below.

```
wls:/offline> os.environ["WL_HOME"]
'C:\\wls12c\\wlserver'

wls:/offline> os.environ["JAVA_HOME"]
'C:\\Java\\jdk1.6.0_34'
```

This WLST trick can be used often, such as when you are configuring resources or creating WebLogic domains. This WLST trick will work on the UNIX platform as well.

Input and Output in WLST

In WLST, we can have the same kind of command line inputs and outputs as in Python and Jython languages. This can be useful when it is required to prepare a huge monitoring report using WLST, or when you work with hundreds of servers or domains and you need to find an automation task with WLST scripts. Normally it is recommended to avoid manual inputs for scripts and instead outsource property values into property files, but it might be the case – e.g. for security sensitive data – where manual input can be quite handy.

Input in WLST

To read a simple string of values, we can use the *raw_input()* built-in function or the *sys.stdin.readline()* method. For reading different data types, such as number values, we can use the *input()* function, which internally calls the *raw_input()* function and applies *eval()* to convert the input value to number values.

```
wls:/offline> x=raw_input('Enter a number:')
Enter a number:4009
wls:/offline> print x*2
40094009
wls:/offline> y=input('Enter a number: ')
Enter a number: 400
wls:/offline> print y*3
1200
```

Let's experiment with the Boolean type of variable in WLST:

```
wls:/offline> b=input('Do you love WLST?')
Do you love WLST?True
wls:/offline> print b
1
wls:/offline> b=input('Do you love WLST?')
Do you love WLST?False
wls:/offline> print b
0
```

Here you enter True or False, but the Boolean variables are stored on WLST SHELL as either zero or one. This is somewhat confusing because regular Boolean types in other languages or in UNIX are the opposite. One represents the True value, and zero represents False. So take care while scripting with the Boolean type variables.

When you have the option to select the data in string format, then go for the *raw_input()* built-in function. The usage of *raw_input()* has the benefit that the input will be treated as string regardless of whether it is a numeric input or not. The value that was read will always be treated as string, which makes the script easier to develop and easier to understand. On the other hand, *input()* will be a good option for when you have to select multiple options for monitoring geographical sites and choose one of them with a numbered input.

Read Variables in WLST with stdin

We have one more option to read the values from the WLST command prompt: using the *sys* module. We can use the *sys.stdin.readline()* method to read the input and assign it to a variable. This will fetch only text data in the variable, so you use this when you want to input the strings.

```
wls:/offline> serv=sys.stdin.readline()
managed3_server
wls:/offline> serv
'managed3_server\n'
wls:/offline> print serv
managed3_server
```

Printing Output

Output can be displayed using the *print* command. Print is a module, which accepts the string as an argument.

Simple string to display:

```
print 'Welcome to WLST!!!!'
```

To display the string and variable combinations in Java Style concatenation using the '+' operator:

```
print   'Server Status '+ stat
```

To display only WLST script variables, you can use comma separated variables. You can use the combination of string in the same line too:

```
print x, y
```

Now, we will see the good old C style formatting for the output:

```
print '%14s %d %f' %(server, freeJvm, throughput)
```

In WLST, we can use the print statement for displaying the data from variable or strings objects. We can display the combination of variables in the same line, which is possible with comma separation or the Java style of concatenation using the plus symbol.

Iterations in WLST Scripts

There are two major types of iterations available in WLST scripting: the for loop and the while loop. But first we will briefly discuss the range function.

The Range Function

When you are using loop, one way to use it is working with a range module. It takes three different arguments and gives different variety of values as output. A range is a built-in function for Python, which simply provides a range:

- Until the given number

- From one particular value to another

- From one value to another with increment by value

Experimenting with the range function will help you to understand all its capabilities.

If the range function is called with a single argument, then this argument is considered to be the upper (excluded) end of the range. In this case the numbers provided as being part of this range will start with the number "0".

```
wls:/offline> R=range(11)
wls:/offline> R
[0, 1, 2, 3, 4, 5, 6, 7, 8, 9, 10]
wls:/offline> R=range(2,10,2)
wls:/offline> R
[2, 4, 6, 8]
wls:/offline> R=range(2,10,3)
wls:/offline> R
[2, 5, 8]
```

while loop control

This loop is same as the C programming style loop. The execution of the while loop should not have any control on the variable that is used to iterate the loop. This means that the initialization of the variable used in the condition must be done before the loop starts. The *loop* command itself defines the condition that needs to be checked in order to determine if the loop should be executed again. Changing of the variables, like increase or decrease, must be done inside the *while loop*.

```
i=0
while i<10:
        print 'jms'+str(i)+'_server'
        i=i+1
```

for loop

The example of a *for loop* is as follows:

```
slist=range(1,11)
for i in slist:
        print 'managed'+str(i)+'_server'
```

WLST Namespace

In WLST, we have the namespace concept that is used to represent a set of modules. To learn more about the namespace in WLST you can try the following:

```
wls:/offline> print __doc__
```

Naming rules

In WLST, you need to follow the same naming rules as in Jython or in Python languages. WLST allows the usage of case sensitive names and arguments of various WLST commands. Argument strings can be enclosed with single or double quotes. In some of the WLST scripts, we need to pass the path as argument and then precede the quote with the letter "r", which indicates that string may contain backslash characters.

```
print 'c:\weblogic\ping\ting'
c:\weblogic\ping       ing

print r'c:\weblogic\ping\ting'
c:\weblogic\ping\ting
```

The identifier name, which is going to be used in the script, must not have invalid characters like a period (.), backslash (\), forward slash (/) etc. It is a must-known fact that while defining the local or global variables and modules:

- Reserved words cannot be defined as namespace

- Variable name must start with alphabet or a underscore (_)

- Identifier names are case sensitive

- Should not use any of operating symbols in namespace

Exiting from WLST

Certain conditions within a script it might be necessary to exit the script immediately. If you are using the WLST shell, then "exit" means returning to the operating system prompt. The *exit()* command will terminate all the open MBean trees and come out to the operating system prompt.

```
exit([defaultAnswer], [exitcode])
```

If the user is still in an edit session, then this method will ask for a user confirmation. In order to avoid the prompting for the confirmation, it is possible to provide the defaultArgument='y'. By default, Jython *exit()* invokes *System.exit(0)* on the current JVM using by WLST shell. If you want to exit the JVM with different exit code, then you can specify that in the optional argument exitCode=9, giving any integer value as an exit code.

Displaying Operations using dir(...)

The *dir* command can be used to display operation names. The following example demonstrates this with the String object. To learn about WLST String operations, use *dir()* with .__class__, which gives all the operations defined for str objects.

```
wls:/offline> dir("".__class__)
['__add__', '__cmp__', '__complex__', '__contains__', '__len__', '__mod__', '__repr__', '__str__',
'alnum', 'alpha', 'capitalize', 'center', 'classDictInit', 'count', 'decimal', 'digit', 'encode',
'endswith', 'expandtabs', 'find', 'index','isalnum', 'isalpha', 'isdecimal', 'isdigit', 'islower',
'isnumeric', 'isspace', 'istitle', 'isunicode', 'isupper', 'join', 'ljust', 'lower', 'lstrip',
'numeric', 'replace', 'rfind', 'rindex', 'rjust', 'rstrip', 'space', 'split', 'splitlines',
'startswith', 'strip', 'swapcase', 'title', 'translate', 'unicode', 'upper', 'zfill']
```

List, Tuple, and Dictionary

The following section will introduce three of the more complex WLST(Jython) data structures: List, Tuple, and Dictionary.

LIST:

A list is a sequence collection of elements and it is like an array of elements. You can assign the values to the List object with square braces.

On a list object we can perform the following operations:

- You can append the elements to the existing list because a list in WLST is a dynamic object.

- You can count and display the number of elements available in the List object using the *count()* method.

- You can pick out the element present in the given index using the *index()* method on the List object.

- It is possible to insert an element into the list.

- It is possible to pop out the last inserted element using *pop()*.

- It is possible to set, in order, the content of list elements using *sort()*.

```
wls:/offline> dir([])
['append', 'count', 'extend', 'index', 'insert', 'pop', 'remove', 'reverse', 'sort']
```

Accessing a List

To display all elements in the list, simply give the name of the list at the prompt or in the print statement. You can access a List object similar to array in C/C++ languages, by giving the index values access the element in the List.

```
wls:/offline> L=['app1','app2','app3']
wls:/offline> L
['app1', 'app2', 'app3']
wls:/offline> L[2]
'app3'
```

Here is an example of adding a new element into the existing list:

```
wls:/offline> L.append('app4')
wls:/offline> L
['app1', 'app2', 'app3', 'app4']
wls:/offline> L.append('web1')
wls:/offline> L
['app1', 'app2', 'app3', 'app4', 'web1']
```

L[i:j] returns a new list, containing the objects between i and j. It would be clearer to say "between i (inclusive) and j (exclusive)".

```
wls:/offline> L[1:3]
['app2', 'app3']
```

In some scripts, we may need the length of the list for iterating or accessing for any other purpose.

```
wls:/offline> len(L)
5
```

Here is an example of searching the element in the list using *index()* command:

```
wls:/offline>L.index('app4')
3
```

Tuple

Tuple is a data structure object that doesn't have any method defined in it. The tuple elements can be enclosed within parentheses. Tuple can be accessed in the same way as a list, because a tuple is an immutable list. It is not possible to append an element or remove an element from a tuple. Tuple objects don't allow you to raise an AttributeError for executing *append()*, *extend()*, *index()*, and *remove()* methods on them.

A tuple can contain items of a mix of data types. A tuple can also contain multiple tuples.

```
wls:/offline> wlurls=(('serverbox101',8981), ('serverbox102',8982))
wls:/offline> wlurls
(('serverbox101', 8981), ('serverbox102', 8982))
wls:/offline> wlurls[0]
('serverbox101', 8981)
wls:/offline> wlurls[0][0]
'serverbox101'
wls:/offline> wlurls[1][1]
8982
```

The tuple is a better option than a list if suitable to your script. A tuple can be used by accessing the elements. Tuples are faster than lists.

Dictionary Objects in WLST

There is a vast requirement of this dictionary (dict) sequence collection in WLST. The dictionary objects are similar to Java Hashtable objects. In order to learn more about dictionaries in WLST, you can use *dir()* command. On a dictionary object, the following operations are available.

```
wls:/offline> dir({})
['clear', 'copy', 'get', 'has_key', 'items', 'keys', 'setdefault', 'update', 'values']
```

The data structure of a dictionary looks similar to a real dictionary. The name of the dictionary will be defined on left side, and the dictionary content will be provided in the curly braces on the right side of the assignment operator.

```
wls:/offline>
urls={'marketing':'http://business.market.com','sales':'http://business.sales.com','cs':'http://busin
ess.customerservice.com'}
wls:/offline> urls
{'cs': 'http://business.customerservice.com', 'marketing': 'http://business.market.com', 'sales':
'http://business.sales.com'}
```

Dictionary is the implementation of a Hashtable-like structure in Jython, which allows the developer to maintain a list of key:value pairs. This data type defines the one-to-one relationship between key and values. To access the dictionary element, we need to use the list operator on the key element that results in the value.

Here in dictionary object we can have key list with not only strings; numbers are also allowed. A dictionary can be copied to a new object using the *copy()* method.

```
wls:/offline> depts=urls.copy()
wls:/offline> depts
{'cs': 'http://business.customerservice.com', 'marketing': 'http://business.market.com', 'sales':
'http://business.sales.com'}
```

On a dictionary object, we can apply the *clear()* method, which will delete all the elements in the dictionary.

```
wls:/offline> urls.clear()
wls:/offline> urls
{}
wls:/offline> depts['cs']
'http://business.customerservice.com'
wls:/offline> depts.keys()
['cs', 'marketing', 'sales']
wls:/offline> depts.values()
['http://business.customerservice.com', 'http://business.market.com',
'http://business.sales.com']
```

To retrieve only the list of keys, the *keys()* method can be used. To get only the list of values, use the *values()* method of the dictionary.

```
wls:/offline> depts.has_key('cs')
1
wls:/offline> depts.has_key('finance')
0
```

The *has_key()* method is used to check if the key element is available in the dictionary object. This method returns a Boolean value that is, True (1) for an existing key element and False (0) if the element does not exist.

Exception Handling in WLST

WLST supports the robustness for the exception handling mechanism. In WLST scripts, it is possible to control the breakouts when an abnormal situation arises. WLST exceptions allow the user to control runtime errors like division by zero. WLST also follows the same syntax as in C++ and Java for an exception handling block.

```
try :
   block statements
except <Exception>, <exceptionRef> : # more than one Exception allowed
   catch block statement
finally:
   cleanup block statement
```

When the WLST interpreter is unable to handle any statement in a block, then it will be terminated on that statement. WLST identifies the exception classes that are inherited from the base exception classes. In WLST, we can define multiple exception classes at single exception block, but it should be separated by comma and enclosed within a parentheses.

If there is no exception raised in the *try* block, then the control reaches the *finally* block without entering the *except* block. The *finally* block is meant for cleanup activities and will be called always. In the *finally* block, it is possible to *disconnect()* from the current connection, call *closeTemplate()*, call *stopRedirecting()*, or call *close()* on file references.

Using the Pass Keyword

To skip any unwanted exceptions, it is possible to use the *pass* keyword. Usually this will be used when the script has loop control flows. The exception could be a bottleneck because if one of the iterations fails, the whole script could get stuck in one of the statements in the block and exit from the execution of that script. While writing WLST scripts, there are some situations where you need a 'do nothing' statement syntactically. That is provided by the *pass* statement.

Raising with Raise

In WLST, *raise* is used to generate or invoke an exception condition. The syntax of this statement allows three comma-separated expressions, which are optional. If no expression is present, WLST will attempt to re-raise the last exception that was raised. This raise statement can be used when we need exception handling with robust scripts. When you pass the expressions to the raise statement, the first two expressions are evaluated to get the objects. These objects are then used to determine the type and value of the exception. Omitted expressions are treated as None. The third expression could be used for traceback objects.

The *raise* keyword is used in exception handling. In the WLST scripts, it is possible to raise any error or exception or user-defined exception. WLST supports Java-based exceptions for generic raise statements with an exception class with a string argument.

```
try:
    raise Exception('SituationalResponse')
except Exception, e:
    print e

java.lang.Exception: SituationalResponse
```

Jython-based WLST Errors

Jython - as any other programming language - also has the capability to deal with errors and exceptions. A useful command is *dumpStack()*, which will display the last exception.

Specifically, this command will display a stack trace from the last exception that occurred while performing a WLST action, and will reset the stack trace. If successful, the *dumpStack* command returns the Throwable object. In the event of an error, the command returns a WLST exception.

The following diagram shows a hierarchy of errors.

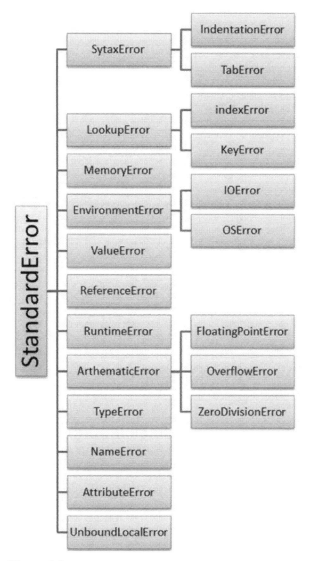

Figure 4.1: *Standard Jython Error Tree*

SyntaxError

This error cannot be handled with the try-except block, because it will be thrown during the script compilation when your syntax is not correct, e.g. missing indentation or improper arguments. The SyntaxError exception could be raised when the script is loaded into the WLST interpreter for parsing. If the script cannot be compiled, WLST will throw a SyntaxError exception and will inform the user where in the script the problem is.

Here is a sample indentation issue that raises the SyntaxError.

```
wls:/offline> try:
...connect('system','weblogic103','t3://adminhost:adminport')
Traceback (innermost last):
  (no code object) at line 0
  File "<console>", line 2
      connect('system','weblogic103','t3://adminhost:adminport')
         ^
SyntaxError: invalid syntax
```

After issuing try block starting, we must use a tab or 4 spaces before the *connect()* command. When the interpreter found that is did not have proper indentation, it raised the SyntaxError.

NameError

WLST will raise the NameError when the name used to do something, like print, is used in some other expression without assigning the value before it was defined. When you are making a first time a script, most of the users encounter these kind of NameErrors.

KeyError

This error can be raised by WLST while using the dictionary objects or map objects, accessed with non-matching key.

```
wls:/offline> urls['b']
Traceback (innermost last):
  File "<console>", line 1, in ?
KeyError: b
```

ValueError

The ValueError is raised by the WLST shell when there is an inappropriate element accessed in a list, such as the value specified for searching in the list with the *index()* method. This requires that you remove the element that does not really exist in the list.

```
wls:/offline> L.index('web2')
Traceback (innermost last):
  File "<console>", line 1, in ?
ValueError: list.index(x): x not in list
AttributeError
wls:/offline> l.remove('web4')
Traceback (innermost last):
  File "<console>", line 1, in ?
ValueError: list.remove(x): x not in list
```

IndexError

The IndexError will be raised by the WLST (Python) shell when the list object, or any sequence object, is accessed with an "out of range" index value.

Here is an example of a list defined with 5 elements:

```
wls:/offline> L
['app1', 'app2', 'app3', 'app4', 'web1']
```

When it is accessed with the "out of range" index value, e.g. 7, then you get the IndexError:

```
wls:/offline> L[7]
Traceback (innermost last):
  File "<console>", line 1, in ?
IndexError: index out of range: 7
```

TypeError

The basic python object types *int*, *str* assignments or expressions, or print statements with concatenation will raise the TypeError.

```
wls:/offline> print 'Number of servers:', 5
Number of servers: 5
wls:/offline>  print 'Number of servers:'+ 5
Traceback (innermost last):
  File "<console>", line 1, in ?
TypeError: cannot concatenate 'str' and 'int' objects
```

WLSTException

The WLSTException is a sub-class of the Java exception class, and it can be thrown when your script or WLST command tries to access the attribute values of current MBeans with the wrong arguments. WLSTException is defined as a Jython class and remember that it is not in the Java class library.

```
wls:/offline>  connect('system','weblogic103','t3://adminhost:adminport')
Connecting to t3://adminhost:adminport with userid system ...
Traceback (innermost last):
  File "<console>", line 1, in ?
  File "<iostream>", line 22, in connect
  File "<iostream>", line 618, in raiseWLSTException
WLSTException: Error occured while performing connect : Error getting the initial context. There is
no server running at t3://adminhost:adminport
Use dumpStack() to view the full stacktrace
This is the top most Exception defined for the WLST scripts. This is extended from regular Java
Exception class.
```

BeanAlreadyExistsException

This is a very common exception that can be thrown by WLST scripts. This exception indicates that the script wants to create a resource that already exists. A very common

---

WLST

scenario is that a script failed due to some exception(s), but has already created some of the resources it should create. If the user corrects the error condition and restarts the script, the resources already created cannot be created again and this exception will be thrown. It is therefore necessary for good scripts to catch this exception for every resource creation if script restarts should be supported. I have experienced this scenario in the following situations:

- Configuring a Managed-Server

- Configuring a new cluster

- Configuring a DataSource

- Configuring a Multi-DataSource

- Configuring a WorkManager

- Configuring a JMS components

Here, you need to UNDO the changes made to that MBean and exit the edit tree. This you can do with *cancelEdit('y')* and *exit()*.

The exception is defined in JMX API, and is thrown when you use the *create()* commands that change existing configuration system resources such as JMS, Managed-Servers, Cluster, JDBC data source, Multi DataSource, etc.

Example:

```
# create a resource
edit()
startEdit()
try:
    < do whatever needed to create your resource >
except BeanAlreadyExistsException:
    # this means the resource or one of the resources already did exist
    < exception handling >

    # do NOT forget to cancel the edit session
    cancelEdit('y')
    exit()
```

The disadvantage here is that you need to open an edit session. The second issue is that you actually need to wrap EACH creation step in a try/catch block, otherwise you will not know which step caused the exception. There are other alternatives to check if an MBean already exists or not. One of them is the *getMBean* function.

Debugging WLST

The best way to identify the WLST script bugs is to use *dumpStack()*. This works best when you are running in the interactive mode. Using *dumpStack()* in a WLST script also works often, but not always.

You can also enable a debug flag when starting the WLST shell:

```
java -Dpython.verbose=debug weblogic.WLST
```

One other option is to use debug("true") or set('DebugEnabled', 'true') in the starting of the WLST script. This will force debug output.

Naming Suggestions for WLST

WLST script can have names that are case sensitive and cannot start with a number. They can contain letters, numbers, and underscore symbols.

Examples:

```
state  State  _state  _2_state_  state_2  StatE
```

Most of us face an issue with what name makes sense for a variable, module, or class while writing the WLST scripts. Just like Java language, you must follow specific naming rules. We can find a keyword list available in WLST with the following commands:

```
wls:/offline> import keyword
wls:/offline> keyword.kwlist
['and', 'assert', 'break', 'class', 'continue', 'def', 'del', 'elif', 'else', 'except', 'exec',
'finally', 'for', 'from', 'global', 'if', 'import', 'in', 'is', 'lambda', 'not', 'or', 'pass',
'print', 'raise', 'return', 'try', 'while', 'yield']
```

- Modules, packages: use lowercase.

- Classes: use Capitalized first letters in the Words; also follow for exceptions that you create.

- Methods, attributes: use lowercase_words

- Local variables: use alphanumeric i, j, sum, x0, etc.

- Globals: use alphanumeric long_descriptive_names

Summary

WLST is the Oracle-preferred and recommended way to administer, manage, change and monitor WebLogic. WLST is a powerful environment based on Jython, which is enriched with many WebLogic commands and WebLogic MBean trees.

Creating Domains with WLST

Creating Domains with WLST

In the first part of the book, I introduced the WebLogic domain as the main administration concept of WebLogic; that is, everything in WebLogic is structured within a domain. Therefore, this first part of the WLST discussion is focused on the domain. We will start with the minimal domain and extend it with more components until we will finally discuss, in the last section of this chapter, a comprehensive but flexible example of how to create a domain with a number of important features.

Introduction to Domains

A domain is the basic administration unit for WebLogic. Each domain has at least one WebLogic instance but can coordinate with more. All resources like JDBC (database connectivity), JMS (messaging), WTC (Tuxedo connectivity), virtual hosts and more are managed together as a single unit.

Besides a dedicated server instance for administrative purposes, a WebLogic domain consists of additional WebLogic Server instances called Managed-Servers. These server instances can be grouped together to form clusters. A domain may have as many clusters as needed. A WebLogic cluster is going to provide scalability and high availability for applications. Clusters can improve performance and provide failover if any of the server instances crash or become unavailable. The servers within a cluster can run on the same machine, known as a vertical cluster, or they can reside on different machines, known as a horizontal cluster. To the end user/client, a cluster appears as a single Oracle WebLogic Server instance.

One of the main responsibilities of the AdminServer is to provide the configuration to all Managed-Server. All configurations will be done on the AdminServer and from the AdminServer distributed to the different Managed-Server(s). Distribution either happens in real-time or at boot time of the Managed-Server, depending on the nature of the configuration change. Besides the static responsibilities, the AdminServer also has dynamic (runtime) responsibilities. One of the runtime responsibilities is to monitor certain parameters like the health of the Managed-Servers or certain central services like JTA. If a domain contains Managed-Servers, then the Managed-Servers are responsible to perform the business logic. The business logic is implemented in application units deployed to these Managed-Servers. Managed-Servers depend on the AdminServer to get the configuration, but Managed-Servers can operate independently of the Administration Server. Managed-Servers will send notifications to the AdminServer in case of state changes so that the AdminServer always has the state of the Managed-Servers.

In the offline mode of WLST, we can configure a simple/customized WebLogic domain. There are two different options for development environment configurations. One is the configuration with a standalone AdminServer in the domain, and the other option is a clustered domain with an AdminServer for administrative purposes and Managed-Servers for application hosting. The second option is the preferred option for all environments, and is also helpful for migration processes. On less powerful machines like personal development machines, the first option becomes handy for development.

Domain Templates

Domain creation is based on templates. Oracle provides a set of templates that are ready to use for constructing domains. Templates are essentially JAR archives with a number of XML files, property files, and other artifacts (e.g. libs you want to automatically distribute). The provided templates are located in the folder WLS_HOME\common\templates\domains for domains and WLS_HOME\common\templates\applications for extensions. The file wls.jar, which is the basic template provided by Oracle, is located under common\templates and will be read while creating a domain using WLST. The new domain will be written using the *writeDomain* command.

Oracle provides a list of tools for creating domains and templates:

- The Configuration Wizard
- The Domain Template Builder
- WLST Offline
- Pack and unpack commands

The *pack* and *unpack* commands provide a simple method for creating domains from the shell; however, they do not enable you to change or extend the contents of your domain. WLST also offers the command *configToScript*, which creates a script based on an existing domain. I recommend being careful with this command as it might not include everything. This command helps to script a new domain based on an existing one, but should only be considered as a starting point for further script development.

Note that starting with WebLogic 12.1.2, the location of the templates has changed.

Template Categories

Templates can be divided into 2 major categories: domain templates and extension templates.

Domain template: This template creates a full domain with potentially all infrastructure components and services. The most used template - wls.jar, which will construct a basic domain - belongs to this category.

Extension template: This template does not define a full domain. Instead, you can define additional applications and/or services you want to add to this domain. This template can only be applied to an already loaded domain template (or configuration). wls_webservice.jar is such an example that adds functionality for advanced Web services, including WSRM, Buffering, and JMS Transport.

You can extend the provided templates with the template builder. Based on real project experiences, I really recommend avoiding this. Whenever possible, try to move all modifications/extensions you want for your domain into an appropriate WLST script. The reason for this involves updates and patches. If you update or patch your WLS installation folder, then you might update your templates if, for example, a template has changed due to a bug correction. In this case you need to re-do all your modifications if changed the template and left it in the default location OR your domain will be based on a potentially buggy template if you saved the modified copy elsewhere. Also, moving to another server may lead to a new installation where you forgot that you changed the default templates. If your modifications are in a WLST script, then they have a much better visibility.

Figure 5.1 shows the content of the basic domain template (wls.jar):

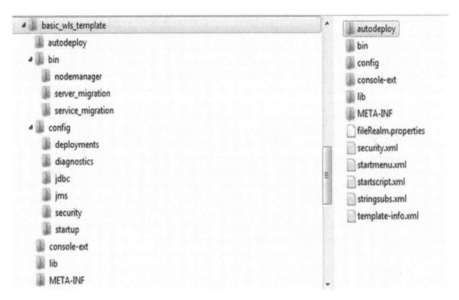

Figure 5.1: *A typical domain template structure*

Templates have to be distinguished between domain templates and extension templates. Domain templates describe the creation of a full domain whereas extension templates add features to a domain. Every template is packed into a JAR file.

Domain templates can be used on their own. In order to use an extension template, you have to either load an existing domain or a domain template first.

The above template consists of a few main XML files that describe the main domain layout and subfolders for resources and extension definitions. The main reason for this is that you can load a template, change and extend it (including libs and deployments), and save it as your own custom template.

Custom templates have great potential to make your scripts and setups easier but - as stated above - there are risks when you update your WebLogic version.

It is possible to create your own templates. Please refer to the links in the reference section at the end of the book for further readings as this topic is out of scope for this book.

Problems and Alternatives to Custom Templates

Using extension templates is basically painless for most environments. But if you want to create your domain with specific settings or additional files, you have different options.

The first option would be to copy the default template (in most cases called wls.jar in the WebLogic template folder) and change the content of the XML description files or add files. This is an easy task and also pretty effective. But this also has some hidden disadvantages. The main disadvantage I have faced while using this approach was that whenever you want to upgrade to another WebLogic version, you MUST NOT forget that you are using a custom domain template based on a specific WebLogic version, even if you have copied and modified it. You also need to re-create another custom template with the same changes, but based on the default WebLogic template from that new version.

This gets even worse if you are dealing with different WebLogic versions in your environment at the same time, which is actually very often the case.

WLST can of course work with templates (see next sections). It is possible to read templates in WLST using the *readtemplate* method. Therefore, a very elegant alternative to the problem mentioned above would be to always use the default template provided by Oracle but change it on the fly after it was opened by WLST. Unfortunately, I have not found a way either documented or undocumented to modify the template files "on-the-fly" without modifying them on disk. As all are XML files, I had expected to get a document object back after reading the template and then get a chance to modify the content using something such as XPath technologies.

Another alternative, which I actually prefer as it eliminates the above problem, is to use the default template, create the basic domain, and after the files have been created use file operation technologies to change the files written to the domain. As WLST domain (=offline) operations have to happen on the box where the domain is created anyway, network is not an issue. This approach is very useful as it eliminates the need to worry about version-dependent custom templates. It has also another benefit as all changes you make are visible in a script and therefore can be documented. If you only modify template files, it is very hard without additional documentation to find out what exactly you have changed and why.

WLST also offers the Jython file system - as it is based on Jython - and OS access functionalities that can be used to modify files. The following little WLST script will show one example. I expect that all UNIX admins might be a bit upset but this is only an example, but I have actually used this in production quite well.

The following WLST script example could be used after domain creation but still as part of the WLST script in order to exchange Xms, Xmx, PermSize and MaxPermSize settings for the AdminServer. For the Managed-Server, this can be configured in the server start section of the domain if a NodeManager is used (recommended). Note that this script will demonstrate how to do system calls. In this case, this script will use a series of *sed* calls in order to modify the setDomainEnv.sh file that was created in the bin directory.

```
< ... readtemplate, do settings, ... writeDomain, ... >

domainLocationBinDir = '/wls_domains/testdomain/bin/'

os.system('sed \'s/\\-Xms256m\\ \\-Xmx512m/\\-Xms1024m\\ \\-Xmx1024m/\' '+
        domainLocationBinDir+'setDomainEnv.sh > '+domainLocationBinDir+'tmp1.sh')
os.system('sed \'s/\\-Xms512m\\ \\-Xmx512m/\\-Xms1024m\\ \\-Xmx1024m/\' '+
        domainLocationBinDir+'tmp1.sh > '+ domainLocationBinDir+'tmp2.sh')
os.system('sed \'s/\\-XX:PermSize=128m/\\-XX:PermSize=196m/\' '+domainLocationBinDir+'tmp2.sh > '
        +domainLocationBinDir+'tmp3.sh')
os.system('sed \'s/\\-XX:PermSize=48m/\\-XX:PermSize=196m/\' '+domainLocationBinDir+'tmp3.sh > '
        +domainLocationBinDir+'tmp4.sh')
os.system('sed \'s/\\-XX:MaxPermSize=128m/\\-XX:PermSize=256m/\' '+domainLocationBinDir+'tmp4.sh > '
        +domainLocationBinDir+'tmp5.sh')
os.system('cp '+domainLocationBinDir+'tmp5.sh '+domainLocationBinDir+'setDomainEnv.sh')
os.system('chmod +x '+domainLocationBinDir+'setDomainEnv.sh')
os.system('rm '+domainLocationBinDir+'tmp*.sh')
```

(Note that the line breaks must be removed in order to run this script)

The same idea of using system calls after the domain creation can be used in order to extend the domain with custom files (like additional MBeans, libs or configuration files). Instead of extending the default WLS template, it is also possible to just create the base domain and then use an os.system('tar ...') tar call in order to extract a prepared tar file on top of the newly created domain.

This approach has several benefits:
  a) It is independent from the WLS template, and
  b) The same command can be integrated in the enroll script on the remote machines so that these required files can also be added to the remote Managed-Servers after the domain was enrolled.

Creation of a Simple Domain

The following example creates a simple test domain with just one server (the Administration Server).

💾 create_simple_domain

```
###################################################################
# Create a very simple domain with only one admin server !!
###################################################################

print 'Creating the domain...'
domainsDirectory='/mydomains';
domainName = 'TestDomain';
readTemplate('/opt/wls/wlserver_10.3/common/templates/domains/wls.jar');

# Setting listen address/port
cd('/Server/AdminServer')
set('ListenAddress','localhost');
set('ListenPort',7001);

# SSL Settings
create('AdminServer','SSL')
cd('SSL/AdminServer')
set('Enabled', 'true');
set('ListenPort',47002);

# Setting the username/password
cd('/Security/base_domain/User/weblogic');
cmo.setName('weblogic');
cmo.setPassword('test1234');

# Set some important domain options
setOption('CreateStartMenu', 'false');
setOption('ServerStartMode', 'prod');
setOption('JavaHome', '/usr/lib/jvm/jre-1.6.0-openjdk.x86_64');

setOption('OverwriteDomain', 'false');

print 'Writing Domain: '+ domainsDirectory+'/'+domainName;
writeDomain( domainsDirectory+'/'+domainName);
closeTemplate();
print 'Domain Created';

connUri = 't3://localhost:7001';
print 'Starting the Admin Server to test system ...';
startServer('AdminServer', domainName , connUri, 'weblogic', 'test1234',
domainsDirectory+'/'+domainName, 'true', 60000, 'false');
print 'Started the Admin Server';

# Connecting to the Admin Server
connect('weblogic','test1234',connUri);
print 'Connected';

print 'Shutting down the Admin Server...';
shutdown();
print 'Exiting...';
exit();
```

Now let us explore the different sections of this script in more detail. Note that the complete script is based on offline WLST, which means that we are basically creating and working on the config.xml file (and others as needed).

First we will read the basic template using *readTemplate(…)* for a domain with the name wls.jar, which is provided with the standard WebLogic installation. This will read in the structure and the necessary MBean definitions into memory and thereby make the MBean structure available for the next steps.

This command will open an existing domain template file, which will then be the basis for creating a new domain. When you navigate in the domain template, you are placed into the configuration bean hierarchy for that domain template, and the prompt is updated to reflect the current location in the configuration hierarchy. WLST traverses the hierarchical structure of the configuration beans using commands such as the *cd* command in a similar way that you would navigate a file system in a UNIX or Windows command shell.

Security settings are always special configuration items. Certain security settings are only available for WLST during domain creation and not while updating a domain. During the design of WLST scripts, which also configures security aspects, it is important to take this into account. Also, certain security aspects are only configurable using the offline mode.

Therefore, in the script section, we can now access the AdminServer MBean and change the values as we require (like port, listener, and SSL settings).

It is very important to define the user and password for the administrative access. Note that this does not create the credentials for the server to log in; it creates the user record in the internal LDAP so that the Administration Server and also Managed-Server can authenticate themselves.

Finally, we set some domain definitions. *ServerStartMode* is an important setting that should always be set to "prod" if the domain is not used for development. Personally I also set my development domains to prod so that I cannot, just by chance, overwrite values.

The final script part starts the Administration Server from the WLST script in order to test if the domain was written correctly and that the server can start.

If you now run this script it will create your domain, start the AdminServer, test the connection, and finally stop the AdminServer again.

💾 start/test_adminserver

```
Initializing WebLogic Scripting Tool (WLST) ...

Welcome to WebLogic Server Administration Scripting Shell

Type help() for help on available commands

Creating the domain...
Writing Domain: /domains/TestDomain
Domain Created
Starting the Admin Server to test system ...
Starting weblogic server ...
WLST-WLS-1352361843103: <Nov 8, 2012 9:04:04 AM CET> <Info> <Security> <BEA-090905> <Disabling
CryptoJ JCE Provider self-integrity check for better startup performance. To enable this check,
specify -Dweblogic.security.allowCryptoJDefaultJCEVerification=true>
WLST-WLS-1352361843103: <Nov 8, 2012 9:04:04 AM CET> <Info> <Security> <BEA-090906> <Changing the
default Random Number Generator in RSA CryptoJ from ECDRBG to FIPS186PRNG. To disable this change,
specify -Dweblogic.security.allowCryptoJDefaultPRNG=true>
WLST-WLS-1352361843103: <Nov 8, 2012 9:04:04 AM CET> <Info> <WebLogicServer> <BEA-000377> <Starting
WebLogic Server with OpenJDK 64-Bit Server VM Version 20.0-b11 from Sun Microsystems Inc.>
[...]
WLST-WLS-1352361843103: <Nov 8, 2012 9:04:22 AM CET> <Notice> <Server> <BEA-002613> <Channel
"Default" is now listening on 127.0.0.1:47001 for protocols iiop, t3, ldap, snmp, http.>
```

```
WLST-WLS-1352361843103: <Nov 8, 2012 9:04:22 AM CET> <Notice> <Server> <BEA-002613> <Channel
"DefaultSecure" is now listening on 127.0.0.1:47002 for protocols iiops, t3s, ldaps, https.>
WLST-WLS-1352361843103: <Nov 8, 2012 9:04:22 AM CET> <Notice> <WebLogicServer> <BEA-000329> <Started
WebLogic Admin Server "AdminServer" for domain "TestDomain" running in Production Mode>
WLST-WLS-1352361843103: <Nov 8, 2012 9:04:22 AM CET> <Notice> <WebLogicServer> <BEA-000365> <Server
state changed to RUNNING>
WLST-WLS-1352361843103: <Nov 8, 2012 9:04:22 AM CET> <Notice> <WebLogicServer> <BEA-000360> <Server
started in RUNNING mode>
Server started successfully.
Started the Admin Server
Connecting to t3://localhost:47001 with userid weblogic ...
Successfully connected to Admin Server 'AdminServer' that belongs to domain 'TestDomain'.

Warning: An insecure protocol was used to connect to the
server. To ensure on-the-wire security, the SSL port or
Admin port should be used instead.

Connected
Shutting down the Admin Server...
Shutting down the server AdminServer with force=false while connected to AdminServer ...
WLST-WLS-1352361843103: <Nov 8, 2012 9:04:40 AM CET> <Alert> <WebLogicServer> <BEA-000396> <Server
shutdown has been requested by weblogic>
WLST-WLS-1352361843103: <Nov 8, 2012 9:04:40 AM CET> <Notice> <WebLogicServer> <BEA-000365> <Server
state changed to SUSPENDING>
WLST-WLS-1352361843103: <Nov 8, 2012 9:04:40 AM CET> <Notice> <HTTP> <BEA-101278> <There are no
active sessions. The Web service is ready to suspend.>
WLST-WLS-1352361843103: <Nov 8, 2012 9:04:40 AM CET> <Notice> <WebLogicServer> <BEA-000365> <Server
state changed to ADMIN>
WLST-WLS-1352361843103: <Nov 8, 2012 9:04:40 AM CET> <Notice> <WebLogicServer> <BEA-000365> <Server
state changed to SHUTTING_DOWN>
WLST-WLS-1352361843103: <Nov 8, 2012 9:04:40 AM CET> <Notice> <Server> <BEA-002607> <Channel
"DefaultSecure" listening on 127.0.0.1:47002 was shutdown.>
WLST-WLS-1352361843103: <Nov 8, 2012 9:04:40 AM CET> <Notice> <Server> <BEA-002607> <Channel
"Default" listening on 127.0.0.1:47001 was shutdown.>
WLST-WLS-1352361843103: Stopped draining WLST-WLS-1352361843103
WLST-WLS-1352361843103: Stopped draining WLST-WLS-1352361843103
WLST lost connection to the WebLogic Server that you were
connected to, this may happen if the server was shutdown or
partitioned. You will have to re-connect to the server once the
server is available.
Disconnected from weblogic server: AdminServer
Disconnected from weblogic server:
Exiting...
```

Note: Starting the AdminServer in a WLST script is nice for testing but is NOT a real production scenario. Under the cover, WLST does a little bit more and especially does not (!) use the start scripts generated in your domain folder.

Especially examine the following line in the script:

```
startServer('AdminServer', domainName , connUri, 'weblogic', 'test1234',
domainsDirectory+'/'+domainName, 'true', 60000, 'false');
```

The script starts the AdminServer and also provides a username and password.

The normal way to start the AdminServer (unless you are using the NodeManager, which is rather uncommon) is to use the generated startWeblogic.sh script, which is generated in your root folder of your new domain.

The addTemplate() Command

The *addTemplate* command is used to load extension templates. This function is similar to "Extend existing domain" in the GUI mode of the domain configuration.

Server Identity

The next step is to start your domain using the startWeblogic.sh script, which is generated in your root folder of your new domain. This will reveal a weakness of the domain generation script of the previous section:

```
[...]
<Nov 8, 2012 8:54:00 AM CET> <Info> <WebLogicServer> <BEA-000377> <Starting WebLogic Server with
OpenJDK 64-Bit Server VM Version 20.0-b11 from Sun Microsystems Inc.>
<Nov 8, 2012 8:54:01 AM CET> <Info> <Management> <BEA-141107> <Version: WebLogic Server 10.3.5.0  Fri
Apr 1 20:20:06 PDT 2011 1398638 >
<Nov 8, 2012 8:54:02 AM CET> <Info> <Security> <BEA-090065> <Getting boot identity from user.>
Enter username to boot WebLogic server:weblogic
Enter password to boot WebLogic server:
<Nov 8, 2012 8:54:14 AM CET> <Notice> <WebLogicServer> <BEA-000365> <Server state changed to
STARTING>
<Nov 8, 2012 8:54:14 AM CET> <Info> <WorkManager> <BEA-002900> <Initializing self-tuning thread pool>
<Nov 8, 2012 8:54:14 AM CET> <Notice> <Log Management> <BEA-170019> <The server log file
/domains/TestDomain/servers/AdminServer/logs/AdminServer.log is opened. All server side log events
will be written to this file.>
<Nov 8, 2012 8:54:18 AM CET> <Notice> <Security> <BEA-090082> <Security initializing using security
realm myrealm.>
<Nov 8, 2012 8:54:22 AM CET> <Notice> <WebLogicServer> <BEA-000365> <Server state changed to STANDBY>
<Nov 8, 2012 8:54:22 AM CET> <Notice> <WebLogicServer> <BEA-000365> <Server state changed to
STARTING>
[...]
] The system is vulnerable to security attacks, since it trusts certificates signed by the demo
trusted CA.>
<Nov 8, 2012 8:54:28 AM CET> <Notice> <Server> <BEA-002613> <Channel "Default" is now listening on
127.0.0.1:47001 for protocols iiop, t3, ldap, snmp, http.>
<Nov 8, 2012 8:54:28 AM CET> <Notice> <Server> <BEA-002613> <Channel "DefaultSecure" is now listening
on 127.0.0.1:47002 for protocols iiops, t3s, ldaps, https.>
<Nov 8, 2012 8:54:28 AM CET> <Notice> <WebLogicServer> <BEA-000329> <Started WebLogic Admin Server
"AdminServer" for domain "TestDomain" running in Production Mode>
<Nov 8, 2012 8:54:28 AM CET> <Notice> <WebLogicServer> <BEA-000365> <Server state changed to RUNNING>
<Nov 8, 2012 8:54:28 AM CET> <Notice> <WebLogicServer> <BEA-000360> <Server started in RUNNING mode>
```

Examine the lines in bold. You need to provide username and password, which might be ok for your private development instance, but as soon as the WebLogic instances are managed by an administrator group or must be started/restarted automatically in production environments, this is not acceptable. The reason is that somehow the AdminServer (same issue exists for the Managed-Server) needs to know what its own identity is as the server process must also authenticate itself.

The WebLogic solution is a file called boot.properties, which contains the user and password for the server itself. During the first start of the server (admin or managed) the password and username in this file will be encrypted. This property file is located in the <domain>/servers/<servername>/security directory.

Let us extend our script so that this file will be generated during domain setup:

🖫 create_simple_domain_(extended)

```
####################################################################
# Create a very simple domain with only one admin server !!
####################################################################

from java.io import FileInputStream
from java.io import File
```

```
print 'Creating the domain...'
domainsDirectory='/user_data/weblogic_domains';
domainName = 'TestDomain';
readTemplate('/opt/wls/wlserver_10.3/common/templates/domains/wls.jar');

# Setting listen address/port
cd('/Server/AdminServer')
set('ListenAddress','localhost');
set('ListenPort',47001);

# SSL Settings
create('AdminServer','SSL')
cd('SSL/AdminServer')
set('Enabled', 'true');
set('ListenPort',47002);

# Setting the username/password
cd('/Security/'+ domainName +'/User/weblogic');
cmo.setName('weblogic');
cmo.setPassword('test1234');

setOption('CreateStartMenu', 'false');
setOption('ServerStartMode', 'prod');
setOption('JavaHome', '/usr/lib/jvm/jre-1.6.0-openjdk.x86_64');
setOption('OverwriteDomain', 'false');

print 'Writing Domain: '+ domainsDirectory+'/'+domainName;
writeDomain( domainsDirectory+'/'+domainName);
closeTemplate();
print 'Domain Created';

# Create boot.properties file !
os.makedirs(domainsDirectory+"/"+domainName+ "/servers/AdminServer/security")
f=open(domainsDirectory+"/"+domainName +
"/servers/AdminServer/security/boot.properties" , 'w')
f.write('username=weblogic')
f.write('password=test1234')
f.flush()
f.close()

connUri = 't3://localhost:47001';
print 'Starting the Admin Server to test system ...';
startServer('AdminServer', domainName , connUri, 'weblogic', 'test1234',
domainsDirectory+'/'+domainName,'true',60000,'false');
print 'Started the Admin Server';

# Connecting to the Admin Server
connect('weblogic','test1234',connUri);
print 'Connected';

print 'Shutting down the Admin Server...';
shutdown();
print 'Exiting...';
exit();
```

Examine the marked section. This script creates the security directory and borrows the "File" API from Java in order to create the boot.properties file.

After the script has finished (remember the AdminServer was started for the connection test) the file contains the encrypted values:

```
password={AES}s5cM1qVtFbJ/nKIgk68K0fV9K6JGpAGExf4rP0Mxsvs\=
username={AES}6F/9mt88/+yxz2bgn0FvunWEJE+CfE1oXe2xGJMM/eg\=
```

Now we have created a minimal domain with nothing else but the AdminServer. However, this domain is ready for use and fully functional. In the next sections we will extend this domain step-by-step in order to accommodate more features and functionalities.

This script will create the same domain as the script in the previous section, but due to the create identity boot file, there won't be any standard input requests for user or password.

Later in the book we will discuss a better and more secure way to work with user credentials at the client side.

Configure Domain and Server Logging Settings

The domain creates log files and every server - including the AdminServer - also creates log files. Especially for production systems, log files must be saved for future reviews. Log files must also be rotated in order to limit size or separate timeframes. For example, this may result in having one log file for each day.

On production systems, it is a good practice to rotate log files once per day. This makes it easy for scheduled processes to move old log files to a backup or log server in order to save disk space and to avoid filling the local disk with logs. For example, rotating logs every day at 2am means that a scheduled process can run at 2:30am and move the old log file away.

The Domain Log File

The following in an example for changing the settings for the domain log.

Offline example for rotating based on time during domain creation:

```
create('TestDomain', 'Log')
cd('/Log/TestDomain')
cmo.setRotationType('byTime')
cmo.setRotationTime('02:00')
cmo.setFileTimeSpan(24)
cmo.setNumberOfFilesLimited(true)
cmo.setFileCount(7)
cmo.setFileMinSize(10000)
```

During domain creation, we need to create the "Log" entry underneath the domain first, otherwise the *cd* command will fail. Then you can set the desired log settings. You can set the rotation time based on size or time, and you can set log file sizes and amount of files, as well as a number of other settings. The settings that are available and which make sense depend on the rotation time.

Offline example for rotating based on size during domain creation:

```
create('TestDomain', 'Log')
cd('/Log/TestDomain')
cmo.setRotationType('bySize')
cmo.setRotateLogOnStartup(false)
cmo.setFileCount(18)
cmo.setNumberOfFilesLimited(false)
cmo.setFileMinSize(10000)
```

For the domain itself, a default (even if empty) LOG branch will be created if not done by you (see above). This means that in this case for an online script, we do not need to create this MBean. Therefore, in the online example below, the create statement is missing. Log file settings must be done on the Edit-MBeanServer, therefore we need to switch to the edit mode first and then we can change these settings.

Online example:

```
connect(...)
edit()
startEdit()
cd('/Log/TestDomain')
cmo.setRotationType('bySize')
cmo.setRotateLogOnStartup(false)
cmo.setFileCount(18)
cmo.setNumberOfFilesLimited(false)
cmo.setFileMinSize(10000)
activate()
disconnect()
```

The Administration Server Logs

Logs for the Administration Server are a little bit different than for the domain. With the AdminServer we are touching a real server, which consists of multiple log files. Not all of them can be configured using WLST-MBeans. The files that can be configured are the server log file and the server access file. These two are located in two different MBeans

Offline example while creating the domain for AdminServer log-settings:

```
# change settings for the server log
cd('/Server/AdminServer')
create('AdminServer', 'Log')
cd('/Servers/AdminServer/Log/AdminServer')

# set rotation type , time and other information
cmo.setRotationType('byTime')
cmo.setRotationTime('02:00')
cmo.setFileTimeSpan(24)
cmo.setNumberOfFilesLimited(true)
cmo.setFileCount(7)
cmo.setRotateLogOnStartup(true)

cd('/Server/'+servername)
create(servername, 'WebServer')
cd('/Server/'+servername+'/WebServer/'+servername)

# now do the same for the access log but you need another mbean
create(servername, 'WebServerLog')
cd('/Server/'+servername+'/WebServer/'+servername+'/WebServerLog/'+servername)
cmo.setRotationTime('02:00')
cmo.setRotationType('byTime')
```

```
cmo.setFileTimeSpan(24)
cmo.setFileCount(14)
cmo.setFileName(serverLogPath+'/access.log')
```

The above script only shows some of the possible settings available for logging. In addition to the above, settings like LogFileRotationDir, filters, and more can be configured.

Changing the Logs of all Managed-Servers

The following is actually an example for a common server farm requirement, especially for production systems. For production systems, it is common to dedicate the AdminServer to administration tasks only and delegate the application work to all the Managed-Servers. This means that usually all Managed-Servers have different log file requirements than the AdminServer.

This script shows two nice WLST features:

- Iterating over all servers of a domain
- Settings options depending on a server name

Example script for changing log settings for all Managed-Servers but NOT for the AdminServer:

```
# connect to the adminserver and start an edit session
connect(...)
edit()
startEdit()

print 'Iterate over the managed servers and set the log settings for all managed servers ';
domainConfig()

# get the list of servers from the config MBean tree
svrs = cmo.getServers()

# switch to the domain runtime tree
domainRuntime()
for server in svrs:
        # Do not set the log settings for the adminserver
        myServerName = server.getName()
        if myServerName != 'AdminServer':
                # set the log settings
                cd('/Servers/'+myServerName+'/Log/'+myServerName)
                cmo.setRotationType('byTime')
                cmo.setRotationTime('02:00')
                cmo.setFileTimeSpan(24)
                cmo.setNumberOfFilesLimited(true)
                cmo.setFileCount(7)
                cmo.setRotateLogOnStartup(true)

# activate the changes
activate()
disconnect()
```

The normal log file MBean for a server is located at:

```
/Servers/<serverName>/Log/<serverName>.
```

For example, for the AdminServer this is /Servers/AdminServer/Log/AdminServer. The log file MBean for HTTP access is located at:

```
/Servers/<serverName>/WebServer/<serverName>/WebServerLog/<serverName>
```

For production and production-like systems, it is necessary to separate the logs from the domain installation. Logs will grow and will likely need other file system access rights. Logs should also be saved on their own file system to protect the domains. For all production systems I have been involved with, logs have been saved outside of the domain file system tree.

In order to change the location of all logs, there are a couple of steps necessary as we are talking about different files. The files involved include

- The domain log
- The AdminServer log
- The AdminServer stdout, stderr
- The AdminServer access log
- The logs of each Managed-Server
- The stdout, stderr of each Managed-Server
- The access log of each Managed-Server

The following table provides an overview what needs to be done in order to really move all logs to a separate location.

domain log	Can be changed via WLST. Should be changed during domain creation:
	Use
	`cd('/Log/<domainName>')`
	`cmo.setFileName(<new log location>)`
	to change the location of this log file

AdminServer log	Can be changed via WLST. Should be changed during domain creation:
	Use
	`[.. mbean creation if needed ...]`
	`cd('/Server/AdminServer/Log/AdminServer')`
	`cmo.setFileName(<new log location and name>)`
	to change the location of this log file

AdminServer stdout, stderr	This cannot be done with WLST as the AdminServer is normally started using the startWeblogic script from the domain Root. What you can do is to overwrite this file during domain creation and add system redirections.

	e.g. for Linux replace the last line this script with
	`${DOMAIN_HOME}/bin/startWebLogic.sh $*  >> <outfile`
	`location> 2>> <errorfile location>`

AdminServer access log	Can be changed via WLST. Should be changed during domain creation:
	Use
	`[.. mbean creation if needed ...]`
	`cd('/Server/AdminServer/WebServer/AdminServer/WebServerLo`
	`g/AdminServer')`
	`cmo.setFileName(<new access log location and name>)`
	to change the location of this log file

logs of each Managed-Server	Can be changed via WLST. Should be changed during domain creation:
	Use
	`[.. mbean creation if needed ...]`
	`cd('/Server/<servername>/Log/<servername>)`
	`cmo.setFileName(<new log location and name>)`
	to change the location of this log file

stdout, stderr of each Managed-Server	This really depends how you start the Managed-Server. If you start the Managed-Server with a script, then you can do the same as described above for the AdminServer out/err If you start the Managed-Server using the NodeManager (which is the preferred way) you can do this via WLST. In this case you need to add two arguments to the ServerStart MBean. (See adding Managed-Server section for more details). You need to add the options -Dweblogic.Stdout=<outfile> and -Dweblogic.Stderr=<errorfile>

access log of each Managed-Server	Can be changed via WLST. Should be changed during domain creation:
	Use
	`[.. mbean creation if needed ...]`
	`cd('/Server/'+servername+'/WebServer/'+servername+'/WebSe`
	`rverLog/'+servername)`
	`cmo.setFileName(<new log path>+'/access.log')`
	to change the location of this log file

Table 5.1: Changing Logs

In production systems, it has worked out well if you combine all logs from one machine in a single place. For example, you can use "/logs" as root folder for all logs and then create a directory for each domain under this root folder. In the domain folder you can place the domain log(s), and in the domain folder you can create a subfolder for each server (including the AdminServer). The creation of these directories can be done with WLST while you configure your domain.

For example:

```
domainLogPath = <logsDirectory>+"/"+<domainName>;
try:
    os.makedirs(domainLogPath);
except:
    print 'Unable to create domain root log path - please check !';
print('Setting Domain Log...');
create(<domainName>, 'Log')
cd('/Log/'+<domainName>)
cmo.setFileName(domainLogPath+'/'+<name of domain log>)
```

Note that the complete domain creation example will contain this.

Configure Domain Log Filters

In every WebLogic domain exists a domain-wide log file. The domain log filter specifies which messages are sent to the domain log. The message must pass all criteria in the filter to be logged. By default, messages are not filtered so that all messages are reported to the log. For example, it is possible to filter by user-id or set a minimum level of severity or filter by subsystem.

The following two scripts show examples of creating log filters for the domain log.

The first example sets a filter in order to filter all events that are ERROR from the local machine or not (!) coming from 'martin':

```
cd('/')
cmo.createLogFilter('LogFilter-F1')

cd('/LogFilters/LogFilter-F1')
cmo.setFilterExpression('(USERID != \'martin\') OR (MACHINE = \'localhost\') AND (SEVERITY =
\'ERROR\')')
```

The second example creates a filter in order to log all events from the subsystem 'test' or from the user 'abcdefg':

```
cd('/')
cmo.createLogFilter('LogFilter-F2')

cd('/LogFilters/LogFilter-F2')
cmo.setFilterExpression('(SUBSYSTEM = \'test\') OR (USERID = \'abcdefg\')')
```

Activate log4j

WebLogic is using an implementation based on the Java Logging APIs by default. Most applications are using log4j. Many administrators have experience in building log file monitors and parsers based on the log4j syntax. The WebLogic log files can be changed to also use log4j.

The following script defines a function that can be used to change the logging implementation to log4j.

The WLST script to enable Log4j Logger on a WebLogic Server is as follows. WebLogic logging services use an implementation based on the Java:

```
def changeLoggingToLog4J(serverName):
    edit()
    startEdit()
    cd ('/Servers/'+serverName+'/Log/'+serverName)
    cmo.setLog4jLoggingEnabled(true)
    save()
    activate()
```

Log4j in WebLogic is available only for server-side and not for client-side logging.

Cluster

Besides the Administration Server, Managed-Servers can be grouped into clusters. Every WebLogic domain can host multiple clusters, but each Managed-Server can only be a member of one cluster (if at all). Every cluster can (but does not need to) include a Managed-Server hosted on different machines. As described in the introduction, there are two different communication models for clusters: Unicast and Multicast.

First of all, let us create one cluster for each communication model with only the necessary configuration parameters.

Creating a unicast cluster:

```
cd('/')
cmo.createCluster('Cluster-UnicastTest')

cd('/Clusters/Cluster-UnicastTest')
cmo.setClusterMessagingMode('unicast')
```

In WLST, switch to root and use this MBean (cmo) to create a new cluster object. Afterwards we are only setting the cluster mode to *unicast*.

Creating a multicast cluster:

```
cd('/')
cmo.createCluster('Cluster-MulticastTest')

cd('/Clusters/Cluster-MulticastTest')
cmo.setClusterMessagingMode('multicast')
cmo.setMulticastAddress('239.192.0.0')
cmo.setMulticastPort(12345)
```

In WLST, switch to root and use this MBean (cmo) to create a new cluster object. Afterwards we are setting the cluster mode to *multicast*. In addition, we need to set the multicast broadcast address and port.

Multicast address: enter the multicast address for the cluster. Cluster members that communicate with each other use this multicast address. The default value is 239.192.0.0. You can choose valid multicast address range of 224.0.0.1 through 239.255.255.255.

Multicast port: enter the multicast port for the cluster. This multicast port is used for cluster members to communicate with each other. The default value is 7001. Here you can use any valid values for multicast ports ranging from 1 through 65534. The ports are not enabled to serve multicast for most machines in real-time. Multicast uses UDP protocol.

Now let us as add another unicast cluster with some more configuration options:

```
cd('/Clusters/Cluster-UnicastTest')
cmo.setNumberOfServersInClusterAddress(3)
cmo.setDefaultLoadAlgorithm('weight-based')
cmo.setClusterType('none')
cmo.setPersistSessionsOnShutdown(false)
cmo.setReplicationChannel('ReplicationChannel')
cmo.setSecureReplicationEnabled(false)
```

NumberOfServersInClusterAddress: This is the amount of servers the cluster will include in the cluster address. This option will not be used if the address is explicitly set. Usually WebLogic maintains this setting automatically.

DefaultLoadAlgorithm: This option specifies the default way load-balancing is used between the appropriate servers of the cluster. This setting only takes effect if it is not overwritten. Options include round-robin (one after the other), weight-based (round-robin with defined weight for each server), or random (random access).

Note the attribute *ClusterType*. This specifies a possibility to cluster between clusters hosted in DIFFERENT WebLogic domains. WebLogic supports three different settings: *none* (own cluster only), *man* (synchronous replication), and *wan* (asynchronous replication).

Here is an example for setting up the cluster in order to replicate to a remote cluster in a different domain:

```
cd('/Clusters/MartinTest_Cluster')
cmo.setClusterType('man')
cmo.setPersistSessionsOnShutdown(false)
cmo.setReplicationChannel('ReplicationChannel')
cmo.setRemoteClusterAddress('192.178.34.123')
cmo.setSecureReplicationEnabled(false)
```

If *wan* is used, which normally means replication across datacenters, the sessions must be stored in a database. Therefore a datasource must be provided for this type of replication:

```
cmo.setClusterType('wan')
cmo.setRemoteClusterAddress('11.22.33.44')
cmo.setDataSourceForSessionPersistence(getMBean('/SystemResources/Prototype_Datasource'))
```

Singleton services are special services you can implement which must be available only once in the whole cluster. Therefore these services will be migrated automatically if the server they are hosted on fails.

Define a singleton service:

```
cd('/')
cmo.createSingletonService('SingletonService-Test')

cd('/SingletonServices/SingletonService-Test')
cmo.setClassName('de.book.test.singleton1')
cmo.setCluster(getMBean('/Clusters/MartinTest_Cluster'))
cmo.setUserPreferredServer(getMBean('/Servers/MartinTest_Domain_MS1'))
set('ConstrainedCandidateServers',jarray.array([ObjectName('com.bea:Name=MartinTest_Domain_MS2,Type=S
erver'), ObjectName('com.bea:Name=MartinTest_Domain_MS1,Type=Server')], ObjectName))
```

New Dynamic Cluster Feature

WebLogic 12.1.2 has added a complete new way of working with clusters. Up to WebLogic 12.1.1, a cluster was defined out of a list of already defined servers. The new feature is called dynamic clusters. The main concept is that the cluster member (servers) will not be defined individually in the WebLogic configuration but will be constructed based on a server template. A server template is basically a blueprint that is used to create Managed-Servers.

With dynamic clusters it is easy to scale up. During setup of the dynamic cluster, the administrator will set the maximum number of server instances you will need to cope with peak loads. WebLogic will then create the different server instances based on the server template and will replace the so-called calculated attributes during the creation.

Calculated attributes include the name of the server and a number of optional values like different ports, destination machines, and network channels (listen ports). Server names, for example, will be constructed out of a given prefix string and an index. The *CalculatedListenPorts* attributes defines how server ports are calculated. Ports that can be calculated include the plain and SSL port for the default channel, replication ports, and other network channels. Port calculations can also be disabled. The cluster configurations *CalculatedMachineNames* and *MachineNameMatchExpression* define the way WebLogic will assign servers to machines.

Here is an example for creating a dynamic cluster:

```
cd('/')
cmo.createCluster('Cluster-12436')

cd('/Clusters/Cluster-12436')
```

```
cmo.setClusterMessagingMode('unicast')

cd('/ServerTemplates/Cluster-12436-Template')
cmo.setCluster(getMBean('/Clusters/Cluster-12436'))

cd('/Clusters/Cluster-12436/DynamicServers/Cluster-12436')
cmo.setServerTemplate(getMBean('/ServerTemplates/Cluster-12436-Template'))
cmo.setMaximumDynamicServerCount(5)
cmo.setCalculatedListenPorts(true)
cmo.setCalculatedMachineNames(false)
cmo.setCalculatedListenPorts(true)
cmo.setServerNamePrefix('Cluster-12436-')
```

Server Templates

Server templates are new configuration items in WLS 12.1.2 which allow an administrator to define a template for a dynamic server. This template can get quite complex as WebLogic offers a huge number of settings for a Managed-Server. This includes general settings like machine, ports, protocols, and network channel. It also includes special dynamic settings like settings for replication group, cluster weight, replication ports, and preferred secondary group. It also can include settings for server services like JMS configurations. In addition to the well-known categories, templates can be used to define configurations in many other aspects of WebLogic, such as security settings.

Here is an example of creating a server template:

```
cd('/')
cmo.createServerTemplate('ServerTemplate-1234')

cd('/ServerTemplates/ServerTemplate-1234')
cmo.setJMSThreadPoolSize(0)
cmo.setXMLRegistry(None)
cmo.setXMLEntityCache(None)

cd('/ServerTemplates/ServerTemplate-1234/TransactionLogJDBCStore/ServerTemplate-1234')
cmo.setEnabled(false)
```

A more complex template will be demonstrated in the following WLST script. Always keep in mind that, more or less, all settings that are available for Managed-Servers can be part of such a template.

```
cd('/')
cmo.createServerTemplate('Cluster-12436-Template')

cd('/ServerTemplates/Cluster-12436-Template')
cmo.setListenPort(7100)

cd('/ServerTemplates/Cluster-12436-Template/SSL/Cluster-12436-Template')
cmo.setListenPort(8100)

cd('/ServerTemplates/Cluster-12436-Template/WebServer/Cluster-12436-Template/WebServerLog/Cluster-
12436-Template')
cmo.setNumberOfFilesLimited(false)

cd('/ServerTemplates/Cluster-12436-Template')
cmo.setListenPort(7100)

cd('/ServerTemplates/Cluster-12436-Template/SSL/Cluster-12436-Template')
cmo.setListenPort(8100)

cd('/ServerTemplates/Cluster-12436-Template')
```

```
cmo.setMachine(getMBean('/Machines/localhost'))
```

Starting Dynamic Clusters

Starting a dynamic cluster will be done in exactly the way as normal clusters.

Complete Example

The following is a complete example of creating a server template and a cluster.

💾 create_server_template/cluster

```
# change to the root folder
cd('/')

# create a new server template
cmo.createServerTemplate('MyDynServer_Template')

# change to the new server template
cd('/ServerTemplates/MyDynServer_Template')
cmo.setListenPort(6000)

# change the SSL port
cd('/ServerTemplates/MyDynServer_Template/SSL/MyDynServer_Template')
cmo.setListenPort(6100)

# set a machine - None means that the adminserver can target the new instances dynamically
cd('/ServerTemplates/MyDynServer_Template')
cmo.setMachine(None)

# create a new dynamic cluster
cd('/')
cmo.createCluster('Cluster-1234')

# configure the cluster
cd('/Clusters/Cluster-1234')
cmo.setClusterMessagingMode('unicast')

# set the template which should be used to create server instances
cd('/ServerTemplates/MyDynServer_Template')
cmo.setCluster(getMBean('/Clusters/Cluster-1234'))

# configure the cluster
cd('/Clusters/Cluster-1234/DynamicServers/Cluster-1234')
cmo.setServerTemplate(getMBean('/ServerTemplates/MyDynServer_Template'))
cmo.setMaximumDynamicServerCount(3)
cmo.setCalculatedListenPorts(true)
cmo.setCalculatedMachineNames(true)
cmo.setCalculatedListenPorts(true)
cmo.setServerNamePrefix('MyDynServer_')

# activate the changes
activate()
```

Limitations

Dynamic clusters also have a number of limitations. Due to its dynamic nature, it is not possible to target a deployment to an individual dynamic server. Also, whole server and service migration are not supported.

Machines and NodeManager

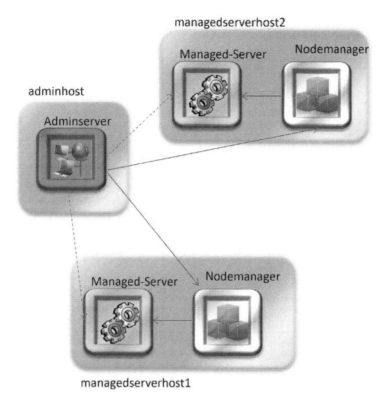

managedserverhost2

Managed-Server   Nodemanager

adminhost

Adminserver

Managed-Server   Nodemanager

managedserverhost1

Figure 5.2: *The Classical NodeManager Managed Domain*

An important configuration within WebLogic is the machine. A machine represents a physical node where Managed-Servers can be located. For the communication between AdminServer and Managed-Server, this concept is rather irrelevant as the AdminServer will contact the Managed-Server over their admin-port. The machine setting and especially the NodeManager configurations for the machines are important for starting the Managed-Servers.

Every machine configuration in WebLogic has exactly one NodeManager. If there is a need for having different NodeManagers on the same physical machine hosting Managed-Servers for the same domain, you need to add multiple machine configurations. The reason for this is that there can be different machine users running the Managed-Servers, which would result in different machine access rights.

WebLogic distinguishes between different types of machines and different types of machines and NodeManagers, which are explained in the subsequent sections. The types are basically distinguished based on their technology (java/script) and on the security (plain/encrypted).

Adding Machines

Normal or generic machines represent a machine type where the underlying operating system is irrelevant. This also means that the amount of settings and especially the available NodeManager types are limited. For example, RSH, SSH NodeManager are only available on UNIX systems.

```
cd('/')
cmo.createMachine('Machine-Other')

cd('/Machines/Machine-Other/NodeManager/Machine-Other')
cmo.setNMType('SSL')
cmo.setListenAddress('myTestMachine1')
cmo.setListenPort(5556)
cmo.setDebugEnabled(false)
```

On normal machines, the only two NodeManager types that are relevant are "Plain" (unencrypted communication) and SSL (secure communication with server certificates).

The machine configuration must include values for the listen address and port number parameters. The machine name is used to identify the machine within the Oracle WebLogic Server domain; it is not required to match the network name for the machine.

- **NodeManager listen address**: Network interface address used by the NodeManager to listen for requests from the AdminServer or WLST scripts.

- **NodeManager listen port**: Listener port for the NodeManager. The default value is 5556.

Adding UnixMachines

The special machine type "Machine-Unix" offers more options because the systems knows that a UNIX based system (UNIX or Linux) is used as the underlying operating system:

```
cd('/')
cmo.createUnixMachine('Machine-Unix')

cd('/Machines/Machine-Unix/NodeManager/Machine-Unix')
cmo.setNMType('SSL')
cmo.setListenAddress('myTestUnixMachine')
cmo.setListenPort(5554)
cmo.setDebugEnabled(false)
```

Configure NodeManager

WebLogic supports a number of different NodeManager types. The available types depend on the underlying operation system. The full list of available types are: SSH, RSH, Plain, SSL, ssh, rsh, ssl, plain, VMM, vmm, VMMS, and vmms.

The most common types are SSL, Plain, and SSH.

Configure an SSL NodeManager

```
cd('/Machines/Machine-UnixSecure/NodeManager/Machine-UnixSecure')
cmo.setNMType('SSH')
cmo.setListenAddress('localhost')
cmo.setListenPort(5556)
cmo.setNodeManagerHome('/opt/wls/nodemanager')
cmo.setDebugEnabled(false)
```

Configure a Plain NodeManager

The next example will configure a plain NodeManager. "Plain" means that the communication with this Java-based NodeManager is not encrypted, and if somebody is sniffing on the wire then this person can record all commands and even unencrypted information like passwords.

```
cd('/Machines/Machine-TestPlain/NodeManager/Machine-TestPlain')
cmo.setNMType('Plain')
cmo.setListenAddress('plainTestMachine')
cmo.setListenPort(5566)
cmo.setDebugEnabled(false)
```

Configure an SSH NodeManager

An SSH NodeManager is a NodeManager version that is available only on Linux/UNIX. It is not based on Java, but it is script-based. The big benefit of this type of NodeManager is that it is independent of the WebLogic version. Note that the Java-based NodeManager versions must use the same WebLogic versions as the domains they are managing, otherwise you get nasty classcast and version exceptions. The script-based NodeManager can work with domains based on different WebLogic versions, which makes it an interesting choice in environments where different WebLogic versions have to be operated on the same hardware.

```
cd('/')
cmo.createMachine('Machine-SSH_Test')

cd('/Machines/Machine-SSH_Test/NodeManager/Machine-SSH_Test')
cmo.setNMType('SSH')
cmo.setListenAddress('testMachineWithSSH')
cmo.setListenPort(5566)
cmo.setNodeManagerHome('/opt/wls/nm')
cmo.setDebugEnabled(false)
```

Securing NodeManager

By default - if activated - the NodeManager uses the WebLogic Demo certificates. In the security chapter you will find more information on how to change this behavior and use your own certificates instead. The problem is that you cannot just reconfigure the NodeManager to use its own certificates, you need to change the AdminServer, and therefore the complete administration communication as well.

Here is an example for the NodeManager configuration (note that these properties must be added to the nodemanager.properties file AND must also be used by the AdminServer):

```
KeyStores=CustomIdentityAndCustomTrust
CustomIdentityKeyStoreFileName=/opt/wls_domains/pki/IdentityKeyStore.jks
CustomIdentityAlias=abcdefg
CustomIdentityKeyStorePassPhrase={3DES}yE1cRhTbYHJdBOQCqwDioA==
CustomIdentityKeyStoreType=JKS
CustomIdentityPrivateKeyPassPhrase={3DES}hMGpokJiInlVzwnK2ri0V2WDyVoxCf3B
```

More details will be provided in the security section.

Starting Servers

There are multiple ways to start Managed-Servers using the NodeManager. The default way is to use the configuration defined in the "server start" sections of the domain configuration. Another way is to tell the NodeManager to use specific scripts.

As the NodeManager must be able to start the Managed-Servers in case of a failure or on machine start (if the NodeManager is powered up during machine start), the arguments must be located in a place on the machine where the NodeManager is running (as the AdminServer might be down). Therefore, a copy of the parameters configured in the domain will be stored under <domain-directory)/servers/<server-name>/data/nodemanagerstartup.properties.

The following are server startup arguments in the file <domain-directory)/servers/<server-name>/data/nodemanagerstartup.properties:

Property	Description
JavaHome	Defines the Java home directory used when starting the server.
Arguments	The arguments used when starting the server.
SSLArguments	These arguments are used when you have enabled the domain-wide administration port.
RestartMax	The number of times NodeManager can attempt to restart the

Property	Description
	server.
RestartDelaySeconds	The number of seconds NodeManager should wait before attempting to restart the server.
ClassPath	The classpath to use when starting a server.
OracleHome	The Oracle home directory to use when starting a server.
AdminURL	The URL of the Administration Server. Note: This value should only be specified in the startup.properties file for a Managed-Server.
AutoRestart	Specifies whether NodeManager can automatically restart this server if it fails.
AutoKillIfFailed	Specifies whether NodeManager should automatically kill the server if its health status is failed.
SecurityPolicyFile	Specifies the security policy file to use when starting this server.
ServerIP	The IP address of the server.

(Source: Oracle Corporation[6])

Table 5.2: Startup Arguments

The default file after a Managed-Server is created, added to a machine, and started for the first time looks like:

```
#Server startup properties
#Tue Nov 13 08:33:14 CET 2012
SSLArguments=-Dweblogic.security.SSL.ignoreHostnameVerification\=false -
Dweblogic.ReverseDNSAllowed\=false
RestartMax=2
RestartDelaySeconds=0
RestartInterval=3600
AdminURL=http\://myadminserverhost.com\:7001
AutoRestart=true
AutoKillIfFailed=false
```

Please note that this example is based on a Managed-Server that has nothing but the default specified in the "ServerStart" section. All arguments in the "ServerStart" section will be copied from the config.xml into this file on the Managed-Server host so that the NodeManager can pick it up. This is one of the main reasons when a NodeManager enroll is needed on remote machines because the NodeManager must be aware of the domain root directories for each domain it should manage.

Here is an example with custom settings:

---

[6] docs.oracle.com/middleware/1212/wls/NODEM/nodemgr_config.htm

```
#Server startup properties
Arguments=-Djava.awt.headless\=true  -Xmx1024m  -XX\:MaxPermSize\=512m -
DmyInstall.dir\=/applications/testapp -DmyLogDir\=/applications/logs/managedserver_1   -
Dweblogic.Stdout\=/applications/logs/managedserver_1.out -
Dweblogic.Stderr\=/applications/logs/managedserver_1.err
JavaHome=/usr/lib/jvm/jre-1.6.0-openjdk.x86_64
SSLArguments=-Dweblogic.security.SSL.ignoreHostnameVerification\=false -
Dweblogic.ReverseDNSAllowed\=false
RestartMax=2
RestartDelaySeconds=0
RestartInterval=3600
BeaHome=/opt/wls
ClassPath=/opt/wls/patch_wls1035/profiles/default/sys_manifest_classpath/weblogic_patch.jar\:/usr/lib
/jvm/jre-1.6.0-
openjdk.x86_64/lib/tools.jar\:/opt/wls/wlserver_10.3/server/lib/weblogic_sp.jar\:/opt/wls/wlserver_10
.3/server/lib/weblogic.jar\:/opt/wls/modules/features/weblogic.server.modules_10.3.5.0.jar\:/opt/wls/
wlserver_10.3/server/lib/webservices.jar\:/opt/wls/modules/org.apache.ant_1.7.1/lib/ant-
all.jar\:/opt/wls/modules/net.sf.antcontrib_1.1.0.0_1-0b2/lib/ant-
contrib.jar\:\:/opt/wls\:/opt/wls/modules/com.oracle.osdt_cert_1.0.0.0.jar\:/opt/wls/modules/com.orac
le.osdt_core_1.0.0.0.jar\:/opt/wls/modules/com.oracle.oraclepki_1.0.0.0.jar
AdminURL=http\://mymanagedserver1.com\:8801
AutoRestart=true
AutoKillIfFailed=false
```

See the later section called "Managed-Server" for more information on how to fill the properties in the config.xml (and therefore the values in this file also) with customer-specific requirements.

Enrollment

For security reasons, but also for initial bootstrapping, every machine that hosts Managed-Servers for a domain (unless they share the root directory with the Administration Server) must be enrolled. Enrollment basically means that the NodeManager knows about the domain and its location and that this bootstrapping will download essential security and configuration files in order to allow the NodeManager to start the Managed-Servers. During startup, the Managed-Servers will communicate with the Administration Server and download updates of the configuration and deployment. But in order to be able to communicate with the Administration Server, the domain security key (=salt file) and other relevant files must be available locally in order to establish the communication with the Administration Server.

The *nmEnroll* command enrolls the machine on which WLST is currently running. WLST must be connected to an Administration Server to run this command; WLST does not need to be connected to NodeManager. This command downloads the following file from the Administration Server: NodeManager secret file (nm_password.properties), which contains the encrypted username and password that is used for server authentication and the SerializedSystemIni.dat file. This command also updates the nodemanager.domains file.

You must run this command once per WebLogic domain per machine unless that domain shares the root directory of the Administration Server. If the machine is already enrolled when you run this command, the NodeManager secret file (nm_password.properties) is refreshed with the latest information from the Administration Server.

WLST command:

```
# enroll server
nmEnroll(domainDirectory, getNmHomeDirectory())
```

Note that this command must be executed on the machine where the NodeManager is running (this means on the machine where the NodeManager should start your Managed-Server). It cannot be executed remotely. During enrollment, basic domain files will be downloaded from the AdminServer.

Domain-Based NodeManager

12.1.2 ++   WebLogic 12.1.2 has added a complete new NodeManager mode. Up to 12.1.1, a NodeManager was basically a machine daemon that could be used by multiple domains to serve as a management agent for server instances.

Starting with 12.1.2, it is possible to create a domain-based NodeManager, which means to align the NodeManager lifecycle management with the domains. The NodeManager is now stored with the domain. The default directory is <domain>/nodemanager. This is done during domain creation. This also means that the domain creation process can be extended to integrate a domain-based NodeManager. This also means that the bin folder of the domain now contains a startNodeManager script. This means that everything needed to run the NodeManager can be embedded into the domain.

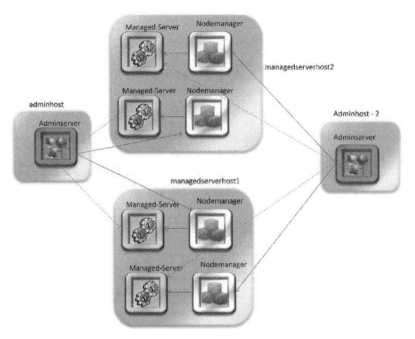

Figure 5.3: *Domain-based NodeManager*

Managed-Server

In addition to having an Administration Server, a domain can have zero or more Managed-Servers. The Managed-Server and Administration Server are similar in the sense that both can host applications; however, only the AdminServer can host the administration console. Managed-Servers host the applications and therefore are actually doing the work. The Administration Server is usually used for administration work and the Managed-Servers are used to host the application.

Every Managed-Server stores a local copy of the domain configuration. When the Managed-Server starts, it connects to the Administration Server to synchronize the configuration. When the configuration changes, the Administration Server sends the changed configuration to the Managed-Servers.

Lifecycle operations like starting and stopping can be performed on the Managed-Server without having an Administration Server running. Of course in this case, the Managed-Server cannot synchronize itself with the Administration Server. This mode is called the Managed-Server independence mode (MSI).

Adding a Managed-Server to the Domain

A Managed-Server can be added to a domain in online or offline modes using WLST. Adding a Managed-Server means create a new Managed-Server for this domain.

Here is an example of how to create a new standalone server (without a cluster):

```
cd('/')
# create a server with the provided name
cmo.createServer('StandaloneTestServer')

# change to the new server mbean
cd('/Servers/StandaloneTestServer')

# set server details like host, port, …
cmo.setListenAddress('myListenAddress')
cmo.setListenPort(7099)

# configure basic server settings
cmo.setListenPortEnabled(true)
cmo.setJavaCompiler('javac')
cmo.setClientCertProxyEnabled(false)
cmo.setCluster(None)

cd('/Servers/StandaloneTestServer/ServerDiagnosticConfig/StandaloneTestServer')
cmo.setWLDFDiagnosticVolume('Low')
```

The NodeManager section contains a description about the server start values and the files used by the NodeManager.

These values can be defined during the creation of a Managed-Server. The same script can be used later on to change them.

```
cd ('ServerStart/TestServer');
set ('Arguments','-Dxyz=3');
set ('BeaHome','/opt/oracle/wls');
set
('ClassPath','/opt/oracle/wls/patch_wls1035/profiles/default/sys_manifest_classpath/weblogic_patch.ja
r:/usr/lib/jvm/jre-1.6.0-
openjdk.x86_64/lib/tools.jar:/opt/oracle/wls/wlserver_10.3/server/lib/weblogic_sp.jar:/opt/oracle/wls
/wlserver_10.3/server/lib/weblogic.jar:/opt/oracle/wls/modules/features/weblogic.server.modules_10.3.
5.0.jar:/opt/oracle/wls/wlserver_10.3/server/lib/webservices.jar:/opt/oracle/wls/modules/org.apache.a
nt_1.7.1/lib/ant-all.jar:/opt/oracle/wls/modules/net.sf.antcontrib_1.1.0.0_1-0b2/lib/ant-
contrib.jar::/opt/oracle/wls:/opt/oracle/wls/modules/com.oracle.osdt_cert_1.0.0.0.jar:/opt/oracle/wls
/modules/com.oracle.osdt_core_1.0.0.0.jar:/opt/oracle/wls/modules/com.oracle.oraclepki_1.0.0.0.jar');
set ('JavaHome', '/usr/lib/jvm/jre-1.6.0-openjdk.x86_64');
```

As referred to in the NodeManager section, these server start arguments are the ideal place to configure the redirection of the standout and stderr log files, as these log files cannot be redirected using MBeans.

In order to redirect the standout and stderr, you need to add 2 parameters to the "Arguments" List:

-Dweblogic.Stdout=<my output log file>
-Dweblogic.Stderr=<my error log file>

The log files (normal log and access log) attributes for the AdminServer, and also the new Managed-Server, can be set using WLST:

```
#################################################################
# Set server log
#################################################################
def configureServerLog(servername):
    try:
        serverLogPath = "data/logs/myTestDomain/"+servername;
        try:
            os.makedirs(serverLogPath);
        except:
            dumpStack()
            print 'Unable to create server ('+servername+') log path - please check !';

        # change to the server and create a log MBean
        cd('/Server/'+servername)
        create(servername, 'Log')

        # change to the new log MBean and configure it
        cd('/Server/'+servername+'/Log/'+servername)
        cmo.setRotationType('byTime')
        cmo.setRotationTime('02:00')
        cmo.setFileTimeSpan(24)
        cmo.setNumberOfFilesLimited(true)
        cmo.setFileCount(14)
        cmo.setFileName(serverLogPath+'/'+servername+'.log')

        # do the same for the access log which lives under a different MBean (=> webserver)
        cd('/Server/'+servername)
        create(servername, 'WebServer')
        cd('/Server/'+servername+'/WebServer/'+servername)
        create(servername, 'WebServerLog')
        cd('/Server/'+servername+'/WebServer/'+servername+'/WebServerLog/'+servername)
        cmo.setRotationTime('02:00')
        cmo.setRotationType('byTime')
        cmo.setFileTimeSpan(24)
        cmo.setFileCount(14)
        cmo.setFileName(serverLogPath+'/access.log')


    except:
        print 'Exception while setting server log options !';
        dumpStack();
        exit();
```

Assigning Managed-Servers to Machines

Managed-Server configurations as done in the previous section are fine as long as you want to start the Managed-Server manually using shell scripts on the same machine as the AdminServer. This is usually not the case. In a normal domain, Managed-Servers are distributed over a number of machines and started using a NodeManager.

In order to start a Managed-Server using the NodeManager, the Managed-Server must be assigned to a machine. The following script assigns a server to a machine:

```
cd('/Servers/StandaloneTestServer')
cmo.setMachine(getMBean('/Machines/localhost'))
```

Assigning Managed-Servers to a Cluster

As discussed before, a WebLogic cluster groups a number of Managed-Servers and offers a range of features like load balancing, failover, etc. In order to participate in a cluster, a Managed-Server must be added to a cluster. Every Managed-Server can participate in at most one cluster at any given time. A Managed-Server does not need to participate in a cluster.

Adding a Managed-Server to a cluster is an easy command in WLST. Just navigate to the Managed-Server MBean and add this Managed-Server to the (existing!) cluster of your choice.

```
cd('/Servers/StandaloneTestServer')
cmo.setCluster(getMBean('/Clusters/MartinTest_Cluster'))
```

Advanced Configurations

Every Managed-Server has a number of additional configurations. This includes overload protection, advanced tuning, settings for web services and more. Most of these options can almost always be left to the default settings. For an impression about the possible settings, the next script will set a few values.

Managed-Server settings:

```
cd('/Servers/TestServer')
cmo.setPeriodLength(60000)
cmo.setManagedServerIndependenceEnabled(true)
```

These two settings are pretty interesting and also pretty important. Especially the property ManagedServerIndependenceEnabled is an important setting for production systems. ONLY (!) if this is set to true, this Managed-Server can be restarted (e.g. from the NodeManager after a system failure) automatically, even if the AdminServer is not running. If for whatever reason you do not want to allow the server to be restarted when the Administration Server is not running (e.g. restriction about the number of Managed-Servers that are allowed to run), then you need to set this value to false.

Login timeout:

```
cd('/Servers/TestServer')

# login timeout for a new non-ssl connection to this server
cmo.setLoginTimeoutMillis(5000)

# login timeout for a new ssl(!) connection to this server
cd('/Servers/StandaloneTestServer/SSL/StandaloneTestServer')
cmo.setLoginTimeoutMillis(25000)
```

Server tuning for dealing with low memory:

```
cd('/Servers/TestServer')

# The threshold level (in percent) that this server uses for logging low memory conditions and
changing the server health state
cmo.setLowMemoryGCThreshold(5)

# granularity level (in percent) that this server uses for logging low memory conditions
cmo.setLowMemoryGranularityLevel(5)

# The amount of time (in seconds) that defines the interval over which this server determines average
free memory values
cmo.setLowMemoryTimeInterval(3600)

# number of times this server samples free memory during the time period specified by
LowMemoryTimeInterval
cmo.setLowMemorySampleSize(10)
```

Tuning for threads and connections:

```
cd('/Servers/TestServer')

# The maximum number of open sockets allowed in server at a given point of time (below 0 = unlimited)
cmo.setMaxOpenSockCount(-1)

# number of seconds after which WebLogic Server periodically scans threads
cmo.setStuckThreadTimerInterval(60)

# number of seconds that a thread must be continually working before this server considers the thread
stuck
cmo.setStuckThreadMaxTime(600)

# number of backlogged, new TCP connection requests that should be allowed for this server
cmo.setAcceptBacklog(300)
```

Settings for native IO:

```
cd('/Servers/TestServer')

# enable native I/O yes or no
cmo.setNativeIOEnabled(true)

# NIO detail settings
cmo.setGatheredWritesEnabled(false)
cmo.setScatteredReadsEnabled(false)
```

Overload Protection

WebLogic has built-in features for detecting, avoiding, and recovering from overload conditions. You can tune your WebLogic Server to take appropriate action during failed or overload states. For example, you can instruct to kill the server process during a failed or overload state so that your NodeManager can restart your server. A Managed-Server can fail as a result of out-of-memory exceptions or stuck application threads, or if one of its services is running into an error condition. A Managed-Server instance can monitor its health. If it detects that an unstable state is reached, it declares itself failed. A server instance declared as failed cannot satisfy administrative or client requests.

When the kernel encounters a panic condition, a predefined action can be taken. The following two actions are available.

Panic Action:

- No-action

- Exit the server process

When the server health monitoring encounters a critical situation and flags the server as failed, one of three predefined actions can be taken automatically (if configured).

Failure Action:

- No-action

- "Force immediate shutdown of this server", meaning that server will shut down completely

- "Suspend server for correction action", meaning that server will go into admin state

The following examples are to demonstrate a number of different property combinations in order to see the different possible settings.

Configuration examples:

```
cd('/Servers/TestServer/OverloadProtection/TestServer')
cmo.setPanicAction('no-action')
cmo.setFailureAction('no-action')
cmo.setSharedCapacityForWorkManagers(65536)
cmo.setFreeMemoryPercentHighThreshold(0)
cmo.setFreeMemoryPercentLowThreshold(0)
cmo.createServerFailureTrigger()

cd('/Servers/TestServer/OverloadProtection/TestServer/ServerFailureTrigger/TestServer')
cmo.setMaxStuckThreadTime(600)
cmo.setStuckThreadCount(0)
```

The next example defines that the panic action is a system exit, which means that the complete server process will not be shutdown gracefully but will be immediately ended:

```
cd('/Servers/TestServer/OverloadProtection/TestServer')
cmo.setPanicAction('system-exit')
cmo.setFailureAction('force-shutdown')
cmo.setSharedCapacityForWorkManagers(65600)
```

The last example will force the server to go into admin state in the case of an overload situation:

```
cd('/Servers/TestServer/OverloadProtection/TestServer')
cmo.setFailureAction('admin-state')
```

Migration and Migratable Targets

Normally in a WebLogic cluster, all services are hosted on all servers of a cluster (homogeneous distribution). This enables transparent failover between servers. The so-called pinned services are hosted on a single server within the cluster.

WebLogic knows about 3 types of pinned services:

- JMS-related services
  - o All JMS services are singleton services.
- The JTA Transaction Recovery Service
  - o Automatically attempts to recover transactions on system startup by parsing all transaction log records for incomplete transactions and completing them.
- User-defined singleton services
  - o Self-written application parts, which must be running exactly once within a cluster.

For these services, failover will fail as there is no backup server with the same service running. For those services, WebLogic supports service migration, as opposed to failover.

Migratable services provide migration policies that define whether the hosted services will be manually migrated (the system default) or automatically migrated from an unhealthy hosting server using the health monitoring subsystem.

Configuration of Migration

Migration and migratable targets are well documented in various sources (please also see link list).

The following example will do the configuration steps:

1. Create a first Managed-Server.
2. Create and configure a cluster.
3. Assign the first server to the cluster.
4. Create the second Managed-Server.
5. Assign the second server to our test cluster.
6. Set auto migration for the first server to false.

7. Set all possible machines (including own!) to which the first service might be migrated.

8. Set all possible migration servers (including own!) to which this service might be migrated.

9. Set all possible JTA migration targets (including own!) to which this service might be migrated.

10. Set auto migration for the second server to false.

11. Set all possible machines (including own!) to which the second service might be migrated.

12. Set all possible migration servers (including own!) to which the second service might be migrated.

13. Set all possible JTA migration targets (including own!) to which the second service might be migrated.

Example script:

🖫 migration

```
cd('/')
# Create a first managed server
cmo.createServer('TestServer1')

cd('/Servers/TestServer1')
cmo.setListenAddress('')
cmo.setListenPort(7001)

cd('/')
# create a cluster
cmo.createCluster('TestCluster')

# configure cluster
cd('/Clusters/TestCluster')
cmo.setClusterMessagingMode('unicast')
cmo.setClusterBroadcastChannel('')

# Assign the first server to the cluster
cd('/Servers/TestServer1')
cmo.setCluster(getMBean('/Clusters/TestCluster'))

cd('/')
# Create a second managed server
cmo.createServer('TestServer2')

cd('/Servers/TestServer2')
cmo.setListenAddress('')
cmo.setListenPort(7001)

# assign the second server also to our testcluster
cmo.setCluster(getMBean('/Clusters/TestCluster'))

cd('/Servers/TestServer1')
cmo.setListenPortEnabled(true)
cmo.setJavaCompiler('javac')
cmo.setClientCertProxyEnabled(false)
cmo.setMachine(getMBean('/Machines/localhost'))

cd('/Servers/TestServer2')
cmo.setListenPortEnabled(true)
cmo.setJavaCompiler('javac')
cmo.setClientCertProxyEnabled(false)
cmo.setMachine(getMBean('/Machines/test12345'))
```

```
cd('/Servers/TestServer1')
# set auto migration for the first server to false
cmo.setAutoMigrationEnabled(false)

# set all possible machines (including own !) to which this service might be migrated
set('CandidateMachines',jarray.array([ObjectName('com.bea:Name=localhost,Type=Machine'),
ObjectName('com.bea:Name=test12345,Type=UnixMachine')], ObjectName))

cd('/MigratableTargets/TestServer1 (migratable)')
# set all possible migration server (including own !) to which this service might be migrated
set('ConstrainedCandidateServers',jarray.array([ObjectName('com.bea:Name=TestServer2,Type=Server'),
ObjectName('com.bea:Name=TestServer1,Type=Server')], ObjectName))

cd('/Servers/TestServer1/JTAMigratableTarget/TestServer1')
# set all possible JTA migration targets (including own !) to which this service might be migrated
set('ConstrainedCandidateServers',jarray.array([ObjectName('com.bea:Name=TestServer2,Type=Server'),
ObjectName('com.bea:Name=TestServer1,Type=Server')], ObjectName))
cmo.setMigrationPolicy('manual')

cd('/Servers/TestServer2')
# set auto migration for the second server to false
cmo.setAutoMigrationEnabled(false)
# set all possible machines (including own !) to which the second service might be migrated
set('CandidateMachines',jarray.array([ObjectName('com.bea:Name=localhost,Type=Machine')],
ObjectName))

# set all possible migration server (including own !) to which this service might be migrated
cd('/MigratableTargets/TestServer2 (migratable)')
set('ConstrainedCandidateServers',jarray.array([ObjectName('com.bea:Name=TestServer1,Type=Server'),
ObjectName('com.bea:Name=TestServer2,Type=Server')], ObjectName))

# set all possible JTA migration targets (including own !) to which the second service might be
migrated
cd('/Servers/TestServer2/JTAMigratableTarget/TestServer2')
set('ConstrainedCandidateServers',jarray.array([ObjectName('com.bea:Name=TestServer1,Type=Server'),
ObjectName('com.bea:Name=TestServer2,Type=Server')], ObjectName))
cmo.setMigrationPolicy('manual')
```

JTA Configurations of the Domain

Domain-level WebLogic offers a set of other options. The following paragraphs show
some examples of the most common settings that can be done on the domain level.
One example is the configuration of domain-wide JTA settings.

Here is a complete Jython method in order to set the transaction timeout:

💾 set_JTA_timeout

```
##################################################################
# Setting Domain JTA Transaction timeout
##################################################################
def setDomainJTATimeout():
    try:
        print 'Setting Domain JTA Transaction timeout...';
        edit();
        startEdit();

        cd('/JTA/'+domainProps.getProperty('domainName'));
        # Maximum amount of time, in seconds, an active transaction
        # is allowed to be in the first phase of a transaction
        cmo.setTimeoutSeconds(300);

        save();
        activate();

    except:
        print 'Exception while setting Domain JTA Transaction timeout !';
        dumpStack();
```

```
    exit();
```

The next Jython method does not only set the transaction timeout, but also many more transaction properties:

set_JTA_properties

```
#################################################################
# Setting Domain JTA Transaction properties
#################################################################
def setDomainJTAProperties():
    try:
        print 'Setting Domain JTA Transaction properties ...';
        edit();
        startEdit();

        cd('/JTA/'+domainProps.getProperty('domainName'));

        # Maximum time, an active transaction is allowed to be in the first phase of a transaction
        cmo.setTimeoutSeconds(300);

        # The maximum number of simultaneous in-progress transactions allowed
        cmo.setMaxTransactions(20000)

        # The time  a transaction manager waits for transactions involving the resource to complete
        cmo.setUnregisterResourceGracePeriod(25)

        # maximum time a transaction manager persists in attempting to complete the second phase
        cmo.setAbandonTimeoutSeconds(80000)

        # Indicates that XA calls are executed in parallel if there are available threads
        cmo.setParallelXAEnabled(true)

        # automatically performs an XA Resource forget for heuristic transaction completions
        cmo.setForgetHeuristics(true)

        # the two-phase commit protocol is used
        cmo.setTwoPhaseEnabled(true)

        # maximum cycles that the transaction manager performs the beforeCompletion synchronization
        cmo.setBeforeCompletionIterationLimit(20)

        # interval the transaction manager creates a new transaction log
        cmo.setCheckpointIntervalSeconds(200)

        # Specifies transport security mode required by WebService Transaction endpoints
        cmo.setSecurityInteropMode('default')
        # XA calls are executed in parallel if there are available threads
        cmo.setParallelXAEnabled(false)

        # Maximum number of concurrent requests to resources allowed for each server
        cmo.setMaxResourceRequestsOnServer(60)

        # transport security mode required by WebService Transaction endpoints
        cmo.setWSATTransportSecurityMode('SSLNotRequired')

        # Maximum allowed time duration, in milliseconds, for XA calls to resources
        cmo.setMaxXACallMillis(100000)

        # maximum time, in seconds, a transaction manager waits for all resource managers to respond
        cmo.setCompletionTimeoutSeconds(0)

        # Maximum duration time, in milliseconds, that a resource is declared dead
        cmo.setMaxResourceUnavailableMillis(1500000)

        save();
        activate();

    except:
        print 'Exception while setting Domain JTA Transaction timeout !';
        dumpStack();
        exit();
```

This example does the same as the first JTA example. The only difference is that this example should provide the reader with a feeling how many different settings only for JTA can set configured using WLST. In normal WLST scripts, only a few - if any - parameters need to be set. This full list is for demonstration purpose only.

Startup and Shutdown Classes

Certain activities in applications cannot be done on the application level, but need to be initialized during the start of WebLogic. Examples for these activities are the installation of additional MBeans required by the applications or for additional monitoring, or the creation of additional management MBeans like security provider.

WebLogic honors these needs with two concepts. The first concept – the so-called startup classes – can be used to implement functionality that must be performed during server startup. This may include MBean registrations or other initializations. The second concept – the so-called shutdown classes – can be used to implement functionality that must be performed during server shutdown. Examples include cleanup activities or shutdown notifications.

Prerequisite for using these features: The classes must be in the class path of the server where these features should be executed. These concepts are available for the Administration Server and Managed-Server.

🖫 configure_startup_class

```
# go into edit mode
edit()
# start edit
startEdit()

# test if the startup class is already configured
# the idea is to get a reference to the startup class mbean. If this mbean does not exit then this
# startup class has not yet been configured in this server and we can create it
cd('/')
startup_class = getMBean('/StartupClasses/TestStartupClass')
if startup_class == None:
    cmo.createStartupClass('TestStartupClass')

# now we can be sure that the startup calss either was already there or has been created
cd('/StartupClasses/TestStartupClass')
# configure classname
cmo.setClassName('com.wlsmonitoringbook.teststartup')

# set the target(s) for this startuo class
set('Targets',jarray.array([ObjectName('com.bea:Name=AdminServer,Type=Server'),
ObjectName('com.bea:Name=Messaging_Cluster,Type=Cluster')], ObjectName))

# define when the class is to be called
cmo.setLoadBeforeAppDeployments(true)
cmo.setLoadBeforeAppActivation(true)
cmo.setDeploymentOrder(1000)
cmo.setFailureIsFatal(true)

# further arguments which will be passed without modification into the init method of the startup
cmo.setArguments('initarg=xyz')
```

This is an example of how to configure a startup class for WebLogic.

The other variation of this class can be called during shutdown. This can be useful for housekeeping and for cleaning up the system, deleting lock files, or performing other actions.

💾 configure_shutdown_class

```
cd('/')
cmo.createShutdownClass('TestShutdownClass')

cd('/Deployments/TestShutdownClass')
cmo.setClassName('com.wlsmonitoringbook.testshutdown')
set('Targets',jarray.array([ObjectName('com.bea:Name=BusinessTier_Cluster,Type=Cluster'),
ObjectName('com.bea:Name=WebTier_Cluster,Type=Cluster')], ObjectName))
cmo.setDeploymentOrder(1000)
```

This is an example of how to configure a shutdown class for WebLogic.

Network Channels

By default, all communication going into a WebLogic Server uses the same communication port or better IP/port. This also means that WebLogic, by default, is listening on the same port with all available protocols for T3, T3S, HTTP, HTTPS, LDAP, SNMP, IIOP, IIOPS cluster and admin communication. For simple domains and networks, this is usually acceptable. But it does not efficiently use the available network resources of bigger machines.

Especially in complex networks or critical environments (like DMZ, NAT hosts, etc.), this default behavior is definitely not sufficient.

WebLogic has the ability to listen to different network endpoints, which allows administrators to restrict communications to certain ports/networks. The resources used in WebLogic are called "channels".

A network channel is a configuration item in WebLogic that defines the communication endpoint of a network connection. This usually includes the protocol used, the IP, and port that WebLogic has to use for the network listener. It might also include additional properties such as login timeout, tunneling support, and (e.g. in case of secure lines) SSL and certificate enforcement.

Configurations of channels obey some general rules:

- Every channel can only be assigned to one WebLogic Server instance.
- Every server instance (Admin or Managed-Server) can have multiple channels.
- Every channel must have a unique combination of listen address, listen port, and protocol (for any individual server).

Figure 5.4 is an example of where channels are definitely needed:

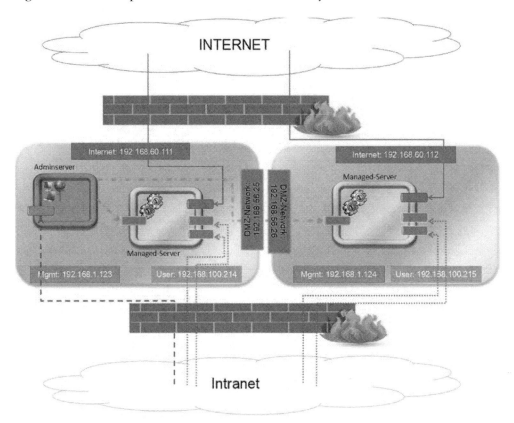

Figure 5.4: *Complex network setup with network channels*

This is the setup of the WebLogic Server running in the DMZ. The administration is done using the admin channel. The heavy-dash network and lines represent the administration communication from the intranet over the intranet firewall on a dedicated administration network to the Administration Servers. The varied-dash network and lines represent the administration communication within the dedicated DMZ network. The solid lines depict the problematic communication from the internet users, which must be particularly secured and restricted (e.g. only HTTPS allowed on this channel). And finally the small-dash lines depict the communication from the intranet users (or batch jobs) coming in over the intranet firewall on the user network. So why are there two small-dash lines and listeners (=channels) on each Managed-Server? Well in this example, I assume that there are clients (e.g. other servers on the intranet calling a web service on these Managed-Servers) calling in using the HTTP protocol. Now let us assume that there are another group of clients (e.g. nightly batch jobs that are only allowed to call in from special server - which also means other firewall rules) and they are using the IIOP protocol. Therefore, both client types do need a dedicated channel as in this example; for security reasons, we do NOT want to expose the default channel.

Note that WebLogic can be configured to use a special channel for the administration communication - the so-called admin channel. The admin channel will be introduced in the security part of this book as it places certain restrictions on security. The following examples will show a number of different channel definitions, with the assumption that the admin communication is still using the default channel

```
# change to the server
cd('/Servers/MartinTest_Domain_MS1')

# create the new network access point
cmo.createNetworkAccessPoint('UnsecureHTTPChannel')

# change to the network access point
cd('/Servers/MartinTest_Domain_MS1/NetworkAccessPoints/UnsecureHTTPChannel')

# configure protocol, port and other settings
cmo.setProtocol('http')
cmo.setListenPort(46912)
cmo.setEnabled(true)
cmo.setHttpEnabledForThisProtocol(true)
cmo.setTunnelingEnabled(false)
cmo.setOutboundEnabled(false)
cmo.setTwoWaySSLEnabled(false)
cmo.setClientCertificateEnforced(false)
```

This is an example of how to create an HTTP channel. This might be useful if you only have web services or a web-application and a firewall in front of this server, which does not allow any other protocol anyway.

T3 example:

```
# change to the server
cd('/Servers/MartinTest_Domain_MS1')

# create the t3 channel
cmo.createNetworkAccessPoint('T3Channel')

# change to the channel and configure it
cd('/Servers/MartinTest_Domain_MS1/NetworkAccessPoints/T3Channel')
cmo.setProtocol('t3')
cmo.setListenPort(46913)
cmo.setEnabled(true)
cmo.setHttpEnabledForThisProtocol(false)
cmo.setTunnelingEnabled(false)
cmo.setOutboundEnabled(false)
cmo.setTwoWaySSLEnabled(false)
cmo.setClientCertificateEnforced(false)
```

This script configures an unsecure T3 network channel.

HTTPS channel:

```
# change to the server
cd('/Servers/MartinTest_Domain_MS1')
```

```
# create the https channel
cmo.createNetworkAccessPoint('SecureHTTPSChannel')

# change to the channel and configure https
cd('/Servers/MartinTest_Domain_MS1/NetworkAccessPoints/SecureHTTPSChannel')
cmo.setProtocol('https')
cmo.setListenPort(46915)
cmo.setEnabled(true)
cmo.setHttpEnabledForThisProtocol(true)
cmo.setTunnelingEnabled(false)
cmo.setOutboundEnabled(false)

# configure SSL and certificate usage
cmo.setTwoWaySSLEnabled(true)
cmo.setClientCertificateEnforced(true)
```

This example configures an HTTPS channel. Note: Here we have additional arguments that specify the usage of SSL and if the client has to provide a certificate. For SSL, a server certificate must be provided (for more details how to set this up, see the security chapters).

IIOP example:

```
# change to the server
cd('/Servers/MartinTest_Domain_MS1')

# create the IIOP channel
cmo.createNetworkAccessPoint('IIOPChannel')

# switch to the IIOP channel and configure it
cd('/Servers/MartinTest_Domain_MS1/NetworkAccessPoints/IIOPChannel')
cmo.setProtocol('iiop')
cmo.setListenPort(46916)
cmo.setEnabled(true)
cmo.setHttpEnabledForThisProtocol(false)
cmo.setTunnelingEnabled(false)
cmo.setOutboundEnabled(false)
cmo.setTwoWaySSLEnabled(false)
cmo.setClientCertificateEnforced(false)
```

The last example configures an IIOP channel for CORBA communications. This protocol can be used with any J2EE client (as it is part of the J2EE standard) or also from non-Java client like C++ processes.

Let us now examine the more complex script that can be used in order to setup the different channels in the diagram. Note that this script only configures the Managed-Servers. This script does not configure an admin channel (please see security chapter for more details on admin channel configuration):

🖫 setup_network_channels

```
# switch to the managed server
cd('/Servers/MartinTest_Domain_MS2')

# create the DMZ network
cmo.createNetworkAccessPoint('DMZ-Network')

# switch to the DMZ network channel
cd('/Servers/MartinTest_Domain_MS2/NetworkAccessPoints/DMZ-Network')

# set the protocol, the DMZ network address and port
cmo.setProtocol('t3')
cmo.setListenAddress('192.168.56.26')
```

```
cmo.setListenPort(20001)
cmo.setEnabled(true)
# configure channel properties
cmo.setHttpEnabledForThisProtocol(false)
cmo.setTunnelingEnabled(false)
cmo.setOutboundEnabled(false)
cmo.setTwoWaySSLEnabled(false)
cmo.setClientCertificateEnforced(false)

# switch back to the server
cd('/Servers/MartinTest_Domain_MS2')

# create the INTERNET channel
cmo.createNetworkAccessPoint('INTERNET')

# switch to the internet channel and configure the https channel
cd('/Servers/MartinTest_Domain_MS2/NetworkAccessPoints/INTERNET')
cmo.setProtocol('https')
cmo.setListenAddress('192.168.60.112')
cmo.setListenPort(20002)
cmo.setEnabled(true)
cmo.setHttpEnabledForThisProtocol(true)
# configure https properties
cmo.setTunnelingEnabled(false)
cmo.setOutboundEnabled(false)
cmo.setTwoWaySSLEnabled(true)
cmo.setClientCertificateEnforced(false)

# again back to the server
cd('/Servers/MartinTest_Domain_MS2')

# create the intranet http access channel
cmo.createNetworkAccessPoint('Intranet_http')

# switch to the channel and configure the http protocol, the correct network address and port
cd('/Servers/MartinTest_Domain_MS2/NetworkAccessPoints/Intranet_http')
cmo.setProtocol('http')
cmo.setListenAddress('192.168.100.215')
cmo.setListenPort(20003)
cmo.setEnabled(true)
cmo.setHttpEnabledForThisProtocol(true)
cmo.setTunnelingEnabled(false)
cmo.setOutboundEnabled(false)
cmo.setTwoWaySSLEnabled(false)
cmo.setClientCertificateEnforced(false)

# last time back to the server
cd('/Servers/MartinTest_Domain_MS2')
# create the access channel for CORBA based applications (like batch clients)
cmo.createNetworkAccessPoint('Intranet_IIOP')
# chage to the IIOP channel and configure again the correct network and port
cd('/Servers/MartinTest_Domain_MS2/NetworkAccessPoints/Intranet_IIOP')
cmo.setProtocol('iiop')
cmo.setListenAddress('192.168.100.215')
cmo.setListenPort(30003)
cmo.setEnabled(true)
cmo.setHttpEnabledForThisProtocol(false)
cmo.setTunnelingEnabled(false)
cmo.setOutboundEnabled(false)
cmo.setTwoWaySSLEnabled(false)
cmo.setClientCertificateEnforced(false)

#######################################################################
# Now do the same for the other managed-server

cd('/Servers/MartinTest_Domain_MS1')
cmo.createNetworkAccessPoint('DMZ-Network')

cd('/Servers/MartinTest_Domain_MS1/NetworkAccessPoints/DMZ-Network')
cmo.setProtocol('t3')
cmo.setListenAddress('192.168.56.25')
cmo.setListenPort(20001)
cmo.setEnabled(true)
cmo.setHttpEnabledForThisProtocol(true)
cmo.setTunnelingEnabled(false)
cmo.setOutboundEnabled(false)
cmo.setTwoWaySSLEnabled(false)
cmo.setClientCertificateEnforced(false)
```

```
cd('/Servers/MartinTest_Domain_MS1')
cmo.createNetworkAccessPoint('INTERNET')

cd('/Servers/MartinTest_Domain_MS1/NetworkAccessPoints/INTERNET')
cmo.setProtocol('https')
cmo.setListenAddress('192.168.60.111')
cmo.setListenPort(20002)
cmo.setPublicPort(40010)
cmo.setEnabled(true)
cmo.setHttpEnabledForThisProtocol(true)
cmo.setTunnelingEnabled(false)
cmo.setOutboundEnabled(false)
cmo.setTwoWaySSLEnabled(false)
cmo.setClientCertificateEnforced(false)
cmo.setPublicPort(20002)

cd('/Servers/MartinTest_Domain_MS1')
cmo.createNetworkAccessPoint('Intranet_http')

cd('/Servers/MartinTest_Domain_MS1/NetworkAccessPoints/Intranet_http')
cmo.setProtocol('http')
cmo.setListenAddress('192.168.100.214')
cmo.setListenPort(20003)
cmo.setEnabled(true)
cmo.setHttpEnabledForThisProtocol(true)
cmo.setTunnelingEnabled(false)
cmo.setOutboundEnabled(false)
cmo.setTwoWaySSLEnabled(false)
cmo.setClientCertificateEnforced(false)

cd('/Servers/MartinTest_Domain_MS1')
cmo.createNetworkAccessPoint('Intranet_IIOP')

cd('/Servers/MartinTest_Domain_MS1/NetworkAccessPoints/Intranet_IIOP')
cmo.setProtocol('iiop')
cmo.setListenAddress('192.168.100.214')
cmo.setListenPort(30003)
cmo.setEnabled(true)
cmo.setHttpEnabledForThisProtocol(false)
cmo.setTunnelingEnabled(false)
cmo.setOutboundEnabled(false)
cmo.setTwoWaySSLEnabled(false)
cmo.setClientCertificateEnforced(false)
```

Summary

We have discussed a special part in a life of a WebLogic domain - its creation. In addition, this chapter has introduced the enrichment of a domain with a number of different WebLogic features that are part of most WebLogic domains. Not all of them are always necessary, but all of them must be considered for each project and a decision must be made if the feature in question is needed for this domain or not.

This section is special in the sense that WebLogic offers automation functions even if no domain - which also means no MBeans - is available. Especially in bigger installations, domain creation must be an automated task so that the setup and maintenance of domains in WebLogic farms can be handled in a professional and timely manner. This so-called offline mode is the essential foundation of automation domain creation.

In the scripts added-on to this book, you can find a comprehensive example that implements a flexible and powerful way to create domains.

Modifying/Extending Domains with WLST

Modifying/Extending Domains with WLST

The last chapter discussed the creation of domains and their essential parts. It depends on the company requirements and system setups if datasources and tuning aspects belong to domain creation or domain extensions. Of course these configuration items can also be part of domain extension. The distinction between them is more based on project experience than technology requirements.

This chapter will discuss additional resources and configuration changes to a WebLogic domain. Even if this is not often used, we should not forget that cleanup operations are also necessary from time to time. Therefore, the last section will introduce some scripts that will delete resources.

Checking for an Existing Edit Session

During domain creation, it is clear that nobody else will work on the domain that was just created. During normal operation, especially in larger admin teams, it might be possible that more than one person wants to make changes on the same domain. Therefore it is advisable to check for an active configuration session before doing your changes.

Extending or changing WebLogic domains always means modifying the domain. Modifications must be done using an edit session and changes will be performed on the Edit-MBeanServer. As different tools and techniques can be used to make changes (AdminConsole, JMX, WLST and others), it is not always easy to recognize when someone else is already doing changes. Whenever changes are required for a given WebLogic domain, it is advisable to check whether someone else is already making changes. Only ONE edit session is allowed at any given time, so you will run into problems (exceptions) if you are trying to open a second session.

WebLogic offers an interface called Configuration Manager that can be used in order to find out whether an active session is already opened or not. You can even find out who is doing changes at the moment. For example, you can use *getCurrentEditor()* to find out who is making changes. You can get the list of inactivated changes using *getUnactivatedChanges()* and you can even find out what is not yet activated. You may also be interested to know how many changes are pending activation (use *len()* on the list to find out).

The following is an example of a function that does a basic check for an active session:

```
def existActiveEditSession():
    # check for existing sessions using the configuration manager
    myConfigurationManager = getConfigManager()
    # try to get an active session.
    # If call succeeds, then a session is available, otherwise an exception is thrown
    try:
        # Test if an active session is available and if yes return it
        myConfigurationManager.getChanges()
        print 'Active edit session found !'

        # test which user is making changes
        userWhoOwnsCurrentEditSession = configmanager.getCurrentEditor()
        print ' The active session belongs to ' + userWhoOwnsCurrentEditSession

        # out of interst, return the number of active changes in the current session
        numberOfUnactivatedChanges numberOfUnactivatedChanges = len(changeList)
        print '   - The actual session has '+str(numberOfUnactivatedChanges)+
              ' not yet activated changes '

        return true
    except:
        # good for us - no active changes found
        print 'No active edit session found !'
        return false
```

But you can get even more information. It is possible to iterate over the list of pending changes and find out what is not yet activated. But be warned: WebLogic has a large and complicated structure for those changes.

The next script is a complete script that uses - same as the domain creation script from the last chapter - property file, userconfig, and key.

🖫 check_session

```
import sys
from java.util import Properties
from java.io import FileInputStream
from java.io import File

pathSeparator = '/';
domainProps = Properties();
userConfigFile = '';
userKeyFile = '';
consoleAction = '';

######################################################################
# Load properties
######################################################################
def intialize():
    global domainProps;
    global userConfigFile;
    global userKeyFile;
    global consoleAction;

    # test arguments
    if len(sys.argv) != 3:
        print 'Usage:  checkforsession.sh <property_file>';
        exit();
```

```
    try:
        domainProps = Properties()

        # load properties and overwrite defaults
        input = FileInputStream(sys.argv[2])
        domainProps.load(input)
        input.close()

        userConfigFile = File(domainProps.getProperty('userconfig'))
        userKeyFile    = File(domainProps.getProperty('userkey'))
    except:
        print 'Cannot load properties  !';
        exit();

    print 'Initialization completed';


###################################################################
# check if session is active
###################################################################
def existActiveEditSession():
    # check for existing sessions using the configuration manager
    myConfigurationManager = getConfigManager()
    # try to get an active session.
    # if call succeeds, then a session is available, otherwise an exception is thrown
    try:
            # Test if an active session is available and if yes return it
            myConfigurationManager.getChanges()
            print 'Active edit session found !'

            # test which user is making changes
            userWhoOwnsCurrentEditSession = myConfigurationManager.getCurrentEditor()
            print '   - The active session belongs to ' + userWhoOwnsCurrentEditSession

            # out of interst, return the number of active changes in the current session
            changeList = myConfigurationManager.getUnactivatedChanges()
            numberOfUnactivatedChanges = len(changeList)
            print '   - The actual session has '+str(numberOfUnactivatedChanges)+
                    ' not yet activated changes '

            print '\n Waiting list of changes:'
            if (numberOfUnactivatedChanges > 0):
                    for nextChange in changeList:
                            print nextChange
            print '\n'

            return 'true'
    except:
            dumpStack()
            # good for us - no active changes found
            print 'No active edit session found !'
            return 'false'


###################################################################
#          Main Code Execution
###################################################################
if __name__ == "main":

        intialize()
        connUri = domainProps.getProperty('adminserverURL)
        print 'Connecting to the Admin Server ('+connUri+')';
        connect(userConfigFile=userConfigFile,userKeyFile=userKeyFile,url=connUri);

        if ('true' == existActiveEditSession()):
            print '\n OH OH session already exists\n'
        else:
            print '\n Good news - session does not yet exist !\n'

        print 'Disconnect from the Admin Server...';
        disconnect();
```

In addition, this script prints out the list of pending changes. Just to give you an impression about the complexity, the test output below shows an example where this script found an active session with one (!) pending change.

```
Initializing WebLogic Scripting Tool (WLST) ...
Welcome to WebLogic Server Administration Scripting Shell

Initialization completed
Connecting to the Admin Server (t3://bookserver.com:7001)
Successfully connected to Admin Server 'AdminServer' that belongs to domain 'MartinTest_Domain'.

Warning: An insecure protocol was used to connect to the
server. To ensure on-the-wire security, the SSL port or
Admin port should be used instead.

Active edit session found !
   - The active session belongs to weblogic
   - The actual session has 1 not yet activated changes

 Waiting list of changes:
javax.management.openmbean.CompositeDataSupport(compositeType=javax.management.openmbean.CompositeTyp
e(name=weblogic.management.mbeanservers.edit.Change,items=((itemName=AttributeName,itemType=javax.man
agement.openmbean.SimpleType(name=java.lang.String)),(itemName=Bean,itemType=javax.management.openmbe
an.CompositeType(name=javax.management.openmbean.CompositeType.ANY,items=((itemName=OpenTypeName,item
Type=javax.management.openmbean.SimpleType(name=java.lang.String)),(itemName=ValueAsString,itemType=j
avax.management.openmbean.SimpleType(name=java.lang.String)),(itemName=ValueAsStringArray,itemType=ja
vax.management.openmbean.ArrayType(name=[Ljava.lang.String;,dimension=1,elementType=javax.management.
openmbean.SimpleType(name=java.lang.String),primitiveArray=false)))),(itemName=NewValue,itemType=jav
ax.management.openmbean.CompositeType(name=javax.management.openmbean.CompositeType.ANY,items=((itemN
ame=OpenTypeName,itemType=javax.management.openmbean.SimpleType(name=java.lang.String)),(itemName=Val
ueAsString,itemType=javax.management.openmbean.SimpleType(name=java.lang.String)),(itemName=ValueAsSt
ringArray,itemType=javax.management.openmbean.ArrayType(name=[Ljava.lang.String;,dimension=1,elementT
ype=javax.management.openmbean.SimpleType(name=java.lang.String),primitiveArray=false)))),(itemName=
OldValue,itemType=javax.management.openmbean.CompositeType(name=javax.management.openmbean.CompositeT
ype.ANY,items=((itemName=OpenTypeName,itemType=javax.management.openmbean.SimpleType(name=java.lang.S
tring)),(itemName=ValueAsString,itemType=javax.management.openmbean.SimpleType(name=java.lang.String)
),(itemName=ValueAsStringArray,itemType=javax.management.openmbean.ArrayType(name=[Ljava.lang.String;
,dimension=1,elementType=javax.management.openmbean.SimpleType(name=java.lang.String),primitiveArray=
false)))),(itemName=Operation,itemType=javax.management.openmbean.SimpleType(name=java.lang.String))
,(itemName=RestartRequired,itemType=javax.management.openmbean.SimpleType(name=java.lang.Boolean)))),
contents={AttributeName=StuckThreadMaxTime,
Bean=javax.management.openmbean.CompositeDataSupport(compositeType=javax.management.openmbean.Composi
teType(name=javax.management.openmbean.CompositeType.ANY,items=((itemName=OpenTypeName,itemType=javax
.management.openmbean.SimpleType(name=java.lang.String)),(itemName=ValueAsString,itemType=javax.manag
ement.openmbean.SimpleType(name=java.lang.String)),(itemName=ValueAsStringArray,itemType=javax.manage
ment.openmbean.ArrayType(name=[Ljava.lang.String;,dimension=1,elementType=javax.management.openmbean.
SimpleType(name=java.lang.String),primitiveArray=false)))),contents={OpenTypeName=javax.management.Ob
jectName, ValueAsString=com.bea:Name=MartinTest_Domain_MS3,Type=Server,
ValueAsStringArray=[Ljava.lang.String;@ddd51a7}),
NewValue=javax.management.openmbean.CompositeDataSupport(compositeType=javax.management.openmbean.Com
positeType(name=javax.management.openmbean.CompositeType.ANY,items=((itemName=OpenTypeName,itemType=j
avax.management.openmbean.SimpleType(name=java.lang.String)),(itemName=ValueAsStringArray,itemType=javax.ma
nagement.openmbean.ArrayType(name=[Ljava.lang.String;,dimension=1,elementType=javax.management.openmb
ean.SimpleType(name=java.lang.String),primitiveArray=false)))),contents={OpenTypeName=java.lang.Integ
er, ValueAsString=6000, ValueAsStringArray=[Ljava.lang.String;@ddd51a7}),
OldValue=javax.management.openmbean.CompositeDataSupport(compositeType=javax.management.openmbean.Com
positeType(name=javax.management.openmbean.CompositeType.ANY,items=((itemName=OpenTypeName,itemType=j
avax.management.openmbean.SimpleType(name=java.lang.String)),(itemName=ValueAsString,itemType=javax.m
anagement.openmbean.SimpleType(name=java.lang.String)),(itemName=ValueAsString,itemType=javax.ma
nagement.openmbean.ArrayType(name=[Ljava.lang.String;,dimension=1,elementType=javax.management.openmb
ean.SimpleType(name=java.lang.String),primitiveArray=false)))),contents={OpenTypeName=java.lang.Integ
er, ValueAsString=
600, ValueAsStringArray=[Ljava.lang.String;@ddd51a7}), Operation=modify, RestartRequired=true})

OH OH session already exists

Disconnect from the Admin Server...
Disconnected from weblogic server: AdminServer
```

The main reason why this output contains so much additional information is the fact that Oracle is using the dynamic datastructures of openMBeans. This is a very flexible way of presenting data, but with the disadvantage of having the data definitions and type definitions also as part of the returned objects.

Datasources

Datasources are very important aspects of domains. All database access is done using datasources. Access to data in databases is configured in WebLogic via JDBC data sources. WebLogic distinguishes between physical datasources and multi-datasources, whereas the latter is basically a container for one or more physical datasources. These datasources are then targeted to a server or cluster and registered in the JNDI tree. Each physical datasource has a connection pool with can be configured and monitored. This chapter will only discuss datasources that are created by the administrator using WLST. This chapter does not discuss datasources created by applications using a deployment plan.

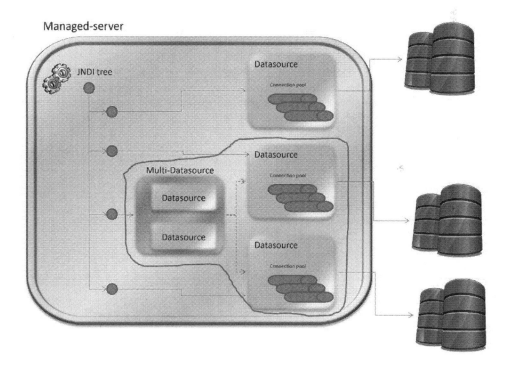

Figure 6.1: *Datasource types*

Note that even if in the diagram a Managed-Server is shown, datasources can also be hosted on the AdminServer. In production systems, however, this is rarely the case as only the Managed-Servers host application components.

WebLogic distinguish between different kinds of datasources.

- Multi-datasources, which are a basically a unit to coordinate a number of real datasources.

- Single NON-XA datasources for database access.

- Single XA datasources, which have different settings than NON-XA datasources.

This section will discuss the automation of datasource creation. We will not (yet) look into datasource monitoring as this will be part of a subsequent chapter.

Creating Standard Datasources

Create a non XA example datasource:

🖫 create_non_XA_datasource

```
cd('/')
# using the create operation on root level to create a new datasource
cmo.createJDBCSystemResource('NonXA_TestDatasource')

# change to the datasource mbean
cd('/JDBCSystemResources/NonXA_TestDatasource/JDBCResource/NonXA_TestDatasource')

# set the name
cmo.setName('NonXA_TestDatasource')

# change to the "JDBCDataSourceParams" mbean of the new datasource and set the JNDI name
cd('/JDBCSystemResources/NonXA_TestDatasource/JDBCResource/NonXA_TestDatasource/JDBCDataSourceParams/
NonXA_TestDatasource')
set('JNDINames',jarray.array([String('jndi/nonXAtest')], String))

# change to the "JDBCDriverParams" mbean of the new datasource and set the connection details like
url , driver and password
cd('/JDBCSystemResources/NonXA_TestDatasource/JDBCResource/NonXA_TestDatasource/JDBCDriverParams/NonX
A_TestDatasource')
cmo.setUrl('jdbc:oracle:thin:@mydbhost.com:1521:TestDB')
cmo.setDriverName('oracle.jdbc.OracleDriver')
cmo.setPassword('db_password');

# change to the JDBCConnectionPoolParams mbean and set connection specific details
cd('/JDBCSystemResources/NonXA_TestDatasource/JDBCResource/NonXA_TestDatasource/JDBCConnectionPoolPar
ams/NonXA_TestDatasource')
cmo.setTestTableName('SQL SELECT 1 FROM DUAL\r\n')
# creating a property for the user name
cd('/JDBCSystemResources/NonXA_TestDatasource/JDBCResource/NonXA_TestDatasource/JDBCDriverParams/NonX
A_TestDatasource/Properties/NonXA_TestDatasource')
cmo.createProperty('user')

# set the user name
cd('/JDBCSystemResources/NonXA_TestDatasource/JDBCResource/NonXA_TestDatasource/JDBCDriverParams/NonX
A_TestDatasource/Properties/NonXA_TestDatasource/Properties/user')
cmo.setValue('dbuser')

# setting transactional options
cd('/JDBCSystemResources/NonXA_TestDatasource/JDBCResource/NonXA_TestDatasource/JDBCDataSourceParams/
NonXA_TestDatasource')
cmo.setGlobalTransactionsProtocol('OnePhaseCommit')

# Finally target the datasource - in this case to a cluster
```

```
cd('/SystemResources/NonXA_TestDatasource')
set('Targets',jarray.array([ObjectName('com.bea:Name=MartinTest_Cluster,Type=Cluster')], ObjectName))
```

Now create 2 XA datasources:

💾 2_XA_example

```
cd('/')
cmo.createJDBCSystemResource('XA_TestDatasource')

cd('/JDBCSystemResources/XA_TestDatasource/JDBCResource/XA_TestDatasource')
cmo.setName('XA_TestDatasource')

cd('/JDBCSystemResources/XA_TestDatasource/JDBCResource/XA_TestDatasource/JDBCDataSourceParams/XA_Tes
tDatasource')
set('JNDINames',jarray.array([String('jndi/xaTest')], String))

cd('/JDBCSystemResources/XA_TestDatasource/JDBCResource/XA_TestDatasource/JDBCDriverParams/XA_TestDat
asource')
cmo.setUrl('jdbc:oracle:thin:@myxadbhost.com:1521:TestXADB')
cmo.setDriverName('oracle.jdbc.xa.client.OracleXADataSource')
cmo.setPassword('db2_password');

cd('/JDBCSystemResources/XA_TestDatasource/JDBCResource/XA_TestDatasource/JDBCConnectionPoolParams/XA
_TestDatasource')
cmo.setTestTableName('SQL SELECT 1 FROM DUAL\r\n')

cd('/JDBCSystemResources/XA_TestDatasource/JDBCResource/XA_TestDatasource/JDBCDriverParams/XA_TestDat
asource/Properties/XA_TestDatasource')
cmo.createProperty('user')

cd('/JDBCSystemResources/XA_TestDatasource/JDBCResource/XA_TestDatasource/JDBCDriverParams/XA_TestDat
asource/Properties/XA_TestDatasource/Properties/user')
cmo.setValue('dbuser')

cd('/JDBCSystemResources/XA_TestDatasource/JDBCResource/XA_TestDatasource/JDBCDataSourceParams/XA_Tes
tDatasource')
cmo.setGlobalTransactionsProtocol('TwoPhaseCommit')

cd('/SystemResources/XA_TestDatasource')
set('Targets',jarray.array([ObjectName('com.bea:Name=MartinTest_Cluster,Type=Cluster')], ObjectName))


cd('/')
cmo.createJDBCSystemResource('XA_TestDatasource2')

cd('/JDBCSystemResources/XA_TestDatasource2/JDBCResource/XA_TestDatasource2')
cmo.setName('XA_TestDatasource2')

cd('/JDBCSystemResources/XA_TestDatasource2/JDBCResource/XA_TestDatasource2/JDBCDataSourceParams/XA_T
estDatasource2')
set('JNDINames',jarray.array([String('jndi/xa_test2')], String))

cd('/JDBCSystemResources/XA_TestDatasource2/JDBCResource/XA_TestDatasource2/JDBCDriverParams/XA_TestD
atasource2')
cmo.setUrl('jdbc:oracle:thin:@myxa2dbhost.com:1521:Test2XADB')
cmo.setDriverName('oracle.jdbc.xa.client.OracleXADataSource')
cmo.setPassword('db3_password');

cd('/JDBCSystemResources/XA_TestDatasource2/JDBCResource/XA_TestDatasource2/JDBCConnectionPoolParams/
XA_TestDatasource2')
cmo.setTestTableName('SQL SELECT 1 FROM DUAL\r\n\r\n')

cd('/JDBCSystemResources/XA_TestDatasource2/JDBCResource/XA_TestDatasource2/JDBCDriverParams/XA_TestD
atasource2/Properties/XA_TestDatasource2')
cmo.createProperty('user')

cd('/JDBCSystemResources/XA_TestDatasource2/JDBCResource/XA_TestDatasource2/JDBCDriverParams/XA_TestD
atasource2/Properties/XA_TestDatasource2/Properties/user')
cmo.setValue('dbuser')

cd('/JDBCSystemResources/XA_TestDatasource2/JDBCResource/XA_TestDatasource2/JDBCDataSourceParams/XA_T
estDatasource2')
cmo.setGlobalTransactionsProtocol('TwoPhaseCommit')

cd('/SystemResources/XA_TestDatasource2')
```

```
set('Targets',jarray.array([ObjectName('com.bea:Name=MartinTest_Cluster,Type=Cluster')], ObjectName))
```

Last, let us create a multi-datasource, which acts as a container/abstraction layer for the 2 XA datasources we just created in the previous script:

```
cd('/')
cmo.createJDBCSystemResource('TestMultiDS')

cd('/JDBCSystemResources/TestMultiDS/JDBCResource/TestMultiDS')
cmo.setName('TestMultiDS')

cd('/JDBCSystemResources/TestMultiDS/JDBCResource/TestMultiDS/JDBCDataSourceParams/TestMultiDS')
set('JNDINames',jarray.array([String('jdbc/multiDS')], String))
cmo.setAlgorithmType('Load-Balancing')
cmo.setDataSourceList('XA_TestDatasource,XA_TestDatasource2')

cd('/SystemResources/TestMultiDS')
set('Targets',jarray.array([ObjectName('com.bea:Name=MartinTest_Cluster,Type=Cluster')], ObjectName))
```

GridLink Datasources

The generic datasource in WebLogic is well suited for most applications. In combination with RAC systems and RAC configurations, the generic datasource has some shortcuts. RAC (Real Application Cluster) means a one-to-many relationship between the database itself and the different database instances. Instances in RAC can be distributed over multiple machines.

In WebLogic 11g, Oracle has introduced a new and advanced feature in order to provide better support for RAC databases. The older multiple datasource approach has its shortcuts and limitations. This is especially true for the multi-datasource, because it is an implementation that relies on WebLogic only (middleware layer) and does not make use of database features like ONS (Oracle Notification Service). On the other hand, multi-datasources are suitable for databases from different vendors.

With version 10.3.4, a new feature has been added to WebLogic that supports RAC natively by responding to FAN events to provide fast connection failover and connection load-balancing. This feature is essentially an extension built into the generic datasource, which uses the RAC integration capabilities of universal connection pool. It requires the administrator to enable FAN and the address(es) of the ONS. It is recommended to upgrade from multi-datasources to this new GridLink feature in the case of real RAC database systems.

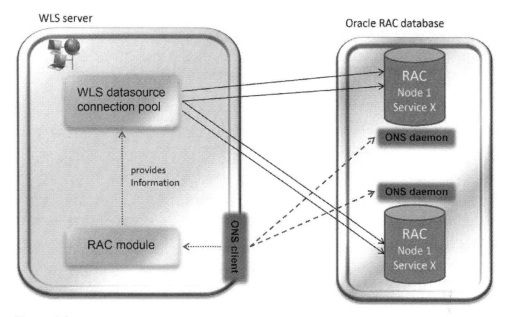

WLS server   Oracle RAC database

Figure 6.2: *GridLink datasource*

GridLink extends the generic datasource with the following features: fast connection failover, runtime connection load balancing, SCAN addresses, and intelligent handling of RAC node outages. FAN stands for "Fast Application Notification". The general concept behind this datasource is that the datasource will get notifications from the Oracle ONS about available RAC nodes, failed nodes, newly activated nodes, and also how these nodes are loaded. Based on this information it is possible for the datasource to select the best RAC node (available and with the smallest load) for new connections. Without FAN, the datasource has no information about which RAC node is actually up or down or heavily loaded, which results in the fact that the datasource has to choose any RAC node out of the list in the connection string until it gets one that is available. The datasource can then effectively adapt its connection pools depending on the state changes received from ONS.

Of course GridLink datasources can be setup and configured using WLST. For WSLT, it is exactly the same as setting up a generic Oracle datasource with a RAC URL. The only extension that we have to add is the activation of FAN and the configuration of the ONS address list:

```
# setup the normal datasource properties (see the above sections)
# this also might include wallets
# ...

# change to oracle params. Note that we must change to the oracle specific
cd('/JDBCSystemResources/myTestDatasource/JDBCResource/myTestDatasource/JDBCOracleParams/myTestDataso
urce')
```

```
# enable FAN
cmo.setFanEnabled(true)
# configure ONS listener address list
cmo.setOnsNodeList('onshost1.book.com:6200,onshost2.book.com:6200')
```

WLS also offers a number of special debug flags for the GridLink feature:

- -Dweblogic.debug.DebugJDBCRAC=true

- -Dweblogic.debug.DebugJDBCONS=true

- -Dweblogic.debug.DebugJDBCUCP=true

Using Parameters in the Scripts

One big disadvantage of the scripts above is the fact that all values are hard-coded into the script. In real production environments, you normally have to setup a large number of datasources with different values. Therefore it is the best approach for any environment to separate the real values from the script and use property files in order to use the same script for many different (datasource) setups.

It is also proven to be a very good approach to write scripts that can configure multiple resources (datasources in this case). This allows you to create one configuration file for each domain.

🖫 configure_datasources

```
##################################################################
# create all datasources
##################################################################
def createAllDatasources():
  try:
        totalDataSource_to_Create=domainProps.get("amountDatasources")

        edit()
        startEdit()
        print 'Creating All DataSources ....'
        i=1
        while (i <= int(totalDataSource_to_Create)) :

            try:
                cd('/')
                datasource_name = get_instance_property('datasource',str(i), 'name');
                datasource_targettype = get_instance_property('datasource',str(i), 'targettype');
                datasource_target = get_instance_property('datasource',str(i), 'target');
                datasource_jndiname  = get_instance_property('datasource',str(i), 'jndiname');
                datasource_driver_class =
                                  get_instance_property('datasource',str(i), 'driver_class');
                datasource_url = get_instance_property('datasource',str(i), 'url');
                datasource_username  = get_instance_property('datasource',str(i), 'username');
                datasource_password  = get_instance_property('datasource',str(i), 'password');
                datasource_maxcapacity  = get_instance_property('datasource',str(i), 'maxcapacity');
                datasource_testquery  = get_instance_property('datasource',str(i), 'testquery');
                # GlobalTransactionsProtocol ONLY for NON-XA datasources possible !!!!
                # values possible: 'None' and 'OnePhaseCommit'  for XA: 'TwoPhaseCommit'
                datasource_globalTransactionsProtocol =
                          get_instance_property('datasource',str(i), 'globalTransactionsProtocol');

                # Creating DataSource
                cmo.createJDBCSystemResource(datasource_name)
                cd('/JDBCSystemResources/' + datasource_name + '/JDBCResource/' + datasource_name)
                cmo.setName(datasource_name)
```

```
                cd('/JDBCSystemResources/' + datasource_name + '/JDBCResource/' + datasource_name
                    + '/JDBCDataSourceParams/' + datasource_name )
                set('JNDINames',jarray.array([String(datasource_jndiname)], String))

                cd('/JDBCSystemResources/' + datasource_name + '/JDBCResource/' + datasource_name
                    + '/JDBCDriverParams/' + datasource_name )
                cmo.setUrl(datasource_url)
                cmo.setDriverName( datasource_driver_class );
                cmo.setPassword(datasource_password);

                cd('/JDBCSystemResources/' + datasource_name + '/JDBCResource/' + datasource_name
                    + '/JDBCConnectionPoolParams/' + datasource_name )
                cmo.setTestTableName(datasource_testquery);

                cd('/JDBCSystemResources/' + datasource_name + '/JDBCResource/' + datasource_name
                    + '/JDBCDriverParams/' + datasource_name + '/Properties/' + datasource_name )
                cmo.createProperty('user')
                cd('/JDBCSystemResources/' + datasource_name + '/JDBCResource/' + datasource_name
                    + '/JDBCDriverParams/' + datasource_name + '/Properties/' + datasource_name
                    + '/Properties/user')
                cmo.setValue(datasource_username);

                cd('/JDBCSystemResources/' + datasource_name + '/JDBCResource/' + datasource_name
                    + '/JDBCDataSourceParams/' + datasource_name )
                cmo.setGlobalTransactionsProtocol(datasource_globalTransactionsProtocol);

                cd('/SystemResources/' + datasource_name );
                set('Targets',jarray.array([ObjectName('com.bea:Name=' + datasource_target
                    + ',Type='+datasource_targettype)], ObjectName))

                print 'DataSource: ',datasource_name,', has been created Successfully !!!'

            except:
                dumpStack();
                print '***** CANNOT CREATE DATASOURCE !!! Check If the DataSource With the Name : ' +
                    datasource_name +' Alreday exists or NOT...'
                print ''

            i = i + 1
        save()
        activate()
except:
    print 'Exception while creating datasources - please check databases !';
    dumpStack();
```

Datasource Security using Wallets

One major challenge in ALL systems, especially in production systems, is security. For databases, this means dealing with access information to the database. Getting access to these databases very often means getting access to confidential/secret and/or personal information. On one hand the WebLogic Server needs credentials in order to connect to the database, but on the other hand nobody else should have it and especially nobody else should see the password in clear text. In most companies, this is an important audit issue.

The big disadvantage of the previous scripts is the fact that the username and especially the password were shown in clear text. Even if these values are stored encrypted in the WebLogic configuration files, they are provided in clear text.

This section describes the usage of the Oracle wallet to store database credentials for WebLogic Server datasource definitions. An Oracle wallet is essentially a keystore that hosts datasource credentials (potentially beside other certificates and entries). In addition, this wallet has the special feature of an autologin which means that the credentials can be used by an Oracle JDBC driver or Oracle client without knowing the wallet password. Without the password, it is not possible to dump the credentials out of the wallet using the keystore or wallet tools.

This approach has a number of benefits:

- Wallets can be provided by the database DBAs and therefore the WebLogic admins do not need to know the passwords as they do not need to configure those into the server.

- Wallets provide a central place for the credentials and can be used by many different servers. Therefore, a credential change done by the DBA results in just updating the wallet and eliminates the need to update all datasources in all servers.

- Wallets therefore support the separation of responsibilities between the DBAs and WebLogic admins.

Besides the benefits, you should never forget that there are also risks. You can see a wallet like a private key. Once somebody has access to it and knows the database URL, he or she has full access without knowing the password or user. Therefore wallets must be secured in the file system as much as possible in order to avoid misuse.

This feature provides even more benefits if combined with the Oracle TNS (Transparent Network Substrate) administrative file to hide the details of the database connection string (host name, port number, and service name) from the datasource definition and instead use an alias. For easier understanding, I will not use the TNS alias extension in this section, but I advise all admins to consider this if an Oracle client is installed on the WebLogic machine. It provides better security and better abstraction.

In order to create a wallet, you need the *mkstore* command from the oracle client.

Step 1: Create a new empty wallet:

```
/data/oracle/product/x.x.x/client/bin/mkstore -wrl /wallet/myWalletDirectoy
-create
```

Step 2: Add credentials to a wallet:

```
/data/oracle/product/x.x.x/client/bin/mkstore -wrl /wallet/myWalletDirectoy
-createCredential <dbJDBC_URL> <dbUser> <dbPassword>
```

Example 1:

Advanced WebLogic Server Automation

mkstore -wrl /wallet/myWalletDirectoy -createCredential localhost:1521:BOOKDB bookuser topSecret

Example 2:
mkstore -wrl /wallet/myWalletDirectoy -createCredential BOOKDBALIAS bookuser topSecret

Note:

- The JDBC URL is everything AFTER the "@" symbol.

- You can add credentials to several distinct databases into one wallet, but you cannot add multiple credentials that point to the same database and just have different schemas.

- Examine the two examples. Example 1 is a "normal" JDBC URL, which is used in most application servers. Example 2 uses an alias, which is defined in the tnsnames.ora.

The JDBC URL will then change to
jdbc:oracle:thin://@databasehost.com:1521:TestDB. Note the "/" in front of the @ symbol.

In the following WLST method, note that a username and password are NOT used. Instead we will set a wallet location as a parameter.

🖫 datasources_wallet

```
##################################################################
# create all datasources
##################################################################
def createAllDatasources():
  try:
        totalDataSource_to_Create=domainProps.get("amountDatasources")

        edit()
        startEdit()
        print 'Creating All DataSources ....'
        i=1
        while (i <= int(totalDataSource_to_Create)) :

          try:
                datasource_name    = get_instance_property('datasource',str(i), 'name');
                datasource_targettype   = get_instance_property('datasource',str(i), 'targettype');
                datasource_target = get_instance_property('datasource',str(i), 'target');
                datasource_jndiname   = get_instance_property('datasource',str(i), 'jndiname');
                datasource_relativeWalletDir
                        = get_instance_property('datasource',str(i), 'relativeWalletDir');
                datasource_driver_class = get_instance_property('datasource',str(i), 'driver_class');
                datasource_url = get_instance_property('datasource',str(i), 'url');
                datasource_maxcapacity   = get_instance_property('datasource',str(i), 'maxcapacity');
                datasource_testquery = get_instance_property('datasource',str(i), 'testquery');
                datasource_globalTransactionsProtocol = get_instance_property('datasource',str(i),
                        'globalTransactionsProtocol');

                # Creating DataSource
                cd('/')
                cmo.createJDBCSystemResource(datasource_name)
                cd('/JDBCSystemResources/' + datasource_name + '/JDBCResource/' + datasource_name)
                cmo.setName(datasource_name)
```

```
            cd('/JDBCSystemResources/' + datasource_name + '/JDBCResource/' + datasource_name
                + '/JDBCDataSourceParams/' + datasource_name )
            set('JNDINames',jarray.array([String(datasource_jndiname)], String))

            cd('/JDBCSystemResources/' + datasource_name + '/JDBCResource/' + datasource_name
                + '/JDBCDriverParams/' + datasource_name )
            cmo.setUrl(datasource_url)
            cmo.setDriverName( datasource_driver_class );

            cd('/JDBCSystemResources/' + datasource_name + '/JDBCResource/' + datasource_name
                + '/JDBCConnectionPoolParams/' + datasource_name )
            cmo.setTestTableName(datasource_testquery);

            # WALLET
            cd('/JDBCSystemResources/' + datasource_name + '/JDBCResource/' + datasource_name
                + '/JDBCDriverParams/' + datasource_name + '/Properties/' + datasource_name )
            cmo.createProperty('oracle.net.wallet_location')

            cd('/JDBCSystemResources/' + datasource_name + '/JDBCResource/' + datasource_name
                + '/JDBCDriverParams/' + datasource_name + '/Properties/' + datasource_name
                + '/Properties/oracle.net.wallet_location')

            cmo.setValue(domainProps.getProperty('walletsDirectory')+
                        '/'+datasource_relativeWalletDir);

            cd('/JDBCSystemResources/' + datasource_name + '/JDBCResource/' + datasource_name
                + '/JDBCDataSourceParams/' + datasource_name )
            cmo.setGlobalTransactionsProtocol(datasource_globalTransactionsProtocol);

            cd('/SystemResources/' + datasource_name )
            set('Targets',jarray.array([ObjectName('com.bea:Name=' + datasource_target
                + ',Type='+datasource_targettype)], ObjectName))

            print 'DataSource: ',datasource_name,', has been created Successfully !!!'
        except:
            dumpStack();
            print '***** CANNOT CREATE DATASOURCE !!! Check If the DataSource With the Name : '
                , datasource_name ,' Alreday exists or NOT...'
            print ''

        i = i + 1
    save()
    activate()
except:
    print 'Exception while creating datasources - please check databases !';
    dumpStack();
```

This script does not look much different than the other scripts, but it has a number of great advantages for production systems. These are some of the advantages:

- No usernames and passwords are necessary in clear text in the scripts

- Wallets can be placed in central (but secured!) locations. Be aware that wallets must be treated like private SSH keys. This also means that database administrators (DBAs) can update wallets without the need of updating every single datasource in all domains.

- Middleware administrators do not need to know the passwords, which eliminate another potential security hole.

- In combination with TNS aliases, the admins do not even know the concrete database URL since the tnsnames.ora is also maintained by the DBAs and aliases can be arbitrary strings.

- All this together dramatically improves security on the middleware layer, provided that the wallets are secured (file system security) in the right way.

JMS Resources

WebLogic provides a complex JMS subsystem, which consists of many different MBeans. The main MBean is the JMSServer, which is basically the container for all other JMS resources. Every WebLogic Server can host multiple JMS servers, which consist of JMS system module resources. These artifacts are stored in the domain's config.xml file.

Base JMS configuration

The base JMS configuration is going to involve the following:

- Persistence store creation with Files: for each Managed-Server where JMS servers are configured, we need to create a File store. As a best practice, create a dedicated folder where all the file stores can be stored per machine. Use the same directory structure for all machines where the file stores configured.

- Persistence store with JDBC: use this when your JMS message persistence requires huge message sizes.

- JMS server: Up to WebLogic 12.1.1 it is necessary to configure one JMS server for each Managed-Server. This of course only applies to all Managed-Servers that should host JMS messaging components. The reason is that up to WebLogic 12.1.1, the deployment target for a JMS server configuration can only be a Managed-Server. Starting with WebLogic 12.1.2 it is possible to target a JMS server also to a cluster.

- JMS module, which may include the following subcomponents: Subdeployment, Connectionfactory, Uniform Distributed queue, and Foreign server.

Persistence store

Initially, we need a JMS persistence store configuration using WLST script. This enables you to configure as many JMS servers and persistence stores as required for an application deployment. The persistence store can be created with File Store or JDBC store options. As per your domain requirement, you can specify the total number in the properties file. Suppose an Architect team decided to use only File Stores. In that case, we can set JDBC total store to 0 so that the loop will be disabled.

Configuring JMS Module

All the configuration changes for JMS will be stored in the config.xml repository and its sub-deployment module descriptor file. The JMS system module can be defined with name, target to servers or cluster, and its related sub-deployments such as Queue or publisher/Subscriber topics.

It is important to understand that one element of a JMS module is a ConnectionFactory. The ConnectionFactory is responsible for providing connectivity to JMS services. If there are different physical machines in the cluster (with respect to CPU power, etc.), then JMS destinations must be distributed destinations with the "Allocate members Uniformly" option set to "false". In this case it is advisable to manually select more physical destination from the high powered machines. The configuring JMS module is going to have various sub-deployment components in it. First, we need to configure the JMS Module name, target to the advanced deployment as sub-deployment.

The JMS module implements the base container, which includes a connection factory and the different JMS destinations (queues or topics). Depending on the infrastructure requirements, it might be necessary to make the connection factory available to all servers in the domain. Queues and topics can be targeted to only a single JMS server if required.

Subdeployment

It is important to configure a subdeployment per JMS Module. The reasons for subdeployments in the JMS area include avoiding network traffic between JMS components, group connection factories, queues and topics, and it simplifies the migration.

A subdeployment is a mechanism by which JMS modules like queues, topics, and connection factories are grouped and targeted to a server resource such as JMS servers, server instances, SAF agents, or a cluster. So there would be two different subdeployments: "Default" is for connection factory, and the other is for resources within the JMS module can be the best practice.

For example, we can group a connection factory with stand-alone queues or topics in a subdeployment targeted to a specific JMS server, which guarantees that all these resources are co-located to avoid extra network traffic. Another advantage of such a configuration would be if the targeted JMS server needs to be migrated to another WebLogic Server instance, then the connection factory and all its connections will also migrate along with the JMS server's destinations. However, when stand-alone queues or topics are members of a subdeployment, a connection factory can only be targeted to the same JMS server.

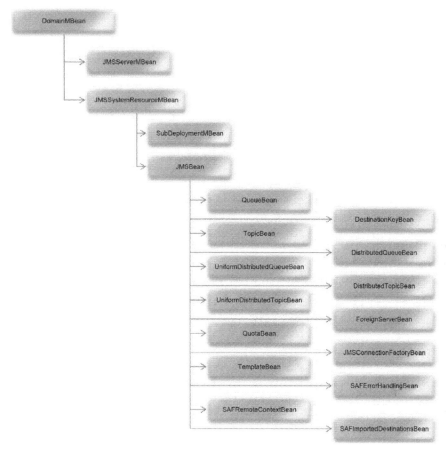

Figure 6.3: *JMS MBean tree*

This MBean...	Configures...
JMSServerMBean	A JMS server is management container for targeted destination resources (queues and topics) in a JMS system. A JMS server's primary responsibility is to maintain information on what persistent store is used for any persistent messages. As a container for targeted destinations, any configuration or run-time changes to a JMS server can affect all of its destinations.
JMSSystemResourceMBean	A JMS system resource is a resource whose definition is part of the system configuration rather than an application.
SubDeploymentMBean	Subdeployments enable administrators to deploy some resources in a JMS module to a JMS server and other JMS resources to a server instance or cluster.
JMSBean	The top of the JMS module bean tree.
DestinationKeyBean	Defines a unique sort order that destinations can apply to arriving messages.
DistributedQueueBean	Defines a set of queues that are distributed on multiple JMS servers, but which are

	accessible as a single, logical queue to JMS clients.
DistributedTopicBean	Defines a set of topics that are distributed on multiple JMS servers, but which are accessible as a single, logical topic to JMS clients.
ForeignServerBean	Defines foreign messaging providers or remote WebLogic Server instances that are not part of the current domain.
JMSConnectionFactoryBean	Defines a set of connection configuration parameters that are used to create connections for JMS clients.
QueueBean	Defines a point-to-point destination type, which are used for asynchronous peer communications. A message delivered to a queue is distributed to only one consumer.
QuotaBean	Controls the allotment of system resources available to destinations.
SAFRemoteContextBean	Defines the URL of the remote server instance or cluster where a JMS destination is exported from
SAFErrorHandlingBean	Defines the action to take when the SAF service
SAFImportedDestinationsBean	Defines a collection of imported store-and-forward (SAF) destinations.
TemplateBean	Defines a set of default configuration settings for multiple destinations.
TopicBean	Defines a publish/subscribe destination type, which are used for asynchronous peer communications. A message delivered to a topic is distributed to all topic consumers.
UniformDistributedQueueBean	Defines a uniformly configured distributed queue, whose members have a consistent configuration of all distributed queue parameters
UniformDistributedTopicBean	Defines a uniformly configured distributed topic, whose members have a consistent configuration of all uniform distributed queue parameters

(Source: Oracle Corporation[7])

Table 6.1: JMS MBeans

Creating Local JMS Resources

This section will explain the creation of the most common scenarios - the creation of JMS components hosted locally in the domain. The different functions in the next script will create the necessary JMS file store, JMS server, and JMS module instances. For the server we can specify the persistent store to use and we can specify logging details (see also previous chapter on logging). The last functions will also create sub-deployments, queues and topics.

The following example scripts show how to create the different local JMS resources.

Example for creating a filestore with a provided name:

```
def createFileStore(fileStoreName, wlsServerName):
    cd('/')
    cmo.createFileStore(fileStoreName)
    cd('/FileStores/'+fileStoreName)
    cmo.setDirectory('/applications/testapplication/myTestApp_filestore')

    # define the target for this filestore
    set('Targets',
        jarray.array([ObjectName('com.bea:Name='+wlsServerName+',Type=Server')], ObjectName))
```

---

[7] docs.oracle.com/middleware/1212/wls/JMXCU/subsystem.htm

Example for creating a JMS server:

```
# this function iterates over all managed-server in a cluster,
# defines a JMS server and target it
def createJMSServer(jmsServerName,fileStoreName,wlsServerName):
    # 1st create the filestore:
    createFileStore(fileStoreName, wlsServerName)
    # now create the server
    cd('/')
    cmo.createJMSServer(jmsServerName)
    cd('/Deployments/'+jmsServerName)
    cmo.setPersistentStore(getMBean('/FileStores/'+fileStoreName))
    set('Targets',
        jarray.array([ObjectName('com.bea:Name='+wlsServerName+',Type=Server')], ObjectName))

    # now we can define threshold values
    cmo.setBytesThresholdHigh(-1)
    cmo.setBytesThresholdLow(-1)
    cmo.setMessagesThresholdHigh(-1)
    cmo.setMessagesThresholdLow(-1)

    # now we can define quotas values
    cmo.setBytesMaximum(-1)
    cmo.setMessagesMaximum(-1)
    cmo.setBlockingSendPolicy('FIFO')
    cmo.setMaximumMessageSize(10000000)

    # configure the log file for this JMS server
    cd('/Deployments/'+jmsServerName+'/JMSMessageLogFile/'+jmsServerName)
    cmo.setRotationType('byTime')
    cmo.setRotateLogOnStartup(false)
    cmo.setRotationTime('00:00')
    cmo.setFileTimeSpan(24)
    cmo.setFileCount(30)
    cmo.setNumberOfFilesLimited(true)
    cmo.setFileName('/applications/testapplication/'+jmsServerName+'.log')
```

Note that up to WebLogic 12.1.1, is was only possible to target a JMSServer to a Managed-Server. This also means that it is necessary to create a JMSServer for each Managed-Server.

The next script function will show how to create a JMS module:

```
def createJMSModule(jmsModuleName, targetType, targetName):
    cd('/')
    cmo.createJMSSystemResource(jmsModuleName)
    cd('/SystemResources/'+jmsModuleName)
    set('Targets',jarray.array([ObjectName('com.bea:Name='+targetName+',Type='+targetType)],
ObjectName))
```

The next script function will show how to create a connection factory:

```
def createJmsConnectionFactory(jmsModuleName, connectionFactoryName, jmsJNDIname):
    cd('/JMSSystemResources/'+jmsModuleName+'/JMSResource/'+jmsModuleName)
    cmo.createConnectionFactory(connectionFactoryName)
    cd('/JMSSystemResources/'+jmsModuleName+'/JMSResource/'+jmsModuleName+
        '/ConnectionFactories/'+connectionFactoryName)
    cmo.setJNDIName(jmsJNDIname)
    cmo.setDefaultTargetingEnabled(true)
    cd('/JMSSystemResources/'+jmsModuleName+'/JMSResource/'+jmsModuleName+'/ConnectionFactories/'
        + connectionFactoryName+'/SecurityParams/'+connectionFactoryName)
    cmo.setAttachJMSXUserId(false)
```

If full XA transaction support is needed, then you have to create a XA enabled connection factory instead of a normal factory:

```
def createJms_XA_ConnectionFactory(jmsModuleName, connectionFactoryName, jmsJNDIname):
    cd('/JMSSystemResources/'+jmsModuleName+'/JMSResource/'+jmsModuleName)
    cmo.createConnectionFactory(connectionFactoryName)
    cd('/JMSSystemResources/'+jmsModuleName+'/JMSResource/'+jmsModuleName+'/ConnectionFactories/'+
        connectionFactoryName)
    cmo.setJNDIName(jmsJNDIname)
    cmo.setDefaultTargetingEnabled(true)
    cd('/JMSSystemResources/'+jmsModuleName+'/JMSResource/'+jmsModuleName+'/ConnectionFactories/'+
        connectionFactoryName+'/SecurityParams/'+connectionFactoryName)
    cmo.setAttachJMSXUserId(false)
    cd('/JMSSystemResources/'+jmsModuleName+'/JMSResource/'+jmsModuleName+'/ConnectionFactories/'+
        connectionFactoryName+'/TransactionParams/'+connectionFactoryName)

    cmo.setTransactionTimeout(3600)
    cmo.setXAConnectionFactoryEnabled(true)
```

The following function will demonstrate how to create a sub-deployment:

```
def createJMSSubDeployment(jmsModuleName,subDeploymentName, targetName):
    cd('/SystemResources/'+jmsModuleName)
    cmo.createSubDeployment(subDeploymentName)
    # target to server or cluster
    cd('/SystemResources/'+jmsModuleName+'/SubDeployments/'+subDeploymentName)
    set('Targets',jarray.array([ObjectName('com.bea:Name='+targetName+',Type=JMSServer')],
        ObjectName))
```

Queues are one of the main concepts of JMS. Queues are basically a one-to-one messaging, which means that the first consumer who reads the message gets it and then the message will be removed from the queue. The message is not read twice.

Example of creating a queue:

```
def createQueue(jmsModuleName, queueName, jndiQueueName, subDeploymentName):
    cd('/JMSSystemResources/'+jmsModuleName+'/JMSResource/'+jmsModuleName)
    cmo.createQueue(queueName)
    cd('/JMSSystemResources/'+jmsModuleName+'/JMSResource/'+jmsModuleName+'/Queues/'+queueName)
    cmo.setJNDIName(jndiQueueName)
    cmo.setSubDeploymentName(subDeploymentName)

def createQueueWithErrorHandling(jmsModuleName, queueName, jndiQueueName,
                                 subDeploymentName, errorQueueName):
    # create the queue
    createQueue(jmsModuleName, queueName, jndiQueueName, subDeploymentName)

    # now add the error handling
    cd('/JMSSystemResources/'+jmsModuleName+'/JMSResource/'+jmsModuleName+'/Queues/'+
        queueName+'/DeliveryFailureParams/'+queueName)
    cmo.setRedeliveryLimit(3)
    cmo.setExpirationPolicy('Redirect')
    cmo.setErrorDestination(getMBean('/JMSSystemResources/'+jmsModuleName+'/JMSResource/'+
                                     jmsModuleName+'/Queues/'+errorQueueName))
```

The other fundamental concept of JMS is topics. A topic is like a newsgroup which means that messages posted to this topic can be read my many consumers until the message gets explicitly removed.

Example of creating a topic:

```
def createTopic(jmsServer, jmsModuleName, topicName, jndiTopicName, subDeploymentName):
    cd('/JMSSystemResources/'+jmsModuleName+'/JMSResource/'+jmsModuleName)
    cmo.createTopic(topicName)
    cd('/JMSSystemResources/'+jmsModuleName+'/JMSResource/'+jmsModuleName+'/Topics/'+topicName)
    cmo.setJNDIName(jndiTopicName)
    cmo.setSubDeploymentName(subDeploymentName)
```

The next script will show the usage of those function definitions. Note that the following script is really just a demonstration of how to use the function. I strongly advise using a script that has all the values outsourced into a property file so that the script itself will implement a generic approach. Normally with outsourced values, the script would make intensive use of loops and generic implementations:

🖫 function_definitions

```
# conncto to the admin server
connect('weblogic','xxxx','t3://localhost:7001')
try:
   # start an edit session
   edit()
   startEdit()
   cd('/')

   # create different instances of JMS servers
   createAnewJMSServer('MyTestServer_1','mytest_filestore_1.store','AdminServer')
   createAnewJMSServer('MyTestServer_2','mytest_filestore_2.store','AdminServer')
   createAnewJMSServer('MyTestServer_3','mytest_filestore_3.store','AdminServer')

   # create different JMS modules
   createJMSModule('testModule_1', 'Server', 'AdminServer')
   createJMSModule('testModule_2', 'Server', 'AdminServer')
   createJMSModule('testModule_3', 'Server', 'AdminServer')

   # now create a number of connection factories on the different modules
   createJmsConnectionFactory('testModule_1', 'connection_1_1', 'jms/connection_1_1')
   createJmsConnectionFactory('testModule_1', 'connection_1_2', 'jms/connection_1_2')
   createJmsConnectionFactory('testModule_1', 'connection_1_3', 'jms/connection_1_3')

   createJmsConnectionFactory('testModule_2', 'connection_2_1', 'jms/connection_2_1')
   createJmsConnectionFactory('testModule_2', 'connection_2_2', 'jms/connection_2_2')

   createJmsConnectionFactory('testModule_3', 'connection_3_1', 'jms/connection_3_1')
   createJmsConnectionFactory('testModule_3', 'connection_3_2', 'jms/connection_3_2')

   # example how to create a XA connection factory
   createJms_XA_ConnectionFactory('testModule_1', 'connection_xa_1_1', 'jms/XA_connection_1_1')

   # create different sub deployments
   createJMSSubDeployment('testModule_1','subDeployment_1', 'MyTestServer_1')
   createJMSSubDeployment('testModule_2','subDeployment_2', 'MyTestServer_2')
   createJMSSubDeployment('testModule_3','subDeployment_3', 'MyTestServer_3')

   # finally create QUEUE destinations
   createQueue('testModule_1', 'Queue_1a', 'jms/Queue_1a', 'subDeployment_1')
   createQueue('testModule_1', 'Queue_1b', 'jms/Queue_1b', 'subDeployment_1')
   createQueue('testModule_1', 'Queue_1c', 'jms/Queue_1c', 'subDeployment_1')
   createQueue('testModule_2', 'Queue_2', 'jms/Queue_2', 'subDeployment_2')
   createQueue('testModule_3', 'Queue_3', 'jms/Queue_3', 'subDeployment_3')

   # create a queue with error handling
   createQueueWithErrorHandling('testModule_1', 'Queue_ERR_1a',
                                'jms/Queue_ERR_1a', 'subDeployment_1', 'Queue_1c')

   # create a TOPIC destination
   createTopic('MyTestServer_1', 'testModule_1', 'Topic_1a', 'jms/Topic_1a', 'subDeployment_1')

   # save changes and activate
   save()
   activate()
except Exception, e:
   print(e)
   dumpStack()

disconnect()
```

Target JMS Server to a Cluster

12.1.2 ++   Starting with WebLogic 12.1.2, it is possible to target a JMSServer to a cluster. This provides a much greater flexibility, especially with respect to the new dynamic cluster feature.

```
# change to domain MBean
cd('/')
# create the JMS Server
cmo.createJMSServer('JMSServer-11')

# change to the new server
cd('/JMSServers/JMSServer-11')

# target it to a cluster - new in 12.1.2 !
set('Targets',jarray.array([ObjectName('com.bea:Name=TestCluster,Type=Cluster')], ObjectName))

# configure the JMSServer
cmo.setPersistentStore(None)
cmo.setTemporaryTemplateResource(None)
cmo.setTemporaryTemplateName(None)
cmo.setProductionPausedAtStartup('false')
cmo.setPagingMessageCompressionEnabled(true)
cmo.setInsertionPausedAtStartup('false')
cmo.setConsumptionPausedAtStartup('false')
cmo.setMessagesMaximum(500000)
cmo.setBytesMaximum(3253223)
```

Creating Distributed Destinations

A distributed destination consists of a number of JMS destinations that are made accessible as a single, logical destination. It has its own entry in the JNDI tree and has members who are normally distributed among the different server of a cluster. Applications that use distributed destinations have much better availability (e.g. 24x7) because load balancing and failover are supported for distributed destinations. WebLogic can balance the messaging load over all members of the distributed destination (if they are running).

Two flavors of distributed destination exist: queues and topics.

The first example shows how to create a distributed queue:

```
def createDistributedUniformQueue(mySystemResource, myJMSResource, mySubDeployment, dQueueName,
dQueueJNDIName):
    # cd into the resource
    cd('JMSSystemResource/'+mySystemResource+'/JmsResource/'+myJMSResource)

    # create uniform distributed queue
    myNewDistributedQueue=create(dQueueName, 'UniformDistributedQueue')
    myNewDistributedQueue.setJNDIName(dQueueJNDIName)
    myNewDistributedQueue.setSubDeploymentName(mySubDeployment)
```

This example shows how to create a distributed topic:

```
def createDistributedUniformTopic(mySystemResource, myJMSResource, mySubDeployment, dTopicName,
dTopicJNDIName):
    # cd into the resource
    cd('JMSSystemResource/'+mySystemResource+'/JmsResource/'+myJMSResource)
```

```
# create uniform distributed topic
myNewDistributedTopic=create(dTopicName, 'UniformDistributedTopic')
myNewDistributedTopic.setJNDIName(dTopicJNDIName)
myNewDistributedTopic.setSubDeploymentName(mySubDeployment)
```

Creating SAF Components

Example situation: An application running in one WebLogic Server wants to send a message using a JMS publisher to a JMS queue or topic hosted on a JMS server, which is running on a remote WebLogic Server. What shall the application do if the remote WebLogic Server, or at least the JMS server, is not running? Durable subscribers are not the solution as the JMS server is not available.

The solution offered by WebLogic is the SAF service. This enables an application to deliver messages reliably between applications, even if the JMS server is down. JMS SAF is transparent to JMS applications; therefore, JMS client code still uses the existing JMS APIs to access remote destinations.

Creating Bridge Components

The Bridge component in WebLogic is a forwarding mechanism that provides messaging integration between different JMS servers, JMS systems hosted in different WebLogic Servers, and even different JMS implementations. A messaging bridge instance forwards messages from the source queue to the destination queue. The messaging bridge communicates with source and target queue using a JCA connector.

The following shows how to create the source destination of the bridge, where the messages are coming from:

```
def createBridgeSourceDestinationQueue(sourceDestinationName, sourceConnectionURL,
sourceFactoryJNDIName, nameOfAdapter):
    cd('/')
    cmo.createJMSBridgeDestination(sourceDestinationName)
    cd('/JMSBridgeDestinations/'+sourceDestinationName)
    cmo.setDestinationType('Queue')
    cmo.setConnectionURL(sourceConnectionURL)
    cmo.setConnectionFactoryJNDIName(sourceFactoryJNDIName)
    cmo.setDestinationJNDIName(sourceDestinationName)
    cmo.setInitialContextFactory('weblogic.jndi.WLInitialContextFactory')
    cmo.setAdapterJNDIName(nameOfAdapter)
```

Next, create the target destination of the bridge, where the messages are going to:

```
def createBridgeSourceDestinationQueue(targetDestinationName, targetConnectionURL,
                                        targetFactoryJNDIName, nameOfAdapter):
    # change to the root MBean (domain)
    cd('/')
    # create a new bridge destination
    cmo.createJMSBridgeDestination(targetDestinationName)
    # change to the new bridge
    cd('/JMSBridgeDestinations/'+targetDestinationName)
    # configure the bridge type - in this case a queue
    cmo.setDestinationType('Queue')
    # configure other bridge relevant attributes
```

```
cmo.setConnectionURL(targetConnectionURL)
cmo.setAdapterJNDIName(nameOfAdapter)
cmo.setConnectionFactoryJNDIName(targetFactoryJNDIName)
cmo.setDestinationJNDIName(targetDestinationName)
cmo.setQOSDegradationAllowed('true')
cmo.setIdleTimeMaximum('60')
cmo.setAsyncEnabled('true')
cmo.setDurabilityEnabled('true')
```

Finally, create the bridge with source and target queue:

```
def createMessagingBridge(newBridgeName, sourceDestinationName, targetDestinationName, newTargetName,
newTargetType):
    cd('/')
    # create bridge
    cmo.createMessagingBridge(newBridgeName,)
    cd('/Deployments/'+newBridgeName')
    # set the target of the bridge
    set('Targets',jarray.array([ObjectName(
        'com.bea:Name='+newTargetName+',Type='+newTargetType+')], ObjectName))

    # very mportant - set source and target queue
    cmo.setSourceDestination(getMBean('/JMSBridgeDestinations/'+sourceDestinationName))
    cmo.setTargetDestination(getMBean('/JMSBridgeDestinations/'+targetDestinationName))

    # configure bridge parameter
    cmo.setStarted(true)
    cmo.setSelector('')
    cmo.setQualityOfService('Exactly-once')
```

Best Practices

It is advisable to avoid a messaging bridge in case the remote JMS provider already provides a secure high-availability implementation. In this case, a bridge would only duplicate this features in an unnecessary way. If the remote provider already provides sufficient quality of service, then JMS clients can directly connect to the remote provider and send the messages directly to remote queues or topics. A message bridge is the WebLogic feature that should be used in cases where the remote provider does not provide the required quality of services, or in cases where the network to the remote provider is not stable enough. Also, it should be taken into account that Oracle recommends using the WebLogic SAF implementation instead of the bridge due to better performance.

The JMS bridge configuration is dependent on local and remote queues or topics. The bridge can be established between the source and target destinations and needs to be created with the following parameters:

- JMS bridge destination

- Connection URL

- JMS ConnectionFactory JNDI name

- JMS destination JNDIName

Once the source and target is configured, you can configure the message bridges. The bridge configuration requires the following:

- Bridge name

- Source destination

- Target destination

- JMS Bridge deployment target Cluster or server

Creating Durable Subscribers

Durable subscribers can be used in pub/sub messaging in order to use persistent messages. These are registered to the JMS server with a well-known name so that subscriptions can be remembered even after a crash. When disconnected, the server will still collect messages for this subscriber and will deliver those after the reconnect. WebLogic JMS offers a comprehensive set of administrative APIs for durable subscriber management.

The following script will create a durable subscriber:

```
def createDurableSubscribers(myServerName, jmsServerName, topicName, durSubName, myClientID):
    # navigate to the server runtime tree
    serverRuntime()

    # navigate to the JMSRuntime on the selected server and then to the JMSServer
    cd('JMSRuntime/'+myServerName)

    # navigate to the JMSServer
    cd('JMSServers/'+jmsServerName)

    # navigate to "MyTopic1" where the durable subscriber will be created
    cd ('Destinations/'+topicName)

    # create a durable subscription with a clientId nd a subscriber name
    cmo.createDurableSubscriber('myclientid1','mydsub1','true',true)
```

Foreign Providers

WebLogic also offers connectivity to JMS queues and topics hosted somewhere else. Most famous example is the integration of MQ series. Durable subscribers can be used in pub/sub messaging in order to use persistent messages. These are registered to the JMS.

Foreign JMS servers can be used as a stand-alone component, similar to messaging bridges. These components target application servers or clusters directly instead of an intermediary component like a JMS server.

Bridges versus Foreign Server

The JMS messaging bridge introduces an extra hop; messages are put into a local destination and then forwarded to the final destination. This is useful when the remote destination is not on a highly available JEE container. The bridge will take the messages even when the remote destination is not available and then forward those with build-in retry logic when the remote destination becomes available.

If the remote destination is highly available (WebLogic JMS or IBM MQ Series), using foreign JMS server is preferable since it directly accesses the final destination without an extra hop. This is mostly preferable for incoming queues on WebLogic 11g and later releases.

Configuring Foreign Server on JMS Module

The foreign server feature makes it possible to map external JMS providers like MQSeries, OpenJMS, or other WebLogic JMS servers to the local JNDI namespace. This would require that it define foreign destinations as local JNDI entries. Once the Foreign Provider is configured within WebLogic, for all practical JMS implementations within the code, it can be called as if it was on a local JNDI lookup. WebLogic will make the remote calls transparent to your code. This allows you to change your destination via configuration on the WebLogic console or through WLST.

Example of how to create a foreign JMS server configuration:

🖫 foreign_JMS_server_configuration

```
def createForeignJMSServer(jmsModuleName,foreignName,foreignConnectionFactoryName,
                           cfnLocalName, cfnRemoteName,connectionURL):
        print 'Start to create foreign JMS server: '+foreignName
        cd('/JMSSystemResources/'+jmsModuleName+'/JMSResource/'+jmsModuleName)
        cmo.createForeignServer(foreignName)

cd('/JMSSystemResources/'+jmsModuleName+'/JMSResource/'+jmsModuleName+'/ForeignServers/'+foreignName)
        cmo.setDefaultTargetingEnabled(true)

        cmo.createForeignConnectionFactory(foreignConnectionFactoryName)
        cd('/JMSSystemResources/'+jmsModuleName+'/JMSResource/'+jmsModuleName+'/ForeignServers/'+
            foreignName+'/ForeignConnectionFactories/'+foreignConnectionFactoryName)
        cmo.setLocalJNDIName(cfnLocalName)
        cmo.setRemoteJNDIName(cfnRemoteName)

cd('/JMSSystemResources/'+jmsModuleName+'/JMSResource/'+jmsModuleName+'/ForeignServers/'+foreignName)
        cmo.setConnectionURL(connectionURL)
        cmo.setInitialContextFactory('com.xyz.jndi.ctx.InitialContextFactoryWrapper')
        cmo.unSet('JNDIPropertiesCredentialEncrypted')

        cmo.createJNDIProperty('factory')
        cd('/JMSSystemResources/'+jmsModuleName+'/JMSResource/'+jmsModuleName+'/ForeignServers/'+
            foreignName+'/JNDIProperties/factory')
        cmo.setValue('com.sun.jndi.fscontext.RefFSContextFactory')

cd('/JMSSystemResources/'+jmsModuleName+'/JMSResource/'+jmsModuleName+'/ForeignServers/'+foreignName)
```

```
        cmo.createJNDIProperty('SECURITY_AUTHENTICATION')
        cd('/JMSSystemResources/'+jmsModuleName+'/JMSResource/'+jmsModuleName+'/ForeignServers/'+
            foreignName+'/JNDIProperties/SECURITY_AUTHENTICATION')
        cmo.setValue('none')

        # setup foreign destinations
        print 'Start to create foreign JMS destinations for server: '+foreignName

        ListJMS = ["foreign_dest1","foreign_dest2","foreign_dest3","foreign_dest4","foreign_dest5"]

        for idJms in range(0, len(ListJMS)):

cd('/JMSSystemResources/'+jmsModuleName+'/JMSResource/'+jmsModuleName+'/ForeignServers/'+foreignName)
            localName = 'jms/' + ListJMS[idJms]
            remoteName = ListJMS[idJms]
            myFD = cmo.createForeignDestination(localName)
            cd('ForeignDestinations')
            myFD.setLocalJNDIName(localName)
            myFD.setRemoteJNDIName(remoteName)
```

The above script only shows the relevant WLST function. The following code part
shows how this function can be used:

```
foreignName                  = 'MyForeignName'
foreignConnectionFactoryName = 'MyForeignConnectionFactoryName'
cfnLocalName                 = 'MyLocalName'
cfnRemoteName                = 'RemoteName'
connectionURL                = 'foreignConnectionURL'

# create Foreign JMS server
createForeignJMSServer(jmsModuleName,foreignName,foreignConnectionFactoryName, cfnLocalName,
                       cfnRemoteName,connectionURL)

print 'Foreign JMS Server: ',foreignName,', has been created Successfully !!!'
```

JMS Quota

WebLogic also supports the concept of constraining resources for JMS. These
constraints - called Quota in WebLogic - can be defined on JMSServer level or even
on a specific destination level. Oracle highly recommends always configuring message
count quotas in order to avoid huge message backlogs and out-of-memory conditions.
Quotas can be defined in many different ways, but usually it is sufficient to define the
maximum number of messages.

Setting FIFO policy Quota on JMS Server level:

```
cd('/Deployments/JMSServer-MS1')

# FIFO prevents the JMS server from delivering smaller messages when larger ones are
# already waiting for space
cmo.setBlockingSendPolicy('FIFO')

# The maximum number of messages that can be stored in this JMS server (-1 = no limits)
cmo.setMessagesMaximum(10000)

# The maximum number of bytes allowed in individual messages on this JMS server
cmo.setMaximumMessageSize(25000)

# The maximum number of bytes that can be stored in this JMS server.
# A value of -1 removes any WebLogic Server limits
cmo.setBytesMaximum(10000000)
```

Setting Preemptive policy Quota on JMS Server level:

```
cd('/Deployments/JMSServer-MS1')

# Preemptive allows smaller send requests to preempt previous larger ones when there is sufficient
space for smaller messages on the destination
cmo.setBlockingSendPolicy('Preemptive')
# The maximum number of messages that can be stored in this JMS server (-1 = no limits)
cmo.setMessagesMaximum(50000)
# The maximum number of bytes allowed in individual messages on this JMS server
cmo.setMaximumMessageSize(25000)

# The maximum number of bytes that can be stored in this JMS server. A value of -1 removes any
WebLogic Server limits
cmo.setBytesMaximum(10000000)
```

JNDI Resources

Foreign JNDI provider in WebLogic enables the administrator to connect different JNDI trees together. JNDI can be roughly compared to a UNIX file system. You have a root directory and underneath you have subfolders. In the different folders (on all levels), you have concrete files. In addition, it is possible to create links in a subtree that are referring other nodes. This is very much like symbolic links in UNIX filesystem. It is also possible to link to other JNDI nameservers, which could also be compared with a mounted filesystem in UNIX.

First, you need to define where this file system is and how to connect (host, user, password, file system type, etc.).

Second, you need to define which folder you want to mount and where this remote folder should appear in your local file system. This is exactly what foreign JNDI providers are good for.

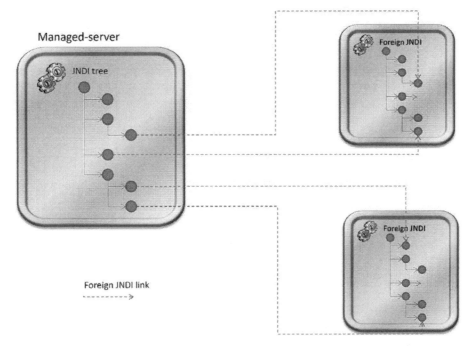

Figure 6.4: *Foreign JNDI resources*

In the following example you will see that we will first define the remote provider with host/port/credentials, and then we will define mount points which are called *links* in WebLogic.

The example uses only one link, but you can define as many as you want. For a better understanding, these links are like mounts on a UNIX file system, which means that they reference entries in the foreign JNDI directory.

💾 JNDI_provider

```
# connect to to the server
connect('weblogic','test1234','t3://localhost:7001')

# start an edit session
edit()
startEdit()

# if the JNDI provider does not exist, then create it
if getMBean("/ForeignJNDIProviders/myTestJNDIProvider") is None:
        foreignJNDIInstance=create('myTestJNDIProvider',"ForeignJNDIProvider")
        foreignJNDIInstance.addTarget(getMBean('/Clusters/WebTier_Cluster'))
        foreignJNDIInstance.setInitialContextFactory('weblogic.jndi.WLInitialContextFactory')
        foreignJNDIInstance.setProviderURL('t3://testhost:7101')
        foreignJNDIInstance.setUser('other_server')
        foreignJNDIInstance.setPassword('other_user')

        # now configuring foreign links
        foreignLinkInstance=foreignJNDIInstance.createForeignJNDILink('MyTestLink')
        foreignLinkInstance.setLocalJNDIName('jndi/local/testserver/TestServerConnectionFactory')
```

```
        foreignLinkInstance.setRemoteJNDIName('jndi/testserver/TestServerConnectionFactory')
else:
        print 'Foreign JNDI provider with the name myTestJNDIProvider already exists !'

activate()
exit()
```

After this script has been executed, we can navigate in WLST to the newly created MBean (or you can use the AdminConsole) and check what has been created:

```
wls:/MartinTest_Domain/serverConfig> cd ('/ForeignJNDIProviders /myTestJNDIProvider')
wls:/MartinTest_Domain/serverConfig/ForeignJNDIProviders/myTestJNDIProvider> ls()
dr--    ForeignJNDILinks
dr--    Targets

-r--    DeploymentOrder                        1000
-r--    InitialContextFactory                  weblogic.jndi.WLInitialContextFactory
-r--    Name                                   myTestJNDIProvider
-r--    Notes                                  null
-r--    Password                               ******
-r--    PasswordEncrypted                      ******
-r--    Properties                             null
-r--    ProviderURL                            t3://testhost:7101
-r--    Type                                   ForeignJNDIProvider
-r--    User                                   other_server

-r-x    freezeCurrentValue                     Void : String(attributeName)
-r-x    isSet                                  Boolean : String(propertyName)
-r-x    unSet                                  Void : String(propertyName)

wls:/MartinTest_Domain/serverConfig/ForeignJNDIProviders/myTestJNDIProvider> ls ('Targets')
dr--    WebTier_Cluster

wls:/MartinTest_Domain/serverConfig/ForeignJNDIProviders/myTestJNDIProvider>                cd
('ForeignJNDILinks/'MyTestLink'')
wls:/MartinTest_Domain/serverConfig/ForeignJNDIProviders/myTestJNDIProvider/ForeignJNDILinks/MyTestLi
nk> ls()

-r--    LocalJNDIName                          jndi/local/testserver/TestServerConnectionFactory
-r--    Name                                   MyTestLink
-r--    Notes                                  null
-r--    RemoteJNDIName                         jndi/testserver/TestServerConnectionFactory
-r--    Type                                   ForeignJNDILink

-r-x    freezeCurrentValue                     Void : String(attributeName)
-r-x    isSet                                  Boolean : String(propertyName)
-r-x    unSet                                  Void : String(propertyName)
```

As I said before and as you can see on the diagram, you can create as many different links as you want for each provider.

Java Mail Sessions

WebLogic Server includes the JavaMail API reference implementation from Sun Microsystems. This API enables applications to use the Internet Message Access Protocol (IMAP) and Simple Mail Transfer Protocol (SMTP) capable mail servers on the internal or external network, depending on firewall and access permissions.

In WebLogic, you can use WLST or JMX (or the Administration Console) to create a mail session instead of doing it in your own code. This configures a javax.mail.Session object and registers it in the WebLogic JNDI tree. Applications can then access the mail session from the JNDI provider.

Even if we define all the settings (see the following example) in the MBean, you can override any properties set in the mail session in your code afterwards. The options in the MBean are used as default options so that you only need to provide options if you need to overwrite them (e.g. mail.from and others).

Property	Description	Default
mail.store.protocol	Protocol for retrieving email. Example: mail.store.protocol=imap	imap
mail.transport.protocol	Protocol for sending email. Example: mail.transport.protocol=smtp	smtp
mail.host	The name of the mail host machine. Example: mail.host=mailserver	localhost
mail.user	Name of the default user for retrieving email. Example: mail.user=wlstbook	Value of the user.name Java system property
mail.protocol.host	Mail host for a specific protocol. For example, you can set mail.SMTP.host and mail.IMAP.host to different machine names.	Value of the mail.host property.
mail.protocol.user	Protocol-specific default user name for logging into protocol specific server. Examples:mail.smtp.user=wlstbook	Value of the mail.user property
mail.from	The default return address. Examples: mail.from=wlsautomation@wlsbook.com	username@host
mail.debug	Set to true to enable JavaMail debug output	False

Table 6.2: Mail Properties

Example script to setup a mail session object in WLS and register it in the JNDI tree:

💾 setup_mail_session

```
# ............... import ......................
from java.util import Properties

####################################################################
def createMailSession():
    try:
        print 'Create EMail session ...';
        edit();
        startEdit();

        cd('/')
        myTestMailMbean = cmo.createMailSession('TestNotificationEmail');
        cd('/MailSessions/TestNotificationEmail');
        set('Targets',jarray.array([ObjectName('com.bea:Name=MartinTest_Cluster,Type=Cluster')],
            ObjectName))
        myTestMailMbean.setJNDIName('mail/TestNotificationEmail');

        properties = java.util.Properties();
        properties.put('mail.to','lector@wlsscriptbook.com');
        properties.put('mail.from','author@wlsscriptbook.com');

        properties.put('mail.transport.protocol','smtp');
        properties.put('mail.smtp.host','mail.wlsscriptbook.com');
        properties.put('mail.smtp.port','25');
        properties.put('mail.smtp.user','username');
        properties.put('mail.smtp.password','password');
        myTestMailMbean.setProperties(properties);
```

```
        save();
        activate();

    except:
        print 'Exception while create EMail session  !';
        dumpStack();
        exit();


# =============================================================
#        Main Code Execution
# =============================================================
if __name__ == "main":
    print '###################################################################';
    print '#                    Test create Mail session                     #';
    print '###################################################################';
    print '';
    connect('weblogic', 'test1234',  't3://localhost:7001');
    createMailSession()
    disconnect();
```

Running the following script will produce the following output. As you can see, the script will connect to the AdminServer, switch to the edit mode, and then create the mail configuration:

```
################################################################################
#                       Test create Mail session                               #
################################################################################

Connecting to t3://localhost:7001 with userid weblogic ...
Successfully connected to Admin Server 'AdminServer' that belongs to domain 'MartinTest_Domain'.

Create EMail session ...
Location changed to edit tree. This is a writable tree with
DomainMBean as the root. To make changes you will need to start
an edit session via startEdit().

For more help, use help(edit)

Starting an edit session ...
Started edit session, please be sure to save and activate your
changes once you are done.
Saving all your changes ...
Saved all your changes successfully.
Activating all your changes, this may take a while ...
The edit lock associated with this edit session is released
once the activation is completed.
Activation completed
Disconnected from weblogic server: AdminServer
```

WorkManager

WebLogic uses a concept called WorkManager in order to prioritize work and maintain threads and thread-pools. WorkManager can be created and configured by the administrator on the WebLogic level or by application developers on the application level (deployment descriptors). Different additional configuration items like maximal thread restriction are available for more detailed configuration of the resource usage and restriction.

For example, you can create scheduling policies for application "a", and another set of policies for application "b". During operation, WebLogic can use these policies to assign pending work and enqueued requests to execution threads. The WorkManager enables you to guarantee that each application will get their chunk of the available resources (threads/connections) or you can limit the amount of resources (e.g. threads).

WorkManagers of Three Different Scopes

WebLogic distinguishes between WorkManagers of three different scopes:

The default WorkManager: This is implemented to handle thread management and perform self-tuning. This instance will be used also by an application if no other WorkManager is configured in the application's deployment descriptors. In most cases the default WorkManager should be sufficient.

Global WorkManagers: These WorkManagers have the scope of the domain and are defined in config.xml. An application can use a Global WorkManager as a blueprint and create its own instance. The work associated with that application can then be distinguished from the work from other applications.

Application-scoped WorkManagers: It is possible to create WorkManagers that are available only to a specific application or module. These can be specified in either weblogic-application.xml, weblogic-ejb-jar.xml, or weblogic.xml.

WorkManager Configuration Items

WorkManager consist of different configuration items. In order to restrict, organize, control or manage work, you need to define WorkManager components. WebLogic offers the following components for WorkManagers:

Constraints:

- Minimum threads constraint
- Maximum threads constraint
- Capacity constraint

Request components:

- Fair share request class
- Response time request class
- Context request class

A constraint defines the minimum or maximum numbers of threads or the total number of requests. The max threads constraint defines the maximum number of concurrent requests allowed. The min threads constraint ensures that the server will always allocate this number of threads. The capacity constraint causes the server to reject requests when it has reached its capacity.

Request classes define the way WebLogic allocates threads to requests. WebLogic offers a number of different request classes out of the box. The *fair share* request class defines the average thread-use time. The *response time* request class defines the requested response time in milliseconds. This value is not applied to each request but to an average. WebLogic also offers a *context* request class that allows the administrator to specify context-based restrictions based on the current user or group, for example.

Example - Create a max threads constraint:

```
cd('/SelfTuning/MartinTestDomain')
create('TestMaxThreads', 'MaxThreadsConstraint')
cd("/SelfTuning/MartinTestDomain/MaxThreadsConstraints/TestMaxThreads")
set("Count", 75)
set('Target', 'TestServer')
```

Example - Create a min threads constraint:

```
cd('/SelfTuning/MartinTestDomain')
create('TestMinThreads', 'MinThreadsConstraint')
cd("/SelfTuning/MartinTestDomain/MinThreadsConstraints/TestMinThreads")
set("Count", 30)
set('Target', 'TestServer')
```

Example - Create a capacity threads constraint:

```
cd('/SelfTuning/MartinTestDomain')
create('TestCapacity', 'Capacity')
cd("/SelfTuning/MartinTestDomain/Capacities/TestCapacity")
set("Count", 100)
set('Target', 'TestServer')
```

Example - Create a fair share request:

```
cd('/SelfTuning/MartinTestDomain')
create('TestFairShare', 'FairShareRequestClass')
cd("/SelfTuning/MartinTestDomain/FairShareRequestClasses/TestFairShare")
set("FairShare", 100)
set('Target', 'TestServer')
```

Example - Create a context request class:

```
cd('/SelfTuning/MartinTestDomain')
create('TestContextReq', 'ContextRequestClass')
cd("/SelfTuning/MartinTestDomain/ContextRequestClasses/TestContextReq")
set('Target', 'TestServer')
```

Example - Create a context case example:

```
create('TestContextCase', 'ContextCase')
cd("/SelfTuning/MartinTestDomain/ContextRequestClasses/TestContextReq/ContextCases/TestContextCase")
set("RequestClassName", "ReqClsName")
set("GroupName", "Deployers")
set("UserName", "maindeployer")
```

Example - Create a response time request class:

```
cd('/SelfTuning/MartinTestDomain')
create('TestResponseTimeReq', 'ResponseTimeRequestClass')
cd("/SelfTuning/MartinTestDomain/ResponseTimeRequestClasses/TestResponseTimeReq")
set("GoalMs", 500)
```

Creating Global WorkManagers

The following is an example script to create a new WorkManager with max threads and a capacity element:

💾 **create_WorkManager**

```
#******************************
# Create a WorkManager
#******************************
def createWorkManager(maxthreads, capacitycount):
    try:
        edit()
        startEdit()

        # change to the domain selftuning instance
        cd('/SelfTuning/'+domainName)

        # create a maxthreads contraint instance
        cmo.createMaxThreadsConstraint('testMaxThreads')
        cd('/SelfTuning/'+domainName+'/MaxThreadsConstraints/testMaxThreads')
        # set count
        cmo.setCount(maxthreads)
        set('Targets',jarray.array([ObjectName('com.bea:Name=MartinTest_Cluster,Type=Cluster')],
            ObjectName))

        # change to the domain selftuning instance
        cd('/SelfTuning/'+domainName)

        # create capacity instance
        cmo.createCapacity('testCapacity')
        cd('Capacities/testCapacity')
        set('Count',capacitycount)
        set('Notes','Defining a capacity instance')
        set('Targets',jarray.array([ObjectName('com.bea:Name=MartinTest_Cluster,Type=Cluster')],
            ObjectName))

        # now create a WorkManager
        cd('/SelfTuning/'+domainName)
        myWorkManager = cmo.createWorkManager('myTestWorkManager')
        cd('/SelfTuning/'+domainName+'/WorkManagers/myTestWorkManager')
        set('Targets',jarray.array([ObjectName('com.bea:Name=MartinTest_Cluster,Type=Cluster')],
            ObjectName))

        # set the maxthreads attribute to the created instance
        cmo.setMaxThreadsConstraint(getMBean('/SelfTuning/'+domainName+
                                '/MaxThreadsConstraints/testMaxThreads'))
        # set the capacity attribute to the created instance
        cmo.setCapacity(getMBean('/SelfTuning/'+domainName+'/Capacities/testCapacity'))

        save()
        activate()
    except Exception, e:
        print 'Error in script:', e
        cancelEdit()
```

Global WorkManager and Applications

If an application does not define its own WorkManager or references a globally defined WorkManager, then WebLogic will perform the following steps during application initialization. EACH application will create its own instance of the WorkManager. This instance is then used to handle the application workload. Due to different instances, the workload of the different applications are separated even if the same WorkManager type is used. This separation also makes it easier for WebLogic to shutdown different applications without affecting the execution environment of other applications. Even if different WorkManager instances are used, it is possible to use shared restrictions like MaxThread so that a maximal thread policy will be applied to the total number of all threads of all instances of this WorkManager type.

The misleading and confusing aspect on this is that if you are creating a global WorkManager, WebLogic creates a different (different ObjectName!) MBean for each application and you can see all those MBeans in the runtime MBean tree. NOTE(!!) that if the new WorkManager is not named "default", then this WorkManager will not be used at all unless it is configured in the deployment descriptor (policy overwrite) that this WorkManager is to be used. If you create multiple global WorkManagers, then you will find multiple WorkManager MBeans underneath each application runtime MBean, which makes monitoring quite difficult.

ThreadPoolRuntimeMBean and WorkManager

Alongside the WorkManager MBeans in the MBean tree, WebLogic offers an MBean (runtime!) that is called ThreadPoolRuntimeMBean. The ThreadPoolRuntimeMBean exists only once, but multiple WorkManagers exist and additional ones can be created (on domain or even application level).

The ThreadPoolRuntimeMBean is basically a summary and represents all of the threads that all of the WorkManagers use altogether.

Example:

```
WorkManagerApplication_1.CompletedRequests = 10
WorkManagerApplication_2.CompletedRequests = 20
WorkManager[weblogic.XXX].CompletedRequests = 30
...

Then the ThreadPoolRuntimeMBean.CompletedRequestCount = 60
```

Virtual Hosts

Virtual hosting allows WebLogic to configure a behavior similar to what is already well known from WebServers like Apache. This features allows the administrator to define a number of hostnames which will be valid hosts that applications hosted on the Managed-Servers are allowed to respond to. This can be very useful if WebLogic hosts application components that are accessible using different Web-URLs. In order to use virtual hosts, all hostnames specified must be valid and resolvable targets in the DNS (Directory Name Service). All DNS lookups of the server names specified must return the IP address that the WebLogic Server instance is listening on. Note that this can also be separated by combining virtual hosting and network channels. If used in a cluster, load balancing allows a better use of the hardware due to distribution, load balancing, and fail-over.

The following script shows an example how to setup a virtual host:

setup_virtual_host

```
# go to root
cd('/')

# create a new virtual host instance
cmo.createVirtualHost('Test_VirtualHost_1')

# go to the new virtual host
cd('/VirtualHosts/Test_VirtualHost_1')

# set the possible host names
set('VirtualHostNames',jarray.array([String('wlsautomation.com'), String('www.wlsautomation.com'),
String('wlst_and_jmx.wlsautomation.com')], String))

# define which network channel this virtual should monitor for incoming requests
cmo.setNetworkAccessPoint('default')

# we can also define log settings for this virtual host in order to separate logs of the different
servers
cd('/VirtualHosts/Test_VirtualHost_1/WebServerLog/Test_VirtualHost_1')
cmo.setRotationType('byTime')
cmo.setRotationTime('02:00')
cmo.setNumberOfFilesLimited(true)
cmo.setFileName('logs/virtualHosts_1/Test_VirtualHost_1/access.log')

# go to the virtual host in order to define the targets
cd('/VirtualHosts/Test_VirtualHost_1')

# define the target(s) for this virtual host
set('Targets',jarray.array([ObjectName('com.bea:Name=AdminServer,Type=Server')], ObjectName))
```

Combining Network Channels and Virtual Hosts

In the previous chapter, we discussed the creation of network channels. Note that the virtual host definition above uses "default" as the NetworkAccessPoint. This means that this virtual host is served with calls coming in over the default channel. In the previous chapter we also discussed why network channels are necessary. We did not discuss how we can use them to restrict access to our applications.

The magic comes with the combination of network channels and virtual hosts. The reason behind it is that WebLogic enables a deployer to target a web application (which can also be part of an enterprise archive (EAR)) not only to a cluster or a Managed-Server, but also to a virtual host.

Please note that it is of course not required to use an EAR application. If the application is deployed as WAR (Web Application Archive), then it is much easier because it is possible to target the complete application to the virtual hosts. I have seen EAR application archives in most projects, therefore this section discusses the more complicated case where the WAR is packaged into an EAR.

The following example will consider a special application that consists (among other components) of different web applications. For various reasons - either serving different domains or access must be provided from different networks - these web applications must be accessible from different networks. A common scenario is that an application consists of the real application component but also has a management/configuration component which must not be accessible from the user network.

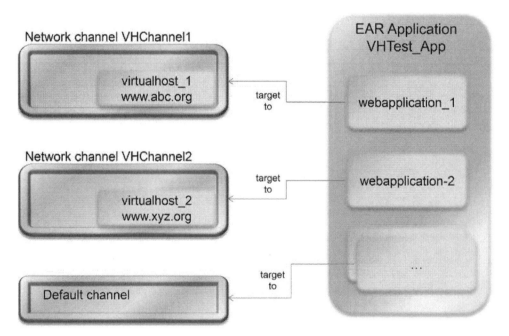

Figure 6.5: *Combining virtual hosts and network channels*

In order to configure this in WebLogic, the following steps must be performed:

- Create the network channel VHChannel1
- Create the virtual host 1 and link it to VHChannel1
- Create the network channel VHChannel2

- Create the virtual host 2 and link it to VHChannel2

- Deploy the application and target only webapplication_1 to virtualhost_1 and target only webapplication_2 to virtualhost_2. It is important here that these two web applications do not have any other target, otherwise they would also be accessible from other network connections.

Example WLST script to setup network channel and virtual hosts:

💾 network_channel_and_virtual_hosts

```
# change to the managed-server where you want to create the services
cd('/Servers/Martin_VirtualHostTest_Domain_MS1')

# create the first channel and allow only the http protocol
cmo.createNetworkAccessPoint('VH1Channel_MS1')
cd('/Servers/Martin_VirtualHostTest_Domain_MS1/NetworkAccessPoints/VH1Channel_MS1')
cmo.setProtocol('http')
cmo.setListenPort(22012)
cmo.setEnabled(true)
cmo.setHttpEnabledForThisProtocol(true)
cmo.setTunnelingEnabled(false)
cmo.setOutboundEnabled(false)
cmo.setTwoWaySSLEnabled(false)
cmo.setClientCertificateEnforced(false)

# create the second channel and allow only the http protocol
cd('/Servers/Martin_VirtualHostTest_Domain_MS1')
cmo.createNetworkAccessPoint('VH2Channel_MS1')

cd('/Servers/Martin_VirtualHostTest_Domain_MS1/NetworkAccessPoints/VH2Channel_MS1')
cmo.setProtocol('http')
cmo.setListenPort(22013)
cmo.setEnabled(true)
cmo.setHttpEnabledForThisProtocol(true)
cmo.setTunnelingEnabled(false)
cmo.setOutboundEnabled(false)
cmo.setTwoWaySSLEnabled(false)
cmo.setClientCertificateEnforced(false)

# change to the root edit mbean as the virtual hosts have to be created on domain level !
cd('/')
# create the first virtual host
cmo.createVirtualHost('VirtualHost-1')
cd('/VirtualHosts/VirtualHost-1')
# link this virtual host to the first network channel
cmo.setNetworkAccessPoint('VH1Channel_MS1')
set('VirtualHostNames',jarray.array([String('www.xyz.org')], String))
set('Targets',jarray.array([ObjectName('com.bea:Name=Martin_VirtualHostTest_Domain_MS1,Type=Server')]
, ObjectName))

# create the second irtual host
cd('/')
cmo.createVirtualHost('VirtualHost-2')
cd('/VirtualHosts/VirtualHost-2')
# link it to the second channel
cmo.setNetworkAccessPoint('VH2Channel_MS1')
set('VirtualHostNames',jarray.array([String('www.abc.org')], String))
set('Targets',jarray.array([ObjectName('com.bea:Name=Martin_VirtualHostTest_Domain_MS1,Type=Server')]
, ObjectName))
```

After the channels and virtual hosts have been created, we need to target the application components. We will discuss deployment later in the book, therefore the following scripts show the rather unusual process of re-targeting the components of an already deployed application.

For the following example, please assume that the application has already been deployed. In order to re-target components, we have to switch in to the application deployments subtree and create a subdeployment MBean entry. This entry can then be targeted to the virtual host.

```
# switch to the application deployment MBean
cd('/AppDeployments/VHTest_App')

# create the first subdeployment for web application 1
cmo.createSubDeployment('webapplication_1')

# switch to the newly created subdeployment
cd('/AppDeployments/VHTest_App/SubDeployments/'webapplication_1)

# target this component to the virtual host 1 only
set('Targets',jarray.array([ObjectName('com.bea:Name=VirtualHost-1,Type=VirtualHost')], ObjectName))

# go back to the application structure root and create the second subdeployment
cd('/AppDeployments/VHTest_App')
cmo.createSubDeployment(''webapplication_2')

# switch to this subdeployment
cd('/AppDeployments/VHTest_App/SubDeployments/'webapplication_2')

# target it to the second virtual host only
set('Targets',jarray.array([ObjectName('com.bea:Name=VirtualHost-2,Type=VirtualHost')], ObjectName))
```

WebLogic Tuxedo Connector (WTC)

The following section provides configuration information to integrate WebLogic with another middleware technology Oracle has inherited from BEA: Tuxedo. Tuxedo is a well-known transaction-based middleware that has existed in the market for a long time.

Overview

The WebLogic Tuxedo Connector (WTC) is the Oracle implementation of an interoperability layer between WebLogic and Tuxedo. WTC enables a bi-directional communication between WebLogic managed-serves and Tuxedo services. WTC provides a new listener (local access points) for incoming connections and remote access points for outgoing connections to Tuxedo services. This connector provides a Java application transaction monitor interface (JATMI) similar to the Tuxedo ATMI. Therefore, this connector provides the functionality to integrate WebLogic-based applications into Tuxedo environments and offers support for transaction integration. One main advantage is that this connector does not require any modifications of the Tuxedo applications.

Using WTC in a WebLogic Cluster

WTC does not support WebLogic clustering natively, which means that the bindings are not replicated to other servers. Every WebLogic Server in the cluster must have its own WTC configuration. This is especially true if multiple Managed-Servers are running on the same machine, because then the local domain ports must be different. Managed-Servers without a WTC configuration will not be able to accept or create WTC configurations.

Configuration MBeans for WTC

WTC configurations consist of a number of different MBeans. The basic container MBean is the WTCServer, which defines the frame for all configurations. A WTCServer can be targeted to one or more Managed-Servers. With a WTCServer it is possible to define a local connection endpoint, which effectively means that a new port will be opened from the WLS server process for incoming connections from Tuxedo services. It also defines remote connections (RemoteTuxDom) for enabling access to remote Tuxedo services (outgoing connections for WebLogic Servers). For these connections you can define imports, which are services of Tuxedo you want to use on the WebLogic side, and exports, which are WebLogic EJBs you want to expose for the Tuxedo side.

MBean Type	Description
WTCServer	Main MBean containing the interoperability attributes required for a connection between WebLogic Server and Tuxedo.
WTCLocalTuxDom	Used to configure available remote Tuxedo domains. You must configure at least one local Tuxedo access point, but you can define more if needed.
WTCRemoteTuxDom	Used to configure connections to remote Tuxedo domains. You may configure multiple remote domains.
WTCExport	Used to configure services exported by a local Tuxedo access point.
WTCImport	Used to configure services imported and available on remote domains.
WTCResources	Specifies global field table classes, view table classes, and application passwords for domains.
WTCPassword	Used to configure information for inter-domain authentication.
WTCtBridgeGlobal	Used to configure information for the transfer of messages between Tuxedo and WebLogic.
WTCtBridgeRedirect	Used to configure source, target, direction, and transport of messages between WebLogic and Tuxedo.

Table 6.3: WTC MBeans

Debug Settings in WebLogic for WTC

The following debug switches are available in WebLogic for WTC:

- Enable debugging for WTC-CORBA runtime
    - o Dweblogic.debug.DebugWTCCorbaEx=true
- Enable debugging for WTC-GWT runtime
    - o Dweblogic.debug.DebugWTCGwtEx=true
- Enable debugging for WTC-JATMI runtime
    - o Dweblogic.debug.DebugWTCJatmiEx=true
- Enable debugging for WTC-tBridge runtime
    - o Dweblogic.debug.DebugWTCtBridgeEx=true
- Enable debugging for WTC Configuration runtime
    - o Dweblogic.debug.DebugWTCConfig=true

Building Blocks for WTC Configurations:

Creating a WTC-Server can be done by calling the appropriate factory method on the domain MBean. This server can then be targeted to one or more servers by using the *addTarget* method.

```
cd ('/')
cmo.createWTCServer('WTCServer_xxx')

cd ('/WTCServers/WTCServer_xxx')
cmo.addTarget(getMBean('/Servers/Martin_VirtualHostTest_Domain_MS1'))
```

A local access point provides the necessary infrastructure so that Tuxedo services can act as clients and call services (EJBs) hosted on WebLogic. Adding a local Tuxedo access point - which means defining a WTC listener in WebLogic - can be done using the following WLST example.

```
cmo.createWTCLocalTuxDom('local_dom_test')
cd ('WTCLocalTuxDoms/local_dom_test')
cmo.setAccessPoint('my_local_endpoint')
cmo.setAccessPointId('WLSTUXID')
cmo.setNWAddr('//localhost:9887')
cmo.setConnectionPolicy('ON_STARTUP')
```

Access point is not a real network listener but a logical name. NWAddr is the real address and listener of the local machine. It is possible to add different local endpoints if needed. This may be required for security reasons (authentication) or different networks.

A remote access point defines the entry point for WTC into a Tuxedo domain. On the Tuxedo side this is the listener configured in the domain gateway of Tuxedo.

Adding a remote Tuxedo access point - which means defining a remote connection endpoint - can be done using the following WLST example.

```
cd ('/WTCServers/WTCServer_xxx')
cmo.createWTCRemoteTuxDom('remote_dom_test')
cd ('WTCRemoteTuxDoms/remote_dom_test')
cmo.setAccessPoint('my_tuxedo_test_system')
cmo.setAccessPointId('TUXREMOTE_1')
cmo.setLocalAccessPoint('my_local_endpoint')
cmo.setNWAddr('//remote.tuxedo.machine:port')
cmo.setFederationName('')
cmo.setFederationURL('')
```

Note that the local access point ID must match the local Tuxedo domain defined in this WTC server configuration.

Now we can define the Tuxedo services we would like to use in our WebLogic-based applications. This is done via import configurations. Note that the local and remote access point must match the local and remote Tuxedo domain configurations (see above):

```
cd ('/WTCServers/WTCServer_xxx')
cmo.createWTCImport('import_test')
cd ('WTCImports/import_test')
cmo.setRemoteName('AI-MSG-IMPxx')
cmo.setLocalAccessPoint('my_local_endpoint')
cmo.setResourceName('AI-MSG-IMPxx')
cmo.setRemoteAccessPointList('my_tuxedo_test_system')
```

We can also define which WebLogic services (EJBs) can be used by Tuxedo clients. In order to do this we need to export EJBs as Tuxedo services:

```
cd ('/WTCServers/WTCServer_xxx')
cmo.createWTCExport('exportEJB_1')
cd ('WTCExports/exportEJB_1')
# The remote name of this service
cmo.setRemoteName('MyRemoteEJBService')
# the local access point used for incoming connections
cmo.setLocalAccessPoint('my_local_endpoint')
# The name used to identify an exported service
cmo.setResourceName('myExportedResource')
# home interface of this EJB
cmo.setEJBName('com.test.ejbservices.MyEJBHome')
```

Security is always a hot topic. You can define different security credentials for the different endpoints. The following script shows how to create a password pair (local and remote passwords) for one remote/local Tuxedo domain combination. Note that you can define a different password set for every local/remote domain combination.

```
cd ('/WTCServers/WTCServer_xxx')
cmo.createWTCPassword('connection_1_security')
cd ('WTCPasswords/connection_1_security')
cmo.setLocalPassword('test1234')
cmo.setLocalPasswordIV('dkfgaskfgakfa')
cmo.setLocalAccessPoint('my_local_endpoint')
cmo.setRemotePassword('test4321')
cmo.setRemotePasswordIV('tzuioldgalsglaasgag')
cmo.setRemoteAccessPoint('my_tuxedo_test_system')
```

Note that you can define passwords for both sides and also define the data for the initial encryption (*IV settings).

Parameterized Script for Flexible and Complex Setups

WTC configurations can get pretty complex, therefore it is highly advisable to use parameterized scripts. The following is an example of such a script to setup more complex WTC server configurations:

🖫 WTC_configuration

```
def createAllWTCServer():
  try:
    totalWTCServer=domainProps.get("wtc.amountserver")

    edit()
    startEdit()
    print 'Creating All WTC server ....'
    i=1
    while (i <= int(totalWTCServer)) :

      try:
      cd('/')
      wtc_name              = get_instance_property('wtc.server',str(i), 'name');
      wtc_targetmanagedserver= get_instance_property('wtc.server',str(i), 'targetmanagedserver');
      wtc_localdomainname   = get_instance_property('wtc.server',str(i), 'localtuxdomain.name');
      wtc_access_point      = get_instance_property('wtc.server',str(i),
                                                    'localtuxdomain.access_point');
      wtc_access_point_id   = get_instance_property('wtc.server',str(i),
                                                    'localtuxdomain.access_point_id');
      wtc_connection_policy = get_instance_property('wtc.server',str(i),
                                                    'localtuxdomain.connection_policy');
      wtc_nwaddr = get_instance_property('wtc.server',str(i), 'localtuxdomain.nw_addr');

      # create WTC server
      cmo.createWTCServer(wtc_name)

      # change to WTC server
      cd ('/WTCServers/'+wtc_name)
      cmo.addTarget(getMBean('/Servers/'+wtc_targetmanagedserver))

      # create local domain configuration
      cmo.createWTCLocalTuxDom(wtc_localdomainname)
      cd ('WTCLocalTuxDoms/'+wtc_localdomainname)
      cmo.setAccessPoint(wtc_access_point)
      cmo.setAccessPointId(wtc_access_point_id)
      cmo.setNWAddr(wtc_nwaddr)
      cmo.setConnectionPolicy(wtc_connection_policy)

      # create remote tux domains
      totalWTCRemoteDomains=get_instance_property('wtc.server',str(i), 'amountremotedomains')

      r=1
      while (r <= int(totalWTCRemoteDomains)) :
        remotetuxdomain_name = get_instance_property('wtc.server',str(i),
                                                     'remotetuxdomain.'+str(r)+'.name');
        remotetuxdomain_access_point = get_instance_property('wtc.server',str(i),
                                                     'remotetuxdomain.'+str(r)+'.access_point');
        remotetuxdomain_access_point_id = get_instance_property('wtc.server',str(i),
                                                     'remotetuxdomain.'+str(r)+'.access_point_id');
        remotetuxdomain_local_access_point = get_instance_property('wtc.server',str(i),
                                                     'remotetuxdomain.'+str(r)+'.local_access_point');
        remotetuxdomain_nw_addr = get_instance_property('wtc.server',str(i),
                                                     'remotetuxdomain.'+str(r)+'.nw_addr');
        remotetuxdomain_federation_url = get_instance_property('wtc.server',str(i),
                                                     'remotetuxdomain.'+str(r)+'.federation_url');
        remotetuxdomain_federation_name = get_instance_property('wtc.server',str(i),
                                                     'remotetuxdomain.'+str(r)+'.federation_name');

        # create remote tux domain
```

```
              cd ('/WTCServers/'+wtc_name)
              cmo.createWTCRemoteTuxDom(remotetuxdomain_name)
              cd ('WTCRemoteTuxDoms/'+remotetuxdomain_name)
              cmo.setAccessPoint(remotetuxdomain_access_point)
              cmo.setAccessPointId(remotetuxdomain_access_point_id)
              cmo.setLocalAccessPoint(remotetuxdomain_local_access_point)
              cmo.setNWAddr(remotetuxdomain_nw_addr)
              cmo.setFederationName(remotetuxdomain_federation_name)
              cmo.setFederationURL(remotetuxdomain_federation_url)

              r = r+1

        # create WTC imports
        totalWTCRImports=get_instance_property('wtc.server',str(i), 'amountimports')

        r=1
        while (r <= int(totalWTCRImports)) :
              import_name = get_instance_property('wtc.server',str(i), 'import.'+str(r)+'.name');
              import_resource_name = get_instance_property('wtc.server',str(i),
                                      'import.'+str(r)+'.resource_name');
              import_remote_name = get_instance_property('wtc.server',str(i),
                                      'import.'+str(r)+'.remote_name');
              import_local_access_point  = get_instance_property('wtc.server',str(i),
                                      'import.'+str(r)+'.local_access_point');
              import_remote_access_point  = get_instance_property('wtc.server',str(i),
                                      'import.'+str(r)+'.remote_access_point');

              # create WTC import
              cd ('/WTCServers/'+wtc_name)
              cmo.createWTCImport(import_name)
              cd ('WTCImports/'+import_name)
              cmo.setRemoteName(import_remote_name)
              cmo.setLocalAccessPoint(import_local_access_point)
              cmo.setResourceName(import_resource_name)
              cmo.setRemoteAccessPointList(import_remote_access_point)

              r = r+1

        # create WTC exports
        totalWTCRImports=get_instance_property('wtc.server',str(i), 'amountexports')

        r=1
        while (r <= int(totalWTCRImports)) :
              export_name  = get_instance_property('wtc.server',str(i), 'export.'+str(r)+'.name');
              export_resource_name     = get_instance_property('wtc.server',str(i),
                                      'export.'+str(r)+'.resource_name');
              export_remote_name      = get_instance_property('wtc.server',str(i),
                                      'export.'+str(r)+'.remote_name');
              export_local_access_point  = get_instance_property('wtc.server',str(i),
                                      'export.'+str(r)+'.local_access_point');
              export_ejbname = get_instance_property('wtc.server',str(i),
                                      'export.'+str(r)+'.ejbname');

              # create WTC export
              cd ('/WTCServers/'+wtc_name)
              cmo.createWTCExport(export_name)
              cd ('WTCExports/'+export_name)
              cmo.setRemoteName(export_remote_name)
              cmo.setLocalAccessPoint(export_local_access_point)
              cmo.setResourceName(export_resource_name)
              cmo.setEJBName(export_ejbname)

              r = r+1

        print 'WTC Server: ',wtc_name,', has been created Successfully !!!'

        except:
        dumpStack();
        print '***** CANNOT CREATE WTC-Server with the Name : ' , wtc_name ,' !'
        print ''

        i = i + 1
    save()
    activate()
except:
    print 'Exception while creating WTC server !';
    dumpStack();
```

Simple example property file (with the potential to get large):

```
wtc.amountserver=1

wtc.server.1.name=myWTCServer_1
wtc.server.1.targetmanagedserver=MS1

wtc.server.1.localtuxdomain.name=myLocalTuxDomain
wtc.server.1.localtuxdomain.access_point=tuxconnector
wtc.server.1.localtuxdomain.access_point_id=LOCTUX_1
wtc.server.1.localtuxdomain.connection_policy=ON_STARTUP
wtc.server.1.localtuxdomain.nw_addr=//localhost:12345

wtc.server.1.amountremotedomains = 1

wtc.server.1.remotetuxdomain.1.name=remoteServer_1
wtc.server.1.remotetuxdomain.1.access_point=remoteServer_1
wtc.server.1.remotetuxdomain.1.access_point_id=REMTUX_1
wtc.server.1.remotetuxdomain.1.local_access_point=tuxconnector
wtc.server.1.remotetuxdomain.1.nw_addr=//remote.tuxedo.host:10000
wtc.server.1.remotetuxdomain.1.federation_url=
wtc.server.1.remotetuxdomain.1.federation_name=

wtc.server.1.amountimports = 1
wtc.server.1.amountexports = 0

wtc.server.1.import.1.name=MyImport_1
wtc.server.1.import.1.resource_name=RESOURCE_1
wtc.server.1.import.1.remote_name=RemoteName_1
wtc.server.1.import.1.local_access_point=tuxconnector
wtc.server.1.import.1.remote_access_point=remoteServer_1
```

This example only creates one WTC server with one remote, one local domain and one import.

Cluster Timer

WebLogic offers a nice feature that allows you to schedule future tasks similar to a cron job. Two flavors of timers exist: local timer and cluster aware timers. Cluster timer ensures that as long as one of the Managed-Servers is still alive, your task can be performed. This enhances your timer implementations with a high availability feature. This so called Job Scheduler enables you to implement a time functionality based on the commonj.timer API that can also be used within a cluster. What you have to do is implement a commonj.timers.TimerListener implementation that can be called for execution. How does it work? Basically it works by serializing the class that will execute the timer implementation to a database. In combination with the leasing feature, it is ensured that exactly one cluster member will be responsible for executing these jobs. The server responsible for this service will check the database every 30 seconds to see if there are new tasks to execute.

In order to use this feature, you need to setup a database (WebLogic provides a DDL that creates a table called WEBLOGIC_TIMERS) and you need to create a datasource in WebLogic. You also need to setup leasing (either consensus or database leasing) which will create a table named ACTIVE.

Last but not least, you need to implement the time functionality, package it up into a JAR file, and (very important!) add this jar file to the system classpath of WebLogic.

WebLogic also offers verbose debugging of the JodScheduler. In order to use this you need to enable:

-Dweblogic.debug.DebugSingletonServices=true -Dweblogic.JobScheduler=true

The following is an example script that can be used to setup such a timer (note that the database and datasource MUST already have been setup):

```
def createClusterJobSchedulerTask(clusterName, jobSchedulerTableName, jobSchedulerDataSource)
    domainConfig()
    edit()
    startEdit()
    cd('/Clusters/' +clusterName)
    # set the table name
    cmo.setJobSchedulerTableName(jobSchedulerTableName)
    save()
    cd('/Clusters/' +clusterName)
    cmo.setDataSourceForJobScheduler(jobSchedulerDataSource)
    save()
    activate()
```

OSGI Integration

| 12.1.2 ++ | Starting with WebLogic 12.1.2, is it possible to integrate OSGI frameworks into the WebLogic Server. See www.osgi.org for background information on OSGI. Applications can get access to these framework implementations by getting them from the JNDI tree.

The WebLogic integration allows you to configure multiple instances of OSGI frameworks, and of course deploy multiple bundles into them. WebLogic provides out of the box the Apache Felix implementation. Features like deploy bundles, enable log, and persistence are available.

The following is an example of creating a new framework instance:

```
startEdit()

# change to the root => domain mbean
cd('/')

# create a new OSGI Framework wth a given name
cmo.createOsgiFramework('OsgiFramework-BookTest')

# change to the newly created MBean and configure it
cd('/OsgiFrameworks/OsgiFramework-BookTest')
set('Targets',jarray.array([ObjectName('com.bea:Name=TestCluster,Type=Cluster')], ObjectName))
cmo.setInitProperties({testprop=something})
set('Targets',jarray.array([ObjectName('com.bea:Name=MS1,Type=Server'),
                            ObjectName('com.bea:Name=MS2,Type=Server')], ObjectName))
cmo.setInitProperties({testprop=something})

activate()
```

Note that we did not create an MBean to deal with an OSGI bundle. WebLogic does not provide an OSGIRuntime framework by default. WebLogic offers the capabilities to host a complete OSGI framework (like Apache-Felix). The framework configuration will then have the information about which OSGI bundles will be loaded into this framework. The runtime configuration discussed above will create and target a complete OSGI framework to the desired server instances.

The frameworks are managed over the *OsgiFrameWorkMBean* MBeans:

```
wls:/testDomain/serverConfig> cd ('OsgiFrameworks')
wls:/testDomain/serverConfig/OsgiFrameworks> ls()
dr--   OsgiFramework-BookTest

wls:/testDomain/serverConfig/OsgiFrameworks> cd ('OsgiFramework-BookTest')
wls:/testDomain/serverConfig/OsgiFrameworks/OsgiFramework-BookTest> ls()
dr--   Targets

-r--   DeployInstallationBundles              populate
-r--   DeploymentOrder                        1000
-r--   DynamicallyCreated                     false
-r--   FactoryImplementationClass             org.apache.felix.framework.FrameworkFactory
-r--   Id                                     0
-r--   InitProperties                         {testprop=something}
-r--   Name                                   OsgiFramework-BookTest
-r--   Notes                                  null
-r--   OrgOsgiFrameworkBootdelegation         null
-r--   OrgOsgiFrameworkSystemPackagesExtra    null
-r--   OsgiImplementationLocation             null
-r--   RegisterGlobalDataSources              true
-r--   RegisterGlobalWorkManagers             true
-r--   Type                                   OsgiFramework

-r-x   freezeCurrentValue                     Void : String(attributeName)
-r-x   getInheritedProperties                 String[] : String[](propertyNames)
-r-x   isInherited                            Boolean : String(propertyName)
-r-x   isSet                                  Boolean : String(propertyName)
-r-x   unSet                                  Void : String(propertyName)
```

Installing OSGI bundles will be done on the frameworks themselves and not via the WebLogic MBean structure.

Cleanup/Delete Resources

In most WebLogic administration books and various websites, the focus for administration and therefore also for automation is always on domain creation/extension/administration and monitoring. The whole topic around resource cleanup and deletion is often left out or forgotten. In fact, the other topics are more common and more popular, but cleanup should not be forgotten.

Many tasks involve cleanup. The following list contains just some examples:

- Physical server goes out of maintenance and will be replaced with new servers. If domains include multiple servers, then you might not want to (or are not allowed to!) delete the whole domain only because a server is exchanged. In this case you should cleanup your domain.

- Applications are no longer needed. In many companies, development and sometimes even testing domains are small domains with one application only, but in production often large domains with many clusters and many applications are used in order to avoid a complicated setup of Administration Servers and "console hopping" for the administrators. Therefore, retiring an application may result in removing the application and all its resources (datasources, JMS servers, mail, etc.) from the larger administration domains.

- Managed-Server must be moved to other machines due to resource problems. This also might result in necessary cleanup.

Cleanup and resource deletion must be done in an active edit session, hence on the edit MBeanServer. After switching to the edit mode, the ROOT (!) object, which is the domain object, provides a large number of methods for resource deletion:

```
destroyRemoteSAFContext(remoteSAFContext:javax.management.ObjectName )
destroyWTCServer(wtcServer:javax.management.ObjectName )
destroyApplication(application:javax.management.ObjectName )
destroyXMLEntityCache(XMLEntityCache:javax.management.ObjectName )
destroySNMPAgentDeployment(mbean:javax.management.ObjectName )
destroyVirtualHost(host:javax.management.ObjectName )
destroyRealm(weblogic.management.configuration.RealmMBean:javax.management.ObjectName )
destroyFileRealm(weblogic.management.configuration.FileRealmMBean:javax.management.ObjectName )
destroyForeignJMSDestination(wsc:javax.management.ObjectName )
destroyJMSBridgeDestination(jmsBridgeDestination:javax.management.ObjectName )
destroyJMSInteropModule(bean:javax.management.ObjectName )
destroyJoltConnectionPool(joltConnectionPool:javax.management.ObjectName )
destroyLogFilter(logFilter:javax.management.ObjectName )
destroyCluster(cluster:javax.management.ObjectName )
destroyJMSConnectionConsumer(wsc:javax.management.ObjectName )
destroyJDBCSystemResource(bean:javax.management.ObjectName )
destroySAFAgent(sAFAgent:javax.management.ObjectName )
destroyLDAPRealm(weblogic.management.configuration.LDAPRealmMBean:javax.management.ObjectName )
destroyErrorHandling(errorHandling:javax.management.ObjectName )
destroyBridgeDestination(bridgeDestination:javax.management.ObjectName )
destroyPathService(pathService:javax.management.ObjectName )
destroyMailSession(ms:javax.management.ObjectName )
destroyMigratableTarget(bean:javax.management.ObjectName )
destroyWLDFSystemResource(bean:javax.management.ObjectName )
destroyJDBCStore(store:javax.management.ObjectName )
destroyJMSServer(jmsServer:javax.management.ObjectName )
destroyWSReliableDeliveryPolicy(policy:javax.management.ObjectName )
destroySingletonService(sc:javax.management.ObjectName )
destroyUnixRealm(weblogic.management.configuration.UnixRealmMBean:javax.management.ObjectName )
destroyStartupClass(sc:javax.management.ObjectName )
destroyEJBContainer()
destroyServer(server:javax.management.ObjectName )
destroyForeignJNDIProvider(provider:javax.management.ObjectName )
destroyWebserviceSecurity(wsc:javax.management.ObjectName )
destroyCustomResource(bean:javax.management.ObjectName )
destroyMessagingBridge(bridge:javax.management.ObjectName )
destroyCachingRealm(weblogic.management.configuration.CachingRealmMBean:javax.management.ObjectName
)
destroyMachine(machine:javax.management.ObjectName )
destroyJMSSystemResource(bean:javax.management.ObjectName )
destroyDomainLogFilter(logFilter:javax.management.ObjectName )
destroyNTRealm(weblogic.management.configuration.NTRealmMBean:javax.management.ObjectName )
destroyShutdownClass(sc:javax.management.ObjectName )
destroyCoherenceClusterSystemResource(bean:javax.management.ObjectName )
destroyMigratableRMIService(bean:javax.management.ObjectName )
destroyFileStore(store:javax.management.ObjectName )
destroyXMLRegistry(registry:javax.management.ObjectName )
destroyCoherenceServer(bean:javax.management.ObjectName )
destroyPasswordPolicy(weblogic.management.configuration.PasswordPolicyMBean:javax.management.ObjectNa
me )
destroyFileT3(fileT3:javax.management.ObjectName )
destroyRDBMSRealm(weblogic.management.configuration.RDBMSRealmMBean:javax.management.ObjectName )
destroyWLECConnectionPool(store:javax.management.ObjectName )
```

The following sections will discuss automation around cleanup and removing resources/elements from domains. Note that application undeployment will be left out as this is discussed in the next chapter together with the other administrative tasks around applications. Therefore it is also not implemented in the provided examples in this chapter.

Delete Datasources

Datasources are an important part of all applications and therefore used in almost all server instances. This means that if applications are no longer needed, the datasources also have to be cleaned up. This is NOT only for cosmetic or resource consumption. Available datasources always mean access to the attached databases! Therefore unused datasources might open a forgotten security hole to your valuable data.

The domain MBean offers a method to remove a datasource (whereas cmo here is the domain MBean):

```
# first delete targets
datasourceInstance.setTargets(None)

# delete
cmo.destroyJDBCSystemResource(datasourceInstance)
```

Delete Filestores

Filestores also have a destroy method that can be used to delete a file store.

```
destroyFileStore(store:javax.management.ObjectName  )
```

Delete JMS Providers

JMS providers are another group of resources which should be cleaned up as soon as the application no longer needs them. The domain MBean offers a method to remove JMS providers (whereas cmo here is the domain MBean). Due to the complex hierarchy and the different JMS elements, WebLogic offers a number of destroy methods for the different JMS elements:

```
# destroy a complete JMS resource
destroyJMSSystemResource(bean:javax.management.ObjectName  )

# destroy one JMS server (and it's subcomponents)
destroyJMSServer(jmsServer:javax.management.ObjectName  )

# destoy a complete message bridge
destroyMessagingBridge(bridge:javax.management.ObjectName  )

# destroy a bridge destination (source or target)
destroyBridgeDestination(bridgeDestination:javax.management.ObjectName  )
destroyJMSBridgeDestination(jmsBridgeDestination:javax.management.ObjectName  )
```

```
# destroy a SAF agent configuration
destroySAFAgent(sAFAgent:javax.management.ObjectName  )

# destroy a foreign JMS destination
destroyForeignJMSDestination(wsc:javax.management.ObjectName  )
```

You may have noticed that in the above list, deletion of queues and topics are not listed. Destroying a queue or a topic is of course also possible with WLST, but not on the root object. You need to navigate to the JMSResource instance first and there you will find the appropriate destroy methods.

Destroying a queue:

```
# navigate to the JMSResource instance
cd('/JMSSystemResources/'+myJMSSystemResource+'/JMSResource/'+myJMSModule)
startEdit()
# destroy the queue by providing the queue mbean
cmo.destroyQueue(getMBean('/JMSSystemResources/'+myJMSSystemResource+'/JMSResource/'+myJMSModule+'/Qu
eues/'+myQueue))
activate()
```

Destroying a topic:

```
# navigate to the JMSResource instance
cd('/JMSSystemResources/'+myJMSSystemResource+'/JMSResource/'+myJMSModule)
startEdit()
# destroy the topic by providing the topic mbean
cmo.destroyTopic(getMBean('/JMSSystemResources/'+myJMSSystemResource+'/JMSResource/'+myJMSModule+'/To
pics/'+myTopic))
activate()
```

Note: destroying distributed destinations is very similar. The methods needed are called destroyDistributedQueue(…) and destroyDistributedTopic(…).

Delete Foreign JNDI Providers

JNDI providers offer access to the JNDI tree of other servers. Once connected to the current server, the content is visible to the application (and administrators). Again, an unused JNDI provider offers insightful knowledge to other servers and therefore might be considered as security hole. Besides this, the current WebLogic Server has to maintain them.

The domain MBean offers a method to remove JNDI providers (whereas cmo here is the domain MBean):

```
cmo.destroyForeignJNDIProvider(foreignProviderInstance)
```

Delete Java Mail Sessions

Access to email gateways (called mail sessions in WebLogic) should be cleaned up if they are no longer needed. The domain MBean offers a method to remove mail sessions (whereas cmo here is the domain MBean):

```
cmo.destroyMailSession(foreignProviderInstance)
```

Delete Managed-Server

Deleting a Managed-Server is not as simple as deleting one of the resources discussed above. In order to do a clean and safe implementation, the automation should first check if the Managed-Server you want to delete still hosts resources or applications. In this case, the resources should be deleted first. If you do not want this then you can overwrite this behavior using the last argument on the command line. Otherwise the Managed-Server can be treated like the other resources. You can delete exactly one server or all if you provide "None" as name. Deleting a Managed-Server means to stop it first, detach it from the cluster (if any) and the machine (if any), and finally delete it:

```
# print name
print 'Managed Server '+nextManagedServerInstance.getName()+' will be destroyed !'

# finally shutdown the server
print "Stopping " + nextManagedServerInstance.getName();

# shutdown the server if this server is not yet in state shutdown
# we need to switch to the domainRuntime in order to find out
domainRuntime()
serverRuntime = getMBean('/ServerLifeCycleRuntimes/'+nextManagedServerInstance.getName())
serverState = serverRuntime.getState()
edit()
print 'Server '+ nextManagedServerInstance.getName()+' is in state ' + serverState
if serverState != 'SHUTDOWN':
    try:
        shutdown(nextManagedServerInstance.getName(),'Server','true',1000,force='true', block='true')
    except:
        pass

    serverState = serverRuntime.getState()
    print 'Server '+ nextManagedServerInstance.getName()+' is NOW in state ' + serverState

# detach from cluster if any
nextManagedServerInstance.setCluster(None)

# detach from machine if any
nextManagedServerInstance.setMachine(None)

# finally delete
cmo.destroyServer(nextManagedServerInstance)
```

Note that we need to switch to the *domainRuntime()* in order to get the server state. If the script issues a shutdown command for a server that is already down, WLST will raise an exception.

Even if you are in an active edit session, you can switch to the domainRuntime / serverRuntime / … MBean tree in order to lookup some information like state. When you switch back, WLST will catch up your already running edit session and continue with this session. IMPORTANT: When switching back, you will be placed in the same tree node of the edit MBeanServer as you had been before.

Delete Cluster

Deleting a cluster should also not be done without checking some prerequisites. The cluster should be empty, which means without any Managed-Servers as members. Finally you should stop the cluster before you delete it. Otherwise the cluster can be treated like the other resources. You can delete exactly one cluster or all if you provide "None" as name. Deleting a cluster means to remove all members (Managed-Servers) first and then delete it:

```
print 'Cluster '+nextClusterInstance.getName()+' will be destroyed !'

# if the cluster still has managed-servers, then detach them from the cluster first !
listOfManagedServer = nextClusterInstance.getServers()
for nextManagedServerInstance in listOfManagedServer:
    # detach from cluster if any
    nextManagedServerInstance.setCluster(None)

# finally delete the cluster
try:
    cmo.destroyCluster(nextClusterInstance)
except Exception, ex:
    print ex
```

Delete Machines

Deleting a machine should also not be done without checking some prerequisites. The machine should not host any Managed-Servers. Otherwise the machine can be treated like the other resources. You can delete exactly one machine or all if you provide "None" as name. Deleting a machine means to detach all hosted Managed-Servers first and then delete it:

```
print 'Machine '+nextMachineInstance.getName()+' will be destroyed !'

# finally delete the machine
cmo.destroyMachine(nextMachineInstance)
```

Deleting the WTC Configuration Components

The WTC components can also be deleted via MBeans from the system. Here we have to distinguish between the WTCServer itself, which can only be destroyed calling the appropriate destroy method on the Domain-MBean, and the other WTC sub-components, which can be destroyed by calling the appropriate methods on the WTCServer MBean.

How to delete a complete WTCServer:

```
edit()
startEdit()
cd ('/')
cmo.destroyWTCServer(getMBean('/WTCServers/WTCServer_xxx'))
save()
activate()
```

Deleting all WTC server components always requires a switch to the WTCServer MBean. Then there are the following destroy methods available:

```
destroyWTCtBridgeGlobal()
destroyWTCExport(expName:javax.management.ObjectName   )
destroyWTCtBridgeRedirect(tBredirect:javax.management.ObjectName   )
destroyWTCPassword(passwdName:javax.management.ObjectName    )
destroyWTCLocalTuxDom(locTuxDomName:javax.management.ObjectName   )
destroyWTCImport(impName:javax.management.ObjectName   )
destroyWTCRemoteTuxDom(remTuxDomName:javax.management.ObjectName   )
```

Complex Example

The following example is a generic script that can be used to remove specific datasources, JMS providers, JNDI providers, mail sessions, Managed-Servers, clusters, or machines from a domain. If the name of the resource is provided, then this script will just delete the specified resource; otherwise this script will delete all resources of this type.

The desired options can be provided as arguments to the script.

💾 deletion_example

```
import sys

# ------------- Check functions ----------------------------

# utility function to check weather a machine still has
# managed-server assigned to it
def machineHostsManagedServer(machineName):
    cd ('/')
    # get list of servers
    listOfManagedServer = cmo.getServers()

    # loop over the server mbeans and if the right one is found (or all if 'None' was provided) delete
it
    already_found = false
    for nextManagedServerInstance in listOfManagedServer:
        # test if machine is defined and if yes if it is the machine in question
        if (nextManagedServerInstance.getMachine()!=None):
            if (nextManagedServerInstance.getMachine().getName() == machineName):
                already_found = true;

    return already_found


# utility function to check weather a cluster still has members
def clusterHasManagedServers(clusterName):
    cd ('/')
    # get the cluster mbean
    clusterMBean = getMBean('/Clusters/'+clusterName)

    # check if the number of servers in the cluster is > 0
    if (len(clusterMBean.getServers()) > 0):
        return true
```

```
        else:
            return false


# -------------- Delete functions ----------------------------

# delete a specific datasource or if 'None' is passed as argument delete all DS
def deleteDataSource(dataSourceName):
    serverConfig()

    # loop over the datasources mbeans and if the right one is found (or all if 'None' was provided)
delete it
    edit()
    startEdit()
    cd ('/')
    listOfDataSources = cmo.getJDBCSystemResources()
    already_found = 'false'
    for datasourceInstance in listOfDataSources:
        # if desired datasource is found OR no name (=None) was provided
        if ((dataSourceName==None) or (dataSourceName == datasourceInstance.getName())):
            # print name
            print 'Datasource '+datasourceInstance.getName()+' will be destroyed !'
            # first delete targets
            datasourceInstance.setTargets(None)
            # delete
            cmo.destroyJDBCSystemResource(datasourceInstance)
            # remember that DataSource was found
            already_found = 'true'

        if ((dataSourceName!=None) and (already_found=='false')):
            print 'DataSource '+ dataSourceName + ' not found'
    save()
    activate()
    serverConfig()


# delete a specific mail session or if 'None' is passed as argument delete all sessions
def deleteMailSessions(mailSessionName):
    serverConfig()

    # loop over the mail mbeans and if the right one is found (or all if 'None' was provided) delete
it
    edit()
    startEdit()
    cd ('/')
    listOfMailSessions = cmo.getJMailSessions()
    already_found = 'false'
    for mailInstance in listOfMailSessions:
        # if desired mail session is found OR no name (=None) was provided
        if ((mailSessionName ==None) or (mailSessionName == mailInstance.getName())):
            # print name
            print Mail Session '+ mailInstance.getName()+' will be destroyed !'
            # first delete targets
            mailInstance.setTargets(None)
            # delete
            cmo.destroyMailSession(mailInstance)
            # remember that Mail Session was found
            already_found = 'true'

        if ((mailSessionName!=None) and (already_found=='false')):
            print Mail Session '+ mailSessionName + ' not found'
    save()
    activate()
    serverConfig()


# delete a specific JNDI provider session or if 'None' is passed as argument delete all provider
def deleteForeignJNDIProvider(providerName):
    serverConfig()

    # loop over the foreign provider mbeans and if the right one is found (or all if 'None' was
provided) delete it
    edit()
    startEdit()
    cd ('/')
    listOfForeignProviders = cmo.getForeignJNDIProviders()
    already_found = 'false'
    for foreignProviderInstance in listOfForeignProviders:
```

```
            # if desired provider is found OR no name (=None) was provided
        if ((providerName==None) or (providerName == foreignProviderInstance.getName())):
                # print name
                print 'Foreign provider '+foreignProviderInstance.getName()+' will be destroyed !'
                # delete
                cmo.destroyForeignJNDIProvider(foreignProviderInstance)
                # remember that Provider was found
                already_found = 'true'

        if ((providerName!=None) and (already_found=='false')):
            print 'Foreign provider '+ providerName + ' not found'
    save()
    activate()
    serverConfig()


# delete a specific managed-server or if 'None' is passed as argument delete all managed-servers
# note that optionally the system can check if datasources, JMS providers or applications are still
# hosted on this server - then it will not delete it unless you pass true for the second option
def deleteManagedServer(managedServerName, deleteAlsoIfDependenciesExist=false):
    serverConfig()

    # loop over the server mbeans and if the right one is found (or all if 'None' was provided) delete
it
    edit()
    startEdit()
    cd ('/')
    listOfManagedServer = cmo.getServers()
    already_found = 'false'
    for nextManagedServerInstance in listOfManagedServer:
        # if desired MS is found OR no name (=None) was provided
        if ((managedServerName==None) or (managedServerName == nextManagedServerInstance.getName())):
            can_be_deleted = 'true';
            if (str(deleteAlsoIfDependenciesExist)=='false'):
                # check for dependencies
                if (managedserverHostsApplications(managedServerName)):
                    can_be_deleted = 'false'
                    print 'Applications still deployed on '+
                        nextManagedServerInstance.getName()+' - cannot delete.'
                if (managedserverHostsDatasources(managedServerName)):
                    can_be_deleted = 'false'
                    print nextManagedServerInstance.getName()+
                        ' still hosts datasources - cannot delete.'
                if (managedserverHostsJMSProviders(managedServerName)):
                    can_be_deleted = 'false'
                    print nextManagedServerInstance.getName()+
                        ' still hosts JMS provider - cannot delete.'

            if (can_be_deleted=='true'):
                # print name
                print 'Managed Server '+nextManagedServerInstance.getName()+' will be destroyed !'

                # finally shutdown the server
                print "Stopping " + nextManagedServerInstance.getName();
                # shutdown the server if this server is not yet in state shutdown
                # we need to switch to the domainRuntime in order to find out
                domainRuntime()
                serverRuntime = getMBean('/ServerLifeCycleRuntimes/'
                                         +nextManagedServerInstance.getName())
                serverState = serverRuntime.getState()
                edit()
                print 'Server '+ nextManagedServerInstance.getName()+' is in state ' + serverState
                if serverState != 'SHUTDOWN':
                    try:
                        shutdown(nextManagedServerInstance.getName(),'Server','true'
                                ,1000,force='true', block='true')
                    except:
                        pass

                    serverState = serverRuntime.getState()
                    print 'Server '+ nextManagedServerInstance.getName()+' is NOW in state '
                        + serverState

                # detach from cluster if any
                nextManagedServerInstance.setCluster(None)
                # detach from machine if any
                nextManagedServerInstance.setMachine(None)
                # finally delete
```

```
                    cmo.destroyServer(nextManagedServerInstance)

              # remember that Provider was found
              already_found = 'true'

    if ((managedServerName!=None) and (already_found=='false')):
        print 'Managed-Server '+ managedServerName + ' not found'
    save()
    activate()
    serverConfig()


# delete a specific cluster or if 'None' is passed as argument delete all clusters
# note that optionally the system can check if managed-servers are still members of this cluster.
# It will not delete it unless you pass true for the second option. In the later case this
# function has to detach the server(s) from the cluster first, otherwise it cannot be deleted
def deleteCluster(clusterName, deleteAlsoIfDependenciesExist=false):
    # loop over the cluster mbeans and if the right one is found
    # (or all if 'None' was provided) delete it
    edit()
    startEdit()
    cd ('/')
    listOfCluster = cmo.getClusters()
    already_found = 'false'
    for nextClusterInstance in listOfCluster:
        # if desired cluster is found OR no name (=None) was provided
        if ((clusterName==None) or (clusterName == nextClusterInstance.getName())):
            can_be_deleted = 'true';
            if (str(deleteAlsoIfDependenciesExist)=='false'):
                # check for dependencies
                if (clusterHasManagedServers(nextClusterInstance.getName())):
                    can_be_deleted = 'false'
                    print 'Cluster '+nextClusterInstance.getName()+
                          ' still has server members - cannot delete.'

            if (can_be_deleted=='true'):
                # print name
                print 'Cluster '+nextClusterInstance.getName()+' will be destroyed !'

                # if the cluster still has managed-servers, then detach them from the cluster first !
                listOfManagedServer = nextClusterInstance.getServers()
                for nextManagedServerInstance in listOfManagedServer:
                    # detach from cluster if any
                    nextManagedServerInstance.setCluster(None)

                # finally delete the cluster
                try:
                    cmo.destroyCluster(nextClusterInstance)
                except Exception, ex:
                    print ex

            # remember that cluster was found
            already_found = 'true'

    if ((clusterName!=None) and (already_found=='false')):
        print 'Cluster '+ clusterName + ' not found'
    save()
    activate()


# delete a specific machine or if 'None' is passed as argument delete all machines
# note that optionally the system can check if managed-servers are still hosted on this machine.
# In this case it will not delete it unless you pass true for the second option
def deleteMachine(machineName, deleteAlsoIfDependenciesExist=false):
    # loop over the machine mbeans and if the right one is found (or all if 'None' was provided)
delete it
    edit()
    startEdit()
    cd ('/')
    listOfMachines = cmo.getMachines()
    already_found = 'false'
    for nextMachineInstance in listOfMachines:
        # if desired machine is found OR no name (=None) was provided
        if ((machineName==None) or (machineName == nextMachineInstance.getName())):
            can_be_deleted = 'true';
            if (str(deleteAlsoIfDependenciesExist)=='false'):
                # check for dependencies
                if (machineHostsManagedServer(nextMachineInstance.getName())):
```

```
                        can_be_deleted = 'false'
                        print 'Machine '+nextMachineInstance.getName()+
                                ' still has server members - cannot delete.'

            if (can_be_deleted=='true'):
                # print name
                print 'Machine '+nextMachineInstance.getName()+' will be destroyed !'
                # finally delete the machine
                cmo.destroyMachine(nextMachineInstance)

            # remember that machine was found
            already_found = true

    if ((machineName!=None) and (already_found=='false')):
        print 'Machine '+ machineName + ' not found'
    save()
    activate()

# ================================================================
#          Main Code Execution
# ================================================================
if __name__ == "main":
    print '#####################################################################';
    print '#                   Weblogic resource deletion                      #';
    print '#####################################################################';
    print 'Usage:  <user> <password> <URL> <resource-type> <None or resource name> <true/false
for deleteIfDep>\n';
    wls_user = sys.argv[1]
    wls_password = sys.argv[2]
    wls_url = sys.argv[3]
    wls_typeForDeletion = sys.argv[4]
    wls_whatShouldBeDeleted = sys.argv[5]    # can be 'None'
    deleteAlsoIfDependenciesExist = sys.argv[6] # can be 'false' (should be) or 'true'

    # connect
    connect(wls_user, wls_password, wls_url)

    if (wls_whatShouldBeDeleted != 'None'):
        whatShouldBeDeleted = wls_whatShouldBeDeleted
    else:
        whatShouldBeDeleted = None

    if (wls_typeForDeletion == 'Machine'):
        deleteMachine(whatShouldBeDeleted,deleteAlsoIfDependenciesExist)
    elif (wls_typeForDeletion == 'Cluster'):
        deleteCluster(whatShouldBeDeleted,deleteAlsoIfDependenciesExist)
    elif (wls_typeForDeletion == 'ManagedServer'):
        deleteManagedServer(whatShouldBeDeleted,deleteAlsoIfDependenciesExist)
    elif (wls_typeForDeletion == 'DataSource'):
        deleteDataSource(whatShouldBeDeleted,deleteAlsoIfDependenciesExist)
    elif (wls_typeForDeletion == 'Mail'):
        deleteMailSessions(whatShouldBeDeleted,deleteAlsoIfDependenciesExist)
    elif (wls_typeForDeletion == 'JNDI'):
        deleteForeignJNDIProvider(whatShouldBeDeleted,deleteAlsoIfDependenciesExist)
    else:
        print '\nUNKOWN resource type: '+wls_typeForDeletion
```

First example: deletion of a cluster.

Commandline to call:

```
wlst.sh ./cleanup.py weblogic test1234 t3://localhost:40001 Cluster MartinTest_Cluster true
```

Result:

```
#######################################################################
#                   Weblogic resource deletion                        #
#######################################################################
Usage:  <user> <password> <URL> <resource-type> <None or resource name> <true/false for deleteIfDep>
```

```
Starting an edit session ...
Started edit session, please be sure to save and activate your
changes once you are done.
Cluster MartinTest_Cluster will be destroyed !
Saving all your changes ...
Saved all your changes successfully.
Activating all your changes, this may take a while ...
The edit lock associated with this edit session is released
once the activation is completed.
Activation completed
```

Second example: deletion of a Managed-Server.

Commandline to call:

```
wlst.sh ./cleanup.py weblogic test1234 t3://localhost:40001 ManagedServer MartinTest_Domain_MS2 false
```

Result:

```
########################################################################
#                    Weblogic resource deletion                        #
########################################################################
Usage:  <user> <password> <URL> <resource-type> <None or resource name> <true/false for deleteIfDep>

Starting an edit session ...
Started edit session, please be sure to save and activate your
changes once you are done.
Managed Server MartinTest_Domain_MS2 will be destroyed !
Stopping MartinTest_Domain_MS2
Location changed to domainRuntime tree. This is a read-only tree with DomainMBean as the root.
For more help, use help(domainRuntime)

You already have an edit session in progress and hence WLST will
continue with your edit session.

Server MartinTest_Domain_MS2 is in state SHUTDOWN
Saving all your changes ...
Saved all your changes successfully.
Activating all your changes, this may take a while ...
The edit lock associated with this edit session is released
once the activation is completed.
Activation completed
```

Third example: deletion of a machine.

Commandline to call:

```
wlst.sh ./cleanup.py weblogic test1234 t3://localhost:40001 Machine localhost  false
```

Result:

```
########################################################################
#                    Weblogic resource deletion                        #
########################################################################
Usage:  <user> <password> <URL> <resource-type> <None or resource name> <true/false for deleteIfDep>

Connecting to t3://localhost:40001 with userid weblogic ...
Successfully connected to Admin Server 'AdminServer' that belongs to domain 'MartinTest_Domain'.

Starting an edit session ...
Started edit session, please be sure to save and activate your
```

```
changes once you are done.
Machine localhost will be destroyed !
Saving all your changes ...
Saved all your changes successfully.
Activating all your changes, this may take a while ...
The edit lock associated with this edit session is released
once the activation is completed.
Activation completed
```

Summary

Like other J2EE servers, WebLogic is based on services that offer abstraction layers to infrastructure services like database access, messaging, transaction integration, directory services, and many more. All these services have to be configured for WebLogic domains and/or individual WebLogic Server instances.

This chapter has discussed the most important services of WebLogic and has shown possible ways to automate their creation, configuration, and also their destruction.

Always be prepared that services you have configured have to be changed or eliminated if these services are no longer needed. I strongly advise everyone to delete unused services, as those services block resources (ports, memory, and others) and also may offer a forgotten backdoor to your application.

A very good practice is also to write WLST scripts that check for the existence of certain resources first. If these resources already exist, either stop the script or delete the old resource and then create the new one. This allows for updating resources and re-running scripts, which may have failed for other reasons.

WebLogic Security Configuration with WLST

WebLogic Security Configuration with WLST

Security is a huge topic that involves many different security technologies and therefore it is out-of-scope of this book to give a comprehensive security description. Oracle has a number of documentation books just for the security layer. Many other books and websites (see reference list) are recommended for further reading in case you need more background information. This chapter will show you how to automate many different aspects of security.

Introduction

The beginning of this chapter will introduce basic security considerations and issues like file system, server/NodeManager connections, and similar issues. Afterwards, many information around PKI (public key infrastructure) and SSL are provided. One security configuration that related to this topic, the configuration of an admin channel, is also provided. Afterwards the important user/group/role management is discussed, which is present in every WebLogic domain. One major part of this chapter is the discussion of the different security providers of a WebLogic realm, especially in the area of authentication, authorization, and role/credential mapping. Information will be also provided on password validation and other providers.

File System Security

WebLogic domains consist of many different files. Some of them contain usernames and passwords for server access, database access, or other resource access. Fortunately WebLogic does a pretty good job in encrypting these passwords with AES. All security is limited somewhere, and WebLogic has a weakness. If somebody gets access to these encrypted passwords and (!) the domain salt file, which is used as key, then all passwords can be easily decrypted.

The next WLST script shows an example of how to decrypt the passwords. This might be helpful for admins who forgot the server access password (boot.properties), but keep in mind that it is a weak point. Therefore, the WebLogic domain and especially the salt file must be secured using file system access rights so that only the executing user (the user that is used to start and run the WebLogic Servers) has access to it.

Example of how to decrypt WebLogic passwords:

```
import os
import weblogic.security.internal.SerializedSystemIni
import weblogic.security.internal.encryption.ClearOrEncryptedService

def decrypt(domainHomeName, encryptedPwd):
    domainHomeAbsolutePath = os.path.abspath(domainHomeName)
    encryptionService = weblogic.security.internal.SerializedSystemIni.
                                getEncryptionService(domainHomeAbsolutePath)
    ces = weblogic.security.internal.encryption.ClearOrEncryptedService(encryptionService)
    clear = ces.decrypt(encryptedPwd)
    print "RESULT:" + clear

try:
        decrypt(sys.argv[1], sys.argv[2])
except:
        print "Unexpected error: ", sys.exc_info()[0]
        dumpStack()
```

This script has two arguments: the first one is the domain home directory and the second the encrypted value. This script will decrypt it and display the decrypted value.

Example:

```
.../bin/wlst.sh ./passwd.py /mydomains/MartinTest_Domain
{AES}tXb+6Cgadh1z1uJVaDHC4K2M31to4BQoTOQeMczGIr8\=
Your environment has been set.
Initializing WebLogic Scripting Tool (WLST) ...
Welcome to WebLogic Server Administration Scripting Shell

RESULT: test1234
```

Access to Server

As you have already seen in some of the scripts already presented in the last chapters, for the *connect* command, the user and password is needed in the WLST scripts. This is one of the most common issues during audits. Fortunately WLST offers a concept for creating a secure (encrypted) user access which can be used from any WLST scripts.

The necessary command is called *storeUserConfig*. In order to use this command you need to do a one-time connect with a clear user/password (I advise for this script to provide the user and password as arguments, so that these values even here do not show up in any script). When connected, you use *storeUserConfig* in order to create the encrypted access values along with a unique key file.

Note: If you ever lose this keyfile, you need to re-generate a new pair of config/key files.

Here is an example script for creating the secret access files (note that the AdminServer must be up and running!):

💾 **secret_access_files**

```
import sys

adminURL = '';
adminUserName = '';
adminPassword = '';
userConfigFile = '';
userKeyFile = '';

# Load properties
def intialize():
        global adminURL;
        global adminUserName;
        global adminPassword;
        global userConfigFile;
        global userKeyFile;

        # test arguments
        if len(sys.argv) != 6:
                print 'Usage: wlst.sh createSecretAccess.py  <admin-URL> <wls_username>
<wls_password> <destUserConfigFile> <destUserKeyFile>';
                exit();

        try:
                adminURL      = sys.argv[1];
                adminUserName = sys.argv[2];
                adminPassword = sys.argv[3];
                userConfigFile= sys.argv[4];
                userKeyFile   = sys.argv[5];
        except:
                print 'Cannot load arguments  !';
                exit();

        print 'Initialization completed';


##################################################################
# Connect to adminserver
##################################################################
def connnectToAdminServer():
        print 'Connecting to the Admin Server ';
        connect(adminUserName, adminPassword, adminURL);

##################################################################
# Create userconfig and key
##################################################################
def creatSecretAccessFiles():
        print 'Create secret access files !';
        storeUserConfig(userConfigFile , userKeyFile);

##################################################################
# disconnect from  adminserver
##################################################################
def disconnectFromAdminserver():
        print 'Disconnect from the Admin Server...';
        disconnect();


# ============================================================
#          Main Code Execution
if __name__ == "main":
        print '';
        intialize();
        connnectToAdminServer();
        creatSecretAccessFiles();
        disconnectFromAdminserver();
```

Example of running this script:

```
/opt/wls/wlserver_10.3/common/bin/wlst.sh    ./createSecretAccess.py    t3://localhost:44001    weblogic
test1234 ./myUserConfig ./myUserSecretKey
Initializing WebLogic Scripting Tool (WLST) ...
Welcome to WebLogic Server Administration Scripting Shell

Starting the initialization process
Initialization completed
Connecting to the Admin Server
Connecting to t3://localhost:7001 with userid weblogic ...
Successfully connected to Admin Server 'AdminServer' that belongs to domain 'MartinTest_Domain'.

Create secret access files !
Creating the key file can reduce the security of your system if it is not kept in a
secured location after it is created. Do you want to create the key file? y or ny
The  username  and  password  that  were  used  for  this  WebLogic  Server  connection  are  stored  in
./myUserConfig and ./myUserSecretKey.
Disconnect from the Admin Server...
Disconnected from weblogic server: AdminServer
```

WLST will always ask you before it creates the security files. This is not possible in automated environments. Therefore, WebLogic provides a command line switch FOR WLST which can be used to disable this question. You need to set -Dweblogic.management.confirmKeyfileCreation=true as a startup property for WLST and this question will never be asked again. But please be aware that these security files have the same security relevance as private certificates!

Resulting myUserConfig file (the keyFile is binary and cannot be displayed here):

```
#WebLogic User Configuration File; 2
#Tue Nov 13 14:27:06 CET 2012
weblogic.management.username={AES}YwaRzRjSz0/nIiJLa5axhOEfw9FCLYjYXcUqsldLt1M\=
weblogic.management.password={AES}8THvUpNltEHjV5HrkM7z0/d6dQgfNpv2CE6ZA0p0F4c\=
```

Now let us test the generated secure files.

First, test connectivity. Note that this script has everything in the two lines of script without any arguments or property files. Nevertheless this script has no user or password in a human readable way:

```
connect(userConfigFile='./myUserConfig',userKeyFile='./myUserSecretKey',url='t3://localhost:7001');
disconnect();
```

Output result:

```
/opt/wls/wlserver_10.3/common/bin/wlst.sh ./testAutomaticConnect.py
Initializing WebLogic Scripting Tool (WLST) ...
Welcome to WebLogic Server Administration Scripting Shell

Connecting to t3://localhost:7001 with userid weblogic ...
Successfully connected to Admin Server 'AdminServer' that belongs to domain 'MartinTest_Domain'.
Disconnected from weblogic server: AdminServer
```

The command *storeUserConfig()* also has a third optional parameter; this parameter has a boolean type value that specifies whether to store the username and password for NodeManager or WebLogic Server. If set to true, then NodeManager's username and password will be stored. This argument default set as nm=false. This option can be useful if you are using NodeManager for your WebLogic domain.

The encryption type can be identified by viewing the userconfig file, where every encrypted value is prefixed with the kind of algorithm used. This encryption in WebLogic 10 is different compared to older versions. WebLogic 11g (10.3) uses the AES (Advanced Encryption Standard) algorithm for encryption; earlier it was DES (Data Encryption Standard).

These files can be used to connect to WebLogic Server instances.

These encrypted files can be used for different purposes in production or development domains in the *connect()* method, such as:

- Start/Stop NodeManager (Production)

- Start/Stop WLS Servers (including AdminServer)

- Deploy/undeploy/redeploy Applications (Production/Development)

- Monitor JMS, JDBC, JVM, ThreadPool (Production)

Access to NodeManager

If you want to access the NodeManager (e.g. for starting the AdminServer directly) you need to know the NodeManager password. This is generated by default and is therefore unknown. However, you can set your own password or query the actual password via WLST.

You can get the NodeManager username using the following WLST script (you need to connect to the AdminServer first):

```
print get('/SecurityConfiguration/tp_domain/NodeManagerUsername')
```

You can also get the NodeManager password using WLST. The password is stored encrypted. In order to display it in a human readable form, you need to enable clear text password display. BE CAREFUL and do not forget to revert this setting back, otherwise your passwords will display in clear text!

Here is a safe script to view NodeManager password (will revert setting afterwards):

```
connect('weblogic','test1234','t3://localhost:7001')
edit()
startEdit()
cd('/SecurityConfiguration/MartinTest_Domain')
#  !! set password display to clear text   - dangerous as this introduces a security issue
cmo.setClearTextCredentialAccessEnabled(true)
save()
activate()

print get('/SecurityConfiguration/MartinTest_Domain/NodeManagerPassword')

# important !  revert clear text display !
```

```
edit()
startEdit()
cd('/SecurityConfiguration/MartinTest_Domain')
#  !! set password display back to encrypted
cmo.setClearTextCredentialAccessEnabled(false)
save()
activate()

disconnect()
exit()
```

Offline script to set the NodeManager password:

```
readDomain('/opt/domains/myTestDomain')
cd("/SecurityConfiguration/myTestDomain'")
cmo.setNodeManagerUsername("<whatever user you want>")
cmo.setNodeManagerPasswordEncrypted("<whatever password you want>")
updateDomain()
```

Script to test if the NodeManager username is correct:

```
nmConnect(domainDir='/opt/domains/myTestDomain', username='<myUserName>', password='<myPassword>')
Connecting to Node Manager ...
Successfully Connected to Node Manager.
nmDisconnect()
Successfully disconnected from Node Manager.
exit()
```

The following parameters can be used for the *nmConnect* command:

- nmConnect([username, password], [host], [port], [domainName], [domainDir], [nmType])

- nmConnect([userConfigFile, userKeyFile], [host], [port], [domainName], [domainDir], [nmType])

PKI/SSL

This chapter discusses the "security on the wire" level of a security architecture. This is concerned with encryption on the wire and making sure that a connection is not tampered ("man-in-the-middle-attack") by authenticating each other.

Introduction to PKI/SSL

The PKI (Private Key Infrastructure) and SSL (Secure Sockets Layer) encryption in WebLogic is only concerned with the encryption on the wire and SSL authentication. This concerns the following aspects:

- Encryption of communication between all involved processes (admin-server, Managed-Server, NodeManager, client like browser, scripts (WLST) customer processes).

- Authentication of the processes:

- o In SSL, servers will present their certificate.

- o Optionally, clients will present their SSL certificate (client certificate). This is independent from other authentication like user login, web service authentication, or others. This is only on SSL level. This also means that the counterpart must have a trust store with all trusted certificates or (much more often used) the trusted issuer certificate(s) as shown in Figure 7.1.

Things to consider while reading the following diagram:

- The AdminServer (it is assumed that in this diagram that it only performs administration tasks) will be contacted from browsers (=> console) using HTTPS and from other admin tools (like WLST or JMX programs) using T3S or IIOPS. In all cases it will present its public key (dashed line). Optionally, clients have to present their client public key that the AdminServer can verify against its trust store (this can be configured in the AdminServer setup).

- The Managed-Server uses the same mechanisms. However, it does not host the admin-console. Clients will contact their deployed applications using HTTPS (for web applications) or T3S/IIOPS for RMI-based applications (like EJB access). It is of course possible for administration tools (not shown in diagram) to also contact the Managed-Server using T3S/IIOPS. NOTE: In this diagram the Managed-Server is depicted using its own certificate. This is usually the case if the Managed-Server is running on a different host than the AdminServer as these certificates (HTTPS/SSL requirements) must be host-dependent. In case these servers are co-located on the same host, they most likely will use the same certificates. Also note that in order for this to work, all certificates must be issued from the same certificate authority or all CA's certificates must be in the trust store. An even more secure option (but trust me: a nightmare for administrators!) would be to create trust stores with the individual certificates.

- The NodeManager can only be contacted using SSL/TCP. The underlying protocol is only based on TCP packets. It will most likely use the same certificates as the Managed-Servers hosted on this host. However, in case the AdminServer/ NodeManager communication is done over a separate ADMIN-LAN, the NodeManager may be listening on a different IP/DNS-name than the Managed-Server. In this case the NodeManager might require its own certificate.

- The different client tools - regardless if used for admin or application communication - can present their client certificate. This can be enforced in the domain configuration. SSL normally requires that the server certificate must be verified, therefore they also need a trust store in order to authenticate the server certificates. Depending on the implementation, this can be disabled on the client but weakens the security of the setup.

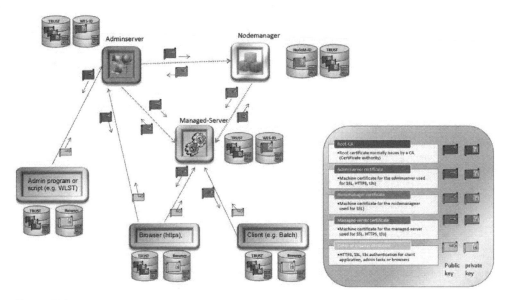

Figure 7.1: *Certificates used in WebLogic*

SSL

SSL (Secure Sockets Layer) is a transport-layer protocol (runs over TCP/IP) and has the following main features:

- Capable of performing

- Data encryption

- Data integrity checking

- Server authentication

- Client authentication

- Designed around a framework

- Standard handshaking protocol for clients and servers

- Pluggable cipher suites for extensibility e.g. SSL_RSA_WITH_RC4_128_MD5

- Can select encryption with or without authentication

SSL is used to protect messages in transit and has many ciphers for different purposes, e.g. message encryption, authentication, message integrity, and encryption strength. In order to establish trust, digital certificates are used. The most common is the format X.509. In a WebLogic environment, everything with regards to SSL-level trust is based on certificates.

Trust establishment protocols (e.g., the SSL "handshake"):

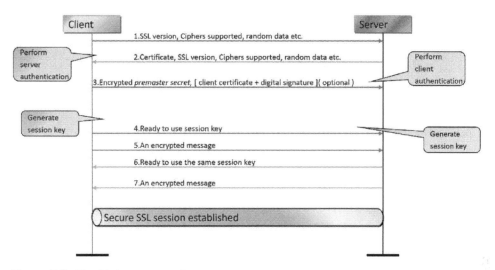

Figure 7.2: *Establishment protocols*

When an entity expects a peer to trust it, the peer requests the entity's certificate(s). The entity supplies a chain of certificates (its own, its Certifying Authority's and others) to the peer.

The peer maintains a list of "trusted certificates" - CAs that it trusts. When a certificate in the entity's certificate chain exactly matches any one of the trusted certificates, trust is established.

Therefore, setting up a trust store involves importing the certificates and also aligning it with the companies trust guidelines. Usually in bigger companies there is a department for certificates, trust, and security guidelines. In order to pass later security audits, it is absolutely advisable to build the certificate stores and trust store according to their guidelines.

Contents of a Digital Certificate (X.509 format):

- Data Section

    o X.509 version

    o Serial number (unique for each certificate from a single CA)

    o CA specific information

- o Public key of the entity (aka 'subject'; if encrypted, cipher used is specified)

- o Distinguished Name (DN) of the issuing CA

- o Validity period of the certificate

- o DN of the subject

- o < optional > certificate extensions

- Signature Section

  - o Cipher used for the creation of the digital signature

  - o Digital Signature of the CA, obtained by creating the hash from all the certificate data and encrypting the hash with the private key of the CA.

Client Authentication (on the server side)

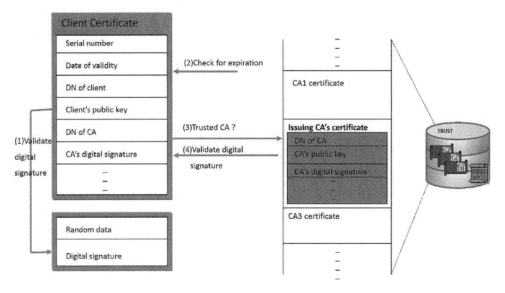

Figure 7.3: *Client Authentication*

Client authentication is the process that the server has to perform to authenticate the client. Client authentication is not mandatory in SSL protocol version 3.0, but the server can do it if desired by demanding that the client provide its certificate. The client authentication mechanism involves performing the above 3 steps. Step 1 validates the digital signature, thereby ensuring that the public key matches the private key used by the client, but it does not authenticate yet. To associate the fact that the public key does belong to the client with the specified DN, steps 3 and 4 are required.

Except for step 1, the rest of the process of authentication is the same as the server authentication.

Server Authentication (on the client side)

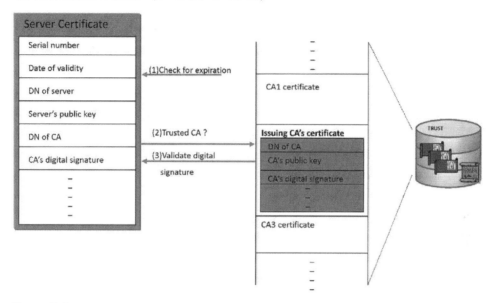

Figure 7.4: *Server Authentication*

Server authentication is the process that the client has to perform to authenticate the server. The server authentication mechanism involves performing the following steps. First, it checks for the validity period of the certificate. If valid, it checks if the CA is found in its known and trusted set of CA's (trust store), stored on the client side. If found, it uses the public key of the CA (extracted from the issuing CA's certificate stored in the local database) and decrypts the digital signature of the CA found in the server's certificate. If the decryption works, then the CA is who it claims to be and the CA is valid and authenticated. In step 2, if the CA is not one of the trusted CA's, then its issuing CA is located on the chain of certificates (if a chain is sent by the server) and the 3 steps are performed on this new CA until a trusted CA is found in the local database. If no trusted CA is found, the authentication fails. There is an optional step 4 performed by many SSL products in which the actual server's domain name is checked with the domain name in the server's certificate to be sure there is no "Man in the middle" attack.

Tools for Certificates

Different tools are available for dealing with certificates. In this section we will only look at the two most important tools that are must-haves for every administrator.

Tools in the JDK

- Keytool
  - o Creates keystores with key entries or trusted certificate lists.
  - o Creates certificate requests or self-signed certificates.

- Jarsigner
  - o Uses information from a keystore to generate or verify digital signatures for JAR files.

Open source tools

- OpenSSL
  - o Creates keys, certificates, or certificate requests.

OpenSSL

The tool OpenSSL can be used in order to create a key pair, create a certificate request, or create a self-signed certificate.

Examples:

```
openssl req -config openssl.cnf2 -new -out my-server.csr
This creates a certificate signing request and a private key

openssl rsa -in privkey.pem -out my-server.key
This removes the passphrase from the private key.

openssl x509 -in my-server.csr -out my-server.cert -req -signkey my-
server.key -days 365
This creates a self-signed certificate that you can use until you get a
"real" one from a certificate authority.
```

Keytool

Private Certificates, Certificate Chains, and Trusted Certificates are very important resources and these resources must be organized and (in case of private certificates) protected. The standard container for certificates and related resources for the JDK are keystores. Keystores are local databases that contain certificates or certificate chains. They can contain protected private certificates and trusted (CA) certificates. Keystores can be created using the JDK keytool.

The program keytool of the JDK manages a keystore of private keys and their associated X.509 certificate chains. It can also manage certificates from trusted entities. Keytool stores the keys and certificates in a so-called keystore. It protects private keys with a password.

There are two different types of entries in a keystore:

1. Key entries
2. Trusted certificate entries

Functionality of the keytool includes:

- Generating a key pair (a public key and private key).

- Reading the certificate or certificate chain from a file.

- Reading (from the keystore) the certificate associated with alias, and storing it in the file cert_file.

- Printing the contents of the keystore.

- Changing the password used to protect the integrity of the keystore contents.

- Changing the password under which the private key identified by alias is protected.

- Deleting from the keystore the entry identified by alias.

- Creating Certificate Requests and self-signed certificates.

Example usages:

Generate public/private key pair and assign an alias:

```
keytool -genkey -alias admin -keysize 1024 -validity 3650 -keypass 123456 -
keystore admin.store -storepass 123456
```

Create a certificate request:

```
keytool -certreq -alias admin -file admin.csr -keypass 123456 -storepass
123456 -keystore admin.store
```

Create a self-signed certificate:

```
keytool -selfcert -alias admin -validity 3650 -keypass 123456 -keystore
admin.store -storepass 123456
```

Certificates can be imported as trusted certificates. Every certificate will be assigned to an alias that must exist when a new certificate is imported. Chains of certificates can be imported.

Import certificates:

```
keytool -import -alias trusted_1 -file trusted_1.cert -keypass 123456 -
keystore admin.store -storepass 123456
```

Create a trust keystore - importing the RootCA certificate:

```
keytool -import  -file rootCA.cer -alias RootCA -keystore trust.jks -
storepass password
```

To verify the contents of the keystore, you can use the below command:

```
Keytool -list -v -keystore <keystore-name> -storepass  <keystore-password>
```

Setting up PKI/SSL on a WebLogic Server

First, set up the PKI and SSL settings of a WebLogic Server. The settings are the same (maybe except filename, alias, and password) for the Administration Server and Managed-Server.

This script will connect to an AdminServer and change the PKI and SSL settings. NOTE that this is a non-dynamic change, which means that the WebLogic Server(s) where you applied the changes must be restarted afterwards.

🖫 change_PKI_SSL_settings

```
# connect to the admin server
connect('weblogic','Welcome1','t3://1.2.3.4:7001')

# go into edit mode
edit()
startEdit()

# change to the adinserver configuration
cd('/Servers/AdminServer')

# change keystore mode to custom and trust - means own keystore and truststore
set('KeyStores','CustomIdentityAndCustomTrust')

# set the keystore with our identity - our private key
set('CustomIdentityKeyStoreFileName','/myfiles/keystores/MartinIdentityKeyStore.jks')
set('CustomIdentityKeyStoreType','jks')
# passphrase for the keystore - remember that the private key is an important security token and must
be protected
# this passthrase will be stored encrypted in WebLogic
set('CustomIdentityKeyStorePassPhrase','passwordForKeystore')

# configure the truststore with either the root CA's or individual public keys which can be trusted
set('CustomTrustKeyStoreFileName','/myfiles/keystores/MartinTrustKeyStore.jks')
set('CustomTrustKeyStoreType','jks')
set('CustomTrustKeyStorePassPhrase','passwordForKeystore')

# switch to the SSL section of the admin-server
```

```
cd('/Servers/AdminServer/SSL/AdminServer')
# Tell weblogic to use keystores for trust
set('IdentityAndTrustLocations','KeyStores')
# Tell the adminserver WHICH certificate of the identity keystore should be used as its server
certificate
set('ServerPrivateKeyAlias','myCertificateAlias')
set('ServerPrivateKeyPassPhrase','MachinePassPhrase')

# disable hostname verifier.  This should only be deactivated if you are on non-production systems
and it
# might be possible that you have to accept certificates which do not belong to the partner's host
set('HostnameVerifier','None')
set('TwoWaySSLEnabled','true')
set('CertAuthenticator','')

# switching this to false means that the server does not force a client to present a client
certificate.
# Should be ok for most (even production) environments
set('ClientCertificateEnforced','false')

save()
activate()
disconnect()
```

For explanation, please see the comments in the script.

SSL basically consists of two different phases. The first phase is used to establish the connection, including trust. Trust on SSL means that the client can trust the server, the server can trust the client, both need to trust each other, or trust is not required. The "one-way" configuration in almost all cases means that the client must trust the server. The server must have a certificate and present this to the client. The client has to have a truststore with the CA's or individual certificates that the client is allowed to trust. The client itself is not required to present a certificate in this case. This in turn means that the server accepts connections from many clients. This is the usual way HTTPS secured connections work over the internet. The rather rare option called "two-way" means that the client also has to present a certificate to the server and that the server needs to establish trust. In this case the server has to maintain a truststore with all valid client certificates or all CA's issuing client certificates. WebLogic Server can be configured to require clients to submit valid and trusted certificates before completing the SSL connection.

WebLogic includes a security concept called "host name verifier". This is an additional level of security for outgoing SSL connections. In addition to trust of the server certificate, this feature verifies that the servername in the URL matches the host name in the server certificate that the server has provided. Only with this option activated the so-called "man-in-the-middle" attack can be detected and avoided. WebLogic enables this feature by default and drops SSL connections if this verification fails.

To pass the hostname verifier, either the host name in the certificate matches the local machine's host name or the URL specifies localhost or the default IP address of the local machine.

WebLogic includes a command-line utility called *ValidateCertChain*. This is a handy Java program that can be used by administrators to check if an existing certificate will be rejected. Note that this is NOT a WebLogic configuration. It is an external command-line tool that can be used by administrators to check certificates or analyze problem situations. This tool is capable of validating different file formats (e.g. PEM, PKCS-12, PKCS-12 keystores, and JKS keystores).

Command-line syntax for this utility:

- java utils.ValidateCertChain -file pemcertificatefilename
- java utils.ValidateCertChain -pem pemcertificatefilename
- java utils.ValidateCertChain -pkcs12store pkcs12storefilename
- java utils.ValidateCertChain -pkcs12file pkcs12filename password
- java utils.ValidateCertChain -jks alias storefilename [storePass]

First steps in PKI/SSL troubleshooting:

One very common problem is when the certificate chain fails the validation. Another very common problem (which will be a periodic nightmare for all administrators) is expired certificates. It is crucial for secured environments to keep an eye on the expiration dates for your certificates.

The command line argument -Dweblogic.security.SSL.enforceConstraints might be used as an immediate help to circumvent the problem, but you must analyze the problem immediately and solve it, otherwise you will run into audit issues.

The *ValidateCertChain* command-line utility can be used to check whether the certificate chains will be accepted.

SSL debugging can be turned on to trace the SSL communication.
Use: -Dssl.debug=true -Dweblogic.StdoutDebugEnabled=true

The following message indicates SSL failure resulting from problems in the certificate chain:

```
<CA certificate rejected. The basic constraints for a CA certificate were
not marked for being a CA, or were not marked as critical>
```

Securing All Servers of a Domain

The same mechanism used in *Chapter 6* for domain creation can be used to configure PKI/SSL for all servers of your domain.

Since you will need to restart all servers after this configuration anyway, it is advisable to shut all of them down first (except the AdminServer of course) and then do the configuration changes. At the end you will also need to shutdown the AdminServer. Then you can do a "normal" full domain restart and you should be fine. Also DO NOT forget to also reconfigure the NodeManager (see next section) before you restart the domain. Otherwise you will fail for every Managed-Server!

The following method will iterate over all servers, get server-specific properties from the provided property list, and configure each server.

💾 **secure_servers**

```
def setPKISSLonAllServers(domainProps):
    print 'Iterate over all managed servers and set PKI / SSL configurations
    domainConfig()
    svrs = cmo.getServers()

    edit()
    startEdit()

    for server in svrs:
        # get server name
        myServerName = server.getName()

        # get server speecific parameter from property list
        id_keystore            = domainProps.getProperty(myServerName+'.id_keystore')
        id_keystorepassphrase  = domainProps.getProperty(myServerName+'.id_keystorepassphrase')
        trust_keystore         = domainProps.getProperty(myServerName+'.trust_keystore')
        trust_keystorepassphrase = domainProps.getProperty(myServerName+'.trust_keystorepassphrase')
        privatekeyalias        = domainProps.getProperty(myServerName+'.privatekeyalias')
        privatekeypassphrase   = domainProps.getProperty(myServerName+'.privatekeypassphrase')

        # change to server directory
        cd('/Servers/'+myServerName)

        # change keystore mode to custom and trust - means own keystore and truststore
        cmo.setKeyStores('CustomIdentityAndCustomTrust')

        # set the keystore with our identity - our private key
        cmo.set('CustomIdentityKeyStoreFileName',id_keystore)
        cmo.set('CustomIdentityKeyStoreType','jks')

        # passphrase for the keystore
        # remember that the private key is an important security token and must be protected
        # this passthrase will be stored encrypted in WebLogic
        cmo.set('CustomIdentityKeyStorePassPhrase',id_keystorepassphrase)

        # configure the truststore with either the root CA's or individual public
        cmo.set('CustomTrustKeyStoreFileName',trust_keystore)
        cmo.set('CustomTrustKeyStoreType','jks')
        cmo.set('CustomTrustKeyStorePassPhrase',trust_keystorepassphrase)

        # switch to the SSL section of the admin-server
        cd('/Servers/'+myServerName+'/SSL/'+myServerName)

        # Tell weblogic to use keystores for trust
        cmo.set('IdentityAndTrustLocations','KeyStores')

        # Tell the server WHICH certificate of the identity keystore should be
        cmo.set('ServerPrivateKeyAlias',privatekeyalias)
```

```
    cmo.set('ServerPrivateKeyPassPhrase',privatekeypassphrase)

    # disable hostname verifier
    cmo.set('HostnameVerifier','None')
    cmo.set('TwoWaySSLEnabled','true')
    cmo.set('CertAuthenticator','')

    # switching this to false means that the server does not force
    # a client to present a client certificate.
    # Should be ok for most (even production) environments
    cmo.set('ClientCertificateEnforced','false')

save()
activate()
```

Securing Nodemanager Access

Securing the NodeManager is important so that the NodeManager will a) use SSL and b) use the correct certificate. As we have changed the AdminServer to use our own certificate and trust only our own trust-list, the standard certificates (demo) of WebLogic (which are also used by default from the NodeManager) are no longer accepted by the AdminServer or Managed-Server.

Therefore, the NodeManager property file must be changed. See highlighted properties for the changes necessary for secure communication:

```
DomainsFile=/infrastructure/nodemanager/nodemanager.domains
LogLimit=0
PropertiesVersion=10.3
javaHome=/opt/jdk/jdk1.6
AuthenticationEnabled=true
NodeManagerHome=/infrastructure/nodemanager
JavaHome=/opt/jdk/jdk1.6
LogLevel=INFO
DomainsFileEnabled=true
StartScriptName=startWebLogic.sh
ListenAddress=
NativeVersionEnabled=true
ListenPort=52000
LogToStderr=true
SecureListener=true
LogCount=1
StopScriptEnabled=false
QuitEnabled=false
LogAppend=true
StateCheckInterval=500
CrashRecoveryEnabled=false
StartScriptEnabled=false
LogFile=/infrastructure/nodemanager/nodemanager.log
LogFormatter=weblogic.nodemanager.server.LogFormatter
ListenBacklog=50

KeyStores=CustomIdentityAndCustomTrust
CustomIdentityKeyStoreFileName=/myfiles/keystores/nodemanager/MyIdentityKeyStore.jks
CustomIdentityAlias=nodemanager_certificate
CustomIdentityKeyStorePassPhrase={3DES}yE1cRhTbYHJdBOQCqwDioA==
CustomIdentityKeyStoreType=JKS
CustomIdentityPrivateKeyPassPhrase={3DES}hMGpokJiIn1VzwnK2ri0V2WDyVoxCf3B
```

You need to set secureListener to "true" in order to listen for SSL communication. We also need to set a keystore with our certificate. Note that you do NOT need to enter those funny looking DES encrypted strings. Instead you have to put the clear text pass phrases into the configuration file. As soon as you restart the NodeManager, the NodeManager will encrypt those values for you.

Place the clear text passphrases in the file, restart the NodeManager, and then check if the NodeManager has encrypted the values. The NodeManager has found and accepted them only if the values are encrypted. Also note that you need to restart the NodeManager BEFORE you try to restart Managed-Servers with modified PKI/SSL settings. These NodeManager settings have to be done on ALL NodeManager hosting Managed-Servers for your domain.

However, there is one aspect that is very important and all administrators must pay attention to. If you change the NodeManager like this, then ALL domains for which the NodeManager maintains Managed-Servers MUST be changed to use our PKI/SSL settings. A mixed mode is impossible. If for some reason you have a mixed mode for your different domains, you have to use different NodeManagers. Every machine can host different NodeManagers listening on different ports. This is necessary for different security requirements of the domain or if the WebLogic domains are based on different WebLogic versions.

WLST Setup for Secure Access

Another common issue is that the administration communication is encrypted using SSL. Therefore the client - in your case the WLST interpreter - has to use either T3S or IIOPS. In both cases the WLST interpreter might need to provide its own SSL certificate, or verify that the server certificate is trusted.

In order to start the WLST with these extended requirements, you need to modify the start script for your WLST environment and add the security parameter. See the example below:

```
java
  [ -Dweblogic.security.SSL.ignoreHostnameVerification=true
  -Dweblogic.security.TrustKeyStore=DemoTrust ]
  [ -Dweblogic.security.JavaStandardTrustKeyStorePassPhrase=password]
    [ -Dweblogic.security.CustomTrustKeyStoreFileName=filename
    -Dweblogic.security.TrustKeystoreType=jks
    [ -Dweblogic.security.CustomTrustKeyStorePassPhrase=password]]
    [ -Dweblogic.security.SSL.hostnameVerifier=classname]
  weblogic.WLST
  [ -loadProperties propertyFilename ]
  [ -skipWLSModuleScanning ]
  [ [-i] filePath.py ]
```

Administration Channel

We have already discussed network channels earlier in *Chapter 6*. We will now be using the same concept and extend it for administration. This actually means that we are telling WebLogic to open a specific port or a complete separated channel (address and port) for administration communication.

Using an administration channel has a lot of advantages with respect to security. The first and biggest benefit is that the admin console will only be reachable over a non-standard port. This means that users cannot just guess the admin URL from their user access. From a "curious" user perspective: Use your application communication (e.g. http://somehost:port/abcdefg/app/start.jsp) and replace it with the default console (e.g. http://somehost:port/console). Then you get the login page. Try weblogic/weblogic or weblogic/Welcome1 and I guarantee that in some cases you might have success.

If the administration channel is used, then the administration channel will listen on a different port than the user communication. Therefore this port is much more difficult to guess. If you also change the context path (e.g. "secretWeapon" instead of "console") then it will be very hard for users to access the console. In addition, another port or even another network listener and other port will allow the admin to set different firewall rules.

Another advantage is that the administrative communication is always secured as SSL and is required as soon as an admin channel is activated (HTTPS, IIOPS, or T3S). In addition, your administrative communication gets its own dedicated thread which means that your admins can still work even if all user threads may be stuck or overloaded. So with an admin port you are able to separate your administrative communication from your application communication.

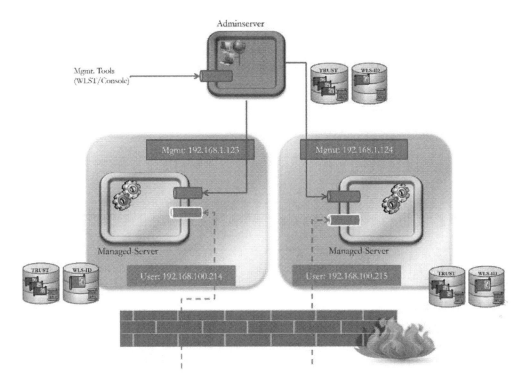

Figure 7.5: *Admin channel usage*

The administration port accepts only secure SSL traffic, and all connections through the port require authentication. This means that all servers (admin and managed) must be configured with SSL support and with a valid certificate (note that invalid or expired certificates may lead to a server crash or forced shutdown during start). This also means that you need to configure ALL servers to support SSL before you should enable the administration port, otherwise communication might not be possible. The administration port is configured on domain-level in order to activate it on all servers, but can be overwritten on each server instance. This is especially necessary if multiple instances are running on the same physical machine.

There are two different ways to configure an administration channel:

- **Port-Only**: The easier way is to enable the administration port on domain level and - if needed - overwrite this port on server level. This means that the same network adapter as the default channel will be used, and WebLogic is just opening another listen port that is secured.

- **Custom channel**: If option "port-only" is not enough for your needs, then you have to configure a custom channel. For this custom channel you can define port and addresses for each server, but you need to set the available protocol for this channel to "admin".

Enable Administration Port

The first example will look at the first option which means that we only enable the administration port and overwrite (optionally) the domain-wide configured port at the Managed-Server level.

VERY important: The following script expects that PKI and SSL (as discussed in the previous section) have already been setup on all servers of this domain.

```
edit()
startEdit()

# change to the edit root -> which is the domain mbean
cd('/')

# enable the administration port
cmo.setAdministrationPortEnabled(true)

# define the domain wide administration port
cmo.setAdministrationPort(9099)

# change to managed-server-1
cd('/Servers/MartinTest_Domain_MS1')

# overwrite the administration port for this server
cmo.setAdministrationPort(10099)
```

Note that in this example all servers in the domain are listening on the admin port 9099, but ONLY (!) the Managed-Server MS1 has a different admin port (10099).

Defining Custom Admin Channel

The second example will use the more complicated approach and define a custom admin channel ON EACH server in the domain.

```
# switch to the admin server
cd('/Servers/AdminServer')
# create a new network channel
cmo.createNetworkAccessPoint('MyCustomAdmin')

# change to the new network channel
cd('/Servers/AdminServer/NetworkAccessPoints/MyCustomAdmin')
# very important:  select the protocol "admin"
cmo.setProtocol('admin')
# set the administration port
cmo.setListenPort(38125)
cmo.setEnabled(true)
cmo.setHttpEnabledForThisProtocol(true)
cmo.setTunnelingEnabled(false)
cmo.setOutboundEnabled(false)
# define that SSL must be used
cmo.setTwoWaySSLEnabled(true)
# disable client side certificates as this is hardly used anyway
cmo.setClientCertificateEnforced(false)
```

```
# set the listener address for the admin channel
cmo.setPublicAddress('192.168.1.120)
cmo.setListenAddress('192.168.1.120')

# change to the first managed server
cd('/Servers/MartinAdminTest_Domain_MS1')
# create a new network channel
cmo.createNetworkAccessPoint('MyMS1Admin')

# change to the new network channel
cd('/Servers/MartinTest_Domain_MS1/NetworkAccessPoints/MyMS1Admin')
# change also protocol to admin and define the port
cmo.setProtocol('admin')
cmo.setListenPort(38115)
cmo.setEnabled(true)
cmo.setHttpEnabledForThisProtocol(true)
cmo.setTunnelingEnabled(false)
cmo.setOutboundEnabled(false)
# define SSL settings
cmo.setTwoWaySSLEnabled(true)
cmo.setClientCertificateEnforced(false)
# et the listener address
cmo.setPublicAddress('192.168.1.123')
cmo.setListenAddress('192.168.1.123')
```

User/Passwords/Groups

The most secure system would shutdown all WLS instances, power off the machines, unplug all cables, lock the machines in a safe, and destroy the key. But of course this system is useless. User, password, groups and roles are the key resources in secure systems. Much effort has to be made in order to setup a secure system where everybody who should be able to do certain actions is able to do so, but also no user will be allowed to undertake actions that are not allowed for this user. This section will introduce automation scripts for the most common tasks with users/groups and roles.

Listing All Users and Groups

Do you really know all your users at all time in all domains? Forgotten user accounts are a pretty nasty backdoor. Therefore listing users and groups and doing a compare to some defined lists should be done periodically. The following script will list all users. In order to make it a bit more interesting, we will list all users - not only from the DefaultAuthenticator, but from all UserAuthenticators:

```
cd('/SecurityConfiguration/'+domainName+'/Realms/myrealm')
allAuthenticationProviders = cmo.getAuthenticationProviders()

print 'List all Users in all Authentication Providers:'
for provider in allAuthenticationProviders:
    if isinstance(provider,UserReaderMBean):
        nextUserAuthenticationProvider = provider
        print 'All users available in provider:'+provider.getName()+' in realm: myrealm'

        cursor = provider.listUsers("*",0)
        while nextUserAuthenticationProvider.haveCurrent(cursor):
            print '   User: ' + nextUserAuthenticationProvider.getCurrentName(cursor)
            nextUserAuthenticationProvider.advance(cursor)
        nextUserAuthenticationProvider.close(cursor)
```

This script will change to the default realm "myrealm". Then we ask for a list of authentication providers. The script will loop over this list and if the provider has users, we will get the user list and print it.

Very similar to users, the following script will list all groups:

```
cd('/SecurityConfiguration/'+domainName+'/Realms/myrealm')
allAuthenticationProviders = cmo.getAuthenticationProviders()

print 'List all Groups in all Authentication Providers:'
for provider in allAuthenticationProviders:
    if isinstance(provider,GroupReaderMBean):
        nextGroupAuthenticationProvider = provider
        print 'All groups available in provider:'+provider.getName()+' in realm: myrealm '

        cursor = provider.listGroups("*",0)
        while nextGroupAuthenticationProvider.haveCurrent(cursor):
            print '    Group: ' + nextGroupAuthenticationProvider.getCurrentName(cursor)
            nextGroupAuthenticationProvider.advance(cursor)
        nextGroupAuthenticationProvider.close(cursor)
```

The principal actions in this script are identical to the user list script listed before.

Last but not least we will list all the user-group membership:

```
cd('/SecurityConfiguration/'+domainName+'/Realms/'+self.realmName)
allAuthenticationProviders = cmo.getAuthenticationProviders()

print 'List users in all groups in all Authentication Providers:'
for provider in allAuthenticationProviders:
    if isinstance(provider,GroupReaderMBean):
        nextGroupAuthenticationProvider = provider
        print 'All user/groups available in provider:'+provider.getName()+' in realm:'+self.realmName

        cursor = nextGroupAuthenticationProvider.listGroups("*",0)
        while nextGroupAuthenticationProvider.haveCurrent(cursor):
            nextGroup = nextGroupAuthenticationProvider.getCurrentName(cursor)
            usersInActualGroup = provider.listAllUsersInGroup(nextGroup,"*",0)
            print '    Group: ' + nextGroupAuthenticationProvider.getCurrentName(cursor)
            for nextUser in usersInActualGroup:
                print '        User: '+nextUser
            nextGroupAuthenticationProvider.advance(cursor)
        nextGroupAuthenticationProvider.close(cursor)
```

Adding Users and Groups

One very common task is the creation of new users and groups. Note that this does not only include administrative users but also application users if these users will not be authenticated using other technologies like SSO, LDAP, ActiveDirectory, etc.

As I said at the beginning, it is highly advisable to keep an open eye (a secure eye) on the users defined in the different domains as forgotten user accounts or user accounts with wrong (too many) permissions can do a lot of damage - wanted or unwanted - to the system.

For audit issues, especially if you activate the security audit logs (see later sections), it is a very good practice (and in many companies required) that every administrator have his/her own account so that it is logged as to who did what. The main WebLogic account, which is used to create the domain, should be generated during domain setup and then secretly hidden with senior management and only used in emergencies and with written permission of that manager.

The following demonstrates how to add a new user to the domain. The user will be added to the default authenticator (which means to the internal LDAP):

```
def createUser(newUserName, newUserPassword, newUserDescription):
    # switch to security configuration
    cd("SecurityConfiguration/MartinTestDomain")

cd("weblogic.security.providers.authentication.DefaultAuthenticator/Security:Name="myrealmDefaultAuth
enticator")

    # create the user
    cmo.createUser(newUserName, newUserPassword, newUserDescription)
```

The above script works but has one disadvantage (especially if you want to add multiple users in one step). If the user already exists, you will get an exception and without proper exception handling your script will exit.

Therefore it is advisable to extend the above script and test if the user exists before you try to create it. Using this check will avoid unnecessary exceptions or script exits:

```
if (cmo.userExists(newUserName)):
    # cannot create !!
    print 'User '+newUserName+' already exists - CANNOT create !'
    return
else:
    # create user
    cmo.createUser(newUserName, newUserPassword, newUserDescription)
```

The next script demonstrates how to add a new group to the domain. A group here is nothing else but a list of users. Grouping helps the administrator keep security rule sets small and stable by defining rules and permissions on a group level.

```
def createGroup(newGroupName, newGroupDescription):
    # switch to security configuration
    cd("SecurityConfiguration/MartinTestDomain")

cd("weblogic.security.providers.authentication.DefaultAuthenticator/Security:Name=myrealmDefaultAuthe
nticator")

    # create the group
    cmo.createGroup(newGroupName, newGroupDescription)
```

Same as with the users, the above script works but has one disadvantage. If the group already exists, you will get an exception and without proper exception handling your script will exit.

Therefore it is advisable to extend the above script and test if the group exists before you try to create it. Using this check will avoid unnecessary exceptions or script exits.

```
if (cmo.groupExists(newGroupName)):
    # cannot create !!
    print 'Group '+newGroupName+' already exists - CANNOT create !'
    return
else:
    # create group
    cmo.createGroup(newGroupName, newGroupDescription)
```

Testing Group Membership

Users are members of groups, and group membership allows users to do certain tasks. Therefore it is important to know who is assigned to which group in order to avoid users getting too many rights.

```
cd('/SecurityConfiguration/'+domainName+'/Realms/myrealm/AuthenticationProviders/DefaultAuthenticator
')
return cmo.isMember(grouName,userName,true)
```

Adding Users to Groups

Groups and users cannot exist independent from each other. In order to use them efficiently, users must be added to groups. One user can of course be member of different groups. In that case you have to do this assignment multiple times - once for each group.

```
def addUserToGroup(groupName, userName):
    # switch to security configuration
    cd("SecurityConfiguration/MartinTestDomain")
    cd("weblogic.security.providers.authentication.DefaultAuthenticator")
    cd("Security:Name="myrealmDefaultAuthenticator")

    # create the user
    cmo.addMemberToGroup(groupName, userName)
```

Again, testing if both group(s) and user(s) exist, or at least proper exception handling exists, should always be added to production-ready scripts.

```
# check if user exists
if (!cmo.userExists(userName)):
print 'User '+userName+' does not exist - CANNOT add '+userName+' to group '+groupName+' !'
    return

# check if group exists
if (!cmo.groupExists(groupName)):
print 'Group '+groupName+' does not exist - CANNOT add '+userName+' to group '+groupName+' !'
    return

# check if already member
if (cmo.isMember(grouName,userName,true):
print 'User '+userName+' is already member of group '+groupName+' !'
    return

# finally :-) add user to group
cmo.addMemberToGroup(groupName, userName)
```

Very similar to what we did during domain creation, it is often very important to create a list of users for all domains. The following script has been proven to be very valuable for administrators who need to setup many domains with the same list of users. The user definitions will be read from a properties file.

```
user_props_file = 'myuserfile.propertied'
print 'Reading user configuration from '+user_props_file;
userFile =  FileInputStream(user_props_file)
userProps.load(userFile)

listAllGroups()

amountOfUsers = int(userProps.getProperty('amountOfUsers'))

nextUser = 1
while (nextUser <= int(amountOfUsers)) :
    nextName        = userProps.getProperty('user.'+str(nextUser)+'.name').strip()
    nextDescription = userProps.getProperty('user.'+str(nextUser)+'.description')
    nextPassword    = userProps.getProperty('user.'+str(nextUser)+'.password')
    nextGroups      = userProps.getProperty('user.'+str(nextUser)+'.groups')

    # create user
    print 'Will create user '+nextName
    createUser(nextName, nextPassword, nextDescription, true)

    # add user to groups
    userGroups = nextGroups.split(',')
    for nextGroup in userGroups:
        print '   Adding user '+nextName+' to group '+nextGroup
        addUserToGroup(nextName, nextGroup.strip())

    nextUser = nextUser + 1
    print '\n'
```

The following example property file will create a number of administration users. This script can of course be used to create application users if those will be authenticated using the DefaultAuthenticator. In case you want to create application users, it is necessary to modify the example property file and use application groups instead of the WebLogic administration groups.

```
amountOfUsers       = 3

user.1.name         = projectAdmin
user.1.description  = Projectinternal admin user
user.1.password     = akfgskfgalg
user.1.groups       = Operators,Deployers,AdminChannelUsers

user.2.name         = projectMonitoring
user.2.description  = Projectinternal monitoring user
user.2.password     = mymonitor4711
user.2.groups       = Monitors,AdminChannelUsers

user.3.name         = projectOperator
user.3.description  = project internal operator user
user.3.password     = doItYourself1234
user.3.groups       = Operators,Deployers,AdminChannelUsers
```

Deleting Users and Groups

In real life systems it is not only necessary to add users, but also to delete users. This might be necessary if a user leaves the company or changes departments. In those cases, the user must no longer have access to the system and information. This is equally true for administrators and users.

The next function will delete a user from the actual realm:

```
# delete a user from the realm
def deleteUser(username):
    # change to default authenticator
```

```
cd ('/SecurityConfiguration/' + domainName +
    '/Realms/myrealm/AuthenticationProviders/DefaultAuthenticator')

# delete user
cmo.removeUser(userName)
```

The next function will delete a group from the actual realm:

```
# delete a group from the realm
def deleteGroup(groupname):
    # change to default authenticator
    cd ('/SecurityConfiguration/' + domainName +
        '/Realms/myrealm/AuthenticationProviders/DefaultAuthenticator')

    # delete group
    cmo.removeGroup(groupname)
```

Last but not least, it is sometimes necessary to change user<->group relationships. Therefore the next function will remove a user from a group:

```
# remove user from group
def removeUserFromGroup(self, username, groupname):
    # change to default authenticator
    cd ('/SecurityConfiguration/' + domainName +
        '/Realms/myrealm/AuthenticationProviders/DefaultAuthenticator')

    # remove user from group
    cmo.removeMemberFromGroup(groupname,username)
```

Changing Users and Groups

Changing a Password

To change a user's password, invoke the *changeUserPassword* method of the UserPasswordEditorMBean, which is extended by the security realm's AuthenticationProvider MBean.

The following WLST online script invokes *changeUserPassword* on the default Authentication Provider:

```
cd('/SecurityConfiguration/'+domainName+'/Realms/'+self.realmName+'/AuthenticationProviders/DefaultAu
thenticator')

# check if user exists
if (cmo.userExists(userName)==0):
print 'User '+userName+' does not exist - CANNOT change password !'
return

# change the password
cmo.changeUserPassword(userName, oldPassword, newPassword)
```

Changing Group Membership of a User

It is sometimes necessary to change the group memberships for an individual user. The reason behind this might be that a user has more rights (add groups), has less rights (remove groups), or changes departments and will get a completely different set of groups.

The following script will get a list of groups for a specific user. To be on the safe side, this script will first remove all current groups that this user has and then add this user to all groups provided:

```
# change the group memberships of this user
# this function will remove the user from all groups and add the user to all groups mentioned in the
parameter
def changeGroupMembershipsOfUser(userName, allNewGroupNames):
   try:
       groupList = returnAllGroupNames()

       # delete user from all groups where this user is member of
       for groupName in groupList:
       print 'test if '+userName+' is member of group '+groupName
       if testIfUserIsMemberOfGroup(groupName, userName)==1:
           # remove user
           removeUserFromGroup(userName, groupName)

       newGroupList = allNewGroupNames.split(',')
       for groupName in newGroupList:
           # add user to group
           print 'Add '+userName+' to group '+groupName
           addUserToGroup(userName, groupName)
   except:
       dumpStack()
```

Role Expressions

Role mapping is the process in which users or groups are mapped to security roles. A security role is a collection of users or groups that have similar permissions to access WebLogic resources. The big difference between roles and groups is that roles are scoped to specific WebLogic resources whereas groups are globally to a domain.

Role Expressions allow the administrator to change/extend existing roles or define new roles. We are not talking about groups but roles.

Example:

```
serverConfig()
cd('/SecurityConfiguration/MartinTest_Domain/Realms/myrealm/RoleMappers/XACMLRoleMapper')
cmo.setRoleExpression('','Admin','Grp(DomainAdmins)|Grp(Administrators)')
```

Protecting User Accounts in a Security Realm

Hot topic for security: How often is a user allowed to enter an invalid password until his/her account gets locked? This is a standard in security to restrict the amount of login tries and also to monitor those failed logins. WebLogic also has the concept of a user lockout. If a user enters the password wrong a couple of times, the account will be locked for a given amount of time.

The *UserLockoutManagerMBean* provides a set of attributes to protect user accounts from intruders. The default configuration for attributes are optimized for strong protection as user accounts are very sensitive configuration items. The level of security can of course be adapted to domain specific needs. This includes increasing or decreasing the level of protection. For example, it is possible to increase the amount of invalid logins before an account will be locked or to change the time period an account is locked after a number of invalid login attempts.

This lockout mechanism can be configured. By default it is enabled. For example, you can set the amount of login tries or the amount of time the account is locked.

The following is an example for the configuration of the user lockout manager:

```
edit()
startEdit()
cd ('/')
userlockoutmanager=cmo.getSecurityConfiguration().getDefaultRealm().getUserLockoutManager()

# lockout activated or not ?
userlockoutmanager.setLockoutEnabled(lockoutEnabled)

# lockout threshold - when gets an account locked
userlockoutmanager.setLockoutThreshold(lockoutThreshold)

# amount (in minutes) how long an account is locked
userlockoutmanager.setLockoutDuration(lockoutDuration)

save()
activate()
```

Another task that can be important for scripting is the ability to test if a user account is locked. The following little script will do that job.

```
cd('/SecurityConfiguration/'+domainName+'/Realms/'+self.realmName)
myLockoutManager = cmo.getUserLockoutManager()
return myLockoutManager.isLockedOut(userName)
```

If a user gets locked then the administrator must be able to unlock this user. The next little script offers exactly this functionality. A locked account will be reactivated.

```
cd('/SecurityConfiguration/'+domainName+'/Realms/'+self.realmName)
myLockoutManager = cmo.getUserLockoutManager()
# clear the lock
myLockoutManager.clearLockout(userName)
print 'User account '+userName+' was unlocked !'
```

Another script that I find quite useful for production is the ability to run over the different domains and list all the user information. This allows the administrator to get information about which user accounts are locked and which are still active.

Note: For the method "returnAllUserNames", please see the complete example. This method will use create an array with a list of user names.

```
alluserNames = returnAllUserNames()

cd('/SecurityConfiguration/'+domainName+'/Realms/'+self.realmName)
myLockoutManager = cmo.getUserLockoutManager()

print 'Lockout-Information about all user acoounts:'
for nextUser in alluserNames:
```

```
print '    User:'+nextUser+'    isLocked:'+str(myLockoutManager.isLockedOut(nextUser))+
'   LoginFailureCount:'+str(myLockoutManager.getLoginFailureCount(nextUser))+
'   LastLoginFailure:'+str(myLockoutManager.getLastLoginFailure(nextUser))
```

The following section will provide examples for invoking *UserLockoutManagerMBean* methods.

Comprehensive User/Group Management Example

The previous sections have demonstrated different aspects of dealing with users and groups. Now let us combine these into one useful production-ready example. In order to demonstrate another way of using WLST, the following example is in the object-oriented style of Jython/WLST. Note that this is not necessary. A normal library with function definitions would do a similar job. However, is it quite nice that you can define classes in Jython and you can use them like in Java.

The following example creates a class which offers the just-discussed features as methods. Afterwards I have provided some possible usages of this class.

🖫 class_definition

```
from weblogic.management.security.authentication import UserReaderMBean
from weblogic.management.security.authentication import GroupReaderMBean
from weblogic.management.security.authentication import UserLockoutManagerMBean
from weblogic.management.security.authentication import UserLockoutManagerMBeanserverRuntime


class UserGroupManagement:

  def __init__(self, realmName):
    self.realmName = realmName

  def __init__(self):
    self.realmName = "myrealm"


  #######################################################
  # PART-1:   List Information
  #######################################################

  # List all users in all authentication providers
  def listAllUsers(self):
    try:
        cd('/SecurityConfiguration/'+domainName+'/Realms/'+self.realmName)
        allAuthenticationProviders = cmo.getAuthenticationProviders()

        print 'List all Users in all Authentication Providers:'
        for provider in allAuthenticationProviders:
            if isinstance(provider,UserReaderMBean):
                nextUserAuthenticationProvider = provider
            print 'All users available in provider:'+provider.getName()+' in realm:'+self.realmName

                cursor = provider.listUsers("*",0)
                while nextUserAuthenticationProvider.haveCurrent(cursor):
                    print '   User: ' + nextUserAuthenticationProvider.getCurrentName(cursor)
                    nextUserAuthenticationProvider.advance(cursor)
                nextUserAuthenticationProvider.close(cursor)
    except:
        dumpStack()
        print "Error in listAllUsers"


  # return all user names in all authentication providers
  def returnAllUserNames(self):
    try:
```

```
        userList = []
        cd('/SecurityConfiguration/'+domainName+'/Realms/'+self.realmName)
        allAuthenticationProviders = cmo.getAuthenticationProviders()
        for provider in allAuthenticationProviders:
              if isinstance(provider,UserReaderMBean):
                    nextUserAuthenticationProvider = provider

                    cursor = provider.listUsers("*",0)
                    while nextUserAuthenticationProvider.haveCurrent(cursor):
                       userList.append(nextUserAuthenticationProvider.getCurrentName(cursor))
                          nextUserAuthenticationProvider.advance(cursor)
                    nextUserAuthenticationProvider.close(cursor)
        return userList
    except:
       dumpStack()
       print "Error in returnAllUserNames"


  # List all groups in all authentication providers
  def listAllGroups(self):
     try:
        cd('/SecurityConfiguration/'+domainName+'/Realms/'+self.realmName)
        allAuthenticationProviders = cmo.getAuthenticationProviders()

        print 'List all Groups in all Authentication Providers:'
        for provider in allAuthenticationProviders:
              if isinstance(provider,GroupReaderMBean):
                    nextGroupAuthenticationProvider = provider
                 print 'All groups available in provider:'+provider.getName()+' in
realm:'+self.realmName
                    cursor = provider.listGroups("*",0)
                    while nextGroupAuthenticationProvider.haveCurrent(cursor):
                          print '   Group: ' + nextGroupAuthenticationProvider.getCurrentName(cursor)
                          nextGroupAuthenticationProvider.advance(cursor)
                    nextGroupAuthenticationProvider.close(cursor)
     except:
        dumpStack()
        print "Error in listAllGroups"


  # return all group names in all authentication providers
  def returnAllGroupNames(self):
     try:
        groupList = []
        cd('/SecurityConfiguration/'+domainName+'/Realms/'+self.realmName)
        allAuthenticationProviders = cmo.getAuthenticationProviders()
        for provider in allAuthenticationProviders:
              if isinstance(provider,GroupReaderMBean):
                    nextGroupAuthenticationProvider = provider

                    cursor = provider.listGroups("*",0)
                    while nextGroupAuthenticationProvider.haveCurrent(cursor):
                          groupList.append(nextGroupAuthenticationProvider.getCurrentName(cursor))
                          nextGroupAuthenticationProvider.advance(cursor)
                    nextGroupAuthenticationProvider.close(cursor)
           return groupList
     except:
        dumpStack()
        print "Error in returnAllGroupNames"



  # List all user in the different groups in all authentication providers
  def listUsersInGroups(self):
     try:
        cd('/SecurityConfiguration/'+domainName+'/Realms/'+self.realmName)
        allAuthenticationProviders = cmo.getAuthenticationProviders()

        print 'List users in all groups in all Authentication Providers:'
        for provider in allAuthenticationProviders:
              if isinstance(provider,GroupReaderMBean):
                    nextGroupAuthenticationProvider = provider
                 print 'All user/groups available in provider:'+provider.getName()+
                      ' in realm:'+self.realmName
                    cursor = nextGroupAuthenticationProvider.listGroups("*",0)
                    while nextGroupAuthenticationProvider.haveCurrent(cursor):
                          nextGroup = nextGroupAuthenticationProvider.getCurrentName(cursor)
                          usersInActualGroup = provider.listAllUsersInGroup(nextGroup,"*",0)
```

```
                        print '   Group: ' + nextGroupAuthenticationProvider.getCurrentName(cursor)
                    for nextUser in usersInActualGroup:
                        print '          User: '+nextUser
                        nextGroupAuthenticationProvider.advance(cursor)
                    nextGroupAuthenticationProvider.close(cursor)
        except:
            dumpStack()
            print "Error in listUsersInGroups"


    #########################################################
    # PART-2:   Create basic security artefacts
    #########################################################

    # create a new user in the default authenticator
    def createUser(self,newUserName, newUserPassword, newUserDescription, deleteUserFirstIfExists):
        try:

cd('/SecurityConfiguration/'+domainName+'/Realms/'+self.realmName+'/AuthenticationProviders/DefaultAu
thenticator')

            if (cmo.userExists(newUserName)):
                if (deleteUserFirstIfExists):
                    print 'User '+newUserName+' already exists - removing old user first !'
                    cmo.removeUser(newUserName)
                else:
                    # cannot create !!
                    print 'User '+newUserName+' already exists - CANNOT create !'
                    return

            # create user
            cmo.createUser(newUserName, newUserPassword, newUserDescription)
        except:
            dumpStack()

    # create a new group in the default authenticator
    def createGroup(self,newGroupName, newGroupDescription, deleteGroupFirstIfExists):
        try:

cd('/SecurityConfiguration/'+domainName+'/Realms/'+self.realmName+'/AuthenticationProviders/DefaultAu
thenticator')

            if (cmo.groupExists(newGroupName)):
                if (deleteGroupFirstIfExists):
                    print 'Group '+newGroupName+' already exists - removing old group first !'
                    cmo.removeGroup(newGroupName)
                else:
                    # cannot create !!
                    print 'Group '+newGroupName+' already exists - CANNOT create !'
                    return

            # create group
            cmo.createGroup(newGroupName, newGroupDescription)

        except:
            dumpStack()


    # add a user to a group. Group membership is very important for correct security rules
    def addUserToGroup(self,userName, groupName):
        try:

cd('/SecurityConfiguration/'+domainName+'/Realms/'+self.realmName+'/AuthenticationProviders/DefaultAu
thenticator')

            # check if user exists
            if (cmo.userExists(userName)==0):
                print 'User '+userName+' does not exist CANNOT add '+userName+' to group '+groupName+' !'
                return

            # check if group exists
            if (cmo.groupExists(groupName)==0):
                print 'Group '+groupName+' does not exist CANNOT add '+userName+' to group '+groupName+' !'
                return

            # check if already member
            if (cmo.isMember(groupName,userName,true)==1):
                print 'User '+userName+' is already member of group '+groupName+' !'
                return
```

```
        # finally :-) add user to group
        cmo.addMemberToGroup(groupName, userName)

    except:
        dumpStack()


# change the password of a user
def changeUserpassword(self,userName, oldPassword, newPassword):
    try:
        cd('/SecurityConfiguration/'+domainName+'/Realms/'+self.realmName+
            '/AuthenticationProviders/DefaultAuthenticator')

        # check if user exists
        if (cmo.userExists(userName)==0):
            print 'User '+userName+' does not exist - CANNOT change password !'
            return

        # change the password
        cmo.changeUserPassword(userName, oldPassword, newPassword)
            print "Changed password of user '+userName+' successfully"
    except:
        dumpStack()


# change the group memberships of this user
# this function will remove the user from all groups and add
# the user to all groups mentioned in the parameter
def changeGroupMembershipsOfUser(self, userName, allNewGroupNames):
    try:
        groupList = returnAllGroupNames()

        # delete user from all groups where this user is member of
        for groupName in groupList:
            print 'test if '+userName+' is member of group '+groupName
            if testIfUserIsMemberOfGroup(groupName, userName)==1:
                # remove user
                removeUserFromGroup(userName, groupName)

        newGroupList = allNewGroupNames.split(',')
        for groupName in newGroupList:
            # add user to group
            print 'Add '+userName+' to group '+groupName
            addUserToGroup(userName, groupName)
    except:
        dumpStack()

#########################################################
# PART-3:   Testing and information
#########################################################

# test if a user exists
def testIfUserExists(self, userName):
    try:
        cd('/SecurityConfiguration/'+domainName+'/Realms/'+self.realmName+
            '/AuthenticationProviders/DefaultAuthenticator')

        return cmo.userExists(newUserName)
    except:
        dumpStack()

# test if a group exists
def testIfGroupExists(self, groupName):
    try:
        cd('/SecurityConfiguration/'+domainName+'/Realms/'+self.realmName+
            '/AuthenticationProviders/DefaultAuthenticator')

        return cmo.groupExists(groupName)
    except:
        dumpStack()


# test if user is member of a group
def testIfUserIsMemberOfGroup(self, groupName, userName):
    try:
        cd('/SecurityConfiguration/'+domainName+'/Realms/'+self.realmName+
            '/AuthenticationProviders/DefaultAuthenticator')
```

```
        return cmo.isMember(groupName,userName,true)
    except:
        dumpStack()


#######################################################
# PART-4:   Delete user and group
#######################################################

# delete a user from the realm
def deleteUser(self, username):
    # change to default authenticator
    cd ('/SecurityConfiguration/' + domainName +
        '/Realms/myrealm/AuthenticationProviders/DefaultAuthenticator')

    # delete user
    cmo.removeUser(userName)

# delete a group from the realm
def deleteGroup(self, groupname):
    # change to default authenticator
    cd ('/SecurityConfiguration/' + domainName +
        '/Realms/myrealm/AuthenticationProviders/DefaultAuthenticator')

    # delete group
    cmo.removeGroup(groupname)


# remove user from group
def removeUserFromGroup(self, username, groupname):
    # change to default authenticator
    cd ('/SecurityConfiguration/' + domainName +
        '/Realms/myrealm/AuthenticationProviders/DefaultAuthenticator')

    remove user from group
    if cmo.isMember(grouname,username,true):
        cmo.removeMemberFromGroup(groupname,username)


#######################################################
# PART-5:   Locking / Unlocking
#######################################################

# test if a user is lockedOut
def testIfUserAccountIsLocked(self, userName):
    try:
        cd('/SecurityConfiguration/'+domainName+'/Realms/'+self.realmName)
        myLockoutManager = cmo.getUserLockoutManager()

        return myLockoutManager.isLockedOut(userName)
    except:
        dumpStack()


# clear the lockedOut of a user and reactivate this user again
def clearUserAccountLock(self, userName):
    try:
        cd('/SecurityConfiguration/'+domainName+'/Realms/'+self.realmName)
        myLockoutManager = cmo.getUserLockoutManager()

        myLockoutManager.clearLockout(userName)
        print 'User account '+userName+' was unlocked !'
    except:
        dumpStack()



# list all user information
def listAllUserLockoutInformation(self):
    try:
        alluserNames = returnAllUserNames()

        cd('/SecurityConfiguration/'+domainName+'/Realms/'+self.realmName)
        myLockoutManager = cmo.getUserLockoutManager()

        print 'Lockout-Information about all user acoounts:'
        for nextUser in alluserNames:
```

WebLogic Security Configuration with WLST

```
            print '    User:'+nextUser+'  isLocked:'+str(myLockoutManager.isLockedOut(nextUser))+
                '   LoginFailureCount:'+str(myLockoutManager.getLoginFailureCount(nextUser))+
                '   LastLoginFailure:'+str(myLockoutManager.getLastLoginFailure(nextUser))

    except:
        dumpStack()


# configure UserLockout Manager
# lockoutEnabled (boolean), lockoutThreshold (int), lockoutDuration (int)
def configureUserLockoutManager(self, lockoutEnabled, lockoutThreshold, lockoutDuration):
    try:
        edit()
        startEdit()
        cd ('/')
        ulm=cmo.getSecurityConfiguration().getDefaultRealm().getUserLockoutManager()

        # lockout activated or not ?
        ulm.setLockoutEnabled(lockoutEnabled)

        # lockout threshold - when gets an account locked
        ulm.setLockoutThreshold(lockoutThreshold)

        # amount (in minutes) how long an account is locked
        ulm.setLockoutDuration(lockoutDuration)

        save()
        activate()
    except:
        dumpStack()


# list all user information
def listAllUserLockoutInformation(self):
    try:

cd('/SecurityConfiguration/'+domainName+'/Realms/'+self.realmName+'/UserLockoutManager/UserLockoutMan
ager')

        print 'Actual lockout-information from the domain '+domainName+' :'
        print '    LockoutEnabled                      : ', get('LockoutEnabled')
        print '    InvalidLoginAttemptsTotalCount      : ',cmo.getInvalidLoginAttemptsTotalCount()
        print '    InvalidLoginUsersHighCount          : ',cmo.getInvalidLoginUsersHighCount()
        print '    LockedUsersCurrentCount             : ',cmo.getLockedUsersCurrentCount()
        print '    LockoutCacheSize                    : ',cmo.getLockoutCacheSize()
        print '    LockoutDuration                     : ',cmo.getLockoutDuration()
        print '    LockoutGCThreshold                  : ',cmo.getLockoutGCThreshold()
        print '    LockoutResetDuration                : ',cmo.getLockoutResetDuration()
        print '    LockoutThreshold                    : ',cmo.getLockoutThreshold()
        print '    LoginAttemptsWhileLockedTotalCount  : '
            ,cmo.getLoginAttemptsWhileLockedTotalCount()
        print '    UnlockedUsersTotalCount             : ',cmo.getUnlockedUsersTotalCount()
        print '    UserLockoutTotalCount               : ',cmo.getUserLockoutTotalCount()
    except:
        dumpStack()
```

The following scripts will show some examples of how to use this class.

The first example shows how to create a user and a group:

```
# connect to the server
connect('weblogic','test1234','t3://localhost:7001')

# create instance
myUserGroupMgmt = UserGroupManagement()

# create a new group
myUserGroupMgmt.createGroup("TestBookGroup","This is group for the book test users", true)

# create a user
myUserGroupMgmt.createUser("TestBookUser", "test1234", "Just another test user", true)

# add the user to the new group
myUserGroupMgmt.addUserToGroup("TestBookUser", "TestBookGroup")
```

The next example will list information from the user management and then test if a special user is locked. If this user is locked, the script will unlock (=clear) this user:

```
# connect to the server
connect('weblogic','test1234','t3://localhost:7001')

# create instance
myUserGroupMgmt = UserGroupManagement()

# list all loacked users
myUserGroupMgmt.listAllUserLockoutInformation()

if (myUserGroupMgmt.testIfUserAccountIsLocked('TestBookUser'):
    print 'User TestBookUser is locked.  Will be unlocked'
    myUserGroupMgmt.clearUserAccountLock('TestBookUser')
else:
    print 'User TestBookUser was not locked.'
```

Result when running this script:

```
Initializing WebLogic Scripting Tool (WLST) ...
Welcome to WebLogic Server Administration Scripting Shell

Connecting to t3://localhost:7001 with userid weblogic ...
Successfully connected to Admin Server "AdminServer" that belongs to domain "base_domain".

Actual lockout-information from the domain base_domain :
    LockoutEnabled                          :  1
    InvalidLoginAttemptsTotalCount          :  0
    InvalidLoginUsersHighCount              :  0
    LockedUsersCurrentCount                 :  0
    LockoutCacheSize                        :  5
    LockoutDuration                         :  30
    LockoutGCThreshold                      :  400
    LockoutResetDuration                    :  5
    LockoutThreshold                        :  5
    LoginAttemptsWhileLockedTotalCount      :  0
    UnlockedUsersTotalCount                 :  0
    UserLockoutTotalCount                   :  0
User TestBookUser was not locked.
```

Internal LDAP Operations

The default location for all user and group configurations is the internal LDAP, which is specific for one WebLogic domain. Every Managed-Server will host a copy of this LDAP in case the AdminServer is not available, and changes are pushed out to the Managed-Server immediately.

We have already seen scripts that can list users and add users (even multiple), but the script always has to deal with concrete users and user lists. WebLogic also offers a possibility to export and import the internal LDAP.

Export users from the internal WebLogic LDAP:

```
connect('weblogic','weblogic', 't3://localhost:8003?)
domainRuntime()
cd('/DomainServices/DomainRuntimeService/DomainConfiguration/TestDomain/SecurityConfiguration/TestDom
ain/DefaultRealm/myrealm/AuthenticationProviders/DefaultAuthenticator')
cmo.exportData('DefaultAtn','/tmp/wlsdata/ldap/export.ldif', Properties())
```

Import users into the internal WebLogic LDAP:

```
connect('weblogic','weblogic', 't3://localhost:8003?)
domainRuntime()
cd('/DomainServices/DomainRuntimeService/DomainConfiguration/NewTestDomain/SecurityConfiguration/NewT
estDomain/DefaultRealm/myrealm/AuthenticationProviders/DefaultAuthenticator')
cmo.importData('DefaultAtn','/tmp/wlsdata/ldap/export.ldif', Properties())
```

External LDAP

Open companies want to use an external LDAP instead of the internal WebLogic LDAP. Many companies maintain all their users and groups in a central LDAP repository.

The following script will create an external LDAP provider. Note that the script does not contain the connect statement in order to establish a connection to the AdminServer. This must be added if you want to run this script standalone.

```
print "****************************************************************";
print " Configuration of an external ldap provider
print "****************************************************************";

# change to edit mode
edit()
startEdit()

## Changing to the realm MBean
cd('/SecurityConfiguration/' + domainName + '/Realms/myRealm')

# Create an LDAP provider -- in this case for openLDAP
cmo.createAuthenticationProvider('myOpenLDAPProvider',
'weblogic.security.providers.authentication.OpenLDAPAuthenticator')

# configure the ldap provider
cd('/SecurityConfiguration/' + domainName +
'/Realms/myRealm/AuthenticationProviders/myOpenLDAPProvider')
cmo.setControlFlag('SUFFICIENT')
cmo.setPrincipal('cn=martin,dc=monitoringbook,dc=consulting,dc=com')
cmo.setHost(monitoringbook.com')
cmo.setGroupBaseDN('ou=groups,dc=monitoringbook,dc=consulting,dc=com')
cmo.setUserBaseDN('ou=users,dc=monitoringbook,dc=consulting,dc=com')

save()
activate()
```

Active Directory Authentication

Many companies are using an active directory for authentication. The following script creates such an authentication provider. The active directory is a widely used system and it is a common scenario that WebLogic-based applications have to check credentials against a central active directory. WebLogic supports this by providing a default authentication provider called *ActiveDirectoryAuthenticator* out of the box.

```
connect('weblogic','weblogic','t3://localhost:7001')
edit()
startEdit()
cmo.getSecurityConfiguration().getDefaultRealm().createAuthenticationProvider('ADAuthenticator',
'weblogic.security.providers.authentication.ActiveDirectoryAuthenticator')
```

```
cmo.getSecurityConfiguration().getDefaultRealm().lookupAuthenticationProvider('ADAuthenticator').setC
ontrolFlag('OPTIONAL')
cd('/SecurityConfiguration')
cd('test_domain')
cd('Realms/myrealm/AuthenticationProviders')
cd('ADAuthenticator')
cmo.setGroupBaseDN('CN=Users,DC=mh-enterpriseconsulting,DC=com')
cmo.setUserBaseDN('CN=Users,DC=mh-enterpriseconsulting,DC=com')
cmo.setAllGroupsFilter('(objectclass=group)')
cmo.setPrincipal('CN=Martin, DC=mh-enterpriseconsulting,DC=com')
cmo.setCredential('< secret >')
cmo.setPort(389)
cmo.setHost('localhost')
save()
activate()
```

RDBMS

By default, WebLogic domains' users and passwords are stored in the internal LDAP. WebLogic also offers a database-based security store based on a relational database. The Oracle Fusion Middleware product family consists of many different and complex products like WebCenter. Some of them require the central RDBMS security store as a central repository. This database offers a central location for user/password configurations, which is very useful if you need to change (or add or remove) users for many domains. It also introduces a new component for administration zoo, which means that we will have new dependencies for our WebLogic domains. Keep in mind that if you use the RDBMS security store, no WebLogic domain will be able to start correctly or authenticate any user if this database is not available. This can be either a network problem or a database problem (or even maintenance window) itself.

The next WLST script shows how to add a RDBMS configuration for a database security store to the security realm.

```
cd('/SecurityConfiguration/'+domainName + '/DefaultRealm/Realm/myrealm')

# create the security store and fill in the database access information
securitDatabaseStore = create("myDatabaseSecurityStore", "RDBMSSecurityStore")
securitDatabaseStore.setUsername('wls_dba')
securitDatabaseStore.setPasswordEncrypted('wls_dba_password')
securitDatabaseStore.setConnectionURL('jdbc:bea:oracle://localhost:1521')
securitDatabaseStore.setDriverName('weblogic.jdbc.oracle.OracleDriver')
securitDatabaseStore.setConnectionProperties('user=wls_dba,portNumber=1521,SID=SECDB,serverName=local
host')
```

Credential Mapping

Credential mapping is the process whereby a system component of an external (legacy) system is contacted to obtain the set of credentials to authenticate users to a target resource. In WebLogic Server, a credential mapping provider is used to provide credential mapping services and bring new types of credentials into the WebLogic Server environment.

The JAAS subject is used by various (security) modules to store security-related information. These are commonly known as credentials. During the authentication process, these credentials are used to authenticate and also authorize the access to special system components or application components. These credentials can include username and password combinations, Kerberos tickets or public key certificates. It is also possible to add additional data to the security credentials like cryptographic keys.

The following script configures the WebLogic PKI Credential Mapping provider:

```
connect('weblogic','Welcome1','t3://127.0.0.1:7071')
edit()
startEdit()
cd('/SecurityConfiguration/MartinTestDomain/DefaultRealm/myrealm/CredentialMappers/Weblogic PKI
Credential Mapping Provider')
set('KeyStoreProvider','SUN')
set('KeyStoreType','JKS')
set('KeyStoreFileName','/keystores/MyIdentityKeyStore.jks')
set('KeyStorePassPhrase','mypassword')
set('UseResourceHierarchy','true')
set('UseInitiatorGroupNames','true')
save()
activate()
```

Security Provider Configurations

Security Providers are modules that provide security service to application to protect WebLogic resource. Types of security providers in WebLogic Server:

- Authentication Provider

- Authorization Provider

- Auditing Providers

- Credential Mapping Provider

- Identity Assertion Provider

- Principal Validation Provider

- Adjudication Providers

- Role Mapping Providers

- Certificate Lookup and Validation Providers

- Keystore Providers

The following sections will examine the different provider and provide scripts, tips and information of how to configure them.

Authentication Provider

WebLogic provides a number of authentication providers. These providers usually differ in the way the user/password is stored or where it is provided (LDAP, JDBC, NTdomain, custom, etc.). All providers try to find a given user in the associated data store and verify that the password is correct.

In addition to the username/password-based authentication providers, WebLogic includes identity assertion providers, which use other security artifacts like certificates or security tokens as credentials.

Types of providers supported by WebLogic include the DefaultAuthenticator (users/groups in WebLogic internal LDAP), different external LDAP providers, Database (JDBC) based authentication, validation of IIOP-CSIv2 and X509 tokens (WebLogic Identity asserter), SAML authentication, the SAML Identity Assertion, which implements a consumer of SAML assertions, and custom authentication and identity asserter.

Every realm in WebLogic must have at least one authentication provider. You can use multiple authentication providers in a security realm. This may be necessary if you want to have SAML-based authentication for your application authentication and the DefaultAuthenticator for your administration.

IMPORTANT: WebLogic has a major weakness in this area as it only allows one security realm to be active; multiple can be configured but only one is active. This means that it is impossible to separate the application authentication process from the administration authentication process. If those are different, the correct combination (and ordering!) of providers is important and necessary. One very important configuration is the JAAS control flags (REQUIRED, REQUISITE, SUFFICIENT, and OPTIONAL) on each of the authentication providers. Providers can be reordered if necessary using WLST (also using the console or JMX).

Example setting the control flag for a provider, in this case the Default-Authenticator:

```
# edit
connect('weblogic','Welcome1','t3://127.0.0.1:7071')
edit()
startEdit()
cd('/SecurityConfiguration/MartinTestDomain/DefaultRealm/myrealm/AuthenticationProviders/DefaultAuthe
nticator')
set('ControlFlag','SUFFICIENT')
save()
activate()
```

In a newly-created domain, only the Default-Authenticator and the Default-IdentityAsserter are configured. If you want to use your own providers, then you first have to create them and afterwards you can configure them. Finally you need to reorder.

Example creating a SAML authentication provider:

```
cd('/SecurityConfiguration/MartinTestDomain/DefaultRealm/myrealm')
cmo.createAuthenticationProvider('Weblogic SAML Authenticator',
'weblogic.security.providers.saml.SAMLAuthenticator')
cd('/SecurityConfiguration/MartinTestDomain/DefaultRealm/myrealm/AuthenticationProviders/Weblogic
SAML Authenticator')
set('ControlFlag','OPTIONAL')
save()
activate()
```

Reorder providers

WebLogic does not offer in its API a method for re-ordering providers. The solution is to provide a list (jarray list) with ALL providers in the order you want them.

```
cd('/SecurityConfiguration/MartinTestDomain/Realms/myrealm')
set('AuthenticationProviders',jarray.array(ObjectName('Security:Name=myrealmDefaultAuthenticator'),
ObjectName('Security:Name=myrealmDefaultIdentityAsserter')], ObjectName))
```

The following example will check if two providers exist. If both exist then this script will change the control flags and reorder the providers.

🖫 check_providers

```
my1stProvider = 'MyOwnCustomAuthenticator'
my2ndProvider = 'MyOwnCustomIdentityAsserter'
my1stProviderControlFlag = 'REQUISITE'
my2ndProviderControlFlag = 'SUFFICIENT'

# Connect to administration server
connect(username, password, url)

# Check if provider-1 provider exists
try:
    cd('/SecurityConfiguration/' + domainName + '/Realms/myrealm/AuthenticationProviders/'
    + my1stProvider)
except:
    print 'The Authentication Provider ' + my1stProvider + ' does not exist.'
    exit()

# Check if provider-2 provider exists
try:
    cd('/SecurityConfiguration/' + domainName + '/Realms/myrealm/AuthenticationProviders/'
    + my2ndProvider)
except:
    print 'The Authentication Provider ' + my2ndProvider + ' does not exist.'
    exit()


print 'Changing the control flags and do a reorder of the providers'

# The changes have to be done on the EDIT mbean
edit()
startEdit()
cd('/')

# get the necessary mbeans.
# A cd(..) is not sufficient as the mbean references will be needed for the reorder
realm = getMBean('/SecurityConfiguration/' + domainName + '/Realms/' + realmName)
prv1 = getMBean('/SecurityConfiguration/' + domainName + '/Realms/' + realmName
            + '/AuthenticationProviders/' + my1stProvider)
prv2 = getMBean('/SecurityConfiguration/' + domainName + '/Realms/' + realmName
```

```
                    + '/AuthenticationProviders/' + my2ndProvider)

# Update 1st provider
prv1.setControlFlag(my1stProviderControlFlag)

# Update 2nd provider
prv2.setControlFlag(my2ndProviderControlFlag)

# Reorder providers
realm.setAuthenticationProviders(jarray.array([prv1,prv2],
weblogic.management.security.authentication.AuthenticationProviderMBean))

# Activate changes
save()
activate(block='true')
print 'Realm has been changed and changes has been activated.'
exit()
```

Delete providers:

Providers that are no longer needed must be deleted. The delete method in WebLogic
is called *destroyAuthenticationProvider*. You need to navigate to your realm, lookup your
provider, and then call the destroy method.

Example:

```
name = 'MyTestAuthenticator';
cd('/SecurityConfiguration/' + domainName + '/Realms/myrealm');
auth = cmo.lookupAuthenticationProvider(name);
cmo.destroyAuthenticationProvider(auth);
```

Identity Asserter

An identity assertion is a specific form of an authentication provider that enables
WebLogic to determine and check the identity of the caller using tokens. The default
WebLogic identity assertion providers support certificate authentication using X509
certificates, SAML assertion tokens, CSIv2 identity assertion, etc.

In order to use X509 based digital certificates for authentication, WebLogic offers the
WebLogic Identity Assertion provider, which can work with X509 certificates and can
map certain fields (like the distinguished name, company, organization or others) to
WebLogic usernames. Normally the distinguished name will be used for this purpose.
The SAML Identity Assertion provider consumes and validates SAML assertions and
checks if the system can trust the assertion.

Example configuration of the default identity asserter and setting the active types to
X.509 certificates:

```
# switch to edit mode
edit()
startEdit()

# change to the default identity serter
cd('/SecurityConfiguration/MartinTestDomain/DefaultRealm/myrealm/AuthenticationProviders/DefaultIdent
ityAsserter')
```

```
# set the active types to x.509 only
set('ActiveTypes',jarray.array(["AuthenticatedUser","X.509"],java.lang.String))

# define the X.509 attribute which should be used for the name
set('DefaultUserNameMapperAttributeType','CN')
set('UseDefaultUserNameMapper','true')
save()
activate()
```

The default identity asserter is configured by default, therefore in the previous example we did not need to create it. All other (WebLogic provided or custom made) identity asserters must be created first before they can be configured.

Example: Create an instance of the SAML identity asserter:

```
# EDIT
connect('weblogic','Welcome1','t3://127.0.0.1:7071')
edit()
startEdit()

# change to the auth. Provider list of the realm
cd('/SecurityConfiguration/MartinTestDomain/DefaultRealm/myrealm/AuthenticationProviders')

# create the identity asserter
create('Weblogic SAML Identity Asserter','weblogic.security.providers.saml.SAMLIdentityAsserterV2')
save()
activate()
```

After an instance of the SAML identity asserter is created, it is necessary to configure one or more asserting parties which define assertion types used by the identity asserter to determine trust.

If WebLogic services are invoked using SAML secured webservices, then it is important to configure WebLogic with all relevant SAML aspects. This means that for each type of incoming call, a so-called SAML profile must be created and registered. A SAML profile contains all information necessary to work with this type of SAML assertion, e.g. profile name, issuer-uri, signing key information and more.

It is possible in WebLogic to configure a list of certificates that will be trusted. The list contains used for validating assertions (WSS/Sender-Vouches) or used for verifying signatures on SAML protocol elements (Browser/POST).

Note that the certificates that can be imported must be in the DER format and cannot be placed in the default WebLogic keystore.

Example of a configuration of the SAML identity asserter and an asserting party:

```
# no edit
cd("/SecurityConfiguration/MartinTestDomain/DefaultRealm/myrealm/AuthenticationProviders/Weblogic
SAML Identity Asserter")
# Import the DER certificate and associate it with the key "mykey"
cmo.registerCertificate("mykey ","/keystores/myapplicationkey.der")

# create a new asserting party (note that this is done in the runtime mode - not edit mode !
ap=cmo.newAssertingParty()
```

```
# set profile type
ap.setProfile('WSS/Sender-Vouches')
ap.setDescription('... something ...')
ap.setEnabled(true)
ap.setTargetURL('default')

# Set issuer URI (which is part of the SAML assertion)
ap.setIssuerURI('http://services.wlst_book.com/wlsID')
ap.setSignedAssertions(true)

# which certificate is used for validation (-> see import above: key only !)
ap.setAssertionSigningCertAlias("mykey")
ap.setGroupsAttributeEnabled(true)
ap.setVirtualUserEnabled(true)

# add asserting party to identity asserter
cmo.addAssertingParty(ap)
disconnect()
```

Note that for whatever reason, WebLogic is using a WebLogic specific transport object instead of MBean methods. This means that ap=cmo.newAssertingParty() is creating a local object (not a remote MBean). Then this object is configured and finally with cmo.addAssertingParty, this object will be sent to the WebLogic Server and the asserting party will be added.

Authorization Provider

Authorization is the process where a decision is made if the actual user has the permission to access the requested resource(s). Authorization is responsible for controlling access to resources based on different information, such as user identity. By default, security realms in newly created domains include the XACML Authorization provider.

Example: Create authorization provider:

```
cd('/SecurityConfiguration/MartinTestDomain/DefaultRealm/myrealm')
cmo.createAuthenticationProvider('MyOwn-Authorization', 'de.monitoringbook.MyAuthorizationProvider')
cd('/SecurityConfiguration/MartinTestDomain/DefaultRealm/myrealm'+
    '/AuthenticationProviders/MyOwn-Authorization')
set('Option1','Some value to be defined')
set('Option2','Some value to be defined')
set('PrintDebugInfo','false')
set('LoginControlFlag','REQUIRED')
```

Example: Create an instance of the XACML authorization provider:

```
edit()
startEdit()
cd('/SecurityConfiguration/' + domainName + '/Realms/' + realmName)
cmo.createAuthorizer('XACMLAuthorizer',
                     'weblogic.security.providers.xacml.authorization.XACMLAuthorizer')
save()
activate(block="true")
```

Password Validation

For security reasons, companies can define password policies like minimum length or maximum number of alphabetic, numeric, or non-alphanumeric characters required. WebLogic must be able to enforce the company policies. In a security realm, this is the job of a Password Validation provider. This is always invoked when a password is created or updated. The Password Validation provider then checks if the new passwords meet the implemented or configured policies. If this is not the case, the password will be rejected. By default, the Default Authentication provider requires a minimum password length of 8 characters. This can be customized.

Example: Create a password validator:

```
edit()
startEdit()
cd('/SecurityConfiguration/' + domainName + '/Realms/myrealm')
cmo.createPasswordValidator('SystemPasswordValidator',
'com.bea.security.providers.authentication.passwordvalidator.SystemPasswordValidator')
save()
activate(block="true")
```

After creation, the validator can be configured. The default system validator offers a wide range of configuration options including password length, min/max of character types, if password can contain username (yes/no), and more.

The default setting requires a password length of at least 8 characters with at least one numeric or special character. Therefore the default password is "Welcome1".

Default settings:

```
wls:/MartinTest_Domain/edit/SecurityConfiguration/MartinTest_Domain/Realms/myrealm/PasswordValidators
/SystemPasswordValidator> ls()
dr--    Realm

-r--    Description                          Password composition checks
-rw-    MaxConsecutiveCharacters             0
-rw-    MaxInstancesOfAnyCharacter           0
-rw-    MaxPasswordLength                     0
-rw-    MinAlphabeticCharacters              0
-rw-    MinLowercaseCharacters               0
-rw-    MinNonAlphanumericCharacters         0
-rw-    MinNumericCharacters                 0
-rw-    MinNumericOrSpecialCharacters        1
-rw-    MinPasswordLength                     8
-rw-    MinUppercaseCharacters               0
-r--    Name                                 SystemPasswordValidator
-r--    ProviderClassName
com.bea.security.providers.authentication.passwordvalidator.SystemPasswordValidatorProviderImpl
-rw-    RejectEqualOrContainReverseUsername  false
-rw-    RejectEqualOrContainUsername         false
-r--    Version                              1.0
```

Example: Set a password policy where each password must have at least 5 alphabetical characters, minimum number of upper case and lower case characters to 2, and in addition restrict the usage of EACH character to 3:

```
# start edit
edit()
startEdit()

# change to default password validator
cd('/SecurityConfiguration/' + domainName +
'/Realms/myrealm/PasswordValidators/SystemPasswordValidator')

cmo.setMaxConsecutiveCharacters(0)
# set the max instance of each character to 3
cmo.setMaxInstancesOfAnyCharacter(3)

# set the minimal number of alphabetic chars to 5
cmo.setMinAlphabeticCharacters(5)

# set the min. of upper case characters to 2
cmo.setMinUppercaseCharacters(2)

# set the min. of lower case characters to 2
cmo.setMinLowercaseCharacters(2)

save()
activate(block="true")
```

After executing this script, the configuration of the system password validator should look like the following:

```
wls:/MartinTest_Domain/serverConfig/SecurityConfiguration/MartinTest_Domain/Realms/myrealm/PasswordVa
lidators/SystemPasswordValidator> ls()
dr--   Realm

-r--   Description                           Password composition checks
-r--   MaxConsecutiveCharacters              0
-r--   MaxInstancesOfAnyCharacter            3
-r--   MaxPasswordLength                      0
-r--   MinAlphabeticCharacters               5
-r--   MinLowercaseCharacters                2
-r--   MinNonAlphanumericCharacters          0
-r--   MinNumericCharacters                  0
-r--   MinNumericOrSpecialCharacters         1
-r--   MinPasswordLength                      8
-r--   MinUppercaseCharacters                2
-r--   Name                                  SystemPasswordValidator
-r--   ProviderClassName
com.bea.security.providers.authentication.passwordvalidator.SystemPasswordValidatorProviderImpl
-r--   RejectEqualOrContainReverseUsername   false
-r--   RejectEqualOrContainUsername          false
-r--   Version                               1.0
```

Example: Define a password policy that requires a password of exactly 10 characters with at least 2 numeric characters:

```
# start edit
edit()
startEdit()

# change to default password validator
cd('/SecurityConfiguration/' + domainName +
'/Realms/myrealm/PasswordValidators/SystemPasswordValidator')

# set min. password to 10
cmo.setMinPasswordLength(10)
# set max. password to 10
cmo.setMaxPasswordLength(10)

# set min of numeric characters to 2
cmo.setMinNumericCharacters(2)

save()
activate(block="true")
```

The next example configures the default password validator to reject passwords that contain the username or even the username in reverse order:

```
# start edit
edit()
startEdit()
# change to default password validator
cd('/SecurityConfiguration/' + domainName +
'/Realms/myrealm/PasswordValidators/SystemPasswordValidator')

# reject password which contains the username in reverse order
cmo.setRejectEqualOrContainReverseUsername(true)

# reject password which contains the username
cmo.setRejectEqualOrContainUsername(true)

save()
activate(block="true")
```

Adjudication

If more than one authorization provider is configured in the domain, it might be possible that different providers will decide differently. In this case the server has a conflict that needs to be solved. This is the job for an adjudication provider. Adjudication involves resolving any authorization conflicts that may occur when more than one Authorization provider is configured. This is done by adding a weight to each authorization provider. Based on the access decisions and the weights the adjudication provider will provide the final PERMIT or DENY decision.

Example of creating an adjudication provider:

```
edit()
startEdit()
cd('/SecurityConfiguration/' + domainName + '/Realms/' + realmName)
cmo.createAdjudicator('DefaultAdjudicator',
                     'weblogic.security.providers.authorization.DefaultAdjudicator')
save()
activate(block="true")
```

Role Mapping

Role mapping providers will provide the list of roles granted to a subject for a given resource. Authorization providers rely on role mapping providers to provide role information in order decide whether access is allowed or not. By default, a WebLogic security realm is configured with the XACML Role Mapping provider that uses XACML. WebLogic invokes each role mapping provider as part of an authorization decision.

Creating a Role Mapping Provider:

```
edit()
startEdit()
cd('/SecurityConfiguration/' + domainName + '/Realms/' + realmName)
cmo.createRoleMapper('DefaultRoleMapper',
'weblogic.security.providers.authorization.DefaultRoleMapper')
```

```
save()
activate(block="true")
```

Configuring a Role Mapping Provider is a difficult task (see XACML section in the next chapter). Configurations are based on XACML policy documents.

A quick look at the possible options and provided methods of the default MBean reveals the complexity:

```
wls:/MartinTest_Domain/serverConfig/SecurityConfiguration/MartinTest_Domain/Realms/myrealm/RoleMapper
s/XACMLRoleMapper> ls()
dr--   Realm

-r--   Description                         WebLogic XACML Role Mapping Provider
-r--   Name                                XACMLRoleMapper
-r--   ProviderClassName
weblogic.security.providers.xacml.authorization.XACMLRoleMapperProviderImpl
-r--   RoleDeploymentEnabled               true
-r--   SupportedExportConstraints          java.lang.String[]
-r--   SupportedExportFormats              java.lang.String[XACML, DefaultRoles]
-r--   SupportedImportConstraints          java.lang.String[]
-r--   SupportedImportFormats              java.lang.String[XACML, DefaultRoles]
-r--   Version                             1.0

-r-x   addPolicy                           Void : String(policy)
-r-x   addPolicy                           Void : String(policy),String(status)
-r-x   addPolicy                           Void :
com.bea.common.security.xacml.policy.Policy
-r-x   addPolicy                           Void :
com.bea.common.security.xacml.policy.Policy,String(status)
-r-x   addPolicySet                        Void : String(set)
-r-x   addPolicySet                        Void : String(set),String(status)
-r-x   addPolicySet                        Void :
com.bea.common.security.xacml.policy.PolicySet
-r-x   addPolicySet                        Void :
com.bea.common.security.xacml.policy.PolicySet,String(status)
-r-x   advance                             Void : String(cursor)
-r-x   close                               Void : String(cursor)
-r-x   deletePolicy                        Void : String(identifier),String(version)
-r-x   deletePolicySet                     Void : String(identifier),String(version)
-r-x   evaluate                            String : String(request)
-r-x   evaluate                            String : String(request),String(store)
-r-x   evaluate                            Void :
String(requestFile),String(responseFile),String(store)
-r-x   exportData                          Void :
String(format),String(filename),java.util.Properties
-r-x   exportResource                      Void : String(filename),String(cn)
-r-x   getCurrentProperties                java.util.Properties : String(cursor)
-r-x   getPolicySetStatus                  String : String(identifier),String(version)
-r-x   getPolicyStatus                     String : String(identifier),String(version)
-r-x   getRegisteredPredicates             String[] : String(nameFilter)
-r-x   getRole                             java.util.Properties :
String(resourceId),String(roleName)
-r-x   getRoleAuxiliary                    String : String(resourceId),String(roleName)
-r-x   getRoleExpression                   String : String(resourceId),String(roleName)
-r-x   getRoleNames                        [[Ljava.lang.String; : String(resourceType)
-r-x   getRoleScopedByResource             java.util.Properties :
String(resourceId),String(roleName)
-r-x   haveCurrent                         Boolean : String(cursor)
-r-x   importData                          Void :
String(format),String(filename),java.util.Properties
-r-x   isRegisteredPredicate               Boolean : String(predicateClassName)
-r-x   isSet                               Boolean : String(propertyName)
-r-x   listAllPolicies                     String :
-r-x   listAllPoliciesAsString             String :
-r-x   listAllPolicySets                   String :
-r-x   listAllPolicySetsAsString           String :
-r-x   listAllRoles                        String : Integer(maximumToReturn)
-r-x   listAllRolesAndURIs                 String[] :
String(application),String(contextPath)
-r-x   listChildRoles                      String :
String(resourceId),Integer(maximumToReturn)
```

```
-r-x    listRepeatingActionsRoles                    String :
String(resourceId),Integer(maximumToReturn)
-r-x    listRoles                                    String :
String(resourceId),Integer(maximumToReturn)
-r-x    listRolesByApplication                       String :
String(applicationName),Integer(maximumToReturn)
-r-x    listRolesByComponent                         String :
String(componentName),String(componentType),String(applicationName),Integer(maximumToReturn)
-r-x    listRolesByResourceType                      String :
String(resourceType),Integer(maximumToReturn)
-r-x    listRolesForResource                         String[] : String(resourceId)
-r-x    modifyPolicy                                 Void : String(policy)
-r-x    modifyPolicy                                 Void : String(policy),String(status)
-r-x    modifyPolicy                                 Void :
com.bea.common.security.xacml.policy.Policy
-r-x    modifyPolicy                                 Void :
com.bea.common.security.xacml.policy.Policy,String(status)
-r-x    modifyPolicySet                              Void : String(set)
-r-x    modifyPolicySet                              Void : String(set),String(status)
-r-x    modifyPolicySet                              Void :
com.bea.common.security.xacml.policy.PolicySet
-r-x    modifyPolicySet                              Void :
com.bea.common.security.xacml.policy.PolicySet,String(status)
-r-x    modifyPolicySetStatus                        Void :
String(identifier),String(version),String(status)
-r-x    modifyPolicyStatus                           Void :
String(identifier),String(version),String(status)
-r-x    readPolicy                                   com.bea.common.security.xacml.policy.Policy :
String(identifier),String(version)
-r-x    readPolicyAsString                           String : String(identifier),String(version)
-r-x    readPolicySet                                com.bea.common.security.xacml.policy.PolicySet :
String(identifier),String(version)
-r-x    readPolicySetAsString                        String : String(identifier),String(version)
-r-x    registerPredicate                            Void : String(predicateClassName)
-r-x    removeRole                                    Void : String(resourceId),String(roleName)
-r-x    roleExists                                   Boolean : String(resourceId),String(roleName)
-r-x    setRoleAuxiliary                             Void :
String(resourceId),String(roleName),String(auxiliary)
-r-x    setRoleExpression                            Void :
String(resourceId),String(roleName),String(expression)
-r-x    unSet                                        Void : String(propertyName)
-r-x    unregisterPredicate                          Void : String(predicateClassName)
```

Credential Mapping

Credential mapping is used to obtain an appropriate set of credentials to authenticate users for a destination resource.

WebLogic provides a PKI credential mapping provider, which maps the security credential of the call initiator (content of the WebLogic subject) and the destination resource to a key pair or public certificate. The PKI credential mapping provider is responsible for getting security information from security keystores. Usually the subject in combination with the requested resource is used to locate the resources in the keystores.

Example for creating the default credential mapper:

```
edit()
startEdit()
cd('/SecurityConfiguration/' + domainName + '/Realms/' + realmName)
cmo.createCredentialMapper('DefaultCredentialMapper',
'weblogic.security.providers.credentials.DefaultCredentialMapper')
save()
activate(block="true")
```

Then configure a PKI Credential Mapping provider on the sending side, and populate it with the keys and certificates to be used for signing. *setKeypairCredential* creates a keypair mapping between the principalName, resourceid, and credential action and the keystore alias and the corresponding password. The following MBean method must be used:

```
setKeypairCredential(type=<remote>, protocol=http, remoteHost=hostname, remotePort=portnumber,
path=/ContextPath/ServicePath,username,Boolean('true'), None, alias, passphrase)
```

Next is an example for the configuration of the PKI credential mapper. Please note that this is done on the runtime MBean tree and NOT on the edit MBean tree:

```
# NO EDIT
cd("/SecurityConfiguration/MartinTestDomain/DefaultRealm/myrealm/CredentialMappers/Weblogic PKI
Credential Mapping Provider")
cmo.setKeypairCredential('type=<remote>, protocol=http, remoteHost=, remotePort=', 'everybody',
                      Boolean('false'), '', 'myapplication', 'mypassword')
```

WebLogic Server also provides the SAML credential mapping provider that can generate SAML 1.1 and 2.0 assertions for authenticated subjects based on a target sites or resources.

Example: Creating a SAML 2 credential mapper:

```
edit()
startEdit()
# switch the list of credential mappers of this realm
cd('/SecurityConfiguration/MartinTestDomain/DefaultRealm/myrealm/CredentialMappers')
# create an instance of the desired credential mapper - in this case SAML v2
create('Weblogic SAML Credential Mapper','weblogic.security.providers.saml.SAMLCredentialMapperV2')
save()
activate()
```

After the credential mapper is created, it can be configured. The configurations needed are the issuer-URI in order to identify the issuer, the valid time period of the assertion, and the key (which is loaded from the keystore, therefore alias and passphrase must be provided).

```
edit()
startEdit()
cd('/SecurityConfiguration/MartinTestDomain/DefaultRealm/myrealm/CredentialMappers/Weblogic SAML
Credential Mapper')
set('IssuerURI','http://myservices.book.com/serviceURL')
set('NameQualifier','myservices.book.com')
set('DefaultTimeToLive','120')
set('DefaultTimeToLiveDelta','-10')
set('SigningKeyAlias','webservice_alias')
set('SigningKeyPassPhrase',',mypassword')
save()
activate()
```

NOTE: "-10" as a TTL delta has the following benefit. If not all system clocks in your server farm are 100% synchronized, it is possible that the sending machine has a time that is slightly before the time of the receiving machine. Therefore the message actually has a negative lifetime.

Relying Parties

A relying party used with a SAML credential mapper is an entry that relies on the information in a SAML assertion. It is possible to control how WebLogic issue SAML assertions.

Example: Create a replying party for a SAML credential mapper:

```
# NO EDIT
cd("/SecurityConfiguration/MartinTestDomain/DefaultRealm/myrealm/CredentialMappers/Weblogic SAML
Credential Mapper")
rp=cmo.newRelyingParty()
rp.setProfile('WSS/Sender-Vouches')
rp.setEnabled(true)
rp.setDescription('rp_00001')
rp.setTargetURL('default')
rp.setTimeToLive(120)
rp.setTimeToLiveOffset(-10)
rp.setSignedAssertions(true)
rp.setKeyinfoIncluded(true)
rp.setGroupsAttributeEnabled(false)
cmo.addRelyingParty(rp)
```

This code shows a weakness of the WebLogic API, which will be more visible in the JMX session. The replying party is a WebLogic-defined object which has to be retrieved from the MBean server, filled with the desired values and finally sent back to WebLogic (*addRelyingParty*). This introduces a client-side dependency to WebLogic code.

Auditing

Auditing involves the collection of information about operating requests and the result of those requests. This information is stored and distributed for the purposes of non-repudiation. This means that the server will create logs that can be used to find out who did what and when. Auditing provider is an optional component and the default realm does not have one.

WebLogic offers a default provider, but other providers can be developed.

Create an instance of the default auditor:

```
cd('/SecurityConfiguration/MartinTest_Domain/Realms/myrealm')
cmo.createAuditor('NewTestDefAuditor', 'weblogic.security.providers.audit.DefaultAuditor')
```

The following script does a couple of configurations.

In order to cleanup the events of the WebLogic standard-out, we will redirect to the security audit provider. This of course requires an audit provider to be configured. As discussed above, WebLogic has a default security audit provider that can be used for this purpose.

The attribute *setConfigurationAuditType* has 4 different values:

- None = Configuration events will neither be written to the server log nor directed to the Security Audit Framework.

- Change Log = Configuration events will be written to the server log.

- Change Audit = Configuration events will be directed to the Security Audit Framework.

- Change Log and Audit = Configuration events will be written to the server log and directed to the Security Audit Framework.

🖫 auditing

```
cd('/')
cmo.setConfigurationAuditType('audit')

# set domain logging configurations
cd('/Servers/AdminServer/Log/AdminServer')
cmo.setLoggerSeverity('Warning')
cmo.setDomainLogBroadcastSeverity('Warning')
cmo.setLogFileSeverity('Info')
cmo.setStdoutSeverity('Info')
cmo.setMemoryBufferSeverity('Debug')

# change to the realm
cd('/SecurityConfiguration/MartinTest_Domain/Realms/myrealm')
# create an auditor instance
cmo.createAuditor('NewTestDefAuditor', 'weblogic.security.providers.audit.DefaultAuditor')

# change to the new auditor
cd('/SecurityConfiguration/MartinTest_Domain/Realms/myrealm/Auditors/NewTestDefAuditor')
# enable information level audit event logging
cmo.setInformationAuditSeverityEnabled(true)
# enable warning level audit event logging
cmo.setWarningAuditSeverityEnabled(true)
# enable failure level audit event logging
cmo.setFailureAuditSeverityEnabled(true)
# enable error level audit event logging
cmo.setErrorAuditSeverityEnabled(true)
cmo.setSeverity('WARNING')
# set active handler entries.  This example sets all handlers available just to demonstrate what is
available
set('ActiveContextHandlerEntries',jarray.array([String('com.bea.contextelement.channel.Address'),
String('com.bea.contextelement.channel.ChannelName'), String('com.bea.contextelement.channel.Port'),
String('com.bea.contextelement.channel.Protocol'),
String('com.bea.contextelement.channel.PublicAddress'),
String('com.bea.contextelement.channel.PublicPort'),
String('com.bea.contextelement.channel.RemoteAddress'),
String('com.bea.contextelement.channel.RemotePort'), String('com.bea.contextelement.channel.Secure'),
String('com.bea.contextelement.ejb20.Parameter'),
String('com.bea.contextelement.entitlement.EAuxiliaryID'),
String('com.bea.contextelement.jmx.AuditProtectedArgInfo'),
String('com.bea.contextelement.jmx.ObjectName'),
String('com.bea.contextelement.jmx.OldAttributeValue'),
String('com.bea.contextelement.jmx.Parameters'), String('com.bea.contextelement.jmx.ShortName'),
String('com.bea.contextelement.jmx.Signature'),
String('com.bea.contextelement.saml.MessageSignerCertificate'),
String('com.bea.contextelement.saml.SSLClientCertificateChain'),
String('com.bea.contextelement.saml.subject.ConfirmationMethod'),
String('com.bea.contextelement.saml.subject.dom.KeyInfo'),
String('com.bea.contextelement.security.ChainPrevailidatedBySSL'),
String('com.bea.contextelement.servlet.HttpServletRequest'),
String('com.bea.contextelement.servlet.HttpServletResponse'),
String('com.bea.contextelement.webservice.Integrity'), String('com.bea.contextelement.wli.Message'),
String('com.bea.contextelement.wsee.SOAPMessage'),
String('com.bea.contextelement.xml.SecurityToken'),
String('com.bea.contextelement.xml.SecurityTokenAssertion')], String))
```

Certification Paths

A standalone certificate is basically useless as anybody can create certificates. Only if a certificate is signed by a trusted authority (called CA) then a certificate becomes a secure entity. As certificate authorities (CAs) can be chained, it is important for WebLogic to ensure that a complete certificate chain is valid and trusted. WebLogic offers a Certification Path provider for this purpose. This module checks the signatures of each certificate in the chain and ensures that none of the certificates in the chain have expired. Only if this is the case AND at least one of the certificates in the chain is issued by one of the server's trusted CAs, the check of the complete chain is considered to be valid. Otherwise the check of the chain will fail.

Example: Creating a certification path provider:

```
edit()
startEdit()
# switch to your realm
cd('/SecurityConfiguration/MartinTestDomain/DefaultRealm/myrealm')
# create a certification path provider
create('WeblogicCertPathProvider','weblogic.security.providers.pk.WebLogicCertPathProvider','CertPath
Providers')
# get the newly created mbean
certPath = getMBean("CertPathProviders/WeblogicCertPathProvider")
# set this as the new default to the realm (remember that co here = realm)
cmo.setCertPathBuilder(certPath)
save()
activate()
```

Example: Setting up an own realm

__Warning:__ It is usually never necessary to create your own security realm. The default security realm is suitable for most tasks and can be extended with providers for your own needs. Furthermore, it can be changed with provider configuration, provider reordering, or more. Therefore it usually does not make sense to create your own security realm.

In case you really want to do it, this section will provide a script that helps you to setup your own security realm based on the information provided in the previous sections. Note that you definitely need to tailor this script to your need.

💾 setup_security_realm

```
edit()
startEdit()

cd('/SecurityConfiguration/MartinTestDomain')
cmo.createRealm('TestRealm')

cd('/SecurityConfiguration/MartinTestDomain/Realms/TestRealm')
cmo.setDeployCredentialMappingIgnored(false)

# Activate that change so that the realm is added to the runtime mbean server
save()
activate(block="true")
```

```
# now create the desired provider, mappers, ...

## setup default authenticator:
cd('/SecurityConfiguration/MartinTestDomain/Realms/TestRealm')
cmo.createAuthenticationProvider('DefaultAuthenticator',
          'weblogic.security.providers.authentication.DefaultAuthenticator')
cd('/SecurityConfiguration/MartinTestDomain/Realms/TestRealm/AuthenticationProviders/DefaultAuthentic
ator')
cmo.setControlFlag('SUFFICIENT')

# identity asserter
cd('/SecurityConfiguration/MartinTestDomain/Realms/TestRealm')
cmo.createAuthenticationProvider('DefaultIdentityAsserter',
          'weblogic.security.providers.authentication.DefaultIdentityAsserter')
cd('/SecurityConfiguration/' + domainName + '/Realms/'+ realmName +
          '/AuthenticationProviders/DefaultIdentityAsserter')
set('ActiveTypes',jarray.array([String('AuthenticatedUser')], String))

# SAML identity asserter
cd('/SecurityConfiguration/MartinTestDomain/Realms/TestRealm')
cmo.createAuthenticationProvider('federation_saml_asserter',
          'weblogic.security.providers.saml.SAMLIdentityAsserterV2')

# create other provider
cd('/SecurityConfiguration/MartinTestDomain/Realms/TestRealm')

# create the default authorization provider which is based on XACML
cmo.createAuthorizer('XACMLAuthorizer',
'weblogic.security.providers.xacml.authorization.XACMLAuthorizer')

# create the default password validator
cmo.createPasswordValidator('SystemPasswordValidator',
          'com.bea.security.providers.authentication.passwordvalidator.SystemPasswordValidator')
# create the default adjudicator
cmo.createAdjudicator('DefaultAdjudicator',
          'weblogic.security.providers.authorization.DefaultAdjudicator')

# create the default role mapping provider
cmo.createRoleMapper('DefaultRoleMapper',
          'weblogic.security.providers.authorization.DefaultRoleMapper')

# create the default credential mapper
cmo.createCredentialMapper('DefaultCredentialMapper',
          'weblogic.security.providers.credentials.DefaultCredentialMapper')

save()
activate(block="true")
```

Domain Web Service Security Settings

If a Web Service has been configured to use security on a message level (encryption and/or digital signatures), the web services runtime has to find out if a web service security configuration is also available for this service. This configuration defines settings such as the usage of a X.509 certificate, the keystore and its entry for encryption, and more. A single security configuration can be associated with many Web services.

Web service security settings are domain configurations. Therefore, in the MBean tree you will find those settings under the root folder of the server configuration rather than under each deployment subtree.

💾 web_service

```
connect('weblogic','Welcome1','t3://127.0.0.1:7071')
edit()
startEdit()

cd('/WebserviceSecurities')
create('default_wss','WebserviceSecurities')

cd('/WebserviceSecurities/default_wss/WebserviceCredentialProviders')
create('Weblogic DK Credential Provider','WebserviceCredentialProviders')

cd('/WebserviceSecurities/default_wss/WebserviceCredentialProviders/Weblogic DK Credential Provider')
set('ClassName','weblogic.wsee.security.wssc.v200502.dk.DKCredentialProvider')
set('TokenType','dk')

cd('/WebserviceSecurities/default_wss/WebserviceCredentialProviders/Weblogic DK Credential
Provider/ConfigurationProperties')
create('ConfidentialityKeyAlias','ConfigurationProperties')
cd('ConfidentialityKeyAlias')
set('Value','myAppAlias')
cd('../ConfidentialityKeyAlias')
set('EncryptValueRequired','false')

cd('/WebserviceSecurities/default_wss/WebserviceCredentialProviders/Weblogic DK Credential
Provider/ConfigurationProperties')
create('ConfidentialityKeyPassword','ConfigurationProperties')
cd('ConfidentialityKeyPassword')
set('EncryptedValue','mypassword')
cd('../ConfidentialityKeyPassword')
set('EncryptValueRequired','true')

cd('/WebserviceSecurities/default_wss/WebserviceCredentialProviders/Weblogic DK Credential
Provider/ConfigurationProperties')
create('ConfidentialityKeyStore','ConfigurationProperties')
cd('ConfidentialityKeyStore')
set('Value','/ MyIdentityKeyStore.jks')
cd('../ConfidentialityKeyStore')
set('EncryptValueRequired','false')

cd('/WebserviceSecurities/default_wss/WebserviceCredentialProviders/Weblogic DK Credential
Provider/ConfigurationProperties')
create('ConfidentialityKeyStorePassword','ConfigurationProperties')
cd('ConfidentialityKeyStorePassword')
set('EncryptedValue','mypassword')
cd('../ConfidentialityKeyStorePassword')
set('EncryptValueRequired','true')

cd('/WebserviceSecurities/default_wss/WebserviceCredentialProviders/Weblogic DK Credential
Provider/ConfigurationProperties')
create('IntegrityKeyAlias','ConfigurationProperties')
cd('IntegrityKeyAlias')
set('Value','myAppAlias')
cd('../IntegrityKeyAlias')
set('EncryptValueRequired','false')

cd('/WebserviceSecurities/default_wss/WebserviceCredentialProviders/Weblogic DK Credential
Provider/ConfigurationProperties')
create('IntegrityKeyPassword','ConfigurationProperties')
cd('IntegrityKeyPassword')
set('EncryptedValue','mypassword')
cd('../IntegrityKeyPassword')
set('EncryptValueRequired','true')

cd('/WebserviceSecurities/default_wss/WebserviceCredentialProviders/Weblogic DK Credential
Provider/ConfigurationProperties')
create('IntegrityKeyStore','ConfigurationProperties')
cd('IntegrityKeyStore')
set('Value','/MyIdentityKeyStore.jks')
cd('../IntegrityKeyStore')
set('EncryptValueRequired','false')

cd('/WebserviceSecurities/default_wss/WebserviceCredentialProviders/Weblogic DK Credential
Provider/ConfigurationProperties')
create('IntegrityKeyStorePassword','ConfigurationProperties')
cd('IntegrityKeyStorePassword')
set('EncryptedValue','mypassword')
cd('../IntegrityKeyStorePassword')
```

```
set('EncryptValueRequired','true')

cd('/WebserviceSecurities/default_wss/WebserviceCredentialProviders/Weblogic DK Credential
Provider/ConfigurationProperties')
create('Length','ConfigurationProperties')
cd('Length')
set('Value','16')
cd('../Length')
set('EncryptValueRequired','false')
save()
activate()
```

Note that these settings are a bit complicated in WLST as you need to create a ConfigurationProperties object. In the case of passwords, you need to set encryption to "true".

Migrating Security Data

Security realms in a WebLogic domain hold different kinds of security data, like policies, users, groups, role expressions and more. If you setup a new domain, you may want to clone the security data from an existing domain. For example, you may want to clone UAT to production. Using this feature you a) do not need to configure all the data again and b) can be sure that you are using the same set of data that you have been using for load and performance tests in the lower-level environment.

Export Data from Security Realms

It is possible to export different aspects of the security realm (authentication, authorization, credential map, and role data) into a file. This enables you to test security configurations and then port them to other domains without the need of recreating all the security data. You can either export all data or selected data from selected providers.

Import Data into Security Realms

This is the contrary operation to export data, which allows you to import security data into a realm or certain providers. Data can be imported to a realm that affects all providers and all data, or can be imported to selected providers. This depends on the scope of the data export.

The following table from the Oracle documentation provides an overview of which data formats are supported for security migration:

WebLogic Provider	Supported Format
WebLogic Authentication provider	DefaultAtn—unpublished format
XACML Authorization Provider	XACML—standard XACML 2.0 format DefaultAtz—unpublished format
WebLogic Authorization Provider	DefaultAtz—unpublished format
XACML Role Mapping Provider	XACML—standard XACML 2.0 format DefaultRoles—unpublished format
WebLogic Role Mapping Provider	DefaultRoles—unpublished format
WebLogic Credential Mapping Provider	DefaultCreds—unpublished format
SAML Identity Asserter V2 SAML Credential Mapping Provider V2	XML Partner Registry—An XML format defined by the SAML partner registry schema JKS Key Store—A key store file format for importing and exporting partner certificates only LDIF Template—LDIF format

(Source: Oracle Corporation[8])

Table 7.1: Security Migration Data Formats

The different security providers available in WebLogic do have different constraints with regards to security data migration. The following overview from the Oracle documentation provides a good overview:

WebLogic Security Provider	Supported Constraints	Description
Default Authentication	users groups	Export all users or all groups
XACML Authorization WebLogic Authorization XACML Role Mapping WebLogic Role Mapping	none	N/A
WebLogic Credential Mapping	passwords	With the constraint passwords=cleartext, passwords will be exported in clear text. Otherwise, they will be exported in encrypted form.

---

[8] docs.oracle.com/middleware/1212/wls/SECMG/security_data_migration.htm

WebLogic Security Provider	Supported Constraints	Description
SAML Identity Asserter V2 SAML Credential Mapping V2	partners	Which partners to import or export. The constraint value can be one of: • all—all partners • none—no partners • list—only listed partners • enabled—only enabled partners • disabled—only disabled partners
SAML Identity Asserter V2 SAML Credential Mapping V2	certificates	Which certificates to import or export. The constraint value can be one of the following: • all—all certificates • none—no certificates • list—only listed certificates • referenced—only certificates referenced by a partner
SAML Identity Asserter V2 SAML Credential Mapping V2	passwords	With the constraint passwords=cleartext, passwords will be exported in clear text. Otherwise, they will be exported in encrypted form.
SAML Identity Asserter V2 SAML Credential Mapping V2	importMode	Specifies how to resolve name conflicts between the imported data and existing data in the SAML registry. The constraint value can be one of the following: • fail—the import operation will fail if conflicts are detected (default) • rename—rename the imported entry that conflicts • replace—replace the existing entry with the conflicting imported entry

(Source: Oracle Corporation[9])

Table 7.2: Security Data Migration

You can use WLST to export and import data from a security provider. In order to use this functionality, you need to get access the RuntimeMBean for the security provider and use its *importData* or *exportData* operation. The following examples will show WLST implementations for exporting and importing security data.

Example for export authentication data based on XACML:

```
def exportAuthenticatorData(securityProviderName, fileName):
    # cd into provider
    cd ('/SecurityConfiguration/'+domainName+'/DefaultRealm/myrealm/AuthenticationProviders/'+
        securityProviderName)
```

---

[9] docs.oracle.com/middleware/1212/wls/SECMG/security_data_migration.htm

```
# export DefaultAtn type of data
cmo.exportData('DefaultAtn',fileName,Properties())
```

Example for import authentication data based on XACML:

```
def importAuthenticatorData(securityProviderName, fileName):
    # cd into provider
    cd ('/SecurityConfiguration/'+domainName+'/DefaultRealm/myrealm/AuthenticationProviders/'+
        securityProviderName)

    # import DefaultAtn type of data
    cmo.importData('DefaultAtn',fileName,Properties())
```

Example for export authorizer data based on XACML:

```
def exportAuthorizerData(securityProviderName, fileName):
    # cd into provider
    cd ('/SecurityConfiguration/'+domainName+'/DefaultRealm/myrealm/Authorizers/'+
        securityProviderName)

    # export XACML type of data
    cmo.exportData('XACML',fileName,Properties())
```

Example for import authorizer data based on XACML:

```
def importAuthorizerData(securityProviderName, fileName):
    # cd into provider
    cd ('/SecurityConfiguration/'+domainName+'/DefaultRealm/myrealm/Authorizers/'+
        securityProviderName)

    # import XACML type of data
    cmo.importData('XACML',fileName,Properties())
```

Example for export rolemapper data: type can either be XACML or DefaultRoles:

```
def exportRoleMapperData(securityProviderName, exportFormat, fileName):
    # cd into provider
    cd ('/SecurityConfiguration/'+domainName+'/DefaultRealm/myrealm/RoleMappers/'+
        securityProviderName)

    # export <exportFormat> type of data
    cmo.exportData(exportFormat,fileName,Properties())
```

Example for import rolemapper data: type can either be XACML or DefaultRoles:

```
def importRoleMapperData(securityProviderName, exportFormat, fileName):
    # cd into provider
    cd ('/SecurityConfiguration/'+domainName+'/DefaultRealm/myrealm/RoleMappers/'+
        securityProviderName)

    # import <exportFormat> type of data
    cmo.importData(exportFormat,fileName,Properties())
```

Example usage of these definitions:

```
connect('weblogic','test1234','t3://localhost:7001')
domainRuntime()
# export authentication data
exportAuthenticatorData("DefaultAuthenticator", "/logs/data_1_DefaultAtn")

# export authorizerdata
exportAuthorizerData("XACMLAuthorizer", "/logs/data_2_xacml")
```

```
# export the rolemapper data in both formats
exportRoleMapperData("XACMLRoleMapper", "XACML", "/logs/data_3_xacml")
exportRoleMapperData("XACMLRoleMapper", "DefaultRoles", "/logs/data_4_DefaultRoles")
```

Example files (note that these are only excerpts due to the large size):

```
cat data_1_DefaultAtn
=========================================================
<...>

dn: cn=Administrators,ou=groups,ou=@realm@,dc=@domain@
memberURL:
ldap:///ou=groups,ou=@realm@,dc=@domain@??sub?(&(objectclass=person)(wlsMemberOf=cn=Administrators,ou
=groups,ou=@realm@,dc=@domain@))
description: Administrators can view and modify all resource attributes and start and stop servers.
objectclass: top
objectclass: groupOfUniqueNames
objectclass: groupOfURLs
cn: Administrators
createTimestamp: 201211201440Z
creatorsName: cn=Admin

dn: uid=weblogic,ou=people,ou=@realm@,dc=@domain@
description: This user is the default administrator.
objectclass: inetOrgPerson
objectclass: organizationalPerson
objectclass: person
objectclass: top
objectclass: wlsUser
cn: weblogic
sn: weblogic
userpassword:: e3NzaGGF9Nm9BSTNsTDRCV0ozV2lNQkdPVzNsbU8yQXo3YWxPY1Q=
uid: weblogic
wlsMemberOf: cn=Administrators,ou=groups,ou=@realm@,dc=@domain@
createTimestamp: 201211201440Z
creatorsName: cn=Admin

<...>
```

cat data_2_xacml
```
=========================================================
<?xml version="1.0" encoding="UTF-8"?>
<PolicySet                                              xmlns="urn:oasis:names:tc:xacml:2.0:policy:schema:os"
PolicySetId="urn:bea:xacml:2.0:export-data:container-policy-set"
PolicyCombiningAlgId="urn:oasis:names:tc:xacml:1.0:policy-combining-algorithm:deny-
overrides"><Description><![CDATA[<MetaData                  xmlns="urn:bea:xacml:2.0:export-data:meta-
data"><WLSMetaData
PolicyId="urn:bea:xacml:2.0:entitlement:resource:type@E@Furl@G@M@Oapplication@Econsoleapp@M@OcontextP
ath@E@Uconsole@M@Ouri@E@Uframework@Uskeletons@Uwlsconsole@Ucss@U@K"          Status="3"><WLSPolicyInfo
wlsCreatorInfo="deploy"/></WLSMetaData><...>
```

data_3_xacml
```
=========================================================
<?xml version="1.0" encoding="UTF-8"?>
<PolicySet                                              xmlns="urn:oasis:names:tc:xacml:2.0:policy:schema:os"
PolicySetId="urn:bea:xacml:2.0:export-data:container-policy-set"
PolicyCombiningAlgId="urn:oasis:names:tc:xacml:1.0:policy-combining-algorithm:deny-
overrides"><Description><![CDATA[<MetaData                  xmlns="urn:bea:xacml:2.0:export-data:meta-
data"><WLSMetaData                        PolicyId="urn:bea:xacml:2.0:entitlement:role:Monitor:"
Status="3"></WLSMetaData><WLSMetaData      PolicyId="urn:bea:xacml:2.0:entitlement:role:Deployer:"
Status="3"></WLSMetaData><WLSMetaData      PolicyId="urn:bea:xacml:2.0:entitlement:role:AppTester:"
Status="3"></WLSMetaData><WLSMetaData       PolicyId="urn:bea:xacml:2.0:entitlement:role:Admin:"
Status="3"></WLSMetaData><WLSMetaData      PolicyId="urn:bea:xacml:2.0:entitlement:role:Anonymous:"
Status="3"></WLSMetaData><WLSMetaData
PolicyId="urn:bea:xacml:2.0:entitlement:role:OracleSystemRole:"<...>
```

data_4_DefaultRoles
```
=========================================================
<...>
dn: cn=::Deployer,ou=ERole,ou=@realm@,dc=@domain@
objectclass: top
```

```
objectclass: ERole
cn: ::Deployer
EExpr:: ZORlcGxveWVycwo=
<...>
```

Connection Filters

Servers are usually protected by firewalls. The big benefit of firewalls is that they can reject unwanted connections based on rules. Rules can be based on source IP/DNS/port, target DNS/IP/port, protocol, or even more. It is highly recommended to use these firewall features - especially for administrative communication - wherever possible. There are also many systems where there is no firewall between the user and the server (intranet). Some resources (e.g. administrative communication, services with sensible or confidential data) must be also protected in those networks.

In case no firewalls are available, WebLogic offers a concept called "connection filter". Connection filters provide network layer access control and allow the server(s) to block unwanted communication based on different criteria.

The default implementation provided by WebLogic offers a number of parameters for each rule. Each rule must contain an action (allow/deny), the localAddress/localPort of the server endpoint, and the client ip/dns/or even domain parts like *.wlsautomation.de (slower!). Optionally, each rule can contain a list of protocols. If no protocols are provided, all protocols are assumed for this rule. Filter rules are evaluated in the order they are defined.

For connection filters it is necessary to enable their usage and to specify which implementation (Java class name) should be used. Unfortunately WebLogic only offers ONE connection filter list for the whole domain instead of offering one filter list for each communication channel (which would include default channel, admin channel, network channels and all this server instance specific). This means that the connection filter list must be designed carefully and should always specify the localAdress and localPort to distinguish between the different server and different channels of the domain.

WebLogic distinguishes between three different types of rules:

Fast rules (most common) are concrete rules that are easy to evaluate. DNS resolutions are cached. Examples include:

```
martin_laptop.wlsautomation.de 127.0.0.1 7001 allow t3s https
192.168.100.0/255.255.254.0 127.0.0.1 7001 allow  #23-bit netmask ; allows all protocols
192.168.110.20 127.0.0.1 7001 deny t3 http
```

Slow rules are incomplete rules and therefore are slower to evaluate. These rules should be avoided if possible. Examples include:

```
*.wlsautomation.de 127.0.0.1 7001 allow t3s https
```

Special rule: For improved security, it is possible to specify a special last rule that blocks all remaining connection requests that do not match any of the previous rules. The default implementation interprets a target address of 0 (0.0.0.0/0) as: "this rule should apply to all IP addresses."

```
0.0.0.0/0  *  *  deny
```

Connection filters can be setup using the admin console, JMX, or WLST. The following script shows an example of how to create and activate rules using the default implementation:

```
# connect to WebLogic
connect('weblogic','test1234','t3://localhost:7001')

# switch to edit mode
edit()
startEdit()

# switch to the domain security configuration mbean (note NOT realm)
cd('/SecurityConfiguration/'+domainName)

# enable the connection filter
cmo.setConnectionLoggerEnabled(true)

# set the filter implementation - in this case the default
cmo.setConnectionFilter('weblogic.security.net.ConnectionFilterImpl')

# set the rules as array of strings
set('ConnectionFilterRules',jarray.array([String('martin_laptop.wlsautomation.de 127.0.0.1 7001 allow
t3s https'),String('192.168.100.0/255.255.254.0 127.0.0.1 7001 allow'),String('192.168.110.20
127.0.0.1 7001 deny t3 http')], String))

# save and activate
save()
activate()
```

Advanced Security using XACML and OPPS

WebLogic has a very fine-grained and complex security system. In most cases you will never need to dig deep into it, but if you have to, the definition of security policies with XACML is a very powerful tool for advanced administrators.

The newer security model of WebLogic - especially in the area of the advanced Oracle tools like OWSM, ESB, OAM and others - is based on policies rather than on providers. This is an additional complex world of its own which can easily fill a book of its own. The following section is only meant to be a brief introduction.

Advanced Role Management using XACML

XACML: Who can access what, under what conditions and for what purpose?

The eXtensible Access Control Markup Language (=XACML) is an OASIS Standard that provides a policy language, a privacy profile, a request and response language, standard data-types, functions, combining algorithms, a RBAC profile, and more.

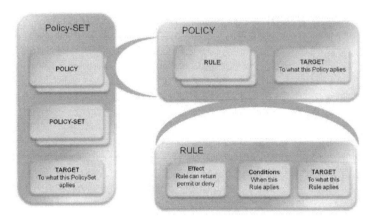

Figure 7.6: *Policy Set, Policy, and Rules*

Please see reference section for further readings and definitions of XACML for detailed introductions and explanations.

XACML Introduction

The following Wikipedia definition provides a good definition of XACML:

XACML stands for eXtensible Access Control Markup Language. The standard defines a declarative access control policy language implemented in XML and a processing model describing how to evaluate authorization requests according to the rules defined in policies.

As a published standard specification, one of the goals of XACML is to promote common terminology and interoperability between authorization implementations by multiple vendors. XACML is primarily an Attribute Based Access Control system (ABAC), where attributes (bits of data) associated with a user or action or resource are inputs into the decision of whether a given user may access a given resource in a particular way. Role-based access control (RBAC) can also be implemented in XACML as a specialization of ABAC.

The XACML model supports and encourages the separation of the authorization decision from the point of use. When authorization decisions are baked into client applications (or based on local machine user-IDs and Access Control Lists (ACLs)), it is very difficult to update the decision criteria when the governing policy changes. When the client is decoupled from the authorization decision, authorization policies can be updated on the fly and affect all clients immediately[10].

XACML and WebLogic

WebLogic makes intensive use of XACML for securing WebLogic resources, especially for expressing authorization policies and role assignments. In a WebLogic realm, there are two main components that use XACML: the XACML Authorization Provider and the XACML Role Mapping Provider.

There are a number of different reasons why you may need to use XACML. First is the ability to create security roles or policies with the admin console limited. If you need more complex roles, then neither the admin console nor the corresponding MBeans of WLST or JMX (see previous chapter) are sufficient. On the other hand you may want to (or need to) express security roles and policies in a standard language. In any of these cases you need to use XACML.

WebLogic also offers an advanced feature that can be used to export your roles and policies to XACML and then import them into other WebLogic domains (see previous chapter). WebLogic documentation offers a number of great pages (online) or chapters (documentation) which introduce XACML.

Whenever you want to secure a resource, you need to decide if you need to create root-level policies or scoped policies:

- A root-level policy applies to all instances of a resource type in your domain.

- A scoped policy applies to a specific resource instance and overrides a root-level policy.

WebLogic makes extensive use of policies and therefore a large number of resources can be secured using policies. This includes administrative resources, application resources, COM/JCA/JDBC/JMS/JNDI/EJB resources, JMX Resources, server resources, work context and web resources. A good overview can be found at http://docs.oracle.com/cd/E11035_01/wls100/secwlres/types.html.

---

[10] en.wikipedia.org/wiki/XACML

WebLogic Resource Identifier

In order to create XACML policies, you need to know what you want to secure or what you want to grant access. WebLogic creates an immutable, unique identifier (ID) whenever a resource is created. This also includes deployment. Every XACML policy must include a resource identifier that specifies the WebLogic ID. This also means that you need to create the source first or deploy your application before you can create a security policy for it.

You need to follow the following steps to create a role or policy:

- Find out which resource you want to secure.

- Get the WebLogic resource ID.

- Create the appropriate XACML policy or role.

- Use WLST (or JMX) to add the role or policy to your realm.

- Finally, verify that the role/policy has been deployed and works.

WebLogic supports all XACML resource identifiers, as described in the XACML 2.0 Core Specification. The following table describes the different resource identifiers and their meanings:

What should be identified	Identifier used
Resource	ID: urn:oasis:names:tc:xacml:1.0:resource:resource-id Be careful: This kind of identifier will only protect one specific resource. Child resources will not be protected
Resource and its ancestors	ID: urn:oasis:names:tc:xacml:2.0:resource:resource-ancestor-or-self
Parent of a resource	ID: urn:oasis:names:tc:xacml:1.0:resource:resource-parent
Ancestor of a resource	ID: urn:oasis:names:tc:xacml:2.0:resource:resource-ancestor

Table 7.3: XACML Resource Identifiers

Policies and WLST

WLST has built-in support for XACML policies. There are two types of XACML documents that can be imported using WLST: Role definitions into the XACML role mapper and authorizer policies into the XACML authorizer.

Add a role policy to the XACML role mapper:

```
# change to the security realm and inside the realm to the XACML role mapper
cd ('SecurityConfiguration/MartinTest_Domain/Realms/myrealm/RoleMappers/XACMLRoleMapper')

# finally apply the policy to the XACML role mapper
cmo.addPolicy(myPolicy)
```

Add a role policyset to the XACML role mapper:

```
# change to the security realm and inside the realm to the XACML role mapper
cd ('SecurityConfiguration/MartinTest_Domain/Realms/myrealm/RoleMappers/XACMLRoleMapper')

# finally apply the policy to the XACML role mapper
cmo.addPolicySet(myPolicySet)
```

Add an authorizer policy to the XACML authorizer:

```
# change to the security realm and inside the realm to the XACML authorizer
cd ('SecurityConfiguration/MartinTest_Domain/Realms/myrealm/Authorizers/XACMLAuthorizer')

# finally apply the policy to the XACML authorizer
cmo.addPolicy(myPolicy)
```

Add an authorizer policyset to the XACML authorizer:

```
# change to the security realm and inside the realm to the XACML authorizer
cd ('SecurityConfiguration/MartinTest_Domain/Realms/myrealm/Authorizers/XACMLAuthorizer')

# finally apply the policy to the XACML authorizer
cmo.addPolicySet(myPolicySet)
```

Example: New Role with Users and Groups

The following example will use a very simple XACML document, which will create a
new role and grant the user "test_1" and the group "group_wlsa" access. Of course
the user and the group must already exist. The new role can then be used to secure
resources.

The following XACML policy will be used.

🖫 XACML_policy

```
<?xml version="1.0" encoding="UTF-8"?>
<Policy
  PolicyId="urn:bea:xacml:2.0:entitlement:role:WLSAutomationUsers:"
RuleCombiningAlgId="urn:oasis:names:tc:xacml:1.0:rule-combining-algorithm:first-applicable">
  <Description>Usr(test_1)|Grp(group_wlsa)</Description>
  <Target>
    <Resources>
      <Resource>
        <ResourceMatch MatchId="urn:oasis:names:tc:xacml:1.0:function:string-equal">
          <AttributeValue
DataType="http://www.w3.org/2001/XMLSchema#string">WLSAutomationUsers</AttributeValue>
          <ResourceAttributeDesignator
            AttributeId="urn:oasis:names:tc:xacml:2.0:subject:role"
            DataType="http://www.w3.org/2001/XMLSchema#string" MustBePresent="true"/>
        </ResourceMatch>
      </Resource>
    </Resources>
    <Actions>
      <Action>
        <ActionMatch MatchId="urn:oasis:names:tc:xacml:1.0:function:anyURI-equal">
```

```
            <AttributeValue
DataType="http://www.w3.org/2001/XMLSchema#anyURI">urn:oasis:names:tc:xacml:2.0:actions:enableRole</A
ttributeValue>
          <ActionAttributeDesignator
            AttributeId="urn:oasis:names:tc:xacml:1.0:action:action-id"
            DataType="http://www.w3.org/2001/XMLSchema#anyURI" MustBePresent="true"/>
        </ActionMatch>
      </Action>
    </Actions>
  </Target>
  <Rule Effect="Permit" RuleId="primary-rule">
    <Condition>
      <Apply FunctionId="urn:oasis:names:tc:xacml:1.0:function:or">
        <!-- users and groups -->
        <Apply FunctionId="urn:oasis:names:tc:xacml:1.0:function:string-is-in">
          <AttributeValue DataType="http://www.w3.org/2001/XMLSchema#string">test_1</AttributeValue>
          <SubjectAttributeDesignator
            AttributeId="urn:oasis:names:tc:xacml:1.0:subject:subject-id"
            DataType="http://www.w3.org/2001/XMLSchema#string"
SubjectCategory="urn:oasis:names:tc:xacml:1.0:subject-category:access-subject"/>
        </Apply>
        <Apply FunctionId="urn:oasis:names:tc:xacml:1.0:function:string-is-in">
          <AttributeValue
DataType="http://www.w3.org/2001/XMLSchema#string">group_wlsa</AttributeValue>
          <SubjectAttributeDesignator
            AttributeId="urn:oasis:names:tc:xacml:2.0:subject:group"
            DataType="http://www.w3.org/2001/XMLSchema#string"
SubjectCategory="urn:oasis:names:tc:xacml:1.0:subject-category:access-subject"/>
        </Apply>
      </Apply>
    </Condition>
  </Rule>
  <Rule Effect="Deny" RuleId="deny-rule"/>
</Policy>
```

With the following WLST script can the above defined policy be added to the domain.

```
# connect to the admin server
connect('weblogic','<password>','t3://<url>')

# change to the security realm and inside the realm to the XACML role mapper
cd ('SecurityConfiguration/MartinTest_Domain/Realms/myrealm/RoleMappers/XACMLRoleMapper')

# open the file which the policy in read mode
myPolicyFile = open('testpolicy.xml','r')

# convert the file content to a XML document
myPolicy = myPolicyFile.read()

# finally apply the policy to the XACML role mapper
cmo.addPolicy(myPolicy)
```

Oracle Platform Security Services (OPSS)

OPSS (Oracle Platform Security Services) is the Oracle implementation of a standards-based security framework. This framework is designed to be portable and to work with many Oracle products. It is based on standard interfaces, supports policy-based security, and can be used for both enterprise and non-enterprise applications. OPSS is the Oracle standard security framework which is, or will be, the preferred security framework for all Oracle products. This framework is also supposed to be portable to other environments.

With the release of Fusion Middleware 11gR1, Oracle has combined the security frameworks used in Oracle Application Server with the security framework used in WebLogic Server into OPSS. OPSS is the foundation for security in Oracle Fusion Middleware and Fusion Applications used across the entire Fusion Middleware Suite and Fusion Applications.

WebLogic has a security framework – as discussed in the previous chapter – based on security providers and other mechanisms. This security framework is domain oriented, which means that it was designed to be used in a WebLogic domain. The setup is not trivial and it does have some shortcuts for recent technology stacks like WebService and SSO. OPSS is heavily based on standard APIs and policies. It is designed to be shared. While the WebLogic's own security framework saves its configuration in the domain configuration file, OPSS uses a policy-based approach and can save its policies in a database. Oracle has some good and comprehensive documents focusing on OPSS.

OPSS supports application life cycle from design, to deployment, to monitoring, etc. Now the security configuration management is exposed through Enterprise Manager - Fusion Middleware Control. It allows administrators to control how security-related artifacts (policies, credentials, etc.) are deployed to the target server.

The following three application security artifacts are of interest during the application deployment process.

Identities - Users and groups and application roles to groups/users mapping. These are defined by a developer during the application development process. In most scenarios, the identities should not be migrated when deploying an application to a remote WLS. Mapping Application role to enterprise groups/users in a remote WLS environment is a post-application deployment task to be done by an administrator.

Policies - Includes application roles and permissions granted to application roles. When deploying the app for the first time, the policies should always be migrated to the Policy store. Upon re-deploying the app, to preserve any application policy modification made in the policy store, the admin should choose the ignore option.

Credentials - Username/password tuples used by the applications. Credentials packaged with the application can be deployed to the remote WLS's credential store. They can also be ignored, which means credentials packaged with the application will not be deployed to the remote WLS's credential store. In this case, the administrator is then expected to create a credential valid for the environment, before the application works as designed by the developer.

OPSS and WLST

WLST has a number of built-in functions for OPSS-related activities. IMPORTANT: These are only available if the appropriate extensions are installed. This is, by default, not the case for WebLogic (up to 10.3.6) but is activated on the WLST version that comes with the Fusion Middleware installation. In some installations you will find multiple, differently configured WLST configurations.

Major MBeans for OPSS:

MBean	Description	MBean-Name
Jps Configuration	Manages domain configuration data, that is in the file jps-config.xml. This MBean provides the only way to modify configuration data.	com.oracle.jps:type=JpsConfig
Credential Store	Manages domain credential data, that is, the store service configured in the default context.	com.oracle.jps:type=JpsCredentialStore
Global Policy Store	Manages global policies in the domain policy store configured in the default context.	com.oracle.jps:type=JpsGlobalPolicyStore
Application Policy Store	Manages application policies in the domain policy store configured in the default context.	com.oracle.jps:type=JpsApplicationPolicyStore
Administration Policy Store	Validates whether a user logged into the current JMX context belongs to a particular role. It does not facilitate any configuration modifications.	com.oracle.jps:type=JpsAdminPolicyStore

(Source: Oracle Corporation[11])

Table 7.4: OPSS MBeans

WLST Extensions for OPSS

OPSS defines a large number of functions for WLST in order to configure different aspects of OPSS. Note that OPSS is not really built into WLST like the core WebLogic functionality. OPSS is rather implemented as a WLST library that provides a number of WLST functions for the most common MBean operations and attributes.

---

[11] docs.oracle.com/cd/E12839_01/core.1111/e10043/apadvadmin.htm

The following three tables provide an overview of some of the WLST functions provided for WLST.

View and manage audit policies and the audit repository configuration:

Function name	Description
getNonJavaEEAuditMBeanName	Display the mBean name for a non-Java EE component.
getAuditPolicy	Display audit policy settings
setAuditPolicy	Update audit policy settings
getAuditRepository	Display audit repository settings
setAuditRepository	Update audit repository settings
listAuditEvents	List audit events for one or all components
exportAuditConfig	Export a component's audit configuration
importAuditConfig	Import a component's audit configuration.

(Source: Oracle Corporation[12])

Table 7.5: Audit Policies

View and manage wallets, JKS keystores, and SSL configuration for Oracle HTTP Server, Oracle WebCache, Oracle Internet Directory, and Oracle Virtual Directory components:

Function name	Description
addCertificateRequest	Generate a certificate signing request in an Oracle wallet
addSelfSignedCertificate	Add a self-signed certificate to an Oracle wallet
changeKeyStorePassword	Change the password to a JKS keystore
changeWalletPassword	Change the password to an Oracle wallet
configureSSL	Set the SSL attributes for a component listener
createKeyStore	Create a JKS keystore
createWallet	Create an Oracle wallet
deleteKeyStore	Delete a JKS keystore
deleteWallet	Delete an Oracle wallet
exportKeyStore	Export a JKS keystore to a file.
exportKeyStoreObject	Export an object from a JKS keystore to a file.
exportWallet	Export an Oracle wallet to a file
exportWalletObject	Export an object from an Oracle wallet to a file
generateKey	Generate a key pair in a JKS keystore
getKeyStoreObject	Display a certificate or other object present in a JKS keystore
getSSL	Display the SSL attributes for a component listener
getWalletObject	Display a certificate or other object present in an Oracle wallet.
importKeyStore	Import a JKS keystore from a file
importKeyStoreObject	Import a certificate or other object from a file to a JKS keystore
importWallet	Import an Oracle wallet from a file.
importWalletObject	Import a certificate or other object from a file to an Oracle wallet.
listKeyStoreObjects	List all objects present in a JKS keystore
listKeyStores	List all JKS keystores configured for a component instance

[12] http://docs.oracle.com/middleware/1212/idm/IDMCR/custom_infra_security.htm

listWalletObjects	List all objects present in an Oracle wallet
listWallets	List all Oracle wallets configured for a component instance
removeKeyStoreObject	Remove a certificate or other object from a component instance's JKS keystore
removeWalletObject	Remove a certificate or other object from a component instance's Oracle wallet

(Source: Oracle Corporation[13])

Table 7.6: Security Functions

WLST security commands used to operate on a domain policy or credential store, and to migrate policies and credentials from a source repository to a target repository:

Function name	Description
listAppStripes	List application stripes in policy store
createAppRole	Create a new application role
deleteAppRole	Remove an application role
grantAppRole	Add a principal to a role
revokeAppRole	Remove a principal from a role
listAppRoles	List all roles in an application
listAppRolesMembers	List all members in an application role
grantPermission	Create a new permission
revokePermission	Remove a permission
listPermissions	List all permissions granted to a principal
deleteAppPolicies	Remove all policies in an application
migrateSecurityStore	Migrate policies or credentials from a source repository to a target repository
listCred	Obtain the list of attribute values of a credential
updateCred	Modify the attribute values of a credential
createCred	Create a new credential
deleteCred	Remove a credential
modifyBootStrapCredentil	Update bootstrap credential store
addBootStrapCredential	Add a credential to the bootstrap credential store
reassociateSecurityStore	Reassociate policies and credentials to an LDAP repository
upgradeSecurityStore	Upgrade security data from data used with release 10.1.x to data used with release 11
createResourceType	Create a new resource type
getResourceType	Fetch an existing resource type
deleteResourceType	Remove an existing resource type
createResource	Create a resource
deleteResource	Remove a resource
listResources	List resources in an application stripe
listResourceActions	List actions in a resource
createEntitlement	Create an entitlement
getEntitlement	List an entitlement
deleteEntitlement	Remove an entitlement.
addResourceToEntitlemen	Add a resource to an entitlement

---

[13] docs.oracle.com/middleware/1212/idm/IDMCR/custom_infra_security.htm

revokeResourceFroEntitle ment	Remove a resource from an entitlement
listEntitlements	List entitlements in an application stripe
grantEntitlement	Create an entitlement
revokeEntitlement	Remove an entitlement
listEntitlement	List an entitlement
listResourceTypes	List resource types in an application stripe

(Source: Oracle Corporation[14])

Table 7.7: Security Functions

Programmatic Authorization Policy Management with OPSS

In the simplistic cases, often the authorization policy management is done using the provided tooling. OPSS provides tooling in the form of EM (EM=Enterprise Manager GUI) and WLST (script) to manage policy.

For more advanced needs, OPSS also provides an API for programmatic policy management. The Policy API is protected by code source permission. Hence applications using the API will need to have the required permission (see FMW Security guide on the code necessary to use the API). What the example assumes is that proper policy access permission is granted beforehand, i.e. the application code running the example has PolicyStoreAccessPermission("context=APPLICATION, name=applicationTest" , "grant").

Here is an example of an OPSS WLST command that needs to be run to grant the required permission. The first entry is the path to the application jar that is making the programmatic API call, the second entry is the application stripe.

Start WLST from <middleware-home>/oracle_common/common/bin/wlst.sh Please note that this is NOT the WLST located in the WebLogic installation folder!

In the WLST shell you can use the following command:

```
grantPermission(codeBaseURL="file:///application/test/PolicySource/-",
            permClass="oracle.security.jps.service.policystore.PolicyStoreAccessPermission",
            permTarget="context=APPLICATION,name=PolicySource#V2.0", permActions="*")
```

There are two basic ways an application can use the example. One is to modify the application policy for itself, the other is to modify the application policy for another application.

---

[14] docs.oracle.com/middleware/1212/idm/IDMCR/custom_infra_security.htm

The latter might be the case when you have authorization management of the application structured as another application. In this case, the code source for the second application needs to be granted the PolicyStoreAccess permission.

1. The first entry is the exploded path where the application is during application development.
2. The second entry is the application stripe which, by default, is applicationname+"#"+"application version".
3. The third entry is the action, which in this case I have a wild card to indicate all actions on the policy. However, in any non-trivial environment, you should use specific actions like "alterAppRole" as specified in the API javadoc.

Deleting Application Policies with WLST

OPSS can automatically delete application policies when the application is undeployed. Now there are also occasions where you might want to delete application policies manually.

Here is a WLST command sample. Note that you need to launch the WLST from the <oracle>/common or general Fusion Middleware installation with the JPS (Java Platform Security) add-ons installed. The WLST provided by the WebLogic Server install does not have these features available:

```
# Connect to Admins server
connect('weblogic','welcome1',"localhost:7001")

# Delete the authZ policy for a an application
deleteAppPolicies(appStripe="TB#V1.0#9")
```

Sample Output:

```
wls:/domain1/serverConfig> deleteAppPolicies(appStripe="TB#V1.0#9")
{appStripe=TB#V1.0#9}
```

Note that the application stripe is a fully qualified name and include the application + the version.

Examples

Oracle has extensive documentation on OPSS and also WLST with OPSS. One very good source is:

http://docs.oracle.com/cd/E23943_01/core.1111/e10043/wlstcmds.htm

Other Security Topics

This section deals with a number of security topics that I consider important to know but did not fit into one of the other subsections in this chapter.

Admin Console Context

What is a very well-known aspect of WebLogic? Well-known facts are, for example, port 7001 and "/console" as context path. Try to search "/console" and "weblogic" and "login" in Google or Bing and you will find quite a few. This means that some admin consoles are available to the whole world over the Internet. And how many might still have "weblogic/weblogic" or "weblogic/Welcome1"?

This something hackers know, whether it be over the Internet or inside a company. One possible solution that WebLogic offers is to change the context root of the console so that it cannot easily be found or guessed. This can be done using the admin console and also via WLST.

```
cd('/')
# change the context path of the console
cmo.setConsoleContextPath('adminaccess')

# Change to the JMX subtree of your domain and change some JMX parameters
cd('/JMX/MartinTest_Domain')
cmo.setManagementEJBEnabled(true)
cmo.setPlatformMBeanServerEnabled(false)
cmo.setPlatformMBeanServerUsed(true)
cmo.setCompatibilityMBeanServerEnabled(true)
cmo.setInvocationTimeoutSeconds(0)

cd('/DeploymentConfiguration/MartinTest_Domain')
cmo.setRemoteDeployerEJBEnabled(false)

cd('/AdminConsole/MartinTest_Domain')
cmo.setCookieName('ADMINCONSOLESESSION')
cmo.setSessionTimeout(3600)
```

As you can see by analyzing this script, WebLogic offers more than just changing the context root. It is also possible to change the HTTP cookie and the session timeout.

Read-only Domain

Different roles in WebLogic allow the user to change attributes of the WebLogic configuration. In order to increase security, it is possible to make a domain read-only. This means that the EDIT MBean tree in the AdminServer will be disabled.

Please be aware of the fact that this has a number of consequences. Many features of the admin console will no longer work. All changes that require an edit session are no longer possible. This setting cannot be revoked in the online mode.

After this change, editing a domain is only possible using the offline mode, which is safer in production. This requires the person who wants to make changes to shut down the domain and log in on the machine where the AdminServer is normally running. This also requires the person to not only have access rights to the physical machine, but also access to the right user on the machine.

In order to change a domain to read-only, you need to set the attribute *EditMBeanServerEnabled* of the JMXMBean. This attribute controls whether JMX clients can access the runtime MBeans as well as read-only configuration MBeans. Note that changes on the runtime MBean tree are still possible, which also includes deployment and undeployment!

Online example:

```
edit()
startEdit()

# switch to the JMX subtree
cd('/JMX/MartinTest_Domain')

# disable the complete edit mode of the domain
set('EditMBeanServerEnabled', 'false')

# save and activate
save()
activate()
```

Offline example:

```
wls:/offline> readDomain('/opt/domains/MartinTest_Domain')
wls:/offline/MartinTest_Domain>cd("JMX")
wls:/offline/MartinTest_Domain/JMX>cd ('/JMX/MartinTest_Domain')
wls:/offline/MartinTest_Domain/JMX/MartinTest_Domain>cmo.setEditMBeanServerEnabled(true)
wls:/offline/MartinTest_Domain/JMX/MartinTest_Domain>updateDomain()
wls:/offline/MartinTest_Domain/JMX/MartinTest_Domain>exit()
```

Bypassing Basic Authentication

Client requests in WebLogic that use HTTP BASIC authentication must pass WebLogic Server authentication, even if access control is not enabled on the target resource. The behavior can be controlled with the flag enforce-valid-basic-auth-credentials. This configures whether or not the system should allow requests with invalid HTTP BASIC authentication to access unsecured resources. You have to be careful with this setting as this affects the complete domain. If you explicitly set the enforce-valid-basic-auth-credentials flag to false, WebLogic Server does not perform authentication for HTTP BASIC authentication client requests for which access control was not enabled for the target resource.

Note that this setting is one of the options that CANNOT be set using the AdminConsole. Therefore you need to either set this offline manually in the config.xml (strongly discouraged) or use WLST.

Example WLST script:

```
connect('weblogic','weblogic','t3://localhost:7001')
edit()
startEdit()
cd('SecurityConfiguration/MartinTest_Domain')
set('EnforceValidBasicAuthCredentials','false')
save()
activate()
```

This change requires a server restart after the change has been activated.

Summary

Security is always a very hot topic for every J2EE application and especially for every J2EE hosting environment like WebLogic. WebLogic offers a broad range of security features bundled in a security realm. All of these features can of course be automated using WLST. Unfortunately the WebLogic security implementation also has a number of disadvantages like the restriction to only one active security realm or that security configurations are not recorded when recording WLST.

Administration Tasks using WLST

Administration Tasks using WLST

The last three chapters discussed various automation abilities around constructing domains, configuring domains, and extending domains. All of these actions normally take place when the domain is created or updated, and not during the day-to-day operation of domains. Now that we have created, configured, and secured our domains, we need to look at common daily tasks for administrators operating these domains. This chapter focuses on lifecycle tasks, such as starting and stopping domains. All the tasks discussed in this chapter are not monitoring tasks, even if of course monitoring aspects are present in almost all scripts. All of these tasks will change the status or even content of the domains.

Server States

In order to understand administration tasks and the corresponding commands in WLST (and also the console), it is important to understand the different server states and the possible state transitions. Figure 8.1 shows an overview of the different state transitions.

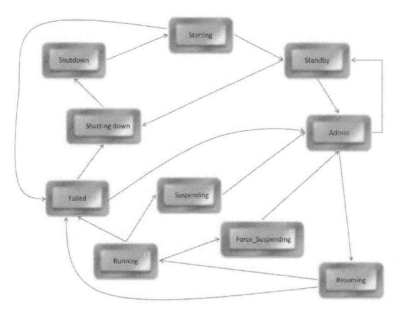

Figure 8.1: *Overview of Different State Transitions*

SHUTDOWN State: In the SHUTDOWN state, the server instance is not running. In the case of a Managed-Server, the configuration can be changed using the AdminServer. When using WLST, there won't be any runtime information available because the process is not running and no listener is opened for any request.

STARTING State: WebLogic Server transitions from SHUTDOWN to STANDBY, as a result of a start command.

STANDBY State: In the STANDBY state, WebLogic does not process any requests and the normal Listen Port is not opened. Only the administration port is open for life cycle requests to move itself to the RUNNING or the SHUTDOWN state.

ADMIN State: In the ADMIN state, WebLogic Servers are available only for administration operations, allowing you to perform server and application-level administration tasks, but are invisible to other cluster members.

RESUMING State: In the RESUMING state, WebLogic moves itself from the STANDBY or ADMIN state to the RUNNING state.

RUNNING State: In the RUNNING state, WebLogic is fully functional, offers its services to clients, and can operate as a cluster-member.

SUSPENDING State: In the SUSPENDING state, WebLogic is transitioning into ADMIN state. If the suspending method is used, WebLogic tries to complete work in progress gracefully.

FORCE_SUSPENDING State: In the FORCE_SUSPENDING state, WebLogic is transitioning into ADMIN state. If the force suspending method is used, WebLogic does not complete work in progress gracefully.

SHUTTING_DOWN State: Using the *shutdown* or *force shutdown* command forces a server to shut down. While the server is shutting down its subsystems, it transitions itself in the SHUTTING_DOWN state where it does not accept application or administration requests.

FAILED State: Every server can fail for several reasons (e.g. out-of-memory). One reason can also be that one of its subsystems became unstable or unusable. If a server detects a failure based on its health monitoring, it declares itself FAILED.

Figure 8.2 is an alternative view provided, which distinguishes between happy states and failure states:

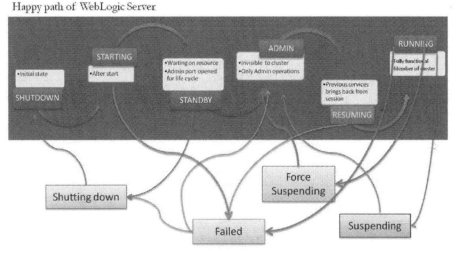

Figure 8.2: *Happy Path View*

Administration Console

The administration console is a very useful tool for development environments in order to experiment with the domain and test the right settings. It is also very common for developers to not be experienced in automation and therefore prefer using the GUI tool instead of the scripting environment.

For higher environments, the console should not be used as an administration tool for configurations and changes or lifecycle operations. It is still useful for visual control though.

This book is all about automation. I want to emphasize though that the console is a very useful tool, but for higher environments, all operations must be audit safe and repeatable. System admins/operators must be able to run and schedule most control and lifecycle operations automatically or on regular basis. In most companies, system administrators need to setup and maintain many WebLogic domains, sometimes hundreds or thousands. Therefore domain setup and configuration must be automated.

Recording

The console has a nice feature that helps developers and administrators create WLST scripts, or at least get some hints for their scripts. The feature is called recording. Recording means that the console records all changes. When the recording is stopped, it will create a WLST script.

Please be aware that these scripts have a number of limitations that will often result in the generation of scripts that have to be manually changed or extended. For security reasons (according to Oracle), the console will not record any changes in the security area. This is really a pity as those changes are sometimes quite hard to script because WebLogic uses (in some cases; see previous chapters) WebLogic proprietary classes or complicated structures, like OpenMBeans.

You always need to check if the generated script does everything you have actually changed. The second aspect you should always keep in mind is that the generated scripts are reflecting the changes at the domain in question only. Scripts should always be written in a generic and flexible way in order to use them for many different domains. Therefore, you should always treat the generated scripts as a guideline for your own scripts.

It should be noted that the recording feature is also available for WLST. This means you can start an interactive WLST shell, connect to an Administration Server, start recording, do your changes, stop the recording, and write the script to a file. Keep in mind that the restrictions as mentioned above do apply here as well.

Activation / Deactivation

Even if you secure the admin access and keep the administrator password secret, the console is a web application and accessible from all machines in this network. In addition, the console is a heavy web application. For production environments, which are automated, it might make sense to disable the console. You still have access through WLST!

In my experience, it has proven very valuable to keep a script that can switch on/off the console so that the console can be reactivated as soon as it will be needed. The console can be activated and deactivated with the operation *setConsoleEnabled*.

The following script can be used to switch the console on or off. You need to adapt this script to your needs if you want to use it as this will a) use the userconfig and userkey file for authentication and b) restart the AdminServer using the generated startWeblogic.sh (see subsequent sections). You can see an example how external programs or scripts can be executed from a WLST script using the Jython *os.system(<myCommand>)* command.

🔲 switch_console

```
import sys
from java.util import Properties
from java.io import FileInputStream
from java.io import File

pathSeparator = '/';
domainProps = Properties();
userConfigFile = '';
userKeyFile = '';
consoleAction = '';

# Load properties
def intialize():
        global domainProps;
        global userConfigFile;
        global userKeyFile;
        global consoleAction;

        # test arguments
        if len(sys.argv) != 4:
                print 'Usage:  wlst.sh adminConsole.py <property_file>  ON/OFF';
                exit();

        try:
                domainProps = Properties()

                # load properties and overwrite defaults
                input = FileInputStream(sys.argv[1])
                domainProps.load(input)
                input.close()

                userConfigFile = sys.argv[2]
                userKeyFile    = sys.argv[3]
                consoleAction  = sys.argv[4]
        except:
                print 'Cannot load properties  !'
```

```
                exit();

        print 'Initialization completed'


# Connect to adminserver
def connnectToAdminServer():
    connUri = domainProps.getProperty('adminURI')
    connect(userConfigFile=userConfigFile,userKeyFile=userKeyFile,url=connUri)
    print 'Connected to '+connUri


# restart the admin server
def restartAdminServer():
    try:
        print 'Shutting down the Admin Server...';
        shutdown(force='true', block='true')

        print 'Start the admin server using start script';
        domainLocation = domainProps.getProperty('domainsDirectory')
                        + pathSeparator + domainProps.getProperty('domainName');
        startScript = domainLocation+ pathSeparator + "startWebLogic.sh"

        myCommand = 'nohup '+startScript+' > '+domainProps.getProperty('domainName')+'.log 2>&1 &'
        print ('The following start command will be used: '+myCommand)
        os.system(myCommand)
        print 'Just in case wait for 10 seconds.'
        java.lang.Thread.sleep(10000)
    except OSError:
        print 'Exception while rstarting the adminserver !'
        dumpStack()


##################################################################
# set console visibility
##################################################################
def setConsoleVisibility():
    try:
        if ('ON' == consoleAction):
            # mark it for edit
            edit()
            # start the edit
            startEdit()
            # set the flag to true
            cmo.setConsoleEnabled(true)
            # save the changes
            save()
            # activate the changes
            activate()
            #  restart admin
            restartAdminServer()
        elif ('OFF' == consoleAction):
            # mark it for edit
            edit()
            # start the edit
            startEdit()
            # set the flag to true
            cmo.setConsoleEnabled(false)
            # save the changes
            save()
            # activate the changes
            activate()
            # restart admin
            restartAdminServer()
        else:
            print ('Operation '+ consoleAction+ ' is not supported !!')
    except OSError:
        print 'Exception while changing the console visibility !'
        dumpStack();


# disconnect from  adminserver
def disconnectFromAdminserver():
        print 'Disconnect from the Admin Server...'
        disconnect();
```

```
if __name__ == "main":
    print ' Toggle Admin Console usability '
    print ''
    intialize()
    connnectToAdminServer()
    setConsoleVisibility()
    disconnectFromAdminserver()
```

This script can be used by admins to switch the administrator console ON or OFF. A deactivated administration console increases security and disburdens the Administration Server.

Server Start

The server of a WebLogic domain can be started using different techniques. The best setup depends on the technical requirements but also on the security/administration guidelines of the company. The following section introduces the different possibilities and will provide best practices information based on real project experience.

Administration Server

The Administration Server can be started in three different ways as explained in the subsequent sections. You can start an Administration Server using a start script or using WLST with or without the NodeManager. All starting mechanisms have their own advantages and disadvantages. Readers are advised to define their own strategy carefully, but keep it simple and stay with one of the discussed methods for your environments.

Using a Startup Script

The Administration Server can be started with a default startup script or with a self-made script. During domain creation, a startup script is created called *startWebLogic.sh*. Note that the script might not have been created if you used a modified template for the domain creation. This script calls another script to set environment variables and finally start the Administration Server. This script can be modified so that the standard output (=out) logfile and error logfile are written to a specified place.

This script starts the Administration Server using the *java weblogic.Server* command, which starts a JVM that is configured to run a WebLogic instance.

Using WLST and NodeManager

The NodeManager is normally used to start Managed-Servers. However, it can also be used to start the Administration Server. The NodeManager was introduced in *Chapter 6*.

Real project usage has shown advantages and disadvantages of using the NodeManager to manage the AdminServer:

The benefits:

- The biggest benefit is that the AdminServer can be started from a script running on a remote host. In case many AdminServers have to be (re-)started on many different machines, all of them can be controlled from a single host talking to the different NodeManagers.

In most projects I have been involved with, the NodeManager was not used to start the AdminServer due to the following reasons.

The disadvantages:

- All AdminServers should always be up and running and therefore it is better to start them up during system boot, including the AdminServer starts using a runlevel start script.

- Usually the AdminServers are running separately from the domain on dedicated hosts with virtual IPs, which can be moved in case of a failure to a different machine. In a usual production setup, the number of machines for the Administration Servers are limited.

- The most common reason is that the generated startup scripts are not used if the NodeManager is used to startup the Administration Server. In many cases the Administration Server is configured with additional libraries, startup parameters, etc., which are configured in the *startWebLogic.sh* script. If the NodeManager is used, these settings must be passed to the NodeManager which is normally more difficult.

The following is a typical procedure using the NodeManager.

The *nmConnect* command can be used to connect to the NodeManager using WLST. The credentials can be given either using a user/password combination or a userconfig/keyfile combination. The following is an example that uses username/password to connect the NodeManager.

```
nmConnect([username, password], [host], [port], [domainName], [domainDir], [nmType])
nmConnect([userConfigFile, userKeyFile], [host], [port], [domainName], [domainDir], [nmType])
```

Example:

```
nmConnect('weblogic', '<pw>', 'localhost',
'5556','Martin_TestDomain','/application/domains/Martin_TestDomain','SSL')
Connecting to Node Manager ...
Successfully connected to Node Manager.
wls:/nm/Martin_TestDomain>
```

The next script demonstrates starting the Administration Server using the *nmStart* command. This command must be provided with the name of the server, the domain directory, and properties.

```
nmStart([serverName], [domainDir], [props], [writer], [serverType])
```

Example:

```
wls:/nm/Martin_TestDomain>nmStart('AdminServer')
starting server AdminServer
Server AdminServer started successfully
wls:/nm/Martin_TestDomain>
```

Next, monitor the status of the server using the NodeManager by entering the *nmServerStatus* command:

```
wls:/nm/Martin_TestDomain>nmServerStatus('AdminServer')
RUNNING
wls:/nm/Martin_TestDomain>
```

Here is an example for starting the NodeManager and then the AdminServer with the NodeManager:

```
print 'Start the NodeManager';
startNodeManager(verbose='false', NodeManagerHome='/opt/wls/nodemanager/xyz', ListenPort='5556');

print 'Wait for a short time to allow the nodemanager to start ...'
os.system("sleep 3")

print 'Connect to the Node Manager';
nmConnect(<user>,<password>, 'localhost', '5556', <domainName>, <domainLocation>, 'plain');

print 'Start the AdminServer using the NodeManager';
nmStart('AdminServer');

print 'Again wait for a short while to allow the AdminServer to start ...'
os.system("sleep 20")   # 20 seconds

print 'Connect to the AdminServer';
connect(<user>, <password>, <url>);
```

It is better and much more secure to use the secret key files as there is no need to provide user and password in the readable script. This is also available for the NodeManager:

```
nmConnect([userConfigFile, userKeyFile], [host], [port], [domainName], [domainDir], [nmType])
```

Example revisited:

```
print 'Start the NodeManager';
startNodeManager(verbose='false', NodeManagerHome='/opt/wls/nodemanager/xyz', ListenPort='5556');

print 'Wait for a short time to allow the nodemanager to start ...'
os.system("sleep 3")

print 'Connect to the Node Manager';
nmConnect(userConfigFile='/opt/domainaccess/testNM/user', userKeyFile='/opt/domainaccess/testNM/key',
'localhost', '5556', <domainName>, <domainLocation>, 'plain');

print 'Start the AdminServer using the NodeManager';
```

```
nmStart('AdminServer');

print 'Again wait for a short while to allow the AdminServer to start ...'
os.system("sleep 20")    # 20 seconds

print 'Connect to the AdminServer';
connect(userConfigFile='/opt/domainaccess/testDomain/user',
userKeyFile='/opt/domainaccess/testDomain/key', <url>);
```

Using WLST without NodeManager

Using the WLST *startServer* command, the Administration Server can be started without using a NodeManager. The server runs in a separate process from WLST, which means that exiting WLST does not shutdown the server.

```
startServer([adminServerName], [domainName], [url], [username], [password],[domainDir], [block],
[timeout], [serverLog], [systemProperties], [jvmArgs])
```

Example:

```
wls:/offline> startServer('AdminServer','MartinTestDomain','t3://myTestServer:12345',
'admin','<pw>5','/application/domains/MartinTestDomain','false', 60000, jvmArgs='-
XX:MaxPermSize=125m, -Xmx512m, -XX:+UseParallelGC')
wls:/offline>
```

Managed-Server

Similar to the AdminServer, WebLogic also offers different ways to start Managed-Servers. However, these differ from the possible ways to start an Administration Server. The big difference is that the Administration Server is already running and can be used (and will be used) to start the Managed-Servers.

Using the start script

Similar to the AdminServer, WebLogic creates a startscript in the bin folder of the domain during domain creation. This can be used to start the different Managed-Servers by calling the script with the Managed-Server's name. This script is called *startManagedWebLogic.sh*.

Using the NodeManager

If the domain is enrolled with the NodeManager and the server start attributes are configured correctly, then WLST can communicate with the NodeManager and start the server based on the configuration.

```
start('MartinTest_Domain_MS1','Server')
```

This requires that the NodeManager on the target machine is started, the domain is enrolled, and the server start attributes are configured.

Using the ServerLifeCycleRuntime

The Managed-Server can also be started using the AdminServer and the *ServerLifeCycleRuntime* of the Managed-Server. This also requires that the NodeManager responsible for this Managed-Server is started.

```
connect('weblogic','xxxxx','t3://localhost:12345')
domainRuntime()
wls:/MartinTest_Domain/domainRuntime>
cd ('/ServerLifeCycleRuntimes/MartinTest_Domain_MS1')
cmo.start()
```

Example: Start All Managed-Servers of a Domain

The following script is an example that is very useful for real production systems. Consider the following situation: You have a maintenance window where you will perform OS updates or database updates. This requires that all Managed-Servers are shut down so that no processes are running on the Managed-Server machines and no requests are issued against the databases. After your maintenance has been finished, you need to loop over all your domains and restart all Managed-Servers.

The following script is doing exactly this. It connects to an AdminServer and loops over all Managed-Servers. All servers that are shut down or failed will be restarted.

🖫 loop_managed_servers

```
# Start all managed servers of a domain

import sys
from java.util import Properties
from java.io import FileInputStream
from java.io import File

domainProps = Properties();
userConfigFile = '';
userKeyFile = '';

# Load properties
def intialize():
        global domainProps;
        global userConfigFile;
        global userKeyFile;

        # test arguments
        if len(sys.argv) != 3:
                print 'Usage:  startAllManagedServers.py  <property_file>';
                exit();

        try:
                domainProps = Properties()

                # load properties and overwrite defaults
                input = FileInputStream(sys.argv[1])
                domainProps.load(input)
                input.close()

                userConfigFile = sys.argv[2]
                userKeyFile =  sys.argv[3]
        except:
                print 'Cannot load properties  !';
                exit();
```

```
        print 'Initialization completed';


# Connect to adminserver - wait max. 10 minutes for connection
def connnectToAdminServer():

        connUri = domainProps.getProperty('adminURL')

        currentcount = 0;
        adminServerIsRunning = 'false';

        while ((adminServerIsRunning=='false')  and (currentcount<30)):
            try:
                    print 'Connecting to the Admin Server ('+connUri+')';
                    connect(userConfigFile=userConfigFile,userKeyFile=userKeyFile,url=connUri);
                    print 'Connected';
                    adminServerIsRunning = 'true';
            except:
                    print 'AdminServer is (not yet) running. Will wait for 10sec.';
                    java.lang.Thread.sleep(10000);
                    currentcount = currentcount +1;

        if (adminServerIsRunning=='false'):
            print 'Could not connect to admin server - script will be exit !'
            exit();


# get Server status
def getMSserverStatus(server):
        try:
            cd('/ServerLifeCycleRuntimes/' +server)
        except:
            print 'oh ohohohoh';
            dumpStack();
        return cmo.getState()


# Start all managed server
def startAllManagedServers():
    try:
                print 'Loop through the managed servers and start all servers ';
                domainConfig()
                svrs = cmo.getServers()

                domainRuntime()
                for server in svrs:
                        # Do not start the adminserver, it's already running
                        if server.getName() != 'AdminServer':
                                # Get state and machine
                                serverState = getMSserverStatus(server.getName())
                                print server.getName() + " is " + serverState
                                # startup if needed
                                if (serverState == "SHUTDOWN") or
                                   (serverState == "FAILED_NOT_RESTARTABLE"):
                                        print "Starting " + server.getName();
                                        start(server.getName(),'Server')
                                        serverState = getMSserverStatus(server.getName())
                                        print "Now " + server.getName() + " is " + serverState;
    except:
        print 'Exception while starting managed servers !';
        dumpStack();


# disconnect from  adminserver
def disconnectFromAdminserver():
        print 'Disconnect from the Admin Server...';
        disconnect();


# =================================================================
#          Main Code Execution
# =================================================================
if __name__== "main":
        print ' Start all managed server of the domain \n';
        intialize();
        connnectToAdminServer();
        startAllManagedServers();
        disconnectFromAdminserver();
```

(Note that line breaks have been introduced for better readability)

Some special notes for this script:

- You can see that the *connect* method has been extended so that the script will try to connect to the AdminServer for a number of times. This script has a fixed number of 30 attempts, but of course this amount should be configurable using a property in a property file. This is useful if, for example, a shell script starts the AdminServer and then immediately starts this script. As the Administration Server needs some time to come up and to initialize, it might be the case that the Administration Server is not yet ready to serve requests when this script tries to connect.

- Note that this script only looks for server in the state SHUTDOWN and FAILED. You may want to extend this script to also start servers that are in the SUSPEND state. This depends on your needs.

- This script tries to start all servers. It might be a very valuable extension if the shutdown script (see the following section) will be extended to save the actual server states to disk before doing the shutdown. The script can be extended in order to start only the server that was running before the shutdown.

Running the script will create the following output:

```
Initializing WebLogic Scripting Tool (WLST) ...
Welcome to WebLogic Server Administration Scripting Shell
Type help() for help on available commands

##############################################################################
#                 Start all managed server of the domain                     #
##############################################################################

Starting the initialization process
Initialization completed
Connecting to the Admin Server (t3://mytestserver.book.com:46901)
Connecting to t3://mytestserver.book.com:46901 with userid weblogic ...
Successfully connected to Admin Server 'AdminServer' that belongs to domain 'MartinTest_Domain'.

Warning: An insecure protocol was used to connect to the
server. To ensure on-the-wire security, the SSL port or
Admin port should be used instead.

Connected
Loop through the managed servers and start all servers
Location changed to serverRuntime tree. This is a read-only tree with DomainMBean as the root.
For more help, use help(domainConfig)

Location changed to domainRuntime tree. This is a read-only tree with DomainMBean as the root.
For more help, use help(domainRuntime)

MartinTest_Domain_MS1 is SHUTDOWN
Starting server MartinTest_Domain_MS1 .....................................................
Server with name MartinTest_Domain_MS1 started successfully
Now MartinTest_Domain_MS1 is RUNNING

MartinTest_Domain_MS2 is SHUTDOWN
Starting server MartinTest_Domain_MS2 ...............................
Server with name MartinTest_Domain_MS2 started successfully
Now MartinTest_Domain_MS2 is RUNNING

MartinTest_Domain_MS3 is SHUTDOWN
Starting server MartinTest_Domain_MS3 ...................................................
```

```
Server with name MartinTest_Domain_MS3 started successfully
Now MartinTest_Domain_MS3 is RUNNING

Disconnect from the Admin Server...
Disconnected from weblogic server: AdminServer
```

NodeManager

WLST also offers functionality to start the NodeManager, which is available in online and offline mode. However, it is mostly used in offline mode. This functionality is only available if the script is running on the host where the NodeManager should start. The WLST function *startNodeManager* can take optional parameters to specify which NodeManager to start. These parameters include NodeManagerHome, ListenAddress, ListenPort, and PropertiesFile.

Example:

```
wls:/offline> startNodeManager(verbose='true',
NodeManagerHome='/opt/infrastructure/nodemanager/nm.4711', ListenPort='9876',
ListenAddress='localhost')
```

Due to the number of options a NodeManager has (which also may include certificates, SSL configuration, etc.), starting the NodeManager using WLST is possible, but it's usually started using shell scripts out of runlevel (UNIX) or Windows services. It is not uncommon to have multiple NodeManagers on the same host. Therefore, the default location/port parameters are usually not the correct ones.

Server Stop

The opposite action to starting the infrastructure is stopping the infrastructure. This includes stopping the AdminServer, the Managed-Server, and also the NodeManager. There are multiple ways to stop the servers. The following section will give a short overview of the different ways and functions available.

Managed-Server

Similar to starting the Managed-Server, WebLogic also offers different ways to stop Managed-Servers. These mechanisms differ from the possibilities to start an Administration Server. The big difference is that the Administration Server is already running and can be used (and will be used) to stop the Managed-Servers.

Using the stopscript

Similar to the start script, WebLogic creates a stopscript in the bin folder of the domain during domain creation. This can be used to stop the different Managed-

Servers by calling the script with the Managed-Server's name. This script is called *stopManagedWebLogic.sh*.

Using the NodeManager

If the domain is enrolled with the NodeManager and the server start attributes are configured correctly, then WLST can communicate with the NodeManager and also stop the server based on the configuration.

```
shutdown(server.getName(),'Server','true',1000,force='true', block='true')
```

This requires that the NodeManager on the target machine is started, that the domain is enrolled, and that the server start attributes are configured.

Using the ServerLifeCycleRuntime

The Managed-Server can also be stopped using the AdminServer and the *ServerLifeCycleRuntime* of the Managed-Server. This also requires that the NodeManager responsible for this Managed-Server is started.

Example for using the interactive mode:

```
connect('weblogic','xxxxx','t3://localhost:12345')
wls:/MartinTest_Domain/serverConfig> domainRuntime()
wls:/MartinTest_Domain/domainRuntime> cd ('ServerLifeCycleRuntimes/MartinTest_Domain_MS1')
wls:/MartinTest_Domain/domainRuntime/ServerLifeCycleRuntimes/MartinTest_Domain_MS1> ls()
dr--   Tasks

-r--    MiddlewareHome                          /opt/weblogic/10.3.6
-r--    Name                                    MartinTest_Domain_MS1
-r--    NodeManagerRestartCount                 0
-r--    State                                   SHUTDOWN
-r--    Type                                    ServerLifeCycleRuntime
-r--    WeblogicHome                            /opt/weblogic/10.3.6/wlserver_10.3

-r-x    forceShutdown                           WebLogicMBean :
-r-x    forceSuspend                            WebLogicMBean :
-r-x    getIPv4URL                              String : String(protocol)
-r-x    getIPv6URL                              String : String(protocol)
-r-x    preDeregister                           Void :
-r-x    resume                                  WebLogicMBean :
-r-x    shutdown                                WebLogicMBean :
-r-x    shutdown                                WebLogicMBean :
Integer(timeout),Boolean(ignoreSessions)
-r-x    start                                   WebLogicMBean :
-r-x    suspend                                 WebLogicMBean :
-r-x    suspend                                 WebLogicMBean :
Integer(timeout),Boolean(ignoreSessions)

wls:/MartinTest_Domain/domainRuntime/ServerLifeCycleRuntimes/MartinTest_Domain_MS1> cmo.shutdown()
```

Instead of the interactive mode, the following script can be used for the same purpose:

```
connect('weblogic','xxxxx','t3://localhost:12345')
domainRuntime()
wls:/MartinTest_Domain/domainRuntime>
```

```
cd ('/ServerLifeCycleRuntimes/MartinTest_Domain_MS1')
cmo.shutdown()
```

AdminServer

Stopping an AdminServer can be achieved using a number of different techniques. Depending on the technique used, different steps have to be taken into consideration. The following possibilities (besides the administration console) are available:

- ServerLifeCycleMBean

- WLST shutdown

- NodeManager shutdown (if started via NodeManager)

- WebLogic generated default scripts

- Operating system capabilities like kill

In the case of stopping the AdminServer, all mechanisms described for Managed-Servers (same function calls, same MBeans) can be used. Please refer to the Managed-Server section above for more details.

NodeManager

WLST offers a function called *stopNodeManager*. This function has a number of restrictions, like special NodeManager configuration *QuitEnabled*. In addition, this function does not take any arguments, so this process of stopping a NodeManager is very uncommon. In highly complex production environments with (potentially) multiple NodeManagers on every box, NodeManagers are almost always started and stopped via scripts at machine start or stop using appropriate runlevel scripts on UNIX or service calls on Windows machines.

Example: Stopping a Complete Domain

The following script will connect to the AdminServer. The script will then iterate over all Managed-Servers. All servers that are not in the state of SHUTDOWN will be asked to shut down. The *shutdown* command in this script uses the force=true option and block=true. Therefore, this script will block and wait until each server is shut down.

This example is very useful for real production systems. For instance, it can be very useful when you need to shut down all servers due to a maintenance window where you will perform OS updates or database updates.

```
# get Server status
def getMSserverStatus(server):
```

```
    try:
        cd('/ServerLifeCycleRuntimes/' +server)
    except:
        print 'oh ohohohoh';
        dumpStack();
    return cmo.getState()


# Stop all managed servers and then also the admin server if wanted
def stopAllServers():
    try:
        print 'Loop through the managed servers and stop all servers ';
        domainConfig()
        svrs = cmo.getServers()

        domainRuntime()
        for server in svrs:
            # Do not stop the adminserver, it's already running
            if server.getName() != 'AdminServer':
                # Get state and machine
                serverState = getMSserverStatus(server.getName())
                print server.getName() + " is " + serverState
                # stop if needed
                if serverState != "SHUTDOWN":
                    print "Stopping " + server.getName();
                    shutdown(server.getName(),'Server','true',1000,force='true', block='true')
                    serverState = getMSserverStatus(server.getName())
                    print "Now " + server.getName() + " is " + serverState;

    except:
        print 'Exception while stopping servers !';
        dumpStack();

    # finally stop the admin server IF wanted
    if ('true' == domainProps.getProperty('stopAdminServerAlso')):
        print 'Stopping the admin server';
        shutdown('AdminServer','Server','true',1000,force='true', block='true')
```

"force=true" is provided to the server so that the server will perform this action regardless of outstanding tasks on the server. "block=true" results in a synchronous call and will block until the shutdown operation has been completed. This is useful if subsequent operations rely on the fact that the shutdown operation has been done. In case you want to shut down a larger number of (managed-) servers, it might be more efficient to use "block=false" so that the shutdown will be performed on all servers in parallel.

This script is also using the userconfig and key files to connect to the Administration Server.

Suspending / Resuming Servers

WebLogic offers two additional functions for state transitioning. Suspending means to bring a running server down into ADMIN state so that the server process is still alive but only accepts administrative calls. Resume is the opposite functionality which brings a server from ADMIN state back into RUNNING state.

Example for suspending a server:

```
connect('weblogic','<pw>','t3://localhost:7001')
domainRuntime()
```

```
cd ('ServerRuntimes/MartinTest_Domain_MS1')
cmo.suspend()
```

Example for resuming a server:

```
connect('weblogic','<pw>','t3://localhost:7001')
domainRuntime()
cd ('ServerRuntimes/MartinTest_Domain_MS1')
cmo.resume()
```

Example for interactive usage:

```
wls:/offline> connect('weblogic','<pw>','t3://localhost:7001')
Connecting to t3://localhost:7001 with userid weblogic ...

wls:/MartinTest_Domain/serverConfig> domainRuntime()
Location changed to domainRuntime tree. This is a read-only tree with DomainMBean as the root.
For more help, use help(domainRuntime)

wls:/MartinTest_Domain/domainRuntime> cd ('ServerRuntimes/MartinTest_Domain_MS1')
wls:/MartinTest_Domain/domainRuntime/ServerRuntimes/MartinTest_Domain_MS1> ls()
<...>
-r--    State                           RUNNING
-r--    StateVal                        2
<...>
-r-x    suspend                         Void : Integer(timeout),Boolean(ignoreSessions)

wls:/MartinTest_Domain/domainRuntime/ServerRuntimes/MartinTest_Domain_MS1> cmo.suspend()
wls:/MartinTest_Domain/domainRuntime/ServerRuntimes/MartinTest_Domain_MS1> ls()
<...>
-r--    State                           ADMIN
-r--    StateVal                        17
<...>

wls:/MartinTest_Domain/domainRuntime/ServerRuntimes/MartinTest_Domain_MS1> cmo.resume()
wls:/MartinTest_Domain/domainRuntime/ServerRuntimes/MartinTest_Domain_MS1> ls()
<...>
-r--    SocketsOpenedTotalCount         4
-r--    State                           RUNNING
-r--    StateVal                        2
<...>
```

Starting / Stopping a Cluster

So far we only discussed starting and stopping of individual servers. In most domains, servers are grouped into clusters where the applications are deployed (targeted) towards a cluster.

WLST also offers functionality to start/stop complete clusters (surprisingly, the administration console does not!) so that the scripts do not need to find out which servers belong to which cluster. Unfortunately WLST does not provide sufficient support for cluster state. The "state" function in WLST can print out the different states of the cluster members but do not return an overall cluster state.

The first example shows the "state" method provided by WLST:

```
# Print state of cluster
def printClusterState(clustername):
    try:
        state(clustername,"Cluster")
```

```
    except Exception, e:
        print 'Error while printing cluster state ',e
        dumpStack()
```

The next example will implement different check functions that check if all members of the cluster - therefore the whole cluster - are either in RUNNING or SHUTDOWN state.

```
# check state of all cluster members if equal to RUNNING
def checkStateOfClusterMembers(clustername,desiredState):
    try:
        domainConfig()
        cd('/')
        servers = cmo.getServers()
        domainRuntime()
        cd('/')
        collectedServers = []
        for server in servers:
            if server.getCluster()!=None and server.getCluster().getName()==clustername:
                serverRuntimeMBean = getMBean('/ServerLifeCycleRuntimes/'+server.getName())
                serverState = serverRuntimeMBean.getState()
                if serverState != desiredState:
                    collectedServers.append(server.getName())

        if len(collectedServers) > 0 :
            # oh oh not in desired state
            return 'false'
        else:
            # ok all servers in desired state
            return 'true'
    except Exception, e:
        print 'Error while checking member states ',e
        dumpStack()
        return 'false'
```

The above function is a general check function. To make it easier for script developers (and easier to remember the different possible values), shortcut functions like the one in the following example are really helpful.

```
################################################################
# check state of all cluster members if equal to RUNNING
################################################################
def checkIfAllServersOfClusterAreRunning(clustername):
    return checkStateOfClusterMembers(clustername, "RUNNING")


################################################################
# check state of all cluster members if equal to desired mode
################################################################
def checkIfAllServersOfClusterAreStopped(clustername):
    return checkStateOfClusterMembers(clustername, "SHUTDOWN")
```

Note that for all other states (e.g. ADMIN) similar functions can be added.

The check method is based on the idea that the script will iterate over all Managed-Servers and check the state for all servers that are members of the cluster in question. Finally, the script will check if all servers are in the desired state or not.

Starting the complete cluster can be done by using the WLST *start* function:

```
################################################################
# Start the Cluster
################################################################
```

```
def startCluster(clustername):
    try:
        start(clustername,"Cluster")
    except Exception, e:
        print 'Error while starting cluster ',e
        dumpStack()
```

Stopping the cluster can be done using the *stop* function.

```
###############################################################
# Stop the Cluster
###############################################################
def shutdownCluster(clustername):
    try:
        shutdown(clustername,"Cluster")
    except Exception, e:
        print 'Error while shutting down cluster ',e
        dumpStack()
```

Often follow-up activities rely on the fact that the cluster has really been stopped and that the stop action was successful. The next implementation shows how to wait until all servers have really reached the stop state:

```
###############################################################
# Stop the Cluster and wait
###############################################################
def shutdownClusterAndWaitForShutdown(clustername):
    if checkIfAllServersOfClusterAreStopped(clustername)=='true':
        print 'Cluster is already down'
        return

    # shutdown
    shutdown(clustername,"Cluster")

    # now wait until all servers are shutdown
    currentcount = 0;

    while ((checkIfAllServersOfClusterAreStopped(clustername)=='false')  and (currentcount<30)):
        print 'Not yet all memebers of cluster in state SHUTDOWN - will wait for 10sec.';
        java.lang.Thread.sleep(10000);
        currentcount = currentcount +1;

    if (checkIfAllServersOfClusterAreStopped(clustername)=='false'):
      print 'Sorry: Could not bring cluster to SHUTDOWN state !'
```

The following code depicts an example of how the functions discussed above can be used. This code can be used to print the state, start the cluster, and finally print the state again:

```
connect('weblogic','<pw>','t3://localhost:40001')

printClusterState('MartinTest_Cluster')

startClusterAndWaitForRunning('MartinTest_Cluster')

printClusterState('MartinTest_Cluster')
```

Result:

```
Initializing WebLogic Scripting Tool (WLST) ...
Connecting to t3://localhost:40001 with userid weblogic ...
Successfully connected to Admin Server 'AdminServer' that belongs to domain 'MartinTest_Domain'.

There are 2 server(s) in cluster: MartinTest_Cluster
```

```
States of the servers are
MartinTest_Domain_MS2---SHUTDOWN
MartinTest_Domain_MS1---SHUTDOWN

Starting        the        following        servers        in        Cluster,        MartinTest_Cluster:
MartinTest_Domain_MS2,MartinTest_Domain_MS1
.................................................
All servers in the cluster MartinTest_Cluster are started successfully.
Location changed to serverRuntime tree. This is a read-only tree with DomainMBean as the root.
For more help, use help(domainConfig)

Location changed to domainRuntime tree. This is a read-only tree with DomainMBean as the root.
For more help, use help(domainRuntime)

There are 2 server(s) in cluster: MartinTest_Cluster

States of the servers are
MartinTest_Domain_MS2---RUNNING
MartinTest_Domain_MS1---RUNNING
```

Force Logfile Rotation

It might sometimes be useful to force log rotation. One possible reason might be that you need to log for investigation or you want to cleanup space and archive the logs. WLST offers a nice function to force a log rotation.

Log directory before the force rotation:

```
bash-3.2$ ls -la /logs/testdomain/AdminServer/
total 776
drwxr-x--- 2 martin martin   4096 Aug 21 16:05 .
drwxr-x--- 5 martin martin   4096 May 28 02:00 ..
-rw-r--r-- 1 martin martin 661477 Aug 18 04:07 AdminServer.err
-rw-r----- 1 martin martin   2323 Aug 21 15:45 AdminServer.log
-rw-r--r-- 1 martin martin  85248 Aug 21 02:00 AdminServer.out
-rw-r----- 1 martin martin      0 May 27 15:09 access.log
```

Calling WLST and force the log file to rotate:

```
bash-3.2$ ./bin/wlst_hist.sh
wls:/offline> connect('weblogic','<pw>','t3://localhost:7100')
Connecting to t3://localhost:7100 with userid weblogic ...
Successfully connected to Admin Server 'AdminServer' that belongs to domain 'testDomain'.

wls:/testDomain/serverConfig> serverRuntime()
Location changed to serverRuntime tree. This is a read-only tree with ServerRuntimeMBean as the root.
For more help, use help(serverRuntime)

wls:/testDomain/serverRuntime> cd('LogRuntime/AdminServer')
wls:/testDomain/serverRuntime/LogRuntime/AdminServer> ls()

-r--   Name                              AdminServer
-r--   Type                              LogRuntime
-r-x   ensureLogOpened                   Void :
-r-x   forceLogRotation                  Void :
-r-x   preDeregister                     Void :

wls:/testDomain/serverRuntime/LogRuntime/AdminServer> cmo.forceLogRotation()
wls:/testDomain/serverRuntime/LogRuntime/AdminServer> exit()
```

Log file directory after executing the above WLST commands:

```
bash-3.2$ ls -la /logs/testdomain/AdminServer/
drwxr-x--- 2 martin martin   4096 Aug 21 16:07 .
drwxr-x--- 5 martin martin   4096 May 28 02:00 ..
```

```
-rw-r--r-- 1 martin martin 661477 Aug 18 04:07 AdminServer.err
-rw-r----- 1 martin martin      0 Aug 21 16:07 AdminServer.log
-rw-r----- 1 martin martin   2323 Aug 21 15:45 AdminServer.log00001
-rw-r--r-- 1 martin martin  86670 Aug 21 16:07 AdminServer.out
-rw-r----- 1 martin martin      0 May 27 15:09 access.log
```

It is of course possible to execute the same as a WLST script instead of step-by-step commands. The following script will do the job for you:

```
def rotateServerLog(servername):
    serverRuntime()
    cd('LogRuntime/'+servername)
    cmo.forceLogRotation()
    print 'Log file of server ' + servername + ' has been rotated !'

connect('weblogic','<pw>','t3://localhost:7001')
rotateServerLog('AdminServer')
```

Datasources

The most common service on all J2EE server are datasources. Almost all J2EE applications need to store and/or retrieve data out of databases. Datasources are the service instances in a J2EE server that offer access to databases.

WebLogic offers a number of administrative tasks around databases that can be of course automated and are discussed in the subsequent sections.

As already mentioned in the create domain section, each datasource consists of a number of different MBeans. For the administration tasks, the *JDBCDataSourcRuntimeMBeans* have to be used. This MBean (see below) offers a number of operations for administration.

⊟   JDBCDataSourcRuntimeMBeans

```
wls:/MartinTest_Domain/serverRuntime/JDBCServiceRuntime/MartinTest_Domain_MS3/JDBCDataSourceRuntimeMB
eans/MyDS> ls()
dr--    JDBCDriverRuntime
dr--    LastTask
dr--    WorkManagerRuntimes

-r--    ActiveConnectionsAverageCount              0
-r--    ActiveConnectionsCurrentCount              0
-r--    ActiveConnectionsHighCount                 1
-r--    ConnectionDelayTime                        299
-r--    ConnectionsTotalCount                      4
-r--    CurrCapacity                               1
-r--    CurrCapacityHighCount                      1
-r--    DatabaseProductName                        Oracle
-r--    DatabaseProductVersion                     Oracle Database 11g Enterprise Edition Release
11.2.0.3.0 - 64bit Production
With the Partitioning, OLAP, Data Mining and Real Application Testing options
-r--    DeploymentState                            2
-r--    DriverName                                 Oracle JDBC driver
-r--    DriverVersion                              11.2.0.2.0
-r--    Enabled                                    true
-r--    FailedReserveRequestCount                  0
-r--    FailuresToReconnectCount                   0
-r--    HighestNumAvailable                        1
-r--    HighestNumUnavailable                      1
-r--    LeakedConnectionCount                      0
-r--    ModuleId                                   MyPersistentBackend
```

```
-r--    Name                                    MyPersistentBackend
-r--    NumAvailable                            1
-r--    NumUnavailable                          0
-r--    PrepStmtCacheAccessCount                0
-r--    PrepStmtCacheAddCount                   0
-r--    PrepStmtCacheCurrentSize                0
-r--    PrepStmtCacheDeleteCount                0
-r--    PrepStmtCacheHitCount                   0
-r--    PrepStmtCacheMissCount                  0
-r--    Properties
{oracle.net.wallet_location=/opt/wallets/martintest}
-r--    ReserveRequestCount                     6
-r--    State                                   Running
-r--    Type                                    JDBCDataSourceRuntime
-r--    VersionJDBCDriver                       oracle.jdbc.OracleDriver
-r--    WaitSecondsHighCount                    0
-r--    WaitingForConnectionCurrentCount        0
-r--    WaitingForConnectionFailureTotal        0
-r--    WaitingForConnectionHighCount           0
-r--    WaitingForConnectionSuccessTotal        0
-r--    WaitingForConnectionTotal               0
-r--    WorkManagerRuntimes                     null

-r-x    clearStatementCache                     Void :
-r-x    dumpPool                                Void :
-r-x    dumpPoolProfile                         Void :
-r-x    forceShutdown                           Void :
-r-x    forceSuspend                            Void :
-r-x    poolExists                              Boolean : String(name)
-r-x    preDeregister                           Void :
-r-x    reset                                   Void :
-r-x    resume                                  Void :
-r-x    shrink                                  Void :
-r-x    shutdown                                Void :
-r-x    start                                   Void :
-r-x    suspend                                 Void :
-r-x    testPool                                String :
```

Start Datasources

One very common task is starting datasources. This might be necessary after a database maintenance window during which the datasources have to be stopped in order to avoid unwanted database traffic.

The *JDBCDataSourcRuntimeMBean* of this datasource offers the method "start" in order to start the datasource.

```
allDSRuntimesOnThisServer =
destinationServerRuntime.getJDBCServiceRuntime().getJDBCDataSourceRuntimeMBeans()
# loop over the runtime mbeans and if the right datasource is found start it
for datasources in allDSRuntimesOnThisServer:
   # if desired datasource is found OR no name (=None) was provided
   if (datasourcename == datasources.getName()):
      datasources.start()
```

Stop Datasources

The contrary task - stopping a datasource - is also often needed. As mentioned earlier, this may be necessary because of a database maintenance window during which the datasources have to be stopped in order to avoid unwanted database traffic. It might also be necessary in a situation where a database error occurs and the administrator/tester wants to make sure that this problem does not occur due to parallel database access. Therefore, all datasources except the one used for testing will be stopped.

The *JDBCDataSourcRuntimeMBean* of this datasource offers the method "shutdown" in order to stop the datasource. In case a graceful stop is not possible or unwanted, a second method is provided called *forceShutdown* in order to stop a datasource immediately.

```
allDSRuntimesOnThisServer =
destinationServerRuntime.getJDBCServiceRuntime().getJDBCDataSourceRuntimeMBeans()
# loop over the runtime mbeans and if the right datasource is found start it
for datasources in allDSRuntimesOnThisServer:
   # if desired datasource is found OR no name (=None) was provided
   if (datasourcename == datasources.getName()):
       datasources.shutdown()

allDSRuntimesOnThisServer =
destinationServerRuntime.getJDBCServiceRuntime().getJDBCDataSourceRuntimeMBeans()
# loop over the runtime mbeans and if the right datasource is found start it
for datasources in allDSRuntimesOnThisServer:
   # if desired datasource is found OR no name (=None) was provided
   if (datasourcename == datasources.getName()):
       datasources.forceShutdown()
```

Test Datasources

Testing datasources is possible using the *testPool* method. In order to use this method, the test-table entry must be defined at the datasource.

```
allDSRuntimesOnThisServer =
destinationServerRuntime.getJDBCServiceRuntime().getJDBCDataSourceRuntimeMBeans()
# loop over the runtime mbeans and if the right datasource is found start it
for datasources in allDSRuntimesOnThisServer:
   # if desired datasource is found OR no name (=None) was provided
   if (datasourcename == datasources.getName()):
       datasources.testPool()
```

Target / Untarget Datasources

There are no direct methods available for targeting and untargeting datasources. Targeting means to assign the datasource to a specific server or a cluster of servers. Untargeting means to remove the datasource from this server or cluster of servers. The combination target/untarget can be used to move datasources and their pools from one server (cluster) to another server (cluster) without losing their configurations.

Untargeting is simply done by setting an empty array of MBean-References (targets) on this datasource.

```
set('Targets',jarray.array([], ObjectName))
```

Targeting the datasource to a new cluster (or servers) is done by providing a list of target MBean references. *targetType* can be either "Server" or "Cluster".

```
set('Targets',jarray.array([ObjectName('com.bea:Name='+newTarget+',Type='+targetType)], ObjectName))
```

Suspend Datasources

Datasources support a "suspend" mode. The *suspend* mode is basically a possible way for the application or the administrator to mark a datasource as disabled without shutting down the server. When a datasource is marked as suspended, applications can no longer use connections maintained by this datasource. Invocations on existing connections will result in an exception. The benefit of the suspend mode is that WebLogic will keep and maintain all connections in the data source exactly as they were before the data source was suspended.

When you use *forceSuspended*, WebLogic marks the datasource as disabled. Connections in use will be disconnected and any ongoing transaction will be rolled back.

Example for suspending the datasource with name stored in the variable *datasourcename*:

```
allDSRuntimesOnThisServer =
destinationServerRuntime.getJDBCServiceRuntime().getJDBCDataSourceRuntimeMBeans()
# loop over the runtime mbeans and if the right datasource is found start it
for datasources in allDSRuntimesOnThisServer:
    # if desired datasource is found OR no name (=None) was provided
    if (datasourcename == datasources.getName()):
        datasources.suspend()
```

Example for force suspending the datasource with name stored in the variable *datasourcename*:

```
allDSRuntimesOnThisServer =
destinationServerRuntime.getJDBCServiceRuntime().getJDBCDataSourceRuntimeMBeans()
# loop over the runtime mbeans and if the right datasource is found start it
for datasources in allDSRuntimesOnThisServer:
    # if desired datasource is found OR no name (=None) was provided
    if (datasourcename == datasources.getName()):
        datasources.forceSuspend()
```

Resume Datasources

Suspended datasources can be reactivated. WebLogic calls this *resume*. When you resume a datasource, WebLogic marks the data source as enabled and allows applications to use connections from the data source.

Example for resuming the datasource with name stored in the variable *datasourcename*:

```
allDSRuntimesOnThisServer =
destinationServerRuntime.getJDBCServiceRuntime().getJDBCDataSourceRuntimeMBeans()
# loop over the runtime mbeans and if the right datasource is found start it
for datasources in allDSRuntimesOnThisServer:
    # if desired datasource is found OR no name (=None) was provided
    if (datasourcename == datasources.getName()):
        datasources.resume()
```

Shrink Datasources

Shrinking a datasource means cleaning up unused connections that otherwise may stay open (depending on the automatic shrink settings).

For example, if you want to free up some connections after a peak period has ended, you can use the shrink operation. When you shrink a datasource, WebLogic reduces the number of connections in the pool to either the initial capacity or the number of connections currently in use (whatever is greater).

Example for shrinking the datasource with name stored in the variable *datasourcename*.

```
allDSRuntimesOnThisServer =
destinationServerRuntime.getJDBCServiceRuntime().getJDBCDataSourceRuntimeMBeans()
# loop over the runtime mbeans and if the right datasource is found start it
for datasources in allDSRuntimesOnThisServer:
    # if desired datasource is found OR no name (=None) was provided
    if (datasourcename == datasources.getName()):
        datasources.shrink()
```

Reset Datasources

Resetting a datasource means to close and recreate all available database connections in a datasource. For example, this may be necessary after the database system has been restarted.

Example for resetting the datasource with name stored in the variable *datasourcename*.

```
allDSRuntimesOnThisServer =
destinationServerRuntime.getJDBCServiceRuntime().getJDBCDataSourceRuntimeMBeans()
# loop over the runtime mbeans and if the right datasource is found start it
for datasources in allDSRuntimesOnThisServer:
    # if desired datasource is found OR no name (=None) was provided
    if (datasourcename == datasources.getName()):
        datasources.reset()
```

Comprehensive Example

All the above discussed administrative tasks for datasources have been compiled into a comprehensive example. The following example introduces a Jython class that takes a datasource name during construction ("None" can be provided for all datasources). It actually provides administrative instances of datasources. This class offers a number of methods for dealing with datasources like start/stop/resume/suspend/target/untarget. Due to its generic nature, this class can be very easily used by all readers.

🖫 datatsource_comprehensive_example

```
# -------------------------------
# CLASS for database operations
# -------------------------------
class DatasourceOperations(object):

    # Contructor which can take a datasourcename. None means all datasources
    def __init__(self, datasourcename=None):
        self.datasourcename = datasourcename


    # ----------------------- Testing ----------------------------------------

    # internal method (for testing one datasource on one specific serverruntime
    def testDatasourceOnDestinationServer(self, destinationServerRuntime):
        # get all datasource runtime mbeans
        allDSRuntimesOnThisServer = destinationServerRuntime.getJDBCServiceRuntime().
                                              getJDBCDataSourceRuntimeMBeans()

        # loop over the runtime mbeans and if the right datasource is found test it
        already_found = false
        for datasources in allDSRuntimesOnThisServer:
            # if desired datasource is found OR no name (=None) was provided
            if ((self.datasourcename==None) or (self.datasourcename == datasources.getName())):
                # print name
                print 'Datasource name is: '+datasources.getName()
                # print state
                print 'State is ' +datasources.getState()
                # test datasource pool
                print datasources.testPool()
                # remember that DS was found
                already_found = true

        if ((self.datasourcename!=None) and (already_found==false)):
            print 'Datasource '+ self.datasourcename + ' not found on server '
                  +destinationServerRuntime.getName()


    # test one specific or all (if passed None as argument) datasources of the connected server
    # note that the argment was passed to the constructor !
    def testDatasourceOnConnectedServer(self):
        # switch to server runtime
        serverRuntime()
        cd ('/')
        # call the test method with the actual (cmo) server runtime
        self.testDatasourceOnDestinationServer(cmo)


    # test one specific or all (if passed None as argument) datasources of the connected server
    # note that the argment was passed to the constructor !
    def testDatasourceOnAllServersInDomain(self):
        if (str(isAdminServer)=='true'):
            domainConfig()
            allServers = cmo.getServers()

            domainRuntime()
            for server in allServers:
                print 'Test Datasources on server: '+server.getName()
                cd ('/ServerRuntimes/'+server.getName())
                # call testDatasourceOnDestinationServer
                self.testDatasourceOnDestinationServer(cmo)
        else:
            print 'testDatasourceOnAllServersInDomain is only available '+
                  'if connected to the adminserver !'
            return


    # ----------------------- Lifecycle ---------------------------------------

    # internal method for lifecycle operations of one datasource on one specific serverruntime
    # lifecycleoperation can be 'start' or 'shutdown' or 'suspend' or 'resume'
    def lifecycleDatasourceOnDestinationServer(self, destinationServerRuntime, lifecycleoperation):
        # get all datasource runtime mbeans
        allDSRuntimesOnThisServer = destinationServerRuntime.getJDBCServiceRuntime().
                                              getJDBCDataSourceRuntimeMBeans()

        # loop over the runtime mbeans and if the right datasource is found start it
```

```
      already_found = false
      for datasources in allDSRuntimesOnThisServer:
          # if desired datasource is found OR no name (=None) was provided
          if ((self.datasourcename==None) or (self.datasourcename == datasources.getName())):
              # print name
              print 'Datasource name is: '+datasources.getName()
              # print state
              actualState = datasources.getState()
              print 'State before operation is: ' + actualState

              if ('start' == lifecycleoperation):
                  # start the server if the server is not already running
                  if (actualState != 'Running'):
                      datasources.start()
                  else:
                      print 'Datasource '+datasources.getName()+' is already running !'
              elif ('shutdown' == lifecycleoperation):
                  # stop the server if the server is not already shutdown
                  if (actualState != 'Shutdown'):
                      datasources.shutdown()
                  else:
                      print 'Datasource '+datasources.getName()+' is already stopped !'
              elif ('resume' == lifecycleoperation):
                  # resume the server if the server is not already running
                  if (actualState != 'Running'):
                      datasources.resume()
                  else:
                      print 'Datasource '+datasources.getName()+' is already running !'
              elif ('suspend' == lifecycleoperation):
                  # suspend the server if the server is not already suspended
                  if (actualState != 'Suspended'):
                      datasources.suspend()
                  else:
                      print 'Datasource '+datasources.getName()+' is already suspended !'
              else:
                  print '!!! Lifecycleoperation '+lifecycleoperation+' is not supported !'

              # print state
              print 'Datasource state is now: ' +datasources.getState()
              already_found = true

      if ((self.datasourcename!=None) and (already_found==false)):
          print 'Datasource '+ self.datasourcename + ' not found on server '
              +destinationServerRuntime.getName()


# lifecycle operations on the connected server only
def lifecycleDatasourceOnConnectedServer(self, lifecycleoperation):
   # switch to server runtime
   serverRuntime()
   cd ('/')
   self.lifecycleDatasourceOnDestinationServer(cmo, lifecycleoperation)


# lifecycle operations on all servers of the domain
def lifecycleDatasourceOnAllServersInDomain(self, lifecycleoperation):
   if (str(isAdminServer)=='true'):
      domainConfig()
      allServers = cmo.getServers()

      domainRuntime()
      for server in allServers:
         print lifecycleoperation+' all datasources on server: '+server.getName()
         try:
            cd ('/ServerRuntimes/'+server.getName())
            # call testDatasourceOnDestinationServer
            self.lifecycleDatasourceOnDestinationServer(cmo, lifecycleoperation)
         except:
            print 'Problem with server '+server.getName()
   else:
      print 'lifecycleoperationDatasourceOnAllServersInDomain('+lifecycleoperation+
            ') is only available if connected to the adminserver !'
      return

# ---------------------- SHORTCUT methods --------------------------------------

def startDatasourceOnAllServersInDomain(self):
   self.lifecycleDatasourceOnAllServersInDomain('start')
```

```
def stopDatasourceOnAllServersInDomain(self):
    self.lifecycleDatasourceOnAllServersInDomain('shutdown')

def suspendDatasourceOnAllServersInDomain(self):
    self.lifecycleDatasourceOnAllServersInDomain('suspend')

def resumeDatasourceOnAllServersInDomain(self):
    self.lifecycleDatasourceOnAllServersInDomain('resume')


def startDatasourceOnConnectedServer(self):
    self.lifecycleDatasourceOnConnectedServer('start')

def stopDatasourceOnConnectedServer(self):
    self.lifecycleDatasourceOnConnectedServer('shutdown')

def suspendDatasourceOnConnectedServer(self):
    self.lifecycleDatasourceOnConnectedServer('suspend')

def resumeDatasourceOnConnectedServer(self):
    self.lifecycleDatasourceOnConnectedServer('resume')


# ----------------------- Target / Untarget methods --------------------------------

# untarget datasource.  Note if "None" was set in the constructor, then all DS will untarget
def untargetDatasource(self):
    if (str(isAdminServer)=='true'):
        serverConfig()
        # edit mode necessary
        edit()
        startEdit()
        # get all datasource config mbeans
        allDSconfigs = cmo.getJDBCSystemResources()

        # loop over all datasources
        already_found = false
        for datasources in allDSconfigs:
            # if desired datasource is found OR no name (=None) was provided
            if ((self.datasourcename==None) or (self.datasourcename == datasources.getName())):
                # print name
                print 'Datasource name is: '+datasources.getName()
                # untarget
                cd('/JDBCSystemResources/'+datasources.getName())
                set('Targets',jarray.array([], ObjectName))
                print ' Datasource has been untargeted !'
                # remember that DS was found
                already_found = true

        if ((self.datasourcename!=None) and (already_found==false)):
            print 'Datasource '+ self.datasourcename + ' not found in this domain !'

        # activate changes
        save()
        activate()

    else:
        print 'untargetDatasource() is only available if connected to the adminserver !'
        return


# target datasource.
# Note if "None" was set in the constructor, then all DS will target to the same target
# target type can be 'Server' or 'Cluster'
def targetDatasource(self, newTarget, targetType='Cluster'):
    if (str(isAdminServer)=='true'):
        serverConfig()
        # edit mode necessary
        edit()
        startEdit()
        # get all datasource config mbeans
        allDSconfigs = cmo.getJDBCSystemResources()

        # loop over all datasources
        already_found = false
        for datasources in allDSconfigs:
```

```
                        # if desired datasource is found OR no name (=None) was provided
            if ((self.datasourcename==None) or (self.datasourcename == datasources.getName())):
                # print name
                print 'Datasource name is: '+datasources.getName()
                # target
                cd('/JDBCSystemResources/'+datasources.getName())
set('Targets',jarray.array([ObjectName('com.bea:Name='+newTarget+',Type='+targetType)], ObjectName))
                print ' Datasource has been targeted to '+targetType+' with the name '+newTarget+' !'
                # remember that DS was found
                already_found = true

        if ((self.datasourcename!=None) and (already_found==false)):
            print 'Datasource '+ self.datasourcename + ' not found in this domain !'

        # activate changes
        save()
        activate()

    else:
        print 'untargetDatasource() is only available if connected to the adminserver !'
        return
```

Note that not all operations have been implemented, but this class can easily be extended for *shrink*, *reset*, *forceShutdown*, and other methods.

First example: Test all datasources of the domain and on all servers, then start all datasources on all servers that are not yet started, and finally run the test again.

```
# test all datasources, then start all which are not started and finally test again
myDS = DatasourceOperations()
myDS.testDatasourceOnAllServersInDomain()
myDS.startDatasourceOnAllServersInDomain()
myDS.testDatasourceOnAllServersInDomain()
```

Result:

```
Connecting to t3://xxxxxx with userid weblogic ...
Successfully connected to Admin Server 'AdminServer' that belongs to domain 'MartinTest_Domain'.

Warning: An insecure protocol was used to connect to the
server. To ensure on-the-wire security, the SSL port or
Admin port should be used instead.

Location changed to serverRuntime tree. This is a read-only tree with DomainMBean as the root.
For more help, use help(domainConfig)

Location changed to domainRuntime tree. This is a read-only tree with DomainMBean as the root.
For more help, use help(domainRuntime)

Test Datasources on server: AdminServer
Test Datasources on server: MartinTest_Domain_MS1
Test Datasources on server: MartinTest_Domain_MS2
Test Datasources on server: MartinTest_Domain_MS3
Datasource name is: MyPersistentBackend
State before operation is Running
None
Test Datasources on server: MartinTest_Domain_MS4
Datasource name is: MyPersistentBackend
State before operation is Running
None

start all datasources on server: AdminServer
start all datasources on server: MartinTest_Domain_MS1
start all datasources on server: MartinTest_Domain_MS2
start all datasources on server: MartinTest_Domain_MS3
Datasource name is: MyPersistentBackend
State before operation is: Running
Datasource MyPersistentBackend is already running !
State is now: Running
```

```
start all datasources on server: MartinTest_Domain_MS4
Datasource name is: MyPersistentBackend
State before operation is: Running
Datasource MyPersistentBackend is already running !
State is now: Running

Test Datasources on server: AdminServer
Test Datasources on server: MartinTest_Domain_MS1
Test Datasources on server: MartinTest_Domain_MS2
Test Datasources on server: MartinTest_Domain_MS3
Datasource name is: MyPersistentBackend
State before operation is Running
None
Test Datasources on server: MartinTest_Domain_MS4
Datasource name is: MyPersistentBackend
State before operation is Running
None
```

Second example: Stop all datasources that are not yet stopped, and then run the test to confirm.

```
myDS = DatasourceOperations()
myDS.stopDatasourceOnAllServersInDomain()
myDS.testDatasourceOnAllServersInDomain()
```

Result:

```
Connecting to t3://xxxx with userid weblogic ...
Successfully connected to Admin Server 'AdminServer' that belongs to domain 'MartinTest_Domain'.

Warning: An insecure protocol was used to connect to the
server. To ensure on-the-wire security, the SSL port or
Admin port should be used instead.

Location changed to serverRuntime tree. This is a read-only tree with DomainMBean as the root.
For more help, use help(domainConfig)

Location changed to domainRuntime tree. This is a read-only tree with DomainMBean as the root.
For more help, use help(domainRuntime)

shutdown all datasources on server: AdminServer
shutdown all datasources on server: MartinTest_Domain_MS1
shutdown all datasources on server: MartinTest_Domain_MS2
shutdown all datasources on server: MartinTest_Domain_MS3
Datasource name is: MyPersistentBackend
State before operation is: Running
State is now: Shutdown
shutdown all datasources on server: MartinTest_Domain_MS4
Datasource name is: MyPersistentBackend
State before operation is: Running
State is now: Shutdown

Test Datasources on server: AdminServer
Test Datasources on server: MartinTest_Domain_MS1
Test Datasources on server: MartinTest_Domain_MS2
Test Datasources on server: MartinTest_Domain_MS3
Datasource name is: MyPersistentBackend
State before operation is Shutdown
Connection test failed with the following exception:
weblogic.common.resourcepool.ResourceDisabledException:  Data   Source   MyPersistentBackend   is   not
active, cannot allocate connections to applications
Test Datasources on server: MartinTest_Domain_MS4
Datasource name is: MyPersistentBackend
State before operation is Shutdown
Connection          test          failed          with          the          following          exception:
weblogic.common.resourcepool.ResourceDisabledException:  Data   Source   MyPersistentBackend   is   not
active, cannot allocate connections to applications
```

Third example: First stop all datasources and then untarget all datasources.

```
# first stop all datasources, then untarget all datasources
myDS = DatasourceOperations()
myDS.stopDatasourceOnAllServersInDomain()
myDS.testDatasourceOnAllServersInDomain()
myDS.untargetDatasource()
```

Result:

```
Connecting to t3://xxxxxxx with userid weblogic ...
Successfully connected to Admin Server 'AdminServer' that belongs to domain 'MartinTest_Domain'.

shutdown all datasources on server: AdminServer
shutdown all datasources on server: MartinTest_Domain_MS1
shutdown all datasources on server: MartinTest_Domain_MS2
shutdown all datasources on server: MartinTest_Domain_MS3
Datasource name is: MyPersistentBackend
State before operation is: Shutdown
Datasource MyPersistentBackend is already stopped !
State before operation is now: Shutdown
shutdown all datasources on server: MartinTest_Domain_MS4
Datasource name is: MyPersistentBackend
State before operation is: Shutdown
Datasource MyPersistentBackend is already stopped !
State is now: Shutdown

Test Datasources on server: AdminServer
Test Datasources on server: MartinTest_Domain_MS1
Test Datasources on server: MartinTest_Domain_MS2
Test Datasources on server: MartinTest_Domain_MS3
Datasource name is: MyPersistentBackend
State before operation is Shutdown
Connection       test       failed       with       the       following       exception:
weblogic.common.resourcepool.ResourceDisabledException:  Data  Source  MyPersistentBackend  is  not
active, cannot allocate connections to applications
Test Datasources on server: MartinTest_Domain_MS4
Datasource name is: MyPersistentBackend
State before operation is Shutdown
Connection       test       failed       with       the       following       exception:
weblogic.common.resourcepool.ResourceDisabledException:  Data  Source  MyPersistentBackend  is  not
active, cannot allocate connections to applications

Location changed to edit tree. This is a writable tree with
DomainMBean as the root. To make changes you will need to start
an edit session via startEdit().

For more help, use help(edit)
You already have an edit session in progress and hence WLST will
continue with your edit session.

Starting an edit session ...
Started edit session, please be sure to save and activate your
changes once you are done.
Datasource name is: MyPersistentBackend
 Datasource has been untargeted !
Saving all your changes ...
Saved all your changes successfully.
Activating all your changes, this may take a while ...
The edit lock associated with this edit session is released
once the activation is completed.
Activation completed
```

Fourth example: Target all datasources (which have been untargeted in the previous example) to another cluster, and finally start and then test the datasources.

```
# target all datasources to the other cluster, then start and test
myDS = DatasourceOperations()
myDS.targetDatasource('WebTier_Cluster')
myDS.startDatasourceOnAllServersInDomain()
myDS.testDatasourceOnAllServersInDomain()
```

Result:

```
Connecting to t3://xxxxxxx with userid weblogic ...
Successfully connected to Admin Server 'AdminServer' that belongs to domain 'MartinTest_Domain'.

Starting an edit session ...
Started edit session, please be sure to save and activate your
changes once you are done.
Datasource name is: MyPersistentBackend
 Datasource has been targeted to Cluster with the name WebTier_Cluster !
Saving all your changes ...
Saved all your changes successfully.
Activating all your changes, this may take a while ...
The edit lock associated with this edit session is released
once the activation is completed.
Activation completed
Location changed to serverRuntime tree. This is a read-only tree with DomainMBean as the root.
For more help, use help(domainConfig)

Location changed to domainRuntime tree. This is a read-only tree with DomainMBean as the root.
For more help, use help(domainRuntime)

start all datasources on server: AdminServer
start all datasources on server: MartinTest_Domain_MS1
Datasource name is: MyPersistentBackend
State before operation is: Running
Datasource MyPersistentBackend is already running !
State is now: Running
start all datasources on server: MartinTest_Domain_MS2
Datasource name is: MyPersistentBackend
State before operation is: Running
Datasource MyPersistentBackend is already running !
State is now: Running
start all datasources on server: MartinTest_Domain_MS3
start all datasources on server: MartinTest_Domain_MS4

Test Datasources on server: AdminServer
Test Datasources on server: MartinTest_Domain_MS1
Datasource name is: MyPersistentBackend
State before operation is Running
None
Test Datasources on server: MartinTest_Domain_MS2
Datasource name is: MyPersistentBackend
State before operation is Running
None
Test Datasources on server: MartinTest_Domain_MS3
Test Datasources on server: MartinTest_Domain_MS4
```

Notes on the 4 examples: If you carefully look at the example output, then you can see that in the first 2 examples, the datasource was only available on the servers 3 and 4; in the last example (after the retargeting), the datasource was only available on servers 1 and 2. The samples provided are actually quite common administration tasks. Whenever you have a maintenance window on your database server and you do not want to shut the complete WLS instances down, you can stop the datasources. After the maintenance window is completed, you can restart the datasources. Moving applications, and in this case datasources, to a different server or different cluster was demonstrated in examples 3 and 4.

JMS Messaging Resources

The following diagram shows the JMS Runtime MBean hierarchy, which begins at *JMSRuntimeMBean*. From this root you can navigate to all the other MBeans in the hierarchy. Some of the MBeans are long lived (as long as the service item is deployed on the server) and others are short lived. Some MBean lifecycles are managed by the administrator; others are by the application.

The complexity of JMS consists of the fact that it involves more than just the runtime state of the configuration items. It also involves the administration/browsing, management, and manipulation of the actual JMS messages themselves.

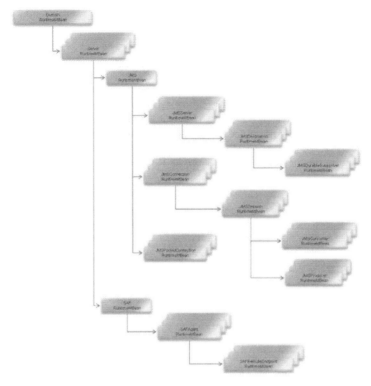

Figure 8.3: *JMS Runtime MBean tree*

Suspend / Resume

There are different scenarios possible where it is necessary to pause/suspend the message consumption or contrarily to resume message consumption. One possible real life scenario could be that the application must go into maintenance mode, and therefore this server must not consume any messages. When the application is fully functional again, the message consumption must be resumed. Another example would be that there are just too many messages at the moment and the server is building up a backlog. In this case, pausing the message consumption might give the server a chance to finish the current workload without the danger of running out of resources due to new messages coming in all the time.

WebLogic offers the JMS feature called "pause/resume messaging operations". You can change the state of the destination in question to "production paused" in WLST by invoking the command *pauseProduction()*. This will prevent new messages being delivered to that destination.

JMSServerRuntimeMBean as well as *JMSDestinationRuntimeMBean* have the methods for pausing and resuming the message processing on any given destination during runtime. When invoking these methods on the JMSServer level, it will be applied to ALL destinations that are configured on this server. If you are invoking these commands on the destination level, only the destination is affected.

The following method will put the server into pause production mode:

```
def serverPauseProduction(jmsServerName):
    # navigate to the JMSRuntime
    cd('JMSRuntime/'+jmsServerName)

    # if not already paused - call pause
    if not cmo.isProductionPaused():
        # pause all destinations on this server
        cmo.pauseProduction()
```

To resume from the pause state, the following method can be used:

```
def serverResumeProduction(jmsServerName):
    # navigate to the JMSRuntime
    cd('JMSRuntime/'+jmsServerName)

    # if paused - call resume
    if cmo.isProductionPaused():
        # resume all destinations on this server
        cmo.resumeProduction()
```

Also, destinations can be put into pause mode:

```
def destinationPauseProduction(jmsServerName, destinationName):
    # navigate to the destination
    cd('JMSRuntime/'+jmsServerName+'/Destinations/'+destinationName)

    # if not already paused - call pause
    if not cmo.isProductionPaused():
        # pause this destination
        cmo.pauseProduction()
```

To resume destinations from paused mode, use the following function:

```
def destinationResumeProduction(jmsServerName, destinationName):
    # navigate to the destination
    cd('JMSRuntime/'+jmsServerName+'/Destinations/'+destinationName)

    # if paused - call resume
    if cmo.isProductionPaused():
        # resume this destination
        cmo.resumeProduction()
```

Example for how to put the server into pause insertion mode:

```
def serverPauseInsertion(jmsServerName):
```

```
# navigate to the JMSRuntime
cd('JMSRuntime/'+jmsServerName)

# if not already paused - call pause
if not cmo.isInsertionPaused():
    # pause insertion on all destinations on this server
    cmo.pauseInsertion()
```

Activate (resume) insertion again:

```
def serverResumeInsertion(jmsServerName):
    # navigate to the JMSRuntime
    cd('JMSRuntime/'+jmsServerName)

    # if paused - call resume
    if cmo.isInsertionPaused():
        # resume insertion on all destinations on this server
        cmo.resumeInsertion()
```

Pause insertion on a specific destination:

```
def destinationPauseInsertion(jmsServerName, destinationName):
    # navigate to the destination
    cd('JMSRuntime/'+jmsServerName+'/Destinations/'+destinationName)

    # if not already paused - call pause
    if not cmo.isInsertionPaused():
        # pause this destination
        cmo.pauseInsertion()
```

Resume insertion on a specific destination:

```
def destinationResumeInsertion(jmsServerName, destinationName):
    # navigate to the destination
    cd('JMSRuntime/'+jmsServerName+'/Destinations/'+destinationName)

    # if paused - call resume
    if cmo.isInsertionPaused():
        # resume insertion on this destination
        cmo.resumeInsertion()
```

Pause consumption on all destinations on this server:

```
def serverPauseConsumption(jmsServerName):
    # navigate to the JMSRuntime
    cd('JMSRuntime/'+jmsServerName)

    # if not already paused - call pause
    if not cmo.isConsumptionPaused():
        # pause consumption on all destinations on this server
        cmo.pauseConsumption()
```

Resume consumption on all destinations:

```
def serverResumeConsumption(jmsServerName):
    # navigate to the JMSRuntime
    cd('JMSRuntime/'+jmsServerName)

    # if paused - call resume
    if cmo.isConsumptionPaused():
        # resume insertion on all destinations on this server
        cmo.resumeConsumption()
```

Pause consumption on a specific destination:

```
def destinationPauseConsumption(jmsServerName, destinationName):
    # navigate to the destination
    cd('JMSRuntime/'+jmsServerName+'/Destinations/'+destinationName)

    # if not already paused - call pause
    if not cmo.isConsumptionPaused():
        # pause this destination
        cmo.pauseConsumption()
```

Resume consumption on a specific destination:

```
def destinationResumeConsumption(jmsServerName, destinationName):
    # navigate to the destination
    cd('JMSRuntime/'+jmsServerName+'/Destinations/'+destinationName)

    # if paused - call resume
    if cmo.isConsumptionPaused():
        # resume insertion on this destination
        cmo.resumeConsumption()
```

Consider the following example: A server instance is configured to consume messages from multiple backends or send messages to different backends (=destinations). If a problematic situation occurs on this server, the administrator needs to examine the issue. If the administrator has identified that a specific backend might have a problem, it might be very helpful to pause all destinations except the one which should be examined. In this case the administrator should pause all destinations by calling pause on the JMS-server level and then call resume only on the destination which he wants to observe.

Browsing Messages

This feature of WebLogic allows you to browse through a list of messages from a queue or topic. You are able to browse through all messages (even if this is not recommended by Oracle due to possible high memory consumption of the associated cursor) or you can restrict your browsing to selected messages or to a single message. This feature is very useful if technical support people or administrators are looking in a list of messages for the source of a problem.

The *JMSServerRuntimeMBean*, *JMSDestinationRuntimeMBean* and *DurableSubscriberRuntimeMBean* provide a number of different API methods for message browsing, depending on your actual need and filtering requirements.

The following methods with respect to message browsing are available on Queue level:

```
<..>/MyTestServer_1/Destinations/testModule_1!Queue_1a> ls()
<...>
-r-x   getCursorEndPosition      Long : String(cursorHandle)
-r-x   getCursorSize             Long : String(cursorHandle)
-r-x   getCursorStartPosition    Long : String(cursorHandle)
-r-x   getItems                  CompositeData[] : String(cursorHandle),Long(start),Integer(count)
-r-x   getMessage                CompositeData : String(cursorHandle),Long(messageHandle)
-r-x   getMessage                CompositeData : String(cursorHandle),String(messageID)
-r-x   getMessage                CompositeData : String(messageID)
```

```
-r-x    getMessages              String : String(selector),Integer(timeout)
-r-x    getMessages              String : String(selector),Integer(timeout),Integer(state)
-r-x    getNext                  CompositeData[] : String(cursorHandle),Integer(count)
-r-x    getPrevious              CompositeData[] : String(cursorHandle),Integer(count)
<...>
```

The first example defines a function that will browse through all messages of a queue:

```
def printAllMessagesFromADestination(nameOfServer, jmsserver, destinationName):
    # chang to the server runtime tree
    serverRuntime()

    # select the JMSRuntime, the JMSServer and finally the destination
    cd('JMSRuntime/'+nameOfServer+'.jms/JMSServers/'+jmsserver+'/Destinations/'+destinationName)

    # we need to instanciate a cursor
    myMessageCursor=cmo.getMessages('true',9999999)

    # how many messages are available in the destination (queue or topic)
    totalAmountOfMessages=cmo.getCursorSize(myMessageCursor)

    # get all messages from the cursor starting from the beginning
    allDestinationMessages=cmo.getItems(myMessageCursor, 1, totalAmountOfMessages)

    # print all the messages' contents
    print allDestinationMessages
```

The second example will query exactly ONE message from the queue and print it:

```
def printMessageFromDestination(nameOfServer, jmsserver, destinationName, messageID):
    # chang to the server runtime tree
    serverRuntime()

    # select the JMSRuntime, the JMSServer and finally the destination
    cd('JMSRuntime/'+nameOfServer+'.jms/JMSServers/'+jmsserver+'/Destinations/'+destinationName)

    # get the message with the provided message ID
    # ID should look similiar to 'ID:<1234.1234567890>'
    myDesiredMessage=cmo.getMessage(messageID)

    # print the message
    print myDesiredMessage
```

Deleting Messages from a Queue

WebLogic offers the possibility for administrators to use WLST (or JMX) to delete messages from queues. There are many situations where this is useful, such as deleting problematic messages that cannot be executed by the server or messages that are identified to harm the server. Message deletion is supported on queues, durable subscriptions, and distributed queues. Note that it is advisable to pause a destination before issuing a delete.

```
def deleteMessageFromDestination(nameOfServer, jmsserver, destinationName, messageSelector):
    # chang to the server runtime tree
    serverRuntime()

    # select the JMSRuntime, the JMSServer and finally the destination
    cd('JMSRuntime/'+nameOfServer+'.jms/JMSServers/'+jmsserver+'/Destinations/'+destinationName)

    # if you want to delete all messages you need to pass "true" to the delete method
    # To delete all the messages pass 'true' as the first argument
    amountOfDeletedMessages = cmo.deleteMessages(messageSelector)

    # print the number of removed messages
    print amountOfDeletedMessages
```

Moving Messages to a Different Queue

WebLogic offers a very interesting feature for administrators. Admins can move messages using WLST or JMX from one destination to another. The reasons for doing so might be to reduce the load on special server, or to eliminate harmful messages without deleting them (putting them on a special queue). Moving messages has a number of restrictions. Please consult the Oracle documentation for a full list of those.

The next example shows a function that will move a number of messages based on a selector from a queue hosted on one JMS server to another queue hosted on a different JMS server.

```
def deleteMessageFromDestination(nameOfServer, jmsSourceServer, jmsTargetServer, sourceName,
targetName, messageSelector):
   # chang to the server runtime tree
   serverRuntime()

   # select the JMSRuntime, the JMSServer and finally the destination
   cd('/JMSRuntime/'+nameOfServer+'.jms")

   # first we need to get a reference to the target server and queue (=destination)
   cd (jmsTargetServer+'/Destinations/'+targetName)
   targetForMovedMessages = cmo.getDestinationInfo()

   # now we sill move to the source server and queue
   cd('/JMSRuntime/'+nameOfServer+'.jms")
   cd (jmsSourceServer+'/Destinations/'+sourceName)

   # rockn roll - let's move the messages based on selector or all if "true" is passed in
   amountOfMovedMessages=cmo.moveMessages(messageSelector,targetForMovedMessages)

   # print
   print str(amountOfMovedMessages)*' messages have been moved from '+sourceName+' to '+targetName
```

Moving messages is a transactional task, which means that all are moved or none.

Transaction Management

It sounds strange but WebLogic offers a number of methods and MBeans to work with transactions. These are of course all runtime MBeans as we are talking about active transaction management. These methods enable the user to monitor and even manage (manipulate) active transactions. Active transactions can be monitored and their outcome can be enforced (commit or rollback). According to Oracle, it is recommended that transaction outcome enforcement should be done on JTA and not JMS level.

First we need to understand what a transaction status means as this status is just an integer number.

```
From javax.transaction.Status:
    STATUS_ACTIVE          = 0;
    STATUS_MARKED_ROLLBACK = 1;
```

```
STATUS_PREPARED        = 2;
STATUS_COMMITTED       = 3;
STATUS_ROLLEDBACK      = 4;
STATUS_UNKNOWN         = 5;
STATUS_NO_TRANSACTION  = 6;
STATUS_PREPARING       = 7;
STATUS_COMMITTING      = 8;
STATUS_ROLLING_BACK    = 9;
```

Please consult the Oracle documentation for a complete picture of the supported operations. The following section will just provide some more common examples. The examples below are assuming that there are messages in the JMS system that are consumed in a "User Transaction" but not committed.

The following example will query all active JMS transaction IDs from the associated JMS server.

```
def queryAllActiveTransactions(nameOfServer, jmsserver):
    # chang to the server runtime tree
    serverRuntime()

    # select the JMSRuntime
    cd('JMSRuntime/'+nameOfServer+'.jms')

    # finally select the desired JMSServer
    cd('JMSServers/'+jmsserver)

    # query all active transactions
    allActiveTransactions=cmo.getTransactions()

    # print them (result: array of transaction IDs)
    print allActiveTransactions

    # finally return them
    return allActiveTransactions
```

When we get the list of all active transaction IDs, then we can print their status or, if provided, the status of a specific transaction. See the above list about the meaning of the status as this script will just print out the integer values.

```
# print JMS transaction status
def printJMSTransactionStatus(nameOfServer, jmsserver, transactionID):
    # get all active transaction IDs
    allActiveTransactions = queryAllActiveTransactions(nameOfServer, jmsserver)

    # if ID provided, print only this transaction, else print all
    if (transactionID==None):
        # print all
        for (nextTransactionID in allActiveTransactions:
            # get status
            nextTransactionStatus = cmo.getTransactionStatus(nextTransactionID)
            # see beginning of section for the different transaction status
            print 'Status of transaction '+nextTransactionID+' is '+ nextTransactionStatus
    else:
        # print only one:
        myTransactionStatus = cmo.getTransactionStatus(transactionID)
        # see beginning of section for the different transaction status
        print 'Status of transaction '+transactionID+' is '+ myTransactionStatus
```

Printing all messages associated with a transaction will print some information about the JMS messages, which are part of the transaction provided. Usually this can be very useful if a transaction got stuck and the administrator needs to know which messages are affected.

```
def queryAllActiveTransactions(nameOfServer, jmsserver, transactionID):
    # change to the server runtime tree
    serverRuntime()

    # select the JMSRuntime and then to the desired server
    cd('JMSRuntime/'+nameOfServer+'.jms/JMSServers/'+jmsserver)

    # create a message cursor for the provided transaction
    myTransactionMessageCursor=cmo.getMessages(transactionID,999999)

    # print the amount of messages
    amountOfMessages = cmo.getCursorSize(myTransactionMessageCursor)
    print 'The transaction '+transactionID+' has '+str(amountOfMessages)+
        ' messages associated with it'

    # print all messages
    print cmo.getItems(myTransactionMessageCursor,0,amountOfMessages)
```

Finally - as mentioned at the beginning of the section - WebLogic offers scripts that can be used to force an outcome of a transaction. The following script will force a rollback of a specific transaction.

```
# force a transaction to rollback
def forceJMSTransactionToRollback(nameOfServer, jmsserver, transactionID):
    # change to the server runtime tree
    serverRuntime()

    # select the JMSRuntime and then to the desired server
    cd('JMSRuntime/'+nameOfServer+'.jms/JMSServers/'+jmsserver)

    # force the rollback of the transaction
    cmo.forceRollback(transactionID)
```

Note that the enforcement of a commit is also possible, but I have never come across a situation in all real life customer projects where the administrator was asked to enforce a commit. Furthermore, enforcement of a commit is difficult as this depends on the overall transaction. So if another resource of this transaction will rollback, then our force to commit will not happen anyway.

JCA Connectors

JCA connectors are - like datasources - resources that are essential for the communication to external systems. The only difference is that JCA connectors are part of a J2EE application, whereas datasources are defined outside of an application on the server/domain level. Nevertheless, connectors have - similar to JDBC resources - a number of lifecycle functions. For JCA connectors, these are limited to resume and suspend. Start/stop can only be done on the application level.

The implementation is slightly different than for datasources. The main MBean, *ConnectorServiceRuntime*, contains functions to resume or suspend on one or all resource adapters. It also maintains lists of active and inactive resource adapters.

```
wls:/MartinTest_Domain/serverRuntime> cd ('ConnectorServiceRuntime/ConnectorService')
wls:/ MartinTest_Domain/serverRuntime/ConnectorServiceRuntime/ConnectorService> ls()
dr--    ActiveRAs
dr--    ConnectionPools
dr--    InactiveRAs
dr--    RAs

-r--    ActiveRACount                        2
-r--    ConnectionPoolCurrentCount           2
-r--    ConnectionPoolsTotalCount            2
-r--    Name                                 ConnectorService
-r--    RACount                              2
-r--    Type                                 ConnectorServiceRuntime

-r-x    getConnectionPool                    WebLogicMBean : String(the)
-r-x    getInboundConnections                WebLogicMBean[] : String(messageListenerType)
-r-x    getRA                                WebLogicMBean : String(jndiName)
-r-x    preDeregister                        Void :
-r-x    resume                               Void : Integer(type)
-r-x    resume                               Void : Integer(type),java.util.Properties
-r-x    resumeAll                            Void :
-r-x    resumeAll                            Void : java.util.Properties
-r-x    suspend                              Void : Integer(type)
-r-x    suspend                              Void : Integer(type),java.util.Properties
-r-x    suspendAll                           Void :
-r-x    suspendAll                           Void : java.util.Properties
```

Note that in this case suspend or resume does not mean that the full resource adapter will be suspended or resumed (this can only be done on the full application level). In this case it means that certain functions of the resource adapter will be resumed or suspended.

The "type" argument in the methods of this MBean are integer values that are defined in the WebLogic interface "weblogic.connector.extensions.Suspendable".

- ALL: Indicates that INBOUND, OUTBOUND & WORK are to be suspended/resumed.

- INBOUND: Indicates that inbound communication is to be suspended/resumed.

- OUTBOUND: indicates that outbound communication is to be suspended/resumed.

- WORK: Indicates that submission of Work is to be suspended/resumed.

So resume in the ConnectorServiceRuntimeMBean means that either all activities (resumeAll) or specific activities based on one of the above type values will be resumed. Optionally you can pass a list of properties to the resource adapter.

Suspend in the ConnectorServiceRuntimeMBean means that either all activities (suspendAll) or specific activities based on one of the above type values will be suspended. Optionally you can pass a list of properties to the resource adapter.

WTC Administration

WebLogic does not offer much in the WTC (WebLogic Tuxedo Connector) area. WTC administration offers the functionality to start/stop connections and suspend/resume services.

In WLST, it is possible to list the available administrative operations that are offered by the WTCRuntime MBean.

🖫 WTCRuntime

```
# connect to the server
connect(...)
# switch to the domain ruuntime
domainRuntime()
# switch to the WTC runtime of a managed-server
cd ('/ServerRuntimes/MS1/WTCRuntime/WTCService')
# list
ls()


-r--    Name                                    WTCService
-r--    Type                                    WTCRuntime

-r-x    getServiceStatus                        Integer :
String(java.lang.String),String(java.lang.String),String(java.lang.String)
-r-x    getServiceStatus                        Integer :
String(localAccessPoint),String(svcName)
-r-x    getServiceStatus                        Integer :
String(localAccessPoint),String(svcName),Boolean(isImport)
-r-x    getServiceStatus                        Integer : String(svcName)
-r-x    getServiceStatus                        Integer : String(svcName),Boolean(isImport)
-r-x    listConnectionsConfigured               weblogic.wtc.gwt.DSessConnInfo[] :
-r-x    preDeregister                           Void :
-r-x    resumeService                           Void :
String(localAccessPoint),String(remoteAccessPointList),String(svcName)
-r-x    resumeService                           Void : String(localAccessPoint),String(svcName)
-r-x    resumeService                           Void :
String(localAccessPoint),String(svcName),Boolean(isImport)
-r-x    resumeService                           Void : String(svcName)
-r-x    resumeService                           Void : String(svcName),Boolean(isImport)
-r-x    startConnection                         Void : String(LDomAccessPointId)
-r-x    startConnection                         Void :
String(LDomAccessPointId),String(RDomAccessPointId)
-r-x    stopConnection                          Void : String(LDomAccessPointId)
-r-x    stopConnection                          Void :
String(LDomAccessPointId),String(RDomAccessPointId)
-r-x    suspendService                          Void :
String(localAccessPoint),String(remoteAccessPointList),String(svcName)
-r-x    suspendService                          Void : String(localAccessPoint),String(svcName)
-r-x    suspendService                          Void :
String(localAccessPoint),String(svcName),Boolean(isImport)
-r-x    suspendService                          Void : String(svcName)
-r-x    suspendService                          Void : String(svcName),Boolean(isImport)
```

As you can see, WTCRuntime offers basic admin operations.

Deployment

Deployment is a very important part of an administrator's or operator's life. Deployment is to take an application created by development and host it on the

---

platform. WebLogic is essentially nothing else than a number of containers (web/ejb/resource) that are useless until applications are deployed (hosted) into those containers.

WebLogic has several different ways to deploy applications:

- Deploy applications using the Admin Console
- Deploy applications using WLST (or JMX)
- Deploy applications using ANT tasks

Overview of Deployment

WebLogic is a J2EE application Server, where you can deploy a variety of deployment units. In this case a deployment unit is a J2EE application. A J2EE application usually means an Enterprise Application (=EAR package), a Web Application (=WAR package) or a standalone J2EE module (an EJB or Resource Adapter package). A deployment package is collection of files that have been organized according to the J2EE specification, packed up in an archive (similar to a directory compressed using a compressor tool like "ZIP") and can be deployed to WebLogic Server.

For each type of deployment unit, the J2EE specification defines both the required files and their location in the respective directory structure of the application or module. Deployment units may include Java classes for EJBs and Servlets, resource adapters, Web pages and supporting files, XML-formatted deployment descriptors, and even other modules.

Oracle WebLogic Server supports deployments that are packaged either as archive files using the jar utility, or as exploded archive directories.

Oracle WebLogic Server supports three deployment methods:

- Automatic (auto)
- Console-based
- Command-based

Auto deployment is applicable when there is need of little change in the application. It is supported in development mode when a single AdminServer exists.

Naming a Deployment

Whenever you deploy a deployment artifact (like an enterprise application) to WebLogic, you have to provide a unique name for this deployment. This unique name is basically an alias for your deployment. If it is necessary to re-deploy, start or stop this deployment package then use the same application name. If you deploy a new deployment package with a name already used, then the old deployment package will be overwritten!

As stated above, a deployment will be identified using a unique name. All subsequent actions will be performed using the unique name. If no name is specified during deployment, WebLogic will choose a default name for you which is either the deployment package file name (for archived deployments) or the top-level directory (for exploded deployments).

Deployment Plan

For the deployment, we can distinguish deployments with and without a deployment plan.

A deployment plan is an optional XML document that resides outside an application archive (jar/ear). It configures an application for deployment to a specific WLS environment. This deployment plan can be created and owned by Administrators or developer for a particular environment.

Why Deployment Plan?

The deployment plan works by setting or overriding deployment property values defined in applications with WebLogic deployment descriptor.

The deployment plan is an optional deployment description, which is very helpful if the same deployment package (application) should be deployed in different WebLogic environments. In this case the same application archive can be used for all environments together with an environment-specific plan descriptor. For example: an application has database access information in the deployment descriptor (which should never be the case but in reality still occurs) and should be deployed to the environments "A", "B", and "C". Then the deployment plan describes which values have to be used for "A", which database details for "B", and which values for "C". The benefit is that for all three environments, the same application archive can be used.

Staging Modes

The staging mode of an application affects its deployment behavior. The deployment staging mode determines how deployment files are made available to target servers that must deploy an application or standalone module. The application's staging behavior is set using DeploymentOptions.setStageMode(stage mode) where the value of stage mode is one of the following:

STAGE	Force copying of files to target servers.
NO_STAGE	Files are not copied to target servers.
EXTERNAL_STAGE	Files are staged manually.

The following table describes the behavior and best practices for using the different deployment staging modes.

Staging Mode	Description
STAGE	The Administration Server first copies the deployment unit source files to the staging directories of target servers. (The staging directory is named stage by default, and it resides under the target server's root directory.) The target servers then deploy using their local copy of the deployment files.
	Applicable when the applications can be targeted to multiple WebLogic Server instances or to a cluster
No_stage	The Administration Server does not copy deployment unit files. Instead, all servers deploy using the same physical copy of the deployment files, which must be directly accessible by the Administration Server and target servers. With nostage deployments of exploded archive directories, WebLogic Server automatically detects changes to a deployment's JSPs or Servlets and refreshes the deployment. (This behavior can be disabled if necessary.)
	Deploying to a single-server domain. • Deploying to a cluster on a multi-homed machine. • Deploying very large applications to multiple targets or to a cluster where deployment files are available on a shared directory. • Deploying exploded archive directories that you want to periodically redeploy after changing content. • Deployments that require dynamic update of elected Deployment Descriptors via the Administration Console
EXTERNAL_STAGE	The Administration Server does not copy deployment files. Instead, the Administrator must ensure that deployment files are distributed to the correct staging directory location before deployment. With external_stage deployments, the AdminServer requires a copy of the deployment files for validation purposes. Copies of the deployment files that reside in target servers' staging directories are not validated before deployment.
	Deployments where you want to manually control the distribution of deployment files to target servers. • Deploying to domains where third-party applications or scripts manage the copying of deployment files to the correct staging directories. • Deployments that do not require dynamic update of selected Deployment Descriptors via the Administration Console • Deployments that do not require partial redeployment of application components

(Source: Oracle Corporation[15])

Table 8.1: Deployment Staging Modes

---

[15] docs.oracle.com/middleware/1212/wls/DEPGD/deploy.htm

WLST and Deployment

As always, deployment should always be a reproducible process, therefore the WLST/JMX method is the preferred way. In this chapter we will concentrate on the WLST deployment

WLST offers a number of predefined functions for applications and application deployment.

WLST function	Description
'deploy'	Deploys an application to a WebLogic Server instance. The deploy command returns a WLSTProgress object that you can access to check the status of the command. In the event of an error, the command returns a WLSTException. Syntax: deploy(appName, path, [targets], [stageMode], [planPath], [options])
'distributeApplication'	Copies the deployment bundle to the specified targets. The deployment bundle includes module, configuration data, and any additional generated code. The distributeApplication command does not start deployment. The distributeApplication command returns a WLSTProgress object that you can access to check the status of the command. In the event of an error, the command returns a WLSTException. Syntax: distributeApplication(appPath, [planPath], [targets], [options])
'getWLDM'	Returns the WebLogic DeploymentManager object. You can use the object methods to configure and deploy applications. WLST must be connected to an Administration Server to run this command. In the event of an error, the command returns a WLSTException. Syntax: getWLDM()
'listApplications'	Lists all applications that are currently deployed to the domain. In the event of an error, the command returns a WLSTException. NOTE that this command will list the application names to stdout. Unfortunately this command will NOT return a list of names. Syntax: listApplications()
'loadApplication'	Load an application and deployment plan Loads an application and deployment plan into memory. The loadApplication command returns a WLSTPlan object that you can access to make changes to the deployment plan. In the event of an error, the command returns a WLSTException. Syntax: loadApplication(appPath, [planPath], [createPlan])
'redeploy'	Reloads classes and redeploys a previously deployed application. The redeploy command returns a WLSTProgress object that you can access to check the status of the command. In the event of an error, the command returns a WLSTException.

	Syntax: redeploy(appName, [planPath], [options])
'startApplication'	Starts an application, making it available to users. The application must be fully configured and available in the domain. The startApplication command returns a WLSTProgress object that you can access to check the status of the command. In the event of an error, the command returns a WLSTException. Syntax: startApplication(appName, [options])
'stopApplication'	Stops an application, making it unavailable to users. The application must be fully configured and available in the domain. The stopApplication command returns a WLSTProgress object that you can access to check the status of the command. In the event of an error, the command returns a WLSTException. Syntax: stopApplication(appName, [block], [timeout])
'undeploy'	Undeploys an application from the specified servers. The undeploy command returns a WLSTProgress object that you can access to check the status of the command. In the event of an error, the command returns a WLSTException. Syntax: undeploy(appName, [targets], [block], [subModuleTargets], [timeout])
'updateApplication'	Update an application configuration using a new deployment plan.

(Source: Oracle Corporation[16])

Table 8.2: WLST Application Functions

Utility Functions Working with Applications

In order to concentrate on the main aspects in the following sections, I have "outsourced" a number of useful helper functions. The following function definitions define useful tools for working with applications and deployment.

Whenever you want to do something with an application (monitoring, deploying, undeploying, start/stop, etc.) it is a good practice to check whether this application is deployed at all in this domain. Note that this script does NOT check if the application is deployed on the current server, it only checks if an application with this name is known to the domain

```
def isApplicationDeployedToDomain(applicationName):
    # get all installed applications
    allInstalledApplicatons=cmo.getAppDeployments()

    # iterator over those applications and compare the name with the provided name
    for nextApplication in allInstalledApplicatons:
        if ( applicationName == nextApplication.getName()):
            return true

    # oh oh nothing found - means false
    return false
```

---

[16] docs.oracle.com/middleware/1212/wls/WLSTC/reference.htm

The following function will create a list of names of all known applications. Again, this lists the names of all applications known to the domain, regardless of which target they are deployed. This is useful for checking names or creating selection menus (for interactive scripts).

```
def getNamesOfAllDeployedApplication():
    listOfDeployedApplicationNames = []

    # get all installed applications
    allInstalledApplicatons=cmo.getAppDeployments()

    # iterator over those applications and compare the name with the provided name
    for nextApplication in allInstalledApplicatons:
        listOfDeployedApplicationNames.append(nextApplication.getName())

    # return list
    return listOfDeployedApplicationNames
```

Starting/Stopping Applications

Applications can be started and stopped. Start/stop does not mean that the application will be deployed or undeployed. Stop means that the application will stop serving customer requests. Start means that the application will start serving customer requests.

Example: In all production environments there are maintenance windows. It might be possible that one Managed-Server hosts a number of applications (however, I would not recommend this as it almost always causes a number of unwanted problems). In this case it might be possible that one application connects to the database doing CRUD (create read update delete) operations while others provide a GUI front end. If the database has to go into maintenance, then the administrators can use the *stopApplication* operation to stop all application parts that are talking to the database (they also can stop the datasource). When the database is available again, they can start the datasources and finally the applications.

Starting applications:

```
progress=startApplication("myTestApplication", block='true')
progress.printStatus()
```

Stopping applications:

```
progress=stopApplication("myTestApplication", block='true')
progress.printStatus()
```

Applications without a Deployment Plan

Deployment without a deployment plan means that the deployment descriptors must have all environment-specific values defined in it. The deployment process will just copy and install the provided application files without modifications.

Applications can be redeployed and deployments can be overwritten. The safest way (depending as always on your application requirements like 24x7) to do a deployment is to undeploy the previous application version before deploying the new version. Before you undeploy an application, you should stop it.

The following script will clean up a WebLogic domain, stop, and then undeploy all applications:

```
def stopAndUndeployAllApplicationsFromDomain():
    # go to the domain config tree
    domainConfig()

    # get list of applications
    myApplicationNames = getNamesOfAllDeployedApplication()

    # go back to domainRuntime
    domainRuntime()

    # iterator over list and undeploy
    for nextApplication in myApplicationNames:
        print 'Stop application '+nextApplication
        # stopApplication(appName, [block], [timeout])
        progress=stopApplication(nextApplication, block='true')
        print 'Now undeploy application '+nextApplication
        # undeploy(appName, [targets], [block], [subModuleTargets], [timeout])
        progress=undeploy(nextApplication, block='true')
        print 'Finished\n'
```

Note that this script will stop and undeploy all applications of this domain.

```
#################################################################
# deploy all applications
#################################################################
def deployAllApplications():
    try:
        amountOfDeployments=domainProps.get("amountDeployments")
        print 'Am:',amountOfDeployments

        print 'Deploy all applications ....'
        i=1
        while (i <= int(amountOfDeployments)) :
            try:
                applicationName = get_instance_property('deployment',str(i),'applicationname');
                sourcepath = get_instance_property('deployment',str(i),'sourcepath');
                deploymentOrderSetting =
                        get_instance_property('deployment',str(i),'deploymentOrder');
                targetsSetting = get_instance_property('deployment',str(i),'targets');

                print 'Start deployment of '+applicationName+' ('+sourcepath+') ';
                deploy(appName=applicationName, path=sourcepath,
                        targets=targetsSetting, upload='true');
            except:
                print '***** deployment of '+applicationname+' ('+sourcepath+') FAILED !';
                print ''
            i = i + 1
    except:
        print 'Exception while deploying all applications !';
        dumpStack();
```

Note that this script will undeploy everything. In case you want to undeploy only a specific application, you have to modify this script in order to take the application name as an argument and stop/undeploy only the desired application.

```
def stopAndUndeployAllApplicationsFromDomain(applicationToUndeploy):
    # go to the domain config tree
```

```
    domainConfig()

    print 'Stop application '+ applicationToUndeploy
    # stopApplication(applicationToUndeploy, [block], [timeout])
    progress=stopApplication(applicationToUndeploy, block='true')
    print 'Now undeploy application '+ applicationToUndeploy
    # undeploy(applicationToUndeploy, [targets], [block], [subModuleTargets], [timeout])
    progress=undeploy(applicationToUndeploy, block='true')
    print 'Finished\n'
```

Note that this application will undeploy the application regardless on which target it is deployed. The undeploy method also knows about the parameter "targets" that let you specify from which target you want to undeploy the application in question.

Applications with a Deployment Plan

A WebLogic Server deployment plan is an optional XML file that configures an application for deployment. The basic idea is that the plan will define property values that would normally be defined in the WebLogic deployment descriptors. It might also overwrite existing values. This means that values defined by developers without knowledge of the destination environment can be overwritten at deployment time by plan values defined by administrators. Deployment plans help administrators to easily modify application deployments to be deployed into to multiple, different WebLogic environments without modifying the packaged WebLogic Server deployment descriptor files. Administrators deploying an application only have to modify the deployment plan. The big benefit is that the original deployment files remain unchanged. It is possible to use a single deployment plan (preferred!) if you know all your environments well. You also may use multiple deployment plans.

Deploy and Deployment Plan Operations

WLST offers a number of deployment operations that can also work with deployment plans. This section will introduce two of them: *loadApplication* and *redeploy*.

loadApplication: This WLST method loads an application and, optionally, a deployment plan into memory and returns a WLSTPlan object that you can use to access and make changes.

The following script loads the myTestApp and its plan into memory and returns a plan object (an object representing a deployment plan) that can be used for various actions.

```
wls:/MartinTest_Domain/serverConfig> appPlan=loadApplication('/opt/application/myTestApp.jar',
'/opt/application/plan.xml')
wls:/MartinTest_Domain/serverConfig> appPlan.showVariables()
```

redeploy: This method allows you to redeploy a previously-deployed application and returns a WLSTProgress instance, which can be used to print the status of the action.

Redeploy example:

```
redeployProgress=redeploy('myTestApp' '/opt/application/plan.xml')
print redeployProgress.getState()
```

Deploy All Applications from a Directory

In order to write deployment scripts that are even more flexible, the following approach can be the solution. Imagine the situation that a production environment has a special folder for each application or environment or whatever grouping of deployment is required. Then it is possible to write a WLST script which can
a)   undeploy all deployed applications,
b)   examine this folder and search for all applications (e.g. all EAR files), and
c)   deploy all EAR files.

Example script:

```
# deploy all applications from deployments directory
def deployAllApplicationsFromDeploymentDirectory(domainName, deploymentsDir, targetCluster):
    try:
        print 'Deploy all EARs for domain '+domainName+' FROM the deployment directory ....'


        for file in os.listdir(deploymentsDir):
            if fnmatch.fnmatch(file, '*.ear'):
                try:
                    sourcefile = deploymentsDir + pathSeparator + file
                    applicationName = file.replace('.ear','').replace('.EAR','')

                    # default = 100
                    deploymentOrderSetting = '100'

                    print '    Start deployment of '+applicationName+
                          ' ('+sourcefile+') for domain '+domainName+' ....'
                    deploy(appName=applicationName, path=sourcefile,
                           targets=targetCluster, upload='true');

                    print '    FINISHED deployment of '+applicationName+
                          ' ('+sourcefile+') for domain '+domainName+' ....\n'

                except:
                    print '    ***** deployment of '+applicationname+' ('+sourcefile+') FAILED !';
                    print ''


    except:
        print 'Exception while deploying all applications for domain '+domainName+' .... !'
        dumpStack();
```

Advantages of this script:

▪   Just drop a new version of this application into this folder. The name of the EAR is not important. Many companies like to have the version number as part of the EAR file name. This is no problem but you need to remember to delete the old version, otherwise the script will try to deploy both versions which is not possible!

▪   Very static and stable script code.

Disadvantages of this approach:

- No deployment order can be specified.

Deploy Directly to the Filesystem

One possible direct deployment would be to just copy the new ear file to a staging location and restart the servers by clearing up the /tmp/cache/stage of Managed-Servers. This will fetch the same result of deploying the new EAR.

While this is an easy and fast approach without WLST or JMX for small and/or controlled domains, my experience from many production environments tells me that there are also many potential issues and disadvantages with this approach.

Potential disadvantages that should not be forgotten include:

- You need access to all the machines.

- You need write access to all the file systems on all the machines.

- For bigger and distributed domains, this approach is more error prone (due to many machines) than a normal WLST or JMX deployment.

- You need domain (or at least Managed-Server) restart.

- In bigger organizations, admin and deployers are often two different groups and therefore the necessary permissions are not given to deployers.

- You have no audit trail in the WebLogic Server logs.

- Deployment can easily be scripted in a WLST script, ant/maven task, and JMX code, even for remote domains where you do not have machine access. But what about your approach if a domain is spread over multiple machines?

- You need a script that has access to several file systems on several hosts, SSH keys++ must be correctly in place, and the network and machines must be reachable.

Side By Side Deployment

It is sometimes necessary to deploy a new version of a software side-by-side with the old version. There are several situations where this might be necessary. One common situation is a 24x7 application with no down time requirement. If you cannot deploy server by server - which means take one server after the other offline for deployment without interrupting the overall application - then it is possible to use side-by-side deployment so that all new connections will already use the new version and only the already-connected clients will use the old version. Of course this task - which most likely has to happen on a (larger) number of servers - can be automated using WLST.

To do this interesting task, the plan for execution is prepared as follows while doing the deployment criteria:

- If the application is new and the version is new (i.e. no other version is in the ACTIVE state with the given appName) the script will deploy the application.

- If one of the versions of the given application is in the ACTIVE state and therefore visible in the console, when the administrator tries to deploy the next version, the script should deactivate the old version and deploy the new version.

- Given that there are already two versions deployed on the domain, one in an ACTIVE state and the other in a RETIRED state, undeploy the RETIRED version with a timeout interval or deploy the new version so that it will make current ACTIVE application to RETIRED and new deployment to ACTIVE.

For implementing the above logic in chronological way, the real challenge lies in the ISSUE with iterations. It is controlled by a *break* statement (still known from good old C programming). In the following example, the flag variable *appFlags* has been used to indicate the status of the application so that we are able to maintain two versions max in the console of the same app.

💾 deploy_applications

```
import sys
#=====================================================
# Function for fresh plain deployment
#=====================================================
def newDeploy(appName,ver):
    print 'Deploying ........'
    deploy(appName,'/path/applications/'+appName+'/'+ver , targets='AdminServer')
    startApplication(appName)

#=====================================================
# Function for finding the  Application Status
#=====================================================
def appstatus(appName, serverName):
    cd('domainRuntime:/AppRuntimeStateRuntime/AppRuntimeStateRuntime')
    #get current real state for app in specific server
    currentState = cmo.getCurrentState(appName, serverName)
    return currentState
#=====================================================
# Undeploy the given application
# Target we can change according to domain and application deployed on
#=====================================================
def unDeploy(appName):
    print 'stopping and undeploying ....'
    stopApplication(appName, targets='AdminServer')
    undeploy(appName, targets='AdminServer')


#=====================================================
# Main program here...
# Target you can change as per your need
#=====================================================
appName = sys.argv[1]
ver     = sys.argv[2]
user    = sys.argv[3]
passwd  = sys.argv[4]
adminurl= sys.argv[5]
```

```
connect(user, passwd, adminurl)
cd('AppDeployments')
appflag=0
y=ls(returnMap='true')
for i in y :
    if i.startswith(appName )  ==1:
        #Checking for the application existence)
        print i
        print appstatus(i,'AdminServer')

if appstatus(i,'AdminServer')=='STATE_RETIRED' :
    appflag=1
    break
elif appstatus(i,'AdminServer')=='STATE_ACTIVE':
    appflag=2
else:
    print ' other Applications are Running '
    pass


if appflag == 1 :
    print 'application having RETIERED STATE ..'
    unDeploy(i)
    print appstatus(i,'AdminServer')
    newDeploy(appName,ver)
    print appstatus(i,'AdminServer')
elif appflag== 2:
    print 'Application exists in ACTIVE state...'
    newDeploy(appName,ver)
    print appstatus(i,'AdminServer')
else:
    print 'new application'
```

When this script is being used in your own environment, note that the targeting of the application (in this case AdminServer only) most likely will vary as in a production domain there should never be an application deployed to the AdminServer. AdminServer deployment is usually only used in development environments. In production or production-similar environments, applications are usually always targeted to a cluster or at least a Managed-Server.

Subdeployment

Normally almost all applications are targeted as a whole to either a cluster or a server (unlikely to a list of servers). This means that the target defined for the application is also used (inherited) for all components.

There are rare cases where it might be necessary to target a part (component) of an application to a different target. This of course is only available for WAR/EJB/RAR modules that are located inside an EAR. The EAR will be deployed with a special target and during deployment - or later - one or multiple components will be targeted differently than the EAR application.

Reasons for doing this may include:

- One component is a web service that has special security requirements and will therefore be targeted to virtual hosts connected to different - more secure - network channels (see the following example).

- One component is a web service that must be accessible from a different network (e.g. administration web service).

- The EJB components should never be invoked directly by external clients. External clients must always use the web services that are also part of the EAR application. This can be easily achieved by using only local interfaces for the EJBs. However, it might be necessary to make direct calls to these EJBs available for batches or administrative tasks using another network.

The following example consists of an EAR application that contains three WAR modules. The domain consists of one cluster with two Managed-Servers. Each Managed-Server has an additional network channel and a virtual host, which is only connected to the additional network channel. The goal will be to target one of the modules (named VH1) not to the cluster but to all virtual hosts. The reason for introducing virtual hosts is the fact that WebLogic can target Web Applications (WAR) only to a server, cluster, or virtual hosts.

Situation: The EAR application is already deployed and completely targeted to the cluster. Now we need a script to re-target one component to the two virtual hosts.

```
# connecto to the admin server
connect('weblogic','< pw >','t3://localhost:7100')

# start an edit session
edit()
startEdit()

# go the application deployments section and here to the application in question
cd ('/AppDeployments/vhtest')

# create a subdeployment for the module (in this case VH1)
cmo.createSubDeployment('VH1')

# change to the subdeployment
cd('SubDeployments/VH1')

# define the targets for this subdeployment
set('Targets',jarray.array([ObjectName('com.bea:Name=MyVirtualHost_MS1,Type=VirtualHost'),
    ObjectName('com.bea:Name=MyVirtualHost_MS2,Type=VirtualHost')], ObjectName))

# save changes and activate them
save()
activate()
```

After this script has been executed, it is possible to examine the result in the MBean tree under "/AppDeployments/vhtest/…". WebLogic also offers an alternative way by looking at the application runtime state information. The above script has changed the application configuration. The real-life state can be queried from the *AppRuntimeStateRuntime* MBean.

IMPORTANT: This MBean reflects the actual state of the application. Even if the above script has been executed and the "AppDeployments" section shows the right content, this does not mean that the life state has already changed. This will be demonstrated in the following sequence of WLST commands.

```
wls:/testDomain/domainRuntime/AppRuntimeStateRuntime/AppRuntimeStateRuntime> ls()

-r--    ApplicationIds                          java.lang.String[vhtest]
-r--    Name                                    AppRuntimeStateRuntime
-r--    Type                                    AppRuntimeStateRuntime

-r-x    getCurrentState                         String :
String(appid),String(moduleid),String(subModuleId),String(target)
-r-x    getCurrentState                         String :
String(appid),String(moduleid),String(target)
-r-x    getCurrentState                         String : String(appid),String(target)
-r-x    getIntendedState                        String : String(appid)
-r-x    getIntendedState                        String : String(appid),String(target)
-r-x    getModuleIds                            String[] : String(appid)
-r-x    getModuleTargets                        String[] : String(appid),String(moduleid)
-r-x    getModuleTargets                        String[] :
String(appid),String(moduleid),String(subModuleId)
-r-x    getModuleType                           String : String(appid),String(moduleid)
-r-x    getRetireTimeMillis                     Long : String(appid)
-r-x    getRetireTimeoutSeconds                 Integer : String(appid)
-r-x    getSubmoduleIds                         String[] : String(appid),String(moduleid)
-r-x    isActiveVersion                         Boolean : String(appid)
-r-x    isAdminMode                             Boolean : String(appid),String(java.lang.String)
-r-x    preDeregister                           Void :

wls:/testDomain/domainRuntime/AppRuntimeStateRuntime/AppRuntimeStateRuntime>
cmo.getModuleIds('vhtest')
array(java.lang.String,['default', 'VH1', 'VH2'])
wls:/testDomain/domainRuntime/AppRuntimeStateRuntime/AppRuntimeStateRuntime>
cmo.getModuleTargets('vhtest','VH1')
array(java.lang.String,['MyCluster'])
wls:/testDomain/domainRuntime/AppRuntimeStateRuntime/AppRuntimeStateRuntime>
cmo.getSubmoduleIds('vhtest','VH1')
array(java.lang.String,[])
```

Note that the command *cmo.getModuleTargets('vhtest','VH1')* still returns the cluster name. Now let us restart the application (or the Managed-Servers). After the restart has been completed, return to the same MBean and issue the command again:

```
wls:/testDomain/domainRuntime/AppRuntimeStateRuntime/AppRuntimeStateRuntime>
cmo.getModuleTargets('vhtest','VH1')
array(java.lang.String,['PrivateVirtualHost_MS1', 'PrivateVirtualHost_MS2'])
wls:/testDomain/domainRuntime/AppRuntimeStateRuntime/AppRuntimeStateRuntime>
```

This time the result is as expected as the state has been updated because of the restart of the application (or Managed-Server).

It is always advisable to use a script that will check if the module is already targeted to the desired destinations. The following script will check if "VH1" is already targeted to the two virtual hosts. If yes, it will not do anything, otherwise it will do the re-targeting.

💾 check_module_targeting

```
import jarray

def retargetApplicationComponent(appName, componentName, newTargetListNames, newTargetListTypes):
    # switch to domain runtime
    domainRuntime()

    # go to app runtime state
    cd ('/AppRuntimeStateRuntime/AppRuntimeStateRuntime')

    # check if appName is in the list of known applications
    appIDs = cmo.getApplicationIds() # ApplicationIds - java.lang.String[vhtest]
    if not (appName in appIDs):
```

```
            print 'PROBLEM:  Application ' + appName + ' is unknown !'
            return

    # get the modules of application
    myModules = cmo.getModuleIds(appName)

    # check if module exists in application
    if not (componentName in myModules):
        print 'PROBLEM:  Module '+componentName+' does not exist in application ' + appName + ' !'
        return

    # ok application and component exist - therefore go ahead

    # test if exactly all targets are already configured
    allDone = true
    myCurrentTargets = cmo.getModuleTargets('vhtest','VH1')
    print 'Actual Targets: ' , myCurrentTargets

    for index, value in enumerate(newTargetListNames):
        print ' ... checking ' , value
        if not (value in myCurrentTargets):
            allDone = false

    # check if current target list is longer than new target list
    if len(myCurrentTargets) > len(newTargetListNames):
        allDone = false

    if allDone:
        print 'The module '+componentName+' is already targeted to the desired list of targets - no
retarget necessary !'
        return

    # ok - this means we need to retarget :-(

    # start edit session
    edit()
    startEdit()

    # go to app deployments configuration
    cd ('/AppDeployments/vhtest')

    # create subdeployment for module and ignore exception if already exist
    try:
        cmo.createSubDeployment('VH1')
    except:
        print 'Ignore submodule creation exception:  please check if submodule already exists'

    # go to the subdeployment
    cd('SubDeployments/VH1')

    # create new array with target ObjectNames
    targetsForDeployment = []

    # convert the argument lists into a Obe´jectName array
    for index, value in enumerate(newTargetListNames):
        nextName =str('com.bea:Name='+value+',Type='+newTargetListTypes[index])
        targetsForDeployment.append(ObjectName(nextName))

    # finally set the targets
    set('Targets',jarray.array(targetsForDeployment, ObjectName))

    # save changes and activate
    save()
    activate()

    # back to domain runtime
    domainRuntime()

    print 'Retarget of '+componentName+' is done !'

if __name__ == "main":
    # connect to the server
    connect('weblogic','<pw>','t3://localhost:7100')

    # retarget
    retargetApplicationComponent('vhtest', 'VH1', ['MyVirtualHost_MS1','MyVirtualHost_MS2'],
                                 ['VirtualHost','VirtualHost'])
```

```
print '\nScript has finished successfully '
```

This function consults the runtime MBean server for the actual runtime configuration and targeting of the applications and their modules. Then the function will check if the module is already targeted to the desired targets. If this is not the case then this method will do the re-targeting.

In order to re-target the module to two servers (instead of two virtual hosts), it is only possible to change the function call to:

```
retargetApplicationComponent('vhtest', 'VH1', ['MS1','MS2'], ['Server','Server'])
```

Note that this script will use MBeans and information from different locations and also from different MBeans (runtime, configuration and edit MBean tree).

List Application Paths

It might be interesting to find out where on the file system the different application files (EAR, WAR, etc.) are located. The actual locations can also be queried from the MBean tree.

List the different deployments:

```
domainConfig()
ls('/AppDeployments')
```

Get the path where this application file is located on the file system:

```
cd('/AppDeployments/<app name>')
print cmo.getAbsoluteSourcePath()
```

If a deployment plan is used, this can also be queried from this MBean and in this case also where the plan is located.

Extended Local Deployment

Another approach for deploying with WLST is shown in the following example provided by Pavan. The following deployment script uses functions from the "os" system library to outsource some tasks to the operating system instead of implementing them in Jython. Please keep in mind that this script will only run on the AdminServer machine as it needs filesystem access. If your deployment server is also the server where the AdminServers are running (rather unusual in big and complex environments, but possible) then this script can be handy.

💾 extended_deployment

```
import os
import time
import sys
from java.util import Date
from java.text import SimpleDateFormat

# define global variables and constants
t = Date()
today=SimpleDateFormat("dd_MMM_HH:mm").format(Date())
user=sys.argv[1]
URL=sys.argv[2]
src="/home/"+user+"/CODE/"
bksrc="/home/"+user+"/CODE_"
dpath="/home/domains/wd"+user
ECODE='\033[0m \n'
G='\033[1;40;32m'
R='\033[1;40;31m'
deploylist=['a_ejb.jar','a_adapter.jar','b_adapter.jar','c.war']

# define the modular functions

def backup():
    try:
        #Creating the Backup with Date And Time
        command = "cp -R "+src+" "+bksrc+today
        os.system(command)
    except:
        print R+'   Code Backup FAILED!! '+ECODE
        print dumpStack()

def getCode():
    try:
            # GETTING THE Fresg Code from build location
            os.system('scp user@hostname:/home/user/Code_Ioc/*.*ar '+src)
            print G+'    THE CODE COPIED SUCCESSFULLY  '+ECODE
    except:
            print R+'    THE CODE COPYING FAILED?!?!?'+ECODE
            print dumpStack()
            exit()
def conn():
    try:
            # CONNECTING TO THE SERVER ....
            connect(userConfigFile=UCF, userKeyFile=UKF, url=URL)
    except:
            print R+'  CONNECTION FAILED....',+ECODE
            print dumpStack()
            exit()
def editing():
        edit()
        startEdit()

def activating():
    save()
    activate()

def stoppingApp():
    deploylist.reverse()
    for s in deploylist:
        try:
            editing()
            progress=stopApplication(s,timeout=360000)
            progress.printStatus()
            activating()
        except:
            print R+'  FAILED TO STOP THE APPLICATION  '+ECODE
            print dumpStack()

    print G+'  APPLICATION STOPPED  '+ECODE

def pUndeploy():
    deploylist.reverse()
    for s in deploylist:
        try:
                editing()
                progress=undeploy(s, timeout=360000)
                progress.printStatus()
```

```
                activating()
        except:
                print R+'  FAILED TO UNDEPLOY THE APPLICATION  '+ECODE
                print dumpStack()
    print G+'  APPLICATION UNDEPLOYED   '+ECODE

# This module is optional
def clearCache():
        try:
                print G+'  CLEARING THE CACHE   '+ECODE
                command = "rm -rf "+dpath+"/servers/"+user+"/tmp/*.*"
                os.system(command)
                print G+'  CLEARED THE CACHE     '+ECODE
        except:
                print R+'  FAILED TO CLEAR CACHE '+ECODE

def pDeploy():
    for s in deploylist:
        try:
                editing()
                progress=deploy(s,src+s,target=user,timeout=360000)
                progress.printStatus()
                activating()
        except:
                print R+'FAILED TO DEPLOY THE APPLICATION'+ECODE
                print dumpStack()
    print G+'  APPLICATION DEPLOYED   '+ECODE

def startingApp():
    for s in deploylist:
        try:
                editing()
                startApplication(s,timeout=360000)
                activating()
        except:
                print R+'FAILED TO START THE APPLICATION '+ECODE
    print G+'APPLICATION STARTED SUCCESSFULLY '+ECODE

if __name__ == "main":
        backup()
        getCode()
        conn()
        stoppingApp()
        pUndeploy()
        clearCache()
        pDeploy()
        startingApp()
        print G+' ....DEPLOYMENET DONE...'+ECODE
```

Summary

This chapter has discussed many different day-to-day actions in an administrator's life in the areas of lifecycle tasks. We have learned how to administer server instances, clusters, and whole domains. We have also discussed how to control services such as datasources and JMS. Finally, we looked at different methods to deploy applications.

All the tasks discussed in this chapter are not monitoring tasks because all of them will change the status or even content of the domains.

Monitoring Domains with WLST

Monitoring Domains with WLST

In the last few chapters we discussed various automation features for constructing domains, configuring domains, and extending domains. In the last chapter we added daily operator and deployer tasks to our automation toolbox. This chapter is all about monitoring. Monitoring involves observing and collecting data for real-time or later analysis. Among all tasks, automation the monitoring tasks add the biggest value for administrators as monitoring is a collection of processes and procedures which a) highly depend on the needs of the actual applications, b) requires that exactly the same steps are performed over and over again, and c) have strict time requirements for when and how often certain tasks must be performed. Without automation, monitoring is practically impossible.

Health and State Information

WebLogic has two special values that are used in many different MBeans. These two values are very often used in monitoring. One is the "state" and the other is the *healthstate* attribute.

Dealing with Health State

Different MBeans return heath state information. This information is provided in a WebLogic proprietary class *weblogic.health.HealthState*. If you print out the return value, you will find numbers associated with each state that are difficult for humans to read and remember. Therefore, the following little function is very useful to translate the health state returned from WebLogic into something that can be written to a log file.

```
def getHealthStateInformation(myState):  # is of type weblogic.health.HealthState
    if(myState.getState()==weblogic.health.HealthState.HEALTH_OK):
        return "HEALTH_OK";
    elif(myState.getState()==weblogic.health.HealthState.HEALTH_WARN):
        return "HEALTH_WARN";
    elif(myState.getState()==weblogic.health.HealthState.HEALTH_CRITICAL):
        return "HEALTH_CRITICAL";
    elif(myState.getState()==weblogic.health.HealthState.HEALTH_FAILED):
        return "HEALTH_FAILED";
    elif(myState.getState()==weblogic.health.HealthState. HEALTH_OVERLOADED):
        return "HEALTH_OVERLOADED";
    else:
```

```
                return "UNKNOWN STATE";
```

State Information

Similar to health state, WebLogic uses state information like RUNNING, ADMIN, FAILED, SHUTDOWN, and others on various occasions. The different states and transitions have been discussed in the previous chapter (Administration Tasks using WLST).

Domain/Server Monitoring

One of the most common monitoring tasks is monitoring the state of the domains and its Managed-Servers. Monitoring state means monitoring the health of the servers themselves and also the deployed applications. Each server has many different values that might be considered for a state. This includes memory settings, transaction queues, connections, JDBC connections, or availability of services. These are important for your application depending on your application requirements.

Server State

The "state" of a server can be defined with a number of different values. This again highly depends on the type and requirements of the deployed application. Examples for important state information could be:

- The overall state of the server.

- The state of the deployed application.

- The state of the resources in use (datasources, JMS, etc.).

- The number of parallel connections to the server, or number of parallel transactions on the server.

- Stuck threads, deadlocks, or other indications observed over a period of time can give valuable indications.

The following script will connect to a WebLogic Server (Admin or Managed-Server) and print the name, state, health, and the number of open sockets (which provides an indication of the number of parallel users in case this is NOT a server-server communication).

```
def printServerBasicInformation(rootDirInTree):
        cd(rootDirInTree)
        print "Basic Server Information:"

        # print Name
        print "    Name ......................... = " + get("Name")
```

```
        # add state
        print "        State ...................... = " + get("State");
        # SocketsOpenedTotalCount
        print "        SocketsOpenedTotalCount ....... = " + str(get("SocketsOpenedTotalCount"));
        # OpenSocketsCurrentCount
        print "        OpenSocketsCurrentCount ....... = " + str(get("OpenSocketsCurrentCount"));
        # AdminServer  - nothe this is BOOLEAN and indicates if this server is the admin server
        print "        isAdminServer ................ = " + str(get("AdminServer"));
        # HealthState
        print "        HealthState ............. = " + getHealthStateInformation(get("HealthState"));
        print("");
```

If you are not dumping it into a file but want to display it on a shell, Jython offers a nice feature of adding colors to the text. The next script will show a method that displays the state in a different color, depending on the server state:

```
def monitorServerState():
    print 'Fetching state of every WebLogic instance'

    serverNames = cmo.getServers()
    domainRuntime()

    for name in serverNames:
        cd("/ServerLifeCycleRuntimes/" + name.getName())
        serverState = cmo.getState()
        if serverState == "RUNNING":
                print 'Server ' + name.getName() + ' is :\033[1;32m' + serverState + '\033[0m'
        elif serverState == "STARTING":
                print 'Server ' + name.getName() + ' is :\033[1;33m' + serverState + '\033[0m'
        elif serverState == "UNKNOWN":
            print 'Server ' + name.getName() + ' is :\033[1;34m' + serverState + '\033[0m'
        else:
                print 'Server ' + name.getName() + ' is :\033[1;31m' + serverState + '\033[0m'
```

Sometimes it is only required to get a summary of the most important server values. The following function provides a summary of the most often queried server values. Please note that the server values that are considered "most important" are heavily dependent on the deployed application.

💾 queried_values_summary

```
def printServerSummary(outputprefix, servername, rootDirInTree):
        cd(rootDirInTree)
        print outputprefix+"Server SUMMARY Information:"

        # print Name
        print outputprefix+"      Name ...... = " + get("Name")
        print outputprefix+"      State ..... = " + get("State");
        print outputprefix+"      HealthState  = " + getHealthStateInformation(get("HealthState"));

        cd (rootDirInTree+"JVMRuntime/"+servername)
        print outputprefix+"      HeapFreeCurrent ................ = " + str(get("HeapFreeCurrent"))

        cd (rootDirInTree+"JTARuntime/JTARuntime")
        # print HealthState
        print outputprefix+"      JTA - HealthState = " +
                        getHealthStateInformation(get("HealthState"));

        # change to ThreadPoolRuntime
        cd (rootDirInTree+"ThreadPoolRuntime/ThreadPoolRuntime")
        print outputprefix+"      ThreadPoolRuntime-HealthState ... = " +
            getHealthStateInformation(get("HealthState"));

        # print CompletedRequestCount
        print outputprefix+"      ThreadPoolRuntime-CompletedRequestCount  = " +
            str(get("CompletedRequestCount"))

        cd(rootDirInTree)
        print outputprefix+"      Datasources:";
```

```
        dataSources = cmo.getJDBCServiceRuntime().getJDBCDataSourceRuntimeMBeans()
        if (len(dataSources) > 0):
            for dataSource in dataSources:
                print outputprefix+"            Datasource-Name..... = "+ dataSource.getName()
                print outputprefix+"            Datasource-State.... = "+ dataSource.getState()
        print("\n\n")
```

The next script is also a nice feature of WebLogic. WebLogic provides information
about when a server was started. For instance, by looping over your server instances
you can find out if there was an outage, if a server has been restarted, and in general
how long your servers are up and running:

💾 server_start_information

```
import os

def ServerState():
  servers = getRunningServerNames()
  domainRuntime()
  currentState=""
  app=""
  # iterate over all servers
  for server in servers:
    try:
      cd("/ServerRuntimes/" + server.getName())
      ActivationTime = cmo.getActivationTime()
      strout=SimpleDateFormat('d MMM yyyy HH:mm:ss').format(java.util.Date(cmo.getActivationTime()))
    except:
      print 'Skipping ..'
    print 'ServerNAME: %4s  %10s' %(server.getName(),strout)
  exit ()

# get the names of all servers in this domain
def getRunningServerNames():
    domainConfig()
    return cmo.getServers()

if __name__ == "main":
    connect (str(user),str(password),str(aserver))
    redirect('Server.log', 'false')
    ServerState()
```

The following script will connect to an AdminServer and query the state of all servers
in a domain. In case that a server is not in running mode, the script will send an email
to a predefined address. Note that this script is using *mailx* and is therefore in the
provided form only usable on Linux/UNIX systems.

💾 query_server_states

```
import os
def sendMail(domain,count,dest,sname):
    str3 = 'Domain:#' + domain +'# Server Name: '+ sname  +', '+ dest +'  @' + str(count)
    cmd = "echo " + str3 + " > /tmp/rw_serverstate_file"
    os.system(cmd)
    os.system('/bin/mailx -s  "Caution, The server state is abnormal  !!! "  operators@test.com  <
/tmp/rw_serverstate_file')
    print '*********  ALTERT MAIL HAS BEEN SENT  ***********'
    cmd = "rm /tmp/rw_serverstate_file"
    os.system(cmd)

def ServerState():
  servers = getRunningServerNames()
  domainRuntime()
  sign="###"
  activecount=0
  problemcount=0
  currentState=""
  app=""
```

```
  for server in servers:
    try:
      cd("/ServerLifeCycleRuntimes/" + server.getName())
      serverState = cmo.getState()
      if serverState == "ADMIN"  :
        resume(server.getName(),block="true")
        sendMail(aserver,app,serverState,server.getName())
        problemcount=problemcount +1
      elif serverState == "FAILED" or serverState == "UNKNOWN"  or serverState == "STARTING":
        sendMail(aserver,app,serverState,server.getName())
        problemcount=problemcount +1
      else:
        activecount=activecount +1
    except:
        print 'Skipping ..'
    print 'ServerNAME: %4s  %10s' %(server.getName(),serverState)
  print 'Total %4s RUNNING :\033[1;31m %4s Problem \033[0m' %(repr(activecount),repr(problemcount))
  exit ()

def getRunningServerNames():
    domainConfig()
    return cmo.getServers()

if __name__ == "main":
    redirect('Server.log', 'false')
    connect (str(user),str(password),str(adminserverURL))
    ServerState()
```
(Script written by Atilla Demirel)

Heap Size and Other VM Monitoring

In bigger production systems, especially in cloud-like systems, many WebLogic Server instances are often running on the same box. This is especially the case if you have dedicated hosts for the Administration Servers. In all cases your physical memory is limited and it is necessary to do some capacity planning. Usually the heap size of your WebLogic Servers are set too high as it is difficult to calculate the right size upfront. You also might experience out-of-memory exceptions on your WebLogic Servers. In this case the memory settings are too small.

The following script will help you do an analysis for the currently-used heap. You can either use this script once to determine the unused resources, or you can run this periodically over a period of time in order to monitor peaks of memory usage. This script is quite handy as it connects to the AdminServer and prints the memory consumption of all running servers of the domain, regardless where they are running.

🖫 get_memory_information
```
########################################################################
#        Get memory information from all servers in your domain        #
########################################################################

# test arguments
if len(sys.argv) != 4:
    print 'Usage:  wlst.sh printMemoryInformation.py <wls_url> <wls_username> <wls_password>';
    exit();

adminURL      = sys.argv[1];
adminUserName = sys.argv[2];
adminPassword = sys.argv[3];

# note: alternatively you could have used security files created by storeconfig

# connect to the admin server
```

```
connect(adminUserName, adminPassword, adminURL),

# get the server namees
serverNames = cmo.getServers()
domainRuntime()

# loop over all servers in the domain
for nextServerName in serverNames:
    try:
        # change to the next server JVM runtime information mbean
        cd("/ServerRuntimes/"+nextServerName.getName()+"/JVMRuntime/"+nextServerName.getName())
        totalMemory = get('HeapSizeCurrent')
            freeMemory  = get('HeapFreeCurrent')
            usedMemory  = (totalMemory - freeMemory)

        print "Memory information for server: "+ nextServerName.getName();
        print "------------------------------------------------------------"
        print 'Total memory allocated : ' + str(totalMemory)
        print 'Free memory            : ' + str(freeMemory)
        print 'Memory in use          : ' + str(usedMemory)
        print '\n';
    except:
        dumpStack()
        print 'Problem getting memory information for server '+ nextServerName.getName();

disconnect();
```

The result of this script might look like:

```
martin@middleware1210:~$ wlst.sh ./printMemoryInformation.py t3://localhost:40001 weblogic test1234

Initializing WebLogic Scripting Tool (WLST) ...

Welcome to WebLogic Server Administration Scripting Shell

Type help() for help on available commands

Connecting to t3://localhost:40001 with userid weblogic ...
Successfully connected to Admin Server 'AdminServer' that belongs to domain 'MartinTest_Domain'.

Warning: An insecure protocol was used to connect to the
server. To ensure on-the-wire security, the SSL port or
Admin port should be used instead.

Location changed to domainRuntime tree. This is a read-only tree with DomainMBean as the root.
For more help, use help(domainRuntime)

Memory information for server: AdminServer
------------------------------------------------------------
Total memory allocated : 328597504
Free memory            : 211795248
Memory in use          : 116802256


Memory information for server: MartinTest_Domain_MS1
------------------------------------------------------------
Total memory allocated : 262602752
Free memory            : 186422248
Memory in use          : 76180504


No stack trace available.
Problem getting memory information for server MartinTest_Domain_MS2
Disconnected from weblogic server: AdminServer
```

In this case, Server MartinTest_Domain_MS2 was not running. Therefore the script could not find a JVM runtime MBean.

NOTE: The available JVM attributes vary from JDK to JDK! A hotspot VM does offer less and different values than a JRockit VM.

JRockit Java Virtual Machine		Hotspot 1.6.0_37 Virtual Machine	
wls:/mydomain/domainruntime/ServerRuntimes/myserver/JVMRuntime/myserver> ls()		wls:/MartinTest_Domain/serverRuntime/JVMRuntime/AdminServer> ls()	
-r--	AllProcessorsAverageLoad	0.0	
-r--	Concurrent	true	
-r--	FreeHeap	15050064	-r-- HeapFreeCurrent	206508240
-r--	FreePhysicalMemory	900702208	-r-- HeapFreePercent	74
-r--	GCHandlesCompaction	true	-r-- HeapSizeCurrent	328597504
-r--	GcAlgorithm	Dynamic GC	-r-- HeapSizeMax	477233152
-r--	Generational	true	-r-- JavaVMVendor	Sun
-r--	HeapFreeCurrent	14742864	Microsystems Inc.	
-r--	HeapFreePercent	5	-r-- JavaVendor	Sun
-r--	HeapSizeCurrent	268435456	Microsystems Inc.	
-r--	HeapSizeMax	268435456	-r-- JavaVersion	1.6.0_37
-r--	Incremental	false	-r-- Name	AdminServer
-r--	JVMDescription	BEA JRockit Java	-r-- OSName	Linux
Virtual Machine			-r-- OSVersion	3.5.0-19-
-r--	JavaVMVendor	BEA Systems, Inc.	generic	
-r--	JavaVendor	BEA Systems, Inc.	-r-- Type	JVMRuntime
-r--	JavaVersion	1.5.0	-r-- Uptime	2092278

Table 9.1: JVM and Hotspot VM

WebLogic has two different possibilities to obtain information from the JVM (Java virtual machine) level. You can either connect to the JVM MBeanServer, or (which I personally prefer) each serverRuntime can have a JVMRuntime subtree in the MBean tree. Depending on the version and type of the virtual machine, this will give you a number of valuable information like free heap, heapsize, or uptime.

The following script will print the Java version and the current heap values, including free heap.

```
def printServerJVMRuntimeInformation(servername,rootDirInTree):
    # change to JVMRuntime
    cd (rootDirInTree+"JVMRuntime/"+servername)
    print "Server JVM Information:"

    # print JavaVendor
    print "     JavaVendor ........................... = " + get("JavaVendor")
    # print JavaVersion
    print "     JavaVersion .......................... = " + get("JavaVersion")
    # print HeapFreeCurrent
    print "     HeapFreeCurrent ...................... = " + str(get("HeapFreeCurrent"))
    # print HeapFreePercent
    print "     HeapFreePercent ...................... = " + str(get("HeapFreePercent"))
    # print HeapSizeCurrent
    print "     HeapSizeCurrent ...................... = " + str(get("HeapSizeCurrent"))
    # print Uptime
    print "     Uptime ............................... = " + str(get("Uptime")/1000)+" seconds"
    print("")
```

Server Resource Monitoring

A J2EE application server like WebLogic consists of many different resources, resource pools, and other runtime artifacts. It is very difficult to document and mention all of them, so this chapter will give an overview of the most common and most important ones with a number of example scripts. At the end a comprehensive example will print the most important server details.

Note that WebLogic does activate or instantiate resource pools as needed (like when a new application is deployed or new WorkManagers are created). Therefore this chapter can only provide basic ideas and general scripts that must be tailored to your actual project and setup need.

Thread Pools

Among the important resources of each WebLogic Server are threads. The amount of threads and especially the amount of parallel execution and pending requests will give you a good indication if the server is operating in a healthy state and if user requests can be executed in a timely manner. If those numbers are getting too high, then the server has too many parallel tasks and needs too much time for scheduling. This also usually means that some dependent services (like databases) do not react on time.

```
def printServerThreadPoolInformation(rootDirInTree):
        # change to ThreadPoolRuntime
        cd (rootDirInTree+"ThreadPoolRuntime/ThreadPoolRuntime")
        print "Server ThreadPool Information:"

        # print Name
        print "     Name ............................. = " + get("Name")
        # print HealthState
        print "        HealthState ............. = " + getHealthStateInformation(get("HealthState"));
        # print CompletedRequestCount
        print "        CompletedRequestCount ................ = " + str(get("CompletedRequestCount"))
        # print ExecuteThreadTotalCount
        print "        ExecuteThreadTotalCount .............. = " + str(get("ExecuteThreadTotalCount"))
        # print ExecuteThreadIdleCount
        print "        ExecuteThreadIdleCount ............... = " + str(get("ExecuteThreadIdleCount"))
        # print HoggingThreadCount
        print "        HoggingThreadCount ................... = " + str(get("HoggingThreadCount"))
        # print PendingUserRequestCount
        print "        PendingUserRequestCount .............. = " + str(get("PendingUserRequestCount"))
        # print QueueLength
        print "        QueueLength .......................... = " + str(get("QueueLength"))
        # print SharedCapacityForWorkManagers
        print "        SharedCapacityForWorkManagers .. = " + str(get("SharedCapacityForWorkManagers"))
        # print StandbyThreadCount
        print "        StandbyThreadCount ................... = " + str(get("StandbyThreadCount"))
        # print Suspended
        print "        Suspended ............................ = " + str(get("Suspended"))
        # print Throughput
        print "        Throughput ........................... = " + str(get("Throughput"))
        print("")
```

The script above monitors the entire thread pool. WebLogic also offers a much more granular concept called WorkManager. Even in a default domain, WebLogic has a number of individual WorkManagers.

```
The following script does monitor an individual WorkManager
# change to the server runtime
serverRuntime()

# get (as an example) the kernel work manager
kenelDefaultWorkManager = getMBean('/WorkManagerRuntimes/weblogic.kernel.Default')

# print some values of default kernel work manager
print 'Pending requests in the default workmanager: ' , wm.getPendingRequests()
print 'Stuck count in the default workmanager: ' , wm.getStuckThreadCount()

# get a custom created work manager mbean
wm = getMBean('/WorkManagerRuntimes/MyOwnWorkManager')
# ... and print some values
print 'MyOwnWorkManager Pending: ' , wm.getPendingRequests()
print 'MyOwnWorkManager stuck count: ' , wm.getStuckThreadCount()
```

MBeans involved in WorkManager:

```
ThreadPoolRuntimeMBean
ExecuteQueueRuntimeMBean
WorkManagerRuntimeMBean
RequestClassRuntimeMBean (a child of WorkManagerRuntimeMBean)
MaxThreadsConstraintRuntimeMBean (a child of WorkManagerRuntimeMBean)
MinThreadsConstraintRuntimeMBean (a child of WorkManagerRuntimeMBean)
```

You can use the interactive mode of WLST to navigate to the WorkManager MBeans and get the runtime values. The following listing provides an example:

```
wls:/MartinTest_Domain/serverRuntime/WorkManagerRuntimes> ls()
dr--   DataRetirementWorkManager
dr--   ImageWorkManager
dr--   JTACoordinatorWM
dr--   JmsAsyncQueue
dr--   JmsDispatcher
dr--   OneWayJTACoordinatorWM
dr--   UserLockout
dr--   WatchManagerEvents
dr--   direct
dr--   weblogic.Rejector
dr--   weblogic.admin.RMI
dr--   weblogic.kernel.Default
dr--   weblogic.kernel.Non-Blocking
dr--   weblogic.kernel.System
dr--   weblogic.logging.DomainLogBroadcasterClient
dr--   weblogic.logging.LogBroadcaster
dr--   wl_oldBootStrap

wls:/MartinTest_Domain/serverRuntime/WorkManagerRuntimes> cd ('weblogic.kernel.Default')
wls:/MartinTest_Domain/serverRuntime/WorkManagerRuntimes/weblogic.kernel.Default> ls()
dr--   MaxThreadsConstraintRuntime
dr--   MinThreadsConstraintRuntime
dr--   RequestClassRuntime

-r--   ApplicationName                          null
-r--   CompletedRequests                        374
-r--   HealthState
Component:null,State:HEALTH_OK,MBean:null,ReasonCode:[]
-r--   MaxThreadsConstraintRuntime              null
-r--   MinThreadsConstraintRuntime              null
-r--   ModuleName                               null
-r--   Name                                     weblogic.kernel.Default
-r--   PendingRequests                          0
-r--   RequestClassRuntime                      null
-r--   StuckThreadCount                         0
-r--   Type                                     WorkManagerRuntime
```

Transaction Pools

Transactions are another very valuable source of information. For the overall health state of the server instance and of the deployed applications, the number of rolled-backs, abandoned, and especially heuristic transactions are very good indicators. Whereas a rolled-back might be absolutely ok, if the business decided not to commit the transactions it might indicate problems. Therefore, WebLogic offers different numbers for the different rollback categories. Especially *TransactionRolledBackResourceTotalCount* (due to resource issues) or *TransactionRolledBackTimeoutTotalCount* (due to maximal duration constraint violation) are indicators for infrastructure and resource issues. Heuristics almost always means problems and in most cases need human intervention in order to repair the damage because this means that atomic operations have only be performed partially.

The following script shows how to monitor transactional values of a server:

```
def printServerJTAInformation(rootDirInTree):
    # change to JTA
    cd (rootDirInTree+"JTARuntime/JTARuntime")
    print "Server Transaction Information:"

    # print Name
    print "      Name ................................ = " + get("Name")
    # print HealthState
    print "      HealthState ........................... = "
        + getHealthStateInformation(get("HealthState"));
    # print TransactionTotalCount
    print "      TransactionTotalCount ................. = "
        + str(get("TransactionTotalCount"))
    # print TransactionCommittedTotalCount
    print "      TransactionCommittedTotalCount ........ = "
        + str(get("TransactionCommittedTotalCount"))
    # print ActiveTransactionsTotalCount
    print "      ActiveTransactionsTotalCount .......... = "
        + str(get("ActiveTransactionsTotalCount"))
    # print TransactionRolledBackTotalCount
    print "      TransactionRolledBackTotalCount ....... = "
        + str(get("TransactionRolledBackTotalCount"))
    # print TransactionRolledBackTimeoutTotalCount
    print "      TransactionRolledBackTimeoutTotalCount . = "
        + str(get("TransactionRolledBackTimeoutTotalCount"))
    # print TransactionRolledBackResourceTotalCount
    print "      TransactionRolledBackResourceTotalCount  = "
        + str(get("TransactionRolledBackResourceTotalCount"))
    # print TransactionAbandonedTotalCount
    print "      TransactionAbandonedTotalCount ........ = "
        + str(get("TransactionAbandonedTotalCount"))
    # print TransactionHeuristicsTotalCount
    print "      TransactionHeuristicsTotalCount ....... = "
        + str(get("TransactionHeuristicsTotalCount"))
    print("");
```

Cluster Monitoring

WebLogic also offers the possibility to monitor the cluster state directly. The following script iterates over all cluster runtimes and prints the health state and the number of alive servers:

```
# connect to admin server
connect(...)

# switch to server runtime
serverRuntime()

# get all cluster runtimes
allCluster = cmo.getClusterRuntimes()

# iterate over all cluster and print name, health and alive servers
for cluster in allCluster:
    print 'Name:'+cluster.getName()+'    HealthState:'+
        getHealthStateInformation(cluster.getHealthState())+
        '    AliveServerCount:'+str(cluster.getAliveServerCount())
```

Each cluster runtime has the following attributes, which can be queried using WLST or JMX:

```
wls:/MartinTest_Domain/serverRuntime> cd ('ClusterRuntime/MyTestCluster')
wls:/MartinTest_Domain /serverRuntime/ClusterRuntime/MyTestCluster'> ls()
dr--    JobSchedulerRuntime
dr--    ServerMigrationRuntime
dr--    UnicastMessaging

-r--    ActiveSingletonServices                 null
-r--    AliveServerCount                        2
-r--    CurrentSecondaryServer                  8874663745593982102S:localhost:[46020,46020,-1,-
1,-1,-1,-1]:SIT_ENV01_Domain:SIT_ENV01_Domain_MS2
-r--    DetailedSecondariesDistribution         null
-r--    ForeignFragmentsDroppedCount            0
-r--    FragmentsReceivedCount                  241037
-r--    FragmentsSentCount                      241230
-r--    HealthState
Component:null,State:HEALTH_OK,MBean:null,ReasonCode:[]
-r--    JobSchedulerRuntime                     null
-r--    MulticastMessagesLostCount              2
-r--    Name                                    MyTestCluster
-r--    PrimaryCount                            0
-r--    ResendRequestsCount                     1
-r--    SecondaryCount                          0
-r--    SecondaryDistributionNames              null
-r--    SecondaryServerDetails                  8874663745593982102S:localhost:[46020,46020,-1,-
1,-1,-1,-1]:SIT_ENV01_Domain:SIT_ENV01_Domain_MS2
-r--    ServerNames                             java.lang.String[MartinTest_Domain_MS2,
MartinTest_Domain_MS1]
-r--    Type                                    ClusterRuntime
```

Network Channel Monitoring

It is also possible to monitor WebLogic network channels. The following script will
iterate over all channels and print actual connection information.

```
def printServerChannelStatus():
    domainConfig()
    allservers = cmo.getServers()

    domainRuntime()

    for server in allservers:
        print 'Server channels for server: '+server
        cd ('/ServerRuntimes/'+server)

            allchannels = cmo.getServerChannelRuntimes()
            for channel in cmo.getServerChannelRuntimes():
                cd ('/ServerRuntimes/'+server+'/ServerChannelRuntimes/'+channel)

                print '    Channel : ' + cmo.getName()
                print '       AcceptCount : '+ (str(cmo.getAcceptCount()))
                print '       ConnectionsCount : '+ (str(cmo.getConnectionsCount()))
                print '       MessagesReceivedCount : '+ (str(cmo.getMessagesReceivedCount()))
                print '       MessagesSentCount : '+ (str(cmo.getMessagesSentCount()))
                print '       BytesSentCount : '+ (str(cmo.getBytesSentCount()))
                print '       BytesReceivedCount : '+ (str(cmo.getBytesReceivedCount()))
```

Service Monitoring

One of the most common monitoring activities is the monitoring of server services.
This includes the monitoring of datasources, JMS services, mail, and other services. A
service is basically everything that is used by one or more applications but is not part
of the application. One concept of J2EE is that services can be used but should not
be provided by the application as they are infrastructure and in almost all cases

depend on the environment in use (e.g. hostnames, ports, user, passwords, etc.). Applications should never worry about those environment details.

Monitoring Datasources

The most common resources are databases. Databases are accessed from a J2EE application by using datasources. Database access means controlling connections, accessing information, and executing statements.

The following script provides a function that prints information about all datasources of the server:

```
def printAllDatasourceInformation():
    print "All Datasource Runtime information:"
    serverRuntime()
    cd('/')
    dataSources = cmo.getJDBCServiceRuntime().getJDBCDataSourceRuntimeMBeans()
    if (len(dataSources) > 0):
        for dataSource in dataSources:
            print "    Name ................................ = "+ dataSource.getName()
            print "    State ............................... = "+ dataSource.getState()
            print "    DeploymentState ....................... = "
                + str(dataSource.getDeploymentState())
            print "    ConnectionsTotalCount ................. = "
                + str(dataSource.getConnectionsTotalCount())
            print "    ActiveConnectionsAverageCount ......... = "
                + str(dataSource.getActiveConnectionsAverageCount())
            print "    ActiveConnectionsCurrentCount ......... = "
                + str(dataSource.getActiveConnectionsCurrentCount())
            print "    ActiveConnectionsHighCount ............ = "
                + str(dataSource.getActiveConnectionsHighCount())
            print "    ConnectionDelayTime ................... = "
                + str(dataSource.getConnectionDelayTime())
            print "    CurrCapacity .......................... = "
                + str(dataSource.getCurrCapacity())
            print "    CurrCapacityHighCount ................. = "
                + str(dataSource.getCurrCapacityHighCount())
            print "    FailedReserveRequestCount ............. = "
                + str(dataSource.getFailedReserveRequestCount())
            print "    FailuresToReconnectCount .............. = "
                + str(dataSource.getFailuresToReconnectCount())
            print "    HighestNumAvailable ................... = "
                + str(dataSource.getHighestNumAvailable())
            print "    HighestNumUnavailable ................. = "
                + str(dataSource.getHighestNumUnavailable())
            print "    LeakedConnectionCount ................. = "
                + str(dataSource.getLeakedConnectionCount())
            print "    WaitingForConnectionCurrentCount ...... = "
                + str(dataSource.getWaitingForConnectionCurrentCount())
            print "    WaitingForConnectionFailureTotal ...... = "
                + str(dataSource.getWaitingForConnectionFailureTotal())
            print "    WaitingForConnectionHighCount ......... = "
                + str(dataSource.getWaitingForConnectionHighCount())
            print "    WaitingForConnectionSuccessTotal ...... = "
                + str(dataSource.getWaitingForConnectionSuccessTotal())
            print "    WaitingForConnectionTotal ............. = "
                + str(dataSource.getWaitingForConnectionTotal())
            print "    WaitSecondsHighCount .................. = "
                + str(dataSource.getWaitSecondsHighCount())
            print("")
```

The next script shows another example of monitoring datasources and datasource pools. This example also shows another nice feature of Jython not yet used in the book, which is to colorize the output. Jython allows the user to place colors on the output text (see \033…).

```
import os

def sendMail(count,dest,datasourcename):
    str3 = 'Pool Name: '+ datasourcename +', '+ dest +' @' + str(count)
    cmd = "echo " + str3 + " > rw_file"
    os.system(cmd)
    os.system('/bin/mailx -s  "Caution, you have a pool problem !!! " atillademirel@gmail.com <
rw_file')


def monitorServerState():
    connect(uname, pwd, url)
    serverNames = getRunningServerNames()
    domainRuntime()
    for sname in serverNames:
      cd("/ServerLifeCycleRuntimes/" + sname.getName())
      serverState = cmo.getState()
      if serverState == "RUNNING"  :
        print 'Now checking '+sname.getName()
        cd("/ServerRuntimes/" + sname.getName())
        cd("JDBCServiceRuntime/" + sname.getName())
        cd("JDBCDataSourceRuntimeMBeans/")
        DSlist=ls(returnMap='true')
        for ds in DSlist:
          cd(ds)
          poolState=cmo.getState()
          if poolState == "Running":
            print ds+"@" + sname.getName() + ' is :\033[1;32m' + poolState + '\033[0m'
          elif poolState == "Suspended":
            print ds+"@" + sname.getName() + ' is :\033[1;31m' + poolState + '\033[0m'
            sendMail(sname.getName(),cmo.getState(),ds)
            cmo.resume()
            poolState=cmo.getState()
            print '\033[1;32m' + ds+"@" + sname.getName() + ' is :' + poolState + '\033[0m'
          elif poolState == "Overloaded":
            print ds + "@" + sname.getName() + ' is :\033[1;36m' + poolState + '\033[0m'
            sendMail(sname.getName(),cmo.getState(),ds)
            cmo.reset()
            poolState=cmo.getState()
            print '\033[1;32m' + ds+"@" + sname.getName() + ' is :' + poolState + '\033[0m'
          elif poolState == "Unhealthy":
            print ds + "@" + sname.getName() + ' is :\033[1;34m' + poolState + '\033[0m'
            sendMail(sname.getName(),cmo.getState(),ds)
            cmo.reset()
            poolState=cmo.getState()
            print '\033[1;32m' + ds+"@" + sname.getName() + ' is :' + poolState + '\033[0m'
          elif poolState == "Shutdown":
            print ds + "@" + sname.getName() + ' is :\033[1;33m' + poolState + '\033[0m'
            sendMail(sname.getName(),cmo.getState(),ds)
            cmo.start()
            poolState=cmo.getState()
            print '\033[1;32m' + ds+"@" + sname.getName() + ' is :' + poolState + '\033[0m'
          else:
            print ds + "@" + sname.getName() + ' is :\033[1;35m' + poolState + '\033[0m'
          cd('..')
    exit()


def getRunningServerNames():
    domainConfig()
    return cmo.getServers()

if __name__ == "main":
    redirect('Server.log', 'false')
    monitorServerState()
```
(Written and provided by Atilla Demirel)

JMS Runtime Monitoring

WLST provides a number of runtime monitoring values on JMS runtime level. The first example prints the overall health state of the JMS runtime system:

```
# print health state of the JMS runtime
def printJMSRuntimeState(myServerName):
    domainRuntime()
    # change to JMS runtime
    cd('/ServerRuntimes/'+myServerName+'/JMSRuntime/'+myServerName+'.jms')

    # print state
    print 'JMSRuntime '+cmo.getName()+' current health state = '+cmo.getHealthState()
```

The second example prints overall connection information of the JMS runtime system. The metrics available are current, high, and total connection count:

```
# print connection details of the JMS runtime system
def printJMSRuntimeInformation(myServerName):
    domainRuntime()
    # change to JMS runtime
    cd('/ServerRuntimes/'+myServerName+'/JMSRuntime/'+myServerName+'.jms')
    rtName = cmo.getName()

    # print connection summary information
    print 'JMSRuntime '+ rtName +' ConnectionsCurrentCount = '
        +str(cmo.getConnectionsCurrentCount())
    print 'JMSRuntime '+ rtName +' ConnectionsHighCount = '+str(cmo.getConnectionsHighCount())
    print 'JMSRuntime '+ rtName +' ConnectionsTotalCount = '
        +str(cmo.getConnectionsTotalCount())
```

Connected Clients, Sessions, Producer and Consumer

For runtime analysis and monitoring, it can be very helpful to monitor who is connected to your JMS servers. WLST offers a pretty powerful API to list all active connections, their sessions, and also the producer and consumer of those sessions. Before we examine the WLST script, let us have a quick look at the MBeans and APIs.

The JMS runtime offers a method called *getConnections* that returns a list of active connections to this JMS runtime. Each of those objects is an instance of *JMSConnectionRuntimeMBean*.

Method	Description
String getClientID()	The client ID for this connection
String getClientIDPolicy()	Gets the ClientIDPolicy on this connection or durable subscriber
String getHostAddress()	The host address of the client JVM as a string
JMSSessionRuntimeMBean[] getSessions()	An array of sessions for this connection.
long getSessionsCurrentCount()	The current number of sessions for this connection
long getSessionsHighCount()	The peak number of sessions for this connection since the last reset
long getSessionsTotalCount()	The number of sessions on this connection since the last reset.

(Source: Oracle Corporation[17])

Table 9.2: Viewing Connections

As you can see, this MBean offers host and client ID information, session information, and also the possibility to view a list of all sessions with the method *getSessions*. All instances of this list are instances of the type *JMSSessionRuntimeMBean*.

Method	Description
String getAcknowledgeMode()	The acknowledge mode
long getBytesPendingCount()	The number of bytes pending (uncommitted and unacknowledged) for this session
long getBytesReceivedCount()	The number of bytes received by this session since the last reset
long getBytesSentCount()	The number of bytes sent by this session since the last reset
long getConsumersCurrentCount()	The current number of consumers for this session
long getConsumersHighCount()	The peak number of consumers for this session since the last reset
long getConsumersTotalCount()	number of consumers instantiated by this session since the last reset.
long getMessagesPendingCount()	The number of messages pending (uncommitted and unacknowledged) for this session
long getMessagesReceivedCount()	The number of messages received by this session since the last reset
long getMessagesSentCount()	The number of bytes sent by this session since the last reset
long getProducersCurrentCount()	The current number of producers for this session
long getProducersHighCount()	The peak number of producers for this session since the last reset.
long getProducersTotalCount()	The number of producers for this session since the last reset
boolean isTransacted()	Indicates whether the session is transacted
JMSConsumerRuntimeMBean[]	An array of consumers for this session

[17]docs.oracle.com/middleware/1212/wls/WLAPI/weblogic/management/runtime/JMSConnectionRuntimeMBean.html

	getConsumers()	
JMSProducerRuntimeMBean[] getProducers()		An array of producers for this session

(Source: Oracle Corporation[18])

Table 9.3: Viewing Sessions

The session MBean provides detailed information about each session which includes throughput in bytes, consumer/producer counts, message information, and other session information like transaction participation. In addition, this MBean provides the ability to get references to all associated producers and consumers with the methods *getConsumers* and *getProducers*.

All consumer MBeans are instances of *JMSConsumerRuntimeMBean*.

Method	Description
long getBytesPendingCount()	The number of bytes pending (uncommitted and unacknowledged) by this consumer
long getBytesReceivedCount()	The number of bytes received by this consumer since the last reset
String getClientID()	The client ID for this connection
String getClientIDPolicy()	The ClientIDPolicy on this connection or durable subscriber
String getDestinationName()	The name of the destination for this consumer
String getMemberDestinationName()	The name of the destination for this consumer
long getMessagesPendingCount()	The number of messages pending (uncommitted and unacknowledged)
long getMessagesReceivedCount()	The number of messages received by this consumer since the last reset
String getSelector()	The selector associated with this consumer, if any
String getSubscriptionSharingPolicy()	The Subscription Sharing Policy on this subscriber
boolean isActive()	Indicates whether the consumer active
boolean isDurable()	Indicates whether the consumer is durable

(Source: Oracle Corporation[19])

Table 9.4: Viewing Consumers

All producer MBeans are instances of *JMSProducerRuntimeMBean*.

---

[18]docs.oracle.com/middleware/1212/wls/WLAPI/weblogic/management/runtime/JMSSessionRuntimeMBean.html

[19]docs.oracle.com/middleware/1212/wls/WLAPI/weblogic/management/runtime/JMSConsumerRuntimeMBean.html

Method	Description
long getBytesPendingCount()	The number of bytes pending (uncommitted and unacknowledged) by this producer
long getBytesSentCount()	The number of bytes sent by this producer since the last reset
long getMessagesPendingCount()	The number of messages pending (uncommitted and unacknowledged) by this producer
long getMessagesSentCount()	The number of messages sent by this producer since the last reset.

(Source: Oracle Corporation[20])

Table 9.5: Viewing Producers

The following script will navigate in the domain MBean tree to the desired server and then print all connections, sessions, and session information of this JMS runtime. Note that it is left up to the reader to extend the information printed for consumers and producers. The method summaries listed above should be a great help.

```
def printConnectedJMSClients(myServerName):
    # switch to the domainRuntime
    domainRuntime()

    # cd into the desired server and then JMS server runtime
    cd('ServerRuntimes/'+myServerName+'/JMSRuntime/'+myServerName+'.jms')

    # get all JMS connections for all JMS servers for this runtime
    # note that all connection instances are of type JMSConnectionRuntimeMBean
    allJMSconnections = cmo.getConnections()

    # print amount
    print 'Actually the '+myServerName+'.jms runtime has '+str(allJMSconnections)+' connections !'

    # now examine all jms connections and get some basic informations
    for nextConnection in allJMSconnections:
        print 'Connection: '+nextConnection.getHostAddress()
            +' with client id = '+nextConnection.getClientID()
        # finally print all sessions associated with this connection
        print '          has actually '+str(nextConnection.getSessionsCurrentCount())
            +' active sessions'
        allConnectionJMSSessions = nextConnection.getSessions()

        # iterate of sessions
        for nextConnectionSession in allConnectionJMSSessions:
            # print some session information
            print '          Session: Active consumers: '
                +str(nextConnectionSession.getConsumersCurrentCount())
            print '                   Active producer: '
                +str(nextConnectionSession.getProducersCurrentCount())
            print '                   Messages: send:'
                +str(nextConnectionSession.getMessagesSentCount())
                +'   received:'+str(nextConnectionSession.getMessagesReceivedCount())
                +'   pending:'+str(nextConnectionSession.getMessagesPendingCount())

            # iterate over producer
            activeJMSProducer = nextConnectionSession.getProducers()
            for nextProducer in activeJMSProducer:
                # ... print information you want -> see API

            # iterate over consumer
            activeJMSConsumers = nextConnectionSession.getConsumers()
            for nextConsumer in activeJMSConsumers:
                # ... print information you want -> see API
```

---

[20]docs.oracle.com/middleware/1212/wls/WLAPI/weblogic/management/runtime/JMSProducerRuntimeMBean.html

JMS Server Monitoring

WLST provides a number of runtime monitoring values on the JMS server level.

```
wls:/MartinTest_Domain/domainRuntime/ServerRuntimes/AdminServer/JMSRuntime/AdminServer.jms/JMSServers
/MyTestServer_3> ls()
-r--   BytesCurrentCount                        0
-r--   BytesHighCount                           0
-r--   BytesPageableCurrentCount                0
-r--   BytesPagedInTotalCount                   0
-r--   BytesPagedOutTotalCount                  0
-r--   BytesPendingCount                        0
-r--   BytesReceivedCount                       0
-r--   BytesThresholdTime                       0
-r--   ConsumptionPaused                        false
-r--   ConsumptionPausedState                   Consumption-Enabled
-r--   DestinationsCurrentCount                 1
-r--   DestinationsHighCount                    1
-r--   DestinationsTotalCount                   1
-r--   HealthState
Component:JMSServer.MyTestServer_1,State:HEALTH_OK,MBean:MyTestServer_1,ReasonCode:[]
-r--   InsertionPaused                          false
-r--   InsertionPausedState                     Insertion-Enabled
-r--   MessagesCurrentCount                     0
-r--   MessagesHighCount                        0
-r--   MessagesPageableCurrentCount             0
-r--   MessagesPagedInTotalCount                0
-r--   MessagesPagedOutTotalCount               0
-r--   MessagesPendingCount                     0
-r--   MessagesReceivedCount                    0
-r--   MessagesThresholdTime                    0
-r--   Name                                     MyTestServer_3
-r--   PagingAllocatedIoBufferBytes             0
-r--   PagingAllocatedWindowBufferBytes         0
-r--   PagingPhysicalWriteCount                 0
-r--   PendingTransactions                      null
-r--   ProductionPaused                         false
-r--   ProductionPausedState                    Production-Enabled
-r--   SessionPoolsCurrentCount                 0
-r--   SessionPoolsHighCount                    0
-r--   SessionPoolsTotalCount                   0
-r--   Transactions                             null
-r--   Type                                     JMSServerRuntime
```

As you can see in the listing above, WLST offers a lot of metrics on JMS server level. This includes various message values, throughput (Bytes*) values, state information and more.

The JMS session offers interesting triple metrics, which include the current number, peak number, and total number of JMS sessions. The following example prints out the current session information of a JMS server:

```
def printJMSSessionInformation(myServerName, myJMSServer):
    domainRuntime()
    cd('ServerRuntimes/'+myServerName+'/JMSRuntime/'+myServerName+'.jms/JMSServers/'+myJMSServer)

    # Print session information
    print 'The SessionPoolsCurrentCount of JMS server '+myJMSServer+' is '
        + str(cmo.getSessionPoolsCurrentCount())
    print 'The SessionPoolsHighCount of JMS server '+myJMSServer+' is '
        + str(cmo.getSessionPoolsHighCount())
    print 'The SessionPoolsTotalCount of JMS server '+myJMSServer+' is '
        + str(cmo.getSessionPoolsTotalCount())
```

JMS Destination Monitoring

WLST has quite an extensive number of metrics for every JMS destination. This includes the monitoring of states, message counts, pending and current message counts, and throughput. Metrics include:

InsertionPausedState, ConsumptionPausedState, ProductionPausedState, State, DurableSubscribers, BytesCurrentCount, BytesHighCount, BytesPendingCount, BytesReceivedCount, BytesThresholdTime, ConsumersCurrentCount, ConsumersHighCount, ConsumersTotalCount, ConsumptionPaused, DestinationType, DurableSubscribers, InsertionPaused, MessagesCurrentCount, MessagesDeletedCurrentCount, MessagesHighCount, MessagesMovedCurrentCount, MessagesPendingCount, MessagesReceivedCount, MessagesThresholdTime, and ProductionPaused.

```
wls:/<...>/JMSServers/MyTestServer_2/Destinations/testModule_2!Queue_2> ls()
dr--    DurableSubscribers

-r--    BytesCurrentCount                      0
-r--    BytesHighCount                         0
-r--    BytesPendingCount                      0
-r--    BytesReceivedCount                     0
-r--    BytesThresholdTime                     0
-r--    ConsumersCurrentCount                  0
-r--    ConsumersHighCount                     0
-r--    ConsumersTotalCount                    0
-r--    ConsumptionPaused                      false
-r--    ConsumptionPausedState                 Consumption-Enabled
-r--    DestinationType                        Queue
-r--    DurableSubscribers                     null
-r--    InsertionPaused                        false
-r--    InsertionPausedState                   Insertion-Enabled
-r--    MessagesCurrentCount                   0
-r--    MessagesDeletedCurrentCount            0
-r--    MessagesHighCount                      0
-r--    MessagesMovedCurrentCount              0
-r--    MessagesPendingCount                   0
-r--    MessagesReceivedCount                  0
-r--    MessagesThresholdTime                  0
-r--    Name                                   testModule_2!Queue_2
-r--    Paused                                 false
-r--    ProductionPaused                       false
-r--    ProductionPausedState                  Production-Enabled
-r--    State                                  advertised_in_cluster_jndi
-r--    Type                                   JMSDestinationRuntime
```

State of a JMS Queue

WLST can print the state of a JMS queue. Every queue does not only have a general state, but also detailed states. The following script prints the different states of a queue.

```
def printQueueState(myServerName, myJMSServer, myQueueName):
    domainRuntime()
    cd('ServerRuntimes/'+myServerName+'/JMSRuntime/'+myServerName
        +'.jms/JMSServers/'+myJMSServer+'/Destinations/'+myQueueName)

    # Print general queue state
    print 'The state of queue '+myQueueName+' is '+ getState()

    # Detail states
    print 'The InsertionPausedState of queue '+myQueueName+' is '+ cmo.getInsertionPausedState()
```

```
print 'The ConsumptionPausedState of queue '+myQueueName+' is '+ cmo.getConsumptionPausedState()
print 'The ProductionPausedState of queue '+myQueueName+' is '+ cmo.getProductionPausedState()
```

Message Count for Certain Queues

The following example is a little script that prints out the number of messages that are actually available in a queue. This might give you an indication of a backlog of work or, especially in the case of error or exception queues, will provide you with information about the number of problems that occurred.

```
def printAmountOfMessagesInDestination(myServerName, myJMSServer, myDestinationName):
    domainRuntime()
    cd('ServerRuntimes/'+myServerName+'/JMSRuntime/'+myServerName+'.jms/JMSServers/'+
        myJMSServer+'/Destinations/'+ myDestinationName)
    # print amount of messages
    print 'The number of messages in the queue/topic '+myDestinationName
        +' is '+str(cmo.getMessagesCurrentCount())
    # print amount of pending messages
    print 'The number of messages in the queue/topic '+myDestinationName
        +' is '+str(cmo.getMessagesPendingCount())
```

Note that there are two different methods on this runtime MBean. The method *getMessagesCurrentCount()* provides the current number of messages on this destination. In addition, a destination might have pending messages. The method *getMessagesPendingCount()* returns the number of pending messages that exist on this destination. A pending message may have either been sent in a transaction and not committed, or received and not committed or acknowledged.

Another example for monitoring all destinations is the following:

💾 monitor_all_destinations

```
# ( Script provided by Andrew Pioro )
import thread
import time
from time import gmtime, strftime


username='weblogic'
password='weblogic123'
wlsUrl='t3://127.0.0.1:7001'


connect(username,password, wlsUrl)

def getTime():
 return strftime("%Y-%m-%d %H:%M:%S", gmtime())

def monitorJms():
 servers = domainRuntimeService.getServerRuntimes();
 if (len(servers) > 0):
    for server in servers:
       jmsRuntime = server.getJMSRuntime();
       jmsServers = jmsRuntime.getJMSServers();
       for jmsServer in jmsServers:
          destinations = jmsServer.getDestinations();
          for destination in destinations:
             try:
                print getTime() , '|' , server.getName() , '|' , jmsServer.getName() , '|' ,
                      destination.getName() , '|' ,destination.getMessagesCurrentCount(), '|' ,
                      destination.getMessagesPendingCount() , '|',
                      destination.getMessagesHighCount() , '|' ,
                      destination.getMessagesReceivedCount() , '|' ,
```

```
                            destination.getMessagesMovedCurrentCount() , '|' ,
                            destination.getConsumersCurrentCount() , '|' ,
                            destination.getConsumersHighCount() , '|' ,
                            destination.getConsumersTotalCount()
            except:
                print 'ERROR_DATA';


print 'Time | ServerName | JMSServerName | DestName | MessagesCurrentCount | MessagesPendingCount |
MessagesHighCount | MessagesReceivedCount | MessagesMovedCurrentCount | ConsumersCurrentCount |
ConsumersHighCount | ConsumersTotalCount';
while 1:
    monitorJms();
    print '';
    java.lang.Thread.sleep(15000);
```
(Script provided by Andrew Pioro)

General Application Monitoring

Every application is represented as an *ApplicationRuntimeMBean* in the runtime MBean trees. All runtime information that is relevant for monitoring is collected by WebLogic and can be queried from the *ApplicationRuntimeMBean* of that application or one of its various child MBeans.

```
def printApplicationInformation(rootDirInTree):
    print('APPLICATION RUNTIME INFORMATION');
    cd(rootDirInTree)
    apps = cmo.getApplicationRuntimes();
    for app in apps:
        print '     Application: ' + app.getName()+ '    -   HealthState: '
                + getHealthStateInformation(app.getHealthState());
```

Application State

Every application consists of one or many application components. Every component has a state (e.g. activated or new) that WebLogic provides through the various component MBeans. You can either use the state values 0-3 or the corresponding, and much more readable name from the WebLogic class:

weblogic.management.runtime.ComponentRuntimeMBean.

The following example prints the status of the component provided as an argument:

```
def printApplicationComponentState(applicationname, componentRuntime):
    myDeploymentState = componentRuntime.getDeploymentState()
    myComponentName   = componentRuntime.getName()

    if myDeploymentState == weblogic.management.runtime.ComponentRuntimeMBean.UNPREPARED:
        print 'Status of component '+myComponentName+' of application '
            +applicationname+' = UNPREPARED'
    elif myDeploymentState == weblogic.management.runtime.ComponentRuntimeMBean.PREPARED:
        print 'Status of component '+myComponentName+' of application '+applicationname+' = PREPARED'
    elif myDeploymentState == weblogic.management.runtime.ComponentRuntimeMBean.ACTIVATED:
        print 'Status of component '+myComponentName+' of application '
            +applicationname+' = ACTIVATED'
    elif myDeploymentState == weblogic.management.runtime.ComponentRuntimeMBean.NEW:
        print 'Status of component '+myComponentName+' of application '+applicationname+'  = NEW'
```

The following function provides the component state as a return value that can then be used in other script parts:

```
def getApplicationComponentState(componentRuntime):
    myDeploymentState = componentRuntime.getDeploymentState()

    if myDeploymentState == weblogic.management.runtime.ComponentRuntimeMBean.UNPREPARED:
        return 'UNPREPARED'
    elif myDeploymentState == weblogic.management.runtime.ComponentRuntimeMBean.PREPARED:
        return 'PREPARED'
    elif myDeploymentState == weblogic.management.runtime.ComponentRuntimeMBean.ACTIVATED:
        return 'ACTIVATED'
    elif myDeploymentState == weblogic.management.runtime.ComponentRuntimeMBean.NEW:
        return 'NEW'
```

The script above can be optimized using the special Jython string feature called "split":

```
x='weblogic.management.runtime.ComponentRuntimeMBean.PREPARED'
x.split('.')[4]
```

The result will be: 'PREPARED'

The following script connects to the Administration Server. It then iterates over all application MBeans and all server MBeans and checks the state of the different applications on the different servers. In case of a problem, this script will send an email using *mailx*.

💾 check_states

```
import os
def sendMail(domain,count,dest,sname):
    str3 = 'Domain:#' + domain +'# Server Name: '+ sname +', '+ dest +' @' + str(count)
    cmd = "echo " + str3 + " > /tmp/rw_file"
    os.system(cmd)
    os.system('/bin/mailx -s "Attention, The application state is abnormal !!! " operators@test.com
< /tmp/rw_file')
    print '*********  ALTERT MAIL HAS BEEN SENT  ***********'
    cmd = "rm  /tmp/rw_file"
    os.system(cmd)

def ServerState():
    servers = getRunningServerNames()
    sign="###"
    activecount=0
    problemcount=0
    cd('domainRuntime:/AppRuntimeStateRuntime/AppRuntimeStateRuntime')
    apps = getAppStatus()
    for app in apps:
      for server in servers:
        cd("/ServerLifeCycleRuntimes/" + server.getName())
        serverState = cmo.getState()
        if serverState == "RUNNING" and server.getName()!="ADMINHOST"  :
          cd('domainRuntime:/AppRuntimeStateRuntime/AppRuntimeStateRuntime')
          currentState = str(cmo.getCurrentState(app, server.getName()))
          if currentState == "STATE_ACTIVE":
            print '%25s,  %25s :\033[1;32m %1s %15s \033[0m' % (app,server.getName(),sign,currentState)
            activecount=activecount + 1
          elif  currentState == "STATE_NEW" or currentState =="None":
            print '%25s,  %25s :\033[1;30m %1s %15s \033[0m' % (app,server.getName(),sign,currentState)
          elif  currentState == "STATE_PREPARED" or  currentState == "STATE_ADMIN"  :
            print '%25s,  %25s :\033[1;31m %1s %15s \033[0m' % (app,server.getName(),sign,currentState)
            try:
              progress=startApplication(app)
            except:
              print 'Skipping ..'
```

Advanced WebLogic Server Automation

```
        sendMail(aserver,app,currentState,server.getName())
        problemcount=problemcount +1
        currentState = str(cmo.getCurrentState(app, server.getName()))
        print '%25s,  %25s :\033[1;30m %1s %15s \033[0m' % (app,server.getName(),sign,currentState)
      else:
        sendMail(aserver,app,currentState,server.getName())
        problemcount=problemcount +1
      print '%25s,  %25s :\033[1;31m %1s %15s \033[0m' % (app,server.getName(),sign,currentState)
  print 'Total %4s STATE_ACTIVE :\033[1;31m %4s Problem \033[0m'
%(repr(activecount),repr(problemcount))
  exit ()

def getAppStatus():
    cd('domainRuntime:/AppRuntimeStateRuntime/AppRuntimeStateRuntime')
    return cmo.getApplicationIds()

def getRunningServerNames():
    domainConfig()
    return cmo.getServers()

if __name__ == "main":
    redirect('Server.log', 'false')
    connect (str(user),str(password),str(adminserverURL))
    ServerState()
```
(Source: Script written by Atilla Demirel)

Monitor Complete Applications

The following script iterates over all applications, and for each application the script retrieves a list of components. Then the script examines all components of the application.

```
connect('weblogic','welcome1','t3://localhost:12345')
serverRuntime()
allApplicationRuntimes = cmo.getApplicationRuntimes();
for application in allApplicationRuntimes:
    print 'Application: ' + application.getName()
    allAppComponents = application.getComponentRuntimes();
    for nextComponent in allAppComponents:
        if (nextComponent.getType() == 'EJBComponentRuntime'):
            printEJBRuntimeInformation(application.getName(),nextComponent)
        if (nextComponent.getType() == 'WebAppComponentRuntime'):
            printWebAppRuntimeInformation(application.getName(),nextComponent)
        if (nextComponent.getType() == 'ConnectorComponentRuntime'):
            printConnectorRuntimeInformation(application.getName(),nextComponent)
```

Note that the methods that are called in this script for the different component types are defined in the subsequent sections of this chapter.

Web Components

Web applications are packed into a *.war file. The principal building blocks of a war file for WebLogic are servlets. Each war file may contain many different servlets and every war file can be integrated into an enterprise archive (EAR). WebLogic provides detailed runtime information about a web application and every different servlet.

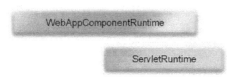

WebAppComponentRuntime

ServletRuntime

The following WLST function will provide information about a web application and all its servlets.

```
def printWebAppRuntimeInformation(applicationName,webAppComponentRuntime):
    myName = webAppComponentRuntime.getName()
    print '\nFound WEB module '+myName+' with current deployment state = ' +
        getApplicationComponentState(webAppComponentRuntime)
    print '     Session information: Session Current Count: '
        + str(webAppComponentRuntime.getOpenSessionsCurrentCount()

    # now look at the submodules
    print '  Servlet overview:'
    myServlets = webAppComponentRuntime.getServlets()
    for nextServlet in myServlets:
        print '      Servlet: ' + nextServlet.getServletName()
            + ', amount invocation: ' +
            str(nextServlet.getInvocationTotalCount())
        print '           invocation time:  average: '
            + str(nextServlet.getExecutionTimeAverage() +
            ' high: ' + str(nextServlet.getExecutionTimeHigh() +
            ' low: ' + str(nextServlet.getExecutionTimeLow() +
            ' total time: ' + str(nextServlet.getExecutionTimeTotal()
```

Note that WebLogic may provide even more information, depending on the domain and application configuration. A web application may even provide information on WorkManagers, page flows, and other runtime information.

Example output:

```
Found WEB module MartinTest_Domain_MS1/myBaseURL with current deployment state = ACTIVATED
    Servlet overview:
        Servlet: TestServlet, amount invocation: 2273
                invocation time:  average: 0 high: 12  low: 0  total time: 571
        Servlet: /data/test/myTestpage_1.jsp, amount invocation: 5
                invocation time:  average: 5 high: 8  low: 4  total time: 26
        Servlet: /data/test/myTestpage_2.jsp, amount invocation: 1327
                invocation time:  average: 1 high: 12  low: 0  total time: 1605
        < ... >
```

Web-sessions

Web sessions do not depend on individual servlets. Therefore, in the above script, web sessions are printed on the web component level rather than the servlet level. WebLogic records a number of interesting values:

```
wls:/MartinTestDomain/serverRuntime/ApplicationRuntimes/xxx/ComponentRuntimes/yyy> ls()
<...>
-r--    OpenSessionsCurrentCount                0
-r--    OpenSessionsHighCount                   0
-r--    ServletReloadCheckSecs                  1
-r--    ServletSessionsMonitoringIds            null
-r--    SessionCookieComment                    null
-r--    SessionCookieDomain                     null
-r--    SessionCookieMaxAgeSecs                 -1
```

```
-r--    SessionCookieName                      JSESSIONID
-r--    SessionCookiePath                      /
-r--    SessionIDLength                        52
-r--    SessionInvalidationIntervalSecs        60
-r--    SessionMonitoringEnabled               false
-r--    SessionTimeoutSecs                     3600
-r--    SessionsOpenedTotalCount               0
-r--    SingleThreadedServletPoolSize          5
<...>
```

Servlets/JSP Information

On the servlet level, WebLogic provides a number of values that can be monitored and/or recorded. The most important are the different execution time values and the number of hits.

```
wls:/MartinTest_Domain/serverRuntime/ApplicationRuntimes/yyy/ComponentRuntimes/test/Servlets/MyServle
t> ls()

-r--    ContextPath                    /yyy
-r--    ExecutionTimeAverage           0
-r--    ExecutionTimeHigh              0
-r--    ExecutionTimeLow               0
-r--    ExecutionTimeTotal             0
-r--    InvocationTotalCount           0
-r--    Name                           FileServlet
-r--    PoolMaxCapacity                0
-r--    ReloadTotalCount               0
-r--    ServletClassName               weblogic.servlet.FileServlet
-r--    ServletName                    FileServlet
-r--    ServletPath                    null
-r--    Type                           ServletRuntime
-r--    URL                            null
-r--    URLPatterns                    null
```

EJB Components

EJB applications are packed into a *.jar file. Each jar file may contain many different EJBs and every EJB-jar file can be integrated into an enterprise archive (EAR). WebLogic provides extensive runtime information about EJB.

Every EJB jar is represented by an *EJBComponentRuntime* MBean, which itself has a health and deployment state. This MBean has appropriate child MBeans for each individual EJB (see diagram), and every individual EJB has child MBeans for specific runtime information. This makes status information and monitoring of EJBs a bit tricky as the MBean hierarchy depends on the EJB type, and not all MBeans may be present.

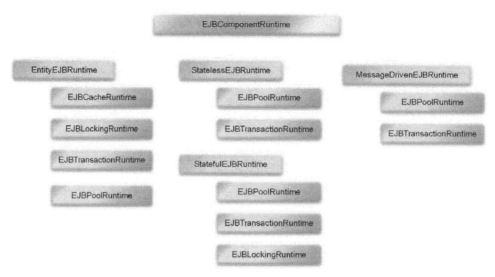

Figure 9.1: *EJB component runtime MBean tree*

Every EJB is represented with an MBean instance that is derived from *EJBComponentRuntime*. Depending on the EJB type, this MBean has a number of its own attributes and a number of sub-MBeans with further information.

The following script prints the most important information from all EJBs found in an EJB module:

💾 EJB_print_information

```
# print EJB information
def printEJBRuntimeInformation(applicationName,ejbComponentRuntime):
    myName = ejbComponentRuntime.getName()
    print '\nFound EJB module '+myName+' with current deployment state = ' +
getApplicationComponentState(ejbComponentRuntime)

    # now look at the submodules
    myEJBs = ejbComponentRuntime.getEJBRuntimes()
    for nextEJB in myEJBs:
        nextEjbType = nextEJB.getType()
        print '    Found EJB module: ' + nextEJB.getName() + ' of type ' + nextEjbType
        if nextEjbType == 'EntityEJBRuntime':
            # transaction information from TransactionRuntime
            myTxRuntime = nextEJB.getTransactionRuntime()
            print '        TransactionInfo:  total:'
                + str(myTxRuntime.getTransactionsCommittedTotalCount())
                +'   rolledback:'+str(myTxRuntime.getTransactionsRolledBackTotalCount())
                +'   timedout:' + str(myTxRuntime.getTransactionsTimedOutTotalCount())

        elif nextEjbType == 'StatelessEJBRuntime':
            # transaction information from TransactionRuntime
            myTxRuntime = nextEJB.getTransactionRuntime()
            print '        TransactionInfo:  total:'
                + str(myTxRuntime.getTransactionsCommittedTotalCount())
                +'   rolledback:'+str(myTxRuntime.getTransactionsRolledBackTotalCount())
                +'   timedout:'
                + str(myTxRuntime.getTransactionsTimedOutTotalCount())
            # pool information from PoolRuntime
            myPoolRuntime = nextEJB.getPoolRuntime()
```

```
        print '      PoolInfo:   totalAccess:'+str(myPoolRuntime.getAccessTotalCount())
            +'    beansInUse:'+str(myPoolRuntime.getBeansInUseCount())
            +'    beansInUseCurrent:'+str(myPoolRuntime.getBeansInUseCurrentCount())
            +'    destroyed:'+str(myPoolRuntime.getDestroyedTotalCount())
            +'    idle:'+str(myPoolRuntime.getIdleBeansCount())
            +'    pooledCurrent:'+str(myPoolRuntime.getPooledBeansCurrentCount())
            +'    timedout:'+str(myPoolRuntime.getTimeoutTotalCount())

        # timer consists of a list of timers
        myTimerRuntime = nextEJB.getTimerRuntime()
        if myTimerRuntime != None:
            print '      Timer information:  Name:'+myTimerRuntime.getName()
                +'    activeTimers:'+str(myTimerRuntime.getActiveTimerCount())
                +'    timeout:'+str(myTimerRuntime.getTimeoutCount())
                +'    cancelled:'+str(myTimerRuntime.getCancelledTimerCount())
                +'    disabled:'+str(myTimerRuntime.getDisabledTimerCount())
    elif nextEjbType == 'StatefulEJBRuntime':
        # transaction information from TransactionRuntime
        myTxRuntime = nextEJB.getTransactionRuntime()
        print '      TransactionInfo:   total:'
            +str(myTxRuntime.getTransactionsCommittedTotalCount())
            +'    rolledback:'+str(myTxRuntime.getTransactionsRolledBackTotalCount())
            +'    timedout:' + str(myTxRuntime.getTransactionsTimedOutTotalCount())
        # cache information from CacheRuntime
        myCacheRuntime = nextEJB.getCacheRuntime()
        print '      CacheInfo:   hits:'+str(myCacheRuntime.getCacheHitCount())
            +'    currentBeans:'+str(myCacheRuntime.getCachedBeansCurrentCount())
            +'    access:'+str(myCacheRuntime.getCacheAccessCount())
        # locking information from LockingRuntime
        myLockingRuntime = nextEJB.getLockingRuntime()
        print '      LockingInfo:   currentCount:'
            + str(myLockingRuntime.getLockEntriesCurrentCount())
            +'    accessCount:'+str(myLockingRuntime.getLockManagerAccessCount())
            +'    timeoutTotalCount:'+str(myLockingRuntime.getTimeoutTotalCount())

    elif nextEjbType == 'MessageDrivenEJBRuntime':
        # transaction information from TransactionRuntime
        myTxRuntime = nextEJB.getTransactionRuntime()
        print '      TransactionInfo:   total:'
            +str(myTxRuntime.getTransactionsCommittedTotalCount())
            +'    rolledback:'+str(myTxRuntime.getTransactionsRolledBackTotalCount())
            +'    timedout:' + str(myTxRuntime.getTransactionsTimedOutTotalCount())
```

Result:

```
Found EJB module myApplicationEJBs.jar with current deployment state = ACTIVATED
    Found EJB module: testStatelessBean of type StatelessEJBRuntime
        TransactionInfo:  total:0    rolledback:0    timedout:0
        PoolInfo:  totalAccess:0    beansInUse:0    beansInUseCurrent:0    destroyed:0    idle:0
            pooledCurrent:0    timedout:0
    Found EJB module: testStateless_2_Bean of type StatelessEJBRuntime
        TransactionInfo:  total:40    rolledback:0    timedout:0
        PoolInfo:  totalAccess:40    beansInUse:0    beansInUseCurrent:0    destroyed:0    idle:1
            pooledCurrent:1    timedout:0
    Found EJB module: testStatefulBean of type StatefulEJBRuntime
        TransactionInfo:  total:0    rolledback:0    timedout:0
        CacheInfo:  hits:0    currentBeans:0    access:0
        LockingInfo:  currentCount:0    accessCount:0    timeoutTotalCount:0
    Found EJB module: testTimerBean of type StatelessEJBRuntime
        TransactionInfo:  total:240722    rolledback:0    timedout:0
        PoolInfo:  totalAccess:240723    beansInUse:0    beansInUseCurrent:0    destroyed:0    idle:1
            pooledCurrent:1    timedout:0
        Timer information:  Name:timer_1    activeTimers:1    timeout:240721    cancelled:0
            disabled:0
    Found EJB module: daemon of type StatelessEJBRuntime
        TransactionInfo:  total:26757    rolledback:0    timedout:0
        PoolInfo:  totalAccess:26759    beansInUse:1    beansInUseCurrent:1    destroyed:0    idle:0
            pooledCurrent:0    timedout:0
        Timer information:  Name:daemon    activeTimers:1    timeout:26756    cancelled:0    disabled:0
```

All MBeans can of course also be queried and listed in interactive mode. The following output of an interactive WLST session demonstrates which attributes can be queried from the different MBeans provided by WebLogic for a stateful session bean type.

```
<...>/ComponentRuntimes/myEJBmodule.jar/EJBRuntimes/myStatefulBean> ls
dr--    CacheRuntime
dr--    LockingRuntime
dr--    Resources
dr--    TransactionRuntime

-r--    EJBName                              myStatefulBean
-r--    Name                                 myStatefulBean
-r--    Type                                 StatefulEJBRuntime

<...>/ComponentRuntimes/myEJBmodule.jar/EJBRuntimes/myStatefulBean> ls
TransactionRuntime/myStatefulBean

-r--    Name                                 myStatefulBean
-r--    TransactionsCommittedTotalCount      0
-r--    TransactionsRolledBackTotalCount     0
-r--    TransactionsTimedOutTotalCount       0
-r--    Type                                 EJBTransactionRuntime

<...>/ComponentRuntimes/myEJBmodule.jar/EJBRuntimes/myStatefulBean>
ls('LockingRuntime/myStatefulBean')

-r--    LockEntriesCurrentCount              0
-r--    LockManagerAccessCount               0
-r--    Name                                 myStatefulBean
-r--    TimeoutTotalCount                    0
-r--    Type                                 EJBLockingRuntime
-r--    WaiterCurrentCount                   0
-r--    WaiterTotalCount                     0

<...>/ComponentRuntimes/myEJBmodule.jar/EJBRuntimes/myStatefulBean> ls('CacheRuntime/myStatefulBean')

-r--    ActivationCount                      0
-r--    CacheAccessCount                     0
-r--    CacheHitCount                        0
-r--    CacheMissCount                       0
-r--    CachedBeansCurrentCount              0
-r--    Name                                 myStatefulBean
-r--    PassivationCount                     0
-r--    Type                                 EJBCacheRuntime
```

JCA Components

Another major component is the resource adapter based on the Java Connector Architecture (JCA). Resource adapters are a complex type of application as they can establish communication to any sort of backend, support transactions, and can use any kind of third party protocol for the communication. They support outgoing and also incoming connections.

This results in another rather complex hierarchy of MBeans for each connector module. The following script shows a function that can provide a number of values and information for a connector module:

```
def printConnectorRuntimeInformation(applicationName,connectorComponentRuntime):
    myName = connectorComponentRuntime.getName()
    print '\nFound JCA modul '+myName+' with current state='+
        connectorComponentRuntime.getState()+'  and deployment state = ' +
        getApplicationComponentState(connectorComponentRuntime)

    # connection pools
    myConPools = connectorComponentRuntime.getConnectionPools()
    for myNextCon in myConPools:
```

```
    print 'ConnectionPool: Name='+myNextCon.getName()+
        ' State='+myNextCon.getState()+
        ' testable='+str(myNextCon.isTestable())+
        ' TransactionSupport='+myNextCon.getTransactionSupport()
    print '                ActiveCurrentCount='
        +str(myNextCon.getActiveConnectionsCurrentCount())+
        ' ActiveHighCount='+str(myNextCon.getActiveConnectionsHighCount())+
        ' FreeCurrentCount='+str(myNextCon.getFreeConnectionsCurrentCount())+
        ' FreeHighCount='+str(myNextCon.getFreeConnectionsHighCount())+
        ' AverageActiveUsage='+str(myNextCon.getAverageActiveUsage())
```

Note that line breaks have in inserted here for better presentation. For the execution of the script, those must be removed.

The following listing provides an impression about the complexity of a connector component and its sub MBeans. In this case, the connection pool:

```
<...>/ComponentRuntimes/MyConnectorComponent> ls()
dr--   ConnectionPools
dr--   ConnectorServiceRuntime
dr--   InboundConnections
dr--   WorkManagerRuntimes

-r--   ActiveVersion                     true
-r--   ActiveVersionId                   null
-r--   ComponentName                     MyConnectorComponent.rar
-r--   Configuration                     ...
-r--   ConfigurationVersion              1.0
-r--   ConfiguredProperties              ...
-r--   ConnectionPoolCount               1
-r--   DeploymentState                   2
-r--   Description                       JCA Implementation of the Test Connector
-r--   Descriptions                      java.lang.String[JCA Implementation of the Test
Connector]
-r--   EISResourceId                     ...
-r--   EISType                           Test Connector
-r--   InboundConnectionsCount           0
-r--   JndiName                          jca/myTestConnector
-r--   Linkref                           null
-r--   ModuleId                          MyConnectorComponent.rar
-r--   Name                              MyConnectorComponent
-r--   Schema                            <?xml version = "1.0" encoding = "UTF-8"?>...
-r--   SpecVersion                       1.5
-r--   State                             Activated
-r--   SuspendedState                    0
-r--   Type                              ConnectorComponentRuntime
-r--   VendorName                        MH-EnterpriseConsulting
-r--   Version                           1.5
-r--   VersionId                         null
-r--   Versioned                         false
```

JCA connectors can have multiple connection pools. The following listing provides a list of possible values that are available for each connection pool.

```
<...>/ComponentRuntimes/MyConnectorComponent> ls ('ConnectionPools/MyConnectorComponent')
-r--   ActiveConnectionsCurrentCount          0
-r--   ActiveConnectionsHighCount             0
-r--   AverageActiveUsage                     0
-r--   CapacityIncrement                      1
-r--   CloseCount                             0
-r--   ConnectionFactoryClassName             com.mh_enterpriseconsulting.test.DataSourceImpl
-r--   ConnectionFactoryName                  null
-r--   ConnectionIdleProfileCount             0
-r--   ConnectionIdleProfiles                 null
-r--   ConnectionLeakProfileCount             0
-r--   ConnectionLeakProfiles                 null
-r--   ConnectionProfilingEnabled             false
-r--   ConnectionsCreatedTotalCount           0
-r--   ConnectionsDestroyedByErrorTotalCount  0
```

```
-r--   ConnectionsDestroyedByShrinkingTotalCount    0
-r--   ConnectionsDestroyedTotalCount               0
-r--   ConnectionsMatchedTotalCount                 0
-r--   ConnectionsRejectedTotalCount                0
-r--   ConnectorEisType                             Test Connector
-r--   CurrentCapacity                              0
-r--   EISResourceId                                ...
-r--   FreeConnectionsCurrentCount                  0
-r--   FreeConnectionsHighCount                     0
-r--   FreePoolSizeHighWaterMark                    0
-r--   FreePoolSizeLowWaterMark                     0
-r--   HighestNumWaiters                            0
-r--   InitialCapacity                              1
-r--   LogFileName                                  null
-r--   LogRuntime                                   null
-r--   MaxCapacity                                  10
-r--   MaxIdleTime                                  0
-r--   Name                                         jca/myTestConnector
-r--   NumUnavailableCurrentCount                   0
-r--   NumUnavailableHighCount                      0
-r--   NumWaiters                                   0
-r--   NumWaitersCurrentCount                       0
-r--   NumberDetectedIdle                           0
-r--   NumberDetectedLeaks                          0
-r--   PoolName                                     jca/myTestConnector
-r--   PoolSizeHighWaterMark                        0
-r--   PoolSizeLowWaterMark                         0
-r--   ProxyOn                                      false
-r--   RecycledTotal                                0
-r--   ResourceAdapterLinkRefName                   null
-r--   ResourceLink                                 null
-r--   ShrinkCountDownTime                          -2407850
-r--   ShrinkPeriodMinutes                          15
-r--   ShrinkingEnabled                             true
-r--   State                                        Running
-r--   Testable                                     false
-r--   TransactionSupport                           LocalTransaction
-r--   Type                                         ConnectorConnectionPoolRuntime
```

WTC Monitoring

As mentioned in an earlier chapter, WebLogic does not offer much in the WTC area. WTC monitoring is included in the additional Oracle product called Oracle Tuxedo System and Application Monitor (TSAM), which is the monitoring solution for Tuxedo applications. Besides some service status information, there is not much offered in WebLogic so far. According to Oracle, the next TSAM version will come with a number of monitoring MBeans for WTC like throughput, requests, and transactions, but unfortunately this will not be part of WebLogic.

In WLST, it is possible to list the available monitoring operations that are offered by the *WTCRuntimeMBean*.

```
# connect to the server
connect(...)
# switch t the domain ruuntime
domainRuntime()
# switch to the WTC runtime of a managed-server
cd ('/ServerRuntimes/MS1/WTCRuntime/WTCService')
# list   (note that in the result below the non-monitoring results have been deleted)
ls()

-r--   Name                                         WTCService
-r--   ServiceStatus
weblogic.wtc.gwt.DServiceInfo[weblogic.wtc.gwt.DServiceInfo@44f686dc,
weblogic.wtc.gwt.DServiceInfo@150ff8e3, weblogic.wtc.gwt.DServiceInfo@4b9d09e2,
```

```
weblogic.wtc.gwt.DServiceInfo@32f3fb36, weblogic.wtc.gwt.DServiceInfo@2ff1b05c,
weblogic.wtc.gwt.DServiceInfo@2471809b, weblogic.wtc.gwt.DServiceInfo@17b252ce,
weblogic.wtc.gwt.DServiceInfo@3c5a5e89, weblogic.wtc.gwt.DServiceInfo@50f49353,
weblogic.wtc.gwt.DServiceInfo@68f457aa, weblogic.wtc.gwt.DServiceInfo@1a78fbb,
weblogic.wtc.gwt.DServiceInfo@1fcd3ed6]
-r--    Type                                  WTCRuntime

-r-x    getServiceStatus                      Integer :
String(java.lang.String),String(java.lang.String),String(java.lang.String)
-r-x    getServiceStatus                      Integer :
String(localAccessPoint),String(svcName)
-r-x    getServiceStatus                      Integer :
String(localAccessPoint),String(svcName),Boolean(isImport)
-r-x    getServiceStatus                      Integer : String(svcName)
-r-x    getServiceStatus                      Integer : String(svcName),Boolean(isImport)
-r-x    listConnectionsConfigured             weblogic.wtc.gwt.DSessConnInfo[] :
...


# call an operation to get the configured connections to Tuxedo domains
cmo.listConnectionsConfigured()
array(weblogic.wtc.gwt.DSessConnInfo, [weblogic.wtc.gwt.DSessConnInfo@14b274ea,
weblogic.wtc.gwt.DSessConnInfo@5019b943, weblogic.wtc.gwt.DSessConnInfo@48d206ca,
weblogic.wtc.gwt.DSessConnInfo@54bbdd1f])
```

Monitoring using SNMP

Simple Network Management Protocol (SNMP) is an "Internet-standard protocol for managing devices on IP networks." Devices that typically support SNMP include routers, switches, servers, workstations, printers, modem racks, and more." It is used mostly in network management systems to monitor network-attached devices for conditions that warrant administrative attention. SNMP is a component of the Internet Protocol Suite as defined by the Internet Engineering Task Force (IETF). It consists of a set of standards for network management, including an application layer protocol, a database schema, and a set of data objects. In typical SNMP uses, one or more administrative computers, called managers, have the task of monitoring or managing a group of hosts or devices on a computer network. Each managed system executes, at all times, a software component called an agent which reports information via SNMP to the manager.[21]

SNMP can be used to collect monitoring information from different WLS instances – Administration Server or Managed-Servers. WebLogic provides integrated support for SNMP. Using WLST or the WebConsole, it is possible for the administrator to configure one or more SNMP agent(s). Monitoring or management tools, which act as SNMP managers, can then connect to these agents in order to get information about resources or state. The internal WebLogic SNMP agent acts as a normal "client" to the WebLogic MBean trees. Hence it can query the different MBeans, collect data, and send this back to the SNMP manager when asked to do so. SNMP requests are based on object identifiers (OIDs). The SNMP agent in WebLogic will map the SNMP OIDs (defined by WebLogic) to the actual MBean. Every WebLogic domain can have multiple SMNP agents.

---

[21] Wikipedia

The following example will create a WebLogic SNMP agent to monitor server runtime state. This consists of 3 major steps, which are creating the SNMP agent, the SNMP string monitor, and finally the SNMP trap destination.

Create the SNMP agent first:

```
# create the SNMP agent
cd('/')
cmo.createSNMPAgentDeployment('MartinTestServerSNMPAgent')
```

Then it is necessary to configure the SNMP agent:

```
# configure the SNMP agent
cd('/SNMPAgent/MartinTestServerSNMPAgent')
cmo.setMasterAgentXPort(700)
cmo.setEnabled(true)
cmo.setInformRetryInterval(10000)
cmo.setSNMPPort(133)
cmo.setLocalizedKeyCacheInvalidationInterval(3600000)
cmo.setPrivacyProtocol('NoPriv')
cmo.setCommunityBasedAccessEnabled(true)
cmo.setMaxInformRetryCount(1)
cmo.setCommunityPrefix('public')
cmo.setSNMPEngineId('MartinTestServerSNMPAgent')
cmo.setAuthenticationProtocol('SHA')
cmo.setSNMPAccessForUserMBeansEnabled(true)
cmo.setInformEnabled(false)
cmo.setSendAutomaticTrapsEnabled(true)
cmo.setSNMPTrapVersion(3)
cmo.setPrivacyProtocol('NoPriv')
set('Targets',jarray.array([ObjectName('com.bea:Name=AdminServer,Type=Server'),
ObjectName('com.bea:Name=BusinessTier_Cluster,Type=Cluster')], ObjectName))
```

Create the SNMP string monitor:

```
cmo.createSNMPStringMonitor('MartinTestSNMPStringMonitor')
```

Configure the string monitor:

```
cd('/SNMPAgent/MartinTestServerSNMPAgent/SNMPStringMonitors/MartinTestSNMPStringMonitor')
cmo.setMonitoredMBeanType('ServerLifeCycleRuntime')
cmo.setMonitoredAttributeName('WeblogicHome')
cmo.setStringToCompare('TestString')
cmo.setPollingInterval(10)
cmo.setMonitoredAttributeName('State')
cmo.setNotifyDiffer(false)
cmo.setNotifyMatch(false)
cmo.setMonitoredMBeanName('MartinTest_Domain')
set('EnabledServers',jarray.array([ObjectName('com.bea:Name=AdminServer,Type=Server'),
ObjectName('com.bea:Name=MartinTest_Domain_MS1,Type=Server'),
ObjectName('com.bea:Name=MartinTest_Domain_MS2,Type=Server')], ObjectName))
```

Create the trap destination:

```
#  create the trap destination
cd('/SNMPAgent/MartinTestServerSNMPAgent')
cmo.createSNMPTrapDestination('TrapDestinationTest1')
```

Configure the trap destination:

```
cd('/SNMPAgent/MartinTestServerSNMPAgent/SNMPTrapDestinations/TrapDestinationTest1')
```

```
cmo.setPort(10000)
cmo.setHost('localhost')
cmo.setCommunity('public')
cmo.setSecurityName('TestSecurity')
cmo.setSecurityLevel('noAuthNoPriv')
```

In a second example, a SNMP agent will be created to monitor a JDBC Connection Pool. We will reuse the SNMP agent created in the first example and we will create a gauge monitor and a trap destination for JDBC monitoring. Therefore, the steps implemented in the following script create a gauge monitor and a trap destination. A gauge monitor observes changes in MBean attributes that are expressed as integers or floating-point.

```
cd('/SNMPAgent/MartinTestServerSNMPAgent')
cmo.createSNMPGaugeMonitor('SNMPGaugeMonitorTest1')

cd('/SNMPAgent/MartinTestServerSNMPAgent/SNMPGaugeMonitors/SNMPGaugeMonitorTest1')
cmo.setMonitoredMBeanType('JDBCConnectionPoolRuntime')
cmo.setMonitoredAttributeName('ActiveConnectionsAverageCount')
cmo.setPollingInterval(10)
cmo.setThresholdLow(0)
cmo.setThresholdHigh(0)

set('EnabledServers',jarray.array([ObjectName('com.bea:Name=AdminServer,Type=Server'),
ObjectName('com.bea:Name=MartinTest_Domain_MS1,Type=Server'),
ObjectName('com.bea:Name=MartinTest_Domain_MS2,Type=Server')], ObjectName))
cd('/SNMPAgent/MartinTestServerSNMPAgent')

cmo.createSNMPTrapDestination('TrapDestination2')

cd('/SNMPAgent/MartinTestServerSNMPAgent/SNMPTrapDestinations/TrapDestination2')
cmo.setPort(162)
cmo.setHost('localhost')
cmo.setCommunity('public')
cmo.setSecurityName('testsec')
cmo.setSecurityLevel('noAuthNoPriv')
```

Virtual Machine Monitoring

WebLogic also offers a more or less hidden secret. A special MBean tree offers information about the virtual machine, information about the operating system, and other low-level information.

This area of the MBean tree can be reached by switching in WLST to the *domainCustom* tree. This tree offers a special subtree that is called *java.lang*. Also, all MBeans *ObjectNames* in this category start with the prefix "java.lang:"

Available information in this subtree can be displayed by running this script:

```
connect('weblogic','< pw >','t3://localhost:7100')
domainCustom()
cd ('java.lang')
ls()
```

Result:

```
drw-    java.lang:Location=AdminServer,name=Code Cache,type=MemoryPool
drw-    java.lang:Location=AdminServer,name=CodeCacheManager,type=MemoryManager
```

```
drw-    java.lang:Location=AdminServer,name=PS Eden Space,type=MemoryPool
drw-    java.lang:Location=AdminServer,name=PS MarkSweep,type=GarbageCollector
drw-    java.lang:Location=AdminServer,name=PS Old Gen,type=MemoryPool
drw-    java.lang:Location=AdminServer,name=PS Perm Gen,type=MemoryPool
drw-    java.lang:Location=AdminServer,name=PS Scavenge,type=GarbageCollector
drw-    java.lang:Location=AdminServer,name=PS Survivor Space,type=MemoryPool
drw-    java.lang:Location=AdminServer,type=ClassLoading
drw-    java.lang:Location=AdminServer,type=Compilation
drw-    java.lang:Location=AdminServer,type=Memory
drw-    java.lang:Location=AdminServer,type=OperatingSystem
drw-    java.lang:Location=AdminServer,type=Runtime
drw-    java.lang:Location=AdminServer,type=Threading
drw-    java.lang:Location=MS1,name=Code Cache,type=MemoryPool
drw-    java.lang:Location=MS1,name=CodeCacheManager,type=MemoryManager
drw-    java.lang:Location=MS1,name=PS Eden Space,type=MemoryPool
drw-    java.lang:Location=MS1,name=PS MarkSweep,type=GarbageCollector
drw-    java.lang:Location=MS1,name=PS Old Gen,type=MemoryPool
drw-    java.lang:Location=MS1,name=PS Perm Gen,type=MemoryPool
drw-    java.lang:Location=MS1,name=PS Scavenge,type=GarbageCollector
drw-    java.lang:Location=MS1,name=PS Survivor Space,type=MemoryPool
drw-    java.lang:Location=MS1,type=ClassLoading
drw-    java.lang:Location=MS1,type=Compilation
drw-    java.lang:Location=MS1,type=Memory
drw-    java.lang:Location=MS1,type=OperatingSystem
drw-    java.lang:Location=MS1,type=Runtime
drw-    java.lang:Location=MS1,type=Threading
```

Threading Information

The threading MBean provides an insight into virtual machine threading. It is possible to get information from the virtual machine about threads, including CPU time, thread counts, and more.

```
connect('weblogic','< pw >','t3://localhost:7100')
domainCustom()
cd ('java.lang/java.lang:Location=AdminServer,type=Threading')
pwd()
ls()
```

Result:

```
'domainCustom:/java.lang/java.lang:Location=AdminServer,type=Threading'
-r--    AllThreadIds                            [J@269c2a55
-r--    CurrentThreadCpuTime                    8090000000
-r--    CurrentThreadCpuTimeSupported           true
-r--    CurrentThreadUserTime                   7860000000
-r--    DaemonThreadCount                       29
-r--    ObjectMonitorUsageSupported             true
-r--    PeakThreadCount                         32
-r--    SynchronizerUsageSupported              true
-rw-    ThreadAllocatedMemoryEnabled            true
-r--    ThreadAllocatedMemorySupported          true
-rw-    ThreadContentionMonitoringEnabled       false
-r--    ThreadContentionMonitoringSupported     true
-r--    ThreadCount                             32
-rw-    ThreadCpuTimeEnabled                    true
-r--    ThreadCpuTimeSupported                  true
-r--    TotalStartedThreadCount                 34
```

This MBean offers a number of interesting values that can be monitored, such as peak number of threads, current number of threads, daemon thread count, and other virtual machine values.

This MBean also offers a number of operations to retrieve values that are not accessible as attributes, or operations to reset the peak thread count value.

```
java.lang:Location=AdminServer,type=Threading
Operation: long  getThreadAllocatedBytes(p0:long  )
Operation: [J  getThreadAllocatedBytes(p0:[J  )
Operation: [J  getThreadCpuTime(p0:[J  )
Operation: long  getThreadCpuTime(p0:long  )
Operation: [J  getThreadUserTime(p0:[J  )
Operation: long  getThreadUserTime(p0:long  )
Operation: [Ljavax.management.openmbean.CompositeData;  dumpAllThreads(p0:boolean  p1:boolean  )
Operation: [J  findDeadlockedThreads()
Operation: [J  findMonitorDeadlockedThreads()
Operation: javax.management.openmbean.CompositeData  getThreadInfo(p0:long  )
Operation: [Ljavax.management.openmbean.CompositeData;  getThreadInfo(p0:[J  )
Operation: javax.management.openmbean.CompositeData  getThreadInfo(p0:long  p1:int  )
Operation: [Ljavax.management.openmbean.CompositeData;  getThreadInfo(p0:[J  p1:int  )
Operation: [Ljavax.management.openmbean.CompositeData;  getThreadInfo(p0:[J  p1:boolean  p2:boolean  )
Operation: void  resetPeakThreadCount()
```

Invoking Operations

Note that this is not the main WebLogic MBean tree; therefore, the *cmo* object is not available. The following example will reset the *PeakThreadCount* attribute by invoking the appropriate operation. As you can see, the attribute is read-only, therefore you have to use the operation instead of the "set" method. This makes sense as the value cannot be reset to a number of your choice. It will be reset to the current number of threads (which is the actual peak).

```
invoke('resetPeakThreadCount',jarray.array([],java.lang.Object),jarray.array([],java.lang.String))
ls()
-r--    AllThreadIds                              [J@7c7174b9
-r--    CurrentThreadCpuTime                      8090000000
-r--    CurrentThreadCpuTimeSupported             true
-r--    CurrentThreadUserTime                     7860000000
-r--    DaemonThreadCount                         20
-r--    ObjectMonitorUsageSupported               true
-r--    PeakThreadCount                           22
-r--    SynchronizerUsageSupported                true
-rw-    ThreadAllocatedMemoryEnabled              true
-r--    ThreadAllocatedMemorySupported            true
-rw-    ThreadContentionMonitoringEnabled         false
-r--    ThreadContentionMonitoringSupported       true
-r--    ThreadCount                               22
-rw-    ThreadCpuTimeEnabled                      true
-r--    ThreadCpuTimeSupported                    true
-r--    TotalStartedThreadCount                   34
```

Note that the thread peak count has been reset from 32 (see the first listing) down to the actual thread count of 22.

Runtime Information

It is interesting to note that it is possible to get information about the VM runtime environment like CLASSAPTH, BOOTCLASSPATH, VM arguments, library path, and more.

```
connect('weblogic','< pw >','t3://localhost:7100')
```

```
domainCustom()
cd ('java.lang/java.lang:Location=AdminServer,type=Runtime')
ls()


-r--   BootClassPath
/opt/java/jre/lib/resources.jar:/opt/java/jre/lib/rt.jar:/opt/java/jre/lib/sunrsasign.jar:/opt/java/j
re/lib/jsse.jar:/opt/java/jre/lib/jce.jar:/opt/java/jre/lib/charsets.jar:/opt/java/jre/lib/modules/jd
k.boot.jar:/opt/java/jre/classes
-r--   BootClassPathSupported                       true
-r--   ClassPath
/opt/wls11g/patch_wls1035/profiles/default/sys_manifest_classpath/weblogic_patch.jar:/opt/java/jre/li
b/tools.jar:/opt/wls11g/wlserver_10.3/server/lib/weblogic_sp.jar:/opt/wls11g/wlserver_10.3/server/lib
/weblogic.jar:/opt/wls11g/modules/features/weblogic.server.modules_10.3.5.0.jar:/opt/wls11g/wlserver_
10.3/server/lib/webservices.jar:/opt/wls11g/modules/org.apache.ant_1.7.1/lib/ant-
all.jar:/opt/wls11g/modules/net.sf.antcontrib_1.1.0.0_1-0b2/lib/ant-
contrib.jar:/opt/wls11g:/opt/wls11g/modules/com.oracle.osdt_cert_1.0.0.0.jar:/opt/wls11g/modules/com.
oracle.osdt_core_1.0.0.0.jar:/opt/wls11g/modules/com.oracle.oraclepki_1.0.0.0.jar
-r--   InputArguments                               java.lang.String[-Dweblogic.Name=MS1, -
Dbea.home=/opt/wls11g, -Djava.security.policy=/opt/wls11g/wlserver_10.3/server/lib/weblogic.policy, -
Dweblogic.management.server=http://localhost:7100, -
Djava.library.path="/opt/java/jre/lib/amd64/server:/opt/java/jre/lib/amd64:/opt/java/jre/../lib/amd64
:/opt/wls11g/patch_wls1035/profiles/default/native:/opt/wls11g/patch_ocp360/profiles/default/native:/
opt/wls11g/wlserver_10.3/server/native/linux/x86_64:/opt/wls11g/wlserver_10.3/server/native/linux/x86
_64/oci920_8:/usr/java/packages/lib/amd64:/usr/lib64:/lib64:/lib:/usr/lib", -
Dweblogic.system.BootIdentityFile=/appdata/domains/testDomain/servers/MS1/data/nodemanager/boot.prope
rties, -Dweblogic.nodemanager.ServiceEnabled=true, -
Dweblogic.security.SSL.ignoreHostnameVerification=false, -Dweblogic.ReverseDNSAllowed=false, -
Djava.awt.headless=true, -Xmx2048m, -XX:MaxPermSize=512m, -
Dweblogic.Stdout=/appdata/logs/testDomain/MS1/MS1.out, -
Dweblogic.Stderr=/appdata/logs/testDomain/MS1/MS1.err, -Djava.library.path=/opt/mqm/lib64]
-r--   LibraryPath                                  /opt/mqm/lib64
-r--   ManagementSpecVersion                        1.2
-r--   Name                                         25272@localhost
-r--   SpecName                                     Java Virtual Machine Specification
-r--   SpecVendor                                   Sun Microsystems Inc.
-r--   SpecVersion                                  1.0
-r--   StartTime                                    1377599725400
-r--   SystemProperties
javax.management.openmbean.TabularDataSupport(tabularType=javax.management.openmbean.TabularType(name
=java.util.Map<java.lang.String,
java.lang.String>,rowType=javax.management.openmbean.CompositeType(name=java.util.Map<java.lang.Strin
g,
java.lang.String>,items=((itemName=key,itemType=javax.management.openmbean.SimpleType(name=java.lang.
String)),(itemName=value,itemType=javax.management.openmbean.SimpleType(name=java.lang.String)))),ind
exNames=(key)),contents={[java.ext.dirs]=javax.management.openmbean.CompositeDataSupport(compositeTyp
e=javax.management.openmbean.CompositeType(name=java.util.Map<java.lang.String,
java.lang.String>,items=((itemName=key,itemType=javax.management.openmbean.SimpleType(name=java.lang.
String)),(itemName=value,itemType=javax.management.openmbean.SimpleType(name=java.lang.String)))),con
tents={key=java.ext.dirs, value=/opt/java/jre/lib/ext:/usr/java/packages/lib/ext}),
[java.security.policy]=javax.management.openmbean.CompositeDataSupport(compositeType=javax.management
.openmbean.CompositeType(name=java.util.Map<java.lang.String, …
-r--   Uptime                                       7558658
-r--   VmName                                       Java HotSpot(TM) 64-Bit Server VM
-r--   VmVendor                                     Sun Microsystems Inc.
-r--   VmVersion                                    20.12-b01
```

Operating System Information

It is also possible to get more information about the underlying operating system, which is normally not available to Java.

```
connect('weblogic','< pw >','t3://localhost:7100')
domainCustom()
cd ('java.lang/java.lang:Location=AdminServer,type=OperatingSystem')
ls()

-r--   Arch                                         amd64
-r--   AvailableProcessors                          24
-r--   CommittedVirtualMemorySize                   1790877696
-r--   FreePhysicalMemorySize                       276557824
-r--   FreeSwapSpaceSize                            107373719552
-r--   MaxFileDescriptorCount                       1024
-r--   Name                                         Linux
```

```
-r--    OpenFileDescriptorCount                  416
-r--    ProcessCpuTime                           73490000000
-r--    SystemLoadAverage                        1.84
-r--    TotalPhysicalMemorySize                  50641022976
-r--    TotalSwapSpaceSize                       107374174208
-r--    Version                                  2.6.18-308.1.1.0.1.el5
```

Information about the underlying machine like physical memory, operating system, and more can be retrieved from this MBean.

Classloading Information

Java applications are compiled from *.java source code into *.class files. Every Java application consists of a number of CLASS files that are loaded into the permanent area of the Java Virtual Machine (JVM). This permanent space is limited. In order to get a baseline for the correct sizing, it might be interesting to know how many classes are loaded into the actual JVM permanent space. Even if this does not say much about the real size, it provides at least an indication of the quantity and the increase rate (if monitored over a period of time). This is possible using the *Classloading* MBean:

```
connect('weblogic','< pw >','t3://localhost:7100')
domainCustom()
cd ('java.lang/java.lang:Location=MS1,type=ClassLoading')
ls()

-r--    LoadedClassCount                         15166
-r--    TotalLoadedClassCount                    15166
-r--    UnloadedClassCount                       0
-rw-    Verbose                                  false
```

Logger Information

WebLogic has a huge number of internal loggers. This information might be useful for fine-grained debug configurations. This area of the MBeanServer also offers information about the different loggers that are available.

The following script demonstrates how to get the list of logger names.

```
connect('weblogic','< pw >','t3://localhost:7100')
domainCustom()
cd ('java.util.logging')
cd ('java.util.logging:Location=AdminServer,type=Logging')
print get('LoggerNames')
```

Result:

```
array(java.lang.String,['weblogic.wsee.policy.checker.PolicyLevelChecker',        'sun.rmi.loader',
'sun.awt.AppContext',                        'javax.enterprise.resource.webservices.jaxws.server',
'javax.management.modelmbean',               'weblogic.wsee.monitoring.WseeClientRuntimeMBeanImpl',
'weblogic.wsee.jaxws.security.AuthorizationTube',
'com.sun.xml.bind.v2.runtime.reflect.opt.AccessorInjector',
'javax.enterprise.resource.webservices.jaxws.server.endpoint',
'com.sun.xml.bind.v2.runtime.reflect.opt.OptimizedAccessorFactory',     'javax.management.mbeanserver',
'com.sun.xml.ws.api.pipe.TubelineAssemblerFactory',
```

```
'javax.enterprise.resource.webservices.jaxws.soap.decoder',                    'sun.rmi.transport.tcp',
'weblogic.utils.classloaders.JarClassFinder',     'weblogic.wsee.reliability2.store.SourceSequenceMap',
'weblogic.wsee.jaxws.WLSTubelineAssemblerFactory',  'weblogic.jws.jaxws.client.ClientIdentityFeature',
'com.sun.xml.bind.v2.runtime.ClassBeanInfoImpl',
'com.sun.xml.ws.transport.http.servlet.ServletAdapter',
'weblogic.wsee.runtime.owsm.OwsmSchedulerHelper',
'weblogic.wsee.reliability2.store.SourceSequenceSenderFactory',        'com.sun.xml.ws.api.pipe.Fiber',
'com.sun.xml.bind.v2.ClassFactory',                 'weblogic.utils.classloaders.ClassPreProcessor',
'com.sun.xml.bind.v2.bytecode.ClassTailor',             'weblogic.wsee.runtime.WebServicesRuntime',
'javax.management.remote.misc',              'global',              'javax.management.remote.timeout',
'com.sun.xml.ws.model.AbstractSEIModelImpl',      'weblogic.wsee.monitoring.WseeRuntimeMBeanDelegate',
'weblogic.wsee.runtime.InMemoryStoreRoutableIDMapper',
'weblogic.wsee.buffer2.api.common.BufferingFeature',
'weblogic.wsee.reliability2.sequence.DestinationSequenceManager',              'javax.activation',
'javax.management.remote.rmi',                                                 'javax.management',
'weblogic.wsee.jaxws.tubeline.standard.WseeServerTube',        'sun.rmi.transport.tcp.proxy',
'javax.enterprise.resource.webcontainer.jsf.config',                  'weblogic.utils.Debug',
'com.sun.xml.ws.server.sei.EndpointMethodHandlerImpl',     'com.sun.xml.ws.server.WSEndpointImpl',
'weblogic.wsee.runtime.JMSStoreRoutableIDMapper',                      'sun.rmi.client.call',
'weblogic.wsee.wstx.wsat.tube.WSATTubelineDeploymentListener',          'com.oracle.wls',
'javax.management.misc',           'sun.rmi.server.call',        'com.sun.xml.ws.addressing.WsaServerTube',
'com.sun.xml.ws.binding.WebServiceFeatureList',    'sun.rmi.transport.misc',     'sun.rmi.client.ref',
'javax.enterprise.resource.webcontainer.jsf',                         'javax.xml.bind',
'weblogic.wsee.jaxws.framework.jaxrpc.EnvironmentFactory',
'weblogic.wsee.reliability2.sequence.SourceSequenceManager',
'weblogic.wsee.reliability2.saf.DestinationSequenceSAFMap',
'weblogic.utils.classloaders.GenericClassLoader',  'com.sun.xml.bind.v2.runtime.reflect.opt.Injector',
'weblogic.wsee.jaxws.tubeline.standard.StandardTubelineDeploymentListener',
'weblogic.wsee.reliability2.store.SequenceMap',
'weblogic.wsee.reliability2.tube.WsrmTubelineDeploymentListener',
'weblogic.wsee.persistence.LogicalStore',       'weblogic.wsee.mc.tube.McTubelineDeploymentListener',
'javax.enterprise.resource.webcontainer.jsf.application',
'com.sun.xml.bind.v2.runtime.reflect.opt.OptimizedTransducedAccessorFactory',
'javax.xml.messaging.saaj.soap',                'weblogic.wsee.reliability2.store.TimedSequenceMap',
'weblogic.wsee.reliability2.sequence.SequenceManager',  'com.sun.xml.ws.transport.http.HttpAdapter',
'weblogic.jws.jaxws.client.async.AsyncClientTransportFeature',        'sun.rmi.server.ref',
'com.sun.xml.ws.addressing.WsaTube',                      'weblogic.wsee.jaxws.WLSContainer',
'weblogic.wsee.buffer2.api.common.BufferingManager', ''])
```

Extended VM Monitoring with 12c

 Starting with 12.1.1, the *domainCustom()* MBean offers some more default MBean subtrees.

The *ls* listing with WebLogic 12.1.1 (and also 12.1.2) reveals that there are new offerings in this area.

```
connect('weblogic',...)
domainCustom()
ls()

drw-    JMImplementation
drw-    com.oracle.jdbc
drw-    com.sun.management
drw-    myWLSMonitoring
drw-    java.lang
drw-    java.nio
drw-    java.util.logging
```

Underneath the JDBC subtree, it is possible to activate/deactivate logging on the JDBC level.

```
cd
('com.oracle.jdbc/com.oracle.jdbc:Location=AdminServer,name=sun.misc.Launcher$AppClassLoader@3aec32de
,type=diagnosability')
ls()
 -rw-    LoggingEnabled                          false
```

The second new category offers information about the Java native IO. Different NIO MBeans might be available, which depend on the JDK used for this server instance.

```
connect('weblogic',...)
domainCustom()
cd ('java.nio')
ls()

drw-    java.nio:Location=AdminServer,name=direct,type=BufferPool
drw-    java.nio:Location=AdminServer,name=mapped,type=BufferPool
drw-    java.nio:Location=MS1,name=direct,type=BufferPool
drw-    java.nio:Location=MS1,name=mapped,type=BufferPool

cd ('java.nio:Location=AdminServer,name=direct,type=BufferPool')
ls()

-r--    Count                               43
-r--    MemoryUsed                          454610
-r--    Name                                direct
-r--    ObjectName
java.nio:Location=AdminServer,name=direct,type=BufferPool
-r--    TotalCapacity                       454610

cd ('../java.nio:Location=AdminServer,name=mapped,type=BufferPool')
ls()

-r--    Count                               0
-r--    MemoryUsed                          0
-r--    Name                                mapped
-r--    ObjectName
java.nio:Location=AdminServer,name=mapped,type=BufferPool
-r--    TotalCapacity                       0
```

Summary

Monitoring is very important for every environment, and therefore important for every J2EE hosting environment like WebLogic. Monitoring has many different aspects, such as gathering information, creating reports, predicting situations (e.g. problems or sales results) and many more. Monitoring without automation is not possible and WLST offers the needed APIs in order to monitor the different system values.

Troubleshooting with WLST CHAPTER

10

Troubleshooting with WLST

Monitoring is a permanent task to observe the server behavior and create reports, but also to anticipate problems. With good monitoring, administrators are often able to anticipate problems before they really occur and can react upfront. Unfortunately problems always exist and in many cases cannot be avoided. Especially in 24x7 system and systems with high volume and high importance, it is absolutely critical to react quickly and have the right tools to find the cause of the problem as soon as possible.

This chapter will discuss a few important tools that can be used/triggered using WLST. Note that these tools are only a subset of the tools that every administrator should know about; it is out of the scope of this book to discuss all of them.

Debugging

Debugging and error analysis is the daily life of every administrator/operator. Normally problems happen in production only and are not reproducible in any test system. Therefore it is important for each administrator to be able to react quickly and have a toolset at hand that allows the gathering of information in a problem situation. This way the administrators - or likely the developers of the application - can analyze and understand what caused the problem and how it can be fixed.

One necessary tool is debugging. WebLogic offers a wide range of debug options that can even be set dynamically on each server at runtime.

Debug Options

WebLogic offers a wide range of possible debug options for the WebLogic Server and its subsystems. These debug options can be set on demand (see next section) while the WebLogic Server is running.

The debug options can be set in the EDIT mode, which means on the Edit-MBeanServer. The following script lists (using *ls()*) the available options that can be set. Please note that non-WebLogic subsystems such as the Oracle JDBC driver might offer additional properties.

```
wls:/MartinTest_Domain/edit> cd ('Servers/AdminServer/ServerDebug/AdminServer')

wls:/MartinTest_Domain/edit/Servers/AdminServer/ServerDebug/AdminServer> ls()
dr--    Server

-rw-    ApplicationContainer                    false
-rw-    ClassChangeNotifier                     false
-rw-    ClassFinder                             false
-rw-    ClassLoader                             false
-rw-    ClassLoaderVerbose                      false
-rw-    ClassloaderWebApp                       false
-rw-    ClasspathServlet                        false
-rw-    DebugAbbreviation                       false
-rw-    DebugAppContainer                       false
-rw-    DebugAsyncQueue                         false
-rw-    DebugBootstrapServlet                   false
-rw-    DebugCertRevocCheck                     false
-rw-    DebugClassRedef                         false
-rw-    DebugClassSize                          false
-rw-    DebugCluster                            false
-rw-    DebugClusterAnnouncements               false

< most items removed in order to reduce the length of the listing >

-rw-    DebugSecurityAdjudicator                false
-rw-    DebugSecurityAtn                        false
-rw-    DebugSecurityAtz                        false
-rw-    DebugSecurityAuditor                    false
-rw-    DebugSecurityCertPath                   false
-rw-    DebugSecurityCredMap                    false
-rw-    DebugSecurityEEngine                    false
-rw-    DebugSecurityEncryptionService          false
-rw-    DebugSecurityJACC                       false
-rw-    DebugSecurityJACCNonPolicy              false
-rw-    DebugSecurityJACCPolicy                 false
-rw-    DebugSecurityKeyStore                   false
-rw-    DebugSecurityPasswordPolicy             false
-rw-    DebugSecurityPredicate                  false
-rw-    DebugSecurityRealm                      false
-rw-    DebugSecurityRoleMap                    false
```

As you can see, WebLogic offers many different options for getting debug output. Many different options are available for debugging different areas of the services, especially in the areas of security, transaction, JMS, JDBC, IIOP, and more.

For example, the following debug attributes are available for the transaction service (JTA).

```
DebugJTAXA                  traces for XA resources
DebugJTANonXA               traces for non-XA resources
DebugJTAXAStackTrace        detailed tracing that prints stack traces at various critical locations
DebugJTA2PC                 traces all 2-phase commit operations
DebugJTA2PCStackTrace       detailed two-phase commit tracing that prints stack traces
DebugJTATLOG                traces transaction logging information
DebugJTAJDBC                traces information about reading/writing JTA records
DebugJTARecovery            traces recovery information
DebugJTAGateway             traces information about imported transactions
DebugJTAGatewayStackTrace   stack traces related to imported transactions
DebugJTANaming              traces transaction naming information
DebugJTANamingStackTrace    traces transaction naming information
DebugJTAResourceHealth      traces information about XA transaction resource health
DebugJTAMigration           traces information about Transaction Log migration
DebugJTALifecycle           traces information about the transaction server lifecycle (initialization,
suspension, resuming, and shutdown)
DebugJTALLR                 traces all Logging Last Resource operations
```

```
DebugJTAHealth            traces information about transaction subsystem health
DebugJTATransactionName   traces transaction names
DebugJTAResourceName      traces transaction resource names
```
(Source: Oracle Corporation[22])

Debugging on Demand

Setting the debug values discussed above can be done using the administration console, and of course also using WLST. The preferred method is WLST because you can switch debug flags on and off as often as you need to. This is very handy, especially if you are running into an error or problem situation and your customer asks you to turn on debugging in order to get more information about what state the server is in and what is actually going on.

Example script for changing a JTA debug flag:

```
# connect to the server
connect('weblogic', '<password>', 't3://localhost:2345')
# switch to edit mode
edit()
# start editing
startEdit()
# change to the debug mbean
cd('Servers/myserver/ServerDebug/myserver')
# change the debug value(s) you need to
set('DebugJTAXA','true')
# save and activate your changes
save()
activate()
```

Administrators will have to change debug flags from time to time and therefore it makes sense to keep the most common changes prepared for future use. The following script defines functions for the different debug areas, and lets the user decide through command line options passed to WLST which set of debug flags the user wants to set to true or false.

🖫 define_debug_area_functions

```
import sys
from java.util import Properties
from java.io import FileInputStream
from java.io import File


domainProps = Properties();
userConfigFile = '';
userKeyFile = '';
groupname = '';
debugvalue = '';


###################################################
# Load properties
###################################################
def intialize():
        global domainProps;
        global userConfigFile;
        global userKeyFile;
```

---

[22] docs.oracle.com/middleware/1212/wls/WLJTA/trbtrx.htm#WLJTA313

```
        global groupname;
        global debugvalue;

        # test arguments
        if len(sys.argv) != 6:
                print 'Usage:  setdebuggroup.py <property_file> <groupname> <debugvalue>'
                exit();

        try:
                domainProps = Properties()

                # load properties and overwrite defaults
                input = FileInputStream(sys.argv[1])
                domainProps.load(input)
                input.close()

                groupname  = sys.argv[2]
                debugvalue = sys.argv[3]

                userConfigFile = sys.argv[4]
                userKeyFile    = sys.argv[5]

        except:
                print 'Cannot load properties  !'
                exit();


###################################
# Connect to adminserver
###################################
def connnectToAdminServer():
     try:
                connUri = domainProps.getProperty('adminURL')

                print 'Connecting to the Admin Server ('+connUri+')'
                connect(userConfigFile=userConfigFile,userKeyFile=userKeyFile,url=connUri)
                print 'Connected'

        except:
                dumpStack();
                print 'Could not connect to admin server - script will exit !'
                exit();


def set_Cluster_DebugFlags():
     set('DebugCluster,                  debugvalue)
     set('DebugClusterAnnouncements,     debugvalue)
     set('DebugClusterFragments,         debugvalue)
     set('DebugClusterHeartbeats,        debugvalue)

def set_EJB_DebugFlags():
     set('DebugEjbCaching,               debugvalue)
     set('DebugEjbCmpDeployment,         debugvalue)
     set('DebugEjbCmpRuntime,            debugvalue)
     set('DebugEjbCompilation,           debugvalue)
     set('DebugEjbDeployment,            debugvalue)
     set('DebugEjbInvoke,                debugvalue)
     set('DebugEjbLocking,               debugvalue)
     set('DebugEjbMdbConnection,         debugvalue)
     set('DebugEjbPooling,               debugvalue)
     set('DebugEjbSecurity,              debugvalue)
     set('DebugEjbSwapping,              debugvalue)
     set('DebugEjbTimers,                debugvalue)

def set_JDBC_DebugFlags():
     set('DebugJDBCConn,                 debugvalue)
     set('DebugJDBCDriverLogging,        debugvalue)
     set('DebugJDBCInternal,             debugvalue)
     set('DebugJDBCONS,                  debugvalue)
     set('DebugJDBCRAC,                  debugvalue)
     set('DebugJDBCREPLAY,               debugvalue)
     set('DebugJDBCRMI,                  debugvalue)
     set('DebugJDBCSQL,                  debugvalue)
     set('DebugJDBCUCP,                  debugvalue)

def set_JMS_DebugFlags():
     set('DebugJMSBackEnd,               debugvalue)
     set('DebugJMSBoot,                  debugvalue)
```

```
        set('DebugJMSCommon,              debugvalue)
        set('DebugJMSConfig,              debugvalue)
        set('DebugJMSDispatcher,          debugvalue)
        set('DebugJMSDistTopic,           debugvalue)
        set('DebugJMSLocking,             debugvalue)
        set('DebugJMSMessagePath,         debugvalue)
        set('DebugJMSModule,              debugvalue)
        set('DebugJMSPauseResume,         debugvalue)
        set('DebugJMSStore,               debugvalue)
        set('DebugJMST3Server,            debugvalue)
        set('DebugJMSWrappers,            debugvalue)
        set('DebugJMSXA,                  debugvalue)

def set_JTA_DebugFlags():
        set('DebugJTA2PC,                 debugvalue)
        set('DebugJTA2PCStackTrace,       debugvalue)
        set('DebugJTAAPI,                 debugvalue)
        set('DebugJTAGateway,             debugvalue)
        set('DebugJTAGatewayStackTrace,   debugvalue)
        set('DebugJTAHealth,              debugvalue)
        set('DebugJTAJDBC,                debugvalue)
        set('DebugJTALifecycle,           debugvalue)
        set('DebugJTAMigration,           debugvalue)
        set('DebugJTANaming,              debugvalue)
        set('DebugJTANamingStackTrace,    debugvalue)
        set('DebugJTANonXA,               debugvalue)
        set('DebugJTAPropagate,           debugvalue)
        set('DebugJTARMI,                 debugvalue)
        set('DebugJTARecovery,            debugvalue)
        set('DebugJTARecoveryStackTrace,  debugvalue)
        set('DebugJTAResourceHealth,      debugvalue)
        set('DebugJTAResourceName,        debugvalue)
        set('DebugJTATLOG,                debugvalue)
        set('DebugJTATransactionName,     debugvalue)
        set('DebugJTAXA,                  debugvalue)
        set('DebugJTAXAStackTrace,        debugvalue)

def set_Security_DebugFlags():
        set('DebugSecurityAdjudicator,    debugvalue)
        set('DebugSecurityAtn,            debugvalue)
        set('DebugSecurityAtz,            debugvalue)
        set('DebugSecurityAuditor,        debugvalue)
        set('DebugSecurityCertPath,       debugvalue)
        set('DebugSecurityCredMap,        debugvalue)
        set('DebugSecurityEEngine,        debugvalue)
        set('DebugSecurityEncryptionService, debugvalue)
        set('DebugSecurityJACC,           debugvalue)
        set('DebugSecurityJACCNonPolicy,  debugvalue)
        set('DebugSecurityJACCPolicy,     debugvalue)
        set('DebugSecurityKeyStore,       debugvalue)
        set('DebugSecurityPasswordPolicy, debugvalue)
        set('DebugSecurityPredicate,      debugvalue)
        set('DebugSecurityRealm,          debugvalue)
        set('DebugSecurityRoleMap,        debugvalue)
        set('DebugSecuritySAML2Atn,       debugvalue)
        set('DebugSecuritySAML2CredMap,   debugvalue)
        set('DebugSecuritySAML2Lib,       debugvalue)
        set('DebugSecuritySAML2Service,   debugvalue)
        set('DebugSecuritySAMLAtn,        debugvalue)
        set('DebugSecuritySAMLCredMap,    debugvalue)
        set('DebugSecuritySAMLLib,        debugvalue)
        set('DebugSecuritySAMLService,    debugvalue)
        set('DebugSecuritySSL,            debugvalue)
        set('DebugSecuritySSLEaten,       debugvalue)
        set('DebugSecurityService,        debugvalue)
        set('DebugSecurityUserLockout,    debugvalue)


if __name__ == "main":
        # connect to the server
        connnectToAdminServer():

        # switch to edit mode
        edit()
        # start editing
        startEdit()
        # change to the debug mbean
        cd('Servers/'+serverName'/ServerDebug/'+serverName)
```

```
# change the debug value(s) you need to
if ('CLUSTER' == groupname):
    set_Cluster_DebugFlags()
elif ('EJB' == groupname):
    set_EJB_DebugFlags()
elif ('JDBC' == groupname):
    set_JDBC_DebugFlags()
elif ('JMS' == groupname):
    set_JMS_DebugFlags()
elif ('JTA' == groupname):
    set_JTA_DebugFlags()
elif ('SECURITY' == groupname):
    set_Security_DebugFlags()

# save and activate your changes
save()
activate()
# Good bye
exit()
```

This script is rather inflexible regarding the number and selection of debug flags. Therefore, it is advisable to refine this script further so that all debug flags and the desired value are stored in a property file. Then the script will just iterate over the entries of this property file and set the configured values for the configured debug flags.

Therefore the next script eliminates this in reading the desired settings - flag name, on/off - from a property file and only sets the desired values. This approach is more flexible and does not overwrite values, which should be kept but also need an additional artefact - a property file.

💾 set_desired_values

```
import sys
from java.util import Properties
from java.io import FileInputStream
from java.io import File

if __name__ == "main":
    myUserConfigFile = sys.argv[1]
    myUserKeyFile = sys.argv[2]
    connUri = sys.argv[3]
    debug_props_file = sys.argv[4]

    debugProps = Properties();
    print 'Reading debugflags from '+debug_props_file;
    debugFile = FileInputStream(debug_props_file)
    debugProps.load(debugFile)

    print 'Connecting to the Admin Server ('+connUri+')';
    connect(userConfigFile=myUserConfigFile,userKeyFile=myUserKeyFile,url=connUri);

    edit()
    startEdit()

    if len(sys.argv) == 5:
        # change to the debug mbean
        cd('Servers/'+serverName+'/ServerDebug/'+serverName)
    elif len(sys.argv) == 6:
        cd('Servers/'+sys.argv[5]+'/ServerDebug/'+sys.argv[5])
    else:
        print 'Wrong number of properties'
        exit()

    # so if all ok, then set all properties

    ls()
```

```
    # iterator over properies
    for prop in debugProps:
        print 'Set '+prop+' to '+debugProps.getProperty(prop)
        set(prop, debugProps.getProperty(prop))

    ls()

    # save and activate your changes
    save()
    activate()
    exit()
```

The following is an example of a property file that can be used for this script:

```
# NOTE: you need to uncomment the values you want to set
#       AND(!!!) of course provide only true or false as value

# Cluster debug values
DebugCluster = true

# EJB debug values
DebugEjbInvoke = true
DebugEjbLocking = true/false
DebugEjbTimers = true/false

# JBDC debug values
DebugJDBCConn = true

# Transaction/JTA debug values
DebugJTAXA = true/false

# Cluster debug values
DebugSecurityAtn = true
DebugSecurityAtz = true
DebugSecurityKeyStore = true/false
DebugSecuritySSL = true/false
```

Debug Options on the Command Line

Most of the debug flags discussed above can also be set as Java virtual machine arguments ("-D" parameters). This might be useful if all your servers on a special machine are started with a shell script and the shell script includes a machine global script that defines these settings. This guarantees you that all servers on a special machine are started with the same debug flags.

I personally do not like those flags much because the Managed-Servers are usually started using the NodeManager, and this means that the list of arguments that have to be configured in the ServerStart section gets very long. It also means that you cannot change them using WLST, therefore a change means changing the domain configuration and restarting the affected servers.

Be careful: Some of those arguments will result in the server logging to the standard output file. Use *RedirectStdoutToServerLogEnabled* in order to redirect standard-out to the server log file in this case (if you need to).

The following list is only a selection of possible command line arguments so that the reader gets an impression of what is possible on the WebLogic command line:

General configuration flags:

```
-Dweblogic.StdoutDebugEnabled=true
-Dweblogic.log.RedirectStdoutToServerLogEnabled=true
```

Security:

```
-Dweblogic.wsee.verbose=*
-Dweblogic.xml.crypto.dsig.verbose
-Dweblogic.xml.crypto.encrypt.verbose=true
-Dweblogic.xml.crypto.dsig.debug=true
-Dweblogic.xml.crypto.dsig.verbose=true
-Dweblogic.wsee.security.debug=true
-Dweblogic.wsee.security.verbose=true
-Dweblogic.xml.crypto.wss.debug=true
-Dweblogic.xml.crypto.wss.verbose=true
-Dweblogic.xml.crypto.keyinfo.debug=true
-Dweblogic.xml.crypto.keyinfo.verbose=true
-Dweblogic.xml.crypto.dsig.debug=true
-Dweblogic.xml.crypto.dsig.verbose=true
-Dweblogic.xml.crypto.encrypt.debug=true
-Dweblogic.xml.crypto.encrypt.verbose=true
-Dweblogic.debug.DebugSecuritySAMLService=true
-Dweblogic.debug.DebugSecuritySAMLCredMap=true
-Dweblogic.debug.DebugSecuritySAMLAtn=true
-Dweblogic.debug.DebugSecuritySAMLLib=true
-Dweblogic.debug.DebugSecuritySAML2Service=true
-Dweblogic.debug.DebugSecuritySAML2CredMap=true
-Dweblogic.debug.DebugSecuritySAML2Atn=true
-Dweblogic.debug.DebugSecuritySAML2Lib=true
-Dweblogic.debug.DebugSecurityCredMap=true
-Dweblogic.log.StdoutSeverity=Debug
-Dweblogic.debug.DebugSecurityAtz=true
-Dweblogic.debug.DebugSecurityAtn=true
-Dweblogic.debug.DebugSecurityAdjudicator=true
-Dweblogic.debug.DebugSecurityRoleMap=true
```

LDAP related debug flags:

```
-Dweblogic.debug.DebugEmbeddedLDAPLogLevel=11
-Dweblogic.debug.DebugEmbeddedLDAP=true
```

WebLogic deployment debug flags:

```
-Dweblogic.debug.DebugConfigurationEdit=true
-Dweblogic.debug.DebugDeploymentTaskRuntime=true
-Dweblogic.debug.DebugDeploymentManagerAdmin=true
-Dweblogic.debug.DebugDeploymentManagerTarget=true
-Dweblogic.debug.DebugDeploymentOperationsAdmin=true
-Dweblogic.debug.DebugDeploymentManagerTargetOperations=true
-Dweblogic.debug.DebugDeploymentServiceApiTargetCalls=true
-Dweblogic.debug.DebugDeploymentServiceApiAdminCalls=true
-Dweblogic.debug.DebugDeploymentServiceApiAdminCallback=true
-Dweblogic.debug.DebugDeploymentServiceApiTargetCallback=true
-Dweblogic.debug.DebugDeploymentServiceStatusUpdatesAdmin=true
-Dweblogic.debug.DebugDeploymentServiceTransport=true
-Dweblogic.debug.DebugDeploymentServiceStatusUpdatesTarget=true
```

Analyzing Problems

One very common task is the analysis of problems. Normally these are problems in production and are not reproducible. This means that the person (developer or analyst) needs runtime information when the server ran into this problem.

Thread Dumps

One very important source of information are thread dumps. Thread dumps help to understand the actual situation of a server and can reveal dead-locks. Creating multiple thread-dumps over a period of time can reveal long-running or even stuck threads.

There are multiple ways to create thread dumps. "Kill -3" is a common one, but this requires that you have access to the machine. Using JVM tools is also a possibility. WebLogic offers a command that can be issued using WLST, which means that this can be issued regardless where the server is running.

The WLST command offered is called *threadDump*. It has the following syntax:

```
threadDump([writeToFile], [fileName], [serverName])
```

The following script will create a threadDump from a server.

🔲 create_threadDump

```
import sys
from java.util import Properties
from java.io import FileInputStream
from java.io import File

# ... global variables
domainProps = Properties();
userConfigFile = '';
userKeyFile = '';
overwrittenServerURL =''

###################################################################
# Load properties
###################################################################
def intialize():
        global domainProps;
        global userConfigFile;
        global userKeyFile;
        global overwrittenServerURL;
        global levelToPrint;

        # test arguments
        if ((len(sys.argv) != 2) and (len(sys.argv) != 3)):
                print 'Usage:  threaddump.py <property_file>';
                print 'OR'
                print 'Usage:  threaddump.py <property_file> <ADMIN-URL overwrite>';
                exit();


        print 'Starting the initialization process';

        try:
                domainProps = Properties()

                # load properties and overwrite defaults
                input = FileInputStream(sys.argv[1])
                domainProps.load(input)
                input.close()

                userConfigFile = domainProps.getProperty('userConfigFile')
                userKeyFile = domainProps.getProperty('userKeyFile ')

                if (len(sys.argv) == 3):
```

```
                    overwrittenServerURL = sys.argv[2];
        except:
                dumpStack()
                print 'Cannot load properties  !';
                exit();

        print 'Initialization completed';


################################################################
# Connect to server
################################################################
def connnectToAdminServer():
        # if NO other URL was provided, the default admin URL from the property file will be used
        if (overwrittenServerURL==''):
            connUri = domainProps.getProperty('adminURL')
        else:
            # Ok, overwrite, this means the URL provided as last argument will be used
            connURI=overwrittenServerURL

        print 'Connecting to the server ('+connUri+')';
        connect(userConfigFile=userConfigFile,userKeyFile=userKeyFile,url=connUri);
        print 'Connected';

if __name__ == "main":
  intialize()
  connnectToAdminServer()

  threadDump()

  disconnect()
```

Another example of how to use the threadDump feature in combination with an email notification is shown in the next example:

💾 threadDump_email_notification

```
import os

def atuning(sname):
    t_limit=15
    cd("/ServerRuntimes/" + sname)
    cd("ThreadPoolRuntime/ThreadPoolRuntime/")
    pr=cmo.getPendingUserRequestCount()
    ql=cmo.getQueueLength()
    queuename=cmo.getName()
    if pr > t_limit :
        tdump(sname,queuename,pr)
    print 'ServerName %-20s# Queuename %-45s Pending Request %-4d Queue %-3d'
        %(sname,queuename,repr(pr),repr(ql))


def tdump(sname,qname,qvalue):
    dump_file= '/tmp/'+sname
    threadDump(writeToFile='true',fileName=dump_file, serverName=sname)
    sendMail("SHADOW",sname,qname,dump_file,qvalue)

def sendMail(count,dest,qname,dumpfile_tmp,qvalue):
    cmd1 = "echo Queue Name:" +  str(qname) + "  Queue Value:" + str(qvalue) + " > rw_tdumpfile"
    cmd2 = "cat " + dumpfile_tmp  + ">>  rw_tdumpfile"
    os.system(cmd1)
    os.system(cmd2)
    os.system('/bin/mailx -s  "Achtung : You have  pending requests " test@gmail.com <  rw_tdumpfile')


def monitorServerState():
    connect(uname, pwd, url)
    t_limit=15
    DSlist=["null"]
    serverNames = getRunningServerNames()
    domainRuntime()
    for sname in serverNames:
      cd("/ServerLifeCycleRuntimes/" + sname.getName())
      serverState = cmo.getState()
      if serverState == "RUNNING"   :
```

```
        print 'Now checking '+sname.getName()
        cd("/ServerRuntimes/" + sname.getName())
        if cmo.getThreadPoolRuntime() is not  None:
          atuning(sname.getName())
        else:
          equeue=cmo.getExecuteQueueRuntimes()
          for names  in  equeue:
             cd("ExecuteQueueRuntimes/" + names.getName())
             executeTTC=cmo.getExecuteThreadTotalCount()
             ETCIC=cmo.getExecuteThreadCurrentIdleCount()
             PRCC=cmo.getPendingRequestCurrentCount()
             queuename=cmo.getName()
             if PRCC > t_limit :
                tdump(sname.getName(),queuename,PRCC)
                print 'ServerName %-20s# Queuename %-45s  \033[1;31m Pending Request %-4d \033[0m  Idle
Thread %3d/%-3d ' %(sname.getName(),queuename,repr(PRCC),repr(ETCIC),repr(executeTTC))
             else:
                print 'ServerName %-20s# Queuename %-45s Pending Request %-4d Idle Thread %3d/%-3d'
%(sname.getName(),queuename,repr(PRCC),repr(ETCIC),repr(executeTTC))
             cd ('../../')
        cd ('../../../../')
     exit()

def getRunningServerNames():
    domainConfig()
    return cmo.getServers()

if __name__ == "main":
    redirect('Server.log', 'false')
    monitorServerState()
```
(Written and provided by Atilla Demirel)

Heap Dumps

Thread dumps are a very valuable source of information. Unfortunately they are not enough to analyze or detect memory leaks. Thankfully Java offers another powerful instrument called heap dump. In this case the complete heap and all allocated objects will be dumped into a file. Be aware that this a) takes some time and b) eats up disk space depending on the size of your heap. In order to analyze and detect memory leaks, you need to take a number of heap dumps over a period of time.

The following script, written and provided by Atilla Demirel, will show you an example of how to use this feature. Thread dump and heap dump in a combination provide a powerful combination to analyze these kind of problems. Fortunately thread dumps can be requested using WLST (if the server is still responding), but in order to create a heap dump you have to run a JVM specific command such as *jmap* for SUN or *jrmcd* for Jrockit. Therefore, the following is a combination of WLST and shell script.

Example: take a HeapDump if limit is greater than x:

💾 **heap_dump**

```
connect ('weblogic','password','t3://adminhost:7700')
heap_limit=5
import os
def sendMail(dumpfile_tmp):
    cmd = "cat " + dumpfile_tmp  + ">>  rw_file "
    os.system(cmd)
    os.system('/bin/mailx -s  "Achtung: There was a heap problem !!! " atillademirel@gmail.com <
rw_file')
```

```
def heapdump(sname,sip):
  from java.io import FileInputStream
  import java.lang
  import os
  import string
  cmd = "ssh -qn " + sip[1] +
        "`` ps -ef | grep java |grep " +str(sname) +" |awk '{print pid= $2}' > /tmp/tmp1.txt``` "
  os.system(cmd)
  propInputStream = FileInputStream("/tmp/tmp1.txt")
  configProps = Properties()
  configProps.load(propInputStream)
  spid = configProps.get("pid")
  cmd1 = "ssh -qn " + sip[1] + "`` /data/hdump.sh "+spid+" `` "
  os.system(cmd1)

def ServerState():
  domainRuntime()
  servers = domainRuntimeService.getServerRuntimes();
  sign="%"
  for server in servers:
   cd("/ServerLifeCycleRuntimes/" + server.getName())
   serverState = cmo.getState()
   if serverState == "RUNNING" :
    cd("/ServerRuntimes/" + server.getName())
    sip=str(cmo.getListenAddress()).split('/')
    cd("JVMRuntime/" + server.getName())
    heapfree=cmo.getHeapFreePercent()
    if heapfree < heap_limit :
     print '%15s :\033[1;31m %15s %1s%2d  \033[0m' % (server.getName(),sip[1],sign,heapfree)
     cmo.runGC()
     heapfree=cmo.getHeapFreePercent()
     print '%15s :\033[1;32m %1s%2d  \033[0m' % (server.getName(),sign,heapfree)
     if heapfree < heap_limit :
      dump_file= '/tmp/'+server.getName()
      threadDump(writeToFile='true',fileName=dump_file, serverName=server.getName())
      sendMail(dump_file)
      heapdump(server.getName(),sip)
      shutdown(server.getName(),timeOut=30,force="true",block="true")
    else:
     print '%15s :\033[1;32m %15s %1s%2d  \033[0m' % (server.getName(),sip[1],sign,heapfree)
  exit ()
def getRunningServerNames():
   domainConfig()
   return cmo.getServers()

if __name__ == "main":
   redirect('Server.log', 'false')
   ServerState()
```

The second part of this example is the corresponding shell script:

💾 heap_dump_shell_script

```
#!/bin/bash

#constants

white='\E[37;40m'
dump_file_dir=/data/dumps

#defult home
JAVA_HOME=/data/jdk617/bin
JROC_HOME=/data/jdk16/bin

TIMESTAMP=`date '+%Y_%m_%d_%H.%M.%S' `
EXPECTED_ARGS=2
E_BADARGS=65

if [ $# -gt 2 -o $# -lt 1 ];then
  ps -ef |grep weblogic.Name|grep -v grep  |sort
  echo -e " $white\033[41m Usage   : `basename $0` pid [optional] -F $white "
  echo -e " $white\033[41m Sample 1: `basename $0` 1234   $white "
  echo -e " $white\033[41m Sample 2: `basename $0` 1234 -F $white "
  exit $E_BADARGS
fi
```

```
hostname=`hostname`
os=`uname`

printf "$s %s #"  $TIMESTAMP  $1

if [ $os == "SunOS" ];then
    servername=` pargs  $1 | grep "Dweblogic.Name" |grep argv | awk '{print $2}' |cut -d= -f2 `
    JAVA_HOME=`pargs $1 |grep bin |grep -v arg  | awk '{print $2}' |cut -d/ -f1-5`
fi

if [ $os == "Linux" ];then
   servername=` tr '\0' '\n' < /proc/$1/environ  |grep SERVER_NAME|grep -v AD |cut -d= -f2  `
   JAVA_HOME=` tr '\0' '\n' < /proc/$1/environ  |grep JAVA_HOME |cut -d= -f2  `
   JAVA_HOME=$JAVA_HOME"/bin"
fi

temp_dir="${dump_file_dir}/${servername}/${TIMESTAMP}"
echo
echo  -e " $white\033[41m $servername      $white "
mkdir  -p ${temp_dir}
file_name=$temp_dir/_$servername.$TIMESTAMP.bin

if [ -f $JAVA_HOME/jmap ]
  then
    $JAVA_HOME/jmap $2  -dump:live,format=b,file=$file_name  $1
  else
    $JAVA_HOME/jrcmd  $1 hprofdump filename=$file_name
fi


if [ $? = 0 ] ; then
echo; echo; echo "Sending mail..."
{ echo "dear friends: i got a heapdump file   $servername@$hostname  $file_name "
} | mailx -s  Caution: i got a heapdump file ' atil]ademirel@gmail.com
echo "Sending mail...: DONE!"

fi
exit 0
```
(Written and provided by Atilla Demirel)

Forced Garbage Collection

Normally you should never force a GC to run for several reasons. The virtual
machine has quite sophisticated implementations of GC and also WebLogic (like
other complex server environments) has built-in strategies for resource management.
Nevertheless, there might be situations where you want to run a GC at a certain time.
This may be for testing or other reasons. Please note again that I strongly discourage
the usage of this script unless it is really necessary.

To force a GC run on a specific server instance, you can use the following script:

```
# connect to the administration server
connect(weblogic,'<password>',url='t3://localhost:40001')

# change to the domain runtime so that you can switch into any server runtime to want
domainRuntime()

# cd into the server runtime
cd('/ServerRuntimes/'+myServer+/JVMRuntime/'+myServer)
print ' Performing Force GC run on server '+myServer

# run the GC
cmo.runGC()

# disconnect from admin server
disconnect()
```

WebLogic Guardian

Guardian is a diagnostic tool for identifying potential problems in your environment before they occur. It also provides specific instructions for resolving them. Guardian itself is a GUI based tool, and in order to use Guardian the guardian agent must be activated in the WebLogic domain. It is also possible to group domains together into groups. Guardian then proceeds against the specified domain(s) and generates a detailed report of potential issues and their remedies.

Activate the Guardian agent:

```
connect('weblogic','test1234','t3://localhost:22123')

# change to edit mode
edit()

# start edit
startEdit()

# change to mbean root
cd ('/')

# configure guardian agent actication yes or no
cmo.setGuardianEnabled(true)

# activate changes
activate()
```

WLDF

Overview

WLDF (WebLogic Diagnostic Framework) is an integrated framework in WebLogic used to collect, save, and analyze runtime data for monitoring or troubleshooting. It provides a number of services that will be executed within (!) the WebLogic Server VM. Using these services, you will be able to gather information that will help you get a detailed view into the runtime performance of your server instances and also inside the deployed applications. It is a very valuable tool for error location and diagnostic operations.

WLDF offers a number of components. One of them is the integration with JRockit, meaning that WLDF can add information to the JRockit Flight Recording file. Capture Diagnostic Image allows the administrator to record a live snapshot that can later be used to analyze problems. The archive feature captures and archives information. Code instrumentation allows the user to collect data at specific operations. The harvester feature allows data collection from standard and custom MBeans. There is also a feature to send out notifications when certain events occur.

WLDF consists of the following:

- Data creators
- Data collectors for the logger and the harvester components
- Archive component
- Accessor component
- Instrumentation component
- Watch and Notification component
- Image Capture component
- Monitoring Dashboard

Data creators collect diagnostic data which is then passed to the components Logger and Harvester. The main server state can also be captured using the image capture component. The Logger and Harvester will use the archive feature in order to persist the collected information. In case there are notifications or watches configured, these components will inform these parts of WLDF. In order to query and use the data, the accessor subsystem will be used.

Configuration

WLDF features are either configured into the server config.xml or into the application deployment descriptors. Basically all will be configured into the server domain configuration and only instrumentation monitors can be defined in application-scoped modules (weblogic-diagnostics.xml file). It is possible to create a diagnostic system module via WLST, which is represented as an instance of a WLDFResourceBean.

Diagnostic Image

A diagnostic image is snapshot of the main server values and saved as a zip. This valuable feature of WLDF can be used to create information that can later be analyzed by the engineering team or a support group.

Example of how to capture an image:

```
# connect to weblogic
connect('weblogic','test1234','t3://localhost:7100')

# switch to the server runtime
serverRuntime()

# change to the image capture runtime bean
cd ('WLDFRuntime/WLDFRuntime/WLDFImageRuntime/Image')

# capture the image
```

```
cmo.captureImage()
```

As we did not provide any file name or location, the image will be saved under <domain>/servers/<server-name>/logs/diagnostic_images

It is also possible to define the image location. The following example will save the image in your home directory:

```
# connect to weblogic
connect('weblogic','test1234','t3://localhost:7100')

# switch to the server runtime
serverRuntime()

# capture and save
imageRuntime = getMBean('/WLDFRuntime/WLDFRuntime/WLDFImageRuntime/Image')
imageRuntime.captureImage('/home/martin/testimage')
```

Example of how to list the images created on a server:

```
# connect to weblogic
connect('weblogic','test1234','t3://localhost:7100')

# switch to the server runtime
serverRuntime()

# Returns a list of all saved image files on this server
allMyImages=getAvailableCapturedImages()

# Returns a list of all saved image files on this server
allMyImages=getAvailableCapturedImages()
if len(allMyImages) > 0:
  # save each diagnostic image
  for myImage in allMyImages:
      # output
      print image
```

Example of how to download all image files:

```
# connect to weblogic
connect('weblogic','test1234','t3://localhost:7100')

# switch to the server runtime
serverRuntime()
# Returns a list of all saved image files on this server
allMyImages=getAvailableCapturedImages()
if len(allMyImages) > 0:
  # save each diagnostic image
  for myImage in allMyImages:
    newFileName='/diag_images/'+myImage
    saveDiagnosticImageCaptureFile(myImage,newFileName)
```

It is also possible to download only a specific entry of an image file. This might be handy if the image file is getting very large or if the data has to be sent via email. The method *saveDiagnosticImageCaptureEntryFile()* has been added to WLST for providing this functionality.

Diagnostic System Module

In order to monitor aspects of your server or some resources, you need to create a system module. It is possible to configure as many system modules as you want for any given server, but only one can be active.

Example of creating a WLDF module:

```
cd('/')
cmo.createWLDFSystemResource('Module-Test')

cd('/SystemResources/Module-Test')
cmo.setDescription('This is a test module')
set('Targets',jarray.array([ObjectName('com.bea:Name=AdminServer,Type=Server'),
ObjectName('com.bea:Name=TestCluster,Type=Cluster')], ObjectName))
```

Diagnostic Archives

An archive is nothing else but a defined place where diagnostic information will be stored. This can either be a directory or a JDBC source. By default, the archive is a directory underneath the <domain>/servers directory: <server>/data/store/diagnostics.

Archives can be file-based or JDBC-based. It is possible to configure the archive settings via WLST.

Example for archive configuration:

```
# connect to weblogic
connect('weblogic','test1234','t3://localhost:7100')

# change to the archive - here at the admin server
cd('/Servers/AdminServer/ServerDiagnosticConfig/AdminServer')

# set the desired configuration values
cmo.setPreferredStoreSizeLimit(1000)
cmo.setStoreSizeCheckPeriod(15)
cmo.setDataRetirementEnabled(true)
cmo.setDiagnosticDataArchiveType('FileStoreArchive')
cmo.setDiagnosticStoreDir('data/store/diagnostics_admin')
cmo.setDiagnosticStoreFileLockingEnabled(true)
```

It is possible to use the built-in function of WLST named *exportDiagnosticDataFromServer()* to query and retrieve WLDF data from the archive.

WLDF Harvester

The WLDF Harvester component can be used to collect and save information from server MBeans. These can either be default WebLogic MBeans or custom MBeans, but they need to be instantiated in the current server instance. The Harvester can only

---

gather information from the runtime MBeanServer, therefore only MBeans registered on the runtime MBeanServer can be used.

A Harvester is created inside a diagnostic module:

```
# change to the module
cd('/WLDFSystemResources/Module-Test/WLDFResource/Module-Test/Harvester/Module-Test')
# it is possible to set sample rates
cmo.setSamplePeriod(200000)
cmo.setEnabled(true)

# create a new harvester instance based on a mbean
cmo.createHarvestedType('weblogic.management.runtime.DomainRuntimeMBean')

# change to it
cd('/WLDFSystemResources/Module-Test/WLDFResource/Module-Test/Harvester/Module-
Test/HarvestedTypes/weblogic.management.runtime.DomainRuntimeMBean')

# configure the harvester
set('HarvestedAttributes',jarray.array([], String))
cmo.setHarvestedInstances(None)
cmo.setNamespace('ServerRuntime')
```

Watch and Notification

This component allows the administrator/user to get notified if defined states of the system or application changes. The notifications are also configured as part of a diagnostic module.

A WLDF watch can inspect data generated from metric collectors, events generated from monitors, or server log files. It can also compare data and can trigger one or more notifications. Every watch is specified as a watch rule which includes a rule, an alarm, and notification handlers.

The following notification types are available: Email, JMS, SNMP traps, or diagnostic images.

Summary

Troubleshooting is a very important set of tools in every administrator's toolbox. Everybody will at some point face a situation where something goes wrong and you need to find out what happened, when and why. This chapter discussed a number of techniques to analyze problem situations. WLST has many potentials strengths in its online and also offline mode to support administrators in analyzing problem situations.

Other WLST Features

Other WLST Features

This chapter presents a collection of WLST features that did not fit well in one of the previous chapters and categories.

JNDI tree

WLST has the ability to browse the JNDI tree of the domain. An interesting fact is that with this WLST feature, not only can you browse the JNDI tree of the server you are connected to, but you can also browse the JNDI tree of all other running (!) Managed-Servers (if you are connected to AdminServer). Note that the usual WLST commands like *cmo* and others do not work.

The following example used the WebLogic example MeDrec server:

🖫 browse_JDNI_tree

```
wls:/medrec/serverConfig>

wls:/medrec/serverConfig> jndi()

wls:/medrec/jndi> ls()
dr--   MedRecServer

wls:/medrec/jndi> cd ('MedRecServer')
wls:/medrec/jndi/MedRecServer> ls()
dr--   com
dr--   ejb
dr--   javax
dr--   jdbc
dr--   mail
dr--   weblogic
-r--   medrecmedrec-facade_jarRmiPatientFacadeBroker_Homeweblogic.rmi.cluster.ClusterableRemoteObject
-r--   mejbmejb_jarMejb_EO                      weblogic.rmi.cluster.ClusterableRemoteObject
-r--   physicianmedrec-
facade_jarRmiPatientFacadeBroker_Homeweblogic.rmi.cluster.ClusterableRemoteObject

wls:/medrec/jndi/MedRecServer> cd ('jdbc')
wls:/medrec/jndi/MedRecServer/jdbc> ls()
-r--   MedRecGlobalDataSourceXA                 weblogic.rmi.cluster.ClusterableRemoteObject

wls:/medrec/jndi/MedRecServer> cd ('javax')
wls:/medrec/jndi/MedRecServer/javax> ls()
dr--   jms
dr--   transaction

wls:/medrec/jndi/MedRecServer/javax> cd ('jms')
wls:/medrec/jndi/MedRecServer/javax/jms> ls()
-r--   QueueConnectionFactory                   weblogic.rmi.cluster.ClusterableRemoteObject
```

```
-r--    TopicConnectionFactory                          weblogic.rmi.cluster.ClusterableRemoteObject

wls:/medrec/jndi/MedRecServer/javax> cd ('transaction')
wls:/medrec/jndi/MedRecServer/javax/transaction> ls()
-r--    TransactionManager
weblogic.transaction.internal.ClientTransactionManagerImpl
-r--    TransactionSynchronizationRegistry
weblogic.transaction.internal.ClientTransactionManagerImpl
-r--    UserTransaction
weblogic.transaction.internal.ClientTransactionManagerImpl
```

If you are connected to a domain with multiple running servers, you can choose which JNDI tree you want to browse.

```
wls:/MartinTest_Domain/serverConfig> jndi()
Location changed to jndi tree. This is a read-only tree with No root.
For more help, use help(jndi)

wls:/MartinTest_Domain/jndi> ls()
dr--    AdminServer
dr--    MartinTest_Domain_MS1
dr--    MartinTest_Domain_MS2

wls:/MartinTest_Domain/jndi> cd ('MartinTest_Domain_MS1')
wls:/MartinTest_Domain/jndi/MartinTest_Domain_MS1> ls()
dr--    javax
dr--    weblogic
```

WLST Running Embedded in the Server

Can WLST scripts execute on the server?

Yes. This can be done by using the embedded mode. Embedded mode requires that you create a startup or shutdown class. In this class you need to create an instance of the WLST interpreter. This instance can be fed with your WLST script. In this case the WLST script will be executed on the server side and will be called before deployment or even before activation (depending on the configuration).

From my long professional and production experience, I strongly discourage you to use this at all! If you need to execute code on the server, then please implement this with normal Java APIs like JMX. This can then be easily executed within a startup class.

On-Demand Deployment of Internal Applications

WebLogic has a number of internal applications that are started during the server start. These applications delay the server startup time and memory footprint, but are already up and running when needed. In day-to-day reality, many of these applications are not needed by most projects. Therefore WebLogic can be configured to delay the startup and deployment of these applications until they are demanded for the first time (on-demand). This reduces the startup time and memory footprint.

We need to distinguish between internal applications with a graphical interface (like the WebLogic console or UDDI) and applications that are services without a GUI. Production-mode domains are by default configured to deploy the internal applications at startup, and development domains for on-demand deployment. This is the reason why the first access to the WebLogic console in a development domain takes a long time.

Configuring on-demand deployment using WLST:

```
connect('weblogic','test1234','t3://localhost:7001')

# change to edit mode
edit()

# start edit
startEdit()

# change to mbean root
cd ('/')

# configure on-demnd or at startup:  false=startup ; true=on demand
cmo.setInternalAppsDeployOnDemandEnabled(false)

# activate changes
activate()
```

Socket using WLST

It is often necessary for WLST scripts to communicate with other systems in order to inform other parties, to archive information, or to download information. This section will give an overview of some of the networking modules that come with Jython, and are therefore available in WLST.

Network Socket with Python/WLST

Internet protocol libraries for Python can be used in WLST. The *gethostname* operation from the socket library can be used to develop more generic scripts.

```
wls:/offline> import socket
wls:/offline> print(socket.gethostname())
wlstautomation.com
```

There are many socket-related modules and built-in functions available. In order to get a better understanding of which functionalities are offered by a special module, it is possible to run the *dir* command on the module to get detailed information about its content.

SMTP

Simple Mail Transfer Protocol (SMTP) is a protocol that is used to send emails. In the context of WebLogic and WLST, we are not talking about receiving or routing emails. Here we are only interested in sending emails, such as notifications for jobs done, alerts, or status reports. This can be done by using the Jython-provided *smtplib* module.

```
wls:/offline> import smtplib
wls:/offline> dir(smtplib)
['CRLF', 'OLDSTYLE_AUTH', 'SMTP', 'SMTPAuthenticationError', 'SMTPConnectError',
 'SMTPDataError', 'SMTPException', 'SMTPHeloError', 'SMTPRecipientsRefused', 'SM
TPResponseException', 'SMTPSenderRefused', 'SMTPServerDisconnected', 'SMTP_PORT'
, 'SSLFakeFile', 'SSLFakeSocket', '__all__', '__doc__', '__file__', '__name__',
'base64', 'encode_base64', 'hmac', 'quoteaddr', 'quotedata', 're', 'rfc822', 'so
cket', 'types']
FTP library in WLST
wls:/offline> import ftplib
wls:/offline> dir(ftplib)
['CRLF', 'Error', 'FTP', 'FTP_PORT', 'MSG_OOB', 'Netrc', '_150_re', '_227_re', '
__all__', '__doc__', '__file__', '__name__', 'all_errors', 'error_perm', 'error_
proto', 'error_reply', 'error_temp', 'ftpcp', 'os', 'parse150', 'parse227', 'par
se229', 'parse257', 'print_line', 'socket', 'string', 'sys', 'test']
```

The main steps are to instantiate a smtplib.SMTP object (providing SMTP server information like host or port) and send the message using the *sendmail* function.

Example for a simple email:

```
import smtplib

sender = 'weblogic_domain_123@mh-enterpriseconsulting.de'
receiver = ['wls_automation@mh-enterpriseconsulting.de']

notification_email = """From: WebLogic Domain 123 <weblogic_domain_123@mh-enterpriseconsulting.de>
To: To Person <wls_automation@mh-enterpriseconsulting.de>
Subject:    Notification of domain Restart

This is an automatically generated message to inform you that the domain <123> has been restarted
Restart was successful
"""

try:
    myEmailObject = smtplib.SMTP('localhost')
    myEmailObject.sendmail(sender, receiver, notification_email)
    print "Successfully sent email"
except SMTPException:
... < do whatever needed in case the notification could not have been send >
```

Jython/WLST also offers functionality to work with the IMAP protocol in order to access emails. For sending notifications, IMAP is not used, as this is mainly used for getting and downloading emails.

```
wls:/offline> import imaplib
wls:/offline> dir(imaplib)
['AllowedVersions', 'CRLF', 'Commands', 'Continuation', 'Debug', 'Flags', 'IMAP4
', 'IMAP4_PORT', 'Int2AP', 'InternalDate', 'Internaldate2tuple', 'Literal', 'Mon
2num', 'ParseFlags', 'Response_code', 'Time2Internaldate', 'Untagged_response',
'Untagged_status', '_Authenticator', '__all__', '__doc__', '__file__', '__name__
', '__version__', '_cmd_log', '_cmd_log_len', '_dump_ur', '_log', '_mesg', 'bina
scii', 'print_log', 'random', 're', 'socket', 'sys', 'time']
```

FTP

Did you ever think of using FTP from WLST? It can be useful in some situations to use the File Transfer Protocol (FTP) to transfer files from WLST scripts. Examples include the automatic upload of log files or error reports, or the automatic download of configuration files from a central server for domain creation. A very useful feature is to keep all your scripts on a central server. In case these scripts must be executed locally and you are not allowed or able to mount the central server, then it might be a very good approach to download the script and execute it so that you always work with the actual script version.

```
wls:/offline> import ftplib
wls:/offline> dir (ftplib)
['CRLF', 'Error', 'FTP', 'FTP_PORT', 'MSG_OOB', 'Netrc', '_150_re', '_227_re', '__all__', '__doc__',
'__file__', '__name__', 'all_errors', 'error_perm', 'error_proto', 'error_reply', 'error_temp',
'ftpcp', 'os', 'parse150', 'parse227', 'parse229', 'parse257', 'print_line', 'socket', 'string',
'sys', 'test'
```

Example of using the *ftplib* in WLST/Jython to download (get) a file:

```
import ftplib
myFTP = ftplib.FTP('ftp.wlsautomationftp.com', 'login', 'password')

try:
    myFTP.setmode('ASCII')
    myFTP.mget('/data/wlstscripts/', 'createdomain.py', '.')
finally:
    myFTP.close()
```

Example of using the *ftplib* in WLST/Jython to upload (put) a file:

```
import ftplib
myFTP = ftplib.FTP('ftp.wlsautomationftp.com', 'login', 'password')
try:
    myFTP.setmode('BINARY')
    myFTP.mput('<domain-lof-dir>', '*.log', '/logs/')
finally:
    myFTP.close()
```

telnet Library in WLST

No, we do not want to implement a telnet session in WLST. However, the telnet functionality can be very useful in order to check if there is a process listening on a certain remote port. For example, it might be very useful to check if the database listener, RMI registry, or a COBRA server is listening before the rest of a WLST script will create and activate a certain resource in WebLogic.

```
wls:/offline> import telnetlib
wls:/offline> dir(telnetlib)
['AO', 'AUTHENTICATION', 'AYT', 'BINARY', 'BM', 'BRK', 'CHARSET', 'COM_PORT_OPTI
ON', 'DEBUGLEVEL', 'DET', 'DM', 'DO', 'DONT', 'EC', 'ECHO', 'EL', 'ENCRYPT', 'EO
R', 'EXOPL', 'FORWARD_X', 'GA', 'IAC', 'IP', 'KERMIT', 'LFLOW', 'LINEMODE', 'LOG
OUT', 'NAMS', 'NAOCRD', 'NAOFFD', 'NAOHTD', 'NAOHTS', 'NAOL', 'NAOLFD', 'NAOP',
'NAOVTD', 'NAOVTS', 'NAWS', 'NEW_ENVIRON', 'NOOPT', 'NOP', 'OLD_ENVIRON', 'OUTMR
K', 'PRAGMA_HEARTBEAT', 'PRAGMA_LOGON', 'RCP', 'RCTE', 'RSP', 'SB', 'SE', 'SEND_
```

```
URL', 'SGA', 'SNDLOC', 'SSPI_LOGON', 'STATUS', 'SUPDUP', 'SUPDUPOUTPUT', 'SUPPRE
SS_LOCAL_ECHO', 'TELNET_PORT', 'TLS', 'TM', 'TN3270E', 'TSPEED', 'TTYLOC', 'TTYP
E', 'TUID', 'Telnet', 'VT3270REGIME', 'WILL', 'WONT', 'X3PAD', 'XASCII', 'XAUTH'
, 'XDISPLOC', '__all__', '__doc__', '__file__', '__name__', 'select', 'socket',
'sys', 'test', 'theNULL']
```

Example showing how to open a telnet session:

```
import telnetlib

telnetHost = 'databaseserver.wlsautomation.com'

myTelnetSession = telnetlib.Telnet(telnetHost, 22)

line1 = myTelnetSession.expect(['>>>'], 1)
```

httplib in WLST

Of course WLST/Jython also provides an implementation of the most common protocol – the HTTP protocol. It is possible to use the module *httplib* for checking sanity, pinging an application, or uploading and downloading files from a webserver (like downloading scripts and configuration files or uploading logs or reports).

```
wls:/offline> import httplib
wls:/offline> dir(httplib)
['BadStatusLine', 'CannotSendHeader', 'CannotSendRequest', 'FakeSocket', 'HTTP',
 'HTTPConnection', 'HTTPException', 'HTTPMessage', 'HTTPResponse', 'HTTPS', 'HTTPSConnection',
'HTTPS_PORT', 'HTTP_PORT', 'ImproperConnectionState', 'IncompleteRead', 'InvalidURL',
'LineAndFileWrapper', 'NotConnected', 'ResponseNotReady', 'SSLFile', 'SharedSocket',
'SharedSocketClient', 'StringIO', 'UnimplementedFileMode', 'UnknownProtocol',
'UnknownTransferEncoding', '_CS_IDLE', '_CS_REQ_SENT', '_CS_REQ_STARTED', '_UNKNOWN', '__all__',
'__doc__', '__file__', '__name__', 'errno', 'error', 'mimetools', 'socket', 'test', 'urlsplit']
```

The main object defined in this module is the *HTTPConnection*:

```
httplib.HTTPConnection('myhost.wlsautomation.de', 80)
```

The following example uses the *GET* method:

```
import httplib
myConnection = httplib.HTTPConnection("myhost.wlsautomation.de")
myConnection.request("GET", "/ping.html")
myResponse = myConnection.getresponse()
print 'Status: ', myResponse.status, '  and reason: ', myResponse.reason
200 OK
```

The next example uses the *POST* method, including some parameters:

```
import httplib, urllib
testparams = urllib.urlencode({'operation': 'ping', 'details': 'true', 'level': 'WARN'})
testheaders = {"Content-type": "application/x-www-form-urlencoded",
...             "Accept": "text/plain"}
myConnection = httplib.HTTPConnection("myhost.wlsautomation.de")
myConnection.request("POST", "/ping/pingmonitor", testparams, testheaders)
myResponse = myConnection.getresponse()
print 'Status: ', myResponse.status, '  and reason: ', myResponse.reason
200 OK
testdata = response.read()
print 'Result from ping: ' + testdata
myConnection.close()
```

For security reasons, it is often necessary to use secure communication (HTTPS). The following examples refines the first example by using HTTPS:

```
import httplib
myConnection = httplib.HTTPSConnection("myhost.wlsautomation.de")
myConnection.request("GET", "/ping.html")
myResponse = myConnection.getresponse()
print 'Status: ' , myResponse.status, '   and reason: ', myResponse.reason
200 OK
```

Not all Jython implementation may have HTTPS (SSL) available. WLST does by default. In order to check it, you can use the following code snippet:

```
import socket
socket.ssl
```

The xmlrpclib Library for WLST

XML-RPC is a Remote Procedure Call method that uses XML and underneath the HTTP protocol as transport.

```
wls:/offline> import xmlrpclib
wls:/offline> dir(xmlrpclib)

['ArrayType', 'Binary', 'Boolean', 'BuiltinFunctionType', 'BuiltinMethodType', 'ClassType',
'CodeType', 'ComplexType', 'DateTime', 'DictProxyType', 'DictType','DictionaryType', 'EllipsisType',
'Error', 'ExpatParser', 'False', 'FastParser',
 'FastUnmarshaller', 'Fault', 'FileType', 'FloatType', 'FrameType', 'FunctionType', 'GeneratorType',
'InstanceType', 'IntType', 'LambdaType', 'ListType', 'LongType', 'MAXINT', 'MININT', 'Marshaller',
'MethodType', 'ModuleType', 'NoneType',
'ObjectType', 'ProtocolError', 'ResponseError', 'SafeTransport', 'Server', 'ServerProxy',
'SgmlopParser', 'SliceType', 'SlowParser', 'StringType', 'StringTypes', 'TracebackType', 'Transport',
'True', 'TupleType', 'TypeType', 'UnboundMethodT
ype', 'UnicodeType', 'Unmarshaller', 'WRAPPERS', 'XRangeType', '_Method', '__doc__', '__file__',
'__name__', '__version__', '_decode', '_stringify', 'binary', 'boolean', 'classDictInit', 'datetime',
'dumps', 'escape', 'getparser', 'loads','operator', 're', 'string', 'time']
```

WebLogic Extension

Later in the JMX part we will discuss Custom MBeans and WebLogic extensions. One open source project called WLHostMachineStats (sourceforge.net/projects/wlhostmchnstats/) offers a very interesting WebLogic extension. This plugin implements additional WebLogic MBeans, which offers more detailed information about the underlying machine and network.

After installation, *domainCustom()* (and also the individual *custom()* areas of each server) will be extended with a new subfolder. Again, note that this is NOT part of WebLogic as delivered by Oracle.

```
# connect to the server
connect(...)

# switch to the custom area
domainCustom()

# switch to the custom mbean
```

```
cd ('wlhostmachinestats/wlhostmachinestats:Location=AdminServer,name=WLHostMachineStats')
ls()

-r--   JVMInstanceCoresUsed                        0.10615711252653928
-r--   JVMInstancePhysicalMemoryUsedMegabytes      1134
-r--   MBeanVersion                                0.2.0
-r--   MonitoredNetworkInferfaceName               eth0
-r--   NativeProcessesCount                        192
-r--   NetworkRxDropped                            0
-r--   NetworkRxErrors                             0
-r--   NetworkRxFrame                              0
-r--   NetworkRxMegabytes                          0
-r--   NetworkRxMillionPackets                     0
-r--   NetworkRxOverruns                           0
-r--   NetworkTxCarrier                            0
-r--   NetworkTxCollisions                         0
-r--   NetworkTxDropped                            0
-r--   NetworkTxErrors                             0
-r--   NetworkTxMegabytes                          0
-r--   NetworkTxMillionPackets                     0
-r--   NetworkTxOverruns                           0
-r--   PhysicalMemoryUsedPercent                   38
-r--   PhysicalSwapUsedPercent                     0
-r--   ProcessorLastMinuteWorkloadAverage          1.36
-r--   ProcessorUsagePercent                       6
-r--   RootFilesystemUsedPercent                   16
-r--   TcpCloseWaitCount                           0
-r--   TcpEstablishedCount                         2
-r--   TcpListenCount                              11
-r--   TcpTimeWaitCount                            0
```

It is possible to get network information, process information, processor information and more. This plug-in internally works with a native library that is loaded via JNI.

Summary

This chapter about WLST highlighted some other WLST features or WLST hints. It is impossible to present everything in one book, so this can only be seen as a selection of additional WLST features.

Part III

WebLogic Automation using Java with the JMX Management API

JMX and WebLogic

JMX and WebLogic

This part of the book will examine the JMX API, MBean layers, and will discuss how JMX can be used to extend domains, setup security, and monitor runtime information. This first chapter of the third part of the book will discuss a number of JMX functions that will be used in all JMX sections of the book. It will also discuss a number of JMX programs that are really helpful tools.

Introduction

Oracle has implemented the complete management layer of WebLogic (with few exceptions) based on JMX management API. There are only a few exceptions, for example parts of the WLST offline mode. This means that in WebLogic, everything is a JMX-MBean. WebLogic distinguishes between different "levels" of MBeans. Basically WebLogic provides a runtime level for actual runtime access (real-time values) and the actual running configuration. WebLogic also provides an "Edit" level that can be used to change the actual runtime information without disturbing the running configuration. Changes can then be propagated into the running MBean server either on-the-fly or, if structural changes are requested, through a server restart.

Different MBean Server Types

WebLogic distinguishes between a number of different MBean servers, such as the Domain MBean server and the EDIT MBeanServer (only available on the AdminServer), as well as the server runtime MBeanServer and special MBeanServer for JNDI and custom MBeans.

Choosing the right MBean server is not too difficult as all of these MBean servers have their specific function. You should always connect to the MBean server that offers you the functionality you currently need. Changing between different MBean servers without disconnect and connect again is not possible. Use the EDIT MBean server to modify the configuration or monitor changes. Keep in mind that all changes done using the EDIT MBean server are not visible or active until they get activated.

For some changes (like port numbers) this activation requires a server restart! Monitoring the server and the actual runtime information can be achieved using the Runtime MBean server. Some properties (like debug) can also be changed on the runtime using the Runtime MBean server. Finally, the Domain runtime server provides a single entry point for domain-wide services and all runtimes of all servers (Admin and all Managed-Servers).

MBean Server Type	JNDI Name	JMX Root Object Name
Domain Runtime MBean Server	weblogic.management.mbeanservers. domainruntime	com.bea:Name=DomainRuntimeService,Type=weblogic.management.mbeanservers.domainruntime.DomainRuntimeServiceMBean
Runtime MBean Server	weblogic.management.mbeanservers.runtime	com.bea:Name=RuntimeService,Type=weblogic.management.mbeanservers.runtime.RuntimeServiceMBean
Edit MBean Server	weblogic.management.mbeanservers.edit	com.bea:Name=EditService,Type=weblogic.management.mbeanservers.edit.EditServiceMBean

(Source: Oracle Corporation[23])
Table 12.1: MBean Servers

It can be very confusing that MBeans with the same name will have a different set of operations and/or attributes in the different MBean servers. Programs running against one MBeanServer might not work when connected to another MBean server. If you get errors that special operations are not found/not available, then you should check which MBean server you are talking to!

The following example demonstrates the different APIs of one of the most important MBeans (the Domain MBean, in this case: com.bea:Name=TestDomain,Type=Domain) in the different (EDIT and Runtime) MBeanServers:

Functionality on the Runtime MBean Server	Functionality on the EDIT MBean Server
| ```
Attribute: VirtualHosts   of Type :
[Ljavax.management.ObjectName;
Attribute: DomainVersion   of Type : java.lang.String
Attribute: ClusterConstraintsEnabled   of Type :
java.lang.Boolean
Attribute: CoherenceClusterSystemResources   of Type :
[Ljavax.management.ObjectName;
Attribute: Servers   of Type : [Ljavax.management.ObjectName;
Attribute: MigratableTargets   of Type :
[Ljavax.management.ObjectName;
Attribute: PasswordPolicies   of Type :
[Ljavax.management.ObjectName;
Attribute: SNMPAgent   of Type : javax.management.ObjectName
Attribute: SNMPAgentDeployments   of Type :
[Ljavax.management.ObjectName;
Attribute: Libraries   of Type : [Ljavax.management.ObjectName;
Attribute: FileStores   of Type : [Ljavax.management.ObjectName;
Attribute: LastModificationTime   of Type : java.lang.Long
Attribute: AdminConsole   of Type : javax.management.ObjectName
Attribute: Parent   of Type : javax.management.ObjectName
Attribute: InternalLibraries   of Type :
[Ljavax.management.ObjectName;
Attribute: SAFAgents   of Type : [Ljavax.management.ObjectName;
Attribute: GuardianEnabled   of Type : java.lang.Boolean
Attribute: ConsoleEnabled   of Type : java.lang.Boolean
``` | ```
Attribute: VirtualHosts   of Type : [Ljavax.management.ObjectName;
Attribute: DomainVersion   of Type : java.lang.String
Attribute: ClusterConstraintsEnabled   of Type : java.lang.Boolean
Attribute: CoherenceClusterSystemResources   of Type :
[Ljavax.management.ObjectName;
Attribute: Servers   of Type : [Ljavax.management.ObjectName;
Attribute: MigratableTargets   of Type : [Ljavax.management.ObjectName;
Attribute: PasswordPolicies   of Type : [Ljavax.management.ObjectName;
Attribute: SNMPAgent   of Type : javax.management.ObjectName
Attribute: SNMPAgentDeployments   of Type : [Ljavax.management.ObjectName;
Attribute: Libraries   of Type : [Ljavax.management.ObjectName;
Attribute: FileStores   of Type : [Ljavax.management.ObjectName;
Attribute: LastModificationTime   of Type : java.lang.Long
Attribute: AdminConsole   of Type : javax.management.ObjectName
Attribute: Parent   of Type : javax.management.ObjectName
Attribute: InternalLibraries   of Type : [Ljavax.management.ObjectName;
Attribute: SAFAgents   of Type : [Ljavax.management.ObjectName;
Attribute: GuardianEnabled   of Type : java.lang.Boolean
Attribute: ConsoleEnabled   of Type : java.lang.Boolean
Attribute: NTRealms   of Type : [Ljavax.management.ObjectName;
Attribute: UnixRealms   of Type : [Ljavax.management.ObjectName;
Attribute: AutoDeployForSubmodulesEnabled   of Type : java.lang.Boolean
Attribute: ProductionModeEnabled   of Type : java.lang.Boolean
Attribute: JoltConnectionPools   of Type : [Ljavax.management.ObjectName;
Attribute: ConfigurationAuditType   of Type : java.lang.String
``` |

---

[23] docs.oracle.com/middleware/1212/wls/JMXCU/understandwls.htm

```
Attribute: NTRealms   of Type : [Ljavax.management.ObjectName;
Attribute: UnixRealms   of Type : [Ljavax.management.ObjectName;
Attribute: AutoDeployForSubmodulesEnabled   of Type :
java.lang.Boolean
Attribute: ProductionModeEnabled   of Type : java.lang.Boolean
Attribute: JoltConnectionPools   of Type :
[Ljavax.management.ObjectName;
Attribute: ConfigurationAuditType   of Type : java.lang.String
Attribute: EmbeddedLDAP   of Type : javax.management.ObjectName
Attribute: SecurityConfiguration   of Type :
javax.management.ObjectName
Attribute: WTCServers   of Type : [Ljavax.management.ObjectName;
Attribute: StartupClasses   of Type :
[Ljavax.management.ObjectName;
Attribute: Machines   of Type : [Ljavax.management.ObjectName;
Attribute: WebAppContainer   of Type :
javax.management.ObjectName
Attribute: Targets   of Type : [Ljavax.management.ObjectName;
Attribute: JMSBridgeDestinations   of Type :
[Ljavax.management.ObjectName;
Attribute: SingletonServices   of Type :
[Ljavax.management.ObjectName;
Attribute: FileRealms   of Type : [Ljavax.management.ObjectName;
Attribute: XMLRegistries   of Type :
[Ljavax.management.ObjectName;
Attribute: JTA   of Type : javax.management.ObjectName
Attribute: ConsoleContextPath   of Type : java.lang.String
Attribute: XMLEntityCaches   of Type :
[Ljavax.management.ObjectName;
Attribute: JPA   of Type : javax.management.ObjectName
Attribute: ConfigurationVersion   of Type : java.lang.String
Attribute: RDBMSRealms   of Type : [Ljavax.management.ObjectName;
Attribute: OCMEnabled   of Type : java.lang.Boolean
Attribute: ExalogicOptimizationsEnabled   of Type :
java.lang.Boolean
Attribute: WSReliableDeliveryPolicies   of Type :
[Ljavax.management.ObjectName;
Attribute: JDBCStores   of Type : [Ljavax.management.ObjectName;
Attribute: MailSessions   of Type :
[Ljavax.management.ObjectName;
Attribute: PathServices   of Type :
[Ljavax.management.ObjectName;
Attribute: CoherenceServers   of Type :
[Ljavax.management.ObjectName;
Attribute: MigratableRMIServices   of Type :
[Ljavax.management.ObjectName;
Attribute: RemoteSAFContexts   of Type :
[Ljavax.management.ObjectName;
Attribute: SystemResources   of Type :
[Ljavax.management.ObjectName;
Attribute: WLECConnectionPools   of Type :
[Ljavax.management.ObjectName;
Attribute: InternalAppDeployments   of Type :
[Ljavax.management.ObjectName;
Attribute: CachingRealms   of Type :
[Ljavax.management.ObjectName;
Attribute: CustomRealms   of Type :
[Ljavax.management.ObjectName;
Attribute: JMSInteropModules   of Type :
[Ljavax.management.ObjectName;
Attribute: LogFilters   of Type : [Ljavax.management.ObjectName;
Attribute: JMX   of Type : javax.management.ObjectName
Attribute: Notes   of Type : java.lang.String
Attribute: Security   of Type : javax.management.ObjectName
Attribute: AdministrationPortEnabled   of Type :
java.lang.Boolean
Attribute: Deployments   of Type : [Ljavax.management.ObjectName;
Attribute: DomainLibraries   of Type :
[Ljavax.management.ObjectName;
Attribute: WLDFSystemResources   of Type :
[Ljavax.management.ObjectName;
Attribute: Realms   of Type : [Ljavax.management.ObjectName;
Attribute: SelfTuning   of Type : javax.management.ObjectName
Attribute: Type   of Type : java.lang.String
Attribute: ArchiveConfigurationCount   of Type :
java.lang.Integer
Attribute: ErrorHandlings   of Type :
[Ljavax.management.ObjectName;
Attribute: ForeignJNDIProviders   of Type :
[Ljavax.management.ObjectName;
Attribute: AdministrationPort   of Type : java.lang.Integer
Attribute: EJBContainer   of Type : javax.management.ObjectName
Attribute: RestfulManagementServices   of Type :
javax.management.ObjectName
Attribute: Log   of Type : javax.management.ObjectName
Attribute: AdministrationMBeanAuditingEnabled   of Type :
java.lang.Boolean
Attribute: LDAPRealms   of Type : [Ljavax.management.ObjectName;
Attribute: ConfigBackupEnabled   of Type : java.lang.Boolean
Attribute: ConsoleExtensionDirectory   of Type : java.lang.String
Attribute: AdministrationProtocol   of Type : java.lang.String
Attribute: CustomResources   of Type :
[Ljavax.management.ObjectName;
Attribute: InternalAppsDeployOnDemandEnabled   of Type :
java.lang.Boolean
Attribute: Clusters   of Type : [Ljavax.management.ObjectName;
Attribute: DeploymentConfiguration   of Type :
javax.management.ObjectName
Attribute: JMSConnectionConsumers   of Type :
[Ljavax.management.ObjectName;
Attribute: AppDeployments   of Type :
[Ljavax.management.ObjectName;
Attribute: ShutdownClasses   of Type :
[Ljavax.management.ObjectName;
Attribute: FileT3s   of Type : [Ljavax.management.ObjectName;
Attribute: JMSServers   of Type : [Ljavax.management.ObjectName;
Attribute: MessagingBridges   of Type :
[Ljavax.management.ObjectName;
Attribute: BasicRealms   of Type : [Ljavax.management.ObjectName;
Attribute: Name   of Type : java.lang.String
Attribute: JDBCSystemResources   of Type :
[Ljavax.management.ObjectName;
Attribute: AdminServerName   of Type : java.lang.String
Attribute: JMSSystemResources   of Type :
[Ljavax.management.ObjectName;
Attribute: WebserviceSecurities   of Type :
[Ljavax.management.ObjectName;
Attribute: BridgeDestinations   of Type :
```

```
Attribute: EmbeddedLDAP   of Type : javax.management.ObjectName
Attribute: SecurityConfiguration   of Type : javax.management.ObjectName
Attribute: WTCServers   of Type : [Ljavax.management.ObjectName;
Attribute: StartupClasses   of Type : [Ljavax.management.ObjectName;
Attribute: Machines   of Type : [Ljavax.management.ObjectName;
Attribute: WebAppContainer   of Type : javax.management.ObjectName
Attribute: Targets   of Type : [Ljavax.management.ObjectName;
Attribute: JMSBridgeDestinations   of Type : [Ljavax.management.ObjectName;
Attribute: SingletonServices   of Type : [Ljavax.management.ObjectName;
Attribute: FileRealms   of Type : [Ljavax.management.ObjectName;
Attribute: XMLRegistries   of Type : [Ljavax.management.ObjectName;
Attribute: JTA   of Type : javax.management.ObjectName
Attribute: ConsoleContextPath   of Type : java.lang.String
Attribute: XMLEntityCaches   of Type : [Ljavax.management.ObjectName;
Attribute: JPA   of Type : javax.management.ObjectName
Attribute: ConfigurationVersion   of Type : java.lang.String
Attribute: RDBMSRealms   of Type : [Ljavax.management.ObjectName;
Attribute: OCMEnabled   of Type : java.lang.Boolean
Attribute: ExalogicOptimizationsEnabled   of Type : java.lang.Boolean
Attribute: WSReliableDeliveryPolicies   of Type : [Ljavax.management.ObjectName;
Attribute: JDBCStores   of Type : [Ljavax.management.ObjectName;
Attribute: MailSessions   of Type : [Ljavax.management.ObjectName;
Attribute: PathServices   of Type : [Ljavax.management.ObjectName;
Attribute: CoherenceServers   of Type : [Ljavax.management.ObjectName;
Attribute: MigratableRMIServices   of Type : [Ljavax.management.ObjectName;
Attribute: RemoteSAFContexts   of Type : [Ljavax.management.ObjectName;
Attribute: SystemResources   of Type : [Ljavax.management.ObjectName;
Attribute: WLECConnectionPools   of Type : [Ljavax.management.ObjectName;
Attribute: InternalAppDeployments   of Type : [Ljavax.management.ObjectName;
Attribute: CachingRealms   of Type : [Ljavax.management.ObjectName;
Attribute: CustomRealms   of Type : [Ljavax.management.ObjectName;
Attribute: JMSInteropModules   of Type : [Ljavax.management.ObjectName;
Attribute: LogFilters   of Type : [Ljavax.management.ObjectName;
Attribute: JMX   of Type : javax.management.ObjectName
Attribute: Notes   of Type : java.lang.String
Attribute: Security   of Type : javax.management.ObjectName
Attribute: AdministrationPortEnabled   of Type : java.lang.Boolean
Attribute: Deployments   of Type : [Ljavax.management.ObjectName;
Attribute: DomainLibraries   of Type : [Ljavax.management.ObjectName;
Attribute: WLDFSystemResources   of Type : [Ljavax.management.ObjectName;
Attribute: Realms   of Type : [Ljavax.management.ObjectName;
Attribute: SelfTuning   of Type : javax.management.ObjectName
Attribute: Type   of Type : java.lang.String
Attribute: ArchiveConfigurationCount   of Type : java.lang.Integer
Attribute: ErrorHandlings   of Type : [Ljavax.management.ObjectName;
Attribute: ForeignJNDIProviders   of Type : [Ljavax.management.ObjectName;
Attribute: AdministrationPort   of Type : java.lang.Integer
Attribute: EJBContainer   of Type : javax.management.ObjectName
Attribute: RestfulManagementServices   of Type : javax.management.ObjectName
Attribute: Log   of Type : javax.management.ObjectName
Attribute: AdministrationMBeanAuditingEnabled   of Type : java.lang.Boolean
Attribute: LDAPRealms   of Type : [Ljavax.management.ObjectName;
Attribute: ConfigBackupEnabled   of Type : java.lang.Boolean
Attribute: ConsoleExtensionDirectory   of Type : java.lang.String
Attribute: AdministrationProtocol   of Type : java.lang.String
Attribute: CustomResources   of Type : [Ljavax.management.ObjectName;
Attribute: InternalAppsDeployOnDemandEnabled   of Type : java.lang.Boolean
Attribute: Clusters   of Type : [Ljavax.management.ObjectName;
Attribute: DeploymentConfiguration   of Type : javax.management.ObjectName
Attribute: JMSConnectionConsumers   of Type : [Ljavax.management.ObjectName;
Attribute: AppDeployments   of Type : [Ljavax.management.ObjectName;
Attribute: ShutdownClasses   of Type : [Ljavax.management.ObjectName;
Attribute: FileT3s   of Type : [Ljavax.management.ObjectName;
Attribute: JMSServers   of Type : [Ljavax.management.ObjectName;
Attribute: MessagingBridges   of Type : [Ljavax.management.ObjectName;
Attribute: BasicRealms   of Type : [Ljavax.management.ObjectName;
Attribute: Name   of Type : java.lang.String
Attribute: JDBCSystemResources   of Type : [Ljavax.management.ObjectName;
Attribute: AdminServerName   of Type : java.lang.String
Attribute: JMSSystemResources   of Type : [Ljavax.management.ObjectName;
Attribute: WebserviceSecurities   of Type : [Ljavax.management.ObjectName;
Attribute: BridgeDestinations   of Type : [Ljavax.management.ObjectName;
Attribute: JDBCDataSourceFactories   of Type : [Ljavax.management.ObjectName;
Attribute: RootDirectory   of Type : java.lang.String
Operation: java.lang.Void
destroyRemoteSAFContext(remoteSAFContext:javax.management.ObjectName  )
Operation: javax.management.ObjectName
createWebserviceSecurity(name:java.lang.String  )
Operation: javax.management.ObjectName  lookupFileStore(name:java.lang.String  )
Operation: javax.management.ObjectName
createUnixRealm(java.lang.String:java.lang.String  )
Operation: java.lang.Void  restoreDefaultValue(attributeName:java.lang.String  )
Operation: javax.management.ObjectName
createJMSSystemResource(name:java.lang.String  descriptorFileName:java.lang.String
)
Operation: java.lang.Void  destroyWTCServer(wtcServer:javax.management.ObjectName
)
Operation: java.lang.Void
destroyApplication(application:javax.management.ObjectName  )
Operation: java.lang.Void
destroyXMLEntityCache(XMLEntityCache:javax.management.ObjectName  )
Operation: javax.management.ObjectName
createJDBCSystemResource(name:java.lang.String
descriptorFileName:java.lang.String  )
Operation: javax.management.ObjectName
lookupCachingRealm(java.lang.String:java.lang.String  )
Operation: java.lang.Void
destroySNMPAgentDeployment(mbean:javax.management.ObjectName  )
Operation: javax.management.ObjectName
lookupJMSInteropModule(name:java.lang.String  )
Operation: javax.management.ObjectName
createBridgeDestination(name:java.lang.String  )
Operation: javax.management.ObjectName  lookupXMLEntityCache(name:java.lang.String
)
Operation: javax.management.ObjectName  lookupCluster(name:java.lang.String  )
Operation: javax.management.ObjectName  createVirtualHost(name:java.lang.String  )
Operation: javax.management.ObjectName
createPasswordPolicy(java.lang.String:java.lang.String  )
Operation: javax.management.ObjectName
lookupDomainLogFilter(name:java.lang.String  )
Operation: javax.management.ObjectName  lookupCustomResource(name:java.lang.String
)
Operation: javax.management.ObjectName  createFileStore(name:java.lang.String  )
Operation: javax.management.ObjectName  createCluster(name:java.lang.String  )
Operation: javax.management.ObjectName
createMigratableTarget(name:java.lang.String  )
Operation: java.lang.Void  destroyVirtualHost(host:javax.management.ObjectName  )
Operation: javax.management.ObjectName  createJDBCStore(name:java.lang.String  )
```

```
[Ljavax.management.ObjectName;
Attribute: JDBCDataSourceFactories   of Type :
[Ljavax.management.ObjectName;
Attribute: RootDirectory  of Type : java.lang.String
Operation: javax.management.ObjectName
lookupFileStore(name:java.lang.String  )
Operation: javax.management.ObjectName
lookupCachingRealm(java.lang.String:java.lang.String  )
Operation: javax.management.ObjectName
lookupJMSInteropModule(name:java.lang.String  )
Operation: javax.management.ObjectName
lookupXMLEntityCache(name:java.lang.String  )
Operation: javax.management.ObjectName
lookupCluster(name:java.lang.String  )
Operation: javax.management.ObjectName
lookupDomainLogFilter(name:java.lang.String  )
Operation: javax.management.ObjectName
lookupCustomResource(name:java.lang.String  )
Operation: javax.management.ObjectName
lookupSAFAgent(name:java.lang.String  )
Operation: javax.management.ObjectName
lookupRemoteSAFContext(name:java.lang.String  )
Operation: javax.management.ObjectName
lookupSNMPAgentDeployment(name:java.lang.String  )
Operation: javax.management.ObjectName
lookupJDBCStore(name:java.lang.String  )
Operation: javax.management.ObjectName
lookupErrorHandling(name:java.lang.String  )
Operation: javax.management.ObjectName
lookupForeignJMSDestination(name:java.lang.String  )
Operation: javax.management.ObjectName
lookupSingletonService(name:java.lang.String  )
Operation: javax.management.ObjectName
lookupShutdownClass(name:java.lang.String  )
Operation: javax.management.ObjectName
lookupCoherenceServer(name:java.lang.String  )
Operation: javax.management.ObjectName
lookupInternalLibrary(name:java.lang.String  )
Operation: javax.management.ObjectName
lookupJDBCDataSourceFactory(name:java.lang.String  )
Operation: javax.management.ObjectName
lookupVirtualHost(name:java.lang.String  )
Operation: javax.management.ObjectName
lookupInternalAppDeployment(name:java.lang.String  )
Operation: javax.management.ObjectName
lookupNTRealm(java.lang.String:java.lang.String  )
Operation: javax.management.ObjectName
lookupPasswordPolicy(java.lang.String:java.lang.String  )
Operation: javax.management.ObjectName
lookupJMSSystemResource(name:java.lang.String  )
Operation: javax.management.ObjectName
lookupLDAPRealm(java.lang.String:java.lang.String  )
Operation: javax.management.ObjectName
lookupFileT3(name:java.lang.String  )
Operation: java.lang.Void  unSet(propertyName:java.lang.String  )
Operation: javax.management.ObjectName
lookupTarget(java.lang.String:java.lang.String  )
Operation: javax.management.ObjectName
lookupWLDFSystemResource(name:java.lang.String  )
Operation: javax.management.ObjectName
lookupJMSDestination(name:java.lang.String  )
Operation: javax.management.ObjectName
lookupJMSBridgeDestination(name:java.lang.String  )
Operation: javax.management.ObjectName
lookupWSReliableDeliveryPolicy(name:java.lang.String  )
Operation: javax.management.ObjectName
lookupForeignJMSConnectionFactory(name:java.lang.String  )
Operation: javax.management.ObjectName
lookupMailSession(name:java.lang.String  )
Operation: javax.management.ObjectName
lookupDomainLibrary(java.lang.String:java.lang.String  )
Operation: javax.management.ObjectName
lookupLogFilter(name:java.lang.String  )
Operation: javax.management.ObjectName
lookupMigratableRMIService(name:java.lang.String  )
Operation: javax.management.ObjectName
lookupWebserviceSecurity(name:java.lang.String  )
Operation: javax.management.ObjectName
lookupCoherenceClusterSystemResource(name:java.lang.String  )
Operation: javax.management.ObjectName
lookupBridgeDestination(name:java.lang.String  )
Operation: javax.management.ObjectName
lookupWTCServer(name:java.lang.String  )
Operation: javax.management.ObjectName
lookupRDBMSRealm(java.lang.String:java.lang.String  )
Operation: javax.management.ObjectName
lookupRealm(java.lang.String:java.lang.String  )
Operation: javax.management.ObjectName
lookupAppDeployment(java.lang.String:java.lang.String  )
Operation: javax.management.ObjectName
lookupWLECConnectionPool(name:java.lang.String  )
Operation: javax.management.ObjectName
lookupJoltConnectionPool(name:java.lang.String  )
Operation: javax.management.ObjectName
lookupApplication(name:java.lang.String  )
Operation: javax.management.ObjectName
lookupSystemResource(java.lang.String:java.lang.String  )
Operation: javax.management.ObjectName
lookupMigratableTarget(name:java.lang.String  )
Operation: javax.management.ObjectName
lookupFileRealm(java.lang.String:java.lang.String  )
Operation: javax.management.ObjectName
lookupJMSConnectionConsumer(name:java.lang.String  )
Operation: javax.management.ObjectName
lookupForeignJNDIProvider(name:java.lang.String  )
Operation: java.lang.Void
freezeCurrentValue(attributeName:java.lang.String  )
Operation: javax.management.ObjectName
lookupLibrary(java.lang.String:java.lang.String  )
Operation: javax.management.ObjectName
lookupServer(name:java.lang.String  )
Operation: javax.management.ObjectName
lookupXMLRegistry(name:java.lang.String  )
Operation: javax.management.ObjectName
lookupJMSServer(name:java.lang.String  )
Operation: javax.management.ObjectName
lookupMachine(name:java.lang.String  )
Operation: javax.management.ObjectName
```

```
Operation: javax.management.ObjectName  createEJBContainer()
Operation: javax.management.ObjectName  lookupSAFAgent(name:java.lang.String  )
Operation: java.lang.Void
destroyRealm(weblogic.management.configuration.RealmMBean:javax.management.ObjectN
ame  )
Operation: java.lang.Void
destroyFileRealm(weblogic.management.configuration.FileRealmMBean:javax.management
.ObjectName  )
Operation: javax.management.ObjectName
lookupRemoteSAFContext(name:java.lang.String  )
Operation: javax.management.ObjectName
lookupSNMPAgentDeployment(name:java.lang.String  )
Operation: java.lang.Void
destroyForeignJMSDestination(wsc:javax.management.ObjectName  )
Operation: java.lang.Void
destroyJMSBridgeDestination(jmsBridgeDestination:javax.management.ObjectName  )
Operation: javax.management.ObjectName  lookupJDBCStore(name:java.lang.String  )
Operation: javax.management.ObjectName  lookupErrorHandling(name:java.lang.String
)
Operation: javax.management.ObjectName
lookupForeignJMSDestination(name:java.lang.String  )
Operation: javax.management.ObjectName
lookupSingletonService(name:java.lang.String  )
Operation: java.lang.Void
destroyJMSInteropModule(bean:javax.management.ObjectName  )
Operation: java.lang.Void
destroyJoltConnectionPool(joltConnectionPool:javax.management.ObjectName  )
Operation: javax.management.ObjectName  lookupShutdownClass(name:java.lang.String
)
Operation: java.lang.Void  destroyLogFilter(logFilter:javax.management.ObjectName
)
Operation: java.lang.Void  destroyCluster(cluster:javax.management.ObjectName  )
Operation: javax.management.ObjectName
lookupCoherenceServer(name:java.lang.String  )
Operation: javax.management.ObjectName
lookupInternalLibrary(name:java.lang.String  )
Operation: java.lang.Void
destroyJMSConnectionConsumer(wsc:javax.management.ObjectName  )
Operation: java.lang.Void
destroyJDBCSystemResource(bean:javax.management.ObjectName  )
Operation: javax.management.ObjectName
lookupJDBCDataSourceFactory(name:java.lang.String  )
Operation: javax.management.ObjectName
createMessagingBridge(name:java.lang.String  )  lookupVirtualHost(name:java.lang.String  )
Operation: javax.management.ObjectName
createForeignJMSConnectionFactory(name:java.lang.String  )
Operation: javax.management.ObjectName  createJMSServer(name:java.lang.String  )
Operation: javax.management.ObjectName
lookupInternalAppDeployment(name:java.lang.String  )
Operation: javax.management.ObjectName
lookupNTRealm(java.lang.String:java.lang.String  )
Operation: javax.management.ObjectName  createPathService(name:java.lang.String  )
Operation: javax.management.ObjectName
lookupPasswordPolicy(java.lang.String:java.lang.String  )
Operation: javax.management.ObjectName
createRealm(java.lang.String:java.lang.String  )  createFileT3(name:java.lang.String  )
Operation: javax.management.ObjectName
createNTRealm(java.lang.String:java.lang.String  )
Operation: javax.management.ObjectName
createJMSBridgeDestination(name:java.lang.String  )
Operation: java.lang.Void  destroySAFAgent(sAFAgent:javax.management.ObjectName  )
Operation: java.lang.Void
destroyLDAPRealm(weblogic.management.configuration.LDAPRealmMBean:javax.management
.ObjectName  )
Operation: java.lang.Void
destroyErrorHandling(errorHandling:javax.management.ObjectName  )
Operation: javax.management.ObjectName
lookupJMSSystemResource(name:java.lang.String  )
Operation: javax.management.ObjectName
lookupLDAPRealm(java.lang.String:java.lang.String  )
Operation: javax.management.ObjectName  lookupFileT3(name:java.lang.String  )
Operation: javax.management.ObjectName  createJMSQueue(name:java.lang.String
destination:javax.management.ObjectName  )
Operation: java.lang.Void
destroyBridgeDestination(bridgeDestination:javax.management.ObjectName  )
Operation: java.lang.Void  unSet(propertyName:java.lang.String  )
Operation: javax.management.ObjectName
lookupTarget(java.lang.String:java.lang.String  )
Operation: javax.management.ObjectName
lookupWLDFSystemResource(name:java.lang.String  )
Operation: javax.management.ObjectName  lookupJMSDestination(name:java.lang.String
)
Operation: java.lang.Void
destroyPathService(pathService:javax.management.ObjectName  )
Operation: java.lang.Void  destroyMailSession(ms:javax.management.ObjectName  )
Operation: javax.management.ObjectName
createCoherenceServer(name:java.lang.String  )
Operation: javax.management.ObjectName
lookupJMSBridgeDestination(name:java.lang.String  )
Operation: javax.management.ObjectName
lookupWSReliableDeliveryPolicy(name:java.lang.String  )
Operation: java.lang.Void
destroyMigratableTarget(bean:javax.management.ObjectName  )
Operation: javax.management.ObjectName
createForeignJMSDestination(name:java.lang.String  )
Operation: javax.management.ObjectName
createCustomRealm(java.lang.String:java.lang.String  )
Operation: javax.management.ObjectName
lookupForeignJMSConnectionFactory(name:java.lang.String  )  lookupMailSession(name:java.lang.String  )
Operation: javax.management.ObjectName
lookupDomainLibrary(java.lang.String:java.lang.String  )
Operation: javax.management.ObjectName  lookupLogFilter(name:java.lang.String  )
Operation: javax.management.ObjectName  createServer(name:java.lang.String  )
Operation: javax.management.ObjectName  createXMLEntityCache(name:java.lang.String
)
Operation: javax.management.ObjectName  createShutdownClass(name:java.lang.String
)
Operation: javax.management.ObjectName
lookupMigratableRMIService(name:java.lang.String  )
Operation: javax.management.ObjectName
lookupWebserviceSecurity(name:java.lang.String  )
Operation: java.lang.Void
destroyWLDFSystemResource(bean:javax.management.ObjectName  )
Operation: javax.management.ObjectName
lookupCoherenceClusterSystemResource(name:java.lang.String  )
```

```
lookupCustomRealm(java.lang.String:java.lang.String  )
Operation: java.lang.Boolean  isSet(propertyName:java.lang.String  )

Operation: javax.management.ObjectName
lookupMessagingBridge(name:java.lang.String  )
Operation: javax.management.ObjectName
lookupJDBCSystemResource(name:java.lang.String  )
Operation: javax.management.ObjectName
lookupStartupClass(name:java.lang.String  )
Operation: javax.management.ObjectName
lookupUnixRealm(java.lang.String:java.lang.String  )
Operation:                            javax.management.ObjectName
lookupPathService(name:java.lang.String  )
```

```
Operation: javax.management.ObjectName
createSingletonService(name:java.lang.String  )
Operation: java.lang.Void  destroyJDBCStore(store:javax.management.ObjectName  )
createWSReliableDeliveryPolicy(name:java.lang.String  )
Operation: javax.management.ObjectName
lookupBridgeDestination(name:java.lang.String  )
Operation: java.lang.Void  destroyJMSServer(jmsServer:javax.management.ObjectName

Operation: java.lang.Void
destroyWSReliableDeliveryPolicy(policy:javax.management.ObjectName  )
createRDBMSRealm(java.lang.String:java.lang.String  )
Operation: java.lang.Void  destroySingletonService(sc:javax.management.ObjectName

Operation: javax.management.ObjectName  createXMLRegistry(name:java.lang.String  )
Operation: javax.management.ObjectName  lookupWTCServer(name:java.lang.String  )
Operation: javax.management.ObjectName  createLogFilter(name:java.lang.String  )
Operation: javax.management.ObjectName
lookupRDBMSRealm(java.lang.String:java.lang.String  )
Operation: javax.management.ObjectName
createWLECConnectionPool(name:java.lang.String  )
Operation: javax.management.ObjectName
lookupRealm(java.lang.String:java.lang.String  )
Operation: java.lang.Void
destroyUnixRealm(weblogic.management.configuration.UnixRealmMBean:javax.management
.ObjectName  )
Operation: javax.management.ObjectName
lookupAppDeployment(java.lang.String:java.lang.String  )
Operation: javax.management.ObjectName
lookupWLECConnectionPool(name:java.lang.String  )
Operation: javax.management.ObjectName
createWLDFSystemResource(name:java.lang.String  )
Operation: javax.management.ObjectName
createSNMPAgentDeployment(name:java.lang.String  )
Operation: javax.management.ObjectName
createJMSDistributedQueueMember(name:java.lang.String
member:javax.management.ObjectName  )
Operation: java.lang.Void  destroyStartupClass(sc:javax.management.ObjectName  )
Operation: javax.management.ObjectName
lookupJoltConnectionPool(name:java.lang.String  )
Operation: javax.management.ObjectName
createForeignJMSDestination(name:java.lang.String
destination:javax.management.ObjectName  )
Operation: javax.management.ObjectName
createJoltConnectionPool(name:java.lang.String  )
Operation: java.lang.Void  destroyEJBContainer()
Operation: java.lang.Void  destroyServer(server:javax.management.ObjectName  )
Operation: javax.management.ObjectName  lookupApplication(name:java.lang.String  )
Operation: javax.management.ObjectName
lookupSystemResource(java.lang.String:java.lang.String  )
Operation: javax.management.ObjectName
lookupMigratableTarget(name:java.lang.String  )
Operation: javax.management.ObjectName
lookupFileRealm(java.lang.String:java.lang.String  )
Operation: javax.management.ObjectName
lookupJMSConnectionConsumer(name:java.lang.String  )
Operation: javax.management.ObjectName
createDomainLogFilter(name:java.lang.String  )
Operation: javax.management.ObjectName
createCachingRealm(java.lang.String:java.lang.String  )
Operation: javax.management.ObjectName  createErrorHandling(name:java.lang.String
)
Operation: javax.management.ObjectName
createJDBCDataSourceFactory(name:java.lang.String  )
Operation: java.lang.Void
destroyForeignJNDIProvider(provider:javax.management.ObjectName  )
Operation: javax.management.ObjectName
lookupForeignJNDIProvider(name:java.lang.String  )
Operation: javax.management.ObjectName
createForeignJMSConnectionFactory(name:java.lang.String
factory:javax.management.ObjectName  )
Operation: java.lang.Void
destroyWebserviceSecurity(wsc:javax.management.ObjectName  )
Operation: javax.management.ObjectName
createJMSSystemResource(name:java.lang.String  )
Operation: java.lang.Void  destroyCustomResource(bean:javax.management.ObjectName  )

Operation: javax.management.ObjectName  createWTCServer(name:java.lang.String  )
Operation: javax.management.ObjectName  createCustomResource(name:java.lang.String
resourceClass:java.lang.String  descriptorBeanClass:java.lang.String  )
Operation: java.lang.Void
destroyMessagingBridge(bridge:javax.management.ObjectName  )
Operation: java.lang.Void
destroyCachingRealm(weblogic.management.configuration.CachingRealmMBean:javax.mana
gement.ObjectName  )
Operation: java.lang.Void  destroyMachine(machine:javax.management.ObjectName  )
Operation: javax.management.ObjectName
createJMSDistributedTopicMember(name:java.lang.String
member:javax.management.ObjectName  )
Operation: java.lang.Void
destroyJMSSystemResource(bean:javax.management.ObjectName  )
Operation: java.lang.Void
destroyDomainLogFilter(logFilter:javax.management.ObjectName  )
Operation: java.lang.Void
destroyNTRealm(weblogic.management.configuration.NTRealmMBean:javax.management.Obj
ectName  )
Operation: javax.management.ObjectName  createSAFAgent(name:java.lang.String  )
Operation: java.lang.Void  freezeCurrentValue(attributeName:java.lang.String  )
Operation: javax.management.ObjectName  createApplication(name:java.lang.String  )
Operation: java.lang.Void  destroyShutdownClass(sc:javax.management.ObjectName  )
Operation: javax.management.ObjectName
lookupLibrary(java.lang.String:java.lang.String  )
Operation: javax.management.ObjectName  createCustomResource(name:java.lang.String
resourceClass:java.lang.String  descriptorBeanClass:java.lang.String
descriptorFileName:java.lang.String  )
Operation: javax.management.ObjectName  lookupServer(name:java.lang.String  )
Operation: javax.management.ObjectName
createForeignJNDIProvider(name:java.lang.String  )
Operation: java.lang.Void
destroyCoherenceClusterSystemResource(bean:javax.management.ObjectName  )
Operation: javax.management.ObjectName  createMachine(name:java.lang.String  )
Operation: javax.management.ObjectName
createCoherenceClusterSystemResource(name:java.lang.String  )
Operation: javax.management.ObjectName
createFileRealm(java.lang.String:java.lang.String  )
Operation: javax.management.ObjectName  lookupXMLRegistry(name:java.lang.String  )
Operation: java.lang.Void
```

```
                                         destroyMigratableRMIService(bean:javax.management.ObjectName  )
                                         Operation: javax.management.ObjectName  lookupJMSServer(name:java.lang.String  )
                                         Operation: javax.management.ObjectName
                                         createJMSInteropModule(name:java.lang.String  )
                                         Operation: java.lang.Void  destroyFileStore(store:javax.management.ObjectName  )
                                         Operation: javax.management.ObjectName
                                         createWLDFSystemResource(name:java.lang.String
                                         descriptorFileName:java.lang.String  )
                                         Operation: javax.management.ObjectName  lookupMachine(name:java.lang.String  )
                                         Operation: javax.management.ObjectName
                                         lookupCustomRealm(java.lang.String:java.lang.String  )
                                         Operation: java.lang.Boolean  isSet(propertyName:java.lang.String  )
                                         Operation: javax.management.ObjectName
                                         createMigratableRMIService(name:java.lang.String  )
                                         Operation: java.lang.Void  destroyXMLRegistry(registry:javax.management.ObjectName
                                         )
                                         Operation: javax.management.ObjectName
                                         createJDBCSystemResource(name:java.lang.String  )
                                         Operation: java.lang.Void  destroyCoherenceServer(bean:javax.management.ObjectName
                                         )
                                         Operation: javax.management.ObjectName
                                         createRemoteSAFContext(name:java.lang.String  )
                                         Operation: java.lang.Void
                                         destroyPasswordPolicy(weblogic.management.configuration.PasswordPolicyMBean:javax.
                                         management.ObjectName  )
                                         Operation: java.lang.Void  destroyFileT3(fileT3:javax.management.ObjectName  )
                                         Operation: javax.management.ObjectName
                                         lookupMessagingBridge(name:java.lang.String  )
                                         Operation: javax.management.ObjectName  createMailSession(name:java.lang.String  )
                                         Operation: java.lang.Void
                                         destroyRDBMSRealm(weblogic.management.configuration.RDBMSRealmMBean:javax.manageme
                                         nt.ObjectName  )
                                         Operation: javax.management.ObjectName
                                         createLDAPRealm(java.lang.String:java.lang.String  )
                                         Operation: javax.management.ObjectName  createStartupClass(name:java.lang.String
                                         )
                                         Operation: javax.management.ObjectName
                                         createJMSConnectionConsumer(name:java.lang.String  )
                                         Operation: javax.management.ObjectName  createJMSTopic(name:java.lang.String
                                         destination:javax.management.ObjectName  )
                                         Operation: javax.management.ObjectName
                                         lookupJDBCSystemResource(name:java.lang.String  )
                                         Operation: javax.management.ObjectName  lookupStartupClass(name:java.lang.String
                                         )
                                         Operation: javax.management.ObjectName
                                         lookupUnixRealm(java.lang.String:java.lang.String  )
                                         Operation: java.lang.Void
                                         destroyWLECConnectionPool(store:javax.management.ObjectName  )
                                         Operation: javax.management.ObjectName  createUnixMachine(name:java.lang.String  )
                                         Operation: java.lang.Void
                                         destroyForeignJMSConnectionFactory(wsc:javax.management.ObjectName  )
                                         Operation: java.lang.Void
                                         destroyJDBCDataSourceFactory(factory:javax.management.ObjectName  )
                                         Operation: javax.management.ObjectName  lookupPathService(name:java.lang.String  )
                                         Operation:                                          java.lang.Void
                                         destroyCustomRealm(weblogic.management.configuration.CustomRealmMBean:javax.manage
                                         ment.ObjectName  )
```

Table 12.2: Functionality of Runtime vs. EDIT MBean Servers

These are common differences. Often the operations are different. In most cases the EDIT MBean version has more operations (especially the "create*" operations).

MBean-Server Overview

The following diagram with the different MBean server types shows the availability of the different MBean Servers. The EDIT and DomainRuntime servers are available only on the Administration Server, whereas each server (including Managed-Servers) has a Runtime MBean server.

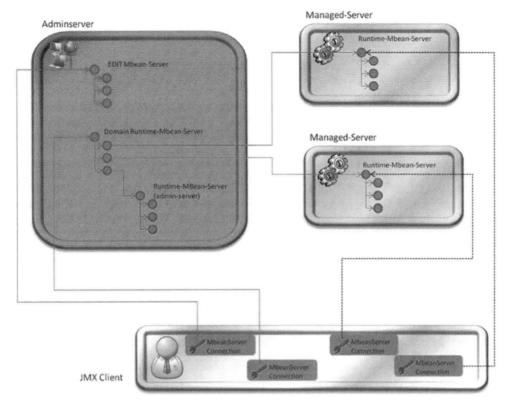

Figure 12.1: *MBean Server Availability*

A JMX client can connect to the different servers. Note that the connections from the client to the Runtime MBean server of the Managed-Servers are represented as black dotted lines. The reason is that Oracle does not recommend this connection. There are a number of disadvantages, but these connections are needed and very helpful in select cases.

As stated above, direct connections to the Managed-Server Runtime MBean server must be considered carefully for the following reasons:

Disadvantages:

- The communication (or administration - depending on your configuration) ports must be accessible directly from the client. Normally this should not be the case. In most systems these ports are protected by firewalls and only accessible from the Administration Server (in case of admin channels). If there are no admin channels defined, then usually a load-balancing mechanism (e.g. F5 load-balancer) or Apache is used to distribute load over the Managed-Servers. If RMI communication is used, then the cluster JNDI mechanisms can be used. In this case, the port might be open directly to the client

- The setup is more complicated for the client as the JMX client has to maintain a list of Managed-Server IP/ports and has to open many more direct connections.

- If the Administration Server is setup to monitor and log administrative access, then this monitor must be installed on all Managed-Servers as well or this communication will bypass the monitoring.

When are these connections useful and necessary?

- If external monitoring systems require Managed-Server level information, then direct connections to the Managed-Server must be used. This is the only way to provide AdminServer-independent access to the information. The reason for this is because guaranteed real-time monitoring is only possible if the JMX (or WLST) client connects to the Managed-Server directly. If the Administration Server fails, then the Managed-Servers might still be operating normally; BUT (!) if the Managed-Servers are monitored using a connection to the Administration Server, the monitor will issue severe alarms. The Administration Server does not have the same level of high-availability requirements that the Managed-Servers have.

- Latency: You need to take into account that monitoring Managed-Servers over the Administration Server introduces an extra network call. Even if this is usually insignificant for normal systems, it can make a difference for real-time systems.

Connecting to MBeanServer

There are different ways to connect to an MBeanServer. This really depends on whether the client is a remote client (other process) or running on the same process (e.g. in the WebLogic Server). For remote clients, this also varies depending on security restrictions.

Remote Connections

A remote connection always requires a remote network link to the MBeanServer. Therefore, these connections require a protocol like IIOP or T3 to be used. In almost all cases, this connection needs security credentials like user/password for authentication. In the case of SSL (or even HTTPS), this may even require (client-) certificates.

Example for a remote connection:

```
String uri = < something like t3://localhost:7001 >
// get protocol from URL string
String protocol = url.substring(0,url.indexOf("://"));
```

```
// get hostname from URL string
String hostname = url.substring(url.indexOf("//")+2, url.indexOf(":",protocol.length()+3));

// get port from URL string
String portString = url.substring(url.indexOf(":",protocol.length()+3)+1,url.length());
int port = Integer.valueOf(portString).intValue();
String mserver = "weblogic.management.mbeanservers.domainruntime";
                // if edit:  "weblogic.management.mbeanservers.edit" :
JMXServiceURL serviceURL = new JMXServiceURL(protocol, hostname, port, "/jndi/" + mserver);
Hashtable h = new Hashtable();
h.put(Context.SECURITY_PRINCIPAL, connectionuser);
h.put(Context.SECURITY_CREDENTIALS, connectionpassword);
h.put(JMXConnectorFactory.PROTOCOL_PROVIDER_PACKAGES,"weblogic.management.remote");
connector = JMXConnectorFactory.connect(serviceURL, h);
connection = connector.getMBeanServerConnection();
```

The example above utilizes the standard JMXServiceURL to create a JMX service URL out of different values, and also utilizes the standard JMXConnectionFactory to establish the connection to the MBeanServer.

Environmental Naming Context Access

JMX access and gathering information from the actual runtime can be used as part of self-written J2EE applications. This is not the focus of this book but at least should be mentioned. An application deployed to a WebLogic Server can make use of the local Runtime MBeanServer using the JNDI tree instead of using a JMX service URL.

Example access from the J2EE application:

```
InitialContext ctx = new InitialContext();
server = (MBeanServer)ctx.lookup("java:comp/env/jmx/runtime");
```

Please note that the access from a J2EE application can be achieved using the environmental naming context (*env*).

In-memory connections to the Runtime MBeanServer

It is also possible to access the different MBean trees (domain and runtime) from startup classes or custom MBeans. As these artifacts are NOT running inside a J2EE application, they cannot use the environmental naming context.

Example access to the server runtime of the server process in which this code is running:

```
public MBeanServer connectToRuntimeService() throws Exception {
    try {
        InitialContext ctx = new InitialContext();
        return (MBeanServer) ctx.lookup("java:comp/jmx/runtime");
    }
    catch (Exception ex) {
            throw new Exception("PROBLEM with connectToRuntimeService: " + ex.getMessage());
    }
}
```

Note that the *env* part of the JNDI name is missing.

The next example shows how to access the domain runtime MBeanServer. This code ONLY works if executed inside the AdminServer process:

```
public MBeanServer connectToDomainRuntimeService() throws Exception {
    try {
        InitialContext ctx = new InitialContext();
        return (MBeanServer) ctx.lookup("java:comp/jmx/domainRuntime");
    }
    catch (Exception ex) {
            throw new Exception("PROBLEM with connectToDomainRuntimeService: " + ex.getMessage());
    }
}
```

Note that WebLogic does NOT offer such a lookup for the EDIT-MBeanServer (like "java:comp/jmx/edit"). Also note that for reasons unknown, it seems that the number of accessible MBeans is different when the MBeanServer is accessed using the InitialContext lookup than when accessed using the JMXConnectionFactory.

Internal WebLogic Protocol Access

WebLogic offers another hidden feature that is very useful. By default, the JMXServiceURL defines remote URLs with hostname and port. Those are therefore not useable when connecting from within the same WebLogic process.

WebLogic defines its own, internal protocol that allows the user to use the standard JMXServiceURL for local connections without looping over the network. This allows the developer to treat local connections in a very similar way as remote connections. The internal protocol is called *"wlx"*.

Example:

```
JMXServiceURL myLocalURL = new JMXServiceURL("wlx", null, 0,
                                "/jndi/weblogic.management.mbeanservers.edit");

connection = JMXConnectorFactory.connect(myLocalURL, params).getMBeanServerConnection();
```

The example above demonstrates the usage. The protocol is *"wlx"*, and host and port are not required. The JNDI name is the same as the name used in the remote connection.

The following code will create a local connection using the *"wlx"* protocol to one of the three MBeanServers:

```
public void connectToAdminServer(boolean edit, boolean domainruntime) throws Exception
{
    String jndiName = "";
    ObjectName service = null;

    if (domainruntime && !edit) {  // DOMAIN-RUNTIME
        jndiName = "/jndi/weblogic.management.mbeanservers.domainruntime";
```

```
        service = new ObjectName("com.bea:Name=DomainRuntimeService,"+
                "Type=weblogic.management.mbeanservers.domainruntime.DomainRuntimeServiceMBean");
}
else if(!edit && !domainruntime) {  // RUNTIME
    jndiName = "/jndi/weblogic.management.mbeanservers.runtime";
    service = new ObjectName("com.bea:Name=RuntimeService,"+
                "Type=weblogic.management.mbeanservers.runtime.RuntimeServiceMBean");
}
else {  // EDIT
    jndiName = "/jndi/weblogic.management.mbeanservers.edit";
    service = new ObjectName("com.bea:Name=EditService,"+
                    "Type=weblogic.management.mbeanservers.edit.EditServiceMBean");
}

Hashtable params = new Hashtable();
params.put("jmx.remote.protocol.provider.pkgs", "weblogic.management.remote");
JMXServiceURL localJMXServiceURL = new JMXServiceURL("wlx", null, 0, jndiName);
connector = JMXConnectorFactory.connect(localJMXServiceURL, params);
connection = connector.getMBeanServerConnection();

...
```

JMX Restrictions

The JMX API of WebLogic is very powerful, but it has less functionality than WLST. WLST is based on JMX, but some parts of WLST are based on other implementation code and can therefore offer a wider range of features. It is important to understand the differences in order to choose the right programming style for the automation. Please also see the summary chapter at the end of the book for further information on this topic.

Summary of features not available in JMX:

- **Domain creation**: JMX can only be used with a running MBeanServer. Therefore in JMX, the AdminServer must be up and running, which also means that the domain must be created. Domain creation is not possible using JMX.

- **Templates**: Similar to creation, nothing related to templates (domain creation, extension, and custom templates) can be used with JMX.

- **Offline mode**: JMX can only be used in online mode. Offline mode is not available in JMX.

- **jndi**: The *jndi()* function of WLST is not available in JMX. Therefore, browsing the JNDI tree content is not possible using JMX.

- **NodeManager**: The complete NodeManager functions are not available with JMX. The NodeManager has an MBean wrapper but the NodeManager itself is a very simple TCP packet-based server.

MBean Tree and Navigation

With WLST, Oracle has organized the MBeans in a filesystem-like structure with subdirectories for parent-child relationships. There are also "soft-links" with the ability to use the *cd* command to jump to other positions in the tree (very similar to what can be done on UNIX using the *ln -s* command). This makes navigation easy, even if there are additional levels in the hierarchy.

With JMX, this simply does not exist. WebLogic has a number of ways to represent "hierarchy" in JMX, but it does not make it very easy. The parent-child relationship is a somewhat hidden in the MBeans, and in most cases cannot be derived from elements of the ObjectName.

There are basically three different ways to implement hierarchy in WebLogic:

1. "parent" attribute

This is the most common approach and basically used in all core server components. MBeans have a "parent" attribute that holds a reference to the father MBean. This means that you need to build an MBean hierarchy from the bottom to the top from all MBeans to their father MBean, unless you have the root MBean of the hierarchy. It is important to understand that there are several root MBeans.

```
com.bea:Location=AdminServer,Name=TestDomain,Type=Log
        Attribute: Parent   of Type : javax.management.ObjectName
        Attribute: RotateLogOnStartup   of Type : java.lang.Boolean
        Attribute: DomainLogBroadcastFilter   of Type : javax.management.ObjectName
        Attribute: RotationTime   of Type : java.lang.String
        Attribute: Type   of Type : java.lang.String
...

com.bea:Location=AdminServer,Name=TestDomain,Type=DeploymentConfiguration
        Attribute: Parent   of Type : javax.management.ObjectName
        Attribute: Type   of Type : java.lang.String
        Attribute: RemoteDeployerEJBEnabled   of Type : java.lang.Boolean

com.bea:Location=AdminServer,Name=AdminServer,Server=AdminServer,Type=OverloadProtection
        Attribute: Parent   of Type : javax.management.ObjectName
        Attribute: Type   of Type : java.lang.String
        Attribute: ServerFailureTrigger   of Type : javax.management.ObjectName
```

2. "realm" attribute

The complete security layer inside a realm is different. For whatever reason, the attribute here is not called "parent", but "realm". When parsing MBeans, it is advisable to search first for the "parent" attribute. If this could not be found, then you need to search for the "realm" attribute in order to know which MBean is the father MBean.

```
Security:Name=myrealm
        Attribute: Authorizers   of Type : [Ljavax.management.ObjectName;
        Attribute: RoleMappers   of Type : [Ljavax.management.ObjectName;
        Attribute: AuthenticationProviders   of Type : [Ljavax.management.ObjectName;
        ...

Security:Name=myrealmDefaultAuthenticator
        Attribute: Realm   of Type : javax.management.ObjectName
```

```
        Attribute: Description   of Type : java.lang.String
        Attribute: Name    of Type : java.lang.String
        Attribute: Version   of Type : java.lang.String
        Attribute: MinimumPasswordLength   of Type : java.lang.Integer
        ...
        Operation: java.lang.Void  setGroupDescription(...)


Security:Location=AdminServer,Name=myrealmXACMLRoleMapper
        Attribute: Realm     of Type : javax.management.ObjectName
        Attribute: Description   of Type : java.lang.String
        Attribute: SupportedExportFormats   of Type : [Ljava.lang.String;
        Attribute: Name    of Type : java.lang.String
        ...
        Operation: java.lang.String  listAllPoliciesAsString()
        ...
```

3. "JDBC"

JDBC datasources have a pretty complex MBean structure (see JDBC). These
MBeans are again different. They neither have a "parent" nor a "realm" attribute.
Here the parent relationship is expressed in an attribute in the ObjectName.

```
com.bea:Name=MySuperDataSource,Type=JDBCSystemResource
        Attribute: Parent of Type : javax.management.ObjectName
        Attribute: Resource of Type : javax.management.ObjectName
        Attribute: Type of Type : java.lang.String
        Attribute: JDBCResource of Type : javax.management.ObjectName
        ...

com.bea:Name=MySuperDataSource,Parent=[TestDomain]/JDBCSystemResources[MySuperDataSource],Path=JDBCRe
source,Type=weblogic.j2ee.descriptor.wl.JDBCDataSourceBean
        Attribute: JDBCDataSourceParams of Type : javax.management.ObjectName
        Attribute: JDBCDriverParams of Type : javax.management.ObjectName
        Attribute: InternalProperties of Type : javax.management.ObjectName
        Attribute: Name of Type : java.lang.String
        Attribute: JDBCConnectionPoolParams of Type : javax.management.ObjectName
        Attribute: JDBCOracleParams of Type : javax.management.ObjectName
        ...

com.bea:Name=MySuperDataSource,Parent=[TestDomain]/JDBCSystemResources[MySuperDataSource],Path=JDBCRe
source[MySuperDataSource]/InternalProperties,Type=weblogic.j2ee.descriptor.wl.JDBCPropertiesBean
        Attribute: Properties of Type : [Ljavax.management.ObjectName;
        ...
```

In the example above, the last MBean (InternalProperties) is the child of the second
MBean (JDBCResource), where it is referenced in the InternalProperties attribute.
The second MBean is the child of the first MBean where it is referenced in the
JDBCResource attribute. The second and third MBeans have a concrete reference as
part of their ObjectName (attribute "Path").

Custom MBeans

WebLogic has a large number of internal MBeans that are registered in one of the
MBean's server discussed earlier. As JMX is THE standard technology for Java-based
management and monitoring, it is also often very useful add to your own MBeans to
the server so that your management tool can access information (or even invoke
operations) using this API.

There are several different ways to extend WebLogic:

Adding custom MBeans to the internal WebLogic tree: This is only possible if WebLogic knows how to deal with those MBeans. One very common example is the implementation of your own security provider. This is necessary if, for example, an SSO implementation must be supported in this WebLogic domain. A custom security provider has to fulfill strict API requirements defined by WebLogic. Therefore, WebLogic understands this implementation (= new MBean). Only MBean types that are defined by WebLogic can be treated that way. These MBeans are installed by just copying the jar file containing the MBean to the lib/mbeantypes folder. It is then possible to access these MBeans from the normal MBean tree(s).

Adding custom MBeans to a server: Completely self-written MBeans are added to the custom MBean server. They can do whatever you implement into it and do not need to follow any WebLogic MBean-type.

Spring Custom MBeans: Creating Custom MBeans using the WebLogic internal Spring framework just requires you to write a POJO-style Java class and create the Spring XML configuration entries. WebLogic will generate the rest.

Adding Custom MBeans as part of an EAR application: Custom MBeans can also be included in an EAR application archive. This allows the bundling of the MBeans with the application. Just note that these MBeans are only available when the application is started. Monitoring tools cannot rely on these MBeans as these MBeans may or may not be accessible depending on the application state and not the server state.

If you want to instantiate your MBeans as part of application deployment, create a WebLogic Server ApplicationLifecycleListener class to register your MBean.

Register Custom MBeans

Registration of custom MBeans requires that you instantiate your MBean, get a connection to the MBean server (usually in the same process), and then register it with an ObjectName.

```
InitialContext ctx = new InitialContext();
ObjectName mymbean = new ObjectName("testMBean:Name=TestAccess,Type=TestAccessMBean");
MBeanServer server = (MBeanServer) ctx.lookup("java:comp/jmx/runtime");
TestMBeanImpl mbean = new TestMBeanImpl();
server.registerMBean(mbean, mymbean);

System.out.println("testMBean:Name=TestAccess,Type=TestAccessMBean - created and registered !");
```

Access Custom MBean

Accessing your custom MBean is very much the same as accessing any other MBean. First, it is necessary to get a connection to the MBean Server. Then you can ask the MBeanServer to invoke operations or access attributes on the desired MBean.

Access within the same process:

```
InitialContext ctx = new InitialContext();
MBeanServer server = (MBeanServer) ctx.lookup("java:comp/env/jmx/runtime");

// get reference to mbean
ObjectName myTestMBean = new ObjectName("testMBean:Name=TestAccess,Type=TestAccessMBean");

// ok, got the reference, now you can access atrributes or invoke operations
server.invoke(myTestMBean,"<operation>",...)
server.getAttribute(myTestMBean, "<attribute-name>");
```

Access Remotely

Remote access is basically the same as local access. The only difference is that you need to establish a remote connection to either the runtime MBean server or the domain-runtime MBean server. In case you need to access custom MBeans hosted in this WebLogic instance, a connection to the runtime MBean server is sufficient. A connection to the domain runtime MBean server is only required if you prefer to access custom MBeans hosted somewhere in your WebLogic domain through a single connection to the AdminServer.

```
String connectionuser = "weblogic";
String connectionpassword = "test1234";
String hostname = "localhost";
int port = 7001;

JMXServiceURL serviceURL = new JMXServiceURL("t3", hostname, port,
"/jndi/weblogic.management.mbeanservers.runtime");

Hashtable<String, String> h = new Hashtable<String, String>();
h.put(Context.SECURITY_PRINCIPAL, connectionuser);
h.put(Context.SECURITY_CREDENTIALS, connectionpassword);
h.put(JMXConnectorFactory.PROTOCOL_PROVIDER_PACKAGES,"weblogic.management.remote");
connector = JMXConnectorFactory.connect(serviceURL, h);
connection = connector.getMBeanServerConnection();

ObjectName myTestMBean = new ObjectName("testMBean:Name=TestAccess,Type=TestAccessMBean");
// ok, got the reference, now you can access attributes or invoke operations
connection.invoke(myTestMBean, "someTestMethod", new Object[] { ... }, new String[]{ ... });
connection.getAttribute(myTestMBean, "<attribute-name>");
```

JMX Programming Styles

Beside the standard Java JMX API, WebLogic offers an API that wraps the WebLogic MBeans. This API offers a convenient way to write JMX code because it is easier to code, type save and can be checked by compilers and IDEs in a better way. On the other hand, this API is not standard, may change with any WebLogic version, and requires the developers to produce non-standard, Oracle-dependent code. Some of these APIs (e.g. MBeanHome) have already been deprecated by Oracle.

For all these reasons, none of the source code examples in this book will use this API. The complete JMX section is based on the JMX standard API. The next code listing will only provide a very small example so that the reader will be able to understand the differences.

Whenever you see JMX code, examine the import statements! You should never see "import weblogic.*" if you want to use 100% standard JMX code. Note that especially in the security provider area (asserting party, relying party), Oracle-defined data structures cannot be fully avoided.

Example for import statements for the Oracle JMX wrapper API:

```
import weblogic.management.runtime.
import weblogic.management.MBeanHome;
import weblogic.management.configuration.DomainMBean;
import weblogic.management.configuration.ServerMBean;
import weblogic.management.configuration.SecurityConfigurationMBean;
import weblogic.management.security.RealmMBean;
import weblogic.management.configuration.SystemResourceMBean;
```

The following code shows some example statements. Note that this is neither a complete method nor running code. It shows a few examples for how to use the API:

```
Environment myEnvironment = new Environment();
myEnvironment.setProviderUrl("t3://localhost:7001");
myEnvironment.setSecurityPrincipal("weblogic");
myEnvironment.setSecurityCredentials("weblogic");
Context myContext = myEnvironment.getInitialContext();
MBeanHome mbeanHome =(MBeanHome)myContext.lookup("weblogic.management.home.localhome");
MBeanServer server = mbeanHome.getMBeanServer();

// get the domain mbean reference
DomainMBean myDomainMBean = mbeanHome.getActiveDomain();

// Get the name of the admin server
String adminName = myDomainMBean.getAdminServerName();

// get all system resources
SystemResourceMBean[] myResources = myDomainMBean.getSystemResources();

// get all server mbean references
ServerMBean serverMbean[] = myDomainMBean.getServers();
```

As you can see in the code examples, the API offers its own class definition for every MBean type. Using this API means that the source code also depends on the WebLogic version, and it is more complicated to write general code that can run against different WebLogic versions.

JMX Base Library for WebLogic

Programming in Java (similar to most other languages) produces a lot of replicated code if you do not factor this out into methods. It is also advisable to reduce your dependencies to specific APIs or technologies by hiding them behind a layer of abstraction. For this book, I will do the same and provide an abstraction layer for the basic JMX operations. These will be implemented in a class called JMXWrapper. All Java code examples in the subsequent chapter will make use of this class. The basic idea is that every instance of this represents (if connected) a connection to a remote server and offers basic operations. One big benefit is that this offers a central place for logging. In many companies, strict audit guidelines exist which require the admins to protocol every action they are doing. This class honors this by logging all activities using log4j.

The following is an internal method to initialize a connection. Here the API allows the distinction between the domain runtime and the edit-MBeanServer. Note that this example shows the remote connection only. Please refer to the previous section for an example using the *"w/x"* protocol.

💾 initialize_connection

```
/**
 * Init and open connection to an MBean server
 *
 */
private void initConnection(boolean editmode,
                            String url,
                            String username,
                            String password,
                            boolean logErrors) throws WLSAutomationException
{
    try {
        isEdit = editmode;
        connectionuser = username;
        connectionpassword = password;

        System.out.println("JMXWrapper:initConnection called !");

        // get protocol from URL string
        protocol = url.substring(0,url.indexOf("://"));

        // get hostname from URL string
        hostname = url.substring(url.indexOf("//")+2, url.indexOf(":",protocol.length()+3));

        // get port from URL string
        portString = url.substring(url.indexOf(":",protocol.length()+3)+1,url.length());

        System.out.println("JMXWrapper:initConnection:    Protocol = "+protocol);
        System.out.println("JMXWrapper:initConnection:    Hostname = "+hostname);
        System.out.println("JMXWrapper:initConnection:    Port     = "+portString);

        Integer portInteger = Integer.valueOf(portString);
        int port = portInteger.intValue();
        String jndiroot = "/jndi/";
        String mserver = (isEdit) ? "weblogic.management.mbeanservers.edit" :
                                    "weblogic.management.mbeanservers.domainruntime";
        JMXServiceURL serviceURL = new JMXServiceURL(protocol, hostname,
            port, jndiroot + mserver);

        System.out.println("URL: "+serviceURL.toString());

        Hashtable h = new Hashtable();
```

```
            h.put(Context.SECURITY_PRINCIPAL, connectionuser);
            h.put(Context.SECURITY_CREDENTIALS, connectionpassword);
            h.put(JMXConnectorFactory.PROTOCOL_PROVIDER_PACKAGES,"weblogic.management.remote");
            connector = JMXConnectorFactory.connect(serviceURL, h);
            connection = connector.getMBeanServerConnection();

            // success
            initialized = true;
        }
        catch (Exception ex)
        {
            initialized = false;
            if (logErrors)
                System.out.println("PROBLEM with JMXWrapper:initConnection: " +
                                    ex.getMessage());
            throw new WLSAutomationException("PROBLEM with JMXWrapper:initConnection: " +
                                    ex.getMessage());
        }
    }
```

The next example sets an attribute on the remote MBean server. Note that this
operation really does changes on the server.

💾 set_attribute

```
public void setAttribute(ObjectName name, Attribute attribute)     throws WLSAutomationException
{
    try {
        System.out.println("JMXWrapper:setAttribute called !");       // Logfile JMX_LAYER !!!

        // Log complete JMX call
        // BE CAREFUL !! as passwords will be visible !!!

        StringBuffer buf = new StringBuffer();

        if (isEdit)
            buf.append("[EDIT-MbeanTree  ] ");
        else // Runtime
            buf.append("[RUNTIME-MBeanTree] ");
        buf.append(" : MBean="+name);
        System.out.println(buf.toString());
        System.out.println("SET "+attribute.getName()+"  to value="+attribute.getValue());

        // do INVOKE
        getConnection().setAttribute(name,attribute);
    }
    catch (Exception ex) {
        throw new WLSAutomationException("PROBLEM with JMXWrapper:setAttribute: " +
                                    ex.getMessage());
    }
}
```

The following gets an attribute from the server. This method queries some
information from the remote server.

💾 get_attribute

```
public Object getAttribute(ObjectName name, String attributeName)     throws WLSAutomationException
{
    try {
        System.out.println("JMXWrapper:getAttribute called !");       // Logfile JMX_LAYER !!!

        // Log complete JMX call
        // BE CAREFUL !! as passwords will be visible !!!

        StringBuffer buf = new StringBuffer();

        if (isEdit)
            buf.append("[EDIT-MBeanTree  ] ");
        else // Runtime
            buf.append("[RUNTIME-MBeanTree] ");
```

```
                buf.append(" : MBean="+name);
                System.out.println(buf.toString());
                System.out.println("GET Attribute="+attributeName);

                // do INVOKE
                return getConnection().getAttribute(name,attributeName);
        }
        catch (Exception ex) {
            throw new WLSAutomationException("PROBLEM with JMXWrapper:getAttribute: " +
                                            ex.getMessage());
        }
}
```

The next example invokes an operation on the remote server. The method in this wrapper implementation allows the user to invoke an operation on the remote server. Beside the specialized *getAttribute()* and *setAttribute()* methods, this method implements to ability to invoke general purpose operations which can, for example, execute changes or return information.

💾 invoke_operation

```
/**
 * Invoke an MBean operation
 */
public Object invoke(ObjectName name, String operationName, Object[] params,
                     String[] signature)  throws WLSAutomationException
{
    try {
        System.out.println("JMXWrapper:invoke called !");     // Logfile JMX_LAYER !!!
        if (params==null)
            params = new Object[0];
        if (signature == null)
            signature = new String[0];

        // Log complete JMX call
        // BE CAREFUL !! as passwords will be visible !!!

        StringBuffer buf = new StringBuffer();

        if (isEdit)
            buf.append("[EDIT-MbeanTree    ] ");
        else // Runtime
            buf.append("[RUNTIME-MbeanTree] ");
        buf.append(" : MBean="+name);
        System.out.println(buf.toString());
        System.out.println("Operation="+operationName);

        // params
        buf = new StringBuffer("    Parameter: ");
        for (int i=0;i<params.length;i++){
            buf.append(((params[i] == null) ? "NULL" : params[i].toString()) +
                        "[" + signature[i] + "] ");
        }
        System.out.println(buf.toString());

        // do INVOKE
        return getConnection().invoke(name, operationName, params, signature);
    }
    catch (Exception ex) {
        throw new WLSAutomationException("PROBLEM with JMXWrapper:invoke: " + ex.getMessage());
    }
}
```

Next is an internal method to start an edit session. This is equivalent to the *edit()* command in WLST.

💾 start_edit_session

```
/**
 * Start an edit session.
 * @return ObjectName
 * @throws WLSAutomationException
 */
private ObjectName startEditSession() throws WLSAutomationException
{
    try {
        System.out.println("JMXWrapper:startEditSession called !");

        // Get the object name for ConfigurationManagerMBean.
        ObjectName cfgMgr = (ObjectName) getAttribute(service,"ConfigurationManager");

        // use the configuration manager in order to start an edit session
        ObjectName domainConfigRoot = (ObjectName)invoke(cfgMgr,
                "startEdit", new Object[] {new Integer(60000),
                new Integer(120000)}, new String[] {"java.lang.Integer",
                "java.lang.Integer"});
        if (domainConfigRoot == null)
        {
            // Couldn't get the lock
            throw new Exception("Somebody else is editing already");
        }
        System.out.println("JMXWrapper:startEditSession finished !");
        return domainConfigRoot;
    }
    catch (Exception ex) {
        System.out.println("PROBLEM with JMXWrapper:startEditSession: " + ex.getMessage(), ex);
        throw new WLSAutomationException("PROBLEM with startEditSession: " + ex.getMessage());
    }
}
```

The following is an internal method in order to start a normal - non edit - session.

💾 start_nonedit_session

```
private ObjectName startNONEditSession() throws WLSAutomationException
{
    try {
        System.out.println("JMXWrapper:startNONEditSession called !");

        ObjectName domainMBean =(ObjectName) getAttribute(service,"DomainConfiguration");
        return domainMBean;
    }
    catch (Exception ex) {
        System.out.println("PROBLEM with JMXWrapper:startNONEditSession: " + ex.getMessage);
        throw new WLSAutomationException("PROBLEM with startNONEditSession: " + ex.getMessage());
    }
}
```

This is the first method you will use on every instance of the class in order to really use it. This method will connect to a WebLogic Server. Depending on the "edit" argument, the wrapper class will open a normal or an edit session.

💾 connect

```
public void connectToAdminServer(boolean edit,
                                 String username,
                                 String password,
                                 String url,
                                 boolean logConnectionProblems
                                 ) throws WLSAutomationException
{
    try {
        System.out.println("JMXWrapper:connectToAdminServer called !");

        initConnection(edit, url, username,password,logConnectionProblems);

        // service depends on edit or NONedit mode
```

```
        service = new ObjectName((edit ?
"com.bea:Name=EditService,Type=weblogic.management.mbeanservers.edit.EditServiceMBean"
:
"com.bea:Name=DomainRuntimeService,Type=weblogic.management.mbeanservers.domainruntime.DomainRuntimeS
erviceMBean")
                        );
    }
    catch (Exception ex) {
        throw new WLSAutomationException("PROBLEM with connectToAdminServer: " + ex.getMessage());
    }
}
```

The following is an internal method in order to activate changes of an edit session prior to a disconnect.

💾 activate_changes

```
    private ObjectName activate() throws WLSAutomationException
    {
        try {
            System.out.println("JMXWrapper:activate called !");

            ObjectName cfgMgr = (ObjectName) getAttribute(service,"ConfigurationManager");
            Object o = invoke(cfgMgr, "save", null, null);
            ObjectName result = (ObjectName) invoke(cfgMgr,"activate",
                            new Object[] {new Long(120000)}, new String[] {"java.lang.Long"});
            return result;
        }
        catch (Exception ex)
        {
            System.out.println("PROBLEM with JMXWrapper:activate: " + ex.getMessage());
            throw new WLSAutomationException("PROBLEM with JMXWrapper:activate: " + ex.getMessage());
        }
    }
```

The next example shows how to disconnect from the AdminServer. In case an edit session has been opened, the activate method (see above) will be called in order to activate all the changes.

💾 disconnect_adminserver

```
public void disconnectFromAdminServer(boolean edit) throws WLSAutomationException
{
    try {
    System.out.println("JMXWrapper:disconnectFromAdminServer called !");

    if (edit)
        activate();

        // Close the connection with the MBean server.
        domainConfigRoot = null;
        try {
            connector.close();
        }
        catch (Exception ex) {
            // ignore
        }

        connector = null;
    }
    catch (Exception ex) {
        System.out.println("PROBLEM with disconnectFromAdminServer: " + ex.getMessage());
        throw new WLSAutomationException("PROBLEM with disconnect: " + ex.getMessage());
    }
}
```

The following function gets a list of the basic domain information. This is a useful help function that will be used in many examples in the following chapters. If a

---

remote client is used, it is always a good practice to collect static data and cache it. This helps avoid unnecessary network traffic, which can also avoid unnecessary delays due to remote calls.

🖫 domain_information

```
public Hashtable<String,String> getMainServerDomainValues() throws WLSAutomationException
{
    try {
        System.out.println("JMXWrapper:getMainServerDomainValues called !");

        Hashtable<String,String> result = new Hashtable<String,String>();
        ObjectName domainMBean =(ObjectName) getAttribute(service,"DomainConfiguration");

        String adminServerName = (String) getAttribute(domainMBean,"AdminServerName");
        String domainName = domainMBean.getKeyProperty("Name");
        String domainRoot = (String) getAttribute(domainMBean,"RootDirectory");

        String configurationVersion = (String) getAttribute(domainMBean,"ConfigurationVersion");

        result.put("adminServerName",adminServerName);
        result.put("domainName",domainName);
        result.put("domainRoot",domainRoot);
        result.put("domainBase",domainRoot.substring(0,domainRoot.length()-(domainName.length()+1)));
        result.put("configurationVersion",configurationVersion);

        return result;
    }
    catch (Exception ex) {
        System.out.println("PROBLEM with getMainServerDomainValues: " + ex.getMessage(), ex);
        throw new WLSAutomationException("PROBLEM with getDomainValues: " + ex.getMessage());
    }
}
```

Next, get the JMX ObjectNames for all Managed-Servers. Many operations need to be performed for all servers, therefore this method will be used quite often.

🖫 get_JMX_objectnames

```
public ArrayList<ObjectName> getManagedServerObjectNames() throws WLSAutomationException
{
    try {
        ArrayList<ObjectName> result = new ArrayList<ObjectName>();

        System.out.println("JMXWrapper:getManagedServerObjectNames called !");

        ObjectName domainMBean =(ObjectName) getAttribute(service,"DomainConfiguration");
        String adminServerName = (String) getAttribute(domainMBean,"AdminServerName");

        ObjectName[] serverRuntimes = (ObjectName[])getAttribute(domainMBean,"Servers");
        for (int i = 0; i < serverRuntimes.length; i++)
        {
            String tmp = serverRuntimes[i].getKeyProperty("Name");
            if (!tmp.equals(adminServerName))
                result.add(serverRuntimes[i]);
        }

        return result;
    }
    catch (Exception ex)
    {
        System.out.println("PROBLEM with getManagedServerObjectNames: " + ex.getMessage(), ex);
        throw new WLSAutomationException("PROBLEM with getMSObjectNames: " + ex.getMessage());
    }
}
```

An often needed bit of information is the status of a specific (Managed) server. The following method will provide this information:

```
public String getServerState(String serverName)  throws WLSAutomationException
{
    try {
        System.out.println("JMXWrapper:getServerState called !");

        ObjectName serverRuntimeObjectName = new ObjectName("com.bea:Name=" + serverName +
        ",Type=ServerLifeCycleRuntime");

        return (String)getAttribute(serverRuntimeObjectName,"State");
    }
    catch (Exception ex)
    {
        System.out.println("PROBLEM with JMXWrapper:getServerState: " + ex.getMessage());
        return "_UNKNOWN_ERROR_";
    }
}
```

Note: It has been proven in many consultancy assignments that such a collection of wrapper functions are very helpful.

Strengths of JMX

Oracle does promote WLST in favor of JMX. This is reflective in the amount of documentation from Oracle and other available sources. There are a number of good reasons (which we will discuss later) for why WLST is a really useful technology. For all online communication, WLST uses JMX under the cover. Nevertheless, the usage of WLST and JMX are quite different. This section will highlight some areas where JMX has distinct advantages over WLST.

Access to multiple WebLogic Servers or domains in parallel

The connect operation is always the most expensive operation. In large environments where many servers and any domains are involved and have to be monitored, concurrent access to multiple servers or domains is not possible with WLST. In WLST, after you issue a *connect* command, WLST will switch to the online mode and operate on the mean tree of the connected server. Based on experience with many real production systems, I know that it is impossible to gather the monitoring data sequentially from all systems.

Imagine 2000+ Managed-Servers in production and you want to get performance/monitoring information from all of them using WLST. You have the following possibilities:

- Connect to one server → get all the data → disconnect → then connect to the next server, etc.

- Start one WLST process for each server.

- Combine 1) and 2) and start one process for a group of servers to reduce the amount of processes.

All options have dramatic disadvantages for production:

- Connect takes a long time. For a large number of servers, this means that one loop to collect data may take a very long time. Resource problems, failed applications or servers must be discovered within minutes or even faster. It is not acceptable for any production system to discover an out-of-memory server failure after 2 hours.

- A WLST process needs a lot of memory since it has to load all the WebLogic classes, the Jython interpreter, and more. Even if you want to monitor the Administration Servers only, you may end up with requirements for hundreds of GB of RAM for only the WLST processes. The second problem is that you have a huge number of processes doing the same - running Jython interpreter, which means that you also need a lot of CPU power and many CPUs to do acceptable monitoring. And who is doing the monitoring of all those WLST processes?

JMX does not have these restrictions. In addition, if you do not need WebLogic proprietary classes (e.g. in the security area some JMX operations return or require WebLogic specific classes) and if you have IIOP enabled on your servers for the administrative access, you do not even need the webglogic.jar files that make your process even smaller.

The following example shows a Java program that can open many connections to different WebLogic Servers in parallel and query some example data. What information is queried in the example is not important (you need to exchange it with your own needs anyway if you wish to reuse this code). It is the ability to connect to many servers in parallel and continuously query data which should be demonstrated.

💾 open_multiple_connections

```
public class ParallelAccessTest {

    public static void main(String[] args)
    {
        JMXThreadTest myJMXThreadTest;
        try {
            // create globalProperties from File
            Properties globalProperties = new Properties();
            globalProperties.load(new FileInputStream(args[0]));
            int counter=1;
            while (globalProperties.getProperty("domain."+counter+".name") != null)
            {
                try {
                    myJMXThreadTest =
                        new JMXThreadTest(counter,
                                globalProperties.getProperty("domain."+counter+".url"),
                                globalProperties.getProperty("domain."+counter+".user"),
                                globalProperties.getProperty("domain."+counter+".password"),
                                Integer.parseInt(globalProperties.getProperty(
                                        ("domain."+counter+"reloadinterval","3"))
                        );

                    myJMXThreadTest.start();
                }
                catch (Exception ex) {
                    ex.printStackTrace();
                }
                counter++;
```

```
          }
        }
      catch (Exception ex) {
         ex.printStackTrace();
      }
   }
}
```

The following implementation is an example of what could be done in each loop. In this example, only when the thread is initialized will a connection to the AdminServer be established. In each loop, information about the Managed-Server, cluster, and deployments will be collected. This should demonstrate the power of multi-threading with different WebLogic domains at the same time.

Of course this example is kept very simple to keep it short. Many improvements should be considered for a real production implementation like reacting to failed server connections in each loop (possibly restart) and many more.

💾 multi-threading_example

```
import java.util.*;
import javax.management.MBeanServerConnection;
import javax.management.ObjectName;
import javax.management.remote.*;
import javax.naming.Context;
import java.io.FileOutputStream;

public class JMXThreadTest extends Thread  {
    // active (if any) mbean server connection
    private MBeanServerConnection connection;

    // connector
    private JMXConnector connector;

    private ObjectName domainRuntimeService = null;

    private ObjectName domainMBean = null;

    private int internalReloadInterval = 0;

    private int id;

    private boolean endOfLoop = false;

    public JMXThreadTest(int _id, String url, String username, String password, int reloadInterval)
    {
        try {
            id = _id;
            internalReloadInterval = reloadInterval;

            // get protocol from URL string
            String protocol = url.substring(0,url.indexOf("://"));

            // get hostname from URL string
            String hostname = url.substring(url.indexOf("//")+2,
                                            url.indexOf(":",protocol.length()+3));

            // get port from URL string
            String portString = url.substring(url.indexOf(":",protocol.length()+3)+1,url.length());

            Integer portInteger = Integer.valueOf(portString);
            int port = portInteger.intValue();
            JMXServiceURL serviceURL = new JMXServiceURL(protocol, hostname, port,
                        "/jndi/weblogic.management.mbeanservers.domainruntime");

            Hashtable h = new Hashtable();
            h.put(Context.SECURITY_PRINCIPAL, username);
            h.put(Context.SECURITY_CREDENTIALS, password);
            h.put(JMXConnectorFactory.PROTOCOL_PROVIDER_PACKAGES, "weblogic.management.remote");
```

```
          connector = JMXConnectorFactory.connect(serviceURL, h);
          connection = connector.getMBeanServerConnection();

          domainRuntimeService = new
ObjectName("com.bea:Name=DomainRuntimeService,Type=weblogic.management.mbeanservers.domainruntime.Dom
ainRuntimeServiceMBean");
          domainMBean =(ObjectName)
                          connection.getAttribute(domainRuntimeService,"DomainConfiguration");


      }
      catch (Exception ex) {
          ex.printStackTrace();
      }
  }


  public void run()  {
     while(!endOfLoop)
     {
        getServersInformation();

        try {
            Thread.currentThread().sleep(internalReloadInterval*1000);
        }
        catch (Exception ex) {
            // ignore
        }
     }

  }



  public void disconnectFromAdminServer()
  {
      try {
          endOfLoop = true;
          connector.close();
          connector = null;
      }
      catch (Exception ex)
      {
          ex.printStackTrace();
      }
  }

  public void getServersInformation()
  {
    try
    {
      FileOutputStream os = new FileOutputStream(domainMBean.getKeyProperty("Name")+".log",true);
      try {

          String domainName = (String) connection.getAttribute(domainMBean,"Name");
          System.out.println("Aufruf Admin-Server Nr.: "+id+" : "+domainName);

          os.write(("\n"+"Domain-Name : " + domainName).getBytes() );
          os.write(("\n"+"  AdminServerName : "+(String)
                          connection.getAttribute(domainMBean,"AdminServerName")).getBytes());
          os.write(("\n"+"  RootDirectory : "+(String)
                          connection.getAttribute(domainMBean,"RootDirectory")).getBytes() );
          os.write(("\n"+"  ProductionModeEnabled : "+((Boolean)
                          connection.getAttribute(domainMBean,"ProductionModeEnabled")).
                          booleanValue() ).getBytes());

          // Managed Server
          os.write(("\n"+"  Managed-Server:").getBytes());
          String adminServerName = (String)
                              connection.getAttribute(domainMBean,"AdminServerName");
          ObjectName[] serverRuntimes = (ObjectName[])connection.
                                  getAttribute(domainMBean,"Servers");
          for (int i = 0; i < serverRuntimes.length; i++) {
              String ms_name = (String) connection.getAttribute(serverRuntimes[i],"Name");
              if (!ms_name.equals(adminServerName)) {
                  os.write(("\n"+"     -> "+ms_name + " : StartupMode = "+(String)
                          connection.getAttribute(serverRuntimes[i],"StartupMode")).getBytes());
                  os.write(("\n"+"        "+ (String)connection.getAttribute(serverRuntimes[i],
```

```
                    "ListenAddress")+":"+((Integer)connection.
                getAttribute(serverRuntimes[i],"ListenPort")).intValue() ).getBytes());
            }
        }

        // Cluster
        os.write(("\n"+"  Cluster:").getBytes());
        ObjectName[] cluster = (ObjectName[])connection.getAttribute(domainMBean,"Clusters");
        for (int i = 0; i < cluster.length; i++)
            os.write(("\n"+"     -> "+(String)
                            connection.getAttribute(cluster[i],"Name")).getBytes());

        // Machines
        os.write(("\n"+"  Machines:").getBytes());
        ObjectName[] machines = (ObjectName[])connection.getAttribute(domainMBean,"Machines");
        for (int i = 0; i < machines.length; i++)
            os.write(("\n"+"     -> "+(String)
                            connection.getAttribute(machines[i],"Name")).getBytes());

        // AppDeployments
        os.write(("\n"+"  AppDeployments:").getBytes());
        ObjectName[] appDeployments = (ObjectName[])
                            connection.getAttribute(domainMBean,"AppDeployments");
        for (int i = 0; i < appDeployments.length; i++)
            os.write(("\n"+"     -> "+(String)
                            connection.getAttribute(appDeployments[i],"Name")).getBytes());
    }
    catch (Exception ex) {
        os.write(("Probleme mit Admin-Server Nr.: "+id).getBytes());
        os.write(ex.getMessage().getBytes());
        disconnectFromAdminServer();
    }
    os.close();
    }
    catch (Exception ex) {
        System.out.println("Probleme mit Admin-Server Nr.: "+id);
        ex.printStackTrace();
        disconnectFromAdminServer();
    }
  }
}
```

In order to use this program, you need to provide a property file with all the domain information.

```
domain.1.name          = Domain_1
domain.1.url           = iiop://myserverhost_1:myserverport_1
domain.1.user          = <user for admin or monitoring access>
domain.1.password      = <password for admin or monitoring access>
domain.1.reloadinterval = 10    # seconds

domain.2.name          = Domain_2
domain.2.url           = iiop://myserverhost_2:myserverport_2
domain.2.user          = <user for admin or monitoring access>
domain.2.password      = <password for admin or monitoring access>
domain.2.reloadinterval = 10    # seconds

domain.3.name          = Domain_3
domain.3.url           = iiop://myserverhost_3:myserverport_3
domain.3.user          = <user for admin or monitoring access>
domain.3.password      = <password for admin or monitoring access>
domain.3.reloadinterval = 10    # seconds
```

If you do not need T3 or even T3S as protocol, you can avoid having the WebLogic classes in your classpath. For real production examples however, it is most likely necessary to have the weblogic.jar files in your classpath.

The above property example has a major weakness: It shows the usernames and passwords in clear text, which is usually prohibited in production systems anyway. For a real production systems, I highly recommend extending this program in order to provide at least user and password (URL might also be requested) in an encrypted way.

Use JMX in J2EE Applications

JMX can be used in your own J2EE applications deployed to any WebLogic Server. This is a standard API and does not introduce vendor lock-in or additional technology stacks (Jython interpreter).

As mentioned earlier, it is possible to write your own custom MBeans or use JMX to query some information about the server instance where the application is hosted.

Access within the same process:

```
InitialContext ctx = new InitialContext();
MBeanServer server = (MBeanServer) ctx.lookup("java:comp/env/jmx/runtime");

// get reference to mbean
ObjectName myRealmMBean = new ObjectName("Security:Name=myrealm");

// ok, got the reference, now you can access attributes or invoke operations
server.getAttribute(myRealmMBean, "Name");
```

This example does a look-up on the runtime MBeanServer in order to get the Name of security realm.

It is also possible to talk to a remote MBeanServer from your J2EE application.

JMX Notifications

JMX offers the concept of notifications. Using notifications means that the remote MBean server - in our case the WebLogic Server - will send a notification to the JMX client as soon as a specific event happens. This could be the change of a state, attribute, or something else.

The following example implements a callback that is listening for state changes of the AdminServer.

```
public class ExampleStateNotification {

    public static void main(String[] args) throws Exception
    {
        JMXWrapperRemote myJMXWrapperRemote = new JMXWrapperRemote();
        myJMXWrapperRemote.connectToAdminServer(false,true,"weblogic", "test1234",
                "t3://localhost:7100");

        ExampleChangeListener listener = new ExampleChangeListener();

        ObjectName myAdminRuntime = myJMXWrapperRemote.getServerRuntime("AdminServer");
        myJMXWrapperRemote.getConnection().addNotificationListener(myAdminRuntime, listener, null,
                                                null);
```

```
            System.out.println("Listener enabled");

            // The following code is used for this example in order to keep it simple
            System.out.println("Please press key to quit. ........");
            System.in.read();
        }
}
```

```
public class ExampleChangeListener implements RemoteNotificationListener
{
  public void handleNotification(Notification newNotify, Object myObject)
  {
    System.out.println("\n Callback handleNotification called");

    if(newNotify instanceof AttributeChangeNotification)   {
        AttributeChangeNotification myChange = (AttributeChangeNotification) newNotify;

        System.out.println("Attribute " + myChange.getAttributeName() + " has been modified from " +
                      myChange.getOldValue() + " to " + myChange.getNewValue());
    }
    else
        System.out.println("Notification of type " + newNotify.getClass().getName() +
                      "  but this is not yet supported !");

    }
}
```

In order to test the above program, please start the WebLogic Server and then start the client program. As soon as the client is running, switch to the WebConsole of WebLogic (or use WLST/JMX) in order to suspend a server. As soon as the suspend command has been issued, you should see a callback notification like the one below.

```
Listener enabled
          Please press key to quit. ........

Callback handleNotification called
Attribute State has been modified from RUNNING to FORCE_SUSPENDING

Callback handleNotification called
Attribute State has been modified from FORCE_SUSPENDING to ADMIN
```

Useful JMX Programs

Programming with JMX requires a good understanding of the MBean structure of WebLogic. WebLogic has a huge number of MBeans and as shown above those MBeans even have different APIs in the different MBean servers. In addition, the documentation from Oracle and information from various websites and blogs do not provide the same level of information as they provide for WLST. A few small utilities are provided that have helped me a lot in writing many different JMX programs in various consultancy projects.

List MBeans

This tool describes a small but very useful tool in order to list all available MBeans with their attributes and operations. Note: Please keep in mind that with all configuration changes and especially new deployments, new MBeans will join the club and therefore running this tool will show a different result set after those administrative changes.

💾 list_available_MBeans

```java
import java.util.*;
import javax.management.*;
import javax.management.ObjectName;
import de.wls_monitoringbook.jmx_access.JMXWrapper;

public class PrintMBeanNames {

    public static void main(String[] args) {
        System.out.println("RUNTIME:");
        System.out.println("-------------------------------------------------");
        printMBeans(false);

        System.out.println("\n\n\n\nEDIT-MBEANServer:");
        System.out.println("-------------------------------------------------");
        printMBeans(true);
    }


    /**
     * Print all MBean information from an MBean server
     * @param edit boolean
     */
    private static void printMBeans(boolean edit) {

        try {
            // adminUser / password / and URL should be provided as commandline parameters
            String adminUser = "weblogic";
            String adminPW = "Weblogic1";
            String adminURL = "t3://localhost:7001";

            // init wrapper
            JMXWrapper myJMXWrapper = new JMXWrapper();

            // connecto server - either runtime or edit mbean server
            myJMXWrapper.connectToAdminServer(edit, adminUser, adminPW,adminURL, true);

            MBeanServerConnection connection = myJMXWrapper.getConnection();
            Set mySet = connection.queryNames(new ObjectName("*:*"), null);
            Iterator it = mySet.iterator();

            while (it.hasNext()) {
                ObjectName myName = (ObjectName) it.next();

                try {
                    System.out.println("--> " + myName.getCanonicalName());

                    // get all attributes
                    MBeanAttributeInfo[] atribs = connection.getMBeanInfo(myName).getAttributes();

                    for (int i = 0; i < atribs.length; i++) {
                        System.out.println("        Attribute: " + atribs[i].getName() +
                                " of Type : " + atribs[i].getType());
                    }

                    // get all operations
                    MBeanOperationInfo[] operations =
                                    connection.getMBeanInfo(myName).getOperations();

                    for (int i = 0; i < operations.length; i++) {
                        System.out.print("        Operation: " +
                                operations[i].getReturnType() + "  " +
                                operations[i].getName() + "(");

                        for (int j = 0; j < operations[i].getSignature().length;j++)
                            System.out.print(operations[i].getSignature()[j].
                                    getName() + ":" +
                                    operations[i].getSignature()[j].
                                    getType() + "  ");

                        System.out.println(")");
                    }
```

```
            } catch (Exception ex) {
                ex.printStackTrace();
            }
        }

        // disconnect
        myJMXWrapper.disconnectFromAdminServer(edit);
    }
    catch (Exception ex) {
        ex.printStackTrace();
    }
  }
}
```

Running the program will create the following result (note that of course the result of a real tool run is much bigger than the example shown below).

RUNTIME:

```
com.bea:Location=AdminServer,Name=ConnectorService,ServerRuntime=AdminServer,Type=ConnectorServiceRun
time
        Attribute: RACount    of Type : java.lang.Integer
        Attribute: Parent    of Type : javax.management.ObjectName
        Attribute: ConnectionPoolCurrentCount    of Type : java.lang.Integer
        Attribute: ConnectionPools    of Type : [Ljavax.management.ObjectName;
        Attribute: Type    of Type : java.lang.String
        Attribute: RAs    of Type : [Ljavax.management.ObjectName;
        Attribute: ActiveRACount    of Type : java.lang.Integer
        Attribute: Name    of Type : java.lang.String
        Attribute: InactiveRAs    of Type : [Ljavax.management.ObjectName; < rest of list removed >
```

EDIT-MBEANServer:

```
------------------------------------------------
Security:Name=myrealmDefaultAdjudicator
        Attribute: Description    of Type : java.lang.String
        Attribute: Name    of Type : java.lang.String
        Attribute: ProviderClassName    of Type : java.lang.String
        Attribute: Realm    of Type : javax.management.ObjectName
        Attribute: RequireUnanimousPermit    of Type : java.lang.Boolean
        Attribute: Version    of Type : java.lang.String
        Operation: java.lang.Boolean  isSet(propertyName:java.lang.String  )
        Operation: java.lang.Void  unSet(propertyName:java.lang.String  )
< rest of list removed >
```

Test MBean Queries

Programming in JMX can make it difficult to find the right MBeans. One good source of information is available through the MBean hierarchy. In almost all cases, the different MBeans are organized in a "parent"-"child" relationship. WLST, for example, organizes the MBeans in a filesystem-like structure. Unfortunately the complete MBean world in WebLogic uses different ways to define a parent-child relationship in the different parts of WebLogic (e.g. the WebLogic core, the JDBC subsystem, and the security area use different ways to define the parent-child relationship). A good understanding of the different MBean relationships really helps a lot when writing JMX programs.

JMX also offers a way of searching for MBeans based on ObjectNames and patterns of ObjectNames. The next utility has been proven to be very useful because you can test your MBean queries against any WebLogic Server you need to. Also keep in mind that the result set will be different (not only in numbers but also the names themselves) depending on which MBean server you are talking to (domain runtime, runtime, edit). This tool also allows the user to select which MBeanServer you want to ask.

🖫 search_MBeans

```
import java.io.IOException;
import java.net.MalformedURLException;
import java.util.*;
import javax.management.MBeanServerConnection;
import javax.management.MalformedObjectNameException;
import javax.management.ObjectName;
import javax.management.remote.JMXConnector;
import javax.management.remote.JMXConnectorFactory;
import javax.management.remote.JMXServiceURL;
import javax.naming.Context;
import java.lang.*;

public class WLSQueryTest
{
    private static MBeanServerConnection connection = null;
    private static JMXConnector connector = null;
    private static ObjectName service = null;


public static void initConnection(String hostname, String portString,String username, String
password) throws Exception
{
    String protocol="t3";
    Integer portInteger=Integer.valueOf(portString);
    int port=portInteger.intValue();
    String jndiroot="/jndi/";
    String mserver=null;

    String myService=System.getProperty("SERVICE","DOMAIN");    // possibe: DOMAIN, RUNTIME, EDIT
        if ("DOMAIN".equalsIgnoreCase(myService))
        {
        service=new
ObjectName("com.bea:Name=DomainRuntimeService,Type=weblogic.management.mbeanservers.domainruntime.Dom
ainRuntimeServiceMBean");
        mserver="weblogic.management.mbeanservers.domainruntime";
    }

        if ("RUNTIME".equalsIgnoreCase(myService))
        {
        service=new
ObjectName("com.bea:Name=RuntimeService,Type=weblogic.management.mbeanservers.runtime.RuntimeServiceM
Bean");
        mserver="weblogic.management.mbeanservers.runtime";
    }

        if ("EDIT".equalsIgnoreCase(myService))
        {
        service=new
ObjectName("com.bea:Name=EditService,Type=weblogic.management.mbeanservers.edit.EditServiceMBean");
        mserver="weblogic.management.mbeanservers.edit";
    }

    System.out.println("    service = " + service);
    System.out.println("    JNDI    = " + jndiroot + mserver);
    System.out.println();
    JMXServiceURL serviceURL=new JMXServiceURL(protocol, hostname,port, jndiroot + mserver);
    Hashtable h=new Hashtable();
    h.put(Context.SECURITY_PRINCIPAL, username);
    h.put(Context.SECURITY_CREDENTIALS, password);
    h.put(JMXConnectorFactory.PROTOCOL_PROVIDER_PACKAGES,"weblogic.management.remote");
    connector=JMXConnectorFactory.connect(serviceURL, h);
    connection=connector.getMBeanServerConnection();
}
```

```
public static void main(String[] args) throws Exception
{
    String hostname=args[0];
    String portString=args[1];
    String username=args[2];
    String password=args[3];
    String queryArgument = args[4];
    System.out.println("Hostname      : " + hostname);
    System.out.println("PortString    : " + portString);
    System.out.println("Username      : " + username);
    System.out.println("Password      : " + password);
    System.out.println("queryArgument : " + queryArgument);

    initConnection(hostname, portString, username, password);

    // query and print result
    Set<ObjectName> beanSet = connection.queryNames(new ObjectName(queryArgument),null );
    System.out.println("\n\nQuery found "+beanSet.size()+" results !");

    ObjectName queryName = null;

    Iterator<ObjectName> i = beanSet.iterator();
    while (i.hasNext())
    {
        queryName = (ObjectName)i.next();
        System.out.println("   --> " + queryName);
    }

    connector.close();
}
```

Examples of calling this tool:

Query an AdminServer:

```
java -DSERVICE=DOMAIN WLSQueryTest localost 7001 weblogic Welcome1
"*:*,Type=ServerRuntime"
```

Query a Managed-Server:

```
java -DSERVICE=RUNTIME WLSQueryTest localost 7011 weblogic Welcome1
"*:*,Type=JTARuntime"
```

Bulk Updates / Bulk Reads

JMX also offers another very interesting feature for performance optimization. It is possible to read or write a whole group of attributes in one method call. This can dramatically reduce the amount of network calls and therefore improve performance if you want to query multiple attributes of the same MBean.

```
    public void getAttributesExample(ObjectName myName)
    {
        String[] attributeNames = new
String[]{"Name","Description","MaxCount","ExecutionTime","NrOfFailures"};

        // get all attributes with Parent
        AttributeList  attrList = myJMXWrapper.getConnection().getAttributes(myName, attributeNames);
        List<Attribute> myAttrList = attrList.asList();

        // Print out all retrieved attributes
        for (int i=0;i<myAttrList.size();i++)
        {
```

```
        Attribute nextAttr = myAttrList.get(i);
        System.out.println("Attribute : "+nextAttr.getName()+" has value: "+nextAttr.getValue());
    }
}
```

Summary

This chapter has given an overview of JMX automation for WebLogic tasks. This section has also provided information about the strengths of JMX that cannot be found in WLST.

Creating Domains with JMX CHAPTER

13

Creating Domains with JMX

JMX is an online API and needs a running MBean server to connect to. This means that the AdminServer must be up and running before you can use JMX. All domain creation scripts and domain template scripts introduced in the WLST part require the WLST OFFLINE mode and therefore cannot be ported to JMX.

If you want to use JMX, then a minimal domain must already be created and the AdminServer must be up and running. The rest of this part of the book assumes at these prerequisites are fulfilled. See the WebLogic overview chapter for more information about domains.

Configure Domain and Server Logging Settings

The domain creates log files and every server - including the AdminServer - creates log files. Especially in production systems, log files must be saved for future review. Log files must be rotated in order to limit size or to separate timeframes. For instance, this may mean having one log file for each day.

In production systems, it is a good practice to rotate log files once per day. This makes it easy for scheduled processes to move old log files to a backup or log server in order to save disk space and avoid the local disk filling up with logs. For example, rotating logs every day at 2am means that a scheduled process can run at 2:30am and move the old log file away.

The Domain Log File

Example for changing the settings for the domain log:

🖫 **domain_log_change_jmx**

```
Mbean needed for the configuration of the domain log file.  The Mbean is shown here in order to give
you an impression about the detailed control which is offered my the WebLogic management APIs
 com.bea:Name=TestDomain,Type=Log
    Attribute: RotateLogOnStartup   of Type : java.lang.Boolean
    Attribute: DomainLogBroadcastFilter   of Type : javax.management.ObjectName
    Attribute: RotationTime   of Type : java.lang.String
```

```
       Attribute: MemoryBufferSize   of Type : java.lang.Integer
       Attribute: Type   of Type : java.lang.String
       Attribute: LoggerSeverity   of Type : java.lang.String
       Attribute: StdoutFormat   of Type : java.lang.String
       Attribute: BufferSizeKB   of Type : java.lang.Integer
       Attribute: ServerLoggingBridgeUseParentLoggersEnabled   of Type : java.lang.Boolean
       Attribute: RedirectStderrToServerLogEnabled   of Type : java.lang.Boolean
       Attribute: StdoutSeverity   of Type : java.lang.String
       Attribute: DomainLogBroadcastSeverity   of Type : java.lang.String
       Attribute: MemoryBufferSeverity   of Type : java.lang.String
       Attribute: StdoutLogStack   of Type : java.lang.Boolean
       Attribute: RedirectStdoutToServerLogEnabled   of Type : java.lang.Boolean
       Attribute: StdoutFilter   of Type : javax.management.ObjectName
       Attribute: Parent   of Type : javax.management.ObjectName
       Attribute: FileTimeSpan   of Type : java.lang.Integer
       Attribute: LogFileRotationDir   of Type : java.lang.String
       Attribute: LoggerSeverityProperties   of Type : java.util.Properties
       Attribute: NumberOfFilesLimited   of Type : java.lang.Boolean
       Attribute: FileCount   of Type : java.lang.Integer
       Attribute: RotationType   of Type : java.lang.String
       Attribute: DomainLogBroadcasterBufferSize   of Type : java.lang.Integer
       Attribute: LogFileFilter   of Type : javax.management.ObjectName
       Attribute: Notes   of Type : java.lang.String
       Attribute: Name   of Type : java.lang.String
       Attribute: MemoryBufferFilter   of Type : javax.management.ObjectName
       Attribute: Log4jLoggingEnabled   of Type : java.lang.Boolean
       Attribute: FileMinSize   of Type : java.lang.Integer
       Attribute: FileName   of Type : java.lang.String
       Attribute: StacktraceDepth   of Type : java.lang.Integer
       Attribute: DateFormatPattern   of Type : java.lang.String
       Attribute: LogFileSeverity   of Type : java.lang.String
```

REMINDER: In order to keep the housekeeping code in all the Java examples to a minimum, almost all examples (except the more complex ones, or complete listings) will avoid the usual exception handling, recover, or even cleanup if necessary. This is not the best programming style and is only chosen in order to reduce the amount code in the listings. The code listings concentrate on the important aspects. It is up to the reader to add the missing Java features like exception handling. The code provided outside of the book (download) will have much better housekeeping.

Java programming example:

💾 domain_log_example

```
import java.util.*;
import javax.management.MBeanServerConnection;
import javax.management.ObjectName;
import javax.management.Attribute;
import javax.management.remote.*;
import de.wls_monitoringbook.jmx_access.JMXWrapper;

public class DomainConfiguration
{
    private JMXWrapper myJMXWrapper;

    private Hashtable<String , String> domainInfo;
    private String domainName = "";

    public DomainConfiguration(JMXWrapper _myJMXWrapper) throws Exception  {
        myJMXWrapper = _myJMXWrapper;

        // get domainInfo
        domainInfo = myJMXWrapper.getMainServerDomainValues();
        domainName = domainInfo.get("domainName");
    }

    /**
     * Configure the attribute and rollover definition of the domain log file
     * @throws Exception
```

```
*/
public void configureDomainLog() throws Exception  {
    // e.g.: com.bea:Name=TestDomain,Type=Log
    ObjectName myLogMBean = new ObjectName("com.bea:Name="+domainName+",Type=Log");

    // set attribute RotationType
    myJMXWrapper.setAttribute(myLogMBean,new Attribute("RotationType",new String("byTime")));

    // set attribute RotationTime
    myJMXWrapper.setAttribute(myLogMBean,new Attribute("RotationTime",new String("02:00")));

    // set attribute FileTimeSpan
    myJMXWrapper.setAttribute(myLogMBean,new Attribute("FileTimeSpan",new Integer(24)));

    // set attribute NumberOfFilesLimited
    myJMXWrapper.setAttribute(myLogMBean,new Attribute("NumberOfFilesLimited",
                        new Boolean(true)));

    // set attribute FileCount
    myJMXWrapper.setAttribute(myLogMBean,new Attribute("FileCount",new Integer(14)));  // 2 weeks

    // set attribute FileName
    myJMXWrapper.setAttribute(myLogMBean,
            new Attribute("FileName","/applications/log/"+domainName+"domainLog.log"));
}


/**
 * Configure various settings of the domain.
 * @throws Exception
 */
public void configureDomain() throws Exception {
    configureDomainLog();
}


public static void main(String[] args) throws Exception
{
    JMXWrapper myJMXWrapper = new JMXWrapper();

  // opens an connection to the "EDIT" MBean tree
    myJMXWrapper.connectToAdminServer(true, // edit
                        "weblogic",
                        "test1234",
                        "t3://localhost:7001",
                        true
                        );
    // create configuration instance
    DomainConfiguration myDomainConfiguration = new DomainConfiguration(myJMXWrapper);

    // configure domain
    myDomainConfiguration.configureDomain();

  // activate changes and close the connection
    myJMXWrapper.disconnectFromAdminServer(true);
}
}
```

This program opens a connection to an AdminServer. Then the method to configure the domain log will be called on the *DomainConfiguration* class, which sets the desired log settings. There are a number of setting you can choose, such as the rotation time based on size or time, the log file sizes, the amount of files, and several others. The settings that are available and which make sense depend on the rotation time.

The Administration Server Logs

Logs for the Administration Server are a little bit different than for the domain. With the AdminServer, we are touching a real server that consists of multiple log files. Not all of them can be configured using MBeans. The files that can be configured are the server log file and the server access file. These are located in two different MBeans.

The following is a JMX example that configures the server log files. Note that only the method added to the *DomainConfiguration* class is shown. This is not a complete Java program!

💾 configure_server_logs_jmx

```java
/**
 * Configure the attribute and rollover definition of a server log file
 * @throws Exception
 */
public void configureServerLog(String servername) throws Exception
{
    // e.g.: com.bea:Name=AdminServer,Server=AdminServer,Type=Log
    ObjectName myLogMBean = new ObjectName("com.bea:Name="+servername+
                                ",Server="+servername+",Type=Log");

    // e.g.: com.bea:Name=AdminServer,Server=AdminServer,Type=WebServerLog,WebServer=AdminServer
    ObjectName myWebserverLogMBean = new ObjectName("com.bea:Name="+servername+",
            Server="+servername+",Type=WebServerLog,WebServer="+servername+"");

    // set attribute RotationType
    myJMXWrapper.setAttribute(myLogMBean,new Attribute("RotationType",new String("byTime")));

    // set attribute RotationTime
    myJMXWrapper.setAttribute(myLogMBean,new Attribute("RotationTime",new String("02:00")));

    // set attribute FileTimeSpan
    myJMXWrapper.setAttribute(myLogMBean,new Attribute("FileTimeSpan",new Integer(24)));

    // set attribute NumberOfFilesLimited
    myJMXWrapper.setAttribute(myLogMBean,new Attribute("NumberOfFilesLimited",
                            new Boolean(true)));

    // set attribute FileCount
    myJMXWrapper.setAttribute(myLogMBean,new Attribute("FileCount",new Integer(14)));  // 2 weeks

    // set attribute FileName
    myJMXWrapper.setAttribute(myLogMBean,
                            new Attribute("FileName","/applications/log/"+
                                    servername+"/"+servername+".log"));

    // now do the same for the access log of the webserver

    // set attribute RotationType
    myJMXWrapper.setAttribute(myWebserverLogMBean,new Attribute("RotationType",
                            new String("byTime")));

    // set attribute RotationTime
    myJMXWrapper.setAttribute(myWebserverLogMBean,new Attribute("RotationTime",
                            new String("02:00")));

    // set attribute FileTimeSpan
    myJMXWrapper.setAttribute(myWebserverLogMBean,new Attribute("FileTimeSpan",new Integer(24)));

    // set attribute NumberOfFilesLimited
    myJMXWrapper.setAttribute(myWebserverLogMBean,new Attribute("NumberOfFilesLimited",
                            new Boolean(true)));

    // set attribute FileCount
    myJMXWrapper.setAttribute(myWebserverLogMBean,new Attribute("FileCount",new Integer(14)));

    // set attribute FileName
    myJMXWrapper.setAttribute(myWebserverLogMBean,
                            new Attribute("FileName","/applications/log/"+
                                    servername+"/access.log"));
}
```

Domain-wide Settings

Some configuration items of WebLogic are defined on the domain level. This means that these settings are not configured in the scope of a specific server instance. These settings apply to all server instances. One common example are the different transactional settings for the JTA transaction service. The following JMX code shows as an example for how the transaction timeout can be changed using a standard JMX call:

```
/**
 * Configure the domain wide JTA attributes
 */
public void configureDomainJTASetting() throws Exception
{
    // e.g.: com.bea:Name=TestDomain,Type=JTA
    ObjectName myJTAMBean = new ObjectName("com.bea:Name="+domainName+",Type=JTA");

    // set attribute TimeoutSeconds
    myJMXWrapper.setAttribute(myJTAMBean,new Attribute("TimeoutSeconds",new Integer(300)));
}
```

Cluster

Managed-Servers can be grouped into clusters. Every WebLogic domain can host multiple clusters, but each Managed-Server can only be a member of one cluster (if at all). Every cluster can (but does not need to) include Managed-Servers hosted on different machines. As described in the introduction, there are two different communication models for clusters: Unicast and Multicast (see the "Cluster" section in *Chapter 5* for more details about the different types).

Example for creating a Unicast cluster with JMX:

```
/**
 * Configure a new cluster
 * @throws Exception
 */
public void createCluster(String clustername) throws Exception
{
    // e.g.: com.bea:Name=TestDomain,Type=Domain
    ObjectName myDomainMBean = new ObjectName("com.bea:Name=" + domainName +",Type=Domain");

    // javax.management.ObjectName  createCluster(name:java.lang.String  )
    ObjectName myNewCluster = (ObjectName)myJMXWrapper.invoke(
            myDomainMBean, "createCluster",new Object[]{new String(clustername)},
            new String[]{String.class.getName()});

    // set attribute ClusterMessagingMode
    myJMXWrapper.setAttribute(myNewCluster,new Attribute("ClusterMessagingMode",
                        new String("unicast")));

    // set attribute FrontendHTTPSPort
    myJMXWrapper.setAttribute(myNewCluster,new Attribute("FrontendHTTPSPort",new Integer(0)));

    // set attribute FrontendHTTPPort
    myJMXWrapper.setAttribute(myNewCluster,new Attribute("FrontendHTTPPort",new Integer(0)));

    // set attribute WeblogicPluginEnabled
    myJMXWrapper.setAttribute(myNewCluster,new Attribute("WeblogicPluginEnabled",
                        new Boolean("false")));
}
```

Machines and NodeManager

An important configuration within WebLogic is the machine. A machine represents a physical node where Managed-Servers can be located. For the communication between the AdminServer and Managed-Server, this concept is rather irrelevant as the AdminServer will contact the Managed-Server over the admin-port. The machine setting and especially the NodeManager configurations for the machines are important for starting the Managed-Servers.

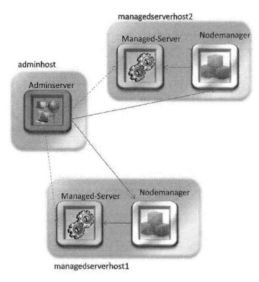

Figure 13.1: *NodeManager Managed Domain*

Every machine configuration in WebLogic has exactly one NodeManager. If there is a need for having different NodeManagers on the same physical machine hosting Managed-Servers for the same domain, you need to add multiple machine configurations. The reason for this may be that different machine users are running the Managed-Servers, which results in different machine access rights.

WebLogic distinguishes between different types of machines and different types of NodeManagers.

The following is an example for creating a UNIX machine with an SSL NodeManager in JMX:

```
public void createUnixMachine(String machinename) throws Exception
{
    // e.g.: com.bea:Name=TestDomain,Type=Domain
    ObjectName myDomainMBean = new ObjectName("com.bea:Name=" + domainName +",Type=Domain");
```

```
    // javax.management.ObjectName  createCluster(name:java.lang.String  )
    ObjectName myNewMachine = (ObjectName)myJMXWrapper.invoke(myDomainMBean,
                            "createUnixMachine",new Object[]{new String(machinename)},
                            new String[]{String.class.getName()});

    // the new mbean will have a name similiar to com.bea:Name=MyTestMachine,Type=UnixMachine
    // also the nodemanager mbean was created: com.bea:Name=MyTestMachine,Type=NodeManager,…

    ObjectName myNodemanagerMBean = new ObjectName("com.bea:Name="+machinename+
                            ",Type=NodeManager,UnixMachine="+machinename);

    // set attribute NMType
    myJMXWrapper.setAttribute(myNodemanagerMBean,new Attribute("NMType",new String("SSL")));

    // set attribute ListenAddress

    myJMXWrapper.setAttribute(myNodemanagerMBean,new Attribute("ListenAddress",
                            new String("myUnixHostName")));

    // set attribute ListenPort
    myJMXWrapper.setAttribute(myNodemanagerMBean,new Attribute("ListenPort",new Integer(4711)));

    // set attribute DebugEnabled
    myJMXWrapper.setAttribute(myNodemanagerMBean,new Attribute("DebugEnabled",new Boolean("false")));
}
```

Managed-Servers

In addition to having an Administration Server, a domain can have zero or more Managed-Servers. Managed-Servers and Administration Server are similar in that both can host applications. However, only the AdminServer can host the administration console. Managed-Servers host the applications and therefore are actually doing the work. The Administration Server is usually used for administration work and the Managed-Servers are used to host the application.

Every Managed-Server stores a local copy of the domain configuration. When the Managed-Server starts, it connects to the Administration Server to synchronize the configuration. When the configuration changes, the Administration Server sends the changed configuration to the Managed-Servers.

Lifecycle operations like starting and stopping can be performed on the Managed-Server without having an Administration Server running. Of course in this case, the Managed-Server cannot synchronize itself with the Administration Server. This mode is called the Managed-Server independence mode (MSI).

Creating a Managed-Server

The following Java method adds a new Managed-Server to the domain and targets it to a machine:

🖫 add_managed-server_jmx

```
public void createManagedServer(String servername, String clustername, String machinename)
    throws Exception
{
    // e.g.: com.bea:Name=TestDomain,Type=Domain
```

```
        ObjectName myDomainMBean = new ObjectName("com.bea:Name=" + domainName +",Type=Domain");

        // javax.management.ObjectName  createCluster(name:java.lang.String  )
        // the new mbean will have a name similiar to com.bea:Name=TestManagdServer,Type=Server
        ObjectName myManagedServerMBean = (ObjectName)myJMXWrapper.invoke(myDomainMBean,
                                                    "createServer",
                                                    new Object[]{new
String(servername)},
                                                    new
String[]{String.class.getName()});

        // and SSL: com.bea:Name=TestManagdServer,Server=TestManagdServer,Type=SSL
        ObjectName myManagedServerSSLMBean = new
ObjectName("com.bea:Name="+servername+",Server="+servername+",Type=SSL");
        // and ServerStart: com.bea:Name=MyTestServer,Server=MyTestServer,Type=ServerStart
        ObjectName myManagedServerServerStartMBean =
                    new
ObjectName("com.bea:Name="+servername+",Server="+servername+",Type=ServerStart");


        // set attribute ListenAddress
        myJMXWrapper.setAttribute(myManagedServerMBean,
                            new Attribute("ListenAddress",
                                    new String("myManagedServerListenerAddress")));

        // set attribute ListenPort
        myJMXWrapper.setAttribute(myManagedServerMBean,new Attribute("ListenPort",new
Integer(10432)));

        // set attribute ListenPortEnabled
        myJMXWrapper.setAttribute(myManagedServerMBean,new Attribute("ListenPortEnabled",new
Boolean(true)));


        // add to machine
        if (machinename != null)
            myJMXWrapper.setAttribute(myManagedServerMBean,
                        new Attribute("Machine",new
ObjectName("com.bea:Name="+machinename+",Type=UnixMachine")));

        // add to cluster
        // set attribute Cluster
        if (clustername != null)
            myJMXWrapper.setAttribute(myManagedServerMBean,new Attribute("Cluster",
                                new ObjectName("com.bea:Name="+clustername+",Type=Cluster")));


        // SSL
        // set attribute ListenPort
        myJMXWrapper.setAttribute(myManagedServerSSLMBean,new Attribute("ListenPort",new
Integer(11111)));

        // set attribute Enabled
        myJMXWrapper.setAttribute(myManagedServerSSLMBean,new Attribute("Enabled",new
Boolean(true)));


        // SERVERSTART
        // note the following paths and file names are only examples !!
        String ms_out = "/logs/domains/"+domainName+"/"+servername+"/"+servername+".out";
        String ms_err = "/logs/domains/"+domainName+"/"+servername+"/"+servername+".err";
        String managedserver_args = "-Djava.awt.headless=true  -Xmx1024 -XX:MaxPermSize=512m -
Dweblogic.Stdout="+ms_out+" -Dweblogic.Stderr="+ ms_err;

        // set attribute Arguments
        myJMXWrapper.setAttribute(myManagedServerServerStartMBean,new
Attribute("Arguments",managedserver_args));

        // set attribute JavaHome
        myJMXWrapper.setAttribute(myManagedServerServerStartMBean,new
Attribute("JavaHome","/opt/jdks/jdk1.6"));
    }
```

Renaming a Managed-Server

Once in a consultancy project, I was faced with the following problem: For a large number of domains and Managed-Servers, the customer wanted to unify the naming of the machines. This does not mean the physical machine names or hostnames on operating system level. I am referring to the machine names in a WebLogic domain definition. The customer did not want to migrate Managed-Servers and he also did not want to re-create/re-configure and re-deploy all the domains, Managed-Servers, and applications in the production environment.

WebLogic does not allow the renaming of machines in a WebLogic domain. Therefore the solution was:

- Iterate over all domains.

- In each domain, iterate over all machines.

- If a machine must be renamed, then create a new machine definition with the new name and copy all configuration attributes from the old machine definition (except the name of course) to the new machine.

- Iterate over all Managed-Servers, and if the machine a Managed-Server was attached to was affected, attach the new machine to that Managed-Server.

- Finally, delete all old machines.

🖫 renaming_machine_jmx

```
public void renameMachineName()  throws WLSAutomationException
{
  // change machine names
  try
  {
    // get domain configuration mbean
    ObjectName domainMBean =(ObjectName)myJMXWrapper.getAttribute(
                         myJMXWrapper.getService(),"DomainConfiguration");

    // get all machines
    ObjectName[] old_machines = (ObjectName[])myJMXWrapper.getAttribute(domainMBean,"Machines");

    // a list of all machines in a hasmap format for better mapping
    HashMap<String,ObjectName> allMachines = new HashMap<String,ObjectName>();

    // a list of all machine names for better mapping and increased performance
    ArrayList<String> allMachineNames = new ArrayList<String>();

    // iterate over all old machine and create the two lists defined
    for (int om=0;om<old_machines.length;om++)
    {
        String nextname = (String)myJMXWrapper.getAttribute(old_machines[om],"Name");
        System.out.println(" Found machine "+nextname+" of type "+old_machines[om].toString());
        allMachines.put(nextname,old_machines[om]);
        allMachineNames.add(nextname);
    }

    // a list to collect all machines which can be deleted
    ArrayList<ObjectName> toBeDeletedMachinesMap = new ArrayList<ObjectName>();

    // a list with all new machines
    HashMap<String,ObjectName> myNewMachines = new  HashMap<String,ObjectName>();

    // iterate over all machines
```

```
        Iterator omIt = allMachines.keySet().iterator();
    while (omIt.hasNext())
    {
      String nextOldName = (String)omIt.next();
      ObjectName nextOldMachine = (ObjectName)allMachines.get(nextOldName);
      System.out.println("Testing machine: "+nextOldName+
                          " with objectname="+nextOldMachine.toString());

      // This is only an example in order to demo this functionality.
      // normally a mapping method which returns the newName if a new name is required
      // String newName = getNewNameIfMachineMustBeRenamed(nextOldName);

      // for demo purpose change all machines and add_TEST to the machine name
      String newName = nextOldName+"_MyTEST";
      if (newName == null)
      {   // for the demo this code will never be reached !!
            System.out.println("Machine "+nextOldName+" MUST NOT be converted !");
      }
      else // ok something to do
      {
        System.out.println("New Name for machine "+nextOldName+" is "+newName);

        // create Machine
        Object  values[] = { newName};
        String  signatur[] = { String.class.getName()};

        if (allMachines.containsKey(newName))
        {
            System.out.println("??? Machine "+newName+" ALREADY EXISTS - using this one !!");
            toBeDeletedMachinesMap.add(nextOldMachine);  // this machine will later be deleted !!
            myNewMachines.put(nextOldName,(ObjectName)allMachines.get(newName));
        }
        else // create a new machine and then copy all values (including nodemanager !!)
        {
            System.out.println("Try to create machine "+newName);
            ObjectName newMachine = (ObjectName)myJMXWrapper.invoke(domainMBean,
                                    "createUnixMachine",values,signatur);
            System.out.println("Created machine"+newName);

            toBeDeletedMachinesMap.add(nextOldMachine);  // this machine will later be deleted !!
            myNewMachines.put(nextOldName,newMachine);

            System.out.println("Copy nodemanager from machine "+nextOldName+" to "+newName);

            // old nodemanager
            ObjectName myOldNodeManager = (ObjectName)myJMXWrapper.getAttribute(nextOldMachine,
                    "NodeManager");
            // new nodemanager
            ObjectName myNewNodeManager = (ObjectName)myJMXWrapper.getAttribute(newMachine,
                    "NodeManager");

            // copy all values from old machine to new machine
            myJMXWrapper.setAttribute(myNewNodeManager,
                    new Attribute("NMType",myJMXWrapper.getAttribute(myOldNodeManager,
                            "NMType")));
            myJMXWrapper.setAttribute(myNewNodeManager,
                    new Attribute("NodeManagerHome",myJMXWrapper.getAttribute(myOldNodeManager,
                            "NodeManagerHome")));
            myJMXWrapper.setAttribute(myNewNodeManager,
                    new Attribute("ListenPort",myJMXWrapper.getAttribute(myOldNodeManager,
                            "ListenPort")));
            myJMXWrapper.setAttribute(myNewNodeManager,
                    new Attribute("Notes",myJMXWrapper.getAttribute(myOldNodeManager,"Notes")));
            myJMXWrapper.setAttribute(myNewNodeManager,
                    new Attribute("Name",myJMXWrapper.getAttribute(myOldNodeManager,"Name")));
            myJMXWrapper.setAttribute(myNewNodeManager,
                    new Attribute("DebugEnabled",myJMXWrapper.getAttribute(myOldNodeManager,
                            "DebugEnabled")));
            myJMXWrapper.setAttribute(myNewNodeManager,
                    new Attribute("ShellCommand",myJMXWrapper.getAttribute(myOldNodeManager,
                            "ShellCommand")));
            myJMXWrapper.setAttribute(myNewNodeManager,
                    new Attribute("ListenAddress",myJMXWrapper.getAttribute(myOldNodeManager,
                            "ListenAddress")));

        }
    }
```

```
    }

        // now as all new machines are created, reconfigure - means retarget the appropriate server
        System.out.println("RECONFIGURE all servers if necessary !");
        ObjectName[] serverRuntimes = (ObjectName[])myJMXWrapper.getAttribute(domainMBean,"Servers");
        for (int i = 0; i < serverRuntimes.length; i++)
        {
            String serverName = serverRuntimes[i].getKeyProperty("Name");
            System.out.println("Try to reconfigure "+serverName);
            // Machine
            try {
                // get the machine of this managed server , if any
                ObjectName server_machine_object = (ObjectName)myJMXWrapper.
                                            getAttribute(serverRuntimes[i],"Machine");
                // if this server is attached to a machine (note adminservers often are not)
                if (server_machine_object!=null)
                {
                    String server_machine_name = (String)myJMXWrapper.
                                        getAttribute(server_machine_object,"Name");

                    // map name and set new machine
                    ObjectName myNewMachineTmpName =
                            (ObjectName)myNewMachines.get(server_machine_name);

                    // if no entry is found in the new machine list - no new machine has been created
                    if (myNewMachineTmpName == null)
                        System.out.println("Server" +serverName+" does NOT need any modifications !");
                    else
                    {
                        // set Machine - re-target the server to the new machine
                        Attribute newMachineAttribute = new Attribute("Machine",myNewMachineTmpName);
                        myJMXWrapper.setAttribute(serverRuntimes[i],newMachineAttribute);
                    }
                }
                else
                    System.out.println("NO machine found for Server = "+serverName);
            }
            catch (Exception ex) {
                System.out.println("Problem in SwitchAllMachinesStep:executeStep "+ex);
                throw new WLSAutomationException(ex.getMessage());
            }
        }

        // destroy all old Machine
        System.out.println("DESTROY all old machines");

        for (int om=0;om<toBeDeletedMachinesMap.size();om++)
        {
          System.out.println("DESTROY "+((ObjectName)toBeDeletedMachinesMap.get(om)).toString());
            Object  values[] = { (ObjectName)toBeDeletedMachinesMap.get(om)};
            String  signatur[] = { javax.management.ObjectName.class.getName()};
            myJMXWrapper.invoke(domainMBean,"destroyMachine",values,signatur);
        }

    }
    catch (Exception ex) {
        throw new WLSAutomationException(ex.getMessage());
    }
}
```

Imagine a domain with 2 machine definitions and in total 6 Managed-Servers (3 on each machine). The following would be the output of this method:

```
Found machine testMachine1 of type com.bea:Name=testMachine1,Type=Machine
Found machine testMachine2 of type com.bea:Name=testMachine2,Type=Machine
Testing machine: testMachine1 with objectname=com.bea:Name=testMachine1,Type=Machine
New Name for machine testMachine1 is testMachine1_MyTEST
Try to create machine testMachine1_MyTEST
Created machinetestMachine1_MyTEST
Copy nodemanager from machine testMachine1 to testMachine1_MyTEST
Testing machine: testMachine2 with objectname=com.bea:Name=testMachine2,Type=Machine
New Name for machine testMachine2 is testMachine2_MyTEST
Try to create machine testMachine2_MyTEST
Created machinetestMachine2_MyTEST
Copy nodemanager from machine testMachine2 to testMachine2_MyTEST
```

```
RECONFIGURE all servers if necessary !
Try to reconfigure AdminServer
NO machine found for Server = AdminServer
Try to reconfigure MartinTest_Domain_MS1
Try to reconfigure MartinTest_Domain_MS2
Try to reconfigure MartinTest_Domain_MS3
Try to reconfigure MartinTest_Domain_MS4
Try to reconfigure MartinTest_Domain_MS5
Try to reconfigure MartinTest_Domain_MS6
DESTROY all old machines
DESTROY com.bea:Name=testMachine1,Type=Machine
DESTROY com.bea:Name=testMachine2,Type=Machine
```

Network Channels

By default, all communication going into a WebLogic Server uses the same communication port or network channel with a special IP address and port. This also means that WebLogic by default is listening on the same port with all available protocols for T3, T3S, HTTP, HTTPS, LDAP, SNMP, IIOP, IIOPS cluster, and admin communication. For simple domains and networks, this is usually acceptable. However, it does not efficiently use the available network resources of bigger machines. In complex networks or critical environments (like DMZ, NAT hosts), this default behavior is definitely not sufficient. Please see the WLST section for a more detailed explanation.

WebLogic has the ability to listen to different network endpoints, which allows administrators to restrict communications to certain ports/networks. The resources used in WebLogic are called "channels". A network channel is a configuration item in WebLogic that defines the communication endpoint of a network connection. This usually includes the protocol, the IP, and the port that WebLogic has to use for the network listener. It might also include additional properties such as login timeout, tunneling support, and (e.g. in case of secure lines) SSL and certificate enforcement.

The first examples creates a channel that only allows the HTTP protocol:

💾 create_network_channel_jmx

```
public void createHTTPNetworkChannel(String serverName, String channelName, int port) throws
WLSAutomationException
{
  try {
    ObjectName myServerRuntime = (ObjectName)myJMXWrapper.invoke(myJMXWrapper.getDomainConfigRoot(),
            "lookupServer",
            new Object[]{new String(serverName)},
            new String[]{String.class.getName()});

    // create new channel with the provided name
    ObjectName myNewChannel = (ObjectName)myJMXWrapper.invoke(myServerRuntime,
            "lookupNetworkAccessPoint",
            new Object[]{new String(channelName)},
            new String[]{String.class.getName()});

    if (myNewChannel != null)
        throw new WLSAutomationException("NetworkChannel "+channelName+" already exists !");

    // now create
    myNewChannel = (ObjectName)myJMXWrapper.invoke(myServerRuntime,
                    "createNetworkAccessPoint",
```

```
                              new Object[]{new String(channelName)},
                              new String[]{String.class.getName()});

  // set protocol to http
  myJMXWrapper.setAttribute(myNewChannel,new Attribute("Protocol",new String("http")));

  // set listener port
  myJMXWrapper.setAttribute(myNewChannel,new Attribute("ListenPort",new Integer(port)));

  // enable
  myJMXWrapper.setAttribute(myNewChannel,new Attribute("Enabled",new Boolean(true)));

  // enable HttpEnabledForThisProtocol
  myJMXWrapper.setAttribute(myNewChannel,new Attribute("HttpEnabledForThisProtocol",
          new Boolean(true)));

  // set OutboundEnabled
  myJMXWrapper.setAttribute(myNewChannel,new Attribute("OutboundEnabled",new Boolean(false)));

  // disable https
  myJMXWrapper.setAttribute(myNewChannel,new Attribute("TwoWaySSLEnabled",new Boolean(false)));
  myJMXWrapper.setAttribute(myNewChannel,new Attribute("ClientCertificateEnforced",
          new Boolean(false)));
}
catch(Exception ex)
{
    throw new WLSAutomationException("Error while createHTTPNetworkChannel ("+channelName+"): "+
                              ex.getMessage());
}
}
```

Very similar, the next method will create a channel for the WebLogic-specific T3 protocol:

💾 create_T3_channel_jmx

```
public void createT3NetworkChannel(String serverName, String channelName, int port) throws
WLSAutomationException
{
  try {
   ObjectName myServerRuntime = (ObjectName)myJMXWrapper.invoke(myJMXWrapper.getDomainConfigRoot(),
          "lookupServer",
          new Object[]{new String(serverName)},
          new String[]{String.class.getName()});

  // create new channel with the provided name
  ObjectName myNewChannel = (ObjectName)myJMXWrapper.invoke(myServerRuntime,
          "lookupNetworkAccessPoint",
          new Object[]{new String(channelName)},
          new String[]{String.class.getName()});

  if (myNewChannel != null)
       throw new WLSAutomationException("NetworkChannel "+channelName+" already exists !");

  // now create
  myNewChannel = (ObjectName)myJMXWrapper.invoke(myServerRuntime,
                      "createNetworkAccessPoint",
                      new Object[]{new String(channelName)},
                      new String[]{String.class.getName()});

  // set protocol to http
  myJMXWrapper.setAttribute(myNewChannel,new Attribute("Protocol",new String("t3")));

  // set listener port
  myJMXWrapper.setAttribute(myNewChannel,new Attribute("ListenPort",new Integer(port)));

  // enable
  myJMXWrapper.setAttribute(myNewChannel,new Attribute("Enabled",new Boolean(true)));

  // enable HttpEnabledForThisProtocol
  myJMXWrapper.setAttribute(myNewChannel,new Attribute("HttpEnabledForThisProtocol",
          new Boolean(false)));

  // set OutboundEnabled
  myJMXWrapper.setAttribute(myNewChannel,new Attribute("OutboundEnabled",new Boolean(false)));
```

```
    // disable https
    myJMXWrapper.setAttribute(myNewChannel,new Attribute("TwoWaySSLEnabled",new Boolean(false)));
    myJMXWrapper.setAttribute(myNewChannel,new Attribute("ClientCertificateEnforced",
            new Boolean(false)));
    }
    catch(Exception ex) {
        throw new WLSAutomationException("Error while createT3NetworkChannel ("+channelName+"): "+
ex.getMessage());
    }
}
```

It is of course also possible to create a CORBA channel, which means enabling the IIOP protocol:

💾 create_CORBA_channel_jmx

```
public void createIIOPNetworkChannel(String serverName, String channelName, int port) throws
WLSAutomationException
{
    try {
        ObjectName myServerRuntime = (ObjectName)myJMXWrapper.invoke(myJMXWrapper.getDomainConfigRoot(),
                "lookupServer",
                new Object[]{new String(serverName)},
                new String[]{String.class.getName()});

        // create new channel with the provided name
        ObjectName myNewChannel = (ObjectName)myJMXWrapper.invoke(myServerRuntime,
                "lookupNetworkAccessPoint",
                new Object[]{new String(channelName)},
                new String[]{String.class.getName()});

        if (myNewChannel != null)
            throw new WLSAutomationException("NetworkChannel "+channelName+" already exists !");

        // now create
        myNewChannel = (ObjectName)myJMXWrapper.invoke(myServerRuntime,
                            "createNetworkAccessPoint",
                            new Object[]{new String(channelName)},
                            new String[]{String.class.getName()});

        // set protocol to http
        myJMXWrapper.setAttribute(myNewChannel,new Attribute("Protocol",new String("iiop")));

        // set listener port
        myJMXWrapper.setAttribute(myNewChannel,new Attribute("ListenPort",new Integer(port)));

        // enable
        myJMXWrapper.setAttribute(myNewChannel,new Attribute("Enabled",new Boolean(true)));

        // enable HttpEnabledForThisProtocol
        myJMXWrapper.setAttribute(myNewChannel,new Attribute("HttpEnabledForThisProtocol",
                new Boolean(false)));

        // set OutboundEnabled
        myJMXWrapper.setAttribute(myNewChannel,new Attribute("OutboundEnabled",new Boolean(false)));

        // disable https
        myJMXWrapper.setAttribute(myNewChannel,new Attribute("TwoWaySSLEnabled",new Boolean(false)));
        myJMXWrapper.setAttribute(myNewChannel,new Attribute("ClientCertificateEnforced",
                new Boolean(false)));
    }
    catch(Exception ex) {
        throw new WLSAutomationException("Error while createIIOPNetworkChannel ("+channelName+"): "+
                ex.getMessage());
    }
}
```

An HTTPS channel requires a few more settings, which define the security requirements of SSL and the usage of client certificates:

🖫 create_HTTPS_channel_jmx

```
public void createHTTPSNetworkChannel(String serverName, String channelName, int port, boolean
enforceClientCert) throws WLSAutomationException
{
  try {
    ObjectName myServerRuntime = (ObjectName)myJMXWrapper.invoke(myJMXWrapper.getDomainConfigRoot(),
             "lookupServer",
             new Object[]{new String(serverName)},
             new String[]{String.class.getName()});

    // create new channel with the provided name
    ObjectName myNewChannel = (ObjectName)myJMXWrapper.invoke(myServerRuntime,
             "lookupNetworkAccessPoint",
             new Object[]{new String(channelName)},
             new String[]{String.class.getName()});

    if (myNewChannel != null)
         throw new WLSAutomationException("NetworkChannel "+channelName+" already exists !");

    // now create
    myNewChannel = (ObjectName)myJMXWrapper.invoke(myServerRuntime,
                     "createNetworkAccessPoint",
                     new Object[]{new String(channelName)},
                     new String[]{String.class.getName()});

    // set protocol to http
    myJMXWrapper.setAttribute(myNewChannel,new Attribute("Protocol",new String("https")));

    // set listener port
    myJMXWrapper.setAttribute(myNewChannel,new Attribute("ListenPort",new Integer(port)));

    // enable
    myJMXWrapper.setAttribute(myNewChannel,new Attribute("Enabled",new Boolean(true)));

    // enable HttpEnabledForThisProtocol
    myJMXWrapper.setAttribute(myNewChannel,new Attribute("HttpEnabledForThisProtocol",
             new Boolean(true)));

    myJMXWrapper.setAttribute(myNewChannel,new Attribute("TunnelingEnabled",new Boolean(false)));

    // set OutboundEnabled
    myJMXWrapper.setAttribute(myNewChannel,new Attribute("OutboundEnabled",new Boolean(false)));

    // enable https
    myJMXWrapper.setAttribute(myNewChannel,new Attribute("TwoWaySSLEnabled",new Boolean(true)));
    myJMXWrapper.setAttribute(myNewChannel,new Attribute("ClientCertificateEnforced",
             new Boolean(enforceClientCert)));
  }
  catch(Exception ex) {
     throw new WLSAutomationException("Error while createHTTPSNetworkChannel ("+channelName+"): "+
             ex.getMessage());
  }
}
```

All the above methods create new channels. It is also possible to add existing channels to other (or new) Managed-Servers and to remove channels from Managed-Servers. This will NOT create or delete channels.

The following will add an existing channel to a Managed-Server:

🖫 add_existing_channel_jmx

```
public void addNetworkChannel(String serverName, ObjectName myChannel)
      throws WLSAutomationException
{
    try {
      ObjectName myServerRuntime =
(ObjectName)myJMXWrapper.invoke(myJMXWrapper.getDomainConfigRoot(),
                "lookupServer",
                new Object[]{new String(serverName)},
                new String[]{String.class.getName()});
```

```
    // add the channel to this server
    myJMXWrapper.invoke(myServerRuntime,
            "addNetworkAccessPoint",
            new Object[]{myChannel},
            new String[]{ObjectName.class.getName()});
    }
    catch(Exception ex) {
        throw new WLSAutomationException("Error while addNetworkChannel : "+ ex.getMessage());
    }
}
```

This will remove an existing channel from a Managed-Server:

💾 remove_existing_channel_jmx

```
public void removeNetworkChannel(String serverName, ObjectName myChannel)
            throws WLSAutomationException
{
    try {
        ObjectName myServerRuntime =
(ObjectName)myJMXWrapper.invoke(myJMXWrapper.getDomainConfigRoot(),
                    "lookupServer",
                    new Object[]{new String(serverName)},
                    new String[]{String.class.getName()});

        // remove the channel to this server
        myJMXWrapper.invoke(myServerRuntime,
            "removeNetworkAccessPoint",
            new Object[]{myChannel},
            new String[]{ObjectName.class.getName()});
    }
    catch(Exception ex)  {
        throw new WLSAutomationException("Error while addNetworkChannel : "+ ex.getMessage());
    }
}
```

Virtual Hosts

The virtual hosting feature of WebLogic provides a similar feature to the Apache
webserver. It is possible to define server names – of course these hostnames must be
known to the DNS (directory name service) – to which WebLogic instances can
respond to. In combination with network channel, it is also possible to define special
IP and port endpoints inside WebLogic that must be used in order to get a response
for certain requests. This feature can also be used in combination with clustering and
load balancing.

The following method shows how to setup a virtual host:

💾 setup_virtual_host_jmx

```
public void createVirtualHost(String virtualhostName,  // name
                        String channelName, // which networkchannel is attached
                        String[] targetServerNames,  // targets
                        String[] networkNames  // on which accept requests
                        ) throws WLSAutomationException
{
    try {

        // e.g.: com.bea:Name=TestDomain,Type=Domain
        ObjectName myDomainMBean = myJMXWrapper.getDomainConfigRoot();

        // lookup and try to find virtual host
```

```
        ObjectName myNewVirtualHost = (ObjectName)myJMXWrapper.invoke(myDomainMBean,
            "lookupVirtualHost",
            new Object[]{new String(virtualhostName)},
            new String[]{String.class.getName()});

        if (myNewVirtualHost != null)
          throw new WLSAutomationException("Virtual host "+virtualhostName+" already exists !");

        // create new virtual host with the provided name
        myNewVirtualHost = (ObjectName)myJMXWrapper.invoke(myDomainMBean,
                            "createVirtualHost",
                            new Object[]{new String(virtualhostName)},
                            new String[]{String.class.getName()});

        // set referenced network channel
        myJMXWrapper.setAttribute(myNewVirtualHost,new Attribute("NetworkAccessPoint",channelName));


        // get servers and set it to virtual host targets
        ObjectName[] myServerRuntimes = new ObjectName[targetServerNames.length];
        for (int i=0;i<targetServerNames.length;i++)
                myS/ServerRuntimes[i] =
(ObjectName)myJMXWrapper.invoke(myJMXWrapper.getDomainConfigRoot(),
                "lookupServer",
                new Object[]{new String(targetServerNames[i])},
                new String[]{String.class.getName()});

        myJMXWrapper.setAttribute(myNewVirtualHost,new Attribute("Targets",myServerRuntimes));

        // set  VirtualHostNames
        myJMXWrapper.setAttribute(myNewVirtualHost,new Attribute("VirtualHostNames",networkNames));
    }
    catch(Exception ex) {
      throw new WLSAutomationException("Error while createVirtualHost ("+virtualhostName+"): "+
ex.getMessage());
    }
}
```

Summary

This chapter has discussed a special part in a life of a WebLogic domain - its creation. JMX does not have much to offer for the birth of a domain, as JMX does not support an "offline" mode like WLST. I have introduced the enrichment of a domain with a number of different WebLogic features that are part of most WebLogic domains. Not all of them are always necessary, but all of them must be considered for each project.

Please keep in mind that JMX can only be used as soon as the base domain was created the AdminServer has been started. The setup and creation of the domain services and configurations can then be done using JMX.

Extending Domains with JMX

Extending Domains with JMX

The last chapter discussed the creation of domains and its essential parts. However, it depends on your requirements and system setups as to whether datasources belong to domain creation or domain extensions. They can also be part of both categories. This is the same for tuning and other aspects.

This chapter will discuss additional resources and configuration changes to a WebLogic domain. Even if this is not used often, we should not forget that cleanup operations are necessary from time to time. Therefore, the last section will also introduce some scripts that will delete resources.

Check for Existing Edit Sessions

Extending or changing WebLogic domains always means modifying the domain. Modifications must be done using an edit session and changes will be performed on the Edit-MBeanServer. Because different tools and techniques can be used to make changes (AdminConsole, WLST, JMX and others), it is not always easy to recognize when somebody else is already making changes. Whenever changes are required for a given WebLogic domain, it is advisable to check if someone else is making changes. Only ONE edit session is allowed at any given time, and you will run into problems (exceptions) if you are trying to open a second session.

WebLogic offers an interface called the Configuration Manager that can be used in order to find out whether an active session is already opened or not. You can even find out who is doing changes at the moment. For example, you can use *getCurrentEditor()* to find out who is making changes. You can get the list of inactivated changes using *getUnactivatedChanges()* and you can even find out what is not yet activated. It may also be useful to see how many changes are pending activation (use *len()* on the list to find out).

The following example does a basic check for an active session:

check_session_jmx

```
public boolean isEditSessionActive() throws WLSAutomationException
{
   boolean sessionFound = false;
   try
   {
      ObjectName myConfigurationManager = new
ObjectName("com.bea:Name=ConfigurationManager,Type=weblogic.management.mbeanservers.edit.Configuratio
nManagerMBean");

      // try to get an active session. If call succeeds, then a session is available, otherwise an
exception is thrown
      CompositeData[] changes =
         (CompositeData[])myJMXWrapper.getAttribute(myConfigurationManager, "UnactivatedChanges");

      if (changes != null && changes.length>0)
      {
      // changes found
      System.out.println("Active edit session found !");

      // who is doing the changes
      String userWhoEdits = (String)myJMXWrapper.getAttribute(myConfigurationManager,
                                          "CurrentEditor");
      System.out.println("   - The actual session is changed by "+ userWhoEdits +" !");

      // number of changes waiting
      System.out.println("   - The actual session has "+changes.length+" not activated changes ");

      sessionFound = true;
      }
      else {
         System.out.println("No active changes found !");
         sessionFound = false;
      }

      return sessionFound;
   }
   catch(Exception ex)
   {
      System.out.println("Error while isEditSessionActive : "+ ex.getMessage());
      throw new WLSAutomationException(ex.getMessage());
   }
}
```

However, you can even get more information. It is possible to iterate over the list of pending changes and to find out what is not yet activated. But be warned: WebLogic has a large and complicated structure for those changes. The following will be returned as the result of setting the transaction timeout in JTA from 3700 to 3800:

```
javax.management.openmbean.CompositeDataSupport(

compositeType=javax.management.openmbean.CompositeType(name=weblogic.management.mbeanservers.edit.Cha
nge,items=((itemName=AttributeName,itemType=javax.management.openmbean.SimpleType(name=java.lang.Stri
ng)),(itemName=Bean,itemType=javax.management.openmbean.CompositeType(name=javax.management.openmbean
.CompositeType.ANY,items=((itemName=OpenTypeName,itemType=javax.management.openmbean.SimpleType(name=
java.lang.String)),(itemName=ValueAsString,itemType=javax.management.openmbean.SimpleType(name=java.l
ang.String)),(itemName=ValueAsStringArray,itemType=javax.management.openmbean.ArrayType(name=[Ljava.l
ang.String;,dimension=1,elementType=javax.management.openmbean.SimpleType(name=java.lang.String),prim
itiveArray=false))))),(itemName=NewValue,itemType=javax.management.openmbean.CompositeType(name=javax
.management.openmbean.CompositeType.ANY,items=((itemName=OpenTypeName,itemType=javax.management.openm
bean.SimpleType(name=java.lang.String)),(itemName=ValueAsString,itemType=javax.management.openmbean.S
impleType(name=java.lang.String)),(itemName=ValueAsStringArray,itemType=javax.management.openmbean.Ar
rayType(name=[Ljava.lang.String;,dimension=1,elementType=javax.management.openmbean.SimpleType(name=j
ava.lang.String),primitiveArray=false))))),(itemName=OldValue,itemType=javax.management.openmbean.Com
positeType(name=javax.management.openmbean.CompositeType.ANY,items=((itemName=OpenTypeName,itemType=j
avax.management.openmbean.SimpleType(name=java.lang.String)),(itemName=ValueAsString,itemType=javax.m
anagement.openmbean.SimpleType(name=java.lang.String)),(itemName=ValueAsStringArray,itemType=javax.ma
nagement.openmbean.ArrayType(name=[Ljava.lang.String;,dimension=1,elementType=javax.management.openmb
ean.SimpleType(name=java.lang.String),primitiveArray=false))))),(itemName=Operation,itemType=javax.ma
nagement.openmbean.SimpleType(name=java.lang.String)),(itemName=RestartRequired,itemType=javax.manage
ment.openmbean.SimpleType(name=java.lang.Boolean)))),
```

```
contents={

AttributeName=TimeoutSeconds,

Bean=javax.management.openmbean.CompositeDataSupport(compositeType=javax.management.openmbean.Composi
teType(name=javax.management.openmbean.CompositeType.ANY,items=((itemName=OpenTypeName,itemType=javax
.management.openmbean.SimpleType(name=java.lang.String)),(itemName=ValueAsString,itemType=javax.manag
ement.openmbean.SimpleType(name=java.lang.String)),(itemName=ValueAsStringArray,itemType=javax.manage
ment.openmbean.ArrayType(name=[Ljava.lang.String;,dimension=1,elementType=javax.management.openmbean.
SimpleType(name=java.lang.String),primitiveArray=false)))),contents={OpenTypeName=javax.management.Ob
jectName, ValueAsString=com.bea:Name=MartinTest_Domain,Type=JTA,
ValueAsStringArray=[Ljava.lang.String;@69fe571f}),

NewValue=javax.management.openmbean.CompositeDataSupport(compositeType=javax.management.openmbean.Com
positeType(name=javax.management.openmbean.CompositeType.ANY,items=((itemName=OpenTypeName,itemType=j
avax.management.openmbean.SimpleType(name=java.lang.String)),(itemName=ValueAsString,itemType=javax.m
anagement.openmbean.SimpleType(name=java.lang.String)),(itemName=ValueAsStringArray,itemType=javax.ma
nagement.openmbean.ArrayType(name=[Ljava.lang.String;,dimension=1,elementType=javax.management.openmb
ean.SimpleType(name=java.lang.String),primitiveArray=false)))),contents={OpenTypeName=java.lang.Integ
er, ValueAsString=3800, ValueAsStringArray=[Ljava.lang.String;@69fe571f}),

OldValue=javax.management.openmbean.CompositeDataSupport(compositeType=javax.management.openmbean.Com
positeType(name=javax.management.openmbean.CompositeType.ANY,items=((itemName=OpenTypeName,itemType=j
avax.management.openmbean.SimpleType(name=java.lang.String)),(itemName=ValueAsString,itemType=javax.m
anagement.openmbean.SimpleType(name=java.lang.String)),(itemName=ValueAsStringArray,itemType=javax.ma
nagement.openmbean.ArrayType(name=[Ljava.lang.String;,dimension=1,elementType=javax.management.openmb
ean.SimpleType(name=java.lang.String),primitiveArray=false)))),contents={OpenTypeName=java.lang.Integ
er, ValueAsString=3700, ValueAsStringArray=[Ljava.lang.String;@69fe571f}),

Operation=modify,

RestartRequired=false}

)
```

Datasources

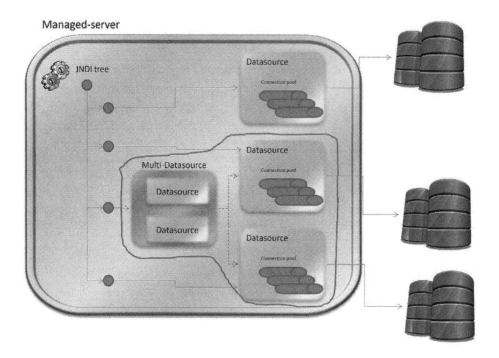

Figure 14.1: *Datasources*

Datasources are very important aspects of domains. All database access is done using datasources. Access to data in databases is configured in WebLogic via JDBC data sources. WebLogic distinguishes between physical datasources and multi-datasources, whereas the latter is basically a container for one or more physical datasources. These datasources are then targeted to a server or cluster and registered in the JNDI tree. Each physical datasource has a connection pool, which can be configured and monitored.

Database security is a very important topic for production systems, administrators, and auditors. Please see WLST section about datasources for a more detailed explanation.

The following Java method creates a datasource using JMX. This method is capable (depending on the parameters) of creating a datasource using the traditional user/password, and also a datasource that uses Oracle wallets.

💾 create_datasource_jmx

```java
/**
 * Create a datasource either using user/password or using wallets
 *
 * @param datasourcename String  Name of the new datasource
 * @param clustername String  Name of the target cluster
 * @param jndiName String  JNDI entry name
 * @param globalTransactionsProtocol String   transaction setting
 * @param drivername String   name of the driver
 * @param url String   database URL - NOTE: in case of wallets don't forget the "/"
 * @param username String  username - ONLY necessary if useWallet=false
 * @param password String  password - ONLY necessary if useWallet=false
 * @param useWallet boolean does this datasource use wallets true/false
 * @param walletlocation String  wallet directory - ONLY necessary if useWallet=true
 * @throws Exception
 */
public void createDataSource(String datasourcename,
                             String clustername,
                             String jndiName,
                             String globalTransactionsProtocol,
                             String drivername,
                             String url,
                             String username,
                             String password,
                             boolean useWallet,
                             String walletlocation) throws Exception
{
    // e.g.: com.bea:Name=TestDomain,Type=Domain
    ObjectName myDomainMBean = new ObjectName("com.bea:Name=" + domainName +",Type=Domain");

    // javax.management.ObjectName   createJDBCSystemResource(name:java.lang.String  )
    ObjectName mySystemResourceMBean = (ObjectName)myJMXWrapper.invoke(myDomainMBean,
                                                   "createJDBCSystemResource",
                                                   new Object[]{new
String(datasourcename)},
                                                   new String[]{String.class.getName()});


    ObjectName myJDBCResourceMBean =
(ObjectName)myJMXWrapper.getAttribute(mySystemResourceMBean,"JDBCResource");
    ObjectName myJDBCDataSourceParamsMBean =
(ObjectName)myJMXWrapper.getAttribute(myJDBCResourceMBean,"JDBCDataSourceParams");
    ObjectName myJDBCDriverParamsMBean =
(ObjectName)myJMXWrapper.getAttribute(myJDBCResourceMBean,"JDBCDriverParams");
    ObjectName myJDBCConnectionPoolParamsMBean =
(ObjectName)myJMXWrapper.getAttribute(myJDBCResourceMBean,"JDBCConnectionPoolParams");

    // set attribute ListenAddress
    myJMXWrapper.setAttribute(myJDBCResourceMBean,new Attribute("Name",datasourcename));

    // set JNDI names
    myJMXWrapper.setAttribute(myJDBCDataSourceParamsMBean,new Attribute("JNDINames",new
String[]{jndiName}));

    // set GlobalTransactionsProtocol
    myJMXWrapper.setAttribute(myJDBCDataSourceParamsMBean,new
Attribute("GlobalTransactionsProtocol",new String(globalTransactionsProtocol)));

    // set TestTableName
    myJMXWrapper.setAttribute(myJDBCConnectionPoolParamsMBean,new Attribute("TestTableName",new
String("SQL SELECT * FROM DUAL")));

    // set URL
    myJMXWrapper.setAttribute(myJDBCDriverParamsMBean,new Attribute("Url",new String(url)));

    // set DriverName
    myJMXWrapper.setAttribute(myJDBCDriverParamsMBean,
                    new Attribute("DriverName",new String(drivername)));

    if (! useWallet)
    {
        // set Password
        myJMXWrapper.setAttribute(myJDBCDriverParamsMBean,
                    new Attribute("Password", new String(password)));

        // user
        ObjectName myJDBCDriverParamsPropertiesMBean = (ObjectName)
                myJMXWrapper.getAttribute(myJDBCDriverParamsMBean, "Properties");
```

```
        ObjectName myUserPropertyMBean = null;
        try {
            myUserPropertyMBean = (ObjectName) myJMXWrapper.invoke(
                    myJDBCDriverParamsPropertiesMBean,
                    "lookupProperty",
                    new Object[] {new String("user")},
                    new String[] {String.class.getName()});
        } catch (Exception ex) {
            // ignore
        }
        if (myUserPropertyMBean == null)
            myUserPropertyMBean = (ObjectName) myJMXWrapper.invoke(
                    myJDBCDriverParamsPropertiesMBean,
                    "createProperty",
                    new Object[] {new String("user")},
                    new String[] {String.class.getName()});
        myJMXWrapper.setAttribute(myUserPropertyMBean, new Attribute("Value",
                    new String(username)));
    }
    else // WALLET !!
    {
        // user
        ObjectName myJDBCDriverParamsPropertiesMBean = (ObjectName)
                myJMXWrapper.getAttribute(myJDBCDriverParamsMBean, "Properties");
        ObjectName myWalletLocationPropertyMBean = null;
        try {
            myWalletLocationPropertyMBean = (ObjectName) myJMXWrapper.invoke(
                    myJDBCDriverParamsPropertiesMBean,
                    "lookupProperty",
                    new Object[] {new String("oracle.net.wallet_locatio")},
                    new String[] {String.class.getName()});
        } catch (Exception ex) {
            // ignore
        }
        if (myWalletLocationPropertyMBean == null)
            myWalletLocationPropertyMBean = (ObjectName) myJMXWrapper.invoke(
                    myJDBCDriverParamsPropertiesMBean,
                    "createProperty",
                    new Object[] {new String("oracle.net.wallet_locatio")},
                    new String[] {String.class.getName()});
        myJMXWrapper.setAttribute(myWalletLocationPropertyMBean, new Attribute("Value",
                    new String(walletlocation)));
    }

    // Note that in this example it is exactly one cluster, but this does not need to be.
    myJMXWrapper.setAttribute(mySystemResourceMBean,new Attribute("Targets",
                    new ObjectName[]{new ObjectName("com.bea:Name="+clustername+",Type=Cluster")} ));
}
```

Datasources in WebLogic use a variety of MBeans, which can make understanding the automation quite complex. The following list contains all the MBeans created for just ONE generic datasource using user/password:

🖫 datasource_MBeans

```
com.bea:Name=MySuperDataSource,Parent=[TestDomain]/JDBCSystemResources[MySuperDataSource],Path=JDBCRe
source[MySuperDataSource]/InternalProperties,Type=weblogic.j2ee.descriptor.wl.JDBCPropertiesBean
 Attribute: Properties   of Type : [Ljavax.management.ObjectName;
 Operation: javax.management.ObjectName  lookupProperty(java.lang.String:java.lang.String  )
 Operation: java.lang.Boolean  isSet(propertyName:java.lang.String )
 Operation: javax.management.ObjectName  createProperty(java.lang.String:java.lang.String  )
 Operation: java.lang.Void
destroyProperty(weblogic.j2ee.descriptor.wl.JDBCPropertyBean:javax.management.ObjectName  )
 Operation: java.lang.Void  unSet(propertyName:java.lang.String  )

com.bea:Name=MySuperDataSource,Type=JDBCSystemResource
 Attribute: Parent   of Type : javax.management.ObjectName
 Attribute: Resource   of Type : javax.management.ObjectName
 Attribute: Type   of Type : java.lang.String
 Attribute: CompatibilityName   of Type : java.lang.String
 Attribute: ModuleType   of Type : java.lang.String
 Attribute: SourcePath   of Type : java.lang.String
 Attribute: JDBCResource   of Type : javax.management.ObjectName
 Attribute: DescriptorFileName   of Type : java.lang.String
```

```
 Attribute: Notes   of Type : java.lang.String
 Attribute: Name   of Type : java.lang.String
 Attribute: SubDeployments   of Type : [Ljavax.management.ObjectName;
 Attribute: DeploymentPrincipalName   of Type : java.lang.String
 Attribute: Targets   of Type : [Ljavax.management.ObjectName;
 Attribute: DeploymentOrder   of Type : java.lang.Integer
 Operation: javax.management.ObjectName  createSubDeployment(name:java.lang.String  )
 Operation: java.lang.Void  destroySubDeployment(subDeployment:javax.management.ObjectName  )
 Operation: java.lang.Boolean  isSet(propertyName:java.lang.String  )
 Operation: javax.management.ObjectName  lookupSubDeployment(java.lang.String:java.lang.String  )
 Operation: java.lang.Void  restoreDefaultValue(attributeName:java.lang.String  )
 Operation: java.lang.Void  freezeCurrentValue(attributeName:java.lang.String  )
 Operation: java.lang.Void  addTarget(target:javax.management.ObjectName  )
 Operation: java.lang.Void  removeTarget(target:javax.management.ObjectName  )
 Operation: java.lang.Void  unSet(propertyName:java.lang.String  )


com.bea:Name=MySuperDataSource,Parent=[TestDomain]/JDBCSystemResources[MySuperDataSource],Path=JDBCRe
source[MySuperDataSource]/JDBCDriverParams/Properties,Type=weblogic.j2ee.descriptor.wl.JDBCProperties
Bean
 Attribute: Properties   of Type : [Ljavax.management.ObjectName;
 Operation: javax.management.ObjectName  lookupProperty(java.lang.String:java.lang.String  )
 Operation: java.lang.Boolean  isSet(propertyName:java.lang.String  )
 Operation: javax.management.ObjectName  createProperty(java.lang.String:java.lang.String  )
 Operation: java.lang.Void
destroyProperty(weblogic.j2ee.descriptor.wl.JDBCPropertyBean:javax.management.ObjectName  )
 Operation: java.lang.Void  unSet(propertyName:java.lang.String  )
 Operation: javax.management.ObjectName  createProperty(java.lang.String:java.lang.String
java.lang.String:java.lang.String  )

com.bea:Name=MySuperDataSource,Parent=[TestDomain]/JDBCSystemResources[MySuperDataSource],Path=JDBCRe
source[MySuperDataSource]/JDBCDataSourceParams,Type=weblogic.j2ee.descriptor.wl.JDBCDataSourceParamsB
ean
 Attribute: GlobalTransactionsProtocol   of Type : java.lang.String
 Attribute: RowPrefetch   of Type : java.lang.Boolean
 Attribute: RowPrefetchSize   of Type : java.lang.Integer
 Attribute: JNDINames   of Type : [Ljava.lang.String;
 Attribute: AlgorithmType   of Type : java.lang.String
 Attribute: ConnectionPoolFailoverCallbackHandler   of Type : java.lang.String
 Attribute: StreamChunkSize   of Type : java.lang.Integer
 Attribute: KeepConnAfterGlobalTx   of Type : java.lang.Boolean
 Attribute: KeepConnAfterLocalTx   of Type : java.lang.Boolean
 Attribute: FailoverRequestIfBusy   of Type : java.lang.Boolean
 Attribute: DataSourceList   of Type : java.lang.String
 Attribute: Scope   of Type : java.lang.String
 Operation: java.lang.Boolean  isSet(propertyName:java.lang.String  )
 Operation: java.lang.Void  addJNDIName(java.lang.String:java.lang.String  )
 Operation: java.lang.Void  removeJNDIName(java.lang.String:java.lang.String  )
 Operation: java.lang.Void  unSet(propertyName:java.lang.String  )

com.bea:Name=MySuperDataSource,Parent=[TestDomain]/JDBCSystemResources[MySuperDataSource],Path=JDBCRe
source[MySuperDataSource]/JDBCConnectionPoolParams,Type=weblogic.j2ee.descriptor.wl.JDBCConnectionPoo
lParamsBean
 Attribute: ProfileType   of Type : java.lang.Integer
 Attribute: ConnectionHarvestTriggerCount   of Type : java.lang.Integer
 Attribute: StatementCacheSize   of Type : java.lang.Integer
 Attribute: TestConnectionsOnReserve   of Type : java.lang.Boolean
 Attribute: RemoveInfectedConnections   of Type : java.lang.Boolean
 Attribute: WrapTypes   of Type : java.lang.Boolean
 Attribute: FatalErrorCodes   of Type : java.lang.String
 Attribute: InactiveConnectionTimeoutSeconds   of Type : java.lang.Integer
 Attribute: TestTableName   of Type : java.lang.String
 Attribute: LoginDelaySeconds   of Type : java.lang.Integer
 Attribute: PinnedToThread   of Type : java.lang.Boolean
 Attribute: ConnectionHarvestMaxCount   of Type : java.lang.Integer
 Attribute: IgnoreInUseConnectionsEnabled   of Type : java.lang.Boolean
 Attribute: SecondsToTrustAnIdlePoolConnection   of Type : java.lang.Integer
 Attribute: DriverInterceptor   of Type : java.lang.String
 Attribute: ConnectionReserveTimeoutSeconds   of Type : java.lang.Integer
 Attribute: JDBCXADebugLevel   of Type : java.lang.Integer
 Attribute: TestFrequencySeconds   of Type : java.lang.Integer
 Attribute: ShrinkFrequencySeconds   of Type : java.lang.Integer
 Attribute: StatementTimeout   of Type : java.lang.Integer
 Attribute: MaxCapacity   of Type : java.lang.Integer
 Attribute: MinCapacity   of Type : java.lang.Integer
 Attribute: CredentialMappingEnabled   of Type : java.lang.Boolean
 Attribute: ConnectionLabelingCallback   of Type : java.lang.String
 Attribute: HighestNumWaiters   of Type : java.lang.Integer
```

```
Attribute: IdentityBasedConnectionPoolingEnabled  of Type : java.lang.Boolean
Attribute: InitSql  of Type : java.lang.String
Attribute: InitialCapacity  of Type : java.lang.Integer
Attribute: StatementCacheType  of Type : java.lang.String
Attribute: ConnectionCreationRetryFrequencySeconds  of Type : java.lang.Integer
Attribute: CapacityIncrement  of Type : java.lang.Integer
Attribute: ProfileHarvestFrequencySeconds  of Type : java.lang.Integer
Operation: java.lang.Void  unSet(propertyName:java.lang.String  )
Operation: java.lang.Boolean  isSet(propertyName:java.lang.String  )

com.bea:Name=MySuperDataSource,Parent=[TestDomain]/JDBCSystemResources[MySuperDataSource],Path=JDBCRe
source,Type=weblogic.j2ee.descriptor.wl.JDBCDataSourceBean
 Attribute: JDBCDataSourceParams  of Type : javax.management.ObjectName
 Attribute: JDBCDriverParams  of Type : javax.management.ObjectName
 Attribute: InternalProperties  of Type : javax.management.ObjectName
 Attribute: Name  of Type : java.lang.String
 Attribute: JDBCXAParams  of Type : javax.management.ObjectName
 Attribute: JDBCConnectionPoolParams  of Type : javax.management.ObjectName
 Attribute: JDBCOracleParams  of Type : javax.management.ObjectName
 Attribute: Version  of Type : java.lang.String
 Operation: java.lang.Boolean  isSet(propertyName:java.lang.String  )
 Operation: java.lang.Void  unSet(propertyName:java.lang.String  )

com.bea:Name=MySuperDataSource,Parent=[TestDomain]/JDBCSystemResources[MySuperDataSource],Path=JDBCRe
source[MySuperDataSource]/JDBCDriverParams,Type=weblogic.j2ee.descriptor.wl.JDBCDriverParamsBean
 Attribute: PasswordEncrypted  of Type : [B
 Attribute: UsePasswordIndirection  of Type : java.lang.Boolean
 Attribute: Password  of Type : java.lang.String
 Attribute: DriverName  of Type : java.lang.String
 Attribute: Properties  of Type : javax.management.ObjectName
 Attribute: UseXaDataSourceInterface  of Type : java.lang.Boolean
 Attribute: Url  of Type : java.lang.String
 Operation: java.lang.Boolean  isSet(propertyName:java.lang.String  )
 Operation: java.lang.Void  unSet(propertyName:java.lang.String  )
com.bea:Name=AdminServer,Server=AdminServer,Type=WLDFServerDiagnostic

com.bea:Name=MySuperDataSource,Parent=[TestDomain]/JDBCSystemResources[MySuperDataSource],Path=JDBCRe
source[MySuperDataSource]/JDBCOracleParams,Type=weblogic.j2ee.descriptor.wl.JDBCOracleParamsBean
 Attribute: OnsWalletFile  of Type : java.lang.String
 Attribute: ConnectionInitializationCallback  of Type : java.lang.String
 Attribute: FanEnabled  of Type : java.lang.Boolean
 Attribute: OnsNodeList  of Type : java.lang.String
 Attribute: UseDatabaseCredentials  of Type : java.lang.Boolean
 Attribute: OracleProxySession  of Type : java.lang.Boolean
 Attribute: OracleEnableJavaNetFastPath  of Type : java.lang.Boolean
 Attribute: OnsWalletPasswordEncrypted  of Type : [B
 Attribute: OracleOptimizeUtf8Conversion  of Type : java.lang.Boolean
 Attribute: OnsWalletPassword  of Type : java.lang.String
 Attribute: AffinityPolicy  of Type : java.lang.String
 Operation: java.lang.Boolean  isSet(propertyName:java.lang.String  )
 Operation: java.lang.Void  unSet(propertyName:java.lang.String  )

com.bea:Name=user,Parent=[TestDomain]/JDBCSystemResources[MySuperDataSource],Path=JDBCResource[MySupe
rDataSource]/JDBCDriverParams/Properties/Properties[user],Type=weblogic.j2ee.descriptor.wl.JDBCProper
tyBean
 Attribute: Value  of Type : java.lang.String
 Attribute: SysPropValue  of Type : java.lang.String
 Attribute: Name  of Type : java.lang.String
 Operation: java.lang.Boolean  isSet(propertyName:java.lang.String  )
 Operation: java.lang.Void  unSet(propertyName:java.lang.String  )

com.bea:Name=MySuperDataSource,Parent=[TestDomain]/JDBCSystemResources[MySuperDataSource],Path=JDBCRe
source[MySuperDataSource]/JDBCXAParams,Type=weblogic.j2ee.descriptor.wl.JDBCXAParamsBean
 Attribute: RecoverOnlyOnce  of Type : java.lang.Boolean
 Attribute: KeepLogicalConnOpenOnRelease  of Type : java.lang.Boolean
 Attribute: ResourceHealthMonitoring  of Type : java.lang.Boolean
 Attribute: NewXaConnForCommit  of Type : java.lang.Boolean
 Attribute: XaRetryDurationSeconds  of Type : java.lang.Integer
 Attribute: XaEndOnlyOnce  of Type : java.lang.Boolean
 Attribute: RollbackLocalTxUponConnClose  of Type : java.lang.Boolean
 Attribute: KeepXaConnTillTxComplete  of Type : java.lang.Boolean
 Attribute: XaTransactionTimeout  of Type : java.lang.Integer
 Attribute: XaRetryIntervalSeconds  of Type : java.lang.Integer
 Attribute: XaSetTransactionTimeout  of Type : java.lang.Boolean
 Attribute: NeedTxCtxOnClose  of Type : java.lang.Boolean
 Operation: java.lang.Boolean  isSet(propertyName:java.lang.String  )
```

JMS Resources

WebLogic provides a complex JMS subsystem, which consists of many different MBeans (see WLST section for more details and MBean hierarchy information). The main MBean is the JMSServer, which is basically the container for all other JMS resources. Every WebLogic Server can host multiple JMS servers, which consist of JMS system module resources.

Create Local JMS Resources with JMX

The section will explain the creation of the most common components - the creation of JMS components hosted locally in the domain. The different methods will create the necessary JMS file store, JMS server, and JMS module instances. For the server, we can specify the persistent store to use and logging details. The last methods will also create subdeployments, queues, and topics.

First we need to create the file store for JMS. Without a file store, most of the create methods will fail as WebLogic cannot persist the changes into the file store.

🖫 create_filestore_jmx

```
    public ObjectName createFileStore(String fileStoreName, String wlsServerName) throws
WLSAutomationException
    {
        try
        {
            // get the domain config root
            ObjectName domainRoot = myJMXWrapper.getDomainConfigRoot();

            // create filesstore and configure it
            ObjectName newFileStore = (ObjectName)myJMXWrapper.invoke(
                    domainRoot,"createFileStore",
                    new Object[]{fileStoreName},new String[]{String.class.getName()});
            myJMXWrapper.setAttribute(newFileStore,
                                new Attribute("Directory",
                                                "/weblogic_domains/MartinTest_Domain"));

            // define targets
            myJMXWrapper.setAttribute(newFileStore, new Attribute("Targets",
                                new ObjectName[]{new ObjectName("com.bea:Name="+wlsServerName+",
                                    Type=Server")}));

            return newFileStore;
        }
        catch(Exception ex)
        {
            System.out.println("Error while createFileStore ("+fileStoreName+"): "+ ex.getMessage());
            throw new WLSAutomationException(ex.getMessage());
        }
    }
```

After the file store is created we can create the JMS server instance. We also need to target the server instance and assign a file store to this server instance:

⊟ JMS_server_instance_jmx

```
public void createAnewJMSServer(String jmsServerName, String fileStoreName, String wlsServerName)
                        throws WLSAutomationException
{
    try {
        // 1st create the filestore:
        ObjectName newFileStore = createFileStore(fileStoreName, wlsServerName);

        // get the domain config root
        ObjectName domainRoot = myJMXWrapper.getDomainConfigRoot();

        // now create the server
        ObjectName newJMSServer = (ObjectName)myJMXWrapper.invoke(domainRoot,"createJMSServer",
                        new Object[]{jmsServerName},new String[]{String.class.getName()});

        // set the persistent store
        myJMXWrapper.setAttribute(newJMSServer, new Attribute("PersistentStore", newFileStore));
        myJMXWrapper.setAttribute(newJMSServer,
                new Attribute("Targets", new ObjectName[]{
                        new ObjectName("com.bea:Name="+wlsServerName+",Type=Server")}));

        // now we can define threshold values
        myJMXWrapper.setAttribute(newJMSServer, new Attribute("BytesThresholdHigh", new Long(-1)));
        myJMXWrapper.setAttribute(newJMSServer, new Attribute("BytesThresholdLow", new Long(-1)));
        myJMXWrapper.setAttribute(newJMSServer, new Attribute("MessagesThresholdHigh",
                                                new Long(-1)));
        myJMXWrapper.setAttribute(newJMSServer, new Attribute("MessagesThresholdLow",
                                                new Long(-1)));

        // now we can define quotas values
        myJMXWrapper.setAttribute(newJMSServer, new Attribute("BytesMaximum", new Long(-1)));
        myJMXWrapper.setAttribute(newJMSServer, new Attribute("MessagesMaximum", new Long(-1)));
        myJMXWrapper.setAttribute(newJMSServer, new Attribute("BlockingSendPolicy", "FIFO"));
        myJMXWrapper.setAttribute(newJMSServer, new Attribute("MaximumMessageSize",
                        new Integer(10000000)));

        // now configure the log file
        // similiar to com.bea:Name=MyTestServer_1,Type=JMSMessageLogFile,JMSServer=MyTestServer_1
        ObjectName newJMSServerLogFile = (ObjectName)myJMXWrapper.getAttribute(newJMSServer,
                "JMSMessageLogFile");

        myJMXWrapper.setAttribute(newJMSServerLogFile, new Attribute("RotationType",
                new String("byTime")));
        myJMXWrapper.setAttribute(newJMSServerLogFile, new Attribute("RotateLogOnStartup",
                new Boolean(false)));
        myJMXWrapper.setAttribute(newJMSServerLogFile, new Attribute("RotationTime",
                new String("00:00")));
        myJMXWrapper.setAttribute(newJMSServerLogFile, new Attribute("FileTimeSpan",
                new Integer(24)));
        myJMXWrapper.setAttribute(newJMSServerLogFile, new Attribute("FileCount", new Integer(25)));
        myJMXWrapper.setAttribute(newJMSServerLogFile, new Attribute("NumberOfFilesLimited",
                new Boolean(true)));
        myJMXWrapper.setAttribute(newJMSServerLogFile, new Attribute("FileName",
                new String(jmsServerName+".log")));
    }
    catch(Exception ex)
    {
        System.out.println("Error while createAnewJMSServer ("+jmsServerName+"): "+
                ex.getMessage());
        throw new WLSAutomationException(ex.getMessage());
    }
}
```

Next, we can create the JMS modules:

💾 create_JMS_modules_jmx

```
public void createJMSModule(String jmsModuleName, String targetType, String targetName)  throws
WLSAutomationException
    {
     try
     {
         // get the domain config root
         ObjectName domainRoot = myJMXWrapper.getDomainConfigRoot();

         // now create the server
         ObjectName newJMSModule = (ObjectName)myJMXWrapper.invoke(domainRoot,
                             "createJMSSystemResource",
                             new Object[]{jmsModuleName},
                             new String[]{String.class.getName()});

         // set the target
         myJMXWrapper.setAttribute(newJMSModule, new Attribute("Targets",
                             new ObjectName[]{new ObjectName("com.bea:Name="+targetName+",
                                                 Type="+targetType)}));
     }
     catch(Exception ex)
     {
         System.out.println("Error while createJMSModule ("+jmsModuleName+"): "+ ex.getMessage());
         throw new WLSAutomationException(ex.getMessage());
     }
    }
```

We can create different resources for the JMS module. One of the necessary resources is a connection factory. Other resources, such as Quotas, can also be defined. The next method shows how to create a connection factory for a JMS module using JMX:

💾 create_connection_factory_jmx

```
public void createJmsConnectionFactory(String jmsModuleName, String connectionFactoryName,
                             String jmsJNDIname) throws WLSAutomationException
{
  try {
     // get the jmsModuleName config root
     ObjectName myJMSModule = new ObjectName("com.bea:Name="+jmsModuleName+",
                                 Type=JMSSystemResource");

     // get the resource
     ObjectName myJMSModuleResource = (ObjectName)myJMXWrapper.getAttribute(myJMSModule,
                                 "JMSResource");

     // create the connection factory
     ObjectName myJMSModuleConnfactory =
                     (ObjectName)(ObjectName)myJMXWrapper.invoke(myJMSModuleResource,
                     "createConnectionFactory",
                     new Object[]{connectionFactoryName},
                     new String[]{String.class.getName()});

     // configure connection factory
     myJMXWrapper.setAttribute(myJMSModuleConnfactory, new Attribute("JNDIName",
                         new String(jmsJNDIname)));
     myJMXWrapper.setAttribute(myJMSModuleConnfactory, new Attribute("DefaultTargetingEnabled",
                         new Boolean(true)));

     // get the security params
     ObjectName mySecParams = (ObjectName)myJMXWrapper.getAttribute(myJMSModuleConnfactory,
                         "SecurityParams");
     // set AttachJMSXUserId
     myJMXWrapper.setAttribute(mySecParams, new Attribute("AttachJMSXUserId", new Boolean(false)));

     // get the default delivery params
     ObjectName myDelivParams = (ObjectName)myJMXWrapper.getAttribute(myJMSModuleConnfactory,
                             "DefaultDeliveryParams");
     // set AttachJMSXUserId
     myJMXWrapper.setAttribute(myDelivParams, new Attribute("DefaultDeliveryMode",
                 new String("Persistent")));
     myJMXWrapper.setAttribute(myDelivParams, new Attribute("DefaultTimeToLive", new Integer(0)));
     myJMXWrapper.setAttribute(myDelivParams, new Attribute("DefaultPriority", new Integer(2)));
  }
```

```
   catch(Exception ex) {
     System.out.println("Error while createJmsConnectionFactory ("+jmsModuleName+":"+
                        connectionFactoryName+"): " + ex.getMessage());
     throw new WLSAutomationException(ex.getMessage());
   }
}
```

If you need to use XA transactions, then you need to create an XA enabled connection factory. This is a normal factory but with special transaction parameters:

💾 XA_enabled_connection_factory_jmx

```
public void createJms_XA_ConnectionFactory(String jmsModuleName, String connectionFactoryName,
                                           String jmsJNDIname)
                                 throws WLSAutomationException
  {
    try {
        // get the jmsModuleName config root
        ObjectName myJMSModule = new ObjectName("com.bea:Name="+jmsModuleName+",
                                       Type=JMSSystemResource");

        // get the resource
        ObjectName myJMSModuleResource = (ObjectName)myJMXWrapper.getAttribute(myJMSModule,
               "JMSResource");

        // create the connection factory
        ObjectName myJMSModuleConnfactory=
                     (ObjectName)(ObjectName)myJMXWrapper.invoke(myJMSModuleResource,
                     "createConnectionFactory",
                     new Object[]{connectionFactoryName},
                     new String[]{String.class.getName()});

        // configure connection factory
        myJMXWrapper.setAttribute(myJMSModuleConnfactory, new Attribute("JNDIName",
                  new String(jmsJNDIname)));
        myJMXWrapper.setAttribute(myJMSModuleConnfactory, new Attribute("DefaultTargetingEnabled",
                  new Boolean(true)));

        // get the security params
        ObjectName mySecParams = (ObjectName)myJMXWrapper.getAttribute(myJMSModuleConnfactory,
                     "SecurityParams");
        // set AttachJMSXUserId
        myJMXWrapper.setAttribute(mySecParams, new Attribute("AttachJMSXUserId",
                           new Boolean(false)));

        // get the transaction params
        ObjectName myTxParams = (ObjectName)myJMXWrapper.getAttribute(myJMSModuleConnfactory,
                     "TransactionParams");
        // configure it
        myJMXWrapper.setAttribute(myTxParams, new Attribute("TransactionTimeout",
                     new Integer(3600)));
        myJMXWrapper.setAttribute(myTxParams, new Attribute("XAConnectionFactoryEnabled",
                     new Boolean(true)));
    }
    catch(Exception ex)
    {
       System.out.println("Error while createJms_XA_ConnectionFactory ("+jmsModuleName+":"+
                  connectionFactoryName+"): "+ ex.getMessage());
       throw new WLSAutomationException(ex.getMessage());
    }
  }
```

Another resource we need to create for a JMS module is a so-called subdeployment. This will also be created for a specific JMSModule:

🖫 subdeployment_jmx

```
public void createJMSSubDeployment(String jmsModuleName, String subDeploymentName, String targetName)
throws WLSAutomationException
    {
        try
        {
            // get the jmsModuleName config root
            ObjectName myJMSModule = new ObjectName("com.bea:Name="+jmsModuleName+",
                                    Type=JMSSystemResource");

            // get the resource
            //ObjectName myJMSModuleResource = (ObjectName)myJMXWrapper.getAttribute(myJMSModule,
                                    "JMSResource");

            // create subdeployment
            ObjectName myJMSModuleSubDeploy =
                            (ObjectName)myJMXWrapper.invoke(myJMSModule,"createSubDeployment",
                                        new Object[]{subDeploymentName},
                                        new String[]{String.class.getName()});

            // target the new subdeployment
            // set the target
            myJMXWrapper.setAttribute(myJMSModuleSubDeploy, new Attribute("Targets",
                    new ObjectName[]{new ObjectName("com.bea:Name="+targetName+",Type=JMSServer")}));
        }
        catch(Exception ex)
        {
            System.out.println("Error while createJMSSubDeployment ("+jmsModuleName+":"+
                    subDeploymentName+"}: " + ex.getMessage());
            throw new WLSAutomationException(ex.getMessage());
        }
    }
```

After the required infrastructure for JMS has been set up, we can finally create the JMS destinations. As we learned in the WLST part, JMS defines two different flavors of destinations: queues and topics.

The next method will show how to implement a queue with JMX. Remember that a queue means that the message is delivered to exactly one subscriber. Whoever reads the message first gets it.

🖫 queue_jmx

```
// Creating queue
public void createQueue(String jmsModuleName, String queueName, String jndiQueueName,
                    String subDeploymentName) throws WLSAutomationException
    {
        try
        {
            // get the jmsModuleName config root
            ObjectName myJMSModule = new ObjectName("com.bea:Name="+jmsModuleName+",
                    Type=JMSSystemResource");

            // get the resource
            ObjectName myJMSModuleResource = (ObjectName)myJMXWrapper.getAttribute(myJMSModule,
                    "JMSResource");

            // create queue
            ObjectName myJMSQueue = (ObjectName)(ObjectName)myJMXWrapper.invoke(myJMSModuleResource,
                    "createQueue",new Object[]{queueName},new String[]{String.class.getName()});

            // configue queue
            myJMXWrapper.setAttribute(myJMSQueue, new Attribute("JNDIName",
                    new String(jndiQueueName)));
            myJMXWrapper.setAttribute(myJMSQueue, new Attribute("SubDeploymentName",
                    new String(subDeploymentName)));
        }
        catch(Exception ex)
        {
```

```
        System.out.println("Error while createQueue ("+jmsModuleName+":"+queueName+"): "+
                        ex.getMessage());
        throw new WLSAutomationException(ex.getMessage());
    }
}
```

JMS means messaging. It is always possible that errors and problems occur during message delivery or message processing. In order to avoid a permanent problem, it is possible to define a so-called error queue, which is a dedicated queue in which the JMS system can move problematic messages. Of course for administrators, this means that this queue must be monitored in order to get notified of error-prone messages.

Creating a queue with error handling:

💾 queue_error_handling_jmx

```
public void createQueueWithErrorHandling(String jmsModuleName, String queueName, String
jndiQueueName, String subDeploymentName, String errorQueueName) throws WLSAutomationException
    {
        try
        {
            // get the jmsModuleName config root
            ObjectName myJMSModule = new ObjectName("com.bea:Name="+jmsModuleName+",
                    Type=JMSSystemResource");

            // get the resource
            ObjectName myJMSModuleResource =
(ObjectName)myJMXWrapper.getAttribute(myJMSModule,"JMSResource");

            // create queue
            ObjectName myJMSQueue = (ObjectName)myJMXWrapper.invoke(myJMSModuleResource,"createQueue",
                            new Object[]{queueName},new String[]{String.class.getName()});

            // configure queue
            myJMXWrapper.setAttribute(myJMSQueue, new Attribute("JNDIName", new
String(jndiQueueName)));
            myJMXWrapper.setAttribute(myJMSQueue, new Attribute("SubDeploymentName", new
String(subDeploymentName)));


            // get the default delivery params
            ObjectName myFailureParams =
(ObjectName)myJMXWrapper.getAttribute(myJMSQueue,"DeliveryFailureParams");
            // set AttachJMSXUserId
            myJMXWrapper.setAttribute(myFailureParams, new Attribute("RedeliveryLimit", new
Integer(3)));
            myJMXWrapper.setAttribute(myFailureParams, new Attribute("ExpirationPolicy", new
String("Redirect")));

            // lookup error queue on SAME module (can be done more generic if error queue is located on
a different module)
            ObjectName errorQueue = (ObjectName)myJMXWrapper.invoke(myJMSModuleResource,"lookupQueue",
                            new Object[]{errorQueueName},new String[]{String.class.getName()});
            // set error queue
            myJMXWrapper.setAttribute(myQueueDeliveryFailureParams, new
Attribute("ErrorDestination",errorQueue));
        }
        catch(Exception ex)
        {
            System.out.println("Error while createQueueWithErrorHandling
("+jmsModuleName+":"+queueName+"): "+ ex.getMessage());
            throw new WLSAutomationException(ex.getMessage());
        }
    }
```

And last but not least, we can also use JMX to create a topic. Remember that a topic means that all subscribers get every message.

Creating a topic:

💾 create_topic_jmx

```
public void createTopic(String jmsModuleName, String topicName, String jndiTopicName, String
subDeploymentName)
                        throws WLSAutomationException
   {
      try {
        // get the jmsModuleName config root
        ObjectName myJMSModule = new
ObjectName("com.bea:Name="+jmsModuleName+",Type=JMSSystemResource");

        // get the resource
        ObjectName myJMSModuleResource =
(ObjectName)myJMXWrapper.getAttribute(myJMSModule,"JMSResource");

         // create topic
         ObjectName myJMSTopic = (ObjectName)myJMXWrapper.invoke(myJMSModuleResource,"createTopic",
                        new Object[]{topicName},new String[]{String.class.getName()});

        // configure topic
        myJMXWrapper.setAttribute(myJMSTopic, new Attribute("JNDIName", new
String(jndiTopicName)));
        myJMXWrapper.setAttribute(myJMSTopic, new Attribute("SubDeploymentName", new
String(subDeploymentName)));
      }
      catch(Exception ex)
      {
        System.out.println("Error while createTopic ("+jmsModuleName+":"+topicName+"): "+
ex.getMessage());
        throw new WLSAutomationException(ex.getMessage());
      }
   }
```

NOTE: It is of course also possible to create Bridge components, distributed destinations, SaF components, durable subscribers, and any other component with JMX. The implementation of these create methods is similar to the code examples shown above. The code depot of the book has the complete methods. Please refer to these sources.

JNDI Resources

Foreign JNDI providers in WebLogic enable the administrator to connect different JNDI trees together (see WLST section for more details).

In the following example, you will see that we will first define the remote provider with host/port/credentials and then define mount points, which are called links in WebLogic. The example uses only one link, but you can define as many as you want:

💾 JNDI_provider_jmx

```
public void createForeignJNDIProvider(String providerName, ObjectName[] targets, java.util.Properties
properties)
         throws WLSAutomationException {
   try {
       // e.g.: com.bea:Name=TestDomain,Type=Domain
       ObjectName myDomainMBean = myJMXWrapper.getDomainConfigRoot();

       ObjectName myProviderMBean = (ObjectName)myJMXWrapper.invoke(myDomainMBean,
               "lookupForeignJNDIProvider",
               new Object[]{new String(providerName)},
```

```
                   new String[]{String.class.getName()});
       if (myProviderMBean==null)  {
           // create
           // Operation: javax.management.ObjectName  createForeignJNDIProvider(name:java.lang.String
)
           myProviderMBean = (ObjectName)myJMXWrapper.invoke(myDomainMBean,
                        "createForeignJNDIProvider",
                        new Object[]{new String(providerName)},
                        new String[]{String.class.getName()});

           //target to cluster
           myJMXWrapper.setAttribute(myProviderMBean, new Attribute("Targets",targets));

           // configure
           if (properties.containsKey("INITIALCONTEXTFACTORY"))
                myJMXWrapper.setAttribute(myProviderMBean,
                             new
Attribute("InitialContextFactory",properties.get("INITIALCONTEXTFACTORY")));

           if (properties.containsKey("PROVIDERURL"))
                myJMXWrapper.setAttribute(myProviderMBean, new
Attribute("ProviderURL",properties.get("PROVIDERURL")));

           if (properties.containsKey("USER"))
                myJMXWrapper.setAttribute(myProviderMBean, new
Attribute("User",properties.get("USER")));

           if (properties.containsKey("PASSWORD"))
                myJMXWrapper.setAttribute(myProviderMBean, new
Attribute("Password",properties.get("PASSWORD")));

           // create and configure JNDI link
           // Operation: javax.management.ObjectName  createForeignJNDILink(name:java.lang.String  )
           ObjectName myForeignLinkMBean = (ObjectName)myJMXWrapper.invoke(myDomainMBean,
                        "createForeignJNDILink",
                        new Object[]{new String(providerName+"_Link")},
                        new String[]{String.class.getName()});

           if (properties.containsKey("LOCALJNDINAME"))
                myJMXWrapper.setAttribute(myForeignLinkMBean,
                             new Attribute("LocalJNDIName",properties.get("LOCALJNDINAME")));

           if (properties.containsKey("REMOTEJNDINAME"))
                myJMXWrapper.setAttribute(myForeignLinkMBean,
                             new Attribute("RemoteJNDIName",properties.get("REMOTEJNDINAME")));
       }
       else
           throw new WLSAutomationException("Foreign JNDI provider "+providerName+" already exist  -
cannot create !");
       }
   catch(Exception ex)
   {
       throw new WLSAutomationException(ex);
   }
}
```

Java Mail Sessions

As requested by the J2EE specification, WebLogic also includes the ability to send emails. WebLogic includes an implementation of the JavaMail API. It is neither a recommended nor good programming style to create mail sessions in your own code. Therefore, WebLogic offers special MBeans that can be used to configure access to mail servers and which provide mail sessions to be used in your own code.

Example program to setup a mail session object in WLS and register it in the JNDI tree:

```
public void createMailSession(String mailSessionName, String jndiName,
         ObjectName[] targets,Properties properties)  throws WLSAutomationExceptio {
   try  {
      // e.g.: com.bea:Name=TestDomain,Type=Domain
      ObjectName myDomainMBean = myJMXWrapper.getDomainConfigRoot();

      // Operation: javax.management.ObjectName  lookupMailSession(name:java.lang.String  )
      ObjectName myMailSessionMBean = (ObjectName)myJMXWrapper.invoke(myDomainMBean,
                   "lookupMailSession",
                   new Object[]{new String(mailSessionName)},
                   new String[]{String.class.getName()});
      if (myMailSessionMBean==null)
      {
      // create
      // Operation: javax.management.ObjectName  createMailSession(name:java.lang.String  )
      myMailSessionMBean = (ObjectName)myJMXWrapper.invoke(myDomainMBean,
                   "createMailSession",
                   new Object[]{new String(mailSessionName)},
                   new String[]{String.class.getName()});

      //target to targets
      // e.g. set('Targets',jarray.array([ObjectName('com.bea:Name=MartinTest_Cluster,Type=Cluster')],
ObjectName))
      myJMXWrapper.setAttribute(myMailSessionMBean, new Attribute("Targets",targets));

      // configure
      myJMXWrapper.setAttribute(myMailSessionMBean, new Attribute("JNDIName",jndiName));
      myJMXWrapper.setAttribute(myMailSessionMBean, new Attribute("Properties",properties));
      }
      else
      throw new WLSAutomationException("Mail session with name "+mailSessionName+" already exist  -
cannot create !");
   }
   catch(Exception ex) {
       throw new WLSAutomationException(ex);
   }
}
```

WorkManager Configuration

In the core of an application server like WebLogic, everything is a work task. Work must be scheduled and in some cases even prioritized. WebLogic used a rather sophisticated concept called WorkManager. WorkManagers control threads, and it is possible to configure WorkManagers with additional information like maximum/minimum thread pool sizes and other settings to work with multiple applications at the same time. You can, for example, create scheduling policies for application "A" and another set of policies for application "B". During operation, WebLogic can use these policies to assign pending work and enqueued requests to execution threads. This means that WorkManagers enable you to guarantee that each application will get their chunk of the available resources (threads/connections), or you can limit the amount of resources like threads.

Each WorkManager can contain following types of components:

▪ Constraints

    o   Minimum threads constraint

    o   Maximum threads constraint

- o Capacity
- Request class
  - o Fair-share
  - o Response-time
  - o Context based
- ShutdownTrigger

The minimum threads constraint makes sure that even with a high workload, there will still be a defined number of threads available to be used for executing tasks. The following method shows how to define a minimum thread constraint in WebLogic:

💾 minimum_thread_constraint_jmx

```
public ObjectName createMinThreadsConstraint(String newName, int count, ObjectName[] targets)
                    throws WLSAutomationException {
   try
   {   // lookup selftuning
       ObjectName mySelfTuning = lookupSelfTuning();

       // check if already created
        ObjectName myMinThreadsConstraint =   (ObjectName)myJMXWrapper.invoke(mySelfTuning,
                    "lookupMinThreadsConstraint",
                    new Object[]{new String(newName)}, new String[]{String.class.getName()});
       if (myMinThreadsConstraint==null){
           // create
           myMinThreadsConstraint = (ObjectName)myJMXWrapper.invoke(mySelfTuning,
                    "createMinThreadsConstraint",
                    new Object[]{new String(newName)}, new String[]{String.class.getName()});
           // configure
           myJMXWrapper.setAttribute(myMinThreadsConstraint,
                                new Attribute("Count",new Integer(count)));
           if (targets != null)
               myJMXWrapper.setAttribute(myMinThreadsConstraint, new Attribute("Targets",targets));

       }
       else
          throw new WLSAutomationException("MinThreadsConstraint with name "+newName+
                                        " already exist  -  cannot create !");

       return myMinThreadsConstraint;
   }
   catch(Exception ex) {
       throw new WLSAutomationException(ex);
   }
}
```

The maximum threads places an upper limit on the amount of threads in the self-tuning thread pool. This limit applies to all WorkManagers that have a link to the same constraint. This constraint has nothing to do with work priorities. The following method shows how to define a maximum thread constraint in WebLogic:

💾 maximum_thread_constraint_jmx

```
public ObjectName createMaxThreadsConstraint(String newName, int count, ObjectName[] targets)
                    throws WLSAutomationException {
   try
   {   // lookup selftuning
       ObjectName mySelfTuning = lookupSelfTuning();
```

```
    // check if already created
      ObjectName myMaxThreadsConstraint =  (ObjectName)myJMXWrapper.invoke(mySelfTuning,
                "lookupMaxThreadsConstraint",
                new Object[]{new String(newName)}, new String[]{String.class.getName()});
    if (myMaxThreadsConstraint==null){
        // create
        myMaxThreadsConstraint = (ObjectName)myJMXWrapper.invoke(mySelfTuning,
                "createMaxThreadsConstraint",
                new Object[]{new String(newName)}, new String[]{String.class.getName()});
        // configure
        myJMXWrapper.setAttribute(myMaxThreadsConstraint,
                                new Attribute("Count",new Integer(count)));

        if (targets != null)
            myJMXWrapper.setAttribute(myMaxThreadsConstraint, new Attribute("Targets",targets));

    }
    else
        throw new WLSAutomationException("MaxThreadsConstraint with name "+newName+
                                " already exist  -  cannot create !");

    return myMaxThreadsConstraint;
}
catch(Exception ex) {
    throw new WLSAutomationException(ex);
}
}
```

The capacity constraint defines the maximum number of requests that can be queued or are executing. The following method shows how to define a capacity constraint in WebLogic:

🖫 capacity_constraint_jmx

```
public ObjectName createCapacity(String newName, int count, ObjectName[] targets)
                throws WLSAutomationException {
  try
  {  // lookup selftuning
    ObjectName mySelfTuning = lookupSelfTuning();

    // check if already created
      ObjectName myCapacity =  (ObjectName)myJMXWrapper.invoke(mySelfTuning,
                "lookupCapacity",
                new Object[]{new String(newName)}, new String[]{String.class.getName()});
    if (myCapacity==null){
        // create
        myCapacity = (ObjectName)myJMXWrapper.invoke(mySelfTuning,
                "createCapacity",
                new Object[]{new String(newName)}, new String[]{String.class.getName()});
        // configure
        myJMXWrapper.setAttribute(myCapacity,
                                new Attribute("Count",new Integer(count)));

        if (targets != null)
            myJMXWrapper.setAttribute(myCapacity, new Attribute("Targets",targets));

    }
    else
        throw new WLSAutomationException("Capacity with name "+newName+
                                " already exist  -  cannot create !");

    return myCapacity;
}
catch(Exception ex) {
    throw new WLSAutomationException(ex);
}
}
```

Request class affects how requests are prioritized. A request class defines a scheduling guideline that WebLogic uses to assign threads to requests. WebLogic offers three different flavors:

---

1. Fair-share

This specifies the average thread-use time required to process requests. It is possible, for example, to define a share of 70 for application 1 and 30 for application 2. These are relative values and not shares in %.

🖫 fair_share_jmx

```
public ObjectName createFairShareRequestClass(String newName, int count, ObjectName[] targets)
               throws WLSAutomationException {
  try
  {   // lookup selftuning
      ObjectName mySelfTuning = lookupSelfTuning();

      // check if already created
        ObjectName myFairShareRequestClass =  (ObjectName)myJMXWrapper.invoke(mySelfTuning,
                "lookupFairShareRequestClass",
                new Object[]{new String(newName)}, new String[]{String.class.getName()});
      if (myFairShareRequestClass==null){
        // create
        myFairShareRequestClass = (ObjectName)myJMXWrapper.invoke(mySelfTuning,
                "createFairShareRequestClass",
                new Object[]{new String(newName)}, new String[]{String.class.getName()});
        // configure
        myJMXWrapper.setAttribute(myFairShareRequestClass,
                                    new Attribute("Count",new Integer(count)));
        if (targets != null)
              myJMXWrapper.setAttribute(myFairShareRequestClass, new Attribute("Targets",targets));

      }
      else
         throw new WLSAutomationException("FairShareRequestClass with name "+newName+
                                          " already exist  -  cannot create !");

      return myFairShareRequestClass;
  }
  catch(Exception ex) {
      throw new WLSAutomationException(ex);
  }
}
```

2. Response-time

This specifies a response time goal in milliseconds. This is not applied to individual requests, but instead applied to the average needed by requests of this WorkManager.

🖫 response_time_jmx

```
public ObjectName createResponseTimeRequestClass(String newName, int count, ObjectName[] targets)
               throws WLSAutomationException {
  try
  {   // lookup selftuning
      ObjectName mySelfTuning = lookupSelfTuning();

      // check if already created
        ObjectName myResponseTimeRequestClass =  (ObjectName)myJMXWrapper.invoke(mySelfTuning,
                "lookupResponseTimeRequestClass",
                new Object[]{new String(newName)}, new String[]{String.class.getName()});
      if (myResponseTimeRequestClass==null){
        // create
        myResponseTimeRequestClass = (ObjectName)myJMXWrapper.invoke(mySelfTuning,
                "createResponseTimeRequestClass",
                new Object[]{new String(newName)}, new String[]{String.class.getName()});
        // configure
        myJMXWrapper.setAttribute(myResponseTimeRequestClass,
                                    new Attribute("Count",new Integer(count)));
        if (targets != null)
```

```
            myJMXWrapper.setAttribute(myResponseTimeRequestClass, new
Attribute("Targets",targets));
        }
        else
            throw new WLSAutomationException("ResponseTimeRequestClass with name "+newName+
                                    " already exist  -  cannot create !");

        return myResponseTimeRequestClass;
    }
  catch(Exception ex) {
        throw new WLSAutomationException(ex);
    }
}
```

3. Context-based

Different request classes can be designed but based on user and/or group information. This means that special user groups can get a higher priority than others. Despite the context request class, it is necessary to create the context mapping sub-MBeans. The following method will create the context request class and – based on the information provided in the list – the context sub-MBeans.

🖫 context_jmx

```
public ObjectName createContextRequestClass(String newName,
                ArrayList<ContextCaseData> myContextList, ObjectName[] targets)
                throws WLSAutomationException {
 try
 { // lookup selftuning
    ObjectName mySelfTuning = lookupSelfTuning();

    // Operation: javax.management.ObjectName  lookupMinThreadsConstraint(name:java.lang.String  )
    ObjectName myContextRequestClass = (ObjectName)myJMXWrapper.invoke(mySelfTuning,
            "lookupContextRequestClass",
            new Object[]{new String(newName)}, new String[]{String.class.getName()});
    if (myContextRequestClass==null) {
    // create
    myContextRequestClass = (ObjectName)myJMXWrapper.invoke(mySelfTuning,
                "createContextRequestClass",
                new Object[]{new String(newName)}, new String[]{String.class.getName()});



    // create all the context sub-MBeans
    for (int i=0;i<myContextList.size();i++) {
        ContextCaseData myData = myContextList.get(i);

        ObjectName newContext = (ObjectName)myJMXWrapper.invoke(myContextRequestClass,
                    "createContextCase",
                    new Object[]{new String("Context_"+i)},
                    new String[]{String.class.getName()});

        myJMXWrapper.setAttribute(newContext, new Attribute("UserName", myData.getUserName()));
        myJMXWrapper.setAttribute(newContext, new Attribute("GroupName", myData.getGroupName()));
        myJMXWrapper.setAttribute(newContext,
                        new Attribute("RequestClassName", myData.getRequestClassName()));
        if (targets != null)
            myJMXWrapper.setAttribute(newContext, new Attribute("Targets",targets));
    }
    if (targets != null)
        myJMXWrapper.setAttribute(myContextRequestClass, new Attribute("Targets",targets));
    }
    else
        throw new WLSAutomationException("ContextRequestClass with name "+newName+" already exist !");

    return myContextRequestClass;
 }
 catch(Exception ex) {
        throw new WLSAutomationException(ex);
```

```
    }
}
```

This method is using an array of context information. The array has the following structure:

```
public class ContextCaseData {
    private String RequestClassName;
    private String GroupName;
    private String UserName;

    public ContextCaseData(String myRequestClassName, String myGroupName, String myUserName) {
            RequestClassName = myRequestClassName;
            GroupName = myGroupName;
            UserName = myUserName;
    }

    public String getRequestClassName() {
            return RequestClassName;
    }

    public String getGroupName() {
            return GroupName;
    }

    public String getUserName() {
            return UserName;
    }
}
```

Cleanup / Delete Resources

In most WebLogic administration books and on various websites, the focus for administration and therefore also for automation is always on domain creation/extension/administration and monitoring. The whole topic around resource cleanup and deletion is often left out or forgotten. In fact, the other topics are more common and more popular, but cleanup should not be forgotten.

Many tasks involve cleanup. The following list contains just some examples:

- Physical servers go out of maintenance and will be replaced with new servers. If domains include multiple servers, then you might not want to (or are not allowed to!) delete the whole domain only because a server is exchanged. In this case you should cleanup your domain.

- Applications are no longer needed. In many companies, development and sometimes testing domains are small domains with one application only; however, in production, large domains with many clusters and many applications are often used in order to avoid a complicated setup of Administration Servers and "console hopping" for the administrators. Therefore, retiring an application may result in removing the application and all its resources (datasources, JMS servers, mail, etc.) from the larger administration domains.

- Managed-Servers must be moved to other machines due to resource problems. This also might result in a necessary cleanup

Cleanup and resource deletion must be done in an active edit session, hence on the edit MBeanServer. After connecting to the EDIT MBeanServer, the domain object provides a large number of methods for resource deletion:

💾 resource_deletion

```
destroyRemoteSAFContext(remoteSAFContext:javax.management.ObjectName )
destroyWTCServer(wtcServer:javax.management.ObjectName )
destroyApplication(application:javax.management.ObjectName )
destroyXMLEntityCache(XMLEntityCache:javax.management.ObjectName )
destroySNMPAgentDeployment(mbean:javax.management.ObjectName )
destroyVirtualHost(host:javax.management.ObjectName )
destroyRealm(weblogic.management.configuration.RealmMBean:javax.management.ObjectName )
destroyFileRealm(weblogic.management.configuration.FileRealmMBean:javax.management.ObjectName )
destroyForeignJMSDestination(wsc:javax.management.ObjectName )
destroyJMSBridgeDestination(jmsBridgeDestination:javax.management.ObjectName )
destroyJMSInteropModule(bean:javax.management.ObjectName )
destroyJoltConnectionPool(joltConnectionPool:javax.management.ObjectName )
destroyLogFilter(logFilter:javax.management.ObjectName )
destroyCluster(cluster:javax.management.ObjectName )
destroyJMSConnectionConsumer(wsc:javax.management.ObjectName )
destroyJDBCSystemResource(bean:javax.management.ObjectName )
destroySAFAgent(sAFAgent:javax.management.ObjectName )
destroyLDAPRealm(weblogic.management.configuration.LDAPRealmMBean:javax.management.ObjectName )
destroyErrorHandling(errorHandling:javax.management.ObjectName )
destroyBridgeDestination(bridgeDestination:javax.management.ObjectName )
destroyPathService(pathService:javax.management.ObjectName )
destroyMailSession(ms:javax.management.ObjectName )
destroyMigratableTarget(bean:javax.management.ObjectName )
destroyWLDFSystemResource(bean:javax.management.ObjectName )
destroyJDBCStore(store:javax.management.ObjectName )
destroyJMSServer(jmsServer:javax.management.ObjectName )
destroyWSReliableDeliveryPolicy(policy:javax.management.ObjectName )
destroySingletonService(sc:javax.management.ObjectName )
destroyUnixRealm(weblogic.management.configuration.UnixRealmMBean:javax.management.ObjectName )
destroyStartupClass(sc:javax.management.ObjectName )
destroyEJBContainer()
destroyServer(server:javax.management.ObjectName )
destroyForeignJNDIProvider(provider:javax.management.ObjectName )
destroyWebserviceSecurity(wsc:javax.management.ObjectName )
destroyCustomResource(bean:javax.management.ObjectName )
destroyMessagingBridge(bridge:javax.management.ObjectName )
destroyCachingRealm(weblogic.management.configuration.CachingRealmMBean:javax.management.ObjectName
)
destroyMachine(machine:javax.management.ObjectName )
destroyJMSSystemResource(bean:javax.management.ObjectName )
destroyDomainLogFilter(logFilter:javax.management.ObjectName )
destroyNTRealm(weblogic.management.configuration.NTRealmMBean:javax.management.ObjectName )
destroyShutdownClass(sc:javax.management.ObjectName )
destroyCoherenceClusterSystemResource(bean:javax.management.ObjectName )
destroyMigratableRMIService(bean:javax.management.ObjectName )
destroyFileStore(store:javax.management.ObjectName )
destroyXMLRegistry(registry:javax.management.ObjectName )
destroyCoherenceServer(bean:javax.management.ObjectName )
destroyPasswordPolicy(weblogic.management.configuration.PasswordPolicyMBean:javax.management.ObjectNa
me )
destroyFileT3(fileT3:javax.management.ObjectName )
destroyRDBMSRealm(weblogic.management.configuration.RDBMSRealmMBean:javax.management.ObjectName )
destroyWLECConnectionPool(store:javax.management.ObjectName )
```

The following sections will discuss automation around cleanup and removing resources/elements from domains. Note that application undeployment will be left out, as this is discussed in the next chapter together with the other administrative tasks around applications. Therefore it is also not implemented in the provided examples in this chapter.

Delete Datasources with JMX

Datasources are an important part of all applications and therefore used in almost all server instances. This means that if applications are no longer needed, the datasources also have to be cleaned up. This is NOT just for cosmetic or resource consumption necessary. Available datasources always mean access to the attached databases! Therefore, unused datasources might open a forgotten security hole to your valuable data.

💾 delete_datasource_jmx

```
public void deleteDataSource(String datasourcename) throws Exception
{
  try
  {
    // e.g.: com.bea:Name=TestDomain,Type=Domain
    ObjectName myDomainMBean = myJMXWrapper.getDomainConfigRoot();

    // Operation: javax.management.ObjectName  lookupJDBCSystemResource(name:java.lang.String  )

    ObjectName mySystemResourceMBean = (ObjectName)myJMXWrapper.invoke(myDomainMBean,
        "lookupJDBCSystemResource",
        new Object[]{new String(datasourcename)},
        new String[]{String.class.getName()});
    if (mySystemResourceMBean!=null) {
        // ok, found => delete it now !
      myJMXWrapper.invoke(myDomainMBean,"destroyJDBCSystemResource",
                          new Object[]{mySystemResourceMBean},new
String[]{ObjectName.class.getName()});
    }
    else
    throw new WLSAutomationException("Datasource "+datasourcename+" does not exist  -  cannot
delete !");
    }
    catch(Exception ex) {
        throw new WLSAutomationException(ex);
    }
}
```

Delete File Stores with JMX

File stores also have a destroy method that can be used to delete a file store:

💾 delete_filestore_jmx

```
public void destroyFileStore(String fileStoreName) throws WLSAutomationException
{
  try {
    // get the domain config root
    ObjectName domainRoot = myJMXWrapper.getDomainConfigRoot();

    // lookup filestore as ObjectName is needed (alternatively you can construct the ObjectName)
    ObjectName myFileStore = (ObjectName)myJMXWrapper.invoke(domainRoot,"lookupFileStore",new
Object[]{fileStoreName},
                                        new String[]{String.class.getName()});

    // destroy filesstore
    myJMXWrapper.invoke(domainRoot,"destroyFileStore",new Object[]{myFileStore},new
String[]{ObjectName.class.getName()});
    }
    catch(Exception ex)
    {
    System.out.println("Error while destroyFileStore ("+fileStoreName+"): "+ ex.getMessage());
    throw new WLSAutomationException(ex.getMessage());
    }
```

Delete JMS Providers with JMX

JMS providers are another group of resources that should be cleaned up as soon as the application no longer needs them. The domain MBean offers a method to remove JMS providers (whereas cmo here is the domain MBean).

Due to the complex hierarchy and the different JMS elements, WebLogic offers a number of destroy methods for the different JMS elements.

Example to destroy a JMS server:

🗄 destroy_JMS_server_jmx

```
public void destroyJMSServer(String jmsServerName) throws WLSAutomationException
{
  try {
    // get the domain config root
    ObjectName domainRoot = myJMXWrapper.getDomainConfigRoot();

    // lookup jmsserver as ObjectName is needed (alternatively you can construct the ObjectName)
    ObjectName myJMSServer = (ObjectName)myJMXWrapper.invoke(domainRoot,"lookupJMSServer",
                                    new Object[]{jmsServerName},new
String[]{String.class.getName()});

    // destroy filesstore
    myJMXWrapper.invoke(domainRoot,"destroyJMSServer",new Object[]{myJMSServer},new
String[]{ObjectName.class.getName()});
  }
  catch(Exception ex)
  {
    System.out.println("Error while destroyJMSServer ("+jmsServerName+"): "+ ex.getMessage());
    throw new WLSAutomationException(ex.getMessage());
  }
}
```

Example to delete a JMS module:

🗄 delete_JMS_module_jmx

```
public void destroyJMSModule(String jmsModuleName)  throws WLSAutomationException
{
  try {
    // get the domain config root
    ObjectName domainRoot = myJMXWrapper.getDomainConfigRoot();

    // lookup jmsmodule as ObjectName is needed (alternatively you can construct the ObjectName)
    ObjectName myJMSModule = (ObjectName)myJMXWrapper.invoke(domainRoot,"lookupJMSSystemResource",
                                    new Object[]{jmsModuleName},new
String[]{String.class.getName()});

    // destroy filesstore
    myJMXWrapper.invoke(domainRoot,"destroyJMSSystemResource",new Object[]{myJMSModule},
                                    new String[]{ObjectName.class.getName()});
  }
  catch(Exception ex)
  {
    System.out.println("Error while destroyJMSModule ("+jmsModuleName+"): "+ ex.getMessage());
    throw new WLSAutomationException(ex.getMessage());
  }
}
```

Example to destroy a connection factory:

💾 destroy_connection_factory_jmx

```
public void destroyJmsConnectionFactory(String jmsModuleName, String connectionFactoryName)  throws
WLSAutomationException
  {
    try
    {
      // get the jmsModuleName config root
      ObjectName myJMSModule = new
ObjectName("com.bea:Name="+jmsModuleName+",Type=JMSSystemResource");

      // get the resource
      ObjectName myJMSModuleResource =
(ObjectName)myJMXWrapper.getAttribute(myJMSModule,"JMSResource");

      // lookup connection factory from module as ObjectName is needed (alternatively you can
construct the ObjectName)
      ObjectName myJMSConnFactory =
(ObjectName)myJMXWrapper.invoke(myJMSModuleResource,"lookupConnectionFactory",
                                    new Object[]{connectionFactoryName},new
String[]{String.class.getName()});

      // destroy the connection factory
      myJMXWrapper.invoke(myJMSModuleResource,"destroyConnectionFactory",new
Object[]{myJMSConnFactory},
                                    new String[]{ObjectName.class.getName()});
    }
    catch(Exception ex)
    {
      System.out.println("Error while destroying JmsConnectionFactory
("+jmsModuleName+":"+connectionFactoryName+"): "
                      + ex.getMessage());
      throw new WLSAutomationException(ex.getMessage());
    }
  }
```

Example to destroy a subdeployment:

💾 destroy_subdeployment_jmx

```
public void destroyJMSSubDeployment(String jmsModuleName, String subDeploymentName) throws
WLSAutomationException
  {
    try
    {
      // get the jmsModuleName config root
      ObjectName myJMSModule = new
ObjectName("com.bea:Name="+jmsModuleName+",Type=JMSSystemResource");

      // lookup sub deplyoment from module as ObjectName is needed (alternatively you can construct
the ObjectName)
      ObjectName myJMSSubDeployment =
(ObjectName)myJMXWrapper.invoke(myJMSModule,"lookupSubDeployment",new Object[]{subDeploymentName},new
String[]{String.class.getName()});

      // destroy the connection factory
      myJMXWrapper.invoke(myJMSModule,"destroySubDeployment",new Object[]{myJMSSubDeployment},new
String[]{ObjectName.class.getName()});
    }
    catch(Exception ex)
    {
      System.out.println("Error while destroyJMSSubDeployment
("+jmsModuleName+":"+subDeploymentName+"): "+ ex.getMessage());
      throw new WLSAutomationException(ex.getMessage());
    }
  }
```

You may have noted that in the above list, the deletion of queues and topics are not listed. Destroying a queue or a topic is of course also possible with JMX, but not on the root object. You need to navigate to the JMSResource instance first and there you will find the appropriate destroy methods.

Destroying a queue:

🖫 destroy_queue_jmx

```
public void destroyQueue(String jmsModuleName, String queueName) throws WLSAutomationException
{
  try
  {
    // get the jmsModuleName config root
    ObjectName myJMSModule = new
ObjectName("com.bea:Name="+jmsModuleName+",Type=JMSSystemResource");

    // get the resource
    ObjectName myJMSModuleResource =
(ObjectName)myJMXWrapper.getAttribute(myJMSModule,"JMSResource");

    // lookup queue from moduleResource as ObjectName is needed (alternatively you can construct
the ObjectName)
    ObjectName myQueue = (ObjectName)myJMXWrapper.invoke(myJMSModuleResource,"lookupQueue",new
Object[]{queueName},new String[]{String.class.getName()});

    // destroy the queue
    myJMXWrapper.invoke(myJMSModuleResource,"destroyQueue",new Object[]{myQueue},new
String[]{ObjectName.class.getName()});
  }
  catch(Exception ex)
  {
    System.out.println("Error while destroyQueue ("+jmsModuleName+":"+queueName+"): "+
ex.getMessage());
    throw new WLSAutomationException(ex.getMessage());
  }
}
```

Destroying a topic:

🖫 destroy_topic_jmx

```
public void destroyTopic(String jmsModuleName, String topicName) throws WLSAutomationException
{
  try
  {
    // get the jmsModuleName config root
    ObjectName myJMSModule = new
ObjectName("com.bea:Name="+jmsModuleName+",Type=JMSSystemResource");

    // get the resource
    ObjectName myJMSModuleResource =
(ObjectName)myJMXWrapper.getAttribute(myJMSModule,"JMSResource");

    // lookup topic from moduleResource as ObjectName is needed (alternatively you can construct
the ObjectName)
    ObjectName myTopic = (ObjectName)myJMXWrapper.invoke(myJMSModuleResource,"lookupTopic",new
Object[]{topicName},new String[]{String.class.getName()});

    // destroy the topic
    myJMXWrapper.invoke(myJMSModuleResource,"destroyTopic",new Object[]{myTopic},new
String[]{ObjectName.class.getName()});
  }
  catch(Exception ex)
  {
    System.out.println("Error while destroyTopic ("+jmsModuleName+":"+topicName+"): "+
ex.getMessage());
    throw new WLSAutomationException(ex.getMessage());
  }
```

Note: destroying distributed destinations is very similar. The methods needed are called *destroyDistributedQueue(…)* and *destroyDistributedTopic(…)*.

Delete Foreign JNDI Providers with JMX

JNDI providers offer access to the JNDI tree of other servers. Once connected to the current server, the content is visible to the application (and administrators). Again, unused JNDI providers offer insight knowledge to other servers and therefore might be considered a security hole. The current WebLogic Server also has to maintain them.

💾 delete_JNDI_provider_jmx

```
public void deleteForeignJNDIProvider(String providerName)   throws WLSAutomationException
{
    try
    {
        // e.g.: com.bea:Name=TestDomain,Type=Domain
        ObjectName myDomainMBean = myJMXWrapper.getDomainConfigRoot();

        ObjectName myProviderMBean = (ObjectName)myJMXWrapper.invoke(myDomainMBean,
                                            "lookupForeignJNDIProvider",
                                            new Object[]{new String(providerName)},
                                            new String[]{String.class.getName()});
        if (myProviderMBean!=null)
        {
            // delete
            // Operation: java.lang.Void  destroyForeignJNDIProvider(provider:javax.management.ObjectName
)
            myJMXWrapper.invoke(myDomainMBean,"destroyForeignJNDIProvider",
                        new Object[]{new String(providerName)},new String[]{String.class.getName()});
        }
        else
            throw new WLSAutomationException("Foreign JNDI provider "+providerName+" does not exist  -
cannot delete !");
    }
    catch(Exception ex) {
        throw new WLSAutomationException(ex);
    }
}
```

Delete Java Mail Sessions with JMX

Access to email gateways (called mail sessions in WebLogic) should be cleaned up if they are no longer needed. The domain MBean offers a method to remove mail sessions (whereas cmo here is the domain MBean):

💾 delete_mail_session_jmx

```
public void deleteMailSession(String mailSessionName)   throws WLSAutomationException {
    try {
        // e.g.: com.bea:Name=TestDomain,Type=Domain
        ObjectName myDomainMBean = myJMXWrapper.getDomainConfigRoot();

        ObjectName myMailSessionMBean = (ObjectName)myJMXWrapper.invoke(myDomainMBean,
                                                "lookupMailSession",
                                                new Object[]{new
String(mailSessionName)},
```

```
                                                          new
String[]{String.class.getName()});
          if (myMailSessionMBean!=null)
          {
            // delete
            // Operation: java.lang.Void  destroyMailSession(ms:javax.management.ObjectName  )
            myJMXWrapper.invoke(myDomainMBean,"destroyMailSession",new Object[]{myMailSessionMBean},
                                        new String[]{ObjectName.class.getName()});
          }
          else
            throw new WLSAutomationException("Mail session with name "+mailSessionName+
                                        " does not exist  -  cannot delete !");
    }
    catch(Exception ex) {
      throw new WLSAutomationException(ex);
    }
}
```

Delete Managed-Servers with JMX

Deleting a Managed-Server is not as simple as deleting one of the resources discussed above. In order to do a clean and safe implementation, the automation should first check if the Managed-Server you want to delete still hosts resources or applications. If so, the resources should be deleted first.

delete_managed-server_jmx

```
public void deleteManagedServer(String managedServerName, boolean deleteAlsoIfDependenciesExist)
throws WLSAutomationException
{
  try
  {
    // e.g.: com.bea:Name=TestDomain,Type=Domain
    ObjectName myDomainMBean = myJMXWrapper.getDomainConfigRoot(); // new ObjectName("com.bea:Name="
+ domainName +",Type=Domain");

    // Operation: javax.management.ObjectName  lookupServer(name:java.lang.String  )
    ObjectName myServer = (ObjectName)myJMXWrapper.invoke(myDomainMBean,"lookupServer",new
Object[]{managedServerName},new String[]{String.class.getName()});

    if (myServer == null)
        throw new WLSAutomationException("Server "+managedServerName+" does not exist !");
    else
    {
        // server exists
        if (! deleteAlsoIfDependenciesExist)
        {
          // check for dependencies
          if (managedserverHostsApplications(managedServerName))
              throw new WLSAutomationException("Applications still deployed on server
"+managedServerName+" - cannot delete !");
          if (managedserverHostsDatasources(managedServerName))
              throw new WLSAutomationException("Datasources still deployed on server
"+managedServerName+" - cannot delete !");
        }

        // ok, can delete
        System.out.println("Managed Server "+managedServerName+" will be destroyed !");

        // detach from cluster if any
        myJMXWrapper.setAttribute(myServer, new Attribute("Cluster", null));
        // detach from machine if any
        myJMXWrapper.setAttribute(myServer, new Attribute("Machine", null));

        // destroy server
        myJMXWrapper.invoke(myDomainMBean,"destroyServer",new Object[]{myServer},new
String[]{ObjectName.class.getName()});
    }

  }
  catch(Exception ex) {
```

```
      throw new WLSAutomationException("Error while deleteManagedServer ("+managedServerName+"): "+
ex.getMessage());
   }
}
```

Delete Cluster with JMX

Deleting a cluster should also not be done without checking some pre-requites. The cluster should be empty, which means without any Managed-Servers as members. Finally, you should stop the cluster before you delete it.

🖫 delete_cluster_jmx

```
public void deleteCluster(String clusterName, boolean deleteAlsoIfDependenciesExist) throws
WLSAutomationException
{
    try
    {
      // e.g.: com.bea:Name=TestDomain,Type=Domain
      ObjectName myDomainMBean = myJMXWrapper.getDomainConfigRoot();

      ObjectName myCluster = (ObjectName)myJMXWrapper.invoke(myDomainMBean,
                "lookupCluster",new Object[]{clusterName},new String[]{String.class.getName()});

      if (myCluster == null)
        throw new WLSAutomationException("Cluster "+clusterName+" does not exist !");
      else
      {
         // cluster exists
         if (! deleteAlsoIfDependenciesExist)
         {
         // check for dependencies
         if (clusterHasManagedServers(clusterName))
             throw new WLSAutomationException("Cluster "+clusterName+" still has server members -
cannot delete !");
         }

         // ok delete cluster
         ObjectName[] clusterMembers = (ObjectName[])myJMXWrapper.getAttribute(myCluster,"Servers");

         if (clusterMembers!=null && clusterMembers.length>0)
         {
            for (int i=0;i<clusterMembers.length;i++)
               myJMXWrapper.setAttribute(clusterMembers[i], new Attribute("Cluster", null));
         }

         // destroy
         System.out.println("Cluster "+clusterName+" will be destroyed !");
         myJMXWrapper.invoke(myDomainMBean,"destroyCluster",new Object[]{myCluster},
                   new String[]{ObjectName.class.getName()});
      }
   }
   catch(Exception ex) {
     throw new WLSAutomationException("Error while deleteCluster ("+clusterName+"): "+
ex.getMessage());
   }
}
```

Delete Machines with JMX

Deleting a machine should also not be done without checking some pre-requites. The machine should not host any Managed-Servers.

💾 delete_machine_jmx

```
public void deleteMachine(String machineName, boolean deleteAlsoIfDependenciesExist) throws
WLSAutomationException
{
  Try {
    // e.g.: com.bea:Name=TestDomain,Type=Domain
    ObjectName myDomainMBean = myJMXWrapper.getDomainConfigRoot();
    ObjectName myMachine = (ObjectName)myJMXWrapper.invoke(myDomainMBean,"lookupMachine",
                                              new Object[]{machineName},new
String[]{String.class.getName()});

    if (myMachine == null)
    throw new WLSAutomationException("Machine "+machineName+" does not exist !");
    else
    {
       // cluster exists
       if (! deleteAlsoIfDependenciesExist)
       {
             // check for dependencies
             if (machineHostsManagedServer(machineName))
                     throw new WLSAutomationException("Machine "+machineName+" still has server
members - cannot delete !");
       }

       // ok delete machine
       ArrayList<ObjectName> machineServers = getServersOfMachine(machineName);
       for (int i=0;i<machineServers.size();i++)
        myJMXWrapper.setAttribute(machineServers.get(i), new Attribute("Machine", null));

       // destroy
       System.out.println("Machine "+machineName+" will be destroyed !");
       myJMXWrapper.invoke(myDomainMBean,"destroyMachine",new Object[]{myMachine},
                   new String[]{ObjectName.class.getName()});
    }
  }
  catch(Exception ex) {
     throw new WLSAutomationException("Error while deleteMachine ("+machineName+"): "+
ex.getMessage());
  }
}
```

Delete Network Channel with JMX

Deleting a network channel can be done easily using JMX:

💾 delete_network_channel_jmx

```
public void deleteNetworkChannel(String serverName, String channelName) throws WLSAutomationException
{
  try {
    ObjectName myServerRuntime = (ObjectName)myJMXWrapper.invoke(myJMXWrapper.getDomainConfigRoot(),
               "lookupServer",
               new Object[]{new String(serverName)},
               new String[]{String.class.getName()});

    // lookup the channel with the provided name
    ObjectName myChannel = (ObjectName)myJMXWrapper.invoke(myServerRuntime,
               "lookupNetworkAccessPoint",
               new Object[]{new String(channelName)},
               new String[]{String.class.getName()});

    if (myChannel != null)
    {
       // now destroy
       myJMXWrapper.invoke(myServerRuntime,
          "destroyNetworkAccessPoint",
          new Object[]{myChannel},
          new String[]{ObjectName.class.getName()});
    }
    else
       throw new WLSAutomationException("NetworkChannel "+channelName+" already exists !");
}
```

```
catch(Exception ex) {
    throw new WLSAutomationException("Error while deleteNetworkChannel ("+channelName+"): "+
ex.getMessage());
  }
}
```

Delete Virtual Host with JMX

Deleting a virtual host can also be done using JMX:

🖫 delete_virtual_host_jmx

```
public void deleteVirtualHost(String virtualhostName) throws WLSAutomationException
{
    try {

        // e.g.: com.bea:Name=TestDomain,Type=Domain
        ObjectName myDomainMBean = myJMXWrapper.getDomainConfigRoot();
        // lookup and try to find virtual host
        ObjectName myVirtualHost = (ObjectName)myJMXWrapper.invoke(myDomainMBean,
                "lookupVirtualHost",
                new Object[]{new String(virtualhostName)},
                new String[]{String.class.getName()});

        if (myVirtualHost != null)
            // destroy virtual host with the provided name
            myJMXWrapper.invoke(myDomainMBean,
                                "destroyVirtualHost",
                                new Object[]{myVirtualHost},
                                new String[]{ObjectName.class.getName()});
        else
         throw new WLSAutomationException("Virtual host "+virtualhostName+" does not exists !");
    }
    catch(Exception ex) {
        throw new WLSAutomationException("Error while destroyVirtualHost ("+virtualhostName+"): "+
ex.getMessage());
    }
}
```

Summary

Like other J2EE servers, WebLogic is based on services that offer abstraction layers to infrastructure services like database access, messaging, transaction integration, directory services, and many more. All these services have to be configured for WebLogic domains and/or individual WebLogic Server instances. This chapter has discussed the most important services of WebLogic and has shown possible ways to automate their creation, configuration, and also their destruction.

Always be prepared to change or eliminate services you have configured if these services are no longer needed. I strongly advise everybody delete unused services as those services block resources (ports, memory, or others) and also may offer a forgotten backdoor to your application.

Security Configuration with JMX

CHAPTER

15

Security Configuration with JMX

A security overview was given in the first part of this book. Security is a huge topic that involves many different security technologies, and therefore it is out-of-scope of this book to give a comprehensive security description. Oracle has a number of documentation books specifically for the security layer. This chapter will show you how to automate many different aspects of security.

For a security overview, please see the introduction section within the WLST part of this book. The security layer is of course 100% identical when accessing it via JMX or WLST.

WebLogic Security Automation with JMX

The beginning this chapter will introduce basic security considerations and issues like file system and server/NodeManager connections. Then information about PKI (public key infrastructure) and SSL is provided. The configuration of an admin channel as it relates to security is also provided. Next, user/group/role management will be discussed, which is important because these are present in every WebLogic domain. Another major part is the discussion of the different security providers of a WebLogic realm, especially in the area of authentication, authorization, and role/credential mapping. Finally, information on password validation and other providers will be covered.

Note that a number of sections provided in the WLST section are NOT presented here. This is because they are either identical or not applicable to JMX, or are just very rarely used with JMX.

JMX Setup for Secure Access with JMX

A common issue is that administration communication is encrypted using SSL. Therefore the client - in your case the JMX interpreter - has to use either T3S or IIOPS. In both cases the JMX interpreter might need to provide its own SSL certificate, or verify that the server certificate is trusted. In order to start the JMX with these extended requirements, you need to modify the start program for your JMX environment and add the security parameter.

In order to connect to an AdminServer or to a Managed-Server using T3S, a number of steps are necessary. First it is necessary to switch from an unsecure protocol to a secure protocol. For JMX, this will normally be either "t3s" or "iiops". The JMX service URL can be specified either as a full string or in parts.

JMX service URL as string:

```
JMXServiceURL serviceURL = new
JMXServiceURL("service:jmx:t3s://mytesthost.test.com:7002/jndi/weblogic.management.mbeanservers.domai
nruntime");
```

JMX service URL specified in separate parts:

```
JMXServiceURL serviceURL = new JMXServiceURL("t3s", "mytesthost.test.com", 7002,
"/jndi/weblogic.management.mbeanservers.domainruntime");
```

Besides the usual *wlfullclient.jar*, which has to be provided to the client application, it is necessary to supply the client with 3 additional JAR files from the WebLogic installation. These are *cryptoj.jar*, *cryptojFIPS.jar*, and for the cipher suites *wlcipher.jar*. Without these jars you will get different sorts of exceptions starting with ClassNotFound up to SSl handshake errors.

Parameters are needed on the commandline in order to specify security behavior. Note that this example works with the demo certificates provided by WebLogic. If you use our own certificates (which is definitely required for production systems) you have to provide your own truststore:

```
-Dweblogic.security.allowCryptoJDefaultJCEVerification=true
-Dweblogic.security.allowCryptoJDefaultPRNG=true
-Dweblogic.security.SSL.ignoreHostnameVerification=true
-Dweblogic.security.TrustKeyStore=CustomTrust
-Dweblogic.security.CustomTrustKeyStoreFileName=<directoy>\DemoTrust.jks
```

For debugging, the following parameters can be set on the VM level:

```
-Dssl.debug=true
-Dweblogic.StdoutDebugEnabled=true
```

The following is an example client to print the name of all clusters. The main point here is the connectivity via a secure protocol:

```
public static void main(String[] rgs) throws Exception
{
    JMXServiceURL serviceURL = new JMXServiceURL("t3s", "mytesthost.test.com", 7002,
            "/jndi/weblogic.management.mbeanservers.domainruntime");
```

```
Hashtable<String, String> h = new Hashtable<String, String>();
h.put(Context.SECURITY_PRINCIPAL, "weblogic");
h.put(Context.SECURITY_CREDENTIALS, "<password>");
h.put(JMXConnectorFactory.PROTOCOL_PROVIDER_PACKAGES,"weblogic.management.remote");

JMXConnector connector = JMXConnectorFactory.connect(serviceURL, h);
MBeanServerConnection connection = connector.getMBeanServerConnection();

// get domain  mbean
ObjectName myDomainMBean = new ObjectName("com.bea:Name=TestDomain,Type=Domain");
// get all cluster mbeans
ObjectName[] allClusters = (ObjectName[])connection.getAttribute(myDomainMBean,"Clusters");

for (int c=0;c<allClusters.length;c++)
    System.out.println("Found cluster: "+ connection.getAttribute(allClusters[c],"Name"));
}
```

User/Passwords/Groups

It requires lot of effort to setup a robust secure system that controls users' actions
based on the role given for whether to deny or allow. This section will show the
reader how to automate the most common tasks with users/groups and roles with
JMX.

Listing All Users and Groups with JMX

In production systems especially, it is important to know about all users who have
access to the WebLogic domains. Forgotten user accounts can be pretty nasty
backdoors. Therefore, listing current users and groups and comparing them to some
defined lists should be done periodically. The following script will list all users. In
order to make it a bit more interesting, we will list all users - not only from the
DefaultAuthenticator, but from all UserAuthenticators.

Tests if a specific method exists on this MBean:

🔲 test_method_exists_jmx

```
private boolean methodExistsOnMBean(String methodName, ObjectName myMBean)
            throws WLSAutomationException
{
   try {
       MBeanInfo myInfo = myJMXWrapper.getConnection().getMBeanInfo(myMBean);

       // get operations, using the operations list from the standard MbeanInfo
       MBeanOperationInfo[] myOps = myInfo.getOperations();
       for (int i=0;i<myOps.length;i++)
         if (myOps[i].getName().equals(methodName))
           return true;

       // oh no - method not found
       return false;
   }
   catch(Exception ex) {
     throw new WLSAutomationException(ex.getMessage());
   }
}
```

The next example returns all user names in all authentication providers:

⊟ return_usernames_jmx

```
public ArrayList<String> returnAllUserNames() throws WLSAutomationException
{
    ArrayList<String> resultList = new ArrayList<String>();

    try {
        ObjectName[] allAuthenticationProviders =
                    (ObjectName[])myJMXWrapper.getAttribute(myRealm, "AuthenticationProviders");

        for (int i=0;i<allAuthenticationProviders.length;i++)
        {
            if ( methodExistsOnMBean("listUsers", allAuthenticationProviders[i]))
            {
                // yes has users (listusers is inherited from UserReaderMBean)

                // get cursor for user listing
                String cursor = (String)myJMXWrapper.invoke(allAuthenticationProviders[i],"listUsers",
                    new Object[]{"*",new Integer(0)},
                    new String[]{String.class.getName(),Integer.class.getName()});

                while ((Boolean)myJMXWrapper.invoke(allAuthenticationProviders[i],"haveCurrent",
                            new Object[]{cursor},
                            new String[]{String.class.getName()}))
                {
                    // add next user to list
                    resultList.add((String)myJMXWrapper.invoke(allAuthenticationProviders[i],
                            "getCurrentName",
                            new Object[]{cursor},new String[]{String.class.getName()}));

                    // advance cursor
                    myJMXWrapper.invoke(allAuthenticationProviders[i],"advance",new Object[]{cursor},
                            new String[]{String.class.getName()});
                }
                // close cursor
                myJMXWrapper.invoke(allAuthenticationProviders[i],"close",new Object[]{cursor},
                        new String[]{String.class.getName()});
            }
        }

        // return list of users
        return resultList;
    }
    catch(Exception ex) {
        System.out.println("Error while returnAllUserNames: "+ ex.getMessage());
        throw new WLSAutomationException(ex.getMessage());
    }
}
```

This program will change to the default realm *myrealm*. Then we ask for a list of authentication providers. The program will loop over this list and if the provider has users, we will get the user list and print it.

NOTE: Other than the WLST version, we cannot easily ask if the MBean is an instance of the UserReader or GroupReader MBean. This cannot be known from the ObjectName alone. Therefore we will use a trick and ask if the MBean has a specific operation. This allows us to keep the code free of WebLogic-specific classes. We will use the standard JMX tools for this check. We also need to use the "cursor" notation, which is not very complicated since the cursor is only a string.

Very similar to users, the following method will return all group names of all authentication providers:

💾 return_groupnames_jmx

```
public ArrayList<String> returnAllGroupNames() throws WLSAutomationException
{
  ArrayList<String> resultList = new ArrayList<String>();

  try {
    ObjectName[] allAuthenticationProviders = (ObjectName[])myJMXWrapper.getAttribute(
              myRealm, "AuthenticationProviders");

    for (int i=0;i<allAuthenticationProviders.length;i++)
    {
      if ( methodExistsOnMBean("listGroups", allAuthenticationProviders[i])) {
        // yes has groups  (listgroups is inherited from GroupReaderMBean)

        // get cursor for user listing
        String cursor = (String)myJMXWrapper.invoke(allAuthenticationProviders[i],"listGroups",
            new Object[]{"*",new Integer(0)},
            new String[]{String.class.getName(),Integer.class.getName()});

        while ((Boolean)myJMXWrapper.invoke(allAuthenticationProviders[i],"haveCurrent",
                                   new Object[]{cursor},
                                   new String[]{String.class.getName()}))
        {
          // add next user to list
          resultList.add((String)myJMXWrapper.invoke(allAuthenticationProviders[i],
                      "getCurrentName",
                      new Object[]{cursor},new String[]{String.class.getName()}));

          // advance cursor
          myJMXWrapper.invoke(allAuthenticationProviders[i],"advance",new Object[]{cursor},
                      new String[]{String.class.getName()});
        }
        // close cursor
        myJMXWrapper.invoke(allAuthenticationProviders[i],"close",new Object[]{cursor},
                      new String[]{String.class.getName()});
      }
    }

    // return list of groups
    return resultList;
  }
  catch(Exception ex)
  {
    System.out.println("Error while returnAllGroupNames: "+ ex.getMessage());
    throw new WLSAutomationException(ex.getMessage());
  }
}
```

The principal actions in this script are identical to the user list script listed before.

And last but not least we will list all the user-group memberships in the different authentication providers:

💾 list_user-group_memberships_jmx

```
public void listUsersInGroups() throws WLSAutomationException
{
  try
  {
    ObjectName[] allAuthenticationProviders = (ObjectName[])myJMXWrapper.getAttribute(
              myRealm, "AuthenticationProviders");

    System.out.println("All user/groups available in realm: myrealm");
    for (int i=0;i<allAuthenticationProviders.length;i++)
    {
      if ( methodExistsOnMBean("listGroups", allAuthenticationProviders[i])) {
        // yes has groups  (listgroups is inherited from GroupReaderMBean)

        // get cursor for user listing
        String cursor = (String)myJMXWrapper.invoke(allAuthenticationProviders[i],"listGroups",
            new Object[]{"*",new Integer(0)},
            new String[]{String.class.getName(),Integer.class.getName()});
```

```
        while ((Boolean)myJMXWrapper.invoke(allAuthenticationProviders[i],"haveCurrent",
                    new Object[]{cursor},
                    new String[]{String.class.getName()}))
    {
        // add next user to list
        String nextGroupName = (String)myJMXWrapper.invoke(allAuthenticationProviders[i],
                        "getCurrentName",
                        new Object[]{cursor},new String[]{String.class.getName()});
        System.out.println("    All user available in group: "+nextGroupName);

        // get all users of this group
        String[] usersInGroup = (String[])myJMXWrapper.invoke(allAuthenticationProviders[i],
            "listAllUsersInGroup",
            new Object[]{nextGroupName,"*",new Integer(0)},
            new String[]{String.class.getName(),String.class.getName(),Integer.class.getName()});

        // print users
        for (int u=0;u<usersInGroup.length;u++)
            System.out.println("            User: "+usersInGroup[u]);

        // advance cursor
        myJMXWrapper.invoke(allAuthenticationProviders[i],"advance",new Object[]{cursor},
                        new String[]{String.class.getName()});
    }
    // close cursor
    myJMXWrapper.invoke(allAuthenticationProviders[i],"close",new Object[]{cursor},
                    new String[]{String.class.getName()});
        }
    }
}
catch(Exception ex) {
    System.out.println("Error while listUsersInGroups: "+ ex.getMessage());
    throw new WLSAutomationException(ex.getMessage());
}
}
```

Adding Users and Groups with JMX

One common task is the creation of new users and groups, which not only includes
administrative users but also application users if these users will not be authenticated
using other technologies like SSO, LDAP, ActiveDirectory or other technologies.

When adding a new user to the domain, the user will be added to the default
authenticator (i.e. to the internal LDAP). It is advisable to test if the user exists before
you try to create it. You will avoid unnecessary exceptions by using this check.

Adding a User

The following is an example to test if a user exists:

```
public boolean testIfUserExists(String userName) throws WLSAutomationException {
    try {
        java.lang.Boolean myValue = (java.lang.Boolean)myJMXWrapper.invoke(myDefaultAuthenticator,
                        "userExists",new Object[]{userName},
                        new String[]{String.class.getName()});
        return myValue;
    }
    catch(Exception ex) {
        System.out.println("Error while testing user: "+ ex.getMessage());
        throw new WLSAutomationException(ex.getMessage());
    }
}
```

The next example creates a new user in the default authenticator:

```
public void createUser(String newUserName, String newUserPassword,
                       String newUserDescription, boolean deleteUserFirstIfExists)
        throws WLSAutomationException
{
  try {
    if (testIfUserExists(newUserName))  {
      if (deleteUserFirstIfExists)  {
        System.out.println("User "+newUserName+" already exists - removing old user first !");
        deleteUser(newUserName);
      }
      else {
        System.out.println("User "+newUserName+" already exists - CANNOT create !");
        return ;
      }
    }

    myJMXWrapper.invoke(myDefaultAuthenticator,"createUser",
        new Object[]{newUserName,newUserPassword,newUserDescription},
        new String[]{String.class.getName(),String.class.getName(),String.class.getName()});
  }
  catch(Exception ex)
  {
    System.out.println("Error while creating user ("+newUserName+"): "+ ex.getMessage());
    throw new WLSAutomationException(ex.getMessage());
  }
}
```

Adding a Group

Next we will demonstrate adding a new group to the domain. A group here is nothing but a list of users. Grouping helps administrators keep security rulesets small and stable by defining rules and permissions on group level.

The following is an example to test if a group exists:

```
public boolean testIfGroupExists(String groupName) throws WLSAutomationException {
  try {
    java.lang.Boolean myValue = (java.lang.Boolean)myJMXWrapper.invoke(myDefaultAuthenticator,
        "groupExists",new Object[]{groupName}, new String[]{String.class.getName()});
    return myValue;
  }
  catch(Exception ex)  {
    System.out.println("Error while testing group: "+ ex.getMessage());
    throw new WLSAutomationException(ex.getMessage());
  }
}
```

The next example creates a new group:

```
public void createGroup(String newGroupName, String newGroupDescription,
                        boolean deleteGroupFirstIfExists) throws WLSAutomationException  {
  try  {
    if (testIfGroupExists(newGroupName)) {
      if (deleteGroupFirstIfExists)  {
        System.out.println("Group "+newGroupName+" already exists - removing old group first !");
        deleteGroup(newGroupName);
      }
      else  {
        System.out.println("Group "+newGroupName+" already exists - CANNOT create !");
        return ;
      }
    }
    myJMXWrapper.invoke(myDefaultAuthenticator,"createGroup",
        new Object[]{newGroupName,newGroupDescription},
        new String[]{String.class.getName(),String.class.getName()});
```

```
    }
  catch(Exception ex)  {
    System.out.println("Error while creating group ("+newGroupName+"): "+ ex.getMessage());
    throw new WLSAutomationException(ex.getMessage());
  }
}
```

Testing Group Membership

Users are members of groups. Group membership allows the user to do certain tasks.
Therefore it is important to know who is assigned to which group in order to avoid
users getting too many rights.

The following example tests if a user is a member of a group:

```
public boolean testIfUserIsMemberOfGroup(String groupName, String userName)
              throws WLSAutomationException {
  try {
    java.lang.Boolean myValue = (java.lang.Boolean)myJMXWrapper.invoke(myDefaultAuthenticator,
                        "isMember",new Object[]{groupName,userName,new Boolean(true)},
                        new String[]{String.class.getName(),String.class.getName(),
                                     Boolean.class.getName()});

    return myValue;
  }
  catch(Exception ex) {
    System.out.println("Error while testing group membership: "+ ex.getMessage());
    throw new WLSAutomationException(ex.getMessage());
  }
}
```

Adding Users to Groups

Groups and users cannot exist independent from each other. In order to use them
efficiently, users must be added to groups. One user can be a member of different
groups. In that case, you have to do this assignment multiple times - once for each
group.

Group membership is very important for correct security rules. The next example
shows how to add a user to a group:

```
public void addUserToGroup(String userName, String groupName) throws WLSAutomationException
{
  try {
    // check if user exists
    if (testIfUserExists(userName)) {
        System.out.println("User "+userName+" does not exist - CANNOT add "+userName+
                           " to group "+groupName+" !");
        return;
    }

    // check if group exists
    if (testIfGroupExists(groupName)) {
        System.out.println("Group "+groupName+" does not exist - CANNOT add "+userName+
                           " to group "+groupName+" !");
        return;
    }

    // check if already member
    if (testIfUserIsMemberOfGroup(groupName, userName)) {
        System.out.println("User "+userName+" is already member of group "+groupName+" !");
        return;
    }
```

```
    // finally :-) add user to group
    myJMXWrapper.invoke(myDefaultAuthenticator,"addMemberToGroup",
              new Object[]{gropName,userName},
              new String[]{String.class.getName(),String.class.getName()});
  }
  catch(Exception ex) {
    System.out.println("Error while adding user ("+userName+") to group ("+groupName+"): "+
                  ex.getMessage());
    throw new WLSAutomationException(ex.getMessage());
  }
}
```

Deleting Users and Groups with JMX

In real systems, it is not only necessary to add users but it is also necessary to delete
the users. This might be necessary if a user leaves the company or changes the
department. In such cases, we must ensure that those users have no access to the
system and information. This is equally true for administrators and users.

The next function will delete a user from the actual realm:

```
public void deleteUser(String userName) throws WLSAutomationException
{
  try
  {
    myJMXWrapper.invoke(myDefaultAuthenticator,"removeUser",new Object[]{userName},
                  new String[]{String.class.getName()});
  }
  catch(Exception ex)
  {
    System.out.println("Error while deleting user ("+userName+"): "+ ex.getMessage());
    throw new WLSAutomationException(ex.getMessage());
  }
}
```

The next function will delete a group from the actual realm:

```
public void deleteGroup(String groupName) throws WLSAutomationException
{
  try
  {
    myJMXWrapper.invoke(myDefaultAuthenticator,"removeGroup",new Object[]{groupName},
                  new String[]{String.class.getName()});
  }
  catch(Exception ex)
  {
    System.out.println("Error while deleting group ("+groupName+"): "+ ex.getMessage());
    throw new WLSAutomationException(ex.getMessage());
  }
}
```

Last but not least, it is sometimes necessary to change user<->group relationships.
The next function will remove a user from a group:

```
public void removeMemberFromGroup(String groupName, String userName) throws WLSAutomationException
{
  try {
    myJMXWrapper.invoke(myDefaultAuthenticator,"removeMemberFromGroup",
                  new Object[]{groupName,userName},
                  new String[]{String.class.getName(),String.class.getName()});
  }
  catch(Exception ex) {
    System.out.println("Error while removing user ("+userName+") from group ("+groupName+"): "+
```

```
                ex.getMessage());
    throw new WLSAutomationException(ex.getMessage());
    }
}
```

Changing User Passwords with JMX

Changing a password is often necessary. To change a user's password, invoke the *changeUserPassword* method of the *UserPasswordEditorMBean*, which is extended by the security realm's *AuthenticationProvider* MBean.

The following JMX online script invokes *changeUserPassword* on the default authentication provider:

```
public void changeUserpassword(String userName, String oldPassword, String newPassword)
        throws WLSAutomationException
{
  try
  {
    if (testIfUserExists(userName))
    {
        myJMXWrapper.invoke(myDefaultAuthenticator,"changeUserPassword",
            new Object[]{userName,oldPassword,newPassword},
            new String[]{String.class.getName(),String.class.getName(),String.class.getName()});
    }
    else
    {
        System.out.println("User "+userName+" does not exists - CANNOT change password !");
    }
  }
  catch(Exception ex)
  {
    System.out.println("Error while changing password of user ("+userName+"): "+ ex.getMessage());
    throw new WLSAutomationException(ex.getMessage());
  }
}
```

Protecting User Accounts in a Security Realm with JMX

Hot topic for security: How often is a user allowed to enter an invalid password until his/her account gets locked? This is a standard in security to restrict the number of login attempts and also to monitor those failed logins. WebLogic also has the concept of a user lockout. If a user enters the passwords a couple of times wrong, the account will be locked for a given amount of time.

The *UserLockoutManagerMBean* provides a set of attributes to protect user accounts from intruders. The default configuration for attributes are optimized for strong protection as user accounts are very sensitive configuration items. The level of security can of course be adapted to domain specific needs. This includes increasing or decreasing the level of protection. For example, it is possible to increase the amount of invalid logins before an account will be locked or to change the time period an account is locked after a number of invalid login attempts.

By default the lockout mechanism is enabled, and there are several ways it can be configured. For example, you can set the number of login attempts and the amount of time the account is locked.

Next is an example configuration of the user lockout manager (note that in this case a connection to the EDIT-MBeanServer is needed):

```
public void configureUserLockoutManager(boolean lockoutEnabled, long lockoutThreshold,
                                  long lockoutDuration)
        throws WLSAutomationException
{
  try {
    ObjectName myLockoutManager = (ObjectName)myJMXWrapper.getAttribute(myRealm,
                                "UserLockoutManager");

      // lockout activated or not ?
    myJMXWrapper.setAttribute(myLockoutManager, new Attribute("LockoutEnabled",
                            new Boolean(lockoutEnabled)));

      // lockout threshold - when gets an account locked
    myJMXWrapper.setAttribute(myLockoutManager, new Attribute("LockoutThreshold",
                            new Long(lockoutThreshold)));

      // amount (in minutes) how long an account is locked
    myJMXWrapper.setAttribute(myLockoutManager, new Attribute("LockoutDuration",
                            new Long(lockoutDuration)));
  }
  catch(Exception ex) {
    System.out.println("Error while configureUserLockoutManager : "+ ex.getMessage());
    throw new WLSAutomationException(ex.getMessage());
  }
}
```

Another task important for automation is the ability to test if a user account is locked:

```
// test if a user is locked out
public boolean testIfUserAccountIsLocked(String userName) throws WLSAutomationException
{
  try
  {
    ObjectName myLockoutManager = (ObjectName)myJMXWrapper.getAttribute(myRealm,
                                "UserLockoutManager");

    return (Boolean)myJMXWrapper.invoke(myLockoutManager,"isLockedOut",new Object[]{userName},
                                new String[]{String.class.getName()});
  }
  catch(Exception ex) {
    System.out.println("Error while testIfUserAccountIsLocked user ("+userName+"): "+
                    ex.getMessage());
    throw new WLSAutomationException(ex.getMessage());
  }
}
```

If a user gets locked, then the administrator must be able to unlock this user. The next little program offers exactly this functionality, reactivating a locked account.

Enabling the user account, i.e. removing the lock of an account so that the user can login again:

```
public void clearUserAccountLock(String userName) throws WLSAutomationException
{
  try {
    ObjectName myLockoutManager = (ObjectName)myJMXWrapper.getAttribute(myRealm,
                                "UserLockoutManager");
```

```
    myJMXWrapper.invoke(myLockoutManager,"clearLockout",new Object[]{userName},
                        new String[]{String.class.getName()});
    }
    catch(Exception ex){
      System.out.println("Error while clearLockout user ("+userName+"): "+ ex.getMessage());
      throw new WLSAutomationException(ex.getMessage());
    }
}
```

Another program that is quite useful for production is the ability to run over the different domains and list all the user information. The administrator will get the information about the user accounts that are locked and still active:

```
// list all user lockout information
public void listAllUserLockoutInformation() throws WLSAutomationException
{
  try {
    ArrayList<String> userList = returnAllUserNames();
    ObjectName myLockoutManager = (ObjectName)myJMXWrapper.getAttribute(myRealm,
                                   "UserLockoutManager");

    System.out.println("Lockout-Information about all user acoounts:");
    for (int i=0;i<userList.size();i++)
      System.out.println("    User:"+userList.get(i)+
        "  isLocked:"+(Boolean)myJMXWrapper.invoke(myLockoutManager,"isLockedOut",
                                new Object[]{userList.get(i)},
                                new String[]{String.class.getName()})
        +"  LoginFailureCount:"+(Long)myJMXWrapper.invoke(myLockoutManager,
                                "getLoginFailureCount",
                                new Object[]{userList.get(i)},new String[]{String.class.getName()})
        +"  LastLoginFailure:"+(Long)myJMXWrapper.invoke(myLockoutManager,"getLastLoginFailure",
                                new Object[]{userList.get(i)},new String[]{String.class.getName()})
        );
  }
  catch(Exception ex) {
    System.out.println("Error while listAllUserLockoutInformation "+ ex.getMessage());
    throw new WLSAutomationException(ex.getMessage());
  }
}
```

Provider Configurations

Security providers are modules that provide a security service to an application in order to protect WebLogic resources. Types of security providers in WebLogic Server include:

- Authentication Provider

- Authorization Provider

- Auditing Providers

- Credential Mapping Provider

- Identity Assertion Provider

- Principal Validation Provider

- Adjudication Providers

- Role Mapping Providers

- Certificate Lookup and Validation Providers
- Keystore Providers

The following sections will examine the different providers and provide scripts, tips, and information for how to configure them.

Authentication Provider

WebLogic provides a number of authentication providers. These providers usually differ in the way the user/password is stored or where it is provided (LDAP, JDBC, NTdomain, custom). All providers try to find a given user in the associated data store and verify that the password is correct.

In addition to the username/password-based authentication providers, WebLogic includes identity assertion providers, which use other security artifacts like certificates or security tokens as credentials.

Example of creating an authentication provider with JMX:

💾 create_authentication_provider_jmx

```
public ObjectName createAuthenticationProvider(String providerName, String providerType)
                throws WLSAutomationException
{
   try
   {
      ObjectName securityRealmMBean =new ObjectName("Security:Name="+realmName);

      // Operation: javax.management.ObjectName  lookupMailSession(name:java.lang.String  )
      ObjectName myAuthenticationProviderMBean = (ObjectName)myJMXWrapper.invoke(securityRealmMBean,
                "lookupAuthenticationProvider",
                new Object[]{new String(providerName)},
                new String[]{String.class.getName()});
      if (myAuthenticationProviderMBean==null)
      {
        // create
        if (providerType==null)
          myAuthenticationProviderMBean = (ObjectName)myJMXWrapper.invoke(securityRealmMBean,
                    "createAuthenticationProvider",
                    new Object[]{providerName},
                    new String[]{String.class.getName()});
        else
          myAuthenticationProviderMBean = (ObjectName)myJMXWrapper.invoke(securityRealmMBean,
                    "createAuthenticationProvider",
                    new Object[]{providerName, providerType},
                    new String[]{String.class.getName(),String.class.getName()});

        // now do configuration
        // TO DO
        return myAuthenticationProviderMBean;
      }
      else
        throw new WLSAutomationException("AuthenticationProvider with name "+providerName+
                                " already exist  -  cannot create !");
   }
   catch(Exception ex) {
     throw new WLSAutomationException(ex);
   }
}
```

Some very important configurations are the JAAS control flags (REQUIRED, REQUISITE, SUFFICIENT, and OPTIONAL) on each of the authentication providers. Providers can be reordered if necessary using JMX (also using the console or JMX).

The next example demonstrates setting the control flag for a provider, in this case the Default-Authenticator:

```
public void setControlFlagForAuthenticationProvider(String providerName, String controlFlag)
        throws WLSAutomationException
{
   try
   {
     ObjectName securityRealmMBean =new ObjectName("Security:Name="+realmName);

     // Operation: javax.management.ObjectName  lookupMailSession(name:java.lang.String  )
     ObjectName myAuthenticationProviderMBean = (ObjectName)myJMXWrapper.invoke(securityRealmMBean,
                  "lookupAuthenticationProvider",
                  new Object[]{new String(providerName)},
                  new String[]{String.class.getName()});
     if (myAuthenticationProviderMBean!=null)
       myJMXWrapper.setAttribute(myAuthenticationProviderMBean,
                          new Attribute("ControlFlag",controlFlag));
     else
       throw new WLSAutomationException("AuthenticationProvider with name "+providerName+
                            " does not exist !");
   }
   catch(Exception ex) {
     throw new WLSAutomationException(ex);
   }
}
```

In a newly-created domain, the Default-Authenticator and the Default-IdentityAsserter are configured. If you want to use your own providers, then you first have to CREATE them and afterwards you can configure them. Finally, you need to reorder.

The next example creates a SAML authentication provider:

```
public ObjectName createDefaultSAMLAuthenticationProvider(String providerName)
               throws WLSAutomationException
 {
   try
   {
     // create identity asserter
     return createAuthenticationProvider(providerName,
                            "weblogic.security.providers.saml.SAMLAuthenticator");
   }
   catch(Exception ex) {
     throw new WLSAutomationException(ex);
   }
 }
```

WebLogic does not offer a method in the API for reordering providers. The solution is to provide a list (jarray list) with all providers in the order you want WebLogic to use.

```
public void reorderProviders(ObjectName[] providerRefs)  throws WLSAutomationException
 {
   try
```

```
  {
      ObjectName securityRealmMBean =new ObjectName("Security:Name="+realmName);

      // reorder only means to set the list of providers as an array
      myJMXWrapper.setAttribute(securityRealmMBean,
                                new Attribute("AuthenticationProviders",providerRefs));
  }
  catch(Exception ex) {
      throw new WLSAutomationException(ex);
  }
}
```

Identity Asserter

An identity assertion is a specific form of an authentication provider that enables WebLogic to determine and check the identity of the caller using tokens. For example, the default WebLogic identity assertion providers support certificate authentication using X509 certificates, SAML assertion tokens, and CSIv2 identity assertion.

The following is an example configuration of the default identity asserter, setting the active types to X.509 certificates:

🖫 **identity_asserter_configuration_jmx**

```
public void configureDefaultIdentityAsserterForX509()   throws WLSAutomationException
{
    try {
        ObjectName securityRealmMBean =new ObjectName("Security:Name="+realmName);

        // Operation: javax.management.ObjectName  lookupMailSession(name:java.lang.String  )
        ObjectName myAuthenticationProviderMBean = (ObjectName)myJMXWrapper.invoke(securityRealmMBean,
                    "lookupAuthenticationProvider",
                    new Object[]{new String("DefaultIdentityAsserter")},
                    new String[]{String.class.getName()});
        if (myAuthenticationProviderMBean!=null)
        {
            // set the active types to x.509 only
            myJMXWrapper.setAttribute(myAuthenticationProviderMBean, new Attribute("ActiveTypes",
                            new String[]{"AuthenticatedUser","X.509"}));
            // define the X.509 attribute which should be used for the name
            myJMXWrapper.setAttribute(myAuthenticationProviderMBean,
                            new Attribute("UseDefaultUserNameMapper",
                            new Boolean(true)));
            myJMXWrapper.setAttribute(myAuthenticationProviderMBean,
                            new Attribute("DefaultUserNameMapperAttributeType","CN"));
        }
        else
          throw new WLSAutomationException("DefaultIdentityAsserter does not exist !");
    }
    catch(Exception ex) {
        throw new WLSAutomationException(ex);
    }
}
```

The default identity asserter is configured by default, therefore in the previous example we did not need to create it. All others (WebLogic-provided or custom-made) must be created first before they can be configured.

The following example creates an instance of the SAML identity asserter:

```
public ObjectName createDefaultSAMLIdentityAsserter(String providerName)
                throws WLSAutomationException
{
  try
  {
    // create identity asserter
    return createAuthenticationProvider(providerName,
                              "weblogic.security.providers.saml.SAMLIdentityAsserterV2");
  }
  catch(Exception ex) {
    throw new WLSAutomationException(ex);
  }
}
```

After an instance of the SAML identity asserter is created, it is necessary to configure one or more asserting parties that define assertion types used by the identity asserter to determine trust.

If WebLogic services are invoked using SAML secured webservices, then it is important to configure WebLogic with all relevant SAML aspects. This means that for each type of incoming call, a so-called SAML profile must be created and registered. A SAML profile contains all information necessary to work with this type of SAML assertion, e.g. profile name, issuer-uri, signing key information and more.

It is possible in WebLogic to configure a list of certificates that will be trusted. The list contains used for validating assertions (WSS/Sender-Vouches) or used for verifying signatures on SAML protocol elements (Browser/POST).

Note that the certificates that can be imported must be in the DER format and cannot be placed in the default WebLogic keystore.

IMPORTANT note: The following methods for creating an asserting party must be called on the RUNTIME MBean tree. The method for creating the identity asserter must be called on the edit MBean tree. This has another impact on programs using these methods. You need to create the identity asserter first on the edit MBean tree, then you need to restart the AdminServer so that the identity asserter gets copied to the runtime MBean tree (restart is required!), and then finally you can create the asserting party.

Example of the configuration of the SAML identity asserter and an asserting party:

💾 identity_asserter_configuration_jmx

```
public ObjectName createAssertingParty(String providerName, Properties myProps)
                throws WLSAutomationException
{
  try
  {
    ObjectName securityRealmMBean =new ObjectName("Security:Name="+realmName);

    ObjectName myIdentityAsserter = (ObjectName)myJMXWrapper.invoke(securityRealmMBean,
        "lookupAuthenticationProvider",
        new Object[]{new String(providerName)},
        new String[]{String.class.getName()});
```

```
        // CreateAssertingParty
        SAMLAssertingParty mySAMLAssertingParty =(SAMLAssertingParty)myJMXWrapper.invoke(
                myIdentityAsserter,
                "newAssertingParty",new Object[0],new String[0]);

        // setAssertingPartyValues
        setAssertingPartyValues(mySAMLAssertingParty, myProps);

        // send object back to JMX Server
        // note that we need to send back an Oracle specific object !
        String[] signature = new String[]{
                            "weblogic.security.providers.saml.registry.SAMLAssertingParty"};
        Object[] myValues  = new Object[]{mySAMLAssertingParty};

        myJMXWrapper.invoke(myIdentityAsserter,"addAssertingParty",myValues,signature);

        return myIdentityAsserter;
    }
    catch(Exception ex) {
      throw new WLSAutomationException(ex);
    }
  }
}
```

Setting the values of the asserting party:

set_values_asserting_party_jmx

```
private void setAssertingPartyValues(SAMLAssertingParty mySAMLAssertingParty, Properties myProps)
            throws WLSAutomationException    {
      String nextValue = null;
      try {
            nextValue = (String)myProps.get("ASSERTERV2_ASSERTIONRETRIEVAL_URL");
            if (nextValue != null && !nextValue.equals(""))
              mySAMLAssertingParty.setAssertionRetrievalURL(nextValue);
            nextValue = (String)myProps.get("ASSERTERV2_AUDIENCE_URI");
            if (nextValue != null && !nextValue.equals(""))
                mySAMLAssertingParty.setAudienceURI(nextValue);
            nextValue = (String)myProps.get("ASSERTERV2_ASSERTION_SIGNING_CERTALIAS");
            if (nextValue != null && !nextValue.equals(""))
              mySAMLAssertingParty.setAssertionSigningCertAlias(nextValue);
            nextValue = (String)myProps.get("ASSERTERV2_DESCRIPTION");
            if (nextValue != null && !nextValue.equals(""))
                mySAMLAssertingParty.setDescription(nextValue);
            nextValue = (String)myProps.get("ASSERTERV2_ENABLED");
            if (nextValue != null && !nextValue.equals(""))
                mySAMLAssertingParty.setEnabled(new Boolean(nextValue));
            nextValue = (String)myProps.get("ASSERTERV2_GROUPSATTRIBUTEENABLED");
            if (nextValue != null && !nextValue.equals(""))
                mySAMLAssertingParty.setGroupsAttributeEnabled(new Boolean(nextValue));
            nextValue = (String)myProps.get("ASSERTERV2_INTERSITETRANSFER_URL");
            if (nextValue != null && !nextValue.equals(""))
              mySAMLAssertingParty.setIntersiteTransferURL(nextValue);
            nextValue = (String)myProps.get("ASSERTERV2_INTERSITETRANSFER_PARAMS");
            if (nextValue != null && !nextValue.equals(""))
            {
                String[] p = new String[1];
                p[0] = nextValue;
                mySAMLAssertingParty.setIntersiteTransferParams(p); //  Array of values expected
            }
            nextValue = (String)myProps.get("ASSERTERV2_ISSUER_URI");
            if (nextValue != null && !nextValue.equals(""))
                mySAMLAssertingParty.setIssuerURI(nextValue);
            nextValue = (String)myProps.get("ASSERTERV2_NAMEMAPPER_CLASS");
            if (nextValue != null && !nextValue.equals(""))
                mySAMLAssertingParty.setNameMapperClass(nextValue);
            nextValue = (String)myProps.get("ASSERTERV2_PROFILE");
            if (nextValue != null && !nextValue.equals(""))
                mySAMLAssertingParty.setProfile(nextValue);
            nextValue = (String)myProps.get("ASSERTERV2_PROTOCOL_SIGNING_CERTALIAS");
            if (nextValue != null && !nextValue.equals(""))
              mySAMLAssertingParty.setProtocolSigningCertAlias(nextValue);
            nextValue = (String)myProps.get("ASSERTERV2_REDIRECT_URIS");
            if (nextValue != null && !nextValue.equals(""))
            {
                String[] p = new String[1];
                p[0] = nextValue;
```

```
                 mySAMLAssertingParty.setRedirectURIs(p);  //  Array of values expected
            }
            nextValue = (String)myProps.get("ASSERTERV2_SIGNED_ASSERTIONS");
            if (nextValue != null && !nextValue.equals(""))
                mySAMLAssertingParty.setSignedAssertions(new Boolean(nextValue));
            nextValue = (String)myProps.get("ASSERTERV2_SOURCE_ID");
            if (nextValue != null && !nextValue.equals(""))
                mySAMLAssertingParty.setSourceId(nextValue);
            nextValue = (String)myProps.get("ASSERTERV2_TARGET_URL");
            if (nextValue != null && !nextValue.equals(""))
                mySAMLAssertingParty.setTargetURL(nextValue);
            nextValue = (String)myProps.get("ASSERTERV2_VIRTUAL_USER_ENABLED");
            if (nextValue != null && !nextValue.equals(""))
                mySAMLAssertingParty.setVirtualUserEnabled(new Boolean(nextValue));

    }
    catch(Exception ex) {
        throw new WLSAutomationException(ex);
    }
}
```

Authorization Provider

Authorization is the process where a decision is made to whether the actual user has the permission to access the requested resource(s). Authorization is responsible for controlling access to resources based on different information, such as user identity. By default, security realms in newly-created domains include the XACML authorization provider.

The following is an example for creating an authorization provider:

💾 create_authorization_provider_jmx

```
public ObjectName createAuthorizer(String providerName, String providerType)
              throws WLSAutomationException {
  try
  {
    ObjectName securityRealmMBean =new ObjectName("Security:Name="+realmName);

    // Operation: javax.management.ObjectName  lookupMailSession(name:java.lang.String  )
    ObjectName myAuthorizerMBean = (ObjectName)myJMXWrapper.invoke(securityRealmMBean,
              "lookupAuthorizer",
              new Object[]{new String(providerName)},
              new String[]{String.class.getName()});
    if (myAuthorizerMBean==null)
    {
      // create
      if (providerType==null)
        myAuthorizerMBean = (ObjectName)myJMXWrapper.invoke(securityRealmMBean,
                  "createAuthorizer",
                  new Object[]{providerName},
                  new String[]{String.class.getName()});
      else
        myAuthorizerMBean = (ObjectName)myJMXWrapper.invoke(securityRealmMBean,
                  "createAuthorizer",
                  new Object[]{providerName, providerType},
                  new String[]{String.class.getName(),String.class.getName()});

      // now do configuration
      // TO DO
      return myAuthorizerMBean;
    }
    else
      throw new WLSAutomationException("Authorizer with name "+providerName+
              " already exist  -  cannot create !");
  }
  catch(Exception ex) {
    throw new WLSAutomationException(ex);
  }
```

```
    }
```

Next is an example for creating the default XACML authorizer:

```
public ObjectName createDefaultXACMLAuthorizationProvider(String providerName)
                throws WLSAutomationException
{
  try
  {
    // create identity asserter
    return createAuthorizer(providerName,
                        "weblogic.security.providers.xacml.authorization.XACMLAuthorizer");
  }
  catch(Exception ex) {
    throw new WLSAutomationException(ex);
  }
}
```

Password Validation

For security reasons, companies can define password policies such as minimum length or maximum number of alphabetic, numeric, or non-alphanumeric characters required. WebLogic must be able to enforce the company policies. In a security realm, this is the job of a Password Validation provider. This is always invoked when a password is created or updated. The Password Validation provider then checks if the new password meets the implemented or configured policies. If this is not the case, the password will be rejected. By default, the Default Authentication provider requires a minimum password length of 8 characters. This can be customized.

Example for creating a password validator:

💾 create_password_validator_jmx

```
public ObjectName createPasswordValidator(String passwordValidatorName, String passwordValidatorType)
                throws WLSAutomationException  {
  try {
    ObjectName securityRealmMBean =new ObjectName("Security:Name="+realmName);

    // Operation: javax.management.ObjectName  lookupMailSession(name:java.lang.String   )
    ObjectName myPasswordValidatorMBean = (ObjectName)myJMXWrapper.invoke(securityRealmMBean,
                "lookupPasswordValidator",
                new Object[]{new String(passwordValidatorName)},
                new String[]{String.class.getName()});
    if (myPasswordValidatorMBean==null)
    {
      // create
      if (passwordValidatorType==null)
        myPasswordValidatorMBean = (ObjectName)myJMXWrapper.invoke(securityRealmMBean,
                    "createPasswordValidator",
                    new Object[]{passwordValidatorName},
                    new String[]{String.class.getName()});
      else
        myPasswordValidatorMBean = (ObjectName)myJMXWrapper.invoke(securityRealmMBean,
                    "createPasswordValidator",
                    new Object[]{passwordValidatorName, passwordValidatorType},
                    new String[]{String.class.getName(),String.class.getName()});
      return myPasswordValidatorMBean;
    }
    else
      throw new WLSAutomationException("PasswordValidator with name "+passwordValidatorName+
                        " already exist  -  cannot create !");
  }
  catch(Exception ex) {
```

```
            throw new WLSAutomationException(ex);
        }
    }
```

Example for creating the default password validator:

```
public ObjectName createDefaultPasswordValidator(String providerName)  throws WLSAutomationException
{
    try {
        // create identity asserter
        return createPasswordValidator(providerName,
            "com.bea.security.providers.authentication.passwordvalidator.SystemPasswordValidator");
    }
    catch(Exception ex) {
        throw new WLSAutomationException(ex);
    }
}
```

After creation, the validator can be configured. The default system validator offers a wide range of configuration options, including password length, min/max of character types, password can contain username yes/no, and more.

The following example sets a password policy where each password must have at least 5 alphabetical characters, minimum number of upper case and lower case characters to 2, and in addition restrict the usage of EACH character to 3:

```
ObjectName myPasswordvalidator= createDefaultPasswordValidator("MyDefPassWordValid") ;
myJMXWrapperRemote.setAttribute(myPasswordvalidator,
                new Attribute("MaxConsecutiveCharacters",new Integer(0)));

// set the max instance of each character to 3
myJMXWrapperRemote.setAttribute(myPasswordvalidator,
                new Attribute("MaxInstancesOfAnyCharacter",new Integer(3)));

// set the minimal number of alphabetic chars to 5
myJMXWrapperRemote.setAttribute(myPasswordvalidator,
                new Attribute("MinAlphabeticCharacters",new Integer(5)));

// set the min. of upper case characters to 2
myJMXWrapperRemote.setAttribute(myPasswordvalidator,
                new Attribute("MinUppercaseCharacters",new Integer(2)));

// set the min. of lower case characters to 2
myJMXWrapperRemote.setAttribute(myPasswordvalidator,
                new Attribute("MinLowercaseCharacters",new Integer(2)));
```

Adjudication

If more than one authorization provider is configured in the domain, it might be possible that different providers will decide differently. In this case, the server has a conflict that needs to be solved. This is the job for an adjudication provider.

Adjudication involves resolving any authorization conflicts that may occur when more than one authorization provider is configured. This is done by adding a weight to each authorization provider. Based on the access decisions and the weights, the adjudication provider will provide the final PERMIT or DENY decision.

The following is an example for creating an adjudication provider. For whatever reason, the adjudicator is the only provider type for which WebLogic does not provide a lookup method! It seems that it is also not possible to create more than one adjudicator.

🖫 create_adjudication_provider_jmx

```
public ObjectName createAdjudicator(String providerName, String providerType)
                throws WLSAutomationException
{
    try
    {
        ObjectName securityRealmMBean =new ObjectName("Security:Name="+realmName);
        ObjectName myAdjudicatorMBean = null;

        // create
        if (providerType==null)
            myAdjudicatorMBean = (ObjectName)myJMXWrapper.invoke(securityRealmMBean,
                        "createAdjudicator",
                        new Object[]{providerName},
                        new String[]{String.class.getName()});
        else
            myAdjudicatorMBean = (ObjectName)myJMXWrapper.invoke(securityRealmMBean,
                        "createAdjudicator",
                        new Object[]{providerName, providerType},
                        new String[]{String.class.getName(),String.class.getName()});
        return myAdjudicatorMBean;
    }
    catch(Exception ex) {
        throw new WLSAutomationException(ex);
    }
}
```

Creating the default adjudication provider:

```
public ObjectName createDefaultAdjudicator(String providerName)  throws WLSAutomationException
{
    try {
        // create identity asserter
        return createAdjudicator(providerName,
            "weblogic.security.providers.authorization.DefaultAdjudicator");
    }
    catch(Exception ex) {
        throw new WLSAutomationException(ex);
    }
}
```

Role Mapping

Role mapping providers will provide the list of roles granted to a subject for a given resource. Authorization providers rely on role mapping providers to provide role information in order to decide whether access is allowed or not. A WebLogic security realm is configured with the XACML Role Mapping provider by default, which uses XACML. WebLogic invokes each role mapping provider as part of an authorization decision.

Creating a role mapping provider:

💾 create_role_mapping_provider_jmx

```
public ObjectName createRoleMapper(String roleMapperName, String roleMapperType)
                 throws WLSAutomationException
{
  try
  {
    ObjectName securityRealmMBean =new ObjectName("Security:Name="+realmName);

    // Operation: javax.management.ObjectName  lookupMailSession(name:java.lang.String  )
    ObjectName myRoleMapperMBean = (ObjectName)myJMXWrapper.invoke(securityRealmMBean,
                "lookupRoleMapper",
                new Object[]{new String(roleMapperName)},
                new String[]{String.class.getName()});
    if (myRoleMapperMBean==null)
    {
      // create
      if (roleMapperType==null)
        myRoleMapperMBean = (ObjectName)myJMXWrapper.invoke(securityRealmMBean,
                "createRoleMapper",
                new Object[]{roleMapperName},
                new String[]{String.class.getName()});
      else
        myRoleMapperMBean = (ObjectName)myJMXWrapper.invoke(securityRealmMBean,
                "createRoleMapper",
                new Object[]{roleMapperName, roleMapperType},
                new String[]{String.class.getName(),String.class.getName()});
      return myRoleMapperMBean;
    }
    else
      throw new WLSAutomationException("RoleMapper with name "+roleMapperName+
              " already exist  -  cannot create !");
  }
  catch(Exception ex) {
    throw new WLSAutomationException(ex);
  }
}
```

The following example shows how to create an instance of the default role mapping provider:

```
public ObjectName createDefaultRoleMapper(String mapperName)  throws WLSAutomationException
{
  try {
    // create identity asserter
    return createRoleMapper(mapperName,
                    "weblogic.security.providers.authorization.DefaultRoleMapper");
  }
  catch(Exception ex) {
    throw new WLSAutomationException(ex);
  }
}
```

Credential Mapping

Credential mapping is used to obtain an appropriate set of credentials to authenticate users for a destination resource.

WebLogic provides a PKI credential mapping provider, which maps the security credential of the call initiator (content of the WebLogic subject) and the destination resource to a key pair or public certificate. The PKI credential mapping provider is responsible for getting security information from security keystores. Usually the subject in combination with the requested resource is used to locate the resources in the keystores.

The following is a general method for creating a credential mapper:

💾 create_credential_mapper_jmx

```
public ObjectName createCredentialMapper(String mapperName, String mapperType)
                 throws WLSAutomationException {
   try
   {
     ObjectName securityRealmMBean =new ObjectName("Security:Name="+realmName);

     // Operation: javax.management.ObjectName  lookupMailSession(name:java.lang.String  )
     ObjectName myCredentialMapperMBean = (ObjectName)myJMXWrapper.invoke(securityRealmMBean,
                 "lookupCredentialMapper",
                 new Object[]{new String(mapperName)},
                 new String[]{String.class.getName()});
     if (myCredentialMapperMBean==null) {
       // create
       if (mapperType==null)
         myCredentialMapperMBean = (ObjectName)myJMXWrapper.invoke(securityRealmMBean,
                     "createCredentialMapper",
                     new Object[]{mapperName},
                     new String[]{String.class.getName()});
       else
         myCredentialMapperMBean = (ObjectName)myJMXWrapper.invoke(securityRealmMBean,
                     "createCredentialMapper",
                     new Object[]{mapperName, mapperType},
                     new String[]{String.class.getName(),String.class.getName()});
       return myCredentialMapperMBean;
     }
     else
       throw new WLSAutomationException("CredentialMapper with name "+mapperName+
                                  " already exist  -  cannot create !");

   }
   catch(Exception ex) {
     throw new WLSAutomationException(ex);
   }
 }
```

Example for creating the default credential mapper:

```
public ObjectName createDefaultCredentialMapper(String mapperName)  throws WLSAutomationException
{
  try {
    return createCredentialMapper(mapperName,
                        "weblogic.security.providers.credentials.DefaultCredentialMapper");
  }
  catch(Exception ex) {
    throw new WLSAutomationException(ex);
  }
}
```

Example for the configuration of the PKI credential mapper:

```
public ObjectName createPKICredentialMapper(String mapperName)  throws WLSAutomationException {
    try {
      return createCredentialMapper(mapperName,
                        "weblogic.security.providers.credentials.PKICredentialMapper");
    }
    catch(Exception ex) {
      throw new WLSAutomationException(ex);
    }
  }
```

WebLogic Server also provides the SAML credential mapping provider, which can generate SAML 1.1 and 2.0 assertions for authenticated subjects based on target sites or resources.

Example for creating a SAML 2 credential mapper:

```
public ObjectName createDefaultSAMLCredentialMapper(String mapperName, Properties myProps)
                throws WLSAutomationException
{
  try
  {
    // create credential mapper
    ObjectName myCredentialMapper = createCredentialMapper(mapperName,
            "weblogic.security.providers.saml.SAMLCredentialMapperV2");

    // first of all configure credential mapper
    if (myProps.containsKey("IssuerURI"))
      myJMXWrapper.setAttribute(myCredentialMapper,
              new Attribute("IssuerURI",(String)myProps.get("IssuerURI")));
    if (myProps.containsKey("NameQualifier"))
      myJMXWrapper.setAttribute(myCredentialMapper,
              new Attribute("NameQualifier",(String)myProps.get("NameQualifier")));
    if (myProps.containsKey("SigningKeyAlias"))
      myJMXWrapper.setAttribute(myCredentialMapper,
              new Attribute("SigningKeyAlias",(String)myProps.get("SigningKeyAlias")));
    if (myProps.containsKey("SigningKeyPassPhrase"))
      myJMXWrapper.setAttribute(myCredentialMapper,
              new Attribute("SigningKeyPassPhrase",(String)myProps.get("SigningKeyPassPhrase")));
    if (myProps.containsKey("DefaultTimeToLive"))
      myJMXWrapper.setAttribute(myCredentialMapper,
              new Attribute("DefaultTimeToLive",
                            Integer.parseInt((String)myProps.get("DefaultTimeToLive"))));
    if (myProps.containsKey("DefaultTimeToLiveDelta"))
      myJMXWrapper.setAttribute(myCredentialMapper,
              new Attribute("DefaultTimeToLiveDelta",
                            Integer.parseInt((String)myProps.get("DefaultTimeToLiveDelta"))));

    return myCredentialMapper;
  }
  catch(Exception ex) {
    throw new WLSAutomationException(ex);
  }
}
```

After the credential mapper is created, it can be configured. The configuration needed include the issuer-URI in order to identify the issuer, the valid time period of the assertion, and the key (which is loaded from the keystore, therefore the alias and passphrase must be provided).

Relying Parties

A relying party used with a SAML credential mapper is an entry that relies on the information in a SAML assertion. It is possible to control how WebLogic issues SAML assertions.

The following example shows the configuration of a relying party for the SAML credential mapper. Note: The following methods for creating a relying party must be called on the RUNTIME MBean tree. The method for creating the credential mapper must be called on the edit MBean tree. This also has an impact on the programs using these methods. You need to create the credential mapper on the edit MBean tree first, then you need to restart the AdminServer so that the credential mapper gets copied to the runtime MBean tree (restart is required!), and then finally you can create the relying party:

💾 create_relying_party_jmx

```
public ObjectName createRelyingParty(String mapperName, Properties myProps)
                  throws WLSAutomationException {
  try {
     ObjectName securityRealmMBean =new ObjectName("Security:Name="+realmName);

     ObjectName myCredentialMapper = (ObjectName)myJMXWrapper.invoke(securityRealmMBean,
        "lookupCredentialMapper",
        new Object[]{new String(mapperName)},
        new String[]{String.class.getName()});

     // create relying party
        SAMLRelyingParty mySAMLRelyingParty =  (SAMLRelyingParty)
                         myJMXWrapper.invoke(myCredentialMapper,
                                             "newRelyingParty",
                                             new Object[0],new String[0]);

        // set the values
        setRelyingPartyValues(mySAMLRelyingParty,myProps);

        // send object back to JMX Server
        String[] signature = new
                        String[]{"weblogic.security.providers.saml.registry.SAMLRelyingParty"};
        Object[] myValues  = new Object[]{mySAMLRelyingParty};

        myJMXWrapper.invoke(myCredentialMapper,"addRelyingParty",myValues,signature);

        return myCredentialMapper;
     }
  catch(Exception ex) {
     throw new WLSAutomationException(ex);
  }
}
```

Now let us inspect a method to configure a relying party:

```
private void setRelyingPartyValues(SAMLRelyingParty mySAMLRelyingParty, Properties myProps)
         throws WLSAutomationException
  {
     String nextValue = null;
     try {
        nextValue = (String)myProps.get("RELYING_PARTY_KEYINFO_INCLUDED");
        if (nextValue != null && !nextValue.equals(""))
          mySAMLRelyingParty.setKeyinfoIncluded(new Boolean(nextValue));

        nextValue = (String)myProps.get("RELYING_PARTY_ASSERTION_CONSUMER_PARAMS");
        if (nextValue != null && !nextValue.equals(""))
           mySAMLRelyingParty.setAssertionConsumerParams(new String[]{nextValue});

        nextValue = (String)myProps.get("RELYING_PARTY_ASSERTIONS_CONSUMER_URL");
        if (nextValue != null && !nextValue.equals(""))
           mySAMLRelyingParty.setAssertionConsumerURL(nextValue);

        nextValue = (String)myProps.get("RELYING_PARTY_AUDIENCE_URI");
        if (nextValue != null && !nextValue.equals(""))
           mySAMLRelyingParty.setAudienceURI(nextValue);

        nextValue = (String)myProps.get("RELYING_PARTY_CREDENTIAL_CACHE_ENABLED");
        if (nextValue != null && !nextValue.equals(""))
           mySAMLRelyingParty.setCredentialCacheEnabled(new Boolean(nextValue));

        nextValue = (String)myProps.get("RELYING_PARTY_DESCRIPTION");
        if (nextValue != null && !nextValue.equals(""))
           mySAMLRelyingParty.setDescription(nextValue);

        nextValue = (String)myProps.get("RELYING_PARTY_DONOT_CACHE_CONDITION");
        if (nextValue != null && !nextValue.equals(""))
           mySAMLRelyingParty.setDoNotCacheCondition(new Boolean(nextValue));

        nextValue = (String)myProps.get("RELYING_PARTY_ENABLED");
        if (nextValue != null && !nextValue.equals(""))
           mySAMLRelyingParty.setEnabled(new Boolean(nextValue));

        nextValue = (String)myProps.get("RELYING_PARTY_GROUPSATTRIBUTE_ENABLED");
        if (nextValue != null && !nextValue.equals(""))
```

```
                    mySAMLRelyingParty.setGroupsAttributeEnabled(new Boolean(nextValue));

            nextValue = (String)myProps.get("RELYING_PARTY_NAMEMAPPER_CLASS");
            if (nextValue != null && !nextValue.equals(""))
                mySAMLRelyingParty.setNameMapperClass(nextValue);

            nextValue = (String)myProps.get("RELYING_PARTY_POSTFORM");
            if (nextValue != null && !nextValue.equals(""))
                mySAMLRelyingParty.setPostForm(nextValue);

            nextValue = (String)myProps.get("RELYING_PARTY_PROFILE");
            if (nextValue != null && !nextValue.equals(""))
                mySAMLRelyingParty.setProfile(nextValue);

            nextValue = (String)myProps.get("RELYING_PARTY_SIGNED_ASSERTIONS");
            if (nextValue != null && !nextValue.equals(""))
                mySAMLRelyingParty.setSignedAssertions(new Boolean(nextValue));

            nextValue = (String)myProps.get("RELYING_PARTY_SSLCLIENT_CERTALIAS");
            if (nextValue != null && !nextValue.equals(""))
                mySAMLRelyingParty.setSSLClientCertAlias(nextValue);

            nextValue = (String)myProps.get("RELYING_PARTY_TARGET_URL");
            if (nextValue != null && !nextValue.equals(""))
                mySAMLRelyingParty.setTargetURL(nextValue);

            nextValue = (String)myProps.get("RELYING_PARTY_TIME_TO_LIVE");
            if (nextValue != null && !nextValue.equals(""))
                mySAMLRelyingParty.setTimeToLive(Integer.parseInt(nextValue));

            nextValue = (String)myProps.get("RELYING_PARTY_TIME_TO_LIVE_OFFSET");
            if (nextValue != null && !nextValue.equals(""))
                mySAMLRelyingParty.setTimeToLiveOffset(Integer.parseInt(nextValue));
    }
    catch(Exception ex) {
        throw new WLSAutomationException(ex);
    }
}
```

The following example of creating a mapper must be called on the **edit** MBeanServer:

```
private static void testCreateSAMLCredentialMapper() throws Exception
{
    Properties myProps = new Properties();
    myProps.setProperty("IssuerURI","http://myservices.book.com/serviceURL");
    myProps.setProperty("NameQualifier","myservices.book.com");
    myProps.setProperty("DefaultTimeToLive","120");
    myProps.setProperty("DefaultTimeToLiveDelta","-10");
    myProps.setProperty("SigningKeyAlias","webservice_alias");
    myProps.setProperty("SigningKeyPassPhrase",",mypassword");

    createDefaultSAMLCredentialMapper("TestSAMLCredMapperWLSTB", myProps);
}
```

The following example of creating a relying party must be called on the **runtime** MBeanServer:

```
private static void testCreateSAMLRelyingParty() throws Exception
{
    Properties myProps = new Properties();
    myProps.setProperty("RELYING_PARTY_PROFILE","WSS/Sender-Vouches");
    myProps.setProperty("RELYING_PARTY_KEYINFO_INCLUDED","true");
    myProps.setProperty("RELYING_PARTY_DESCRIPTION","rp_wlsbook");
    myProps.setProperty("RELYING_PARTY_ENABLED","true");
    myProps.setProperty("RELYING_PARTY_GROUPSATTRIBUTE_ENABLED","false");
    myProps.setProperty("RELYING_PARTY_SIGNED_ASSERTIONS","true");
    myProps.setProperty("RELYING_PARTY_TARGET_URL","default");
    myProps.setProperty("RELYING_PARTY_TIME_TO_LIVE","100");
    myProps.setProperty("RELYING_PARTY_TIME_TO_LIVE_OFFSET","-15");

    createRelyingParty("TestSAMLCredMapperWLSTB", myProps);
}
```

Auditing

Auditing involves the collection of information about operating requests and the result of those requests. This information is stored and distributed for the purposes of non-repudiation. This means that the server will create logs that can be used to find out who has done what and when. An auditing provider is an optional component and the default realm does not have one. WebLogic offers a default provider, but your own providers can be developed.

The following shows how to create an instance of the default auditor:

💾 create_auditor_instance_jmx

```
public ObjectName createAuditor(String providerName, String providerType)
                  throws WLSAutomationException {
   try
   {
      ObjectName securityRealmMBean =new ObjectName("Security:Name="+realmName);

      // Operation: javax.management.ObjectName  lookupMailSession(name:java.lang.String  )
      ObjectName myAuditorMBean = (ObjectName)myJMXWrapper.invoke(securityRealmMBean,
                  "lookupAuditor",
                  new Object[]{new String(providerName)},
                  new String[]{String.class.getName()});
      if (myAuditorMBean==null)
      {
        // create
        if (providerType==null)
          myAuditorMBean = (ObjectName)myJMXWrapper.invoke(securityRealmMBean,
                      "createAuditor",
                      new Object[]{providerName},
                      new String[]{String.class.getName()});
        else
          myAuditorMBean = (ObjectName)myJMXWrapper.invoke(securityRealmMBean,
                      "createAuditor",
                      new Object[]{providerName, providerType},
                      new String[]{String.class.getName(),String.class.getName()});
        return myAuditorMBean;
      }
      else
        throw new WLSAutomationException("Auditor with name "+providerName+
              " already exist  -  cannot create !");

   }
   catch(Exception ex) {
      throw new WLSAutomationException(ex);
   }
}
```

Certification Paths

A standalone certificate is basically useless as anybody can create certificates. Only if a certificate is signed by a trusted authority (called CA) then a certificate becomes a secure entity. As certificate authorities (CAs) can be chained, it is important for WebLogic to ensure that a complete certificate chain is valid and trusted. WebLogic offers a Certification Path provider for this purpose. This module checks the signatures of each certificate in the chain and ensures that none of the certificates in the chain have expired. Only if this is the case AND at least one of the certificates in the chain is issued by one of the server's trusted CAs, the check of the complete chain is considered to be valid. Otherwise the check of the chain will fail.

Example for creating a certification path provider:

💾 create_certification_path_provider_jmx

```
public ObjectName createCertPathProvider(String providerName, String providerType)
                throws WLSAutomationException {
  try
  {
    ObjectName securityRealmMBean =new ObjectName("Security:Name="+realmName);

    // Operation: javax.management.ObjectName  lookupMailSession(name:java.lang.String  )
    ObjectName myCertPathProviderMBean = (ObjectName)myJMXWrapper.invoke(securityRealmMBean,
                "lookupCertPathProvider",
                new Object[]{new String(providerName)},
                new String[]{String.class.getName()});
    if (myCertPathProviderMBean==null)
    {
      // create
      if (providerType==null)
        myCertPathProviderMBean = (ObjectName)myJMXWrapper.invoke(securityRealmMBean,
                    "createCertPathProvider",
                    new Object[]{providerName},
                    new String[]{String.class.getName()});
      else
        myCertPathProviderMBean = (ObjectName)myJMXWrapper.invoke(securityRealmMBean,
                    "createCertPathProvider",
                    new Object[]{providerName, providerType},
                    new String[]{String.class.getName(),String.class.getName()});
      return myCertPathProviderMBean;
    }
    else
      throw new WLSAutomationException("CertPathProvider with name "+providerName+
                " already exist  -  cannot create !");
  }
  catch(Exception ex) {
    throw new WLSAutomationException(ex);
  }
}
```

Delete Providers

Providers that are no longer needed must be deleted. The delete method in WebLogic is called *destroyXXXProvider*. You need to navigate to your realm, lookup your provider, and then call the destroy method.

Example for deleting an authentication provider:

💾 delete_authentication_provider_jmx

```
public void deleteAuthenticationProvider(String providerName)  throws WLSAutomationException {
  try
  {
    ObjectName securityRealmMBean =new ObjectName("Security:Name="+realmName);

    // Operation: javax.management.ObjectName  lookupMailSession(name:java.lang.String  )
    ObjectName myAuthenticationProviderMBean = (ObjectName)myJMXWrapper.invoke(securityRealmMBean,
                "lookupAuthenticationProvider",
                new Object[]{new String(providerName)},
                new String[]{String.class.getName()});
    if (myAuthenticationProviderMBean!=null)
    {
      // delete MBean
```

```
        myAuthenticationProviderMBean = (ObjectName)myJMXWrapper.invoke(securityRealmMBean,
                        "destroyAuthenticationProvider",
                        new Object[]{providerName},
                        new String[]{String.class.getName()});
    }
    else
      throw new WLSAutomationException("Provider with name "+providerName+
              " does not exist  -  cannot delete !");
  }
  catch(Exception ex) {
    throw new WLSAutomationException(ex);
  }
}
```

Example for deleting an authorization provider:

💾 delete_authorization_provider_jmx

```
public void deleteAuthorizer(String authorizerName)  throws WLSAutomationException {
  try {
    ObjectName securityRealmMBean =new ObjectName("Security:Name="+realmName);

    // Operation: javax.management.ObjectName  lookupMailSession(name:java.lang.String  )
    ObjectName myAuthorizerMBean = (ObjectName)myJMXWrapper.invoke(securityRealmMBean,
                "lookupAuthorizer",
                new Object[]{new String(authorizerName)},
                new String[]{String.class.getName()});
    if (myAuthorizerMBean!=null)
    {
      // delete MBean
      myAuthorizerMBean = (ObjectName)myJMXWrapper.invoke(securityRealmMBean,
                        "destroyAuthorizer",
                        new Object[]{authorizerName},
                        new String[]{String.class.getName()});
    }
    else
      throw new WLSAutomationException("Authorizer with name "+authorizerName+
              " does not exist  -  cannot delete !");
  }
  catch(Exception ex) {
    throw new WLSAutomationException(ex);
  }
}
```

Example for deleting an adjudicator:

💾 delete_adjudicator_jmx

```
public void deleteAdjudicator(String adjudicatorName)  throws WLSAutomationException {
  try
  {
    ObjectName securityRealmMBean =new ObjectName("Security:Name="+realmName);

    // Operation: javax.management.ObjectName  lookupMailSession(name:java.lang.String  )
    ObjectName myAdjudicatorMBean = (ObjectName)myJMXWrapper.invoke(securityRealmMBean,
                "lookupAdjudicator",
                new Object[]{new String(adjudicatorName)},
                new String[]{String.class.getName()});
    if (myAdjudicatorMBean!=null) {
      // delete MBean
      myAdjudicatorMBean = (ObjectName)myJMXWrapper.invoke(securityRealmMBean,
                    "destroyAdjudicator",
                    new Object[]{adjudicatorName},
                    new String[]{String.class.getName()});
    }
    else
      throw new WLSAutomationException("Adjudicator with name "+adjudicatorName+
              " does not exist  -  cannot delete !");
  }
  catch(Exception ex) {
    throw new WLSAutomationException(ex);
  }
}
```

Example for deleting an auditor:

💾 delete_auditor_jmx

```
public void deleteAuditor(String auditorName)  throws WLSAutomationException {
   try {
      ObjectName securityRealmMBean =new ObjectName("Security:Name="+realmName);

      // Operation: javax.management.ObjectName  lookupMailSession(name:java.lang.String  )
      ObjectName myAuditorMBean = (ObjectName)myJMXWrapper.invoke(securityRealmMBean,
                     "lookupAuditor",
                     new Object[]{new String(auditorName)},
                     new String[]{String.class.getName()});
      if (myAuditorMBean!=null) {
        // delete MBean
        myAuditorMBean = (ObjectName)myJMXWrapper.invoke(securityRealmMBean,
                           "destroyAuditor",
                           new Object[]{auditorName},
                           new String[]{String.class.getName()});
      }
      else
        throw new WLSAutomationException("Auditor with name "+auditorName+
                " does not exist  -  cannot delete !");
   }
   catch(Exception ex) {
      throw new WLSAutomationException(ex);
   }
}
```

Example for deleting a certificate path provider:

💾 delete_certificate_path_provider_jmx

```
public void deleteCertPathProvider(String providerName)  throws WLSAutomationException {
   try {
      ObjectName securityRealmMBean =new ObjectName("Security:Name="+realmName);

      // Operation: javax.management.ObjectName  lookupMailSession(name:java.lang.String  )
      ObjectName myCertPathProviderMBean = (ObjectName)myJMXWrapper.invoke(securityRealmMBean,
                     "lookupCertPathProvider",
                     new Object[]{new String(providerName)},
                     new String[]{String.class.getName()});
      if (myCertPathProviderMBean!=null)
      {
        // delete MBean
        myCertPathProviderMBean = (ObjectName)myJMXWrapper.invoke(securityRealmMBean,
                           "destroyCertPathProvider",
                           new Object[]{providerName},
                           new String[]{String.class.getName()});
      }
      else
        throw new WLSAutomationException("CertPathProvider with name "+providerName+
                " does not exist  -  cannot delete !");
   }
   catch(Exception ex) {
      throw new WLSAutomationException(ex);
   }
}
```

Example for deleting a credential mapper:

💾 delete_credential_mapper_jmx

```
public void deleteCredentialMapper(String mapperName)  throws WLSAutomationException {
   try {
      ObjectName securityRealmMBean =new ObjectName("Security:Name="+realmName);

      // Operation: javax.management.ObjectName  lookupMailSession(name:java.lang.String  )
      ObjectName myCredentialMapperMBean = (ObjectName)myJMXWrapper.invoke(securityRealmMBean,
                     "lookupCredentialMapper",
                     new Object[]{new String(mapperName)},
```

```
                        new String[]{String.class.getName()});
        if (myCredentialMapperMBean!=null)
        {
            // delete MBean
            myCredentialMapperMBean = (ObjectName)myJMXWrapper.invoke(securityRealmMBean,
                        "destroyCredentialMapper",
                        new Object[]{mapperName},
                        new String[]{String.class.getName()});
        }
        else
            throw new WLSAutomationException("CredentialMapper with name "+mapperName+
                    " does not exist  - cannot delete !");

    }
    catch(Exception ex) {
        throw new WLSAutomationException(ex);
    }
}
```

Example for deleting a password validator:

🔲 **delete_password_validator_jmx**

```
public void deletePasswordValidator(String passwordValidatorName)   throws WLSAutomationException
{
    try
    {
        ObjectName securityRealmMBean =new ObjectName("Security:Name="+realmName);

        // Operation: javax.management.ObjectName  lookupMailSession(name:java.lang.String  )
        ObjectName myPasswordValidatorMBean = (ObjectName)myJMXWrapper.invoke(securityRealmMBean,
                    "lookupPasswordValidator",
                    new Object[]{new String(passwordValidatorName)},
                    new String[]{String.class.getName()});
        if (myPasswordValidatorMBean!=null)
        {
            // delete MBean
            myPasswordValidatorMBean = (ObjectName)myJMXWrapper.invoke(securityRealmMBean,
                        "destroyPasswordValidator",
                        new Object[]{passwordValidatorName},
                        new String[]{String.class.getName()});
        }
        else
            throw new WLSAutomationException("PasswordValidator with name "+passwordValidatorName+
                                        " does not exist  - cannot delete !");

    }
    catch(Exception ex) {
        throw new WLSAutomationException(ex);
    }
}
```

Example for deleting a role mapper:

🔲 **delete_role_mapper_jmx**

```
public void deleteRoleMapper(String roleMapperName)   throws WLSAutomationException {
    try {
        ObjectName securityRealmMBean =new ObjectName("Security:Name="+realmName);

        // Operation: javax.management.ObjectName  lookupMailSession(name:java.lang.String  )
        ObjectName myRoleMapperMBean = (ObjectName)myJMXWrapper.invoke(securityRealmMBean,
                    "lookupRoleMapper",
                    new Object[]{new String(roleMapperName)},
                    new String[]{String.class.getName()});
        if (myRoleMapperMBean!=null)
        {
            // delete MBean
            myRoleMapperMBean = (ObjectName)myJMXWrapper.invoke(securityRealmMBean,
                        "destroyRoleMapper",
                        new Object[]{roleMapperName},
                        new String[]{String.class.getName()});
        }
```

```
        else
          throw new WLSAutomationException("RoleMapper with name "+roleMapperName+
                " does not exist  -  cannot delete !");
    }
    catch(Exception ex) {
       throw new WLSAutomationException(ex);
    }
  }
```

Migrating Security Data

Security realms in a WebLogic domain hold different kinds of security data, like policies, users, groups, role expressions and more. If you setup a new domain, you may want to clone the security data from an existing domain, e.g. clone UAT to production. Using this feature you a) do not need to configure all the data again and b) can be sure that you are using the same set of data that you have been using for load and performance tests in the lower level environment.

Export Data from Security Realms

It is possible to export different aspects of the security realm (authentication, authorization, credential map, and role data) into a file. This enables you to test security configurations and then port them to other domains without the need of recreating all the security data. You can either export all data or selected data from selected providers.

The following is an example for exporting authentication data based on XACML:

🖫   export_authentication_data_jmx

```
public void exportAuthenticatorData(String securityProviderName, String fileName)
          throws WLSAutomationException {
    try {
      ObjectName securityRealmMBean =new ObjectName("Security:Name="+realmName);

      ObjectName myAuthenticationProviderMBean = (ObjectName)myJMXWrapper.invoke(securityRealmMBean,
                "lookupAuthenticationProvider",
                new Object[]{new String(securityProviderName)},
                new String[]{String.class.getName()});
      if (myAuthenticationProviderMBean!=null)
      {
            // export DefaultAtn type of data
            myJMXWrapper.invoke(myAuthenticationProviderMBean, "exportData",
                  new Object[]{"DefaultAtn",fileName, new Properties()},
                  new String[]{String.class.getName(),String.class.getName(),
                              Properties.class.getName()});
      }
      else
         throw new WLSAutomationException("Provider with name "+securityProviderName+
                  " does not exist !");
    }
    catch(Exception ex) {
       throw new WLSAutomationException(ex);
    }
}
```

Next is an example for exporting authorizer data based on XACML:

💾 export_authorizer_data_jmx

```
public void exportAuthorizerData(String securityProviderName, String fileName)
            throws WLSAutomationException {
    try {
        ObjectName securityRealmMBean =new ObjectName("Security:Name="+realmName);

        ObjectName myAuthorizerMBean = (ObjectName)myJMXWrapper.invoke(securityRealmMBean,
                    "lookupAuthorizer",
                    new Object[]{new String(securityProviderName)},
                    new String[]{String.class.getName()});
        if (myAuthorizerMBean!=null)
        {
            // export DefaultAtn type of data
            myJMXWrapper.invoke(myAuthorizerMBean, "exportData",
                    new Object[]{"XACML",fileName, new Properties()},
                    new String[]{String.class.getName(),String.class.getName(),
                            Properties.class.getName()});
        }
        else
            throw new WLSAutomationException("Authorizer with name "+securityProviderName+
                    " does not exist !");
    }
    catch(Exception ex) {
        throw new WLSAutomationException(ex);
    }
}
```

Example for exporting rolemapper data; type can either be XACML or DefaultRoles:

💾 export_rolemapper_data_jmx

```
public void exportRoleMapperData(String roleMapperName, String exportFormat, String fileName)
            throws WLSAutomationException
{
    try
    {
        ObjectName securityRealmMBean =new ObjectName("Security:Name="+realmName);

        ObjectName myRoleMapperMBean = (ObjectName)myJMXWrapper.invoke(securityRealmMBean,
                "lookupRoleMapper",
                new Object[]{new String(roleMapperName)},
                new String[]{String.class.getName()});
        if (myRoleMapperMBean!=null)
        {
            // export <exportFormat> type of data
            // cmo.exportData(exportFormat,fileName,Properties())
            myJMXWrapper.invoke(myRoleMapperMBean, "exportData",
                    new Object[]{exportFormat,fileName, new Properties()},
                    new String[]{String.class.getName(),String.class.getName(),
                            Properties.class.getName()});
        }
        else
            throw new WLSAutomationException("RoleMapper : "+roleMapperName+" does not exist !");
    }
    catch(Exception ex) {
        throw new WLSAutomationException(ex);
    }
}
```

Import Data into Security Realms

This is the contrary operation to export data, which allows you to import security data
into a realm or certain providers. Data can be imported into a realm that affects all
providers or all data can be imported into the selected providers. This depends on the
scope of the data export.

You can use JMX to export and import data from a security provider. In order to use this functionality, you need to get access the RuntimeMBean for the security provider and use its *importData* or *exportData* operation.

The following is an example for importing authentication data based on XACML:

💾 import_authentication_data_jmx

```
public void importAuthenticatorData(String securityProviderName, String fileName)
            throws WLSAutomationException
{
    try
    {
        ObjectName securityRealmMBean =new ObjectName("Security:Name="+realmName);

        ObjectName myAuthenticationProviderMBean = (ObjectName)myJMXWrapper.invoke(securityRealmMBean,
                "lookupAuthenticationProvider",
                new Object[]{new String(securityProviderName)},
                new String[]{String.class.getName()});
        if (myAuthenticationProviderMBean!=null)
        {
                // import DefaultAtn type of data
                myJMXWrapper.invoke(myAuthenticationProviderMBean,"importData",
                    new Object[]{"DefaultAtn",fileName, new Properties()},
                    new String[]{String.class.getName(),String.class.getName(),
                                Properties.class.getName()});
        }
        else
            throw new WLSAutomationException("Provider: "+securityProviderName+" does not exist !");
    }
    catch(Exception ex) {
        throw new WLSAutomationException(ex);
    }
}
```

Next is an example for importing authorizer data based on XACML:

💾 import_authorizer_data_jmx

```
public void importAuthorizerData(String securityProviderName, String fileName)
            throws WLSAutomationException
{
    try
    {
        ObjectName securityRealmMBean =new ObjectName("Security:Name="+realmName);

        ObjectName myAuthorizerMBean = (ObjectName)myJMXWrapper.invoke(securityRealmMBean,
                "lookupAuthorizer",
                new Object[]{new String(securityProviderName)},
                new String[]{String.class.getName()});
        if (myAuthorizerMBean!=null)
        {
                // # export DefaultAtn type of data
                myJMXWrapper.invoke(myAuthorizerMBean, "importData",
                    new Object[]{"XACML",fileName, new Properties()},
                    new String[]{String.class.getName(),String.class.getName(),
                                Properties.class.getName()});
        }
        else
            throw new WLSAutomationException("Authorizer:"+securityProviderName+"  does not exist !");
    }
    catch(Exception ex) {
        throw new WLSAutomationException(ex);
    }
}
```

Example for importing rolemapper data; type can either be XACML or DefaultRoles:

```
public void importRoleMapperData(String roleMapperName, String exportFormat, String fileName)
        throws WLSAutomationException
{
  try
  {
    ObjectName securityRealmMBean =new ObjectName("Security:Name="+realmName);

    ObjectName myRoleMapperMBean = (ObjectName)myJMXWrapper.invoke(securityRealmMBean,
            "lookupRoleMapper",
            new Object[]{new String(roleMapperName)},
            new String[]{String.class.getName()});
    if (myRoleMapperMBean!=null)
    {
        // import <exportFormat> type of data
        myJMXWrapper.invoke(myRoleMapperMBean,"importData",
            new Object[]{exportFormat,fileName, new Properties()},
            new String[]{String.class.getName(),String.class.getName(),
                    Properties.class.getName()});
    }
    else
        throw new WLSAutomationException("RoleMapper "+roleMapperName+"  does not exist !");

  }
  catch(Exception ex) {
    throw new WLSAutomationException(ex);
  }
}
```

Working with Policies

Working with policies is a broad and complicated topic that could easily fill a book of its own. This section discusses a simple example of how to install an XACML policy into an authentication provider.

Import a Security Policy

By default, security policies are based on XACML. See *Chapter 7: Advanced Security with XACML* for a more detailed description on XACML and policies. It is sometimes necessary to grant special users more rights than they normally would have based on their roles and groups.

Example: Starting, stopping, and other administration operations on a datasource require "Administrator" rights or at least "Operator" rights. It might be necessary in some cases to do this from the application. The following example grants the user "SpecialTestUser" the right to administer the datasource "Testdatasource", but only between 9PM and 5AM.

This example shows that it is possible to grant application users the right to do certain administration tasks, and that it is even possible to restrict these rights to certain times (dates and/or hours). For a better understanding, this example also shows how the installed policy will be displayed in the WebLogic console.

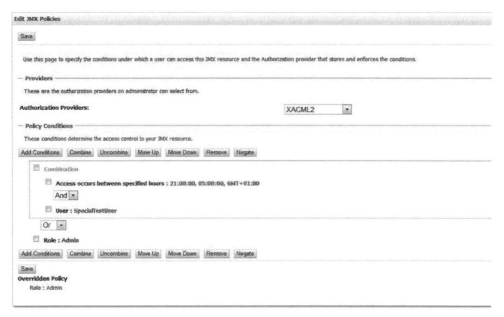

Figure 15.1: *Policy displayed in the WebLogic console*

The following JMX code can be used to install the policy into the authorization provider. As there is no easy way to check if a specific policy is installed, the code will first try to add the policy to the security provider. In case of an exception, the following code will modify the policy. Note that "catch(Exception ex)" is done here to keep the code simple. Many different exceptions may occur, such as policy invalid or others; real production code must therefore have better exception handling.

🖫 install_policy_jmx

```
// Main security realm MBean
ObjectName securityRealmMBean =new ObjectName("Security:Name=myrealm");

// get correct authorizer
myAuthorizationMBean = (ObjectName)myJMXWrapper.invoke(securityRealmMBean, "lookupAuthorizer",
                        new Object[]{new String(authorizationProviderName)},
                        new String[]{String.class.getName()});

if (myAuthorizationMBean!=null) {
   try {
      myJMXWrapper.invoke(myAuthorizationMBean,
         "addPolicy",
         new Object[]{myPolicy},
         new String[]{String.class.getName()});
   }
   catch( Exception ex) {
      System.out.println("Policy already exists - will modify it !");
      myJMXWrapper.invoke(myAuthorizationMBean,
         "modifyPolicy",
         new Object[]{myPolicy},
         new String[]{String.class.getName()});
   }
}
else
   System.out.println("AuthorizationProvider: "+authorizationProviderName+"  does not exist !");
```

The following XML code depicts the XACML policy that can be used. Note that "Testdatasource" for the datasource and "SpecialTestUser" for the username must be changed if you want to use it. Also, remember that it is necessary to apply this policy for each datasource individually.

💾 XACML_policy

```
<Policy
PolicyId="urn:bea:xacml:2.0:entitlement:resource:type@E@Fjmx@G@M@Ooperation@Einvoke@M@Oapplication@ETestDatasource@M@Om
beanType@Eweblogic.management.runtime.JDBCDataSourceRuntimeMBean" RuleCombiningAlgId="urn:oasis:names:tc:xacml:1.0:rule-
combining-algorithm:first-applicable">

<Description>{?weblogic.entitlement.rules.TimePredicate(21:0:0,5:0:0,GMT+01:00}&amp;Usr(SpecialTestUser)}|Rol(Admin)</D
escription>
  <Target>
    <Resources>
      <Resource>
        <ResourceMatch MatchId="urn:oasis:names:tc:xacml:1.0:function:string-equal">
          <AttributeValue DataType="http://www.w3.org/2001/XMLSchema#string">
            type=&lt;jmx&gt;, operation-invoke, application-TestDatasource,
mbeanType=weblogic.management.runtime.JDBCDataSourceRuntimeMBean
          </AttributeValue>
          <ResourceAttributeDesignator AttributeId="urn:oasis:names:tc:xacml:2.0:resource:resource-ancestor-or-self"
DataType="http://www.w3.org/2001/XMLSchema#string" MustBePresent="true"/>
        </ResourceMatch>
      </Resource>
    </Resources>
  </Target>
  <Rule RuleId="primary-rule" Effect="Permit">
    <Condition>
      <Apply FunctionId="urn:oasis:names:tc:xacml:1.0:function:or">
        <Apply FunctionId="urn:oasis:names:tc:xacml:1.0:function:and">
          <Apply FunctionId="urn:oasis:names:tc:xacml:1.0:function:or">
            <Apply FunctionId="urn:oasis:names:tc:xacml:1.0:function:integer-greater-than-or-equal">
              <Apply FunctionId="urn:bea:xacml:2.0:function:dateTime-secondsOfDay">
                <Apply FunctionId="urn:oasis:names:tc:xacml:1.0:function:dateTime-subtract-dayTimeDuration">
                  <Apply FunctionId="urn:oasis:names:tc:xacml:1.0:function:dateTime-add-dayTimeDuration">
                    <Apply FunctionId="urn:oasis:names:tc:xacml:1.0:function:dateTime-one-and-only">
                      <EnvironmentAttributeDesignator AttributeId="urn:oasis:names:tc:xacml:1.0:environment:current-
dateTime" DataType="http://www.w3.org/2001/XMLSchema#dateTime" MustBePresent="true"/>
                    </Apply>
                    <AttributeValue DataType="http://www.w3.org/TR/2002/WD-xquery-operators-
20020816#dayTimeDuration">PT1H</AttributeValue>
                  </Apply>
                  <Apply FunctionId="urn:bea:xacml:2.0:function:dayTimeDuration-timeZoneOffset"></Apply>
                </Apply>
              </Apply>
              <AttributeValue DataType="http://www.w3.org/2001/XMLSchema#integer">75600</AttributeValue>
            </Apply>
            <Apply FunctionId="urn:oasis:names:tc:xacml:1.0:function:integer-less-than">
              <Apply FunctionId="urn:bea:xacml:2.0:function:dateTime-secondsOfDay">
                <Apply FunctionId="urn:oasis:names:tc:xacml:1.0:function:dateTime-subtract-dayTimeDuration">
                  <Apply FunctionId="urn:oasis:names:tc:xacml:1.0:function:dateTime-add-dayTimeDuration">
                    <Apply FunctionId="urn:oasis:names:tc:xacml:1.0:function:dateTime-one-and-only">
                      <EnvironmentAttributeDesignator AttributeId="urn:oasis:names:tc:xacml:1.0:environment:current-
dateTime" DataType="http://www.w3.org/2001/XMLSchema#dateTime" MustBePresent="true"/>
                    </Apply>
                    <AttributeValue DataType="http://www.w3.org/TR/2002/WD-xquery-operators-
20020816#dayTimeDuration">PT1H</AttributeValue>
                  </Apply>
                  <Apply FunctionId="urn:bea:xacml:2.0:function:dayTimeDuration-timeZoneOffset"></Apply>
                </Apply>
              </Apply>
              <AttributeValue DataType="http://www.w3.org/2001/XMLSchema#integer">18000</AttributeValue>
            </Apply>
          </Apply>
          <Apply FunctionId="urn:oasis:names:tc:xacml:1.0:function:string-is-in">
            <AttributeValue DataType="http://www.w3.org/2001/XMLSchema#string">
              SpecialTestUser
            </AttributeValue>
            <SubjectAttributeDesignator AttributeId="urn:oasis:names:tc:xacml:1.0:subject:subject-id"
DataType="http://www.w3.org/2001/XMLSchema#string"/>
          </Apply>
        </Apply>
        <Apply FunctionId="urn:oasis:names:tc:xacml:1.0:function:string-is-in">
          <AttributeValue DataType="http://www.w3.org/2001/XMLSchema#string">Admin</AttributeValue>
          <SubjectAttributeDesignator AttributeId="urn:oasis:names:tc:xacml:2.0:subject:role"
DataType="http://www.w3.org/2001/XMLSchema#string"/>
        </Apply>
      </Apply>
    </Condition>
  </Rule>
  <Rule RuleId="deny-rule" Effect="Deny"></Rule>
</Policy>
```

Access Security - Words of Warning

Every security has some weak points. This section will discuss two possible ways that allow application developers to circumvent security restrictions and gain more access than they should have. These examples have been added to the book in order to make administrators aware of these possibilities but **not** for you to use them!

Password Security

In *Chapter 7* we discussed the possibility to decrypt the user/password that is used for the server to authenticate itself. This user is a member of the "Administrator" group. Well the script shown in *Chapter 7* has the dependency that you need to access the machine and file system and also read access to the domain files, which is not so often the case.

It is of course also possible to incorporate this code as standard Java code into your server-side application. One option to use this code is to implement a startup class that decrypts the user/password of the boot.properties and prints it to the log (see example). If a user really wants to hide this action, these log entries will be masked so that administrators won't see them. Even advanced users could use a WebService call or something else to even send the unencrypted credentials to somewhere.

Example of a startup class:

💾 startup_class_jmx

```
public class StartSpecialTest {

    public static void main(String[] args) {
        try {
            // get access to the MBean server for root directory and server-name
            MBeanServer server = (MBeanServer)
                        (new InitialContext()).lookup("java:comp/jmx/runtime");
            ObjectName service = new ObjectName("com.bea:Name=RuntimeService,"+
                            "Type=weblogic.management.mbeanservers.runtime.RuntimeServiceMBean");
            ObjectName domainMBean =(ObjectName) server.getAttribute(service,"DomainConfiguration");
            String serverName = (String) server.getAttribute(service,"ServerName");
            String domainRoot = (String) server.getAttribute(domainMBean,"RootDirectory");

            // test if boot id file has been changed (e.g. when starting via nodemanager)
            String bootIdentityFile = System.getProperty("weblogic.system.BootIdentityFile");

            // if not set, construct default one with the values from the mbean tree
            if (bootIdentityFile==null)  // create filename from mbean information
                bootIdentityFile = domainRoot + "/servers/"+serverName+"/security/boot.properties";

            // load boot properties file
            Properties bootProperties = new Properties();
            bootProperties.load(new FileInputStream(bootIdentityFile));

            ClearOrEncryptedService ces = new ClearOrEncryptedService(
                                SerializedSystemIni.getEncryptionService(domainRoot));

            // decrypt user
            System.out.println("SPECIAL: User="+ces.decrypt(bootProperties.getProperty("username")));

            // decrypt password
```

```
            System.out.println("SPECIAL: PW  ="+ces.decrypt(bootProperties.getProperty("password")));
        }
        catch (Exception e) {
            // ignore exceptions to avoid traces in the logs ;-)
        }
    }
}
```

In order to use this functionality, a startup class (in the config.xml) must be defined. (Of course you can use WLST or JMX to create this entry as already discussed in the book):

```
<startup-class>
   <name>StartSpecialTest</name>
   <target>AdminServer</target>
   <class-name> com.wlsautomation.specialtest.StartSpecialTest</class-name>
</startup-class>
```

As this code does not depend on any specific privileges, it is even possible to hide this code in a servlet or ejb call so that the user can get the information back. As you know, the MBean tree (in case of a Managed-Server) also offers all the information about the admin location and port, which could also be retrieved. The code is also flexible enough to run in the AdminServer (usually default boot.properties location) and also in the Managed-Server where the boot.properties location might be different when the server was started by a NodeManager.

Solution for the administrators: This code will always run. There is not much administrators can do against it. However, there are some steps that can be taken by the infrastructure layout in order to make this information close to useless:

- Use admin channels for the administrative communication. This means that the user will not be able to use the gained access information to access over the same network endpoint via HTTP or T3 (console on AdminServers or WLST/JMX on all servers).

- Never allow application deployment and/or startup classes to be targeted on AdminServers. Exceptions must have good reasons and code reviews.

- Use firewall, network separation, or connection filters to restrict admin access (admin channels) to the administration group only.

- Log all administrative access (with client information!) and monitor those logs for strange/unexpected client addresses.

- Disallow file access from non-WebLogic classes.

Create Your Own Admin Access

The method above to decrypt the admin access is actually in the legal grey area. There is another option that can be used in a startup class of WebLogic. In this case you have to use a startup class. The following example cannot be used in a servlet or ejb implementation due to the fact that the code must run with administrator privileges, and for startup classes this is the case.

The idea is that inside the startup class I can create my own admin user and add it to the administrator group. The code can be written in a way that this startup functionality will only be executed under certain circumstances, which means that you even have a sleeping back door. A complementary shutdown class can then be used to remove the user from the admin group and even delete the user when the AdminServer is going down. This reduces the risk that an audit run will detect this. All administrators should be aware that of course the name of the startup class in this case will be on purpose misleading - as in my following example. So never trust startup classes unless you know exactly what they are doing!

Example of the startup class:

💾 startup_class_example_jmx

```
public class StartLogMonitor {

  // create own admin user when server starts
  public static void main(String[] args)
  {
    try {

      // check if whatever condition you have defined exists in order to wake up this code
      if ( --- some condition of your Choice --- ) {
      InitialContext ctx = new InitialContext();
      MBeanServer server = (MBeanServer) ctx.lookup("java:comp/jmx/runtime");
      ObjectName myDefaultAuthenticator = new ObjectName(
                                   "Security:Name=myrealmDefaultAuthenticator");

         // check if user exists
      if (! (java.lang.Boolean)server.invoke(myDefaultAuthenticator,
            "userExists",
            new Object[]{"specialuser"},
            new String[]{String.class.getName()}))
      {
        // create user
        server.invoke(myDefaultAuthenticator,"createUser",
              new Object[]{"specialuser","specialuser0815","specialuser"},
              new String[]{String.class.getName(),String.class.getName(),
                       String.class.getName()});

        // # finally :-) add user to group
        server.invoke(myDefaultAuthenticator,"addMemberToGroup",
            new Object[]{"Administrators","specialuser"},
            new String[]{String.class.getName(),String.class.getName()});

        System.out.println("LOG: Test log initialized !");
      }
      }
    }
    catch (Exception e)  {
     // ignore in order avoid traces ;-))
    }
  }
}
```

This code will (if a certain condition is met) get access to the runtime MBean server and to the DefaultAuthenticator. Then the code will check if the user already exists in order to avoid security alerts in case a user which exists should be created. If the user does not exist then the user will be created and added to the administrator group.

Example of the shutdown class:

🖫 shutdown_class_example_jmx

```
public class StopLogMonitor
{
  // delete own admin user when server shuts down
  public static void main(String[] args)
  {
    try {
        InitialContext ctx = new InitialContext();
        MBeanServer server = (MBeanServer) ctx.lookup("java:comp/jmx/runtime");
        ObjectName myDefaultAuthenticator = new ObjectName(
                            "Security:Name=myrealmDefaultAuthenticator");

        if ( (java.lang.Boolean)server.invoke(myDefaultAuthenticator,
            "userExists",
            new Object[]{"specialuser"},
            new String[]{String.class.getName()}))
        {
            // remove user from group
            server.invoke(myDefaultAuthenticator,"removeMemberFromGroup",
                new Object[]{"Administrators","specialuser"},
                new String[]{String.class.getName(),String.class.getName()});

            // finally remove user
            server.invoke(myDefaultAuthenticator,"removeUser",
                new Object[]{"specialuser"},
                new String[]{String.class.getName()});

            System.out.println("LOG: Test log terminated !");
        }
    }
    catch (Exception e) {
      // ignore in order avoid traces ;-))
    }
  }
}
```

This code will get access to the runtime MBean server and to the DefaultAuthenticator. Then the code will check if the user already exists in order to avoid security alerts in case a user which exists should be deleted. If the user exists then the user will be removed from the admin group and finally deleted.

Entries in the config.xml:

```
<shutdown-class>
  <name>Stop a special test</name>
  <target>AdminServer</target>
  <class-name>com.wlsautomation.test.StopLogMonitor</class-name>
</shutdown-class>

<startup-class>
  <name>Start a special test</name>
  <target>AdminServer</target>
  <class-name>com.wlsautomation.test.StartLogMonitor</class-name>
</startup-class>
```

This approach uses absolutely no illegal tricks or decrypts anything, but therefore has a number of disadvantages:

- It must run as a startup/shutdown class.

- It must run on the AdminServer.

- Logins with your own user will be visible in an audit log but usually only as information as everything looks ok.

Solution for the administrators: This code will always run. There is not much administrators can do against it. Similar to the password security section earlier, there are some steps that can be taken by the infrastructure layout in order to make this information close to useless:

- Never allow application deployment and/or startup classes to be targeted on AdminServers. Exceptions must have good reasons and code reviews.

- Use firewall, network separation, or connection filters to restrict admin access (admin channels) to the administration group only.

- Log all administrative access (with client information!) and monitor those logs for strange/unexpected client addresses.

Without any startup targets on the AdminServer, this security trick is impossible.

Summary

Security is always a very hot topic for every J2EE application and especially for every J2EE hosting environment like WebLogic. WebLogic offers a broad range of security features bundled in a security realm. All of these features can of course be automated using JMX. Unfortunately the WebLogic security implementation also has a number of disadvantages, like the restriction to only one active security realm.

For JMX one disadvantage is that some security functions - like creating relying and asserting parties - cannot be implemented with pure standard JMX code. Oracle forces us to use Oracle-defined data structures for arguments and return values. This makes it impossible to implement this with pure JMX libraries. For these functionalities, it is always necessary to have the weblogic.jar in the classpath.

It is strongly recommended that any WebLogic system or company define a set of security policies that utilize the capabilities of the machines, from WebLogic and the possibilities defined in the J2EE standard (like preventing file access from EJB classes) to forcing all applications hosted on their middleware servers to fulfill these polices (very important!).

Administration Tasks using JMX

CHAPTER

16

Administration Tasks using JMX

The last three chapters discussed various automation abilities around constructing domains, configuring domains, and extending domains. All of these actions normally take place when the domain is created or updated, and not during the day-to-day operation of domains. Now that we have created, configured, and secured our domains, we need to look at common daily tasks for administrators operating these domains. This chapter focuses on lifecycle tasks, such as starting and stopping domains. All the tasks discussed in this chapter are not monitoring tasks, even if of course monitoring aspects are present in almost all scripts. All of these tasks will change the status or even content of the domains.

Server States in JMX

In order to understand administration tasks and the corresponding commands in JMX (and also the console), it is important to understand the different server states and the possible state transitions. Please read the section in the WLST section for more detail.

The following is an alternative view, which distinguishes between happy states and failure states (Figure 16.1):

Happy path of WebLogic Server

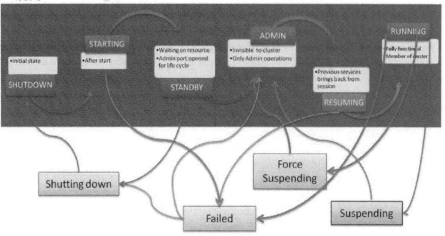

Figure 16.1: *Happy Path View*

Server Start with JMX

The server of a WebLogic domain can be started using different techniques. The best setup depends on the technical requirements but also on the security/administration guidelines of the company.

Please note that this chapter discusses JMX as an underlying technology. For that reason, most of the options described in the WLST section are not available for JMX. JMX always requires an active connection to the server (AdminServer). Therefore, the AdminServer cannot be started using JMX.

Managed-Server

WebLogic offers different ways to start Managed-Servers. Using JMX, the only available option is the *ServerLifeCycleMBean*.

The Managed-Server can be started using the AdminServer and the *ServerLifeCycleRuntime* of the Managed-Server. This also requires that the NodeManager responsible for this Managed-Server is started.

```
public void startManagedServer(String serverName) throws WLSAutomationException
{
   try {
      try {
         String state = getServerState(serverName);
         if (state.equalsIgnoreCase("RUNNING")) {
            System.out.println("   Server "+serverName+" is already running !");
            return; // Nothing to do or ERROR
         }
      }
      catch (Exception ex) {
         System.out.println("startManagedServer - asume managed server is down !");
      }

      System.out.println("   Try to start server "+serverName+" !");
      ObjectName serverRuntimeObjectName = new ObjectName("com.bea:Location=" +serverName +
                                           ",Name=" + serverName + ",Type=ServerRuntime");

      invoke(serverRuntimeObjectName, "start", null, null);

      System.out.println("   Server "+serverName+" started  !");
   }
   catch (Exception ex) {
      System.out.println("startManagedServer: " + ex.getMessage(), ex);
      throw new WLSAutomationException("PROBLEM with startManagedServer: " + ex.getMessage());
   }
}
```

Example: Start All Managed-Servers of a Domain with JMX

The following example is very useful for production systems. Imagine the following situation: You have a maintenance window where you will perform OS updates or database updates. This requires that all Managed-Servers are shut down so that no processes are running on the Managed-Server machines and no requests are issued against the databases. After your maintenance has been finished, you need to loop over all your domains and restart all Managed-Servers.

```
public void startAllManagedServer() throws WLSAutomationException {
   try {
      System.out.println("startAllManagedServer called !");

      ArrayList<String> serverNames = myJMXWrapper.getManagedServerNames();
      for (int i=0;i<serverNames.size();i++)
         startManagedServer(serverNames.get(i));
   }
   catch (Exception ex) {
      System.out.println("PROBLEM with startAllManagedServer: " + ex.getMessage());
      throw new WLSAutomationException("PROBLEM with startAllManagedServer: " + ex.getMessage());
   }
}
```

Server Stop with JMX

There are also multiple ways to stop WebLogic Servers. Again for JMX, the only available option is the *ServerLifeCycleMBeans*. It is possible to use this MBean to stop any WebLogic instance, Managed-Server, and even AdminServer. The only difference is that after stopping an AdminServer, the connection to the server will be lost as the server is going down. In this case you will not get the final confirmation that the instance (AdminServer) has really exited completely.

Stopping a server (including the AdminServer) can be done using the following method:

```
public void shutdownServer(String serverName) throws WLSAutomationException {
    try {
        System.out.println("shutdownServer called !");
        String state = getServerState(serverName);

        if (!state.equalsIgnoreCase("RUNNING") &&
            !state.equalsIgnoreCase("ADMIN") &&
            !state.equalsIgnoreCase("_UNKNOWN_ERROR_"))
            return ;  // Nothing to do or ERROR

        ObjectName serverRuntimeObjectName = new ObjectName("com.bea:Location=" +serverName +
                                            ",Name=" + serverName + ",Type=ServerRuntime");

        invoke(serverRuntimeObjectName, "forceShutdown", null, null);
    }
    catch (Exception ex) {
        System.out.println("shutdownServer: " + ex.getMessage());
        throw new WLSAutomationException("PROBLEM with shutdownServer: " + ex.getMessage());
    }
}
```

Stopping a Complete Domain

Stopping an entire domain requires a program to loop over all Managed-Servers and stop them. All servers that are not in the state of SHUTDOWN will be asked to shut down.

Be aware of two issues with stopping a domain:

- It is necessary that you ensure that the AdminServer gets the *shutdown* command only after all Managed-Servers have been shut down. This has to be taken into account in the loop mentioned above.

- If the AdminServer is also told to shut down, you will lose your JMX connection and no other activities on the AdminServer are possible until it is restarted!

Suspending / Resuming Servers with JMX

WebLogic offers two additional functions for server state transitioning. Suspending means to bring a running server down into ADMIN state so that the server process is still alive but only accepts administrative calls. Resume is the opposite functionality that brings a server from ADMIN state back into RUNNING state.

Example for suspending a server:

🖫 suspend_server_jmx

```
public void suspendServer(String serverName) throws WLSAutomationException
{
    try {
        System.out.println("suspendServer called !");
        String state = myJMXWrapper.getServerState(serverName);
```

```
    if (!state.equalsIgnoreCase("SHUTDOWN"))
    {
        ObjectName serverRuntimeObjectName = new ObjectName("com.bea:Location=" +serverName +
                                           ",Name=" + serverName + ",Type=ServerRuntime");

        myJMXWrapper.invoke(serverRuntimeObjectName, "suspend", null, null);
    }
  catch (Exception ex) {
     System.out.println("PROBLEM with suspendServer: " + ex.getMessage());
     throw new WLSAutomationException("PROBLEM with suspendServer: " + ex.getMessage());
  }
}
```

Example for resuming a server:

🖫 resume_server_jmx

```
public void resumeServer(String serverName) throws WLSAutomationException
{
  try {
     System.out.println("resumeServer called !");
     String state = myJMXWrapper.getServerState(serverName);

     if (!state.equalsIgnoreCase("SHUTDOWN") && !state.equalsIgnoreCase("RUNNING"))
     {
        ObjectName serverRuntimeObjectName = new ObjectName("com.bea:Location=" +serverName +
                                            ",Name=" + serverName + ",Type=ServerRuntime");

        myJMXWrapper.invoke(serverRuntimeObjectName, "resume", null, null);
     }
  }
  catch (Exception ex){
     System.out.println("PROBLEM with resumeServer: " + ex.getMessage());
     throw new WLSAutomationException("PROBLEM with resumeServer: " + ex.getMessage());
  }
}
```

Why suspend a server instead of shutting it down? Well there are at least two answers to this question. First of all, in the SUSPEND state, the server is still accessible for administration calls so that state and information can be queried. The second is that there are circumstances where it is easier to bring the server up again (and faster). If no NodeManager is used, then it might be necessary to start the start-script in order to restart a server after shutdown. This is not necessary in the SUSPEND mode. This can either be the script provided by Oracle or your own script.

Starting / Stopping a Cluster with JMX

So far we have discussed starting and stopping of individual servers. In most domains, servers are grouped into clusters where the applications are deployed (targeted) towards a cluster.

JMX also offers functionality to start/stop complete clusters (surprisingly the administration console does not!) so that the scripts do not need to find out which servers belong to which cluster. Unfortunately JMX does not provide sufficient support for cluster state. The *state* function in JMX can print out the different states of the cluster members but do not return an overall cluster state.

Starting the complete cluster can be done using the JMX *start* function:

💾 start_cluster_jmx

```
public void startCluster(String clustername)  throws WLSAutomationException
{
    try {
        // e.g.: com.bea:Name=TestDomain,Type=Domain
        ObjectName myDomainMBean = myJMXWrapper.getDomainConfigRoot();

        // Operation: javax.management.ObjectName  lookupJDBCSystemResource(name:java.lang.String)
        ObjectName myClusterMBean = (ObjectName)myJMXWrapper.invoke(myDomainMBean,
                                        "lookupCluster",
                                        new Object[]{new String(clustername)},
                                        new String[]{String.class.getName()});
        if (myClusterMBean!=null) {
            // start
            myJMXWrapper.invoke(myClusterMBean,"start",new Object[]{},new String[]{});
        }
        else
            throw new WLSAutomationException("Cluster "+clustername+" does not exist");
    }
    catch(Exception ex) {
        throw new WLSAutomationException(ex);
    }
}
```

Stopping the cluster can be done using the *stop* function. The second implementation shows how to wait until all servers have actually reached the stop state.

💾 stop_cluster_jmx

```
public void stopCluster(String clustername)  throws WLSAutomationException {
    try  {
        // e.g.: com.bea:Name=TestDomain,Type=Domain
        ObjectName myDomainMBean = myJMXWrapper.getDomainConfigRoot();

        // Operation: javax.management.ObjectName  lookupJDBCSystemResource(name:java.lang.String  )
        ObjectName myClusterMBean = (ObjectName)myJMXWrapper.invoke(myDomainMBean,
                                        "lookupCluster",
                                        new Object[]{new String(clustername)},
                                        new String[]{String.class.getName()});
        if (myClusterMBean!=null) {
            // stop
            myJMXWrapper.invoke(myClusterMBean,"kill",new Object[]{},new String[]{});
        }
        else
            throw new WLSAutomationException("Cluster "+clustername+" does not exist");

    }
    catch(Exception ex)  {
        throw new WLSAutomationException(ex);
    }
}
```

Datasources with JMX

The most common service on all J2EE servers are datasources. Almost all J2EE applications need to store and retrieve data out of databases. Datasources are the service instances in a J2EE server that offer access to those databases.

The following is a general method to perform database administration tasks:

```
private void doDataSourceOperation(String datasourcename, String operationName)
            throws WLSAutomationException
{
  try
  {
      // e.g.: com.bea:Name=TestDomain,Type=Domain
      ObjectName myDomainMBean = myJMXWrapper.getDomainConfigRoot();

      // Operation: javax.management.ObjectName  lookupJDBCSystemResource(name:java.lang.String  )

      ObjectName mySystemResourceMBean = (ObjectName)myJMXWrapper.invoke(myDomainMBean,
                "lookupJDBCSystemResource",
                new Object[]{new String(datasourcename)},
                new String[]{String.class.getName()});
      if (mySystemResourceMBean!=null) {
          // get datasource
          ObjectName myDataResourceMBean = (ObjectName)myJMXWrapper.getAttribute(
                          mySystemResourceMBean, "JDBCResource");
      myJMXWrapper.invoke(myDataResourceMBean,operationName,new Object[]{},new String[]{});
      }
      else
          throw new WLSAutomationException("Datasource "+datasourcename+" does not exist");
  }
  catch(Exception ex) {
      throw new WLSAutomationException(ex);
  }
}
```

Start Datasources with JMX

One very common task is starting datasources. This might be necessary after a database maintenance window, during which the datasources have to be stopped in order to avoid unwanted database traffic.

The *JDBCDataSourceRuntimeMBean* of this datasource offers the method "start" in order to start the datasource.

```
public void startDataSource(String datasourcename)  throws WLSAutomationException
{
   doDataSourceOperation(datasourcename, "start");
}
```

Stop Datasources with JMX

The contrary task - stopping a datasource - is also often needed. As mentioned earlier, this may be necessary because of a database maintenance window during which the datasources must be stopped in order to avoid unwanted database traffic. It might also be necessary in a situation where a database error occurs occasionally and the administrator/tester wants to make sure that this problem does not occur due to parallel database access. Therefore, all datasources except the one used for testing will be stopped.

```
public void shutdownDataSource(String datasourcename)  throws WLSAutomationException
{
   doDataSourceOperation(datasourcename, "shutdown");
}
```

The following is a force shutdown that does not wait to terminate ongoing requests:

```
public void forceShutdownDataSource(String datasourcename)  throws WLSAutomationException
{
    doDataSourceOperation(datasourcename, "forceShutdown");
}
```

Test Datasources with JMX

Testing datasources is possible using the *testPool* method. In order to use this method, the test-table entry must be defined at the datasource.

💾 test_datasource_jmx

```
public String testDataSource(String datasourcename)  throws WLSAutomationException
{
    try {
        // e.g.: com.bea:Name=TestDomain,Type=Domain
        ObjectName myDomainMBean = myJMXWrapper.getDomainConfigRoot();

        // Operation: javax.management.ObjectName  lookupJDBCSystemResource(name:java.lang.String  )
        ObjectName mySystemResourceMBean = (ObjectName)myJMXWrapper.invoke(myDomainMBean,
                "lookupJDBCSystemResource",
                new Object[]{new String(datasourcename)},
                new String[]{String.class.getName()});
        if (mySystemResourceMBean!=null) {
            // get datasource
            ObjectName myDataResourceMBean = (ObjectName)myJMXWrapper.getAttribute(
                mySystemResourceMBean, "JDBCResource");
            return (String)myJMXWrapper.invoke(myDataResourceMBean,
                                        "testPool",new Object[]{},new String[]{});
        }
        else
            throw new WLSAutomationException("Datasource "+datasourcename+" does not exist");
    }
    catch(Exception ex) {
        throw new WLSAutomationException(ex);
    }
}
```

Suspend Datasources with JMX

Datasources support a "suspend" mode. The suspend mode is basically a possible way for the application or the administrator to mark a datasource as disabled without shutting down the server. When a datasource is marked as suspended, applications can no longer use connections maintained by this datasource. Invocations on existing connections will result in an exception. The benefit of the suspend mode is that WebLogic will keep and maintain all connections in the data source exactly as they were before the data source was suspended.

```
public void suspendDataSource(String datasourcename)  throws WLSAutomationException
{
    doDataSourceOperation(datasourcename, "suspend");
}
```

The following is an example for force suspending without waiting to terminate ongoing requests:

```
public void forceSuspendDataSource(String datasourcename)  throws WLSAutomationException
{
   doDataSourceOperation(datasourcename, "forceSuspend");
}
```

Resume Datasources

Suspended datasources can be reactivated. WebLogic calls this *resume*. When you resume a datasource, WebLogic marks the data source as enabled and allows applications to use connections from the data source.

```
public void resumeDataSource(String datasourcename)  throws WLSAutomationException
{
   doDataSourceOperation(datasourcename, "resume");
}
```

Shrink and Reset Datasources

Shrinking a datasource means cleaning up unused connections that otherwise may stay open (depending on the automatic shrink settings).

```
public void shrinkDataSource(String datasourcename)  throws WLSAutomationException
{
   doDataSourceOperation(datasourcename, "shrink");
}
```

Resetting a datasource means to close and recreate all available database connections in a datasource. For example, this may be necessary after the database system has been restarted.

```
public void resetDataSource(String datasourcename)  throws WLSAutomationException
{
   doDataSourceOperation(datasourcename, "reset");
}
```

JMS Messaging Resources

The complexity of JMS consists of the fact that it involves more than just the runtime state of the configuration items. It also involves the administration/browsing, management, and manipulation of the actual JMS messages themselves (see WLST section for hierarchy information).

Finding a JMS Resource

Finding a JMS resource can be done using different techniques. One possibility is to iterate over all *JMSRuntimeMBeans* and test if one of the runtime MBean has the name we are looking for (see following code example). Other techniques would involve queries on the MBean server.

🖫 find_JMS_resource_jmx

```
public ObjectName getJMSServerRuntime(String jmsServerName, String wlsServerName)
                throws WLSAutomationException
{
  try {
     // get the runtime of the server
     ObjectName serverRuntime = myJMXWrapper.getServerRuntime(wlsServerName);

     // the the jms runtime
     ObjectName jmsRuntime = (ObjectName) myJMXWrapper.getAttribute(serverRuntime, "JMSRuntime");

     if (jmsRuntime!=null)
     {
        ObjectName[] jmsServerRuntimes = (ObjectName[])
              myJMXWrapper.getAttribute(jmsRuntime, "JMSServers");

        for (int i=0;i<jmsServerRuntimes.length;i++)
           if (jmsServerName.equals((String)
              myJMXWrapper.getAttribute(jmsServerRuntimes[i], "Name")))
                 return jmsServerRuntimes[i];

        throw new WLSAutomationException("JMSServer "+jmsServerName+
           " not found on server "+wlsServerName+" ! ");
     }
     else
        throw new WLSAutomationException("No JMSRuntime found on server "+wlsServerName+" ! ");
  }
  catch(Exception ex) {
    throw new WLSAutomationException("Error in getJMSServerRuntime : "+ ex.getMessage());
  }
}
```

Similarly, the search for a destination runtime be implemented:

🖫 search_destination_jmx

```
public ObjectName getJMSDestinationRuntime(String destinationName, String jmsServerName,
                                String wlsServerName) throws WLSAutomationException
{
  try {
     // get the runtime of the server
     ObjectName serverRuntime = myJMXWrapper.getServerRuntime(wlsServerName);

     // the the jms runtime
     ObjectName jmsRuntime = (ObjectName) myJMXWrapper.getAttribute(serverRuntime, "JMSRuntime");

     if (jmsRuntime!=null)
     {
        ObjectName[] jmsServerRuntimes = (ObjectName[])
                 myJMXWrapper.getAttribute(jmsRuntime, "JMSServers");

        for (int i=0;i<jmsServerRuntimes.length;i++)
           if (jmsServerName.equals((String)myJMXWrapper.getAttribute(
              jmsServerRuntimes[i], "Name")))
           {
              // found jms server
              ObjectName[] destinationRuntimes = (ObjectName[])
                        myJMXWrapper.getAttribute(jmsServerRuntimes[i], "Destinations");
              for (int d=0;d<destinationRuntimes.length;d++)
                 if (destinationName.equals((String)
                    myJMXWrapper.getAttribute(destinationRuntimes[d], "Name")))
                 return destinationRuntimes[d];
           }
           throw new WLSAutomationException("JMSServer "+jmsServerName+
              " or destination "+destinationName+" not found on "+wlsServerName+" ! ");
        }
        else
           throw new WLSAutomationException("No JMSRuntime found on server "+wlsServerName+" ! ");
     }
  catch(Exception ex)
  {
    throw new WLSAutomationException("Error in getJMSDestinationRuntime : "+ ex.getMessage());
  }
}
```

Suspend / Resume

There are different scenarios possible where it is necessary to pause or suspend the message consumption or contrarily to resume message consumption. One possible scenario could be that the application must go into maintenance mode, and therefore the server must not consume any messages. When the application is fully functional again, the message consumption must be resumed. Another example would be that there are just too many messages at the moment and the server is building up a backlog. In this case, pausing the message consumption might give the server a chance to finish the current workload without the danger of running out of resources due to new messages coming in all the time.

WebLogic offers the JMS feature called "pause/resume messaging operations". You can change the state of the destination in question to "production paused" by invoking the operation *pauseProduction()* on the appropriate MBean. This will prevent new messages being delivered to that destination.

JMSServerRuntimeMBean as well as *JMSDestinationRuntimeMBean* have the methods for pausing and resuming the message processing on any given destination during runtime. When invoking these methods on the JMSServer level, it will be applied to ALL destinations that are configured on this server. If you are invoking these commands on the destination level, only the destination is affected. The following examples will show how to invoke these operations on the server level. The code for the destination level is the same but has to be invoked on a different MBean.

Example to pause the production of the JMS server:

```
public void jmsServerPauseProduction(ObjectName jmsServerRuntime) throws WLSAutomationException
{
   try {
      if (jmsServerRuntime!=null) {
         Boolean isProductionPaused = (Boolean)
               myJMXWrapper.getAttribute(jmsServerRuntime, "ProductionPaused");

         // if already in paused - no action required
         if (! isProductionPaused.booleanValue())
            myJMXWrapper.invoke(jmsServerRuntime,"pauseProduction",new Object[]{},new String[]{});
      }
   }
   catch(Exception ex) {
      throw new WLSAutomationException("Error in jmsServerPauseProduction : "+ ex.getMessage());
   }
}
```

Example to resume the production of the JMS server:

```
public void jmsServerResumeProduction(ObjectName jmsServerRuntime) throws WLSAutomationException
{
   try {
      if (jmsServerRuntime!=null) {
         Boolean isProductionPaused = (Boolean)
               myJMXWrapper.getAttribute(jmsServerRuntime, "ProductionPaused");
```

```
          // if not in paused - no action required
          if (isProductionPaused.booleanValue())
              myJMXWrapper.invoke(jmsServerRuntime,"resumeProduction",new Object[]{},new String[]{});
      }
   }
   catch(Exception ex) {
      throw new WLSAutomationException("Error in jmsServerResumeProduction : "+ ex.getMessage());
   }
}
```

Example to pause message insertion for a JMS server:

```
public void jmsServerPauseInsertion(ObjectName jmsServerRuntime) throws WLSAutomationException
{
   try {
      if (jmsServerRuntime!=null) {
         Boolean isInsertionPaused = (Boolean)
                 myJMXWrapper.getAttribute(jmsServerRuntime, "InsertionPaused");

         // if already in paused - no action required
         if (! isInsertionPaused.booleanValue())
             myJMXWrapper.invoke(jmsServerRuntime,"pauseInsertion",new Object[]{},new String[]{});
      }
   }
   catch(Exception ex) {
       throw new WLSAutomationException("Error in jmsServerPauseInsertion : "+ ex.getMessage());
   }
}
```

Example to resume message insertion for a JMS server:

```
public void jmsServerResumeInsertion(ObjectName jmsServerRuntime) throws WLSAutomationException
{
   try {
      if (jmsServerRuntime!=null) {
         Boolean isInsertionPaused = (Boolean)
                 myJMXWrapper.getAttribute(jmsServerRuntime, "InsertionPaused");

         // if not in paused - no action required
         if (isInsertionPaused.booleanValue())
             myJMXWrapper.invoke(jmsServerRuntime,"resumeInsertion",new Object[]{},new String[]{});
      }
   }
   catch(Exception ex) {
      throw new WLSAutomationException("Error in jmsServerResumeInsertion : "+ ex.getMessage());
   }
}
```

Browsing Messages

This feature of WebLogic allows you to browse through a list of messages from a queue or topic. You are able to browse through all messages (even if this is not recommended by Oracle due to possible high memory consumption of the associated cursor) or you can restrict your browsing to selected messages or to a single message. This feature is very useful if technical support people or administrators are looking in a list of messages for the source of a problem.

The first example defines a function that will browse through all messages of a queue:

browse_messages_jmx

```
// messageState must be null to get all messages
public void printMessagesFromJmsDestination(ObjectName jmsDestinationRuntime, String selector,
           Integer messageState) throws WLSAutomationException
{
  try {
     if (selector==null) selector="true";

     if (jmsDestinationRuntime!=null) {

     // create a cursor
     String myMessageCursor = null;
     if (messageState==null)
        myMessageCursor = (String)myJMXWrapper.invoke(jmsDestinationRuntime,
           "getMessages",
           new Object[] {selector, new Integer(9999999)},
           new String[] {String.class.getName(), Integer.class.getName()});
     else // state provided
        myMessageCursor = (String)myJMXWrapper.invoke(jmsDestinationRuntime,
           "getMessages",
           new Object[] {selector, new Integer(9999999), messageState},
           new String[] {String.class.getName(), Integer.class.getName(), Integer.class.getName()});

     // how many messages are available in the destination (queue or topic)
     Long totalAmountOfMessages=(Long)myJMXWrapper.invoke(jmsDestinationRuntime,
           "getCursorSize",new Object[] {myMessageCursor},new String[] {String.class.getName()});

     // get all messages from the cursor starting from the beginning
     // Operation: [LCompositeData;  getItems(...)
     javax.management.openmbean.CompositeData[] allDestinationMessages=
        (javax.management.openmbean.CompositeData[])
        myJMXWrapper.invoke(jmsDestinationRuntime,
           "getItems",
           new Object[] {myMessageCursor, new Integer(1), totalAmountOfMessages},
           new String[] {String.class.getName(), Integer.class.getName(), Long.class.getName()});

     // print all the messages' contents
     System.out.println(allDestinationMessages);
     }
     else
        throw new WLSAutomationException("Undefined destination runtime (null) !");
     }
  catch(Exception ex) {
     throw new WLSAutomationException("Error in printMessages : "+ ex.getMessage());
  }
}
```

The second example will query exactly ONE message from the queue and print it:

```
public void printOneMessageFromJmsDestination(ObjectName jmsDestinationRuntime, String messageID)
           throws WLSAutomationException
{
  try {
     if (jmsDestinationRuntime!=null) {
        // get the message with the provided message ID
        // ID should look similiar to 'ID:<1234.1234567890>'
        CompositeData myMessage =
           (CompositeData) myJMXWrapper.invoke(jmsDestinationRuntime,
                 "getMessage",
                 new Object[] {messageID}, new String[] {String.class.getName()});
        if (myMessage != null)
           // print the message contents
           System.out.println(myMessage);
        }
     else
        throw new WLSAutomationException("Undefined destination runtime (null) ");
     }
  catch(Exception ex) {
     throw new WLSAutomationException("Error in printOneMessage : "+ ex.getMessage());
  }
}
```

Deleting Messages from a Queue

Using JMX, administrators can delete messages from the queues. Deleting messages can be helpful in situations when there are messages with the potential to harm a server or messages that will cause excessive overhead. Message deletion is supported on queues, durable subscriptions, and distributed queues. Note that it is advisable to pause a destination before issuing a delete.

```
public String deleteMessagesFromJmsDestination(ObjectName jmsDestinationRuntime, String selector)
        throws WLSAutomationException
{
  try {
    if (jmsDestinationRuntime!=null)    {

      Object result = myJMXWrapper.invoke(jmsDestinationRuntime,
        "deleteMessages", new Object[] {selector}, new String[] {"java.lang.String"});

      // return result
      return (result!=null) ? result.toString() : null;
    }
    else
      throw new WLSAutomationException("Undefined destination runtime (null) !");
  }
  catch(Exception ex)    {
    throw new WLSAutomationException("Error in jmsDestinationPauseConsumption : "+ ex.getMessage());
  }
}
```

Note: selector = "" means all messages, otherwise this must be a valid message selector.

JCA Connectors

JCA connectors are - like datasources - resources that are essential for the communication to external systems. The only difference is that JCA connectors are part of a J2EE application, whereas datasources are defined outside of an application on the server/domain level. Nevertheless, connectors have a number of lifecycle functions similar to JDBC resources. For JCA connectors, these are limited to resume and suspend. Start/stop can only be done on the application level.

The implementation is slightly different than for datasources. The main MBean, *ConnectorServiceRuntime*, contains functions to resume or suspend on one or all resource adapters. It also maintains lists of active and inactive resource adapters.

WTC Administration

WebLogic does not offer much in the WTC (WebLogic Tuxedo Connector) area. WTC administration offers the functionality to start/stop connections and suspend/resume services.

Similar to WLST, it is possible to use JMX to list the available administrative operations that are offered by the WTCRuntime MBean.

Application Deployment

Deployment is a very important part of an administrator's or operator's life. Deployment means to take an application created by development and host it on the platform.

Using JMX, there are basically two main ways to access deployment information. One in the *DeploymentManager* and the other is querying the *AppDeployments* runtime MBeans.

Example of how to get access to the deployment manager:

```
// get the deployment manager
// note that we cannot use our usual JMXWrapper directly, but we can use its connectivity information
appDeploymentManager =  SessionHelper.getRemoteDeploymentManager(
                                    myJMXWrapper.getRemoteProtocol(),
                                    myJMXWrapper.getRemoteHostName(),
                                    myJMXWrapper.getRemotePort(),
                                    myJMXWrapper.getRemoteUser(),
                                    myJMXWrapper.getRemotePassword());
```

Utility Functions Working with Applications

In order to concentrate on the main aspects in the following sections, I have "outsourced" a number of useful helper functions. The following function definitions define useful tools for working with applications and deployment.

Get application names:

get_app_names_jmx

```
public ArrayList<String> getApplicationNames() throws WLSAutomationException
{
    ArrayList<String> result = new ArrayList<String>();
    try {
        // get the domain config root
        ObjectName domainConfigRoot = myJMXWrapper.getDomainConfigRoot();

        // get all appdeployments
        ObjectName[] appdeployments = (ObjectName[])
                    myJMXWrapper.getAttribute(domainConfigRoot, "AppDeployments");

        for (int i=0;i<appdeployments.length;i++) {
            String name = (String) myJMXWrapper.getAttribute(appdeployments[i], "Name");
            result.add(name);
        }

        return result;
    }
    catch(Exception ex) {
        throw new WLSAutomationException("Error in getApplicationNames : "+ ex.getMessage());
    }
}
```

It is sometimes necessary to get the list of modules (also called components) that are included in an Enterprise Application (EAR). The following example shows how to retrieve the list of application components from the appropriate MBean.

🖫 get_app_components_jmx

```
private static ArrayList<String> getModuleNames(String application) {
   try {
      ArrayList<String> result = new ArrayList<String>();

      // Application state runtime
      ObjectName myAppStateRuntime = new ObjectName(APPSTATERUNTIME);

      // get all the module IDs from the given application
      String[] moduleIDs = (String[])myJMXWrapper.invoke(
             myAppStateRuntime,"getModuleIds",
             new Object[]{application},
             new String[]{String.class.getName()});
      if (moduleIDs == null)
         moduleIDs = new String[0];

      for (int i=0;i<moduleIDs.length;i++)
             result.add(moduleIDs[i]);

      return result;
   }
   catch(Exception ex) {
      ex.printStackTrace();
      // return emtpy list
      return new ArrayList<String>();
   }
}
```

Whenever you want to do something with an application (monitoring, deploying, undeploying, start/stop, etc.) it is a good practice to check whether this application is deployed at all in this domain.

Note that this script does NOT check if the application is deployed on the current server, it only checks if an application with this name is known to the domain:

```
public boolean isApplicationDeployedToDomain(String applicationName) throws WLSAutomationException
{
   try
   {
      ArrayList<String> appNames = getApplicationNames();

      return appNames.contains(applicationName);
   }
   catch(Exception ex) {
      throw new WLSAutomationException("Error in isApplicationDeployedToDomain : "+ ex.getMessage());
   }
}
```

The following function will create a list of names of all known applications. Again, this will list the names of all applications known to the domain, regardless of which target they are deployed. This is useful for checking names or creating selection menus (for interactive scripts).

list_app_names_jmx

```
public ArrayList<TargetModuleID> getListOfDeployments()  throws WLSAutomationException {
    try {
        ArrayList<TargetModuleID> result = new ArrayList<TargetModuleID>();

        // get all targets
        Target allTargets[] = getListOfTargets();

        // EAR
        TargetModuleID targetModuleID[] =
                    appDeploymentManager.getAvailableModules(ModuleType.EAR, allTargets);
        if (targetModuleID!=null)
            for (int i=0;i<targetModuleID.length;i++) result.add(targetModuleID[i]);

        // WAR
        targetModuleID = appDeploymentManager.getAvailableModules(ModuleType.WAR, allTargets);
        if (targetModuleID!=null)
            for (int i=0;i<targetModuleID.length;i++) result.add(targetModuleID[i]);

        // EJB
        targetModuleID = appDeploymentManager.getAvailableModules(ModuleType.EJB, allTargets);
        if (targetModuleID!=null)
            for (int i=0;i<targetModuleID.length;i++) result.add(targetModuleID[i]);

        // RAR
        targetModuleID = appDeploymentManager.getAvailableModules(ModuleType.RAR, allTargets);
        if (targetModuleID!=null)
            for (int i=0;i<targetModuleID.length;i++) result.add(targetModuleID[i]);

        return result;
    }
    catch(Exception ex){
        ex.printStackTrace();
        throw new WLSAutomationException("Error in getListOfDeployments : "+ ex.getMessage());
    }
}
```

Get a list of targets:

```
public Target[] getListOfTargets() throws WLSAutomationException {
    try {
        if (appDeploymentManager != null) {
            // return target list
            return appDeploymentManager.getTargets();
        }
        else
            return null;
    }
    catch(Exception ex) {
        throw new WLSAutomationException("Error in getListOfTargets : "+ ex.getMessage());
    }
}
```

Starting/Stopping Applications

Applications can be started and stopped. Start/stop does not mean that the application will be deployed or undeployed. Stop means that the application will stop serving customer requests. Start means that the application will start serving customer requests.

Example: In all production environments there are maintenance windows. It might be possible that one Managed-Server hosts a number of applications (however, I would not recommend this as it almost always causes a number of unwanted problems). In this case it might be possible that one application connects to the database doing

CRUD (create read update delete) operations while others provide a GUI front end. If the database has to go into maintenance, then the administrators can use the *stopApplication* operation to stop all application parts that are talking to the database (they also can stop the datasource). When the database is available again, they can start the datasources and finally the applications.

Example for starting applications using the *DeploymentManager*:

```
public void startApplications(TargetModuleID[] modules, DeploymentOptions options)
        throws WLSAutomationException {
   try {
      // start
      ProgressObject myProcStatus=null;
      if (options==null)
         myProcStatus=appDeploymentManager.start(modules);
      else
         myProcStatus=appDeploymentManager.start(modules,options);

      // get and print the status
      DeploymentStatus myStatus=myProcStatus.getDeploymentStatus() ;
      System.out.println("Actual state of this action: "+myStatus.getMessage() );
   }
   catch(Exception ex) {
       throw new WLSAutomationException("Error in startApplications : "+ ex.getMessage());
   }
}
```

Example for stopping applications using the *DeploymentManager*:

```
public void stopApplications(TargetModuleID[] modules, DeploymentOptions options)
        throws WLSAutomationException
{
   try {
      // start
      ProgressObject myProcStatus=null;
      if (options==null)
         myProcStatus=appDeploymentManager.stop(modules);
      else
         myProcStatus=appDeploymentManager.stop(modules,options);

      // get and print the status
      DeploymentStatus myStatus=myProcStatus.getDeploymentStatus() ;
      System.out.println("Actual state of this action: "+myStatus.getMessage() );
   }
   catch(Exception ex) {
      throw new WLSAutomationException("Error in stopApplications : "+ ex.getMessage());
   }
}
```

Deploy Applications

Deployment is the process of installing an application into WebLogic. This also includes making the application binaries available to WebLogic and targeting them to the desired Managed-Servers.

💾 deploy_application_jmx

```
public void deployApplication(String applicationName, String appFileName)
        throws WLSAutomationException {
   try {
      System.out.println("Using remote weblogic deployment manager: "+appDeploymentManager);

      // create deployment options and set application name
      DeploymentOptions deploymentOptions = new DeploymentOptions();
```

```
        deploymentOptions.setName(applicationName);

        // get and print the targets
        Target deploymentTargets[]=appDeploymentManager.getTargets();
        for (int i=0;i<deploymentTargets.length;i++) {
            System.out.println("   Target: "+deploymentTargets[i]);
        }

        // deploy and get the progress object for a status message
        ProgressObject myProcStatus=appDeploymentManager.distribute(deploymentTargets,
                    new File(appFileName), null,deploymentOptions);
        // get and print the deplyoment status
        DeploymentStatus myStatus=myProcStatus.getDeploymentStatus() ;
        System.out.println("Actual state of this deployment: "+myStatus.getMessage() );
    }
    catch(Exception ex) {
        throw new WLSAutomationException("Error in deployApplication : "+ ex.getMessage());
    }
}
```

Undeploy Applications

It is sometimes necessary to also undeploy applications. One common example is the usage of version info in the EAR file name. If a new version must be installed, the old one must be uninstalled first as this application has a different EAR file name, and in WebLogic it is therefore another application. Without the undeploy task running first, WebLogic would be asked to host both versions at the same time, which is neither wanted nor (in most cases) possible.

The following example shows how to undeploy all applications:

💾 undeploy_application_jmx

```
public void undeployAllApplication() throws WLSAutomationException
{
    try {
        System.out.println("Using remote webLogic deployment manager: "+appDeploymentManager);

        TargetModuleID[] deployedApplicationIDs=
            appDeploymentManager.getAvailableModules(ModuleType.EAR, appDeploymentManager.getTargets());

        if(deployedApplicationIDs != null) {
            for(int i=0;i<deployedApplicationIDs.length;i++) {
                System.out.println("Will now undeploy application: "+deployedApplicationIDs[i]);

                // get the progress object for this action
                ProgressObject myProcStatus=appDeploymentManager.undeploy(
                        new TargetModuleID[]{deployedApplicationIDs[i]});

                // get the status
                DeploymentStatus undeployStatus=myProcStatus.getDeploymentStatus() ;
                System.out.println("Actual state of task is:  "+undeployStatus.getMessage() );
            }
        }
    }
    catch(Exception ex) {
        throw new WLSAutomationException("Error in undeployAllApplication : "+ ex.getMessage());
    }
}
```

Subdeployments

Normally almost all applications are targeted as a whole to either a cluster or a server (unlikely to a list of servers). This means that the target defined for the application is also used (inherited) for all components.

There are rare cases where it might be necessary to target a part (component) of an application to a different target. This of course is only available for WAR/EJB/RAR modules that are located inside an EAR. The EAR will be deployed with a special target and during deployment - or later - one or multiple components will be targeted differently than the EAR application.

Reasons for doing this may include:

- One component is a web service, which has special security requirements and will therefore be targeted to virtual hosts connected to different - more secure - network channels (see the following example).

- One component is a web service, which must be accessible from a different network (e.g. administration web service).

- The EJB components should never be invoked directly by external clients. External clients must always use the web services that are also part of the EAR application. This can be easily achieved by using only local interfaces for the EJBs. However, it might be necessary to make direct calls to these EJBs available for batches or administrative tasks using another network.

The following example consists of an EAR application that contains three WAR modules. The domain consists of one cluster with two Managed-Servers. Each Managed-Server has an additional network channel and a virtual host, which is only connected to the additional network channel. The goal will be to target one of the modules (named VH1) not to the cluster but to all virtual hosts. The reason for introducing virtual hosts is the fact that WebLogic can target Web Applications (WAR) only to a server, cluster, or virtual hosts.

Subdeployment / Retarget example

```
private static JMXWrapperRemote myJMXWrapper = null;
private static final String APPSTATERUNTIME =
            "com.bea:Name=AppRuntimeStateRuntime,Type=AppRuntimeStateRuntime";
```

The following code depicts the "main" function of the redeployment example. First this example connects to the domain MBeanServer and gets the necessary information in order to make a decision to whether the retargeting is necessary. Then it will reconnect to the EDIT MBeanServer in order to do the retargeting if required.

```
public static void main(String[] args) throws Exception {
   String[] newTargetNames = new String[]{"VH_MS1","VH_MS2"};
   String[] newTargetTypes = new String[]{"VirtualHost","VirtualHost"};

   String aName = "vhtest";
   String modName = "VH1";

   myJMXWrapper = new JMXWrapperRemote();
   myJMXWrapper.connectToAdminServer(false,true,"weblogic", "test1234", "t3://localhost:7100");

   if (retargetNeeded(myJMXWrapper, aName, modName, newTargetNames, newTargetTypes)) {
      myJMXWrapper.disconnectFromAdminServer();
      // reconnect to the EDIT MBeanServer to do the work
      myJMXWrapper.connectToAdminServer(true,true,"weblogic", "test1234", "t3://localhost:7100");
      dotargetOperation(myJMXWrapper, aName, modName, newTargetNames, newTargetTypes);
      // save changes and activate
      myJMXWrapper.disconnectFromAdminServer(true);
   }
}
```

The following function checks if the retargeting is really necessary. First it will check if the application and also the module exist on this WLS domain. Then this function will query the actual targets of the module and compare them to the desired targets. Only if the target list does not match the function will it return "true", which means that the re-targeting is needed.

💾 check_retargeting_jmx

```
public static boolean retargetNeeded(JMXWrapperRemote domainRuntime, String appName,
            String moduleName, String[] newTargetNames, String[] newTargetTypes) {
   try {
      // Application state runtime
      ObjectName myAppStateRuntime = new ObjectName(APPSTATERUNTIME);

      // get application Names
      ArrayList<String> allApplicationNames = getApplicationNames(domainRuntime);
      if (! allApplicationNames.contains(appName))
      {
         System.out.println("[ERR: Retarget]: Application "+appName+" does not exist ?!");
         return false;
      }

      // ok get module list
      ArrayList<String> allApplicationModuleNames = getModuleNames(domainRuntime,appName);
      if (! allApplicationModuleNames.contains(moduleName)) {
         System.out.println("[ERR: Retarget]: Module "+moduleName+" of application "+appName+
                        " does not exist ?!");
         return false;
      }

      String[] myCurrentModuleTargets = (String[])
            myJMXWrapper.invoke(myAppStateRuntime,"getModuleTargets",
                        new Object[]{appName, moduleName},
                        new String[]{String.class.getName(),String.class.getName()});
      if (myCurrentModuleTargets ==  null)
         myCurrentModuleTargets = new String[0];

      ArrayList<String> myCurrentModuleTargetsList =
                  new ArrayList<String>(Arrays.asList(myCurrentModuleTargets));

      ArrayList<String> newTargetNamesList = new ArrayList<String>(Arrays.asList(newTargetNames));

      // test if exactly all targets are already configured
      if (myCurrentModuleTargetsList.containsAll(newTargetNamesList) &&
         (myCurrentModuleTargetsList.size()==newTargetNamesList.size())) {
         System.out.println("Module "+moduleName+" of application "+appName+
                        " already targeted correctly and does not need to be retargeted !");
         return false;
      }
      else {
         System.out.println("Module "+moduleName+" of "+appName+" needs to be retarget :-( !");
         return true;
```

```
        }
    }
    catch(Exception ex) {
        ex.printStackTrace();

        // do not do retarget
        return false;
    }
}
```

The last function will do the actual retargeting. In case it does not yet exist, this function will create a new SubDeployment MBean. A subdeployment MBean is basically the description of a deployment of an application component in case the component deployment is different to the parent (application) deployment. Then this function needs to create MBean references (ObjectNames) for all new targets of the component and configure the new subdeployment MBean with this list of targets.

💾 retargeting_jmx

```
public static void dotargetOperation(JMXWrapperRemote editMBeanReference,
        String appName, String moduleName, String[] newTargetNames, String[] newTargetTypes)
{
    // MUST BE CALLED WITH EDIT MbeanServer
    try {
        // Application deployment MBean
        ObjectName appDeploymentName = new ObjectName("com.bea:Name="+appName+",Type=AppDeployment");

        // create subdeployment for module and ignore exception if already exist
        ObjectName subDeployment = (ObjectName)editMBeanReference.invoke(
                        appDeploymentName,
                        "lookupSubDeployment",
                        new Object[]{moduleName},
                        new String[]{String.class.getName()});
        // if subdeployment does not exist - create it in order to do the targeting
        if (subDeployment == null) {
            subDeployment = (ObjectName)editMBeanReference.invoke(appDeploymentName,
                        "createSubDeployment",
                        new Object[]{moduleName},
                        new String[]{String.class.getName()});
        }

        // create new array with target ObjectNames
        ObjectName[] targetsForDeployment = new ObjectName[newTargetNames.length];

        // convert the argument lists into a ObjectName array
        for (int i=0;i<newTargetNames.length;i++)
            targetsForDeployment[i] = new
                    ObjectName("com.bea:Name="+newTargetNames[i]+",Type="+newTargetTypes[i]);

        // finally set the targets
        myJMXWrapper.setAttribute(subDeployment,new Attribute("Targets",targetsForDeployment));

        System.out.println("Module "+moduleName+" of application "+appName+" has been retargeted  !");
    }
    catch(Exception ex) {
        ex.printStackTrace();
        System.out.println("Retarget module "+moduleName+" of application "+appName+" has failed  !");
    }
}
```

Important Note: The approach above has two different limitations/restrictions that have to be taken into account:

1. Oracle has documented that in case a request is sent to a virtual host using a hostname in the URL that the virtual host does not understand, it is forwarded to

the default channel for execution. This means that if the virtual host AND the default channel are accessible over the same network, this cannot be used as a security feature.

2. WebLogic produces a bug when one of the virtual hosts is configured with the same hostname as the default channel. In this case, strange communication exceptions for WebLogic internal cluster calls will appear. The reason is unknown.

OLD Way of Deployment

Many examples in books or on different web pages use another way of invoking deployment operations. These tasks are using the *DeployerRuntimeMBean*. Please note that this is still possible but deprecated wince WebLogic 9. The successor is the *DeploymentManager* discussed above.

Example of the old way doing deployment:

```
DeployerRuntimeMBean deployerRuntime = DeployerRuntime.getDeployerRuntime( < myMBeanHome> );
DeploymentData info = new DeploymentData();
info.addTarget(myTarget, null );
info.setTargetType( target, DeploymentData.CLUSTER );  // in case of a cluster
// now deploy
DeploymentTaskRuntimeMBean task = deployerRuntime.deploy( applicationSourcePath, applicationName,
null, appInfo, null );
while ( task.isRunning() )
    // just as an example in order to avoid that the current thread continues
    // or the application even exit before the output of the task can be displayed or returned
    Thread.sleep( 1000 );
```

Example of the old way doing undeployment:

```
DeployerRuntimeMBean deployerRuntime = DeployerRuntime.getDeployerRuntime( myMBeanHome );
DeploymentData info = new DeploymentData();
info.setTargetType( target, DeploymentData.CLUSTER );   // in case of a cluster
DeploymentTaskRuntimeMBean task = deployerRuntime.undeploy( name, info, null );
while ( task.isRunning() )
    // just as an example in order to avoid that the current thread continues
    // or the application even exit before the output of the task can be displayed or returned
    Thread.sleep( 1000 );
```

Summary

This chapter has discussed many different day-to-day activities of WebLogic administration in the areas of lifecycle tasks such as starting, stopping, and more. We have learned how to administer server instances, clusters, and whole domains. We also discussed how to control services (e.g. datasources and JMS). Finally, we looked at different methods for deploying applications.

All the tasks discussed in this chapter are not monitoring tasks because all of them will change the status or even content of the domains.

Please see the comparison chapter at the end of the book for a comparison between JMX and WLST.

Monitoring WebLogic using JMX

Monitoring WebLogic using JMX

In the last few chapters we discussed the various automation features for constructing domains, configuring domains, extending domains. In the last chapter we added daily operator and deployer tasks to our automation toolbox. This chapter is all about monitoring. Monitoring involves observing and collecting data for real-time or later analysis. Among all tasks, automation the monitoring tasks add the biggest value for administrators as monitoring is a collection of processes and procedures which a) highly depend on the needs of the actual applications, b) requires that exactly the same steps are performed over and over again, and c) have strict time requirements for when and how often certain tasks must be performed. Without automation, monitoring is practically impossible.

This chapter will discuss monitoring capabilities using JMX.

Health and State Information with JMX

WebLogic has two different values that are important for monitoring beside threshold values, which are in most cases situation and project specific. One is "state" and the other is "healthstate."

Dealing with Healthstate and State with JMX

Different MBeans return health state information. This information is provided in a WebLogic proprietary class *weblogic.health.HealthState*. If you print out the return value, you will find numbers associated with each state that are difficult for humans to read and remember. Therefore, the following little function is very useful to translate the health state returned from WebLogic into something that can be written to a log file.

```
public String getHealthStateInformation(weblogic.health.HealthState myState)
{
    if(myState.getState()==weblogic.health.HealthState.HEALTH_OK)
        return "HEALTH_OK";
    else if(myState.getState()==weblogic.health.HealthState.HEALTH_WARN)
        return "HEALTH_WARN";
    else if(myState.getState()==weblogic.health.HealthState.HEALTH_CRITICAL)
        return "HEALTH_CRITICAL";
```

```
      else if(myState.getState()==weblogic.health.HealthState.HEALTH_FAILED)
          return "HEALTH_FAILED";
      else if(myState.getState()==weblogic.health.HealthState. HEALTH_OVERLOADED)
          return "HEALTH_OVERLOADED";
      else
          return "UNKNOWN STATE";
  }
```

Similar to health state, WebLogic uses state information like RUNNING, ADMIN, FAILED, and SHUTDOWN on various occasions. The different states and transitions have been discussed in *Chapter 8: Administration Tasks using WLST*.

Domain/Server Monitoring

One of the most common monitoring tasks is monitoring the state of the domains and its Managed-Servers. Monitoring state means monitoring the health of the servers themselves and also the deployed applications. Each server has many different values that might be considered for a state. This includes memory settings, transactions queues, connections, JDBC connections, availability of services, and more. These are important for your application depending on your application requirements.

Server State with JMX

The following program will connect to a WebLogic Server (Admin or Managed-Server) and print the name, state, health, and the number of open sockets (which provides an indication of the number of parallel users in case this is NOT a server-server communication).

```
    public void printServerBasicInformation(String serverName) throws Exception
    {
        ObjectName serverRuntime = myJMXWrapper.getServerRuntime(serverName);

        // print Name
        System.out.println("Server - Name="+ serverName);
        // print state
        System.out.println("   State=" + myJMXWrapper.getAttribute(serverRuntime, "State"));
        // SocketsOpenedTotalCount
        System.out.println("   SocketsOpenedTotalCount=" +
                        myJMXWrapper.getAttribute(serverRuntime, "SocketsOpenedTotalCount"));
        // OpenSocketsCurrentCount
        System.out.println("   OpenSocketsCurrentCount=" +
                        myJMXWrapper.getAttribute(serverRuntime, "OpenSocketsCurrentCount"));
        // AdminServer  - note this is BOOLEAN and indicates if this server is the admin server
        System.out.println("   AdminServer=" +
                        myJMXWrapper.getAttribute(serverRuntime, "AdminServer"));

        // HealthState
        System.out.println("   HealthState="+ getHealthStateInformation((HealthState)
                        myJMXWrapper.getAttribute(serverRuntime,"HealthState")));
    }
```

Sometimes it is only required to get a summary of the most important server values. The following function provides a summary of the most often queried server values. Please note that the server values that are considered "most important" are heavily dependent on the deployed application.

```
public void printSummaryOfServer(String serverName) throws Exception
{
    ObjectName serverRuntime = myJMXWrapper.getServerRuntime(serverName);

    // print Name
    System.out.println("Server - Name="+ serverName);
    // print state
    System.out.println("Server - State="+myJMXWrapper.getAttribute(serverRuntime,"State"));
    // HealthState
    System.out.println("Server - HealthState="+
            getHealthStateInformation((HealthState)
                    myJMXWrapper.getAttribute(serverRuntime, "HealthState")));

    ObjectName jvmRuntime = (ObjectName) myJMXWrapper.getAttribute(serverRuntime, "JVMRuntime");
    // print HeapFreeCurrent
    System.out.println("JVM - HeapFreeCurrent="+
                    myJMXWrapper.getAttribute(jvmRuntime,"HeapFreeCurrent"));


    ObjectName jtaRuntime = (ObjectName) myJMXWrapper.getAttribute(serverRuntime, "JTARuntime");
    // HealthState
    System.out.println("JTA - HealthState="+ getHealthStateInformation((HealthState)
                    myJMXWrapper.getAttribute(jtaRuntime, "HealthState")));
    // print TransactionTotalCount
    System.out.println("JTA - TransactionTotalCount="+
                    myJMXWrapper.getAttribute(jtaRuntime,"TransactionTotalCount"));


    ObjectName threadPoolRuntime = (ObjectName)
                    myJMXWrapper.getAttribute(serverRuntime, "ThreadPoolRuntime");
    // HealthState
    System.out.println("Threadpool - HealthState="+ getHealthStateInformation((HealthState)
                    myJMXWrapper.getAttribute(threadPoolRuntime, "HealthState")));
    // print CompletedRequestCount
    System.out.println("Threadpool - CompletedRequestCount="+
                    myJMXWrapper.getAttribute(threadPoolRuntime,"CompletedRequestCount"));

    // datasources
    String nextName = null;
    ObjectName nextOName = null;
    HashMap<String, ObjectName> dsList = getDatasourceNames(serverName);
    Iterator it = dsList.keySet().iterator();
    while (it.hasNext())
    {
        nextName = (String)it.next();
        nextOName = dsList.get(nextName);

        // print Enabled
        System.out.println("Datasource:"+nextName+" Enabled",
                        myJMXWrapper.getAttribute(nextOName,"Enabled"));
        // print State
        System.out.println("Datasource:"+nextName+" State",
                        myJMXWrapper.getAttribute(nextOName,"State"));
    }

    // applications
    HashMap<String, ObjectName> appList = getApplicationNames(serverName,true);
    it = appList.keySet().iterator();
    while (it.hasNext())
    {
        nextName = (String)it.next();
        System.out.println("Application "+nextName+" State ",
                        myWLSMonitoringUtils.getHealthStateInformation((HealthState)
                        myJMXWrapper.getAttribute(appList.get(nextName), "HealthState")));
    }
}
```

Heap Size and Other VM Monitoring with JMX

In larger production systems, especially in cloud-like systems, many WebLogic Server instances are often running on the same box. This is especially the case if you have dedicated hosts for the Administration Servers. In all cases your physical memory is limited and it is necessary to do some capacity planning. Usually the heap size of your WebLogic Servers are set too high as it is difficult to calculate the right size upfront. You might also experience out-of-memory exceptions on your WebLogic Servers. In this case the memory settings are too small.

The following method will print the Java version and the current heap values, including free heap. Note that the attributes and operations provided by this MBean depend on the JVM type, which means that the Hotspot VM has other attributes/operations besides the JRockit VM.

```
public void printServerJVMRuntimeInformation(String serverName) throws Exception
{
    ObjectName serverRuntime = myJMXWrapper.getServerRuntime(serverName);
    ObjectName jvmRuntime = (ObjectName) myJMXWrapper.getAttribute(serverRuntime, "JVMRuntime");

    // print JavaVendor
    System.out.println("   JavaVendor=" + myJMXWrapper.getAttribute(jvmRuntime, "JavaVendor"));
    // print JavaVersion
    System.out.println("   JavaVersion=" + myJMXWrapper.getAttribute(jvmRuntime, "JavaVersion"));
    // print HeapFreeCurrent
    System.out.println("   HeapFreeCurrent=" +
                myJMXWrapper.getAttribute(jvmRuntime, "HeapFreeCurrent"));
    // print HeapFreePercent
    System.out.println("   HeapFreePercent=" +
                myJMXWrapper.getAttribute(jvmRuntime, "HeapFreePercent"));
    // print HeapSizeCurrent
    System.out.println("   HeapSizeCurrent=" +
                myJMXWrapper.getAttribute(jvmRuntime, "HeapSizeCurrent"));
    // print Uptime
    System.out.println("   Uptime=" + myJMXWrapper.getAttribute(jvmRuntime, "Uptime"));
}
```

Server Resource Monitoring with JMX

A J2EE application server like WebLogic consists of many different resources, resource pools, and other runtime artifacts. It is very difficult to document and mention all of them, so this chapter will give an overview of the most common and most important ones with a number of example scripts. At the end a comprehensive example will print the most important server details.

Note that WebLogic does activate or instantiate resource pools as needed (like when a new application is deployed or new WorkManagers are created). Therefore this chapter can only provide basic ideas and general scripts that must be tailored to your actual project and setup needs.

Thread Pools

Among the important resources of each WebLogic Server are threads. The amount of threads and especially the amount of parallel execution and pending requests will give you a good indication if the server is operating in a healthy state and if user requests can be executed in a timely manner. If those numbers are getting too high, then the server has too many parallel tasks and needs too much time for scheduling. This also usually means that some dependent services (like databases) do not react on time.

🖫 monitor_thread_pool_jmx

```
public void printServerThreadPoolInformation(String serverName) throws Exception
{
    ObjectName serverRuntime = myJMXWrapper.getServerRuntime(serverName);
    ObjectName threadPoolRuntime = (ObjectName)
                    myJMXWrapper.getAttribute(serverRuntime, "ThreadPoolRuntime");

    // print CompletedRequestCount
    System.out.println("    CompletedRequestCount=" +
                    myJMXWrapper.getAttribute(threadPoolRuntime, "CompletedRequestCount"));
    // print ExecuteThreadTotalCount
    System.out.println("    ExecuteThreadTotalCount=" +
                    myJMXWrapper.getAttribute(threadPoolRuntime, "ExecuteThreadTotalCount"));
    // print ExecuteThreadIdleCount
    System.out.println("    ExecuteThreadIdleCount=" +
                    myJMXWrapper.getAttribute(threadPoolRuntime, "ExecuteThreadIdleCount"));
    // HealthState
    System.out.println("    HealthState="+ myWLSMonitoringUtils.getHealthStateInformation(
                    (HealthState)myJMXWrapper.getAttribute(threadPoolRuntime,"HealthState")));
    // print HoggingThreadCount
    System.out.println("    HoggingThreadCount=" +
                    myJMXWrapper.getAttribute(threadPoolRuntime, "HoggingThreadCount"));
    // print PendingUserRequestCount
    System.out.println("    PendingUserRequestCount=" +
                    myJMXWrapper.getAttribute(threadPoolRuntime, "PendingUserRequestCount"));
    // print QueueLength
    System.out.println("    QueueLength=" +
                    myJMXWrapper.getAttribute(threadPoolRuntime, "QueueLength"));
    // print SharedCapacityForWorkManagers
    System.out.println("    SharedCapacityForWorkManagers=" +
                myJMXWrapper.getAttribute(threadPoolRuntime, "SharedCapacityForWorkManagers"));
    // print StandbyThreadCount
    System.out.println("    StandbyThreadCount=" +
                    myJMXWrapper.getAttribute(threadPoolRuntime, "StandbyThreadCount"));
    // print Suspended
    System.out.println("    Suspended=" +
                    myJMXWrapper.getAttribute(threadPoolRuntime, "Suspended"));
    // print Throughput
    System.out.println("    Throughput=" +
                    myJMXWrapper.getAttribute(threadPoolRuntime, "Throughput"));
}
```

The script above monitors the entire thread pool. WebLogic also offers a much finer concept called WorkManager. Even in a default domain, WebLogic has only the default WorkManager, but it is possible to create any number of individual WorkManagers (see the WorkManager discussion in *Chapter 6* for more information).

Transaction Pools

Transactions are another very valuable source of information. For the overall health state of the server instance and of the deployed applications, the number of rolled-backs, abandoned, and especially heuristic transactions are very good indicators. Whereas a rolled-back might be absolutely ok, if the business decided not to commit the transactions it might indicate problems. Therefore, WebLogic offers different numbers for the different rollback categories. Especially TransactionRolledBackResourceTotalCount (due to resource issues) or TransactionRolledBackTimeoutTotalCount (due to maximal duration constraint violation) are indicators for infrastructure and resource issues. Heuristics almost always means problems and in most cases need human intervention in order to repair the damage because this means that atomic operations have only be performed partially.

The following method shows how to monitor transactional values of a server:

🖫 monitor_transactional_values_jmx

```
public void printServerJTAInformation(String serverName) throws Exception
{
    ObjectName serverRuntime = myJMXWrapper.getServerRuntime(serverName);
    ObjectName jtaRuntime = (ObjectName) myJMXWrapper.getAttribute(serverRuntime, "JTARuntime");

    // HealthState
    System.out.println("   HealthState="+ getHealthStateInformation((HealthState)
                     myJMXWrapper.getAttribute(jtaRuntime,"HealthState")));
    // print TransactionTotalCount
    System.out.println("   TransactionTotalCount=" +
                     myJMXWrapper.getAttribute(jtaRuntime, "TransactionTotalCount"));
    // print TransactionCommittedTotalCount
    System.out.println("   TransactionCommittedTotalCount=" +
                     myJMXWrapper.getAttribute(jtaRuntime, "TransactionCommittedTotalCount"));
    // print ActiveTransactionsTotalCount
    System.out.println("   ActiveTransactionsTotalCount=" +
                     myJMXWrapper.getAttribute(jtaRuntime, "ActiveTransactionsTotalCount"));
    // print TransactionRolledBackTotalCount
    System.out.println("   TransactionRolledBackTotalCount=" +
                     myJMXWrapper.getAttribute(jtaRuntime, "TransactionRolledBackTotalCount"));
    // print TransactionRolledBackTimeoutTotalCount
    System.out.println("   TransactionRolledBackTimeoutTotalCount=" +
               myJMXWrapper.getAttribute(jtaRuntime, "TransactionRolledBackTimeoutTotalCount"));
    // print TransactionRolledBackResourceTotalCount
    System.out.println("   TransactionRolledBackResourceTotalCount=" +
               myJMXWrapper.getAttribute(jtaRuntime, "TransactionRolledBackResourceTotalCount"));
    // print TransactionAbandonedTotalCount
    System.out.println("   TransactionAbandonedTotalCount=" +
               myJMXWrapper.getAttribute(jtaRuntime, "TransactionAbandonedTotalCount"));
    // print TransactionHeuristicsTotalCount
    System.out.println("   TransactionHeuristicsTotalCount=" +
               myJMXWrapper.getAttribute(jtaRuntime, "TransactionHeuristicsTotalCount"));
}
```

Cluster Monitoring

WebLogic also offers the possibility to monitor the cluster state. Unfortunately this cannot be done directly as WebLogic does not know about the *cluster runtime* MBean type and therefore the following method will retrieve the list of cluster names and the list of servers belonging to each cluster from the configuration MBean. Then the code will iterate over all the servers of one cluster and collect their actual runtime state. The overall cluster state is computed out of the combined state of all Managed-Servers.

🖫 monitor_cluster_state_jmx

```
public void printClusterStates() throws Exception
{
    ObjectName myDomainMBean = myJMXWrapper.getDomainConfigRoot();

    System.out.println("Cluster state information:");
    ObjectName[] allClusters = (ObjectName[])myJMXWrapper.getAttribute(myDomainMBean,"Clusters");
```

```
for (int c=0;c<allClusters.length;c++)
{
  // use 1st cluster !!!
  // get cluster member
  ObjectName[] clusterServer = (ObjectName[])myJMXWrapper.getAttribute(allClusters[c],"Servers");
  String nextName = (String)myJMXWrapper.getAttribute(allClusters[c],"Name");

  int amountClusterServerRunning = 0;
  int amountClusterServerShutdown = 0;
  int amountClusterServerNotWorkingOrFailed = 0;

  // iterate over cluster member
  for (int i=0; i<clusterServer.length;i++)
  {
    String nextState =  myJMXWrapper.getServerState((String)
                                    myJMXWrapper.getAttribute(clusterServer[i],"Name"));

    if ("RUNNING".equalsIgnoreCase(nextState))
        amountClusterServerRunning++;
    else if ("SHUTDOWN".equalsIgnoreCase(nextState))
        amountClusterServerShutdown++;
    else // all other states
        amountClusterServerNotWorkingOrFailed++;
  }

  if (clusterServer.length == amountClusterServerRunning)  // all running
    System.out.println(" Cluster "+nextName+" has the state: RUNNING" );
  else if (clusterServer.length == amountClusterServerShutdown)  // all shutdown or failed :-((
    System.out.println(" Cluster "+nextName+" has the state: SHUTDOW" );
  else if (clusterServer.length == amountClusterServerNotWorkingOrFailed) // shutdown or failed
    System.out.println(" Cluster "+nextName+" has the state: NOT WORKING OR FAILED");
  else  if (amountClusterServerRunning>0) // partly running
    System.out.println(" Cluster "+nextName+" has the state: PARTLY RUNNING" );
  else
    System.out.println(" Cluster "+nextName+" has the state: NOT WORKING OR FAILED" );
}

// if cluster list is empty
if (allClusters.length==0)
{
  // no cluster ?!?!?!
  System.out.println("NO Cluster configured" );
}
}
```

WorkManager Monitoring

WebLogic uses a concept called WorkManager in order to prioritize work and maintain threads and thread-pools. WorkManager can be created and configured by the administrator on the WebLogic level or by application developers on the application level (deployment descriptors). Different additional configuration items like maximal thread restriction are available for more detailed configuration of the resource usage and restriction. See the WorkManager section in *Chapter 6* for more details.

WorkManager consist of different configuration items. In order to restrict, organize, control, or manage work, you need to define WorkManager components. WebLogic offers the following components for WorkManagers:

Constraints:

- Minimum threads constraint

- Maximum threads constraint

- Capacity constraint

Request components:

- Fair share request class

- Response time request class

- Context request class

The following JMX code shows how to monitor values from the different WorkManagers and their subcomponents:

```
mySet = myJMXWrapper.getConnection().queryNames(new
     ObjectName("*:*,ServerRuntime="+mainDomainValues.get("serverName")+",Type=WorkManagerRuntime"),
     null);
Iterator it = mySet.iterator();
System.out.println("All WorkManagerRuntime MBeans !");
while (it.hasNext()) {
   printOneWorkManagerInfo((ObjectName) it.next());
}
```

This code shows an interesting JMX query that will retrieve all WorkManager runtime MBeans from the MBeanServer. After retrieving the MBeans, it is possible to display all the details:

💾 WorkManager_runtime_MBeans_jmx

```
public void printOneWorkManagerInfo(ObjectName wmRuntime) throws Exception {
   System.out.println("\nWorkmanager : "+wmRuntime.toString());

   String name   = (String) myJMXWrapper.getAttribute(wmRuntime, "Name");
   String health = getHealthStateInformation((HealthState)
                 myJMXWrapper.getAttribute(wmRuntime,"HealthState"));
   long completedRequests = (Long)myJMXWrapper.getAttribute(wmRuntime, "CompletedRequests");
   int pendingRequests = (Integer)myJMXWrapper.getAttribute(wmRuntime, "PendingRequests");
   int stuckThreadCount = (Integer)myJMXWrapper.getAttribute(wmRuntime, "StuckThreadCount");

   System.out.println("    Name: "+ name);
   System.out.println("    Healthstate: "+ health);
   System.out.println("    CompletedRequests: "+ completedRequests);
   System.out.println("    PendingRequests: "+ pendingRequests);
   System.out.println("    StuckThreadCount: "+ stuckThreadCount);

   // get the different subcomponent
   ObjectName myMaxThreadsConstraintRuntime =
            (ObjectName)myJMXWrapper.getAttribute(wmRuntime, "MaxThreadsConstraintRuntime");
   ObjectName myMinThreadsConstraintRuntime =
            (ObjectName)myJMXWrapper.getAttribute(wmRuntime, "MinThreadsConstraintRuntime");
   ObjectName myRequestClassRuntime =
            (ObjectName)myJMXWrapper.getAttribute(wmRuntime, "RequestClassRuntime");

   if (myMaxThreadsConstraintRuntime != null) {
      String maxContraintName = (String)
            myJMXWrapper.getAttribute(myMaxThreadsConstraintRuntime, "Name");
      int maxContraintDeferredRequests = (Integer)
            myJMXWrapper.getAttribute(myMaxThreadsConstraintRuntime, "DeferredRequests");
      int maxContraintExecutingRequests = (Integer)
            myJMXWrapper.getAttribute(myMaxThreadsConstraintRuntime, "ExecutingRequests");

      System.out.println("    MaxThreadsConstraint: Name: "+maxContraintName+" DeferredRequests: "+
```

```
                         maxContraintDeferredRequests+"     ExecutingRequests: "+
                         maxContraintExecutingRequests);

    String maxONname=myMaxThreadsConstraintRuntime.getKeyProperty("Name");
    if (maxONname != null) {
       // try to get config mbean
       Set<ObjectName> mySet = myJMXWrapper.getConnection().queryNames(
                         new ObjectName("*:*,Name="+maxONname+",Type=MaxThreadsConstraint"), null);
       if (! mySet.isEmpty()) {
          // get first
          ObjectName myFirstConfigName = (ObjectName) mySet.iterator().next();
          // get count
          int maxCount = (Integer)myJMXWrapper.getAttribute(myFirstConfigName, "Count");
          System.out.println("            -> max limit = "+maxCount);
       }
       else {
          System.out.println("            -> no config mbean found !");
       }
    }
 }
 else {
    System.out.println("   MaxThreadsConstraint not defined !");
 }

 if (myMinThreadsConstraintRuntime != null) {
    String minContraintName = (String)
          myJMXWrapper.getAttribute(myMinThreadsConstraintRuntime, "Name");
    long minContraintOutOfOrderExecutionCount = (Long)
          myJMXWrapper.getAttribute(myMinThreadsConstraintRuntime, "OutOfOrderExecutionCount");
    int minContraintPendingRequests = (Integer)
          myJMXWrapper.getAttribute(myMinThreadsConstraintRuntime, "PendingRequests");
    long minContraintCompletedRequests = (Long)
          myJMXWrapper.getAttribute(myMinThreadsConstraintRuntime, "CompletedRequests");
    long minContraintMaxWaitTime = (Long)
          myJMXWrapper.getAttribute(myMinThreadsConstraintRuntime, "MaxWaitTime");
    int minContraintMustRunCount = (Integer)
          myJMXWrapper.getAttribute(myMinThreadsConstraintRuntime, "MustRunCount");

    long minContraintCurrentWaitTime = (Long)
          myJMXWrapper.getAttribute(myMinThreadsConstraintRuntime, "CurrentWaitTime");
    int minContraintExecutingRequests = (Integer)
          myJMXWrapper.getAttribute(myMinThreadsConstraintRuntime, "ExecutingRequests");

    System.out.println("   MinThreadsConstraint: Name = "+ minContraintName);
    System.out.println("                         OutOfOrderExecutionCount = "
                     + minContraintOutOfOrderExecutionCount);
    System.out.println("                         PendingRequests = "
                     + minContraintPendingRequests);
    System.out.println("                         CompletedRequests = "
                     + minContraintCompletedRequests);
    System.out.println("                         MaxWaitTime = " + minContraintMaxWaitTime);
    System.out.println("                         MustRunCount = " + minContraintMustRunCount);
    System.out.println("                         CurrentWaitTime = "
                     + minContraintCurrentWaitTime);
    System.out.println("                         ExecutingRequests = "
                     + minContraintExecutingRequests);

    String minONname=myMinThreadsConstraintRuntime.getKeyProperty("Name");
    if (minONname != null) {
       // try to get config mbean
       Set<ObjectName> mySet = myJMXWrapper.getConnection().queryNames(
                         new ObjectName("*:*,Name="+minONname+",Type=MinThreadsConstraint"), null);
       if (! mySet.isEmpty()) {
          // get first
          ObjectName myFirstConfigName = (ObjectName) mySet.iterator().next();
          // get count
          int minCount = (Integer)myJMXWrapper.getAttribute(myFirstConfigName, "Count");
          System.out.println("            -> min limit = "+minCount);
       }
       else {
          System.out.println("            -> no config mbean found !");
       }
    }
 }
 else
    System.out.println("   MinThreadsConstraint not defined !");

 if (myRequestClassRuntime != null) {
```

```
long reqClassTotalThreadUse = (Long)
            myJMXWrapper.getAttribute(myRequestClassRuntime, "TotalThreadUse");
double reqClassInterval = (Double)
            myJMXWrapper.getAttribute(myRequestClassRuntime, "Interval");
long reqClassCompletedCount = (Long)
            myJMXWrapper.getAttribute(myRequestClassRuntime, "CompletedCount");
long reqClassVirtualTimeIncrement = (Long)
            myJMXWrapper.getAttribute(myRequestClassRuntime, "VirtualTimeIncrement");
long reqClassThreadUseSquares = (Long)
            myJMXWrapper.getAttribute(myRequestClassRuntime, "ThreadUseSquares");
long reqClassDeltaFirst = (Long)myJMXWrapper.getAttribute(myRequestClassRuntime, "DeltaFirst");
int reqClassPendingRequestCount = (Integer)
            myJMXWrapper.getAttribute(myRequestClassRuntime, "PendingRequestCount");
long reqClassDeltaRepeat = (Long)
            myJMXWrapper.getAttribute(myRequestClassRuntime, "DeltaRepeat");
long reqClassMyLast = (Long)myJMXWrapper.getAttribute(myRequestClassRuntime, "MyLast");
String reqClassRequestClassType = (String)
        myJMXWrapper.getAttribute(myRequestClassRuntime, "RequestClassType");
String reqClassName = (String)myJMXWrapper.getAttribute(myRequestClassRuntime, "Name");

System.out.println("    RequestClass:  Name = "+reqClassName+
                " is of type "+reqClassRequestClassType);
System.out.println("                        TotalThreadUse = "+reqClassTotalThreadUse);
System.out.println("                        Interval = "+reqClassInterval);
System.out.println("                        CompletedCount = "+reqClassCompletedCount);
System.out.println("                        VirtualTimeIncrement = "+reqClassVirtualTimeIncrement);
System.out.println("                        ThreadUseSquares = "+reqClassThreadUseSquares);
System.out.println("                        DeltaFirst = "+reqClassDeltaFirst);
System.out.println("                        PendingRequestCount = "+reqClassPendingRequestCount);
System.out.println("                        DeltaRepeat = "+reqClassDeltaRepeat);
System.out.println("                        MyLast = "+reqClassMyLast);
}
else {
    System.out.println("    RequestClass not defined !");
}
}
```

Transaction Monitoring with JMX

Transactions are one of the most important and most often used resources on a J2EE server. WebLogic offers a broad range of configuration options to configure transactions, which also includes rather unknown values such as abandoning transactions or XA call timeouts. WebLogic also offers recovery strategies for transactions of a failed server, which includes server migration or manual activities. Starting with 12c, WebLogic also offers the ability to outsource the transaction log (TLog) into a database.

What is rather unknown is the fact that WebLogic also offers monitoring on transactions and resources. This includes views of transaction statistics, views for XA and non-XA resources, current transactions, and more. This monitoring can be done using the WebConsole, WLST, or JMX.

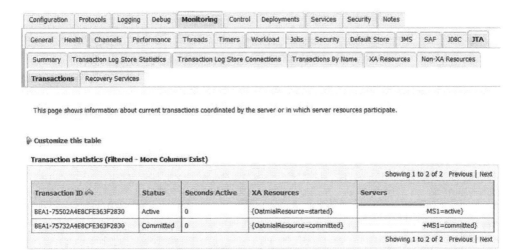

Figure 17.1: *Transaction monitoring in WLS*

Transaction MBean

The transactional subsystem in WebLogic consists of a number of different MBeans that provide runtime information about transactions. Every live transaction is represented in WebLogic using an object that implements the *weblogic.management.runtime.JTATransaction* interface.

```
public interface JTATransaction extends Serializable

 String getCoordinatorURL()
         The URL of the coordinating server.
 String getName()
         The name of the transaction as defined by the application that started the transaction.
 Map getResourceNamesAndStatus()
         The collection of participating resource names and their status for the transaction.
 int getSecondsActiveCurrentCount()
         The time in seconds for which the transaction has been active.
 String[] getServers()
         The servers that participate in the transaction.
 Map getServersAndStatus()
         The collection of participating servers and their status for the transaction.
 String getStatus()
         The current status of the transaction.
 Map getUserProperties()
         The user-defined properties associated with the transaction.
 Xid getXid()
         The transaction ID assigned by the transaction manager.
```

The main transaction MBeans include:

- JTARecoveryRuntimeMBean

- JTAStatisticsRuntimeMBean

- JTATransactionStatisticsRuntimeMBean

- JTARuntimeMBean

- TransactionNameRuntimeMBean

- NonXAResourceRuntimeMBean

- TransactionResourceRuntimeMBean

Transaction Monitoring

The main MBean used for transaction monitoring is the *JTARuntimeMBean*. This MBean offers a variety of information about each active transaction. Each transaction is represented by an object of the type *JTATransaction*, which represents actual runtime data about a transaction.

The following table shows the methods for interfacing *weblogic.management.runtime.JTATransaction*:

Method	Description
getCoordinatorURL()	The URL of the coordinating server
getName()	The name of the transaction as defined by the application that started the transaction
getResourceNamesAndStatus()	The collection of participating resource names and their status for the transaction.
getSecondsActiveCurrentCount()	The time in seconds for which the transaction has been active
getServers()	The servers that participate in the transaction
getServersAndStatus()	The collection of participating servers and their status for the transaction
getStatus()	The current status of the transaction
getXid()	transaction ID assigned by the transaction manager

(Source: Oracle Corporation)

Table 17.1: weblogic.management.runtime.JTATransaction Methods

The next example will discuss a function that will query all active transactions from the transaction runtime and print their status, time active, and also the participating servers. For this example, the following methods from *weblogic.management.runtime.JTARuntimeMBean* are being used:

Method	Description
getJTATransaction(String xid)	Gets the JTATransaction object for the transaction with the specified Xid
getJTATransactions()	Get a list of all transaction objects
getTransactionsOlderThan(Integer seconds)	Interesting method to get a list of all transactions which are older than a given time. Very handy to detect long running transactions

Table 17.2: weblogic.management.runtime.JTARuntimeMBean Methods

Implementation of the method:

query_active_transactions_jmx

```
@SuppressWarnings("rawtypes")
public void printActiveJTATransactionValues() throws Exception {
    ObjectName serverRuntime =
        myJMXWrapper.getServerRuntime(myJMXWrapper.getMainServerDomainValues().get("serverName"));

    ObjectName jtaRuntime = (ObjectName) myJMXWrapper.getAttribute(serverRuntime, "JTARuntime");

    // all active transactions
    JTATransaction[] allActiveTransactions =
        (JTATransaction[])myJMXWrapper.getAttribute(jtaRuntime, "JTATransactions");
    //allActiveTransactions
    if (allActiveTransactions != null)
        for (int i=0;i<allActiveTransactions.length;i++) {
            System.out.println("\nTransaction Nr.: "+
                        i+"\n======================================\n");

            // transaction details
            //The transaction ID assigned by the transaction manager.
            try {
                System.out.println("XID :"+
                    allActiveTransactions[i].getXid().getGlobalTransactionId().toString());
            }
            catch(Exception ex) {
                System.out.println("XID : XID_wrong_or_missing");
            }

            //The current status of the transaction.
            System.out.println("Status :"+allActiveTransactions[i].getStatus());

            //The URL of the coordinating server.
            System.out.println("CoordinatorURL :"+allActiveTransactions[i].getCoordinatorURL());

            // The name of the transaction as defined by the application that started the transaction.
            System.out.println("Name :"+allActiveTransactions[i].getName());

            //The time in seconds for which the transaction has been active.
            System.out.println("SecondsActive :" +
                        allActiveTransactions[i].getSecondsActiveCurrentCount());

            String[] txServers = allActiveTransactions[i].getServers();
            if (txServers==null) txServers = new String[0];

            //The servers that participate in the transaction.
            StringBuffer txServerNames = new StringBuffer();
            for (int s=0;s<txServers.length;s++)
                txServerNames.append(txServers[s]+" ");

            // add
            System.out.println("Servers :"+txServerNames.toString());

            // The collection of participating resource names and their status for the transaction.
            Map mapResourceNamesAndStatus = allActiveTransactions[i].getResourceNamesAndStatus();
            if (mapResourceNamesAndStatus!=null)
                System.out.println("ResourceNamesAndStatus :"+printMap(mapResourceNamesAndStatus));
            else
                System.out.println("ResourceNamesAndStatus ----");
```

```
    // The collection of participating servers and their status for the transaction.
    Map mapServersAndStatus = allActiveTransactions[i].getServersAndStatus();
    if (mapServersAndStatus!=null)
       System.out.println("ServersAndStatus :"+printMap(mapServersAndStatus));
    else
       System.out.println("ServersAndStatus ----");

    // The user-defined properties associated with the transaction.
    Map mapUserProperties = allActiveTransactions[i].getUserProperties();
    if (mapUserProperties!=null)
        System.out.println("Properties :"+printMap(mapUserProperties));
    else
        System.out.println("Properties: ----");
   }
}
```

This function can be particularly useful in order to find long-running transactions and their involved resource manager.

Resource Monitoring with JMX

Transactions coordinate the usage of resources. WebLogic honors this by providing MBeans for resources used by transactions. For the next example, the following method from *weblogic.management.runtime.JTARuntimeMBean* will be used, which returns the different resource MBeans:

Method	Description
getTransactionResourceRuntimeMBeans()	Returns a list of ResourceRuntime MBeans. Each of the returned MBean provides statistic values for a resource.

Table 17.3: weblogic.management.runtime.JTARuntimeMBean Method

The runtime MBean for resource monitoring (*TransactionResourceRuntimeMBean*) and its parent interfaces offer the following methods used in the following code example. Besides health state and name, a number of very interesting values are provided that help to identify potential issues. The different heuristic values are especially valuable indicators for whether the resource can perform the transactions well.

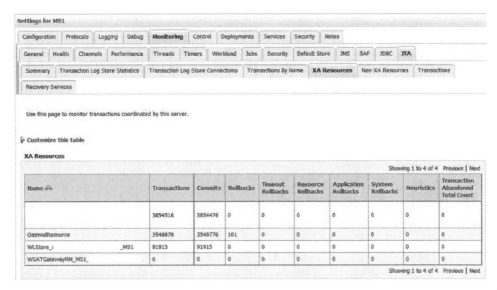

Figure 17.2: *WLS Resource Monitoring*

The following methods from the *TransactionResourceRuntimeMBean* are used in the subsequent code example:

Method	Description
getHealthState()	The health state of the Resource
getResourceName()	The resource name
getTransactionHeuristicCommitTotalCount()	The number of transactions for which this resource has returned a heuristic commit decision
getTransactionHeuristicHazardTotalCount()	The number of transactions for which this resource has reported a heuristic hazard decision
getTransactionHeuristicMixedTotalCount()	The number of transactions for which this resource has reported a heuristic mixed decision
getTransactionHeuristicRollbackTotalCount()	The number of transactions for which this resource has returned a heuristic rollback decision
getTransactionCommittedTotalCount()	The total number of transactions committed since the server was started
getTransactionHeuristicsTotalCount()	The number of transactions that completed with a heuristic status since the server was started.
getTransactionRolledBackTotalCount()	The number of transactions that were rolled back since the server was started
getTransactionTotalCount()	The total number of transactions processed

(Source: Oracle Corporation)

Table 17.4: TransactionResourceRuntimeMBean Methods

The following is an implementation example for a method that prints the statistic information from the different transactional resources:

```
public  void printXAResourceInformationValues() throws Exception
{
    ObjectName serverRuntime =
        myJMXWrapper.getServerRuntime(myJMXWrapper.getMainServerDomainValues().get("serverName"));

    ObjectName jtaRuntime = (ObjectName) myJMXWrapper.getAttribute(serverRuntime, "JTARuntime");

    // all XA Resources transactions
    TransactionResourceRuntimeMBean[] allXAResources =
        (TransactionResourceRuntimeMBean[])myJMXWrapper.getAttribute(jtaRuntime,
        "TransactionResourceRuntimeMBeans");

    //all XA resources
    if (allXAResources != null)
        for (int i=0;i<allXAResources.length;i++)
        {
            System.out.println("\nXA Resource Nr.: "+i);

            // resource details

            // The resource name
            System.out.println("ResourceName: "+
                        myJMXWrapper.getAttribute(serverRuntime, "ResourceName"));

            // The number of tx for which this resource has returned a heuristic commit decision
            System.out.println("TransactionHeuristicCommitTotalCount: "+
                myJMXWrapper.getAttribute(serverRuntime, "TransactionHeuristicCommitTotalCount"));

            // The number of tx for which this resource has reported a heuristic hazard decision
            System.out.println("TransactionHeuristicHazardTotalCount: "+
                myJMXWrapper.getAttribute(serverRuntime, "TransactionHeuristicHazardTotalCount"));

            // The number of transactions for which this resource has reported a heuristic mixed decision
            System.out.println("TransactionHeuristicMixedTotalCount: "+
                myJMXWrapper.getAttribute(serverRuntime, "TransactionHeuristicMixedTotalCount"));

            // The number of tx for which this resource has returned a heuristic rollback decision
            System.out.println("TransactionHeuristicRollbackTotalCount: "+
                myJMXWrapper.getAttribute(serverRuntime, "TransactionHeuristicRollbackTotalCount"));

            // The total number of transactions committed since the server was started.
            System.out.println("TransactionCommittedTotalCount: "+
                myJMXWrapper.getAttribute(serverRuntime, "TransactionCommittedTotalCount"));

            System.out.println("TransactionHeuristicsTotalCount: "+
                myJMXWrapper.getAttribute(serverRuntime, "TransactionHeuristicsTotalCount"));

            // TransactionRolledBackTotalCount
            System.out.println("TransactionRolledBackTotalCount: "+
                myJMXWrapper.getAttribute(serverRuntime, "TransactionRolledBackTotalCount"));

            // The total number of transactions processed.
            System.out.println("TransactionTotalCount: "+
                    myJMXWrapper.getAttribute(serverRuntime, "TransactionTotalCount"));
        }
}
```

Network Channels with JMX

By default, all communication going into a WebLogic Server uses the same communication port or better IP/port. This also means that WebLogic is listening on the same port with all available protocols for T3, T3S, HTTP, HTTPS, LDAP, SNMP, IIOP, IIOPS cluster, and admin communication. For simple domains and networks, this is usually acceptable. However, it does not efficiently use the available network resources of bigger machines.

A network channel is a configuration item in WebLogic that defines the communication endpoint of a network connection. This usually includes the protocol, IP, and port that WebLogic has to use for the network listener. It might also include additional properties such as login timeout, tunneling support, and (in case of secure lines) SSL and certificate enforcement.

Monitoring network channel means querying network information like bytes received/sent or other values:

🖫 monitor_network_channel_jmx

```
public void printNetworkChannelInformation() throws Exception {
    Hashtable<String,String> mainDomainValues = myJMXWrapper.getMainServerDomainValues();

    ObjectName serverRuntime = myJMXWrapper.getServerRuntime(mainDomainValues.get("serverName"));

    // get all the different channel runtime mbeans
    ObjectName[] serverChannelRuntimes = (ObjectName[])
            myJMXWrapper.getAttribute(serverRuntime, "ServerChannelRuntimes");

    for (int i=0;i<serverChannelRuntimes.length;i++) {
        String channelName = (String)myJMXWrapper.getAttribute(serverChannelRuntimes[i], "Name");
        String channelURL = (String)myJMXWrapper.getAttribute(serverChannelRuntimes[i], "PublicURL");

        long channelAcceptCount = (Long)
            myJMXWrapper.getAttribute(serverChannelRuntimes[i], "AcceptCount");
        long channelActiveConnectionsCount = (Long)
            myJMXWrapper.getAttribute(serverChannelRuntimes[i], "ConnectionsCount");
        long channelBytesReceivedCount = (Long)
            myJMXWrapper.getAttribute(serverChannelRuntimes[i], "BytesReceivedCount");
        long channelBytesSentCount = (Long)
            myJMXWrapper.getAttribute(serverChannelRuntimes[i], "BytesSentCount");
        long channelMessagesReceivedCount = (Long)
            myJMXWrapper.getAttribute(serverChannelRuntimes[i], "MessagesReceivedCount");
        long channelMessagesSentCount = (Long)
            myJMXWrapper.getAttribute(serverChannelRuntimes[i], "MessagesSentCount");

        System.out.println("Channelname: "+channelName+"   (URL="+channelURL+")");
        System.out.println("            Total connections count = "+channelAcceptCount);
        System.out.println("            Actual connected connections = "
                    +channelActiveConnectionsCount);
        System.out.println("            BytesReceived = "+channelBytesReceivedCount);
        System.out.println("            BytesSent = "+channelBytesSentCount);
        System.out.println("            MessagesReceived = "+channelMessagesReceivedCount);
        System.out.println("            MessagesSent = "+channelMessagesSentCount);
        System.out.println("\n");
    }
}
```

Service Monitoring

One of the most common monitoring activities is the monitoring of server services. This includes the monitoring of datasources, JMS services, mail, and other services. A service is basically everything used by one or more applications but is not part of the application. One concept of J2EE is that services can be used but should not be provided by the application as they are infrastructure and in almost all cases depend on the environment in use (e.g. hostnames, ports, user, passwords, etc.). Applications should never worry about those environment details.

Monitoring Datasources with JMX

The most common resources are databases. Databases are accessed from a J2EE application by using datasources. Database access means controlling connections, accessing information, and more.

The following method shows a way to find all datasources deployed on a particular server. In order to find these datasources, the program is using the *JDBCServiceRuntime* of the server in question.

```
public HashMap<String, ObjectName> getDatasourceNames(String serverName) throws Exception
{
    HashMap<String, ObjectName> myResultList = new HashMap<String, ObjectName>();

    ObjectName jdbcServerRuntime = new ObjectName("com.bea:Name="+serverName+
                            ",ServerRuntime="+serverName+",Type=JDBCServiceRuntime");

    ObjectName[] allDatasourceRuntimeMBeans = (ObjectName[])
            myJMXWrapper.getAttribute(jdbcServerRuntime,"JDBCDataSourceRuntimeMBeans");

    String nextDatasourceName = null;
    for (int i=0;i<allDatasourceRuntimeMBeans.length;i++)
    {
        nextDatasourceName =
                (String)myJMXWrapper.getAttribute(allDatasourceRuntimeMBeans[i],"Name");

        myResultList.put(nextDatasourceName,allDatasourceRuntimeMBeans[i]);
    }

    return myResultList;
}
```

Once the datasource name is known, you can use the next method in order to print a number of important values from that datasource.

⊟ print_datasource_values_jmx

```
public void printDatasourceInformation(String datasourceName, ObjectName jdbcRuntimeMBean)
        throws Exception
{
    // print Name
    System.out.println("DATASOURCE:   Information about the datasource: "+datasourceName);

    System.out.println("   Enabled="+ myJMXWrapper.getAttribute(jdbcRuntimeMBean, "Enabled") +
                "    State="+ myJMXWrapper.getAttribute(jdbcRuntimeMBean, "State") );
    // print ActiveConnectionsHighCount
    System.out.println("   ActiveConnectionsHighCount="+
                myJMXWrapper.getAttribute(jdbcRuntimeMBean, "ActiveConnectionsHighCount"));
    // print ActiveConnectionsCurrentCount
    System.out.println("   ActiveConnectionsCurrentCount=" +
                myJMXWrapper.getAttribute(jdbcRuntimeMBean, "ActiveConnectionsCurrentCount"));
    // print ActiveConnectionsAverageCount
    System.out.println("   ActiveConnectionsAverageCount=" +
                myJMXWrapper.getAttribute(jdbcRuntimeMBean, "ActiveConnectionsAverageCount"));
    // print ConnectionsTotalCount
    System.out.println("   ConnectionsTotalCount=" +
                myJMXWrapper.getAttribute(jdbcRuntimeMBean, "ConnectionsTotalCount"));
    // print CurrCapacity
    System.out.println("   CurrCapacity=" +
                myJMXWrapper.getAttribute(jdbcRuntimeMBean, "CurrCapacity"));
    // print CurrCapacityHighCount
    System.out.println("   CurrCapacityHighCount=" +
                myJMXWrapper.getAttribute(jdbcRuntimeMBean, "CurrCapacityHighCount"));
    // print HighestNumAvailable
    System.out.println("   HighestNumAvailable=" +
                myJMXWrapper.getAttribute(jdbcRuntimeMBean, "HighestNumAvailable"));
```

```
        // print LeakedConnectionCount
        System.out.println("   LeakedConnectionCount=" +
                    myJMXWrapper.getAttribute(jdbcRuntimeMBean, "LeakedConnectionCount"));

        // print FailuresToReconnectCount
        System.out.println("   FailuresToReconnectCount=" +
                    myJMXWrapper.getAttribute(jdbcRuntimeMBean, "FailuresToReconnectCount"));

        // print WaitSecondsHighCount
        System.out.println("   WaitSecondsHighCount=" +
                    myJMXWrapper.getAttribute(jdbcRuntimeMBean, "WaitSecondsHighCount"));
        // print WaitingForConnectionCurrentCount
        System.out.println("   WaitingForConnectionCurrentCount=" +
                    myJMXWrapper.getAttribute(jdbcRuntimeMBean, "WaitingForConnectionCurrentCount"));
        // print WaitingForConnectionFailureTotal
        System.out.println("   WaitingForConnectionFailureTotal=" +
                    myJMXWrapper.getAttribute(jdbcRuntimeMBean, "WaitingForConnectionFailureTotal"));
        // print WaitingForConnectionTotal
        System.out.println("   WaitingForConnectionTotal=" +
                    myJMXWrapper.getAttribute(jdbcRuntimeMBean, "WaitingForConnectionTotal"));
        // print WaitingForConnectionHighCount
        System.out.println("   WaitingForConnectionHighCount=" +
                    myJMXWrapper.getAttribute(jdbcRuntimeMBean, "WaitingForConnectionHighCount"));
    }
```

JMS Runtime Monitoring with JMX

JMX provide a number of runtime monitoring values on JMS runtime level. The first example prints the overall health state of the JMS runtime system:

```
// prints the overall health state of the JMS runtime system
public void printJMSRuntimeState(String myServerName)  throws WLSAutomationException
{
   try
   {
      ObjectName serverRuntime = myJMXWrapper.getServerRuntime(myServerName);

      // get JMS runtime object reference
      ObjectName myJMSRuntime = (ObjectName) myJMXWrapper.getAttribute(serverRuntime, "JMSRuntime");

      // print state
      String health = getHealthStateInformation((weblogic.health.HealthState)
                         myJMXWrapper.getAttribute(myJMSRuntime, "HealthState"));
      String name = (String)myJMXWrapper.getAttribute(myJMSRuntime, "Name");
      System.out.println("JMSRuntime "+name+" current health state = "+health);
   }
   catch(Exception ex)
   {
      throw new WLSAutomationException("Error in printJMSRuntimeState : "+ ex.getMessage());
   }
}
```

The second example prints overall connection information of the JMS runtime system. The metrics available are current, high, and total connection count:

```
public void printJMSRuntimeInformation(String myServerName)  throws WLSAutomationException
{
   try
   {
      ObjectName serverRuntime = myJMXWrapper.getServerRuntime(myServerName);

      // get JMS runtime object reference
      ObjectName myJMSRuntime = (ObjectName) myJMXWrapper.getAttribute(serverRuntime, "JMSRuntime");
      String name = (String)myJMXWrapper.getAttribute(myJMSRuntime, "Name");

      // System.out.println(connection summary information
      System.out.println("JMSRuntime "+name+" ConnectionsCurrentCount = "+
                      myJMXWrapper.getAttribute(myJMSRuntime, "ConnectionsCurrentCount"));
      System.out.println("JMSRuntime "+name+" ConnectionsHighCount = "+
                      myJMXWrapper.getAttribute(myJMSRuntime, "ConnectionsHighCount"));
```

```
        System.out.println("JMSRuntime "+name+" ConnectionsTotalCount = "+
                             myJMXWrapper.getAttribute(myJMSRuntime, "ConnectionsTotalCount"));
    }
    catch(Exception ex)
    {
        throw new WLSAutomationException("Error in printJMSRuntimeState : "+ ex.getMessage());
    }
}
```

It is possible to define a number of JMSServers, therefore some of the following methods require a list of all configured JMSServers for a given ServerRuntime.

```
public Hashtable<String, ObjectName> getListOfJMSServerFromRuntime(ObjectName myJMSRuntime)
                             throws WLSAutomationException
{
    try
    {
        Hashtable<String, ObjectName> result = new Hashtable<String, ObjectName>();

        ObjectName[] jmsServers = (ObjectName[])
                myJMXWrapper.getAttribute(myJMSRuntime, "JMSServers");
        for (int i=0;i<jmsServers.length;i++)
        {
            String nextName = (String)myJMXWrapper.getAttribute(jmsServers[i], "Name");
            result.put(nextName, jmsServers[i]);
        }

        // return list
        return result;
    }
    catch(Exception ex)
    {
        throw new WLSAutomationException("Error in printJMSRuntimeState : "+ ex.getMessage());
    }
}
```

Connected Clients, Sessions, Producer and Consumer with JMX

For runtime analysis and usage monitoring, it can be very helpful to monitor who is connected to your JMS servers. JMX offers a pretty powerful API to list all active connections, their sessions, and also the producer and consumer of those sessions. Before we examine the JMX script, let us have a quick look at the MBeans and APIs.

The JMS runtime offers a method called *getConnections* that returns a list of active connections to this JMS runtime. Each of those objects is an instance of *JMSConnectionRuntimeMBean*. Please see *Chapter 9: Monitoring Domains with WLST* for more details.

The following program will navigate in the domain MBean tree to the desired server and then print all connections, sessions, and session information of this JMS runtime. Note that it is left up to the reader to extend the information printed for consumers and producers.

The following example prints information about connected JMS clients:

🖫 print_connections_jmx

```
public void printConnectedJMSClients(String myServerName) throws WLSAutomationException
{
    try
    {
        ObjectName serverRuntime = myJMXWrapper.getServerRuntime(myServerName);

        // get JMS runtime object reference
        ObjectName myJMSRuntime = (ObjectName) myJMXWrapper.getAttribute(serverRuntime, "JMSRuntime");

        // get all JMS connections for all JMS servers for this runtime
        // note that all connection instances are of type JMSConnectionRuntimeMBean
        ObjectName[] jmsConnections = (ObjectName[])
                myJMXWrapper.getAttribute(myJMSRuntime, "Connections");

        // amount
        System.out.println("Actually the "+myServerName+".jms runtime has " +
                        jmsConnections.length + " connections !");

        // now examine all jms connections and get some basic informations
        for (int i=0;i<jmsConnections.length;i++)
        {
            System.out.println("Connection: "+
                    myJMXWrapper.getAttribute(jmsConnections[i], "HostAddress")+
                    " with client id = "+myJMXWrapper.getAttribute(jmsConnections[i], "ClientID"));
            // print all sessions associated with this connection
            System.out.println(" has actually "+myJMXWrapper.getAttribute(jmsConnections[i],
                        "SessionsCurrentCount") +
                        " active sessions");

            // get all sessions
            ObjectName[] allConnectionJMSSessions = (ObjectName[])
                    myJMXWrapper.getAttribute(jmsConnections[i], "Sessions");

            // iterate of sessions
            for (int session=0;session<allConnectionJMSSessions.length;session++)
            {
                // print some session information
                System.out.println(" Session: Active consumers: "+
                myJMXWrapper.getAttribute(allConnectionJMSSessions[session], "ConsumersCurrentCount"));

                System.out.println(" Active producer: "+
                myJMXWrapper.getAttribute(allConnectionJMSSessions[session], "ProducersCurrentCount"));

                System.out.println(" Messages: send:"+
                    myJMXWrapper.getAttribute(allConnectionJMSSessions[session], "MessagesSentCount")+
                    " received:"+myJMXWrapper.getAttribute(allConnectionJMSSessions[session],
                    "MessagesReceivedCount")+
                    " pending:"+myJMXWrapper.getAttribute(allConnectionJMSSessions[session],
                    "MessagesPendingCount"));

                // iterate over producer
                ObjectName[] activeJMSProducer = (ObjectName[])
                        myJMXWrapper.getAttribute(allConnectionJMSSessions[session], "Producers");
                for(int producer=0;producer<activeJMSProducer.length;producer++)
                {
                    // ... System.out.println(information you want -> see API);
                }

                // iterate over consumer
                ObjectName[] activeJMSConsumers = (ObjectName[])
                        myJMXWrapper.getAttribute(allConnectionJMSSessions[session], "Consumers");
                for(int consumer=0;consumer<activeJMSConsumers.length;consumer++)
                {
                    // ... System.out.println(information you want -> see API);
                }
            }
        }
    }
    catch(Exception ex)
    {
        throw new WLSAutomationException("Error in printJMSRuntimeState : "+ ex.getMessage());
    }
}
```

JMS Server Monitoring with JMX

JMX provides a number of runtime monitoring values and metrics on the JMS server level. This includes various message values, throughput (Bytes*) values, state information, and more.

The JMS session offers interesting triple metrics, which include the current number, peak number, and total number of JMS sessions. The following example prints out the current session information of a JMS server:

🖫 current_session_information_jmx

```
public void printSessionPoolInformation(String myServerName, String myJMSServer)  throws
WLSAutomationException
{
  try
  {
    ObjectName serverRuntime = myJMXWrapper.getServerRuntime(myServerName);

    // get JMS runtime object reference
    ObjectName myJMSRuntime = (ObjectName) myJMXWrapper.getAttribute(serverRuntime, "JMSRuntime");

    ObjectName myJMSServerReference = getListOfJMSServerFromRuntime(myJMSRuntime).get(myJMSServer);
    if (myJMSServerReference==null)
    {
            System.out.println("JMS Server "+myJMSServer+" does not exit !");
    }
    else
    {
            System.out.println("The SessionPoolsCurrentCount of JMS server "+myJMSServer+" is "+
                    myJMXWrapper.getAttribute(myJMSRuntime, "SessionPoolsCurrentCount"));
            System.out.println("The SessionPoolsHighCount of JMS server "+myJMSServer+" is "+
                    myJMXWrapper.getAttribute(myJMSRuntime, "SessionPoolsHighCount"));
            System.out.println("The SessionPoolsTotalCount of JMS server "+myJMSServer+" is "+
                    myJMXWrapper.getAttribute(myJMSRuntime, "SessionPoolsTotalCount"));
    }
  }
  catch(Exception ex)
  {
    throw new WLSAutomationException("Error in printJMSRuntimeState : "+ ex.getMessage());
  }
}
```

JMS Destination Monitoring

JMX has an extensive number of metrics for every JMS destination. This includes the monitoring of states, message counts, pending and current message counts, and throughput.

JMX can print the state of a JMS queue. Every queue not only has a general state, but also detailed states. The following script prints the different states of a queue.

🖫 print_states_jmx

```
public void printQueueState(String myServerName, String myJMSServer, String myQueueName)
        throws WLSAutomationException
{
  try
  {
    ObjectName myQueue = getJMSDestinationRuntime(myQueueName, myJMSServer, myServerName);
```

```
    if (myQueue != null)
    {
            System.out.println("Information about the queue: "+myQueueName);
            // Detail states
            System.out.println("The InsertionPausedState of queue "+myQueueName+" is "+
                    myJMXWrapper.getAttribute(myQueue, "InsertionPausedState"));
            System.out.println("The ConsumptionPausedState of queue "+myQueueName+" is "+
                    myJMXWrapper.getAttribute(myQueue, "ConsumptionPausedState"));
            System.out.println("The ProductionPausedState of queue "+myQueueName+" is "+
                    myJMXWrapper.getAttribute(myQueue, "ProductionPausedState"));
    }
  }
  catch(Exception ex)
  {
    throw new WLSAutomationException("Error in printJMSRuntimeState : "+ ex.getMessage());
  }
}
```

Message Count for Certain Queues

The following example is a script that prints out the number of messages that are actually available in a queue. This might give you an indication of a backlog of work or, especially in the case of error or exception queues, will provide you with the information about the number of problems that occurred.

💾 message_count_jmx

```
public void printAmountOfMessagesInDestination(String myServerName,
                                               String myJMSServer,
                                               String myDestinationName)
        throws WLSAutomationException
{
  try
  {
    ObjectName myDestination = getJMSDestinationRuntime(myDestinationName,
                        myJMSServer, myServerName);

    // System.out.println(amount of messages
    System.out.println("The number of messages in the queue/topic "+myDestinationName +" is "+
                    myJMXWrapper.getAttribute(myDestination, "MessagesCurrentCount"));
    // System.out.println(amount of pending messages
    System.out.println("The number of messages in the queue/topic "+myDestinationName +" is "+
                    myJMXWrapper.getAttribute(myDestination, "MessagesPendingCount"));
  }
  catch(Exception ex)
  {
    throw new WLSAutomationException("Error in printJMSRuntimeState : "+ ex.getMessage());
  }
}
```

Note that there are two different methods on this runtime MBean. The method *getMessagesCurrentCount()* provides the current number of messages on this destination. In addition, a destination might have pending messages. The method *getMessagesPendingCount()* returns the number of pending messages that exist on this destination. A pending message may have either been sent in a transaction and not committed, or received and not committed or acknowledged.

General Application Monitoring

Every application is represented as an application runtime MBean in the runtime MBean trees. All runtime information that is relevant for monitoring is collected by WebLogic and can be queried from the application runtime MBean of that application or one of its various child MBeans.

The following method shows a way to find all application runtimes of the server you are connected to. Note that this method will only return the EAR applications and will most likely not be the complete list of deployed applications. EAR is the J2EE notion of an enterprise application, but WebLogic counts all deployments that are marked as "application" as an application deployment, which also includes WAR, EJB-JAR, and others.

💾 find_application_runtimes_jmx

```
public HashMap<String, ObjectName> getApplicationNames(String serverName) throws Exception
{
    HashMap<String, ObjectName> myResultList = new HashMap<String, ObjectName>();

    ObjectName serverRuntime = myJMXWrapper.getServerRuntime(serverName);

    ObjectName[] allApplicationRuntimeMBeans = (ObjectName[])
            myJMXWrapper.getAttribute(serverRuntime,"ApplicationRuntimes");

    String nextApplicationName = null;
    for (int i=0;i<allApplicationRuntimeMBeans.length;i++)
    {
        nextApplicationName = (String)
                        myJMXWrapper.getAttribute(allApplicationRuntimeMBeans[i],"Name");

        Boolean isEAR = (Boolean) myJMXWrapper.getAttribute(allApplicationRuntimeMBeans[i],"EAR");
        if (isEAR)
            myResultList.put(nextApplicationName,allApplicationRuntimeMBeans[i]);

        return myResultList;
    }
}
```

Application State

Every application consists of one or many application components. Every component has a state (activated, new, or others) that WebLogic provides through the various component MBeans. You can either use the state values 0-3 or the corresponding, and much more readable name from the WebLogic class:
weblogic.management.runtime.ComponentRuntimeMBean.

The following method shows how to print basic information about a deployed application, which includes the name, version, and healthstate.

```
public void printApplicationInformation(String applicationName,ObjectName applicationRuntimeMBean)
        throws Exception
{
    // print Name
    System.out.println(" Application information for component: "+applicationName);
```

```
    // print ApplicationName
    System.out.println("   ApplicationName=" +
                myJMXWrapper.getAttribute(applicationRuntimeMBean, "ApplicationName"));
    // print ApplicationVersion
    System.out.println("   ApplicationVersion=" +
                myJMXWrapper.getAttribute(applicationRuntimeMBean, "ApplicationVersion"));
    // print EAR
    System.out.println("   EAR=" + myJMXWrapper.getAttribute(applicationRuntimeMBean, "EAR"));
    // HealthState
    System.out.println("   HealthState="+ getHealthStateInformation((HealthState)
                myJMXWrapper.getAttribute(applicationRuntimeMBean,"HealthState")));
}
```

Every application in WebLogic is composed of components. As every component can be targeted to different targets (servers, clusters, virtual hosts, etc.), every component hast its own deployment state that can be queried from WebLogic by using the following method:

```
public String getApplicationComponentState(ObjectName componentRuntime)  throws Exception
{
    int myDeploymentState = (Integer)myJMXWrapper.getAttribute(componentRuntime, "DeploymentState");

    if (myDeploymentState == weblogic.management.runtime.ComponentRuntimeMBean.UNPREPARED)
        return "UNPREPARED";
    else if (myDeploymentState == weblogic.management.runtime.ComponentRuntimeMBean.PREPARED)
        return "PREPARED";
    else if (myDeploymentState == weblogic.management.runtime.ComponentRuntimeMBean.ACTIVATED)
        return "ACTIVATED";
    else if (myDeploymentState == weblogic.management.runtime.ComponentRuntimeMBean.NEW)
        return "NEW";

    return "UNKNOWN";
}
```

Monitor Complete Applications

The following script iterates over all components of an application and then calls the appropriate method to gather and print runtime information about all the components of the application.

```
public void printApplicationMonitoringInformation(ObjectName applicationRuntimeMBean)
        throws Exception
{
    // get component runtimes
    ObjectName[] componentRuntimes =  (ObjectName[])
                myJMXWrapper.getAttribute(applicationRuntimeMBean, "ComponentRuntimes");

    for (int compNumber=0; compNumber < componentRuntimes.length; compNumber++)
    {
        String componentType = (String)
                        myJMXWrapper.getAttribute(componentRuntimes[compNumber], "Type");
        String name = (String) myJMXWrapper.getAttribute(componentRuntimes[compNumber], "Name");
        if (componentType.toString().equals("WebAppComponentRuntime"))
        {
            printWebAppComponentInformation(name,componentRuntimes[compNumber]);
            printServletInvocationCountInformation(componentRuntimes[compNumber]);
        }
        else if (componentType.toString().equals("EJBComponentRuntime"))
            printEJBInformation(componentRuntimes[compNumber], true);

        if (componentType.toString().equals("ConnectorComponentRuntime"))
        {
            printConnectorMonitoringValues(componentRuntimes[compNumber]);
        }
    }
}
```

Web Components

Web applications are packed into a *.war file. The principal building blocks of a war file for WebLogic are servlets. Each war file may contain many different servlets and every war file can be integrated into an enterprise archive (EAR). WebLogic provides detailed runtime information about a web application and every different servlet.

The following JMX function will provide a list of web component names of an application. This can be useful if you want to analyze all the web components or if you want to find out which web components are part of this application.

```
public HashMap<String, ObjectName> getWebComponentNames(ObjectName applicationRuntimeMBean)
                               throws Exception
{
   HashMap<String, ObjectName> myResultList = new HashMap<String, ObjectName>();

   // get component runtimes
   ObjectName[] componentRuntimes =  (ObjectName[])
                    myJMXWrapper.getAttribute(applicationRuntimeMBean, "ComponentRuntimes");

   for (int compNumber=0; compNumber < componentRuntimes.length; compNumber++)
   {
      String componentType = (String)
                         myJMXWrapper.getAttribute(componentRuntimes[compNumber], "Type");
      if (componentType.toString().equals("WebAppComponentRuntime"))
      {
         String name = (String) myJMXWrapper.getAttribute(componentRuntimes[compNumber], "Name");
         myResultList.put(name,componentRuntimes[compNumber]);
      }
   }
   return myResultList;
}
```

Web-sessions

Web sessions do not depend on individual servlets. Therefore, in the above script web sessions are printed on the web component level rather than the servlet level. WebLogic records a number of interesting values:

```
public void printWebAppSessionInformation(String webappName,ObjectName webAppComponentRuntime)
          throws Exception
{
   // print Name
   System.out.println(" Webapplication information for component: "+webappName);
   // print ContextRoot
   System.out.println("   ContextRoot=" +
                   myJMXWrapper.getAttribute(webAppComponentRuntime, "ContextRoot"));
   // print Status
   System.out.println("   Status=" + myJMXWrapper.getAttribute(webAppComponentRuntime, "Status"));
   // print OpenSessionsCurrentCount
   System.out.println("   OpenSessionsCurrentCount=" +
                   myJMXWrapper.getAttribute(webAppComponentRuntime, "OpenSessionsCurrentCount"));
   // print OpenSessionsHighCount
   System.out.println("   OpenSessionsHighCount=" +
                   myJMXWrapper.getAttribute(webAppComponentRuntime, "OpenSessionsHighCount"));
   // print SessionsOpenedTotalCount
   System.out.println("   SessionsOpenedTotalCount=" +
                   myJMXWrapper.getAttribute(webAppComponentRuntime, "SessionsOpenedTotalCount"));
}
```

Servlets/JSP Information

On the servlet level, WebLogic provides a number of values that can be monitored and/or recorded. The most important are the different execution time values and the number of hits.

servlet_values_jmx

```
public void printServletInvocationCountInformation(ObjectName webAppComponentRuntime)
          throws Exception
{
   // calculcate the total summary of all calls
   long invocationTotal = 0;

   // get all servlet MBeans
   ObjectName[] servletRuntimes = (ObjectName[])
              myJMXWrapper.getAttribute(webAppComponentRuntime, "Servlets");

   for (int servletNumber=0; servletNumber<servletRuntimes.length; servletNumber++)
   {
      String nextName = (String)myJMXWrapper.getAttribute(servletRuntimes[servletNumber], "Name");
      int contextInvocationTotalCount =
          (Integer)myJMXWrapper.getAttribute(servletRuntimes[servletNumber], "InvocationTotalCount");

      // sum up
      invocationTotal += contextInvocationTotalCount;

      // print to list
      System.out.println("       Servlet:"+nextName+"  Invocations:"+
                        new Integer(contextInvocationTotalCount));
   }

   // print SUMMARY to list
   System.out.println("  Overall-InvocationTotalCount" + new Long(invocationTotal));
}
```

EJB Components

EJB applications are packed into a *.jar file. Each jar file may contain many different EJBs and every EJB-jar file can be integrated into an enterprise archive (EAR). WebLogic provides extensive runtime information about EJB. Please see the WLST section for MBean trees and descriptions.

Every EJB jar (not individual EJB!) is represented by an MBean instance that is derived from *EJBComponentRuntime*. This MBean offers a list of MBeans that represent the individual MBeans in this archive.

The following method is a simple example that iterates over all EJBs defined in this EJB-jar (*EJBComponentRuntime*) and prints the name of the EJB and its type.

EJB_print_information_jmx

```
public HashMap<String, ObjectName> getEJBComponentNames(ObjectName applicationRuntimeMBean)
                            throws Exception
{
   HashMap<String, ObjectName> myResultList = new HashMap<String, ObjectName>();

   // get component runtimes
   ObjectName[] componentRuntimes = (ObjectName[])
```

```
                  myJMXWrapper.getAttribute(applicationRuntimeMBean, "ComponentRuntimes");

    for (int compNumber=0; compNumber < componentRuntimes.length; compNumber++)
    {
        String componentType = (String)
                    myJMXWrapper.getAttribute(componentRuntimes[compNumber], "Type");
        if (componentType.toString().equals("EJBComponentRuntime"))
        {
            String name = (String) myJMXWrapper.getAttribute(componentRuntimes[compNumber], "Name");
            myResultList.put(name,componentRuntimes[compNumber]);
        }
    }
    return myResultList;
}
```

The J2EE specification defines four different types of EJB components. These four
components - message driven, stateless, stateful, and entity EJBs - have very different
natures and purposes. WebLogic reflects this by providing different MBean types for
each of these EJB types. All are derived from *EJBRuntimeMBean*.

The following JMX method iterates over all EJBs of an EJB component (which for
WebLogic is a jar file containing one or more EJB definitions) and prints runtime
information of each of these EJBs. Due to the different EJB types, this method has to
distinguish the different EJB types. Please note that System.out is definitely not the
best way of doing monitoring. The reader is highly encouraged to exchange the
System.out with whatever monitoring and logging process you are doing.

💾 EJB_print_runtime_jmx

```
public void printEJBInformation(ObjectName ejbComponentRuntime, boolean printDetails)
            throws Exception
{
    String myName = (String)myJMXWrapper.getAttribute(ejbComponentRuntime, "Name");
    System.out.println("Found EJB modul "+myName+" with current deployment state = " +
                    getApplicationComponentState(ejbComponentRuntime));

    // now look at the submodules
    ObjectName[] myEJBs = (ObjectName[])myJMXWrapper.getAttribute(ejbComponentRuntime, "EJBRuntimes");

    for (int i=0;i<myEJBs.length;i++)
    {
        String ejbName = (String)myJMXWrapper.getAttribute(myEJBs[i], "Name");
        String ejbType = (String)myJMXWrapper.getAttribute(myEJBs[i], "Type");
        System.out.println("   EJB: "+ejbName+" is of type "+ejbType);

        if (printDetails)
        {
            // all have transactions
            //transaction information from TransactionRuntime
            ObjectName myTxRuntime = (ObjectName)
                    myJMXWrapper.getAttribute(myEJBs[i], "TransactionRuntime");
            System.out.println("   TransactionInfo: total:"+
                    myJMXWrapper.getAttribute(myTxRuntime, "TransactionsCommittedTotalCount")+
                    "rolledback:"+myJMXWrapper.getAttribute(myTxRuntime,
                    "TransactionsRolledBackTotalCount")+
                    " timedout:" +myJMXWrapper.getAttribute(myTxRuntime,
                    "TransactionsTimedOutTotalCount"));

            if ("StatelessEJBRuntime".equals(ejbType)) {
                // pool information from PoolRuntime
                ObjectName myPoolRuntime = (ObjectName)
                                    myJMXWrapper.getAttribute(myEJBs[i], "PoolRuntime");
                System.out.println("   PoolInfo: totalAccess:"+
                    myJMXWrapper.getAttribute(myPoolRuntime, "AccessTotalCount")+
                    "   beansInUse:"+myJMXWrapper.getAttribute(myPoolRuntime, "BeansInUseCount")+
                    "   beansInUseCurrent:"+myJMXWrapper.getAttribute(myPoolRuntime,
                    "BeansInUseCurrentCount")+
```

```java
                     "    destroyed:"+myJMXWrapper.getAttribute(myPoolRuntime, "DestroyedTotalCount")+
                     "    idle:"+myJMXWrapper.getAttribute(myPoolRuntime, "IdleBeansCount")+
                     "    pooledCurrent:"+myJMXWrapper.getAttribute(myPoolRuntime,
                     "PooledBeansCurrentCount")+
                     "    timedout:"+myJMXWrapper.getAttribute(myPoolRuntime, "TimeoutTotalCount"));

            // timer consists of a list of timers
            ObjectName myTimerRuntime = (ObjectName)
                    myJMXWrapper.getAttribute(myEJBs[i], "TimerRuntime");
            if (myTimerRuntime != null)
              System.out.println("    Timer information: Name:"+
                    myJMXWrapper.getAttribute(myTimerRuntime, "Name")+
                    "    activeTimers:"+myJMXWrapper.getAttribute(myTimerRuntime, "ActiveTimerCount")+
                    "    timeout:"+myJMXWrapper.getAttribute(myTimerRuntime, "TimeoutCount")+
                    "    cancelled:"+myJMXWrapper.getAttribute(myTimerRuntime, "CancelledTimerCount")+
                    "    disabled:"+myJMXWrapper.getAttribute(myTimerRuntime, "DisabledTimerCount"));
        }
        else if ("StatefulEJBRuntime".equals(ejbType)) {
            // cache information from CacheRuntime
            ObjectName myCacheRuntime = (ObjectName)
                    myJMXWrapper.getAttribute(myEJBs[i], "CacheRuntime");
            System.out.println("    CacheInfo: hits:"+
                    myJMXWrapper.getAttribute(myCacheRuntime, "CacheHitCount")+
                    "    currentBeans:"+myJMXWrapper.getAttribute(myCacheRuntime,
                    "CachedBeansCurrentCount")+
                    "    access:"+myJMXWrapper.getAttribute(myCacheRuntime, "CacheAccessCount"));

            // locking information from LockingRuntime
            ObjectName myLockingRuntime = (ObjectName)
                    myJMXWrapper.getAttribute(myEJBs[i], "LockingRuntime");
            System.out.println("    LockingInfo: currentCount:"+
                myJMXWrapper.getAttribute(myLockingRuntime, "LockEntriesCurrentCount")+
                "    accessCount:"+myJMXWrapper.getAttribute(myLockingRuntime, "LockManagerAccessCount")+
                "    timeoutTotalCount:"+myJMXWrapper.getAttribute(myLockingRuntime,
                "TimeoutTotalCount"));
        }
        else if ("EntityEJBRuntime".equals(ejbType))
        {
            ObjectName entityPool = (ObjectName)myJMXWrapper.getAttribute(myEJBs[i], "PoolRuntime");

            System.out.println("    PooledBeansCurrent ="+
                myJMXWrapper.getAttribute(entityPool,"PooledBeansCurrentCount")+
                "    AccessTotal ="+ myJMXWrapper.getAttribute(entityPool,"AccessTotalCount")+
                "    DestroyedTotal ="+ myJMXWrapper.getAttribute(entityPool,"DestroyedTotalCount")+
                "    IdleBeans ="+ myJMXWrapper.getAttribute(entityPool,"IdleBeansCount")+
                "    BeansInUse ="+ myJMXWrapper.getAttribute(entityPool,"BeansInUseCount")+
                "    BeansInUseCurrent ="+
                myJMXWrapper.getAttribute(entityPool,"BeansInUseCurrentCount")+
                "    WaiterTotal ="+ myJMXWrapper.getAttribute(entityPool,"WaiterTotalCount")+
                "    WaiterCurrent ="+ myJMXWrapper.getAttribute(entityPool,"WaiterCurrentCount")+
                "    TimeoutTotal ="+ myJMXWrapper.getAttribute(entityPool,"TimeoutTotalCount"));
        }
        else if ("MessageDrivenEJBRuntime".equals(ejbType)) {
            // print the mdb status
            System.out.println("    ConnectionStatus = "+
                        myJMXWrapper.getAttribute(myEJBs[i], "ConnectionStatus");
            // print status of the MDB
            System.out.println("    MDBStatus = "+myJMXWrapper.getAttribute(myEJBs[i], "MDBStatus");
            // client id
            System.out.println("    JmsClientID = "+myJMXWrapper.getAttribute(myEJBs[i], "JmsClientID");
            // count of processed messages
            System.out.println("    ProcessedMessageCount = "+
                        myJMXWrapper.getAttribute(myEJBs[i], "ProcessedMessageCount");
            // amout of suspended messages
            System.out.println("    SuspendCount = "+
                        myJMXWrapper.getAttribute(myEJBs[i], "SuspendCount");
            // healthstate of MDB
            System.out.println("    HealthState="+getHealthStateInformation((HealthState)
                        myJMXWrapper.getAttribute(myEJBs[i],"HealthState")));

            // pool information from PoolRuntime
            ObjectName myPoolRuntime = (ObjectName)myJMXWrapper.getAttribute(myEJBs[i], "PoolRuntime");
            System.out.println("    PoolInfo: totalAccess:"+
                myJMXWrapper.getAttribute(myPoolRuntime, "AccessTotalCount")+
                "    beansInUse:"+myJMXWrapper.getAttribute(myPoolRuntime, "BeansInUseCount")+
                "    beansInUseCurrent:"+myJMXWrapper.getAttribute(myPoolRuntime,
                "BeansInUseCurrentCount")+
                "    destroyed:"+myJMXWrapper.getAttribute(myPoolRuntime, "DestroyedTotalCount")+
```

```
            "    idle:"+myJMXWrapper.getAttribute(myPoolRuntime, "IdleBeansCount")+
            "    pooledCurrent:"+myJMXWrapper.getAttribute(myPoolRuntime,
            "PooledBeansCurrentCount")+
            "    timedout:"+myJMXWrapper.getAttribute(myPoolRuntime, "TimeoutTotalCount"));
         // timer consists of a list of timers
         ObjectName myTimerRuntime = (ObjectName)
                                        myJMXWrapper.getAttribute(myEJBs[i], "TimerRuntime");
         if (myTimerRuntime != null)
            System.out.println("   Timer information: Name:"+
                  myJMXWrapper.getAttribute(myTimerRuntime, "Name")+
                  "   activeTimers:"+myJMXWrapper.getAttribute(myTimerRuntime, "ActiveTimerCount")+
                  "   timeout:"+myJMXWrapper.getAttribute(myTimerRuntime, "TimeoutCount")+
                  "   cancelled:"+myJMXWrapper.getAttribute(myTimerRuntime, "CancelledTimerCount")+
                  "   disabled:"+myJMXWrapper.getAttribute(myTimerRuntime, "DisabledTimerCount"));
      }
   }
 }
}
```

JCA Components

Another major component is the resource adapter based on the Java Connector
Architecture (JCA). Resource adapters are a complex type of application as they can
establish communication to any sort of backend, support transactions, and can use
any kind of third party protocol for the communications. JCA components support
outgoing and also incoming connections.

This results in another rather complex hierarchy of MBeans for each connector
module. The following script shows a function that can provide a number of values
and information for a connector module. The first method can be used to get a list of
JCA components for a specific application. Note that the runtime is always WebLogic
Server-specific. If the JCA component has a different target list than the application,
the target list will be different for different Managed-Servers.

💾 get_JCA_component_list

```
public HashMap<String, ObjectName> getJCAConnectorRuntimes(ObjectName applicationRuntimeMBean)
                              throws Exception
{
    HashMap<String, ObjectName> myResultList = new HashMap<String, ObjectName>();

    // get component runtimes
    ObjectName[] componentRuntimes = (ObjectName[])
            myJMXWrapper.getAttribute(applicationRuntimeMBean, "ComponentRuntimes");

    for (int compNumber=0; compNumber < componentRuntimes.length; compNumber++)
    {
        String componentType =
            (String)myJMXWrapper.getAttribute(componentRuntimes[compNumber], "Type");

        if (componentType.toString().equals("ConnectorComponentRuntime"))
        {
            String name = (String) myJMXWrapper.getAttribute(componentRuntimes[compNumber], "Name");
            myResultList.put(name,componentRuntimes[compNumber]);
        }
    }
    return myResultList;
}
```

The following method will examine a concrete JCA component and print out some
connector values:

🖫 print_JCA_connector_values

```
public void printConnectorMonitoringValues(ObjectName connectorRuntime) throws Exception
{
    String myName = (String)myJMXWrapper.getAttribute(connectorRuntime, "Name");
    System.out.println("Found Connector modul "+myName+
            " with current deployment state = " + getApplicationComponentState(connectorRuntime));

    int myDeploymentState = (Integer) myJMXWrapper.getAttribute(connectorRuntime,"DeploymentState");
    String d_state = "UNKNOWN";

    if (myDeploymentState == weblogic.management.runtime.ComponentRuntimeMBean.UNPREPARED)
        d_state = "UNPREPARED";
    else if(myDeploymentState == weblogic.management.runtime.ComponentRuntimeMBean.PREPARED)
        d_state = "PREPARED";
    else if(myDeploymentState == weblogic.management.runtime.ComponentRuntimeMBean.ACTIVATED)
        d_state = "ACTIVATED";
    else if(myDeploymentState == weblogic.management.runtime.ComponentRuntimeMBean.NEW)
        d_state = "NEW";

    // add T_DeploymentState
    System.out.println("  DeploymentState: "+ d_state);


    ObjectName[] myConPools = (ObjectName[])
                        myJMXWrapper.getAttribute(connectorRuntime,"ConnectionPools");
    if (myConPools.length > 0)
    {
     // monitor only first pool !

        System.out.println("  ActiveConCurrent: "+
            myJMXWrapper.getAttribute(connectorRuntime, "ActiveConnectionsCurrentCount"));
        System.out.println("  ActiveConHigh: "+
            myJMXWrapper.getAttribute(connectorRuntime, "ActiveConnectionsHighCount"));
        System.out.println("  ConCreatedTotal: "+
            myJMXWrapper.getAttribute(connectorRuntime, "ConnectionsCreatedTotalCount"));
        System.out.println("  ConRejectedTotal: "+
            myJMXWrapper.getAttribute(connectorRuntime, "ConnectionsRejectedTotalCount"));
        System.out.println("  ConDestroyedTotal: "+
            myJMXWrapper.getAttribute(connectorRuntime, "ConnectionsDestroyedTotalCount"));
        System.out.println("  FreeConCurrent: "+
            myJMXWrapper.getAttribute(connectorRuntime, "FreeConnectionsCurrentCount"));
        System.out.println("  FreeConHigh: "+
            myJMXWrapper.getAttribute(connectorRuntime, "FreeConnectionsHighCount"));
        System.out.println("  AverageActiveUsage: "+
            myJMXWrapper.getAttribute(connectorRuntime, "AverageActiveUsage"));
        System.out.println("  CloseCount: "+
            myJMXWrapper.getAttribute(connectorRuntime, "CloseCount"));
        System.out.println("  ConnectionsDestroyedByErrorTotalCount: "+
            myJMXWrapper.getAttribute(connectorRuntime, "ConnectionsDestroyedByErrorTotalCount"));
        System.out.println("  ConnectionsDestroyedByShrinkingTotalCount: "+
            myJMXWrapper.getAttribute(connectorRuntime,
                                "ConnectionsDestroyedByShrinkingTotalCount"));
        System.out.println("  ConnectionsMatchedTotalCount: "+
            myJMXWrapper.getAttribute(connectorRuntime,
                                "ConnectionsMatchedTotalCount"));
        System.out.println("  CurrentCapacity: "+
            myJMXWrapper.getAttribute(connectorRuntime, "CurrentCapacity"));
        System.out.println("  MaxCapacity: "+
            myJMXWrapper.getAttribute(connectorRuntime, "MaxCapacity"));
        System.out.println("  MaxIdleTime: "+
            myJMXWrapper.getAttribute(connectorRuntime, "MaxIdleTime"));
        System.out.println("  NumUnavailableCurrentCount: "+
            myJMXWrapper.getAttribute(connectorRuntime, "NumUnavailableCurrentCount"));
        System.out.println("  NumUnavailableHighCount: "+
            myJMXWrapper.getAttribute(connectorRuntime, "NumUnavailableHighCount"));
        System.out.println("  NumWaiters: "+
            myJMXWrapper.getAttribute(connectorRuntime, "NumWaiters"));
        System.out.println("  NumWaitersCurrentCount: "+
            myJMXWrapper.getAttribute(connectorRuntime, "NumWaitersCurrentCount"));
        System.out.println("  RecycledTotal: "+
            myJMXWrapper.getAttribute(connectorRuntime, "RecycledTotal"));
        System.out.println("  ShrinkCountDownTime: "+
            myJMXWrapper.getAttribute(connectorRuntime, "ShrinkCountDownTime"));
        System.out.println("  ShrinkPeriodMinutes: "+
            myJMXWrapper.getAttribute(connectorRuntime, "ShrinkPeriodMinutes"));
    }
}
```

WTC Monitoring

WebLogic does not offer much in the WTC area. WTC monitoring is included in the additional Oracle product called Tuxedo System and Application Monitor (TSAM), which is the monitoring solution for Tuxedo applications. Besides some service status information, there is not much offered in WebLogic so far. From a monitoring perspective, it is possible to monitor the status of the WTC connections and the status of the different services like IMPORT services.

The class *WTCServiceStatus* defines the different status values. It also contains converter functions that can convert the integer values to string representations of the different status values.

The service status can be one of the following:

- AVAILABLE - The imported or exported service is available.

- SUSPENDED - The imported or exported service is suspended.

- UNAVAILABLE - The imported or exported service status is not available.

- UNKNOWN - The imported or exported service status is unknown.

The service type can be one of the following:

- IMPORT - The service is imported from a foreign domain.

- EXPORT - The service is exported to a foreign domain.

The main MBean for monitoring is the *WTCRuntime* MBean. The main parts for the monitoring are:

```
com.bea:Name=WTCService,ServerRuntime=MS1,Type=WTCRuntime
        Attribute: ServiceStatus    of Type : [Lweblogic.wtc.gwt.DServiceInfo;
        Attribute: Name    of Type : java.lang.String
        Operation: java.lang.Integer  getServiceStatus(localAccessPoint:java.lang.String
                                                svcName:java.lang.String
                                                isImport:java.lang.Boolean  )
        Operation: [Lweblogic.wtc.gwt.DSessConnInfo;  listConnectionsConfigured()
        Operation: java.lang.Integer  getServiceStatus(…)
        Operation: java.lang.Integer  getServiceStatus(svcName:java.lang.String
                                                isImport:java.lang.Boolean  )
        Operation: java.lang.Integer  getServiceStatus(localAccessPoint:java.lang.String
                                                svcName:java.lang.String  )
        Operation: java.lang.Integer  getServiceStatus(svcName:java.lang.String  )
        Operation: java.lang.Void  startConnection(LDomAccessPointId:java.lang.String
                                                RDomAccessPointId:java.lang.String  )
```

The following method demonstrates the monitoring values for WebLogic 11g and 12c.

```
public void monitorWTC() throws Exception {
    // get main values
    Hashtable<String,String> mainValues = myJMXWrapper.getMainServerDomainValues();

    // go to MBean
    ObjectName serverRuntime = myJMXWrapper.getServerRuntime(mainValues.get("serverName"));

    ObjectName wtcRuntime = (ObjectName) myJMXWrapper.getAttribute(serverRuntime, "WTCRuntime");

    // list connections configured
    DSessConnInfo[] myWTCConnectionInfos = (DSessConnInfo[])
                        myJMXWrapper.invoke(wtcRuntime,"listConnectionsConfigured",
                                        new Object[]{},new String[]{});

    System.out.println("DSessConnInfo:");
    for (int i=0;i<myWTCConnectionInfos.length;i++) {
        DSessConnInfo nextDSessConnInfo = myWTCConnectionInfos[i];
        System.out.println("DSessConnInfo-"+i);
        System.out.println("    "+nextDSessConnInfo.getLocalAccessPointId());
        System.out.println("    "+nextDSessConnInfo.getRemoteAccessPointId());
        System.out.println("    "+nextDSessConnInfo.getConnected());
    }

    // get all service information
    DServiceInfo[] allDServiceInfos = (DServiceInfo[])
                            myJMXWrapper.getAttribute(wtcRuntime, "ServiceStatus");

    System.out.println("\n\nDServiceInfos:");
    for (int i=0;i<allDServiceInfos.length;i++) {
        System.out.println("DSessConnInfo-"+i);
        System.out.println("    "+allDServiceInfos[i].getLocalAccessPoint());
        System.out.println("    "+allDServiceInfos[i].getServiceName());
        System.out.println("    "+
                        WTCServiceStatus.svcTypeToString(allDServiceInfos[i].getServiceType()));
        System.out.println("    "+WTCServiceStatus.statusToString(allDServiceInfos[i].getStatus()));
    }
}
```

More Complex Monitoring Examples

This section will discuss a number of more complex monitoring examples. Note that it is neither possible nor easy to read and to publish the full source code in this section of the book. The code will be provided in full with the WLST/JMX toolbox. This section will describe the ideas and provide some example source snippets.

Monitoring All Major Resources

The last sections have discussed the different possibilities to monitor application aspects. Of course monitoring solutions have to combine all those aspects into a comprehensive monitoring solution. These solutions always have to fulfill application-specific requirements. For example, real-time banking systems have completely different requirements than massive batch systems or industrial machines. Therefore, the source codes provided in this section can only be a guideline and example for your own monitoring solution.

Pushing Monitoring Data

In the previous section we discussed a JMX program that prints some key runtime values from the server, from the different main resources, and from the installed applications. Monitoring always means creating load, and also almost always means polling information. In this section I want to show you some example code that you can use to push monitoring data.

The idea is to create a WebLogic startup class and host the monitoring code there. Then, configurable either using Custom MBeans or via arguments to the server, this implementation can push the monitoring data to a configurable data collector. The example here is kept simple due to space restriction and will just do it periodically. It is possible to use more advanced techniques like notifications to get informed when the data has changed and therefore need to be pushed again. It would also be possible, if permitted by the business requirements, to utilize time periods with less machine load to push the data to the monitoring system.

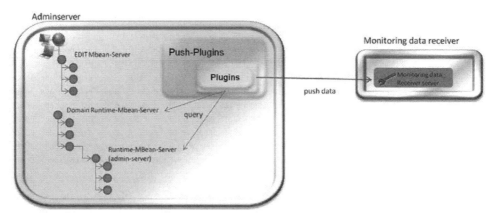

Figure 17.3: *Push model*

The implementation of this push model consists of 4 different components:

- The WebLogic startup class in order to initiate the plug-in.

- A custom MBean, which allows the configuration of this plug-in via standard JMX.

- A data collector thread, which will actually collect the desired monitoring data.

- Push implementations, which can push the data to the desired destination.

The code is too lengthy for the book even in this simple example, so the following code snippets are only the most relevant parts of the above 4 components.

The following class implements a WebLogic startup class (must have a main method) that connects to the internal runtime MBean server and instantiates a thread. This periodically polls information from the internal runtime MBean server and pushes the information to an external monitoring server (or writes to a file).

```
public class PushExampleStartup
{
    /**
     * @param args
     */
    public static void main(String[] args)
    {
        System.out.println("PushExample-Monitoring was loaded");
        try {
                new PushExampleMBeanImpl(new JMXWrapperLocal());
        }
        catch (Exception e) {
          e.printStackTrace();
        }
    }
}
```

There is one additional configuration necessary in order to instruct WebLogic to execute this code during startup. This feature is called Startup-Class in WebLogic. The following configuration part of config.xml demonstrates how to configure WebLogic in order to execute this code on the AdminServer and on the two Managed-Servers TestMS1 and TestMS2:

```
<startup-class>
  <name>ExampleMonitor</name>
  <target>AdminServer,TestMS1,TestMS2</target>
  <class-name>com.example.wls.pushmonitoring.PushExampleStartup</class-name>
</startup-class>
```

Standard MBeans consist of an interface definition and an implementation class with defined naming rules. Example interface definition:

🖫 interface_definition_jmx

```
public interface PushExampleMBean
{
    /**
     * Is plugin enabled - means does plugin record periodically the runtime values and report them
     * @return String
     */
    public String getEnabled();

    /**
     * VERY IMPORTANT:  Activates or deactivates the gathering and pushing
     * @param enabled String
     */
    public void setEnabled(String enabled);


    /**
     * Interval in seconds how often the information are collected and reported
     * @return interval
     */
    public int getUpdateIntervalInSeconds();
```

```
/**
 * Set the  interval how often the runtime information should be gathered and reported
 * @param intervalInSeconds int
 */
public void setUpdateIntervalInSeconds(int intervalInSeconds);

/**
 * GEt the destination URL:
 * @return the destination URL
 */
public String getDestinationURL();


/**
 * Set the destination URL:
 */
public void setDestinationURL(String destinationURL);
}
```

The MBean implementation in our example has a number of functionalities implemented. Please note that in larger implementations, these functionalities should be implemented in different classes and need to be implemented in a more flexible and general way. The following code listings are only part of this class due to its size:

💾 implement_constructor_jmx

```java
public class PushExampleMBeanImpl extends StandardMBean implements PushExampleMBean
{
    ...

    public PushExampleMBeanImpl(JMXWrapperLocal _JMXWrapper) throws Exception {
        super(PushExampleMBean.class, false);

        try
        {
            System.out.println("WLSMonitoringMBean - Init called");

            myJMXWrapper = _JMXWrapper;
            myJMXWrapper.connectToAdminServer(false,null,null,null);
            mainDomainValues = myJMXWrapper.getMainServerDomainValues();

            ObjectName mymbean = new
                    ObjectName("pushMonitoring:Name=ExamplePushInformation,Type=ExamplePushPlugin");

            // now register in MBeanServer
            ((MBeanServer)myJMXWrapper.getConnection()).registerMBean(this, mymbean);
            System.out.println("Push-Monitoring:  PushExampleMBean - MBean registered");

            // if running on adminserver -> change to domainruntime
            String isCurrentServerAnAdminServer = mainDomainValues.get("connectedToAdminServer");

            if ("true".equalsIgnoreCase(isCurrentServerAnAdminServer))  // is Admin
            {
                myJMXWrapper.disconnectFromAdminServer();
                myJMXWrapper.connectToAdminServer(true,null,null,null);
                connectedToAdmin = true;
                System.out.println("Monitoring:  Connection changed to DomainRuntime as "+
                            "THIS is the admin server !");
            }

            // example implementation in order to start data thread
            setEnabled(getEnabled());

            System.out.println("PushExample-Monitoring:  init completed");
        }
        catch(Exception ex) {
            ex.printStackTrace();
            throw ex;
        }
    }
```

The above method implements the constructor of our MBean, which is called during WLS server startup. First this method will connect to the ServerRuntime MBean tree and query some basic WLS information (see *mainDomainValues()* function). If this code is running inside the AdminServer, the plug-in will do a reconnect to the *DomainRuntime* in order to monitor domain level values.

Finally, the plug-in will check if it should be enabled. In this case, the data collector thread must be started.

🖫 plug-in_check_jmx

```
/**
 * Is plugin enabled - means does plugin record periodically the runtime values and report them
 * @return boolean
 */
public String getEnabled()
{
  return pluginEnabled ? "true" : "false" ;
}


public void setEnabled(String newEnabledValue)
{
    // set value
  pluginEnabled = Boolean.parseBoolean(newEnabledValue);


    if (pluginEnabled==true)    // ENABLE
    {
        if (myPushExampleThread != null)
        {
            System.out.println("Monitoring is already active !!");
        }
        else
        {
            System.out.println("Monitoring will be started !!");
            myPushExampleThread = new PushExampleThread(this);
            myPushExampleThread.setDaemon(true);
            myPushExampleThread.start();
        }
    }
    else  // DISABLE
    {
        if (myPushExampleThread == null)
        {
            System.out.println("Monitoring is already disabled !!");
        }
        else
        {
            // setting enabled to false is enough - will be picked up by thread
            System.out.println("Monitoring will be disabled !!");
            myPushExampleThread.interrupt();
            myPushExampleThread = null;
        }
    }

}
```

The data collector thread will periodically collect (depending on the configured interval) the desired data and push them to the destination. In this small example, the data collector will only collect domain values (if connected to the AdminServer) and server values. Of course this must be extended to your own needs.

💾 push_data_jmx

```
public class PushExampleThread extends Thread
{
    private PushExampleMBeanImpl myMBean = null;

    private PushExampleDestinations myPushExampleDestination= null;

    public PushExampleThread(PushExampleMBeanImpl _myMBean) {
      myMBean = _myMBean;
      myPushExampleDestination = new PushExampleDestinations(myMBean);
    }


    public void run()
    {
      try
      {
          // do pushing while plugin is enabled
          while (myMBean.getEnabled().equalsIgnoreCase("true"))
          {
              int waitSeconds = myMBean.getUpdateIntervalInSeconds();
              // wait
              try {
                  Thread.sleep(waitSeconds*1000);
              }
              catch (Exception ex) {
                  continue;
              }

              // still enabled ?
              if (myMBean.getEnabled().equalsIgnoreCase("true"))
              {
                  // get monitoring values and push to destination

                  // if admin => push domain data
                  if (myMBean.isConnectedToAdmin())
                          myPushExampleDestination.pushData("DOMAIN", myMBean.getDomainData());

                  // push server data
                  myPushExampleDestination.pushData("SERVER", myMBean.getServerData());
              }
          }
      }
      catch (Exception ex)
      {
          ex.printStackTrace();
      }
    }
}
```

The following method demonstrates a simple implementation of getting basic domain data. Note that for demonstration and simplicity, the method will only look at the 1st cluster (if at least one is available).

💾 get_domain_data_jmx_(partial)

```
public HashMap<String, String> getDomainData() throws Exception
{
    HashMap<String, String> myResultList = new HashMap<String, String>();

    // add domain name
    myResultList.put("DomainName", (String)mainDomainValues.get("domainName"));

    ArrayList<String> msServerNames = myJMXWrapper.getManagedServerNames();

    int amountOfMSServer = msServerNames.size();
    int amountRunning = 0;
    int amountShutdown = 0;
    int amountFailedAdmin = 0;

    // iterator over server list and get server info
    for (int i=0; i<amountOfMSServer;i++)
    {
```

```
            String nextState =  myJMXWrapper.getServerState(msServerNames.get(i));

        if ("RUNNING".equalsIgnoreCase(nextState))
                amountRunning++;
        else if ("SHUTDOWN".equalsIgnoreCase(nextState) ||
                "SHUTTING_DOWN".equalsIgnoreCase(nextState))
                amountShutdown++;
        if ("UNKNOWN".equalsIgnoreCase(nextState) ||
            "FAILED_NOT_RESTARTABLE".equalsIgnoreCase(nextState) ||
                "FAILED".equalsIgnoreCase(nextState) ||
                "FAILED_RESTARTING".equalsIgnoreCase(nextState) ||
                "FORCE_SHUTTING_DOWN".equalsIgnoreCase(nextState)
            )
                amountFailedAdmin++;
    }

    // looking only at first cluster for demonstration reasons
    // e.g.: com.bea:Name=TestDomain,Type=Domain
    ObjectName myDomainMBean = new ObjectName("com.bea:Name=" +
            (String)mainDomainValues.get("domainName") +",Type=Domain");

    ObjectName[] allClusters = (ObjectName[])myJMXWrapper.getAttribute(myDomainMBean,"Clusters");

    if (allClusters.length > 0)
    {
        // use 1st cluster !!!
        // get cluster member
        ObjectName[] clusterServer =
                    (ObjectName[])myJMXWrapper.getAttribute(allClusters[0],"Servers");
        int amountClusterServerRunning = 0;
        int amountClusterServerShutdown = 0;
        int amountClusterServerNotWorkingOrFailed = 0;

        // iterate over cluster member
        for (int i=0; i<clusterServer.length;i++)
        {
            String nextState =  myJMXWrapper.getServerState(
                            (String)myJMXWrapper.getAttribute(clusterServer[i],"Name"));

            if ("RUNNING".equalsIgnoreCase(nextState))
                    amountClusterServerRunning++;
            else if ("SHUTDOWN".equalsIgnoreCase(nextState))
                    amountClusterServerShutdown++;
            else // all other states
                    amountClusterServerNotWorkingOrFailed++;
        }

     // NOTE: In this example: Only looking at 1st cluster
            if (clusterServer.length == amountClusterServerRunning)  // all running
                    myResultList.put("ClusterState", "RUNNING");
            else if (clusterServer.length == amountClusterServerShutdown)
                    // all shutdown or failed :-((
                    myResultList.put("ClusterState", "SHUTDOW");
            else if (clusterServer.length == amountClusterServerNotWorkingOrFailed)
                    // all shutdown or failed :-((
                    myResultList.put("ClusterState", "NOT WORKING OR FAILED");
            else  if (amountClusterServerRunning>0) // partly running
                    myResultList.put("ClusterState", "PARTLY RUNNING");
            else
                    myResultList.put("ClusterState", "NOT WORKING OR FAILED");
    }
    else
    {
            // no cluster ?!?!?!
            myResultList.put("ClusterState", "NO Cluster configured");
    }

    // add values to result list
    myResultList.put("NrServers",       ""+amountOfMSServer);
    myResultList.put("SrvRunning",      ""+amountRunning);
    myResultList.put("SrvFailedAdmin", ""+amountFailedAdmin);
    myResultList.put("SrvDown",         ""+amountShutdown);

    return myResultList;
}
```

Also for demonstration purposes, the method will produce a string-based HashMap, which usually is not flexible enough for production implementation.

Finally, it is also necessary to implement the functionality to push the collected data to the monitoring infrastructure. This might be just a log file or remote server access via HTTP, IIOP, T3, WebService, or something else. As this depends on individual needs, the provided example only prints out the values to System.out:

🖫 push_data_jmx_(partial)

```
public class PushExampleDestinations
{
    // this is only a dummy implementation as it does nothing but print the values to system.out.
    // depending on the supported destinations (e.g. http, file, corba(iiop), webservice
    // appropriate endpoint communication must be implemented here

    private PushExampleMBeanImpl myPushExampleMBeanImpl = null;

    public PushExampleDestinations(PushExampleMBeanImpl myBean) {
        myPushExampleMBeanImpl = myBean;

        // get connection URL an initialize appropriate backend connectivity
        // this should be outsourced into own classes according to the well known design patterns

        // e.g. String connURI = myPushExampleMBeanImpl.getDestinationURL();
        // if (connURI.startswith('http://') ....       http backend
        // else if (connURI.startswith("iiop://") ....  corba backend
        // ...
    }


    // only simple example to write out data
    public void pushData(String dataCategory, HashMap<String, String> data) {
        System.out.println("\nMonitoring Data - Push simulation:\n===============\n");
        System.out.println("    Category: " + dataCategory);

        Iterator<String> it = data.keySet().iterator();

        while (it.hasNext()) {
        String name = it.next();
        String value = data.get(name);
        System.out.println("                    "+name+" = "+value);
        }
    }

}
```

This example plug-in will produce the following log entries if installed on an AdminServer:

```
Monitoring Data - Push simulation:
====================================================

    Category: DOMAIN
            ClusterState = SHUTDOW
            NrServers = 2
            SrvDown = 2
            SrvRunning = 0
            DomainName = _test_1_OMS
            SrvFailedAdmin = 0

Monitoring Data - Push simulation:
====================================================

    Category: SERVER
            Uptime = 545966
            PendingUserRequestCount = 0
            Thread_HealthState = HEALTH_OK
```

```
JTA_HealthState = HEALTH_OK
CompletedRequestCount = 1035
TransactionRolledBackTotalCount = 0
TransactionAbandonedTotalCount = 0
HeapFreeCurrent = 911276576
HealthState = HEALTH_OK
TransactionTotalCount = 0
ActivationTime = 1370421329056
Name = AdminServer
TransactionCommittedTotalCount = 0
QueueLength = 0
State = RUNNING
Throughput = 3.4965034965034967
ExecuteThreadTotalCount = 5
SocketsOpenedTotalCount = 0
OpenSocketsCurrentCount = 0
ActiveTransactionsTotalCount = 0
HeapSizeCurrent = 1029046272
```

Access to Custom MBeans

WebLogic offers a huge number of MBeans that provide configuration and runtime information of nearly everything WebLogic. JMX and MBeans are *the* standard in the Java world, and therefore it is good to also utilize this standard to provide management and monitoring information about your own application. It is possible to extend the WebLogic MBeans with custom MBeans that can provide information about your own application. For example, a system that provides information about books could provide MBeans that offer information about searches, the number of failed searches, and even invalid or intrusive search requests. With other MBeans it might be possible to restrict access to certain categories, certain times, or other restrictions.

One security issue is that, by default, attribute changes or operations on MBeans (and also custom MBeans) are only allowed for privileged users. A normal application user will not be allowed to do that. However, every MBean has a so-called resourceId in WebLogic. To be precise, every operation and every attribute accessor has its own resourceId. Based on this resource ID, it is possible to grant non-privileged users access to restricted aspects of your MBean.

To keep the example simple, the following code shows a very simple standard MBean and how a standard non-privileged user called "martin" gets the rights granted to change the attribute "Information".

MBean interface and implementation:

```
package com.wlsautomation.customaccess;

public interface TestMBean {
    public String getInformation();
    public void setInformation(String info);
    public void invokeTestMethod();
}

package com.wlsautomation.customaccess;
```

```
import javax.management.StandardMBean;

public class TestMBeanImpl extends StandardMBean implements TestMBean
{

    private String info = "This is just a test";

    public TestMBeanImpl() {
        super(TestMBean.class, false);
    }

    public String getInformation() {
        return info;
    }

    public void invokeTestMethod() {
        // just some dummy test method
        info = info.toUpperCase();
    }

    public void setInformation(String newinfo) {
        info = newinfo;
    }
}
```

MBean registration class:

```
public class RegisterMBeanInTree
{
  // register the mbean when application starts.
  public static void main(String[] args)
  {
      try {
          InitialContext ctx = new InitialContext();
          ObjectName mymbean = new ObjectName("testMBean:Name=TestAccess,Type=TestAccessMBean");
          MBeanServer server = (MBeanServer) ctx.lookup("java:comp/jmx/runtime");
          TestMBeanImpl mbean = new TestMBeanImpl();
          server.registerMBean(mbean, mymbean);

          System.out.println("MBean created and registered !");
      }
      catch (Exception e) {
              e.printStackTrace();
      }
  }
}
```

The following WLST script (could of course also be JMX) should be executed:

```
connect('martin','martin1234','t3://localhost:7001')
custom()
cd ('testMBean/testMBean:Name=TestAccess,Type=TestAccessMBean')
ls()
set('Information','dgdsgsdsdgsdgsdg')
ls()
```

Without an additional security policy, the script shown above will raise the following
error:

```
wls:/testdomain/custom/testMBean/testMBean:Name=TestAccess,Type=TestAccessMBean>
set('Information','wewwe')
This Exception occurred at Thu Jul 27 13:16:56 CEST 2013.
weblogic.management.NoAccessRuntimeException: Access not allowed for subject: principals=[martin], on
ResourceType: TestAccessMBean Action: write, Target: Information
        at weblogic.rjvm.ResponseImpl.unmarshalReturn(ResponseImpl.java:234)
        at weblogic.rmi.internal.BasicRemoteRef.invoke(BasicRemoteRef.java:223)
        at javax.management.remote.rmi.RMIConnectionImpl_1035_WLStub.setAttribute(Unknown Source)
        at weblogic.management.remote.common.RMIConnectionWrapper$14.run(ClientProviderBase.java:842)
        at weblogic.security.acl.internal.AuthenticatedSubject.doAs(AuthenticatedSubject.java:363)
        at weblogic.security.service.SecurityManager.runAs(SecurityManager.java:146)
```

```
. . .
WLSTException: Error occured while performing set : Error setting attribute Information : Access not
allowed for subject: principals=[martin], on ResourceType: TestAccessMBean Action: write, Target:
Information
```

It is necessary to apply a specific security policy, shown in the final script example below. After applying the following script (which could be JMX), the script/program above which failed at the first try will now run successfully.

```
connect('weblogic','test1234','t3://localhost:7001')
cd('SecurityConfiguration/testdomain/Realms/myrealm/Authorizers/XACMLAuthorizer')
cmo.createPolicy('type=<jmx>,operation=set,application=,mbeanType=TestAccessMBean,target=setInformati
on','{Usr(martin)}')
```

Summary

Monitoring is very important for every environment, and therefore also important for every J2EE hosting environment like WebLogic. Monitoring has many different aspects, such as gathering information, creating reports, predicting situations, and many more. Monitoring also has a number of tough requirements in certain real-time situations, such as when observing many WebLogic domains/Managed-Servers/applications at the same time, or when collecting information and feeding it into other systems. JMX is very well suited for monitoring tasks due to its native Java API and the power of Java.

Troubleshooting with JMX

Troubleshooting with JMX

Monitoring is a permanent task to observe server behavior, generate reports, and anticipate problems. With good monitoring, administrators are often able to anticipate problems before they really occur and can react upfront. However, problems are inevitable and in many cases cannot be avoided. Especially in 24x7 systems and systems with high volumes and high importance, it is absolutely critical to react quickly and to have the right tools to find the cause of the problem as soon as possible.

Debugging

Debugging and error analysis are part of the daily routine of every administrator/operator. Normally issues that occur in production systems may not be easily reproduced in the testing systems. It is important for every administrator to have a set of tools handy in order to quickly gather traces or snapshots at the time of the issue. This will be very useful to analyze and understand the root cause of the issue. Based on the findings, administrators or developers can determine how to fix the problem and avoid it in the future.

Debugging on Demand

WebLogic offers a wide range of possible debug options for the WebLogic Server and its subsystems. These debug options can be set on demand while the WebLogic Server is running.

Setting the debug values discussed above can be done using the administration console and also using JMX. The preferred method is JMX as you can switch debug flags on and off as often as you need to. This is very handy, especially if you are running into an error or troublesome situation and your customer asks you to turn on debugging in order to get more information.

The next method shows a flexible way to read the desired settings - flag name, on/off - from a property file and set the desired values. This approach is very flexible as it does not overwrite values that should be kept. However, it needs an additional property file.

💾 set_debug_flags_jmx

```
public void setDebugFlags(String serverName, Properties debugProps) throws WLSAutomationException
{
   try {
      // get the server runtime(!)
      ObjectName myServer = (ObjectName)myJMXWrapper.invoke(myJMXWrapper.getDomainConfigRoot(),
         "lookupServer",
         new Object[]{new String(serverName)},
         new String[]{String.class.getName()});

      // get the ServerDebug mbean
      ObjectName myServerDebugMBean = (ObjectName)myJMXWrapper.getAttribute(myServer, "ServerDebug");

      // iterate of debugProps and set them !
      Iterator it = debugProps.keySet().iterator();
      while (it.hasNext())
      {
         String nextkey = (String)it.next();
         String nextvalue = debugProps.getProperty(nextkey);

         // set debug value
         myJMXWrapper.setAttribute(myServerDebugMBean, new Attribute(nextkey,new Boolean(nextvalue)));
         System.out.println("Setting "+nextkey+" to value "+nextvalue);
      }
   }
   catch(Exception ex) {
      throw new WLSAutomationException("Error while getThreadDump of server "+serverName+" : "+
ex.getMessage());
   }
}
```

The following is an example of a property file that turns 6 debug flags on.

```
#####################################
# EJB debug values
DebugEjbInvoke = true

#####################################
# JBDC debug values
DebugJDBCConn = true
DebugJDBCSQL = true

#####################################
# Security debug values
DebugSecurityAtn = true
DebugSecurityAtz = true
DebugSecuritySSL = true
```

Analyzing Problems

One very common task is the analysis of problems. Normally these are problems in production and are not easily reproduced. This means that the person (developer or analyst) needs runtime information for when the server ran into the problem.

Thread Dumps

Thread dumps are an important source of information. Thread dumps help to understand the actual situation of a server and can reveal dead-locks. Creating multiple thread dumps over a period of time can reveal long-running or even stuck threads.

There are multiple ways to create thread dumps. "Kill -3" is a common one, but this requires that you have access to the machine. Using JVM tools is also a possibility. WebLogic also offers a command that can be issued using JMX, meaning that this can be issued regardless of where the server is running.

```
public String getThreadDump(String serverName) throws WLSAutomationException
{
    try {
        // get the server runtime(!)
        ObjectName serverRuntime = myJMXWrapper.getServerRuntime(serverName);

        // get JVMRuntime of that server
        ObjectName jvmRuntime = (ObjectName)myJMXWrapper.getAttribute(serverRuntime, "JVMRuntime");

        // finally retun the threaddump
        return (String)myJMXWrapper.getAttribute(jvmRuntime, "ThreadStackDump");
    }
    catch(Exception ex) {
        throw new WLSAutomationException("Error while getThreadDump of server "+serverName+" : "+
ex.getMessage());
    }
}
```

See the tools chapter for additional tools around thread dumps like JConsole and Samurai.

Forced Garbage Collection

Normally you should never force a GC to run for several reasons. The virtual machine has quite sophisticated implementations of GC, and WebLogic (like other complex server environments) also has built-in strategies for resource management.

Nevertheless, there might be situations where you want to run a GC at a certain time. This might be for testing or other reasons. Please note again that I strongly discourage the usage of this script unless it is really necessary.

To force a GC run on a specific server instance, you can use the following method:

```
public void forceGarbageCollection(String serverName) throws Exception
{
    serverRuntime = myJMXWrapper.getServerRuntime(serverName);
    ObjectName jvmRuntime = (ObjectName) myJMXWrapper.getAttribute(serverRuntime, "JVMRuntime");

    // run garbage collector
    myJMXWrapper.invoke(jvmRuntime,"runGC",new Object[]{},new String[]{});
}
```

Summary

Troubleshooting is a very important set of tools in every administrator's toolbox. Sooner or later, everybody will face a situation where something goes wrong and you need to find out what happened, when, and why. This chapter discussed a number of techniques to analyze a problem situation. As long as it is still possible to communicate with the AdminServer or MBean server, JMX is a good technology for analyzing a problem situation.

Part IV

Looking Beyond

Looking Beyond

Looking Beyond

The complete book is dedicated to the WebLogic automaton technologies WLST and JMX. These come as part of WebLogic and do not require any additional tools, neither from open source nor from commercial companies. This does not mean that there aren't other technologies or tools around that are closely related to these technologies.

Introduction

This chapter provides an overview of some of these tools. Please note that it is impossible to introduce all tools – there are just too many – and it is also impossible to describe them in detail. For most of them it would be possible to write a book for just that tool. Please consider this chapter as an overview of a number of selected tools and technologies only.

WLST and JMX require software development. Most administrators will think about *vi* or other text editors for this purpose. However, there are more advanced tools out there that can be used to develop WLST and JMX.

This chapter groups the tools into a number of categories. Besides development and editing tools, there are tools for monitoring, troubleshooting, and related technologies.

The last section focuses on "the family." This means that the last section of this chapter will discuss other members of the Oracle Fusion Middleware product family. Even this family is too large to introduce all members; therefore a selection has been made.

WLST/Jython Tools

This section describes tools that support the development and also execution and debugging of WLST scripts.

OEPE

Most administrators and developers use *vi* or Jython/Python tools. OEPE is the answer from Oracle to support the development and testing of WLST.

Features include:

- WLST/Jython/Python Source Editor
- Syntax highlighting, validation
- Code completion
- WLST Templates
- MBean Navigator for browsing MBeans
- WLST Execution and Console in Eclipse
- WLST integrated Help
- Support for both online and offline modes

After starting OEPE, the first step is to create a new project. If you already have an existing project, you can enhance this project with WLST support. If you create a new project, then you may choose "Dynamic Web Project" as this has most (but not all) features enabled that you need for WLST.

You need to add the "Facet" WLST to your project in order to work with WLST script. Go to *Project Facets* and enable the *Oracle WebLogic Scripting Tools Support* (Figure 19.1).

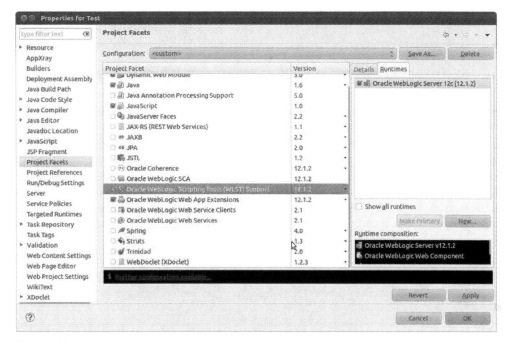

Figure 19.1: *Adding WLST support to OEPE project*

After enabling this facet of OEPE, a new folder will be added to your project. By default it is called "wlst" and will be used to host your WLST scripts.

It is now possible to add WLST scripts by using the context menu (see Figure 19.2).

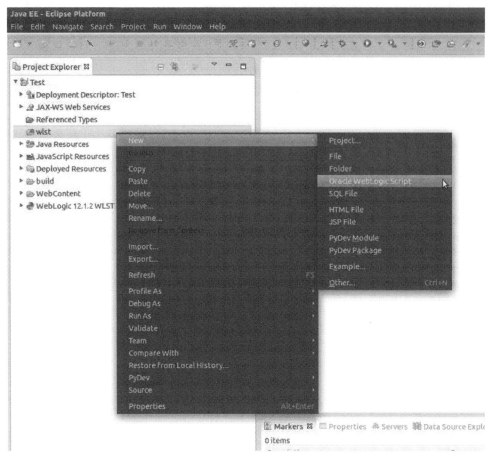

Figure 19.2: *Add WLST scripts to the project*

After adding a WLST script to the project, a default script with a typical command sequence will be added to the project. Then you can use the Jython/WLST editor of OEPE to edit your script.

OEPE will colorize your code and also offers command help (what WLST offers with the *help* command).

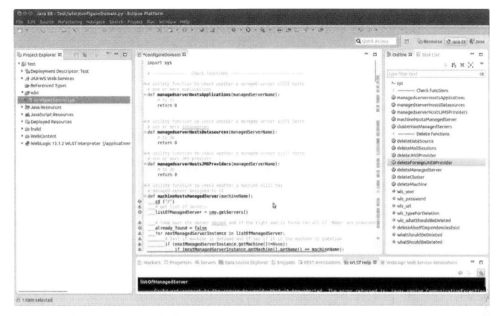

Figure 19.3: *OEPE WLST editor*

OEPE offers two different ways to display command help. By clicking on a command, the frame below the editor will display the help information for this command.

OEPE also offers a pop-up window with the help information if the mouse is hovered over the command.

The next screenshot will depict both help views. The command has been selected to display the help in the frame underneath and the mouse has been moved over the command in order to see the pop-up window.

Figure 19.4: *OEPE – WLST help information*

OEPE does not only offer editing features. Scripts can also be executed (and debugged) directly from the OEPE-IDE. The context menu of the script file offers different *RUN-AS* and *Debug-As* options.

It is possible to create so-called *Run-Configurations* with predefined settings for execution.

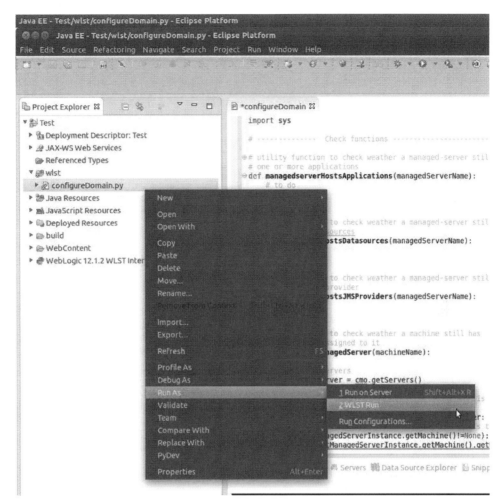

Figure 19.5: *Run-As options for WLST scripts in OEPE*

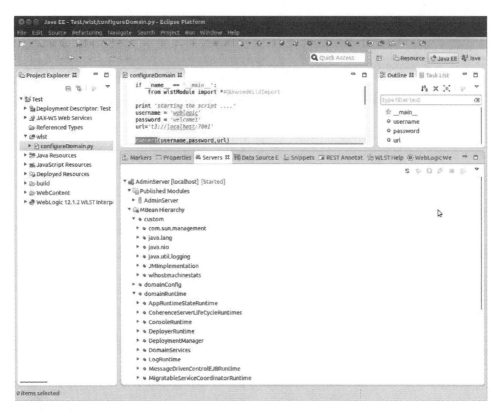

Figure 19.6: *OEPE MBean Browser*

If connections to remote or local WebLogic Servers are configured within OEPE, it is also possible to browse the different MBean hierarchies. The screenshot above depicts this feature of OEPE.

Please refer to the Oracle documentation for a more detailed description of the aforementioned features and of all other features of OEPE.

JMX Tools

JMX is integrated in the Java Virtual Machine. Therefore, every Java application has the standard Java APIs available. Most tools introduced in this category are JMX explorer or tools to make it easier to work with JMX. The only exception is MX4J.

MX4J

MX4J is an Open Source implementation of the Java Management Extensions technology, for both JSR 3 (JMX) and JSR 160 (JMX Remote API).[24]

JConsole

JConsole is a graphical monitoring tool to monitor Java Virtual Machine (JVM) and Java applications both on a local or remote machine.

JConsole is a graphical MBean browser that allows the user to connect to the MBeanServer, browse the MBeans, get/set attributes, or invoke operations. The number of operations permitted to be invoked using JConsole depends on the security configuration of the remote server. It also might be the case that different users have different rights and are allowed to see a different subset of the available MBeans.

The JConsole is part of the JDK and therefore knows about the default connectivity. In order to use it with WebLogic, it is necessary to extend the CLASSPATH of the JConsole with the WebLogic provider and WebLogic classes, which are needed for the protocol provider and also for WebLogic proprietary classes.

Example how to start JConsole on Windows:

```
@echo off

set JAVA_HOME=C:\Program Files\Java\jdk1.6.0_31
set PATH=%JAVA_HOME%\bin;%PATH%

set WLFULCLIENT=H:\99_Downloads\wlfullclient.jar

echo "%JAVA_HOME%\lib\jconsole.jar;%JAVA_HOME%\lib\tools.jar;%WLFULCLIENT%"
jconsole -J-Djava.class.path="%JAVA_HOME%\lib\jconsole.jar;%JAVA_HOME%\lib\tools.jar;%WLFULCLIENT%" -
J-Djmx.remote.protocol.provider.pkgs=weblogic.management.remote -debug
```

In order to use JConsole, it is necessary to establish a connection to the MBeanServer.

---

[24] sourceforge.net/projects/mx4j

Figure 19.7: *Establish MBean Server connection*

In order to establish an MBean-Server connection, it is necessary to provide the MBeanServer URL and user/password credentials.

As WebLogic has a number of different MBeanServers, as discussed in previous chapters of this book, it is important to provide the correct service URL to JConsole in order to connect to the correct MBeanServer.

Possible service URLs include:

```
Runtime MBean Server:
service:jmx:iiop://<some IP>:<port>/jndi/weblogic.management.mbeanservers.runtime

Domain Runtime MBean Server:
service:jmx:iiop://<some IP>:<port>/jndi/weblogic.management.mbeanservers.domainruntime

Edit MBean Server:
service:jmx:iiop://<some IP>:<port>/jndi/weblogic.management.mbeanservers.edit
```

After connecting to the MBeanServer, it is possible to browse the MBeans and access attributes (get/set). Usually the MBeans are organized into a hierarchy, but this highly depends on the remote MBean structure. WebLogic has a rather large and deep hierarchy (see JMX chapters).

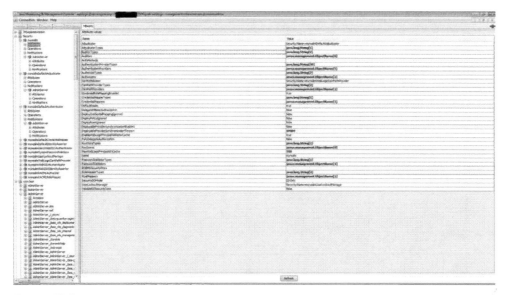

Figure 19.8: *Browsing MBeans and accessing attributes*

It is also possible to invoke operations (if the user has the appropriate permissions). The following screenshot shows the way JConsole offers the various operations available on an MBean.

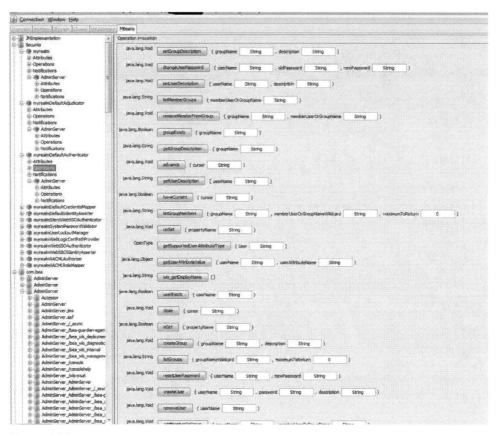

Figure 19.9: *Invoking MBean operations*

So far we discussed the way JConsole can access information and invoke operations. Many values in WebLogic are changing as they reflect the actual status of some server aspects. These monitoring values can also be displayed in charts in order to visualize the ways they are changing.

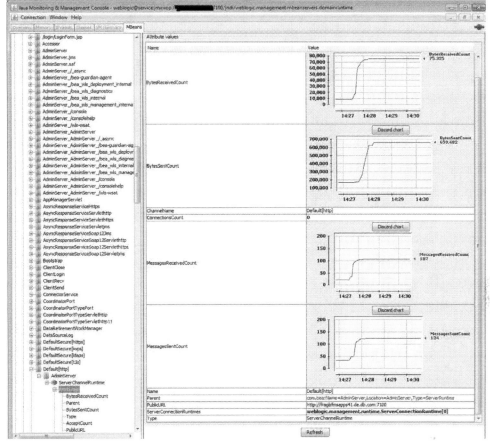

Figure 19.10: *Examples of charts in JConsole*

Finally, one powerful feature of JConsole is the ability to connect to different MBeanServers at the same time – like connecting to different WebLogic domains which together form an application (i.e. frontend, router, service bus, and backend). It is possible to monitor different values of the different remote servers.

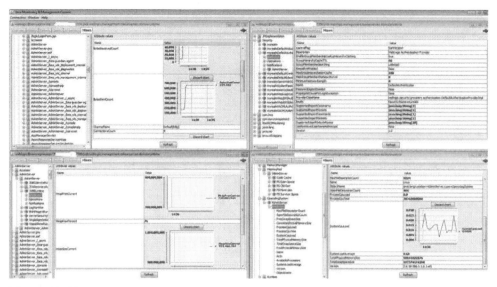

Figure 19.11: *Multiple JConsole connections*

Admin4J

Admin4J provides a base set of administrative support for custom Java EE applications including the following: exception management, thread contention alerts, memory usage alerts, application error reporting, and runtime logger administration.[25]

Admin4J provides the following support features:

- "Track and summarize exceptions generated by applications so the most severe issues are more easily identified.

- Detect thread contention problems at runtime. Problems are logged and administrators optionally notified.

- Detect memory issues at runtime. Problems are logged and administrators optionally notified.

- Track and display performance metrics.

- Provides a SQL Performance Measurement page.

- Identify the most frequently executed code ("Hot Spots") in web applications.

---

[25] sourceforge.net/projects/admin4j/

- Provides a Log Level administration page to change log levels at runtime. Currently supports log4j and JDK logging.

- Provides a Web-Based File Explorer administration page with optional security features to limit display and change capabilities.

- Provides a Java EE Filter to automatically detect application errors. Problems are logged and administrators optionally notified.

- Provides a web-based JMX browser for environments that don't expose JMX ports for remote browsing."[26]

jmx4perl

"Jmx4Perl provides an alternate way of accessing Java JEE Server management interfaces that are based on JMX (Java Management Extensions). It is an agent-based approach where a small Web application deployed on the application server provides HTTP/JSON-based access to JMX MBeans registered within the application server. It is set up from a handful of Perl modules, which can be integrated seamlessly in your own programs. It also includes a Nagios plug-in, check_jmx4perl, a jmx4perl command line tool for remote JMX queries and operations, and a readline-based JMX shell j4psh, with context sensitive command completion and syntax highlighting."[27]

MC4J

MC4J is a Swing application for remote monitoring and administration using Java Management Extensions (JMX). It includes support for all major application servers and advanced features such as live attribute graphing and customizable dashboards.[28]

Unfortunately it looks like MC4J is no longer under active development.

Automation Tools

This section introduces tools that are used to automate special tasks like deployment, artifact creation, and more.

---

[26] admin4j.net/
[27] freecode.com/projects/jmx4perl
[28] sourceforge.net/projects/mc4j/

Ant

"Apache Ant is a Java library and command-line tool whose mission is to drive processes described in build files as targets and extension points dependent upon each other. The main known usage of Ant is the build of Java applications. Ant supplies a number of built-in tasks allowing to compile, assemble, test and run Java applications. Ant can also be used effectively to build non Java applications, for instance C or C++ applications. More generally, Ant can be used to pilot any type of process which can be described in terms of targets and tasks. Ant is written in Java. Users of Ant can develop their own 'antlibs' containing Ant tasks and types, and are offered a large number of ready-made commercial or open-source 'antlibs'."[29]

WebLogic also offers a number of such Ant tasks with an *antlib* provided by Oracle. The Ant tasks provided by Oracle include running WLST scripts from Ant, using weblogic.Deployer functionality, or creating and administering WebLogic.

The following code snippets are some examples. Please refer to the Apache and Oracle documentation for further details.

Invoking WLST scripts

WebLogic offers the ability to either run embedded WLST scripts (provided within the build.xml) or to execute external WLST scripts. It is definitely advisable to separate the build.xml from the WLST script in this case in order to maintain and develop both of them separately.

There are situations where you need to invoke WLST scripts from Ant scripts. This includes:

- Configure WebLogic resources with Ant

- Server Control using Ant

- Monitoring using Ant

Example of the Ant build.xml:

```
<project default="FetchManagedServer" name="WLST project">
  <property file="wlstbuild.properties">

  <taskdef classname="weblogic.ant.taskdefs.management.WLSTTask" name="wlst">
    <classpath>
      <pathelement location="${weblogic.lib.dir}/weblogic.jar">
    </pathelement></classpath>
  </taskdef>
```

---

[29] ant.apache.org

```
<target name="FetchManagedServer">
  <wlst debug="false" executescriptbeforefile="true" failonerror="false" filename="./test.py">
     <script>
  connect('weblogic','welcome1','t3://localhost:6100')
    </script>
  </wlst>
  </target>
</property></project>
```

Sample WLSTbuild.properties file:

```
weblogic.home.dir=/opt/server/weblogic/wlserver_10.3
weblogic.lib.dir=${weblogic.home.dir}/server/lib
wlst.script.source=/scripts/test.py
```

Sample Jython script to be invoked from the Ant script:

```
# Started recording all user actions at Tue Dec 18 22:41:59 IST 2012
svrs = cmo.getServers()
print 'Servers in the domain are'
for x in svrs:
        print x.getName()
```

wldeploy Ant Task

Oracle offers the *weblogic.Deployer* operations as Ant tasks. The attributes must be specified in an Ant build.xml file. In combination with other WebLogic tasks this enables administrators to build complex Ant build files which may include WebLogic deploy and administrative operations and more.

Example of deploying an application to a single server instance:

```
<target name="deploy">
    <wldeploy
      action="deploy" verbose="true" debug="true"
      name="MyTestApplication" source="/application/ears/"
      user="weblogic" password="test1234"
      adminurl="t3://localhost:7001" targets="MS1" />
  </target>
```

Example of undeploying an application:

```
<target name="undeploy">
    <wldeploy
      action="undeploy" verbose="true" debug="true"
      name="MyTestApplication"
      user="weblogic" password="test1234"
      adminurl="t3://localhost:7001" targets="myserver"
      failonerror="false" />
  </target>
```

Example of deploying a library file:

```
<target name="deploy">
    <wldeploy action="deploy" name="myLibrary"
      source="/application/libs/" library="true"
      user="weblogic" password="test1234"
      verbose="true" adminurl="t3://localhost:7001"
      targets="TestCluster" />
```

```
    </target>
```

Ant Tasks for Configuration and Administration

The Ant task allows you to start, reboot, or shutdown a WebLogic Server. It is also possible to create a new single-server domain and/or extend domains with new configuration items like datasources, JavaMail, or JMS configuration.

Example of starting a server (must be current directory):

```
<target name="wlserver-default">
  <wlserver/>
</target>
```

Example of starting a specific instance (local host):

```
<target name="start-server">
  <wlserver dir="./config" host="127.0.0.1" port="7001" action="start"/>
</target>
```

Connect to a server instance:

```
<target name="connect-server">
  <wlserver host="testserver.wlsautomation.de" port="11231" username="weblogic" password="test1234"
action="connect"/>
</target>
```

Example of creating a new single-server domain and then starting the AdminServer:

```
<target name="new-server">
  <delete dir="/applications/server/wls/testdomain"/>
  <mkdir dir="/applications/server/wls/testdomain"/>
  <wlserver dir="/applications/server/wls/testdomain" host="testserver.wlsautomation.de" port="11231"
  generateConfig="true" username="weblogic" password="test1234" action="start"/>
</target>
```

Example of creating a JDBC connection pool and then a datasource:

```
<create type="JDBCConnectionPool" name="TestBookConnectionPool" property="testbookpool">
  <set attribute="CapacityIncrement" value="1"/>
  <set attribute="DriverName" value="oracle.driver.JDBCDriver"/>
  <set attribute="InitialCapacity" value="1"/>
  <set attribute="MaxCapacity" value="10"/>
  <set attribute="Password" value="db1234"/>
  <set attribute="Properties" value="user=myDBUser"/>
  <set attribute="RefreshMinutes" value="0"/>
  <set attribute="ShrinkPeriodMinutes" value="15"/>
  <set attribute="ShrinkingEnabled" value="true"/>
  <set attribute="TestConnectionsOnRelease" value="false"/>
  <set attribute="TestConnectionsOnReserve" value="false"/>
  <set attribute="URL"  value="jdbc:oracle:thin@dbserver.wlsautomation.de:1521:service"/>
  <set attribute="Targets" value="TestCluster"/>
</create>
```

Example of creating a datasource:

```
<create type="JDBCTxDataSource" name="TestBookDataSource">
  <set attribute="JNDIName" value="jndi/TestBookDataSource"/>
  <set attribute="PoolName" value="TestBookConnectionPool"/>
```

```
    <set attribute="Targets" value="TestCluster"/>
</create>
```

Example of rebooting a server (which must be done through the AdminServer):

```
<wlserver
    adminserverurl="t3://test.wlsautomation.de:11521"
    username="weblogic"
    password="test1234"
    servername="MS1"
    action="reboot"
    noExit="true"/>
```

Please consult the Oracle documentation for a full list of possible Ant tasks and attributes.

Maven

"Maven is a build automation tool used primarily for Java projects. Maven serves a similar purpose to the Apache Ant tool, but it is based on different concepts and works in a different manner. Like Ant it can also be used to build and manage projects written in C#, Ruby, Scala, and other languages. The Maven project is hosted by the Apache Software Foundation, where it was formerly part of the Jakarta Project. Maven uses an XML file to describe the software project being built, its dependencies on other external modules and components, the build order, directories, and required plug-ins. It comes with pre-defined targets for performing certain well-defined tasks such as compilation of code and its packaging. Maven dynamically downloads Java libraries and Maven plug-ins from one or more repositories such as the Maven 2 Central Repository, and stores them in a local cache. This local cache of downloaded artifacts can also be updated with artifacts created by local projects. Public repositories can also be updated. Maven is built using a plug-in-based architecture that allows it to make use of any application controllable through standard input."[30]

In WebLogic 12.1.2, Oracle has added the following features to the Maven plug-in included with WebLogic Server:

- Maven archetypes to create new projects.

- Plug-ins for Maven in order to build projects for different target runtimes.

- Maven POMs that describe the Oracle-provided dependency JAR files – for client libraries, APIs, things needed during the build process, etc.

- A Maven plug-in that allows you to populate a (local or remote) Maven repository.

---

[30] www.en.wikipedia.org/wiki/Apache_Maven

As this is a complex topic of its own, it is out of the scope of this book to provide a detailed tutorial. For a detailed Maven example, please see docs.oracle.com/middleware/1212/wls/WLPRG/maven.htm.

Bmap4j

Bmap4j is a framework for the management and processing of batch jobs in Java. Bmap4j is a Java-based framework, with which - together with a Java EE application server - a modern batch transaction processing platform can be built.

The platform required for processing large amounts of data in batch processing mode (Batch Transaction Processing, BTP) has various different aspects when compared to the one used in online processing mode (Online Transaction Processing, OLTP). Bmap4j was developed specifically to achieve the highest possible use within an enterprise environment in the areas of management and processing.[31]

For more details, please see www.bmap4j.org/en/fundamentals/architecture.html.

Over a well-defined JMX interface batch jobs can be controlled and queried for status. Bmap4j provides functions to optimize batch execution in J2SE and J2EE environments.

Batch jobs can be run within a WebLogic Server process as part of an Enterprise Application. The framework can of course also be used to run batches against WebLogic. For more details, please see www.bmap4j.org/en/index.html.

Troubleshooting Tools

Troubleshooting will always be necessary for an application, server, cluster, or even the whole grid. The following section will introduce some selected tools to support administrators and developers in analyzing problems.

Guardian

Each Guardian client has a list of known domains. A domain is called *active* when the client application can connect to it and when the Guardian agent is available for evaluation. Two different flavors of the client exist: the better known GUI interface, which provides a richer functionality, and a command-line interface. Only the command line interface provides automated scripting capabilities.

---

[31] www.bmap4j.org/en/index.html

On the domain side, a Guardian agent is required. This agent will install as web application (WAR) and can be queried by the client using HTTP or HTTPS. The agent will use JMX to query different MBeans and MBeanServers and report the results back to the client. (See WLST troubleshooting chapter for an example on how to install the agent).

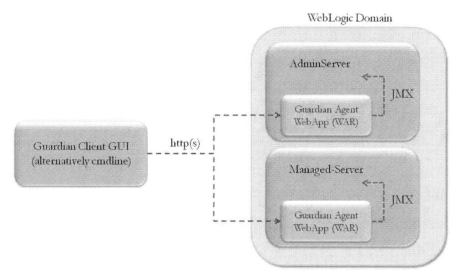

Figure 19.12: *Guardian architecture*

Guardian has a large number of so-called bundles. A bundle is basically a collection of typical error conditions/settings. If a bundle is used for evaluation, then Guardian will check if the problems described in the bundle exist in the selected domains:

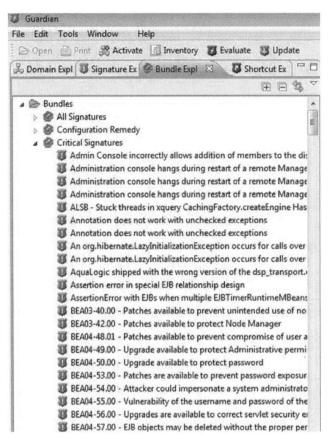

Figure 19.13: *Example list of critical signatures*

After the Guardian starts, you will see the Explorer view. Here you can add domains to your inventory and also group domains into logical groups of your choice.

Every time you evaluate a domain, a new evaluation summary is created and added to the domain's history folder. If you double-click an Evaluation Summary, an Evaluation Summary Editor opens in the Document pane. This summary displays all items found when the domain was evaluated against the selected bundle signatures.

Figure 19.14: *Evaluation Overview*

One interesting aspect of Guardian is that it has all information ready to help you to open support cases with Oracle.

Unfortunately the Guardian as a standalone tool is no longer developed, as its functionality will be integrated into the OEM (Oracle Enterprise Manager) Management Pack. The product still works against WebLogic 11g and 12c, and even if the signature catalog will not be updated it is still quite helpful to identify typical problem configurations.

Mission Control

"The JRockit Mission Control tools suite includes tools to monitor, manage, profile, and eliminate memory leaks in your Java application without introducing the performance overhead normally associated with tools of this type." Please see www.oracle.com/technetwork/middleware/jrockit/overview/index-090630.html.

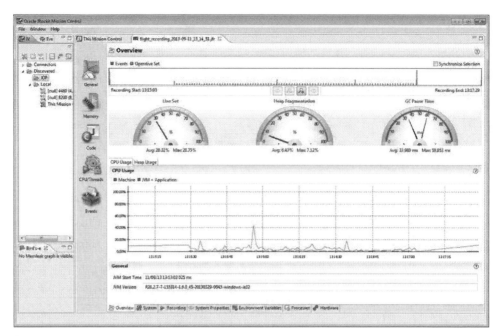

Figure 19.15: *Example of a flight recording in Mission Control*

The next screenshot shows a thread and CPU analysis that was recorded during the flight recording.

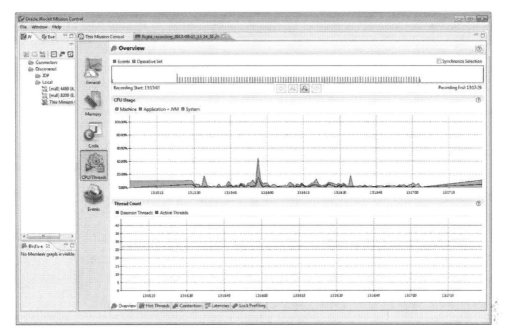

Figure 19.16: *CPU and Thread Analysis in Mission Control*

Mission Control also provides many other views, analysis features, and data collectors. Please see the Oracle documentation for a complete description. An interesting overview can be found at:

www.oracle.com/technetwork/middleware/jrockit/overview/missioncontrol-whitepaper-june08-1-130357.pdf

JVisualVM

Java VisualVM combines several monitoring, troubleshooting, and profiling utilities into a single tool, like jmap, jinfo, jstat and jstack. With the available plug-in API, other tools can be added. See visualvm.java.net for more information.

After starting VisualVM, the tool discovers all local VMs that are available. It is possible to right click on the items found underneath "Local" and then select "Open" in order to attach to this VM. It is also possible to attach to remote VMs or to connect using JMX to an MBeanServer.

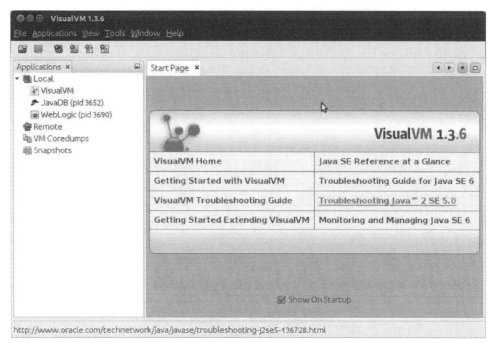

Figure 19.17: *Start screen of VisualVM with Java Process list*

After the tool has been attached to a virtual machine, the user will have different tabs with different functionality available. One common view is the Monitor, which provides an overall picture of the process status:

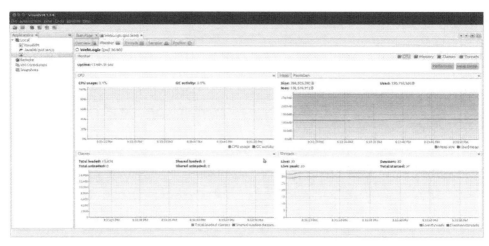

Figure 19.18: *Monitor view of VisualVM*

Another common and important view is the live Thread view. This view has also sub-tabs "Table" and "Details," which provide a detailed view with data about all threads:

Figure 19.19: *Live Thread Overview in VisualVM*

The "Table" view of the threads section provides some interesting data about thread states and the times each thread has been in which state.

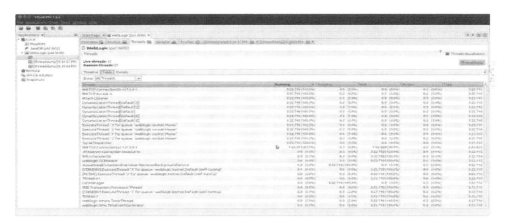

Figure 19.20: *Table view with thread details in VisualVM*

VisualVM also supports sampling of the processes. Sampling of CPU usage and memory usage is supported. Note that this has a performance impact on the running system.

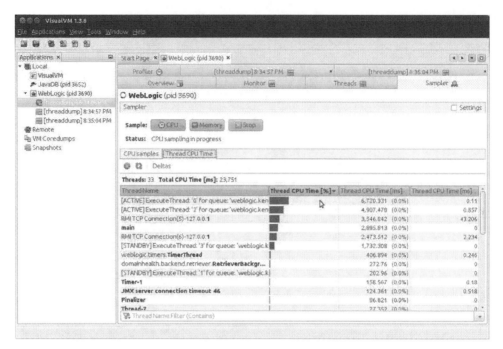

Figure 19.21: *CPU sampling in VisualVM*

It is possible to take one or more thread dumps. Each thread dump will be displayed in its own tab. The thread dump tab itself has multiple views:

Figure 19.22: *Summary view of a thread dump*

This view provides summary data of all threads found in that process.

Another feature of VisualVM is the ability to create heap dumps. This will basically dump the heap and all its content into a file and can then be analyzed by the tool.

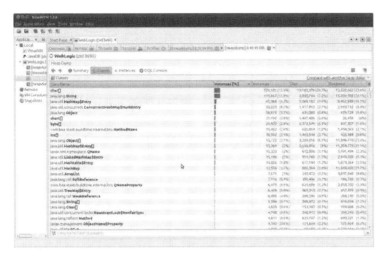

Figure 19.23: *Classes view of a heap dump*

This view lists all the different classes used in this process and the number and size of their instances. Comparing multiple heap dumps may reveal memory leaks in certain areas, but this has to be analyzed with caution.

VisualVM has a number of other views and features, such as remote connections to processes, MBean views, and plug-in options. Please see the documentation for a full list of features.

Samurai

Samurai is a tabbed GUI application for working with thread dumps and other virtual machine data. The main feature of Samurai is the very useful thread analyzer. Samurai will color idle threads in gray, blocked threads in red, and all the running threads in green. One of the strong features of Samurai is the capability to read multiple thread dumps from a single log file. It is therefore possible to take multiple thread dumps and then load this file into Samurai, and Samurai will compare all those thread dumps. In fact the full power of Samurai can only be used if you provide the tool with more than one thread dump.

Legend:

Figure 19.24: *Colors codes in Samurai*

Samurai offers three different views for thread dumps. The default view is the table overview. In most cases you will be interested in the table view and the sequence view. This view can be used to decide quickly (based on the colors) which thread you need to examine. This is really a big benefit. Especially look for threads in red!

Features provided by Samurai:

- Analyze log files and filter out all thread dumps from a log, regardless of other messages.

- Color code thread states.

- Compare different thread dumps and detects possible deadlocks and hanging situations.

- Visualize the "-verbose:gc" log.

- Works as a GUI-based "tail -f".

The next screenshot shows the table view provided by Samurai.

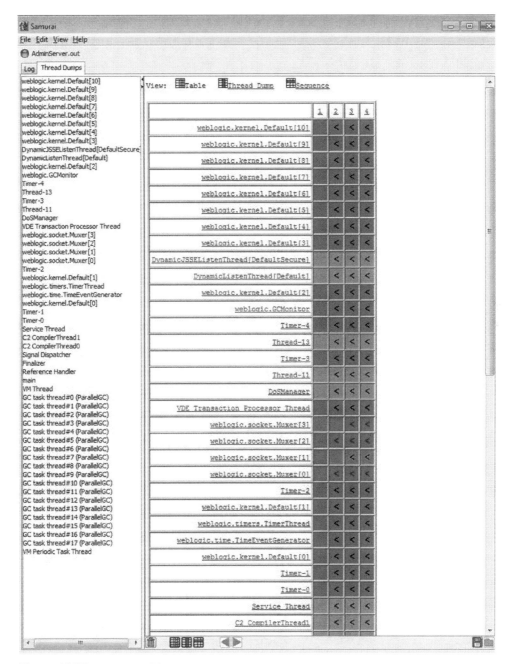

Figure 19.25: *Samurai table view*

By selecting one thread in the left-hand list or clicking on the colorized view, Samurai will show you the details of this thread. If multiple thread dumps are available, then all occurrences of this thread will be shown. The tool will also colorize this view.

Figure 19.26: *Thread sequence view of Samurai*

Thread Dump Analyzer (TDA)

The Thread Dump Analyzer (TDA) is another tool similar to Samurai to parse log files for thread dumps. The program parses log files and displays all thread dumps found in the log.

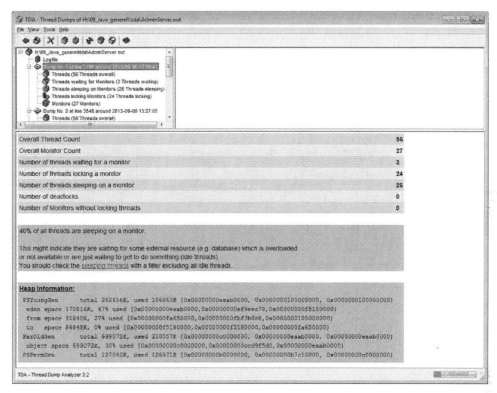

Figure 19.27: *TDA Thread dump view*

The default view is the thread dump summary view, which provides an overview of the amount of threads and possible problems.

TDA also offers more detailed views for each thread dump. The following screenshot shows the detailed thread list view of TDA.

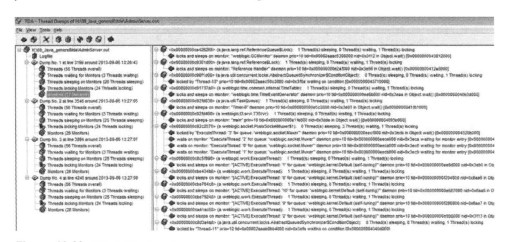

Figure 19.28: *TDA Thread details view*

TDA also offers a detailed view on all monitors found. This is very helpful so that you do not need to collect them from the log file:

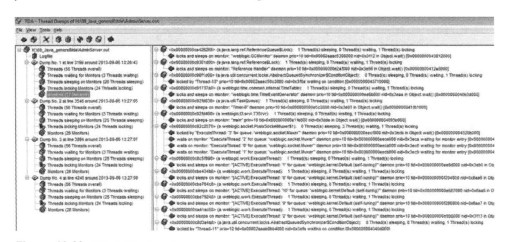

Figure 19.29: *TDA Monitor view*

JConsole Plug-in

The TDA can also be used as a plug-in in JConsole or VisualVM in order to request thread dumps from a remote virtual machine. The thread dumps are retrieved from the remote server and then parsed locally. Then they can be analyzed just like running a standalone application.

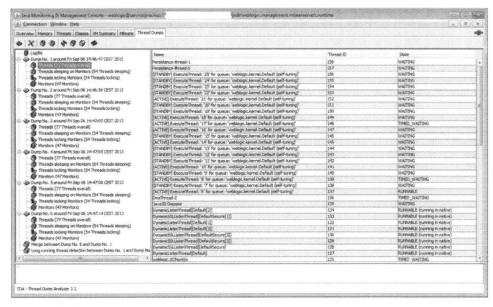

Figure 19.30: *JConsole with TDA plug-in*

Example: Start JConsole with the TDA plug-in:

```
jconsole -pluginpath ./tda.jar
```

Log File Colorizer

This utility color-codes log files or console output from JBoss, WebLogic, WebSphere, and DAS application servers. Output originating from ATG is also recognized and colored appropriately. This utility greatly aids in reading and interpreting log files.[32]

It is very helpful to see, based on colors, where there are errors. This is especially useful when errors are only a single line and not full stack traces, as it is easy to overlook them in larger log files.

See sourceforge.net/projects/atglogcolorizer for source, download and more details.

---

[32] sourceforge.net

Integration with Monitoring Tools

This section lists a number of monitoring tools that can be used with WebLogic. Please note that it is neither possible to list all nor to explain them in detail. Please consult the documentation/websites of the different tools for more information.

OEM

Oracle Enterprise Manager (OEM) is the management and monitoring solution from Oracle. Originated from database management and monitoring, this tool has evolved in order to manage the complete infrastructure, including middleware and in combination with SUN's OpsCenter. Oracle is trying to move all management tools into OEM, or at least provide a version of all tools with can be plugged into OEM (e.g. the Tuxedo monitor TSAM).

OEM offers management and monitoring features for WebLogic and other Fusion Middleware products, but also for non-Oracle middleware technology. Support includes: WebLogic, SOA Suite, Coherence, Identity Management, WebCenter, Web Tier, Business Intelligence, Exalogic Elastic Cloud, GlassFish Server, and others.

For WebLogic, Oracle offers WebLogic and SOA management packs as OEM extensions. See www.oracle.com/technetwork/oem/soa-mgmt/ds-em12c-wls-mgmt-pack-ee-15524 for a description.

Applications Manager

Applications Manager automatically diagnoses, notifies, and corrects performance and availability problems not only with WebLogic Servers, but also with the servers and applications in the entire IT infrastructure.[33]

AppDynamics

AppDynamics automatically discovers and monitors application code running on WebLogic and provides deep visibility of how it executes through the JVM in production. This enables users to understand where latency is spent and how system resources like CPU and memory are consumed by an application and business transactions.[34]

---

[33] www.manageengine.com/products/applications_manager/weblogic-management.html
[34] www.appdynamics.com/solutions/appdynamics-java-monitoring/oracle-weblogic-monitoring

up.time

up.time provides a monitoring environment for WebLogic. Main features include the availability of applications and servers, alerting problems, mapping system performance and server behavior, profiling, diagnostics, monitoring, and reporting. For more details please see: www.uptimesoftware.com/weblogic.php.

Hyperic

Hyperic is application monitoring and performance management for virtual, physical, and cloud infrastructures. Hyperic provides dynamic domain auto-discovery, and granular monitoring and control of every component deployable into WebLogic.[35]

Nimsoft

Nimsoft is a widely-used system monitoring tool. It provides support for WebLogic, and can continually monitor and report on critical performance data within WebLogic environments. It also provides centralized, agentless WebLogic monitoring (domains, servers, clusters, and more).

For details please see: www.ca.com/us/collateral/solution-briefs/na/ca-nimsoft-monitor-oracle-weblogic.aspx

ITRS Geneos

Geneos is the monitoring solution from ITRS. It is a hub<->agent system where the hub is called *gateway* and the agents are called *netprobes*. Many different monitoring features like log file parsing, SQL, processes, and system information (called samplers) are available out of the box. Geneos also provides a JMX sampler, which allows the monitoring tool to connect to JMX-enabled systems and query MBeans. This might work well for small applications, but in all our tests it was insufficient for WebLogic and its huge amount of MBeans. The main reason is the architecture behind it. Geneos also offers an XML-RPC API, which is a powerful mechanism to feed data into the monitoring system and then define rules and alerts on this data. This offers a powerful feature for WebLogic monitoring. See the JMX monitoring chapter for an example of feeding data into monitoring systems. This in combination with the XML-RPC API of Geneos allows the definition of powerful Geneos WebLogic monitoring. For more details see: www.itrsgroup.com

---

[35] www.hyperic.com

Nagios

Nagios is an open source software application for system monitoring, network monitoring, and infrastructure monitoring. Nagios offers monitoring and alerting services for servers, switches, applications, and services. It alerts the users when things go wrong and alerts them a second time when the problem has been resolved.[36]

Nagios offers many different features for system and application monitoring, and uncounted plugins from the commercial and open-source communities. A number of different plugins for WebLogic monitoring exist.

For different Nagios plugins with regards to WebLogic and monitoring, please see:

```
http://exchange.nagios.org/directory/Plugins/Java-Applications-and-Servers/Weblogic
http://code.google.com/p/wlsagent/
http://sourceforge.net/projects/nagchkweblogic/
```

Standalone Monitoring Tools

Tools in this category do not require JMX/WLST configurations or plug-ins; these run standalone.

DomainHealth

DomainHealth is an open source "zero-config" monitoring tool for WebLogic. It collects important server metrics over time, archives these into CSV files, and provides a simple web interface for viewing graphs of current and historical statistics.[37] Since version 1.0, it also offers the optional capability to collect and show Processor, Memory, and Network statistics from the underlying host Operating System and Machine that WebLogic is running on. This additional data is only available if DomainHealth is used in combination with another open source tool called WLHostMachineStats.

DomainHealth uses JMX to query MBeans from the domain runtime server and from the different server runtimes. It also uses WLDF under the cover for more advanced data queries.

---

[36] Wikipedia

[37] sourceforge.net/apps/mediawiki/domainhealth/index.php?title=Introduction_to_the_Domain_Health_monitoring_tool

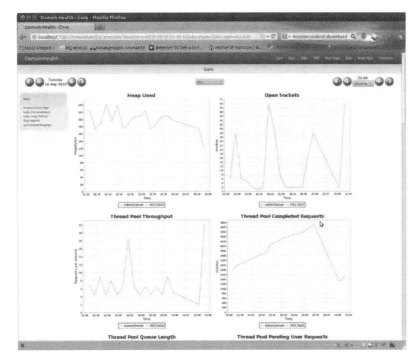

Figure 19.31: *Domain Screen of DomainHealth*

Figure 19.32: *Host screen of DomainHealth*

Note: this is only available with WLHostMachineStats enabled.

WLDF monitoring - which is part of WebLogic - is a comparable tool to DomainHealth. Paul Done has provided the following explanation on how to choose one for different situations.

Use DomainHealth (with its built-in WLDF harvesting mechanism) rather than the WLDF Console Extension, in situations where some of the following factors are advantageous:

1. **Zero-configuration**. An administrator does not have to first work out and configure the server objects to monitor. An administrator does not have to spend time creating a complex WLDF module with the correct object types, names, and attributes in it. An administrator does not have to work out what graphs to plot and then configure specific graphs for each server in the domain for every new environment (e.g. Test, Pre-Prod, Prod1, and Prod2).

2. **Minimal performance impact on Managed-Servers**. Obtains a set of statistics once and ONLY once, regardless of how many times you come back to view the

same statistics in the graphs. The background statistics collection work is driven from the AdminServer, once per minute, lasting far less than a second.

3. **Tools friendly storage of statistics in CSV files**. Administrators can open the CSVs in MS Excel or Open Office for offline analysis and graphing. Using CSV files rather than WebLogic Persistent File Stores on the AdminServer has no detrimental performance impact. It doesn't matter if it takes 10 microseconds or 100 milliseconds to persist the set of statistics - timeliness only has to be to the nearest minute. The file I/O for writing data to CSV files on the AdminServer is not in the 'flight-path' of transactions that happen to be racing through the Managed-Servers.

4. **Minimal administrator workstation pre-requisites**. Doesn't require Java Applet support on the administrator's workstation; it's browser-friendly and just uses very simple HTML and PNG images to display graphs.

5. **Hot deployable**. Deployable to an already running domain for diagnosis of currently occurring problems, without needing to restart the AdminServer.

6. **Statistics don't constantly scroll whilst trying to analyze them**. Administrators can focus in on the current window of time or a historic window of time, in a graph, without it continuously refreshing and moving to a later time. A simple set of navigation buttons is provided to move backwards or forwards in time or just go to the most current time.

7. **Statistics can be viewed for non-running Managed-Servers**. If a Managed-Server has just died, graphs of its recent statistics can still be viewed to help diagnose the failure cause, without first requiring the Managed-Server to be recovered and re-started.

Use the WLDF Console Extension rather than DomainHealth when some of the following factors are advantageous:

1. **Infinitely configurable**. Administrators get to choose exactly what server resources they want to monitor.

2. **Fine-grained statistics capture**. Statistics are gathered and displayed at a much higher frequency than just once every minute.

3. **Comes with WebLogic**. No need for an administrator to seek corporate approval to download and provision a 3rd party open source application into the organization's WebLogic environment.

4. **Statistics can be retrieved for the periods of time when the AdminServer was down**. As long as an administrator has previously configured a WLDF module with the right harvested objects and attributes, statistics can still be

retrieved retrospectively by the console's graphs, following a period of time when the AdminServer was down and unable to contact the Managed-Servers.

Many thanks to Paul Done who granted me permission to use material from the tool web pages and his blog. (See pauldone.blogspot.de/2011/10/new-release-of-domainhealth-10.html for more details)

Other Tools

The following section summarizes a selection of other interesting tools related to management and monitoring that do not fit well into another category.

Queue Message Admin

Developing Queue Message admin GUI-based tools for OpenMQ (GlassFish JMS) / Oracle WebLogic MQ. The name of tool is QBrowserV2. It aims to implement functionality such as New Message Create/Send, Delete Messages, Forward Messages, and Subscribe TOPICs. See sourceforge.net/projects/qbrowserv2 for more information.

LoadUI

LoadUI is an Open Source Load Testing solution that is free and cross-platform. With a visual, drag-and-drop interface, it allows you to create, configure, and redistribute your Load Tests interactively and in real-time.[38]

LoadUI offers support for WebLogic. A tutorial can be found at www.loadui.org/Server-monitoring/weblogic-server-monitor.html

Other Fusion Middleware Products

WebLogic is the foundation of the Fusion Middleware product family (see www.oracle.com/us/products/middleware/026134.pdf for an overview). WebLogic as the JEE application server offers all the features also discussed in this book. In addition, WebLogic is the basis for most of the other components of Fusion Middleware.

Besides WebLogic and Coherence as foundation technologies, Fusion Middleware also provides SOA components (e.g. SOA SuiteOracle, Service Bus (ESB), BPEL

---

[38] www.loadui.org

Process Manager, B2B Integration, Event Processing, Business Rules, Governance, and more), WebCenter as a portal solution, Identity Management (e.g. Oracle Access Management (OAM)), business intelligence, and business management components.

Oracle has therefore developed extensions not only for WebLogic itself but also for WLST (and JMX) in order to support these extended functionalities. This section of the book can by no means provide a thorough or even complete overview. It is only meant to introduce WLST/JMX capabilities of some of the Fusion Middleware components.

OWSM

Oracle Web Services Manager (WSM) is a comprehensive solution for securing and managing service-oriented architectures (SOA). It allows IT managers to centrally define policies that govern web services operations such as access control (authentication, authorization), logging and content validation, and then attach these policies to one or multiple web services with no modification to existing web services required. In addition, Oracle WSM collects runtime data to monitor access control, message integrity, message confidentiality, quality of service (defined in service-level agreements (SLAs)) and displays that information in graphical charts. Oracle WSM brings enterprises better control and visibility over their SOA deployments.[39]

Key features of Oracle WSM include the Policy Manager and Policy Enforcements.

Policy Manager

Policy Manager is a graphical tool for building new security and operation policies, storing policies, and managing distribution and updates to runtime policy enforcement points (gateways and agents). Policy Manager allows administrators to configure operational rules and propagate them to the appropriate enforcement components across an application deployment of any scale and complexity. [40]

Enforcement

To ensure maximum deployment flexibility, Oracle WSM provides two kinds of policy enforcement components: Gateways and Agents. Gateways are deployed in front of a group of applications or services. Gateways can intercept inbound requests to these applications in order to enforce policy steps defined in the Policy Manager, adding application security and other operation rules to applications that are already

---

[39] www.oracle.com/us/corporate/Acquisitions/oblix/owsm-10gr3-fov-1-087696.html
[40] www.oracle.com/us/corporate/Acquisitions/oblix/owsm-10gr3-fov-1-087696.html

deployed. Agents provide "last-mile" security by running directly into an application or service. [41]

The Agent approach of OWSM means that each WLS server has an OWSM agent deployed that checks policies before a call leaves the process and when a call arrives at the server.

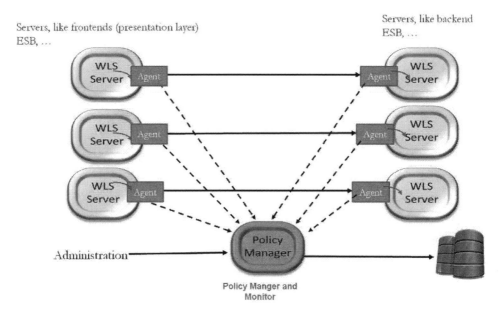

Figure 19.33: *OWSM Agent approach*

Another approach, which is rather uncommon as this will be replaced by the Oracle Access Manager, is the usage of a central gateway. This has less configuration items but introduces additional process and network calls:

---

[41] www.oracle.com/us/corporate/Acquisitions/oblix/owsm-10gr3-fov-1-087696.html

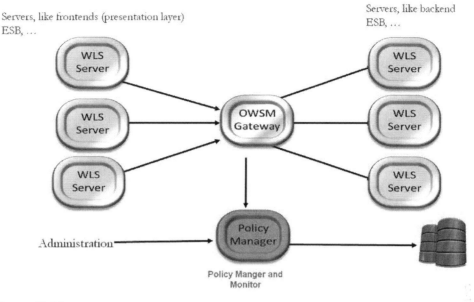

Figure 19.34: *OWSM Gateway Approach*

OWSM uses a pipeline approach, which means that a sequence of (different) categories of policies is evaluated in a defined sequence. Of course the order is different when executed in a client (outgoing message) or in a server (incoming message).

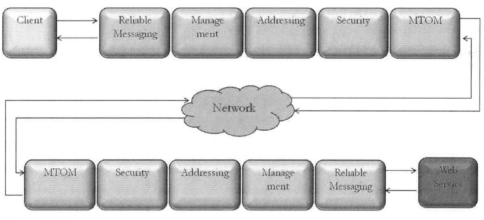

Figure 19.35: *OWSM Pipeline*

Running OWSM WLST Commands

The most common issue people seem to run into is trying to run the OWSM WLST commands from the wrong location. You need to run the WLST commands from "oracle_common/common/bin/wlst.sh"

(For example: /home/Oracle/Middleware/oracle_common/common/bin/wlst.sh)

Custom WLST command	Command description
listWebServices	List the Web service information for an application, composite, or domain.
listWebServicePorts	List the Web service ports for a Web service application or SOA composite.
listWebServiceConfiguration	List Web services and port configuration for an application or SOA composite.
setWebServiceConfiguration	Set or change the Web service port configuration for a Web service application or SOA composite.
listWebServiceClients	List Web service client information for an application, SOA composite, or domain.
listWebServiceClientPorts	List Web service client ports information for an application or SOA composite.
listWebServiceClientStubProperties	List Web service client port stub properties for an application or SOA composite.
setWebServiceClientStubProperty	Set, change, or delete a single stub property of a Web service client port for an application or SOA composite.
setWebServiceClientStubProperties	Configure the set of stub properties of a Web service client port for an application or SOA composite.
listAvailableWebServicePolicies	Display a list of all the available Oracle Web Services Manager (WSM) policies by category or subject type.
listWebServicePolicies	List Web service port policy information for a Web service in an application or SOA composite.
attachWebServicePolicy	Attach a policy to a Web service port of an application or SOA composite.
attachWebServicePolicies	Attach multiple policies to a Web service port of an application or SOA composite.
enableWebServicePolicy	Enable or disable a policy attached to a port of a Web service application or SOA composite.
enableWebServicePolicies	Enable or disable multiple policies attached to a port of a Web service application or SOA composite.
detachWebServicePolicy	Detach an Oracle WSM policy from a Web service port of

	an application or SOA composite.
detachWebServicePolicies	Detach multiple Oracle WSM policies from a Web service port of an application or SOA composite.
listWebServiceClientPolicies	List Web service client port policies information for an application or SOA composite.
attachWebServiceClientPolicy	Attach an Oracle WSM policy to a Web service client port of an application or SOA composite.
attachWebServiceClientPolicies	Attach multiple policies to a Web service client port of an application or SOA composite.
enableWebServiceClientPolicy	Enable or disable a policy of a Web service client port of an application or SOA composite.
enableWebServiceClientPolicies	Enable or disable multiple policies of a Web service client port of an application or SOA composite.
detachWebServiceClientPolicy	Detach a policy from a Web service client port of an application or SOA composite.
detachWebServiceClientPolicies	Detach multiple policies from a Web service client port of an application or SOA composite.
setWebServicePolicyOverride	Configure the Web service port policy override properties of an application or SOA composite.
createPolicySet	Create a new, empty policy set.
listPolicySets	Lists the policy sets in the repository.
clonePolicySet	Clone a new policy set from an existing policy set.
displayPolicySet	Display the configuration of a specified policy set.
modifyPolicySet	Specify an existing policy set for modification in the current session.
enablePolicySet	Enable or disable a policy set.
enablePolicySetPolicy	Enable or disable a policy attachment for a policy set using the policy's URI.
setPolicySetDescription	Specify a description for the policy set selected within a session.

(Source: Oracle Corporation[42])

Table 19.1: Custom WLST Commands

Using JMX to Configure the OWSM

If the automation is embedded into other programs, then it might be a better architecture to use JMX automation. As documentation on this topic is very hard to

---

[42] docs.oracle.com/cd/E21764_01/web.1111/e13813/custom_webservices.htm

find – if at all – this section provides some JMX code functions that demonstrate how to automate OWSM using JMX. All MBeans used in automation require the Oracle Java Platform Security (JPS) to be added to the domain. This requires a change in the WebLogic domain creation as the JPS templates must be added to the domain.

Setting up a normal WebLogic domain with the OWSM agent involves the following steps:

- Setup all WebLogic artifacts like PKI, SSL, security settings, etc.

- Create and configure a JPS keystore.

- Setup the issuer.

- Setup trustedDNS.

- Define an entry in the keystore for which user will be used to access the OWSM manager.

- Define the OSWM Manager location and which entry of the keystore should be used for authentication.

- Complete additional OWSM configurations like cache and binding interceptor configurations.

Create and Configure a JPS Keystore

Note that this has nothing to do with the PKI keystore. This is a keystore created under the JPS (Java Platform Security) environment.

🖫 configure_JPS_keystore

```
String operation_name = "addKeyStoreService";
ObjectName myObjectName = new ObjectName(com.oracle.jps:type=JpsConfig);

// Example values
String param_path = "/opt/keystores/oswm/test.jks";
String param_typ = "JKS";
String param_pwd = "myKeystorePassword";
String param_signAlias = "mySignAlias";
String param_signPwd = "myPwd";
String param_encAlias = "myEncryptionAlias";
String param_encPwd = "myEncrPassword";

// try to remove old service KEYSTORE.  This has proven to be necessary in case another keystore
// already exists. Reason unknown
try {
    myJMXWrapper.invoke(myObjectName,"removeServiceType",
        new Object[] { null, "KEY_STORE" },
        new String[] { String.class.getName(), String.class.getName() });
}
catch (Exception ex) {
    // Log but ignore exception
    System.out.println("Exception "+ex.getMessage()+" while deleting old keystore -> can be IGNORED
!");
}

HashMap<String,String> myMap = new HashMap<String,String>();
myMap.put("keystore.csf.map", "oracle.wsm.security");
```

```
PortableMap myOracleMap = new PortableMap(myMap);

//create keystore
System.out.println("Creating Keystore !");
myJMXWrapper.invoke(myObjectName, operation_name,
    new Object[] { null,
    param_path,
    param_typ,
    param_pwd.toCharArray(),
    param_signAlias,
    param_signPwd.toCharArray(),
    param_encAlias,
    param_encPwd.toCharArray(),
    myOracleMap.toCompositeData(PortableMap.toCompositeType())
},
new String[] { String.class.getName(),
    String.class.getName(),
    String.class.getName(),
    "[C",
    String.class.getName(),
    "[C",
    String.class.getName(),
    "[C",
    "javax.management.openmbean.CompositeData"
});

System.out.println("Keystore configuration has been created !");
```

OWSM Issuer Configuration

As this is all based on policies, it is necessary to setup (in all WLS servers) a list of issuer URIs that this WLS instance will trust. It is possible to define as many issuers URIs as you need. The following example will only define one.

define_issuer_URI

```
System.out.println("Setup Issuer URIs");

String[] myURIs = new String[]{"http://services.wlst_automation.de/wlstbook/MyPartner"};

myJMXWrapper.invoke(
    new ObjectName("com.oracle.jps:type=JpsConfig"),
    "updateSAMLLoginModule",
    new Object[] { "SAML",   // Context
    "saml.loginmodule",      // name of login module
    "required",              // ControlFlag
    new Boolean(true),       // set debug to true
    new Boolean(true),       // add roles
    null,
    myURIs)
},
new String[] { String.class.getName(),
    String.class.getName(),
    String.class.getName(),
    Boolean.class.getName(),
    Boolean.class.getName(),
    javax.management.openmbean.CompositeData,
    "[Ljava.lang.String;"
});
```

Do not forget to persist your changes, otherwise they will be lost. It is necessary to issue a second call just to persist your changes:

```
myJMXWrapper.invoke(new ObjectName("com.oracle.jps:type=JpsConfig"),
    "persist",new Object[0],new String[0]);
```

Looking Beyond

OWSM Issuer - Trusted DNs

In the previous step, we defined which issuer URIs we trust. It is also necessary to setup the issuer URI that the WebLogic instance will use when secure calls based on OSWM policies are made. So here we setup which issuer URI will be submitted with an outgoing call. Together with the issuer URI, it is necessary to define which certificate will be used to sign the request. Unfortunately OWSM uses a very strange way of defining this. It does not use (as most may expect) the keystore alias, but instead uses the distinguished name (DN) of the certificate.

This code also demonstrates the complexity of developing OSWM automations, as OSWM is using open MBeans.

🖫 OWSM_issuer

```
String issuer_uri = "http://services.wlst_automation.de/wlstbook/ThatIsMe"
ObjectName myObjectName    = new ObjectName("oracle.j2ee.config:name=pap,type=PolicyAccessorConfig");
String parameter_name ="SamlSvTrustedDns";
String value ="wlst_automation@mh-enterpriseconsulting.de, CN=WLST, OU=PRODUCTION, O=MH-
EnterpriseConsulting, C=DE";


// Build openmbean structure
String[] itemNames = new String[]{"key", "value"};
CompositeType rowInTabular = new CompositeType("java.util.Map<java.lang.String,
java.util.List<java.lang.String>>","java.util.Map<java.lang.String,
java.util.List<java.lang.String>>",
        itemNames,itemNames,
        new OpenType[]{SimpleType.STRING, new ArrayType(1,SimpleType.STRING)} );

TabularType myMapTabularType = new TabularType("IssuerURIs", "List of IssuerURIs", rowInTabular, new
String[]{"key"});

TabularDataSupport tabularSupport = null;

// try to get from server, if null create new
tabularSupport = (TabularDataSupport)myJMXWrapper.getAttribute(myObjectName,parameter_name);

if (tabularSupport == null)
    tabularSupport = new TabularDataSupport(myMapTabularType);

// compile data
CompositeData compositeData = new CompositeDataSupport(rowInTabular,
        itemNames,
        new Object[]{issuer_uri, new String[]{value}});

tabularSupport.put(compositeData);

// set Attribute
myJMXWrapper.setAttribute(myObjectName,new Attribute(parameter_name, tabularSupport));
```

Accessor User Configuration

The OWSM Manager is a remote process, therefore it is necessary to authenticate incoming requests. The following code will setup the user/password credentials that will be used to authenticate calls from this OWSM agent against the manager.

💾 OWSM_user_configuration

```
String key_value    = "myOWSMaccesskey";
String alias        = "oracle.wsm.security";
String user         = "MyOWSMaccessUser";
String password     = "lfhajfh3297562935jdhso325z";

ObjectName myObjectName = new ObjectName("com.oracle.jps:type=JpsCredentialStore");

// Use an WebLogic class to create th correct credentials
// package to be used:  oracle.security.jps.mas.mgmt.jmx.credstore
PortableCredential cred = new PortablePasswordCredential(user,password.toCharArray(),"OWSM Access
UserInfo");

// key and alias exists ?
boolean alreadyExists = (Boolean) myJMXWrapper.invoke(myObjectName,"containsCredential",
        new Object[] { alias, key_value },
        new String[] { String.class.getName(), String.class.getName() });

// check if alias and key exists and if yes, delete it
if (alreadyExists) {
        myJMXWrapper.invoke(myObjectName,"deleteCredential",
            new Object[] { alias, key_value },
            new String[] { String.class.getName(), String.class.getName() });
}

//create a password credential
myJMXWrapper.invoke(myObjectName, operation_name,
        new Object[] { alias, key_value, cred.toCompositeData(null) },
        new String[] { String.class.getName(), String.class.getName(),CompositeData.class.getName()
});

System.out.println("Alias="+alias+" , Key="+key_value+" has been created !");
```

Policy Manager Access Configuration

The next activity is to define the access information of the manager. Every OSWM agent must be configured with the information for where the manager can be found. This requires the definition of two properties. One property with the URL of the manager, and another property with the information for which credentials should be used for authentication (see above). The properties are created on the MBean oracle.j2ee.config:name=pap,type=PolicyAccessorConfig. Here we also have to use the complicated open MBean structure:

```
mbean=oracle.j2ee.config:name=pap,type=PolicyAccessorConfig
parameterName=PolicyAccessor
propertyName=java.naming.provider.url
propertyValue=t3://endOfTheWorld.org:4711
```

and then:

```
mbean=oracle.j2ee.config:name=pap,type=PolicyAccessorConfig
parameterName=PolicyAccessor
propertyName=jndi.lookup.csf.key
propertyValue=owsmaccesskey
```

JMX function definition:

```
public void addMapProperty(String parameterName, String propertyName, String propertyValue) {
    try {
        // Try to get Properties
        TabularData tabularSupport =
                (TabularData)myJMXWrapper.getAttribute(myObjectName,parameterName);
```

```
String[] itemNames;
CompositeType rowInTabular;
// Build opeenmbean structure
TabularType myMapTabularType;

if(tabularSupport==null)  // then create new structure
{
    itemNames = new String[]{"key", "value"};
    rowInTabular = new CompositeType("xxx","xxxx",
                                     itemNames,itemNames,
                                     new OpenType[]{SimpleType.STRING, SimpleType.STRING} );
    // Build opeenmbean structure
    myMapTabularType = new TabularType("yyy", "yyy", rowInTabular, new String[]{"key"});

    tabularSupport = new TabularDataSupport(myMapTabularType);
}
else {
    itemNames = new String[]{"key", "value"};
    myMapTabularType = tabularSupport.getTabularType();
    rowInTabular = myMapTabularType.getRowType();
}

// compile data
CompositeData compositeData = new CompositeDataSupport(rowInTabular,
        itemNames, new Object[]{propertyName, propertyValue});

if (tabularSupport.containsKey(new Object[]{propertyName})) {
        // remove first
        tabularSupport.remove(new Object[]{propertyName});
}


tabularSupport.put(compositeData);

// set Attribute
myJMXWrapper.setAttribute(
                new ObjectName("oracle.j2ee.config:name=pap,type=PolicyAccessorConfig"),
                new Attribute(propertyName, tabularSupport));
}
catch (Exception ex) {
    System.err.println("Problem in addMapProperty");
    throw new Exception(ex.getMessage());
}
}
```

Configurations

The OWSM agent setup may also contain a number of additional settings and configurations. The following example shows how to configure the settings of the binding interceptor (in the console these settings can be found on the interceptor bindings tab). These settings reuse the JMX function *addMapProperty*, defined above.

```
mbean=oracle.j2ee.config:name=BindingSecurityInterceptor,type=PolicyAccessorConfig.InterceptorConfig,
                        PolicyAccessorConfig=pap
parameterName=ConfigProperties
propertyName=agent.expire.time
propertyValue=100
```

```
mbean=oracle.j2ee.config:name=BindingSecurityInterceptor,type=PolicyAccessorConfig.InterceptorConfig,
                        PolicyAccessorConfig=pap
parameterName=ConfigProperties
propertyName=agent.clock.skew
propertyValue=15
```

```
mbean=oracle.j2ee.config:name=BindingSecurityInterceptor,type=PolicyAccessorConfig.InterceptorConfig,
                        PolicyAccessorConfig=pap
parameterName=ConfigProperties
propertyName=agent.nonce.ttl
propertyValue=25000
```

OSWM Manager – Database Migration

For database migration, it might be necessary to dump all policies defined in the OWSM database and import them in the new manager. The following function shows how to do this.

The first step is to export all policy sets and, in our example, dump them to a file:

🖫 export_policy_sets

```
ObjectName myObjectName = new
        ObjectName("oracle.wsm:Location=AdminServer,name=WSMDocumentManager,type=Repository");

String export_directory = "/data/owsm/export";

StringBuffer buf = new StringBuffer();

System.out.println("Export all Policy Sets");

IDocumentManager idm = JMX.newMXBeanProxy(myJMXWrapper.getConnection(), myObjectName,
IDocumentManager.class);
RepositoryCommands wsm_rcs = new RepositoryCommands(idm);

String retString = wsm_rcs.beginRepositorySession();

// Step 1:  Export all policy sets !

List<String> ps_names = wsm_rcs.listPolicySets(null);
for (int i=0;i<ps_names.size();i++)
{
    String psName = ps_names.get(i).trim();

    // ignore this entry.
    if (! "Global Policy Sets in Repository:".equals(psName)) {
        buf.append("POLICYSET-Name = "+psName+"\n=======================================\n");

        List<String> polSet = wsm_rcs.displayPolicySet(psName);
        for (int ps = 0; ps < polSet.size(); ps++)
            buf.append("        " + polSet.get(ps)+"\n");
    }
}

System.out.println("END - List all Policy Sets");

// abort session. No need to commit as we did not change anything
wsm_rcs.abortRepositorySession();

// write in File
FileUtils.writeFile(export_directory+"/_all_policy_sets.txt",buf.toString());
```

The second step is to export all single policies. This is a bit more complicated, as we have to break it up into two steps. First of all we need to compile a list of policy names and then construct a search string to export them:

🖫 export_single_policies

```
String[] signature = new String[] {"java.lang.String"};       // mode = "WRITE_ALWAYS"
Object[] params = new Object[]{ null};

String[] nameList = (String[])myJMXWrapper.invoke(myObjectName, "retrieveDocumentNames",
                params, signature);

ArrayList<String> myPolicyDocs = new ArrayList<String>();

for (int i=0;i<nameList.length;i++)
    if (nameList[i].startsWith("/policies/")) {
        System.out.println"Found policy: "+nameList[i]);
```

```
          myPolicyDocs.add(nameList[i]);
     }

// now construct the search string
String searchString = null;
if (myPolicyDocs.size() != 0) {
    searchString = "|";
    for (int i=0;i<wespeDocs.size();i++)
        searchString=searchString+"("+ myPolicyDocs.get(i)+")";
}

// now export the policies
String[] signatureExport = new String[]
                       {"java.lang.String","javax.management.openmbean.TabularData"};
Object[] paramsExport = new Object[]{ searchString, null};

// read the policies
Map myPolicies = (Map)myJMXWrapper.invoke(myObjectName, "retrieveDocuments", paramsExport,
                                 signatureExport);

Iterator it = myPolicies.values().iterator();
while (it.hasNext()) {
    javax.management.openmbean.CompositeDataSupport  myVal =
                       (javax.management.openmbean.CompositeDataSupport)it.next();
    Iterator it2 = myVal.values().iterator();
    while (it2.hasNext()) {
        String nextPolicyName     = (String)it2.next();  // read name
        String nextPolicyDocument = (String)it2.next();  // read policy document

        FileUtils.writeFile(export_directory+"/"+ nextPolicyName+".policy",nextPolicyDocument);
    }
}
```

OWSM Manager

Up to now we have discussed how to setup a WebLogic domain with the OWSM agent. This section describes how to setup the OWSM Manager. This section will only describe OSWM-specific actions. The setup of PKI, security providers, and other aspects will not be discussed here.

User Access

In the previous section we discussed how to setup the credentials to connect to the OWSM Manager. On the manager side we need to setup the appropriate user. It is necessary to create the appropriate user and add this user to the WebLogic group "OracleSystemGroup". Please see the security sections for a description of user creation.

Install All Policies

Before the OWSM Manager can be used, it is important to import all required policies into the OWSM database. The following example assumes that each policy is saved in its own file and will install all policies found in the given directory:

```
ObjectName myMBean = new
            ObjectName("oracle.wsm:LocationAdminServer,name=WSMDocumentManager,type=Repository ");

// assume that all policy file names are provided in the policy_filenames list
```

```
// read in the file content and save it as strings
String[] policy_signatures = new String[policy_filenames.length];
for (int i=0;i<policy_filenames.length;i++)
    policy_signatures[i] = FileUtils.readFile(dirname+"/"+policy_filenames[i]);

String[] signature = new String[] {"java.lang.String",       // typ = "policies"
                                   "[Ljava.lang.String;",
                                   "java.lang.String"};       // mode = "WRITE_ALWAYS"

Object[] params = new Object[]{ "policies", policy_signatures, "WRITE_ALWAYS"};

// write all policies
myJMXWrapper.invoke(myMBean, "writeDocuments", params, signature);
```

Cleanup the OSWM Database

It may also sometimes be necessary to clean the OWSM database. A good practice is to delete the old policies before a policy update is imported into the database, that way there will definitely be no conflict.

The following JMX code will remove all policies from the OWSM database:

```
ObjectName myObjectName    = new
ObjectName("oracle.wsm:Location=AdminServer,name=WSMDocumentManager,type=Repository");

String[] signature = new String[] {"java.lang.String"};

// get the names of the policies
String[] nameList = (String[])myJMXWrapper.invoke(myObjectName, "retrieveDocumentNames",
                new Object[]{ null}, signature);

System.out.println("Policies found :");
for (int i=0;i<nameList.length;i++)
   if (nameList[i].startsWith("/policies/"))
      System.out.println("      "+nameList[i]);


ArrayList<String> myPolicyDocs = new ArrayList<String>();
for (int i=0;i<nameList.length;i++)
    myPolicyDocs.add(nameList[i]);

// build the search string
String searchString = null;
if (myPolicyDocs.size() != 0) {
   searchString = "|";
   for (int i=0;i<wespeDocs.size();i++)
       searchString=searchString+"("+wespeDocs.get(i)+")";
}

if (searchString != null) {
   // delete
   myJMXWrapper.invoke(myObjectName, "deleteDocuments", new Object[]{ searchString}, signature);
}
```

Oracle ESB

An Enterprise Service Bus (ESB) is an architecture concept for the interaction and communication between distributed services. ESB has a number of additional features and services, as an ESB implementation is often used as the main backbone and integration layer of an EAI (Enterprise Application Integration) infrastructure or of a SOA (Service Oriented Architecture) infrastructure.

Therefore, an ESB has additional services like monitoring and controlling messages, message routing, filtering, transforming, event handling, queuing, security checking and mapping, and many more. Please consult the extensive documentation on ESB concepts and implementations available.

Oracle ESB is the implementation from Oracle which provides an ESB implementation for SOA and EDA (Event Driven Architecture). It is basically an application deployed on WebLogic, and therefore inherits all the features of WebLogic discussed in this book. In addition, Oracle has provided extended functionality for WLST and JMX to interact with the ESB, such as administration, deployment of projects/services, and much more. A good introduction with diagrams can be found at:

docs.oracle.com/cd/E14571_01/doc.1111/e15020/introduction.htm

The OSB has a number of important root MBeans:

- *ALSBConfigurationMBean* for managing and manipulating resources in your OSB domain.

- *ServiceDomainMBean* for monitoring statistics for service.

List projects of the ESB:

```
def connectToAdminServer():
    connect(...)

def listAllESBService():
    myESB = findService(ALSBConfigurationMBean.NAME,
                        ALSBConfigurationMBean.TYPE)
    allReferences = myESB.getRefs(com.bea.wli.config.Ref.DOMAIN)

    for nextReference in allReferences:
        # test if project reference
        if nextReference.getTypeId() == com.bea.wli.config.Ref.PROJECT_REF:
            print 'Found project with name = ' + str(nextReference.getProjectName())

# main code
connectToAdminServer()
domainRuntime()
listAllESBService()
```

A similar function to list all proxy services can be implemented like this:

```
def listAllESBService():
    myESB = findService(ALSBConfigurationMBean.NAME,
                        ALSBConfigurationMBean.TYPE)
    allReferences = myESB.getRefs(com.bea.wli.config.Ref.DOMAIN)

    for nextReference in allReferences:
        # test if project reference
        if nextReference.getTypeId() == "ProxyService":
            print 'Found next proxy service with name = ' + nextReference.getFullName()
```

A similar function to list all business services can be implemented like this:

```
def listAllESBService():
    myESB = findService(ALSBConfigurationMBean.NAME,
                        ALSBConfigurationMBean.TYPE)
    allReferences = myESB.getRefs(com.bea.wli.config.Ref.DOMAIN)

    for nextReference in allReferences:
        # test if project reference
        if nextReference.getTypeId() == "BusinnessService":
            print 'Found next proxy service with name = ' + nextReference.getFullName()
```

Oracle Service Bus provides a mechanism to export the project artifacts and provides a facility to create an environment-specific customization file using the Service Bus Console[43]. Deployment processes have to be automated across multiple environments, i.e. Development, Test, User Acceptance Testing (UAT), Staging, and Production. The automation of the deployment can be done using WLST or JMX.

The following script will:

- Load the properties file

- Connect to server

- Read the project jar file (sbconfig.jar)

- Create and start and ALSB change session

- Obtain *ALSBConfigurationMBean* instance

- Perform update operations in the session

- Execute environment customization file

🖫 ESB_deployment

```
import wlstModule
from com.bea.wli.sb.management.configuration import SessionManagementMBean
from com.bea.wli.sb.management.configuration import ALSBConfigurationMBean
from com.bea.wli.config import Ref
from com.bea.wli.config.customization import Customization
from java.io import FileInputStream
from java.util import HashMap
from java.util import ArrayList
from java.util import HashSet

import sys

#=========================================================================================
# Entry function to deploy project configuration and resources
#         into a ALSB domain
#=========================================================================================

def importToALSBDomain():
        try:
                # Declare Variables
                sessionMBean = None
                alsbConfigurationMBean = None


                # Connect to Server
                print 'Connecting to server: ', adminUrl
                connectToServer(connectMethod)
```

---

[43] www.insemble.com/oracleservicebus-deployment.html

```
                        print 'Starting import of:', importJar, "on ALSB Admin Server:", adminUrl

                        # Read import jar file
                        print 'Read import jar file'
                        theBytes = readBinaryFile(importJar)
                        print 'Import file read successfully', importJar

                        # Create unique session name
                        print 'Creating unique session name'
                        sessionName = createSessionName()
                        print 'Created session name :', sessionName

                        # Create and start session
                        print 'Creating SessionMBean'
                        sessionMBean = getSessionMBean(sessionName)
                        print 'SessionMBean started new session'

                        # obtain the ALSBConfigurationMBean instance that operates
                        # on the session that has just been created. Notice that
                        # the name of the mbean contains the session name.
                        print 'Create ALSBConfiguration'
                        alsbConfigurationMBean = findService(String(ALSBConfigurationMBean.NAME
                                        + ".").concat(sessionName), ALSBConfigurationMBean.TYPE)
                        print "ALSBConfiguration MBean found", alsbConfigurationMBean

                        # Perform updates or read operations in the session using alsbSession

                        # Upload Jar File
                        print 'Uploading Jar file'
                        alsbConfigurationMBean.uploadJarFile(theBytes)
                        print 'Jar Uploaded'

                        print 'ALSB Project will now get imported'
                        alsbJarInfo = alsbConfigurationMBean.getImportJarInfo()

                        alsbImportPlan = alsbJarInfo.getDefaultImportPlan()

                        alsbImportPlan.setPassphrase(passphrase)

                        operationMap=HashMap()

                        operationMap = alsbImportPlan.getOperations()

                        print 'Default importPlan'
                        printOpMap(operationMap)

                        alsbImportPlan.setPreserveExistingEnvValues(false)
                        alsbImportPlan.setPreserveExistingOperationalValues(false)

                        print 'Modified importPlan'
                        printOpMap(operationMap)
                        importResult = alsbConfigurationMBean.importUploaded(alsbImportPlan)

                        printDiagMap(importResult.getImportDiagnostics())

                        if importResult.getFailed().isEmpty() == false:
                                print 'One or more resources could not be imported properly'
                                raise


                        #customize if a customization file is specified
                        #affects only the created resources
                        if customFile != None :
                                print 'Loading customization File', customFile
                                iStream = FileInputStream(customFile)
                                customizationList = Customization.fromXML(iStream)
                                alsbConfigurationMBean.customize(customizationList)

                        sessionMBean.activateSession(sessionName,
                                                "ALSBImport Operation Completed Successfully")

                        print "Deployment of : " + importJar + " successful"
        except:
                print "Unexpected error:", sys.exc_info()[0]
                if sessionMBean != None:
                        sessionMBean.discardSession(sessionName)
                raise
```

```
#========================================================================
# Utility function to print the list of operations
#========================================================================
def printOpMap(map):
    set = map.entrySet()
    for entry in set:
        op = entry.getValue()
        print op.getOperation(),
        ref = entry.getKey()
        print ref
    print


#========================================================================
# Utility function to print the diagnostics
#========================================================================
def printDiagMap(map):
    set = map.entrySet()
    for entry in set:
        diag = entry.getValue().toString()
        print diag
    print


#========================================================================
# Connect to the Admin Server
#========================================================================

def connectToServer(connnectMethod):
    if connectMethod == "boot":
        connect(url=adminUrl, adminServerName=adminServer)
    else:
        connect(userConfigFile=configFile, userKeyFile=keyFile, url=adminUrl)

    domainRuntime()

#========================================================================
# Utility function to read a binary file
#========================================================================
def readBinaryFile(fileName):
    file = open(fileName, 'rb')
    bytes = file.read()
    return bytes


#========================================================================
# Utility function to create an arbitrary session name
#========================================================================
def createSessionName():
    sessionName = String("ALSBImportScript-"+Long(System.currentTimeMillis()).toString())
    return sessionName


#========================================================================
# Utility function to load a session MBeans
#========================================================================
def getSessionMBean(sessionName):
    # obtain session management mbean to create a session.
    # This mbean instance can be used more than once to
    # create/discard/commit many sessions
    sessionMBean = findService(SessionManagementMBean.NAME,SessionManagementMBean.TYPE)

    # create a session
    sessionMBean.createSession(sessionName)

    return sessionMBean

# MAIN section
try:
    # import the service bus configuration
    importToALSBDomain()

except:
    print "Unexpected error: ", sys.exc_info()[0]
    dumpStack()
    raise
```

(Source: www.insemble.com/oracleservicebus-deployment.html)

Looking Beyond

This script shows an example of deployment to an ESB. It also demonstrates the usage of two of the main MBeans *ALSBConfigurationMBean* and *SessionManagementMBean*.

JMX and Oracle ESB

Of course the ESB can also be accessed using JMX. The first code example shows two different ways to define the ObjectNames of the Mbeans, which have to be used for access.

Direct definition:

```
ObjectName alsbConfigurationName = new ObjectName(
    "com.bea:Name=ALSBConfiguration,Type="+
    "com.bea.wli.sb.management.configuration.ALSBConfigurationMBean");

ObjectName xbusName = new ObjectName(
    "com.bea:Name=Config.XBus Kernel,Type=com.bea.wli.config.mbeans.ConfigMBean");

ObjectName sessionManagementName = new ObjectName(
    "com.bea:Name=SessionManagement,Type="+
    "com.bea.wli.sb.management.configuration.SessionManagementMBean");
```

Querying the object names from the domain runtime MBeanServer:

```
// obtain the ALSBConfigurationMBean that operates on the session that has just been created
// ************************************************************************************************
Object  opParams_findService[] = {
        "ALSBConfiguration." + sessionName,
        "com.bea.wli.sb.management.configuration.ALSBConfigurationMBean",
        null};

String  opSig_findService[] = { String.class.getName(),
                                String.class.getName(),
                                String.class.getName()};

//  Invoke operation
ObjectName myALSBConfigurationName = (ObjectName)
        myJMXWrapper.invoke(domainRuntimeService,
                            "findService",
                            opParams_findService,
                            opSig_findService);
```

The following example exports the list of all resources of a given project:

```
ArrayList<String> result = new ArrayList<String>();
Ref tmp;
String tmpPrjName;

MBeanServerConnection mbsc = myJMXWrapper.getConnection();

// call getRefs ->
Object  opParams[] = { Ref.getDomainRef()};
String  opSig[] = { Ref.class.getName()};

//  Invoke operation
Set<Ref> myReferences = (Set<Ref>)mbsc.invoke(alsbConfigurationName, "getRefs", opParams, opSig);

System.out.println("Found "+myReferences.size()+" References !");

String resourceOnly = null;

Iterator<Ref> it = myReferences.iterator();
```

```
while (it.hasNext()) {
   tmp = it.next();
   tmpPrjName = tmp.getProjectName();

   if ( ! ( (projectName!=null) && !projectName.equals(tmpPrjName)))
      if  (!(tmp.isProjectRef() && !tmpPrjName.equalsIgnoreCase("Wespe")))
      {
         // eliminate projectname AND leading "/"
         resourceOnly = tmp.getFullName().
                            substring(tmpPrjName.length()+1,tmp.getFullName().length());
         if (resourceOnly.indexOf("/") != -1)
            resourceOnly = resourceOnly.substring(0, resourceOnly.indexOf("/"));

         if (!result.contains(resourceOnly))
            result.add(resourceOnly);
      }
}
```

The following example imports a project into the ESB:

```
String projectName = "TestProject";
String prjDirectory = "/opt/orj/testPrj";

MBeanServerConnection mbsc = myJMXWrapper.getConnection();

ObjectName domainRuntimeService = myJMXWrapper.getService();

// obtain the raw bytes that make up the configuration jar file
byte[] bytesOfSBConfigJar = FileUtils.readBINFile(prjDirectory);

// create a session
String sessionName = "session." + System.currentTimeMillis();

Object  opParams_createsession[] = { sessionName};
String  opSig_createsession[] = { String.class.getName()};

// Invoke operation
mbsc.invoke(sessionManagementName, "createSession", opParams_createsession, opSig_createsession);
System.out.println("Session "+sessionName+" created !");

// obtain the ALSBConfigurationMBean that operates on the session that has just been created
Object  opParams_findService[] = {
        "ALSBConfiguration." + sessionName,
        "com.bea.wli.sb.management.configuration.ALSBConfigurationMBean",
        null};
String  opSig_findService[] = { String.class.getName(), String.class.getName(),
                                String.class.getName()};

// Invoke operation
ObjectName myALSBConfigurationName = (ObjectName)
        mbsc.invoke(domainRuntimeService, "findService", opParams_findService, opSig_findService);


// import configuration into the session.
// First we upload the jar file, which will stage it temporarily.
Object  opParams_uploadJarFile[] = { bytesOfSBConfigJar};
String  opSig_uploadJarFile[] = { bytesOfSBConfigJar.getClass().getName()};
// Invoke operation
mbsc.invoke(myALSBConfigurationName, "uploadJarFile", opParams_uploadJarFile, opSig_uploadJarFile);


// Pass null to importUploaded method to mean the default import plan.
Object  opParams_importUploaded[] = { null};
String  opSig_importUploaded[] = { ALSBImportPlan.class.getName()};
// Invoke operation
ImportResult result = (ImportResult)mbsc.invoke(
            myALSBConfigurationName,
            "importUploaded",
            opParams_importUploaded,
            opSig_importUploaded);

// print out status
if (result.getImported().size() > 0) {
   System.out.println("The following resources have been successfully imported.");
   for (Ref ref : result.getImported())
```

```
        System.out.println("\t\t" + ref);
    }

    if (result.getFailed().size() > 0) {
        System.out.println("The following resources have failed to be imported.");

        for (Map.Entry e : result.getFailed().entrySet()) {
            Ref ref = (Ref)e.getKey();
            System.out.println("\t\t" + ref + ". reason: " + e.getValue());
        }
    }
}
if (result.getFailed().size() > 0) {
    // discard the changes to the session

    Object  opParams_discardSession[] = { sessionName};
    String  opSig_discardSession[] = { String.class.getName()};
    //  Invoke operation
    mbsc.invoke(sessionManagementName,
                "discardSession",
                opParams_discardSession,
                opSig_discardSession);
}
else {
    // activate the session
    Object  opParams_activateSession[] = { sessionName, "Imported by TestTool"};
    String  opSig_activateSession[] = { String.class.getName(), String.class.getName()};

    //  Invoke operation
    mbsc.invoke(sessionManagementName,
                "activateSession",
                opParams_activateSession,
                opSig_activateSession);
}
```

OAM

"Oracle Access Manager (OAM) is the foundation of the new Oracle Access Management platform. Access Manager provides the core functionality of Web Single Sign On (SSO), authentication, authorization, centralized policy administration and agent management, real-time session management and auditing. Built as a 100% Java solution, Access Manager is extremely scalable to handle Internet scale deployments and works with existing heterogeneous environments in the enterprise with agents certified on hundreds of web servers and application servers. Access Manager provides rich functionality, extreme scalability and high availability thereby increasing security, improving user experience and productivity and enhancing compliance while reducing total cost of ownership."

Key Features of Access Manager include:

- Simplified Web Single Sign On (SSO)

- Authentication and Authorization

- Centralized Policy Administration

- Advanced Session Management

- Streamlined Agent Management

- Native Password Management

- Windows Native Authentication

- Comprehensive Auditing and Logging[44]

A good overview with a descriptive diagram can be found at:

www.oracle.com/technetwork/middleware/id-mgmt/overview/am-11gr2-technical-white-paper-1696397.pdf

OAM and WLST

Like most other members of the Fusion Middleware family, OAM provides a number of configuration and administration tasks as WLST extensions. These extensions are implemented as custom commands in WLST and can therefore be used in your own WLST scripts for automated tasks as an alternative to the OAM WebConsole.

The following table describes the different custom commands added to WLST for OAM.

Custom WLST command	Command description
listOAMAuthnProviderParams	List the parameters set for an Oracle Access Manager authentication or identity assertion provider.
createOAMIdentityAsserter	Create a new identity asserter.
updateOAMIdentityAsserter	Update an existing identity asserter.
createOAMAuthenticator	Create a new authenticator.
deleteOAMAuthnProvider	Delete an existing authentication provider.
updateOAMAuthenticator	Update an existing authenticator.
addOAMSSOProvider	Add a new SSO provider.
displayTopology	List the details of deployed Oracle Access Manager Servers.
displayOamServer	Display Oracle Access Manager Server configuration details.
createOamServer	Create an entry for an Oracle Access Manager Server configuration.
editOamServer	Edit the entry for an Oracle Access Manager Server configuration.
deleteOamServer	Delete the named Oracle Access Manager Server

---

[44] www.oracle.com/technetwork/middleware/id-mgmt/index-090417.html

Custom WLST command	Command description
	configuration.
displayOssoAgent	Display OSSO Agent configuration details.
editOssoAgent	Edit OSSO Agent configuration details.
deleteOssoAgent	Delete the named OSSO Agent configuration.
displayWebgateAgent	Display 10g WebGate Agent configuration details.
editWebgateAgent	Edit 10g WebGate Agent registration details.
deleteWebgateAgent	Delete the named 10g WebGate Agent configuration.
changeLoggerSetting	Change Logger Settings.
changeConfigDataEncryptionKey	Regenerate the configuration data encryption key and re-encrypt data.
displayUserIdentityStoreConfig	Display a user identity store registration.
editUserIdentityStoreConfig	Edit a user identity store registration.
createUserIdentityStoreConfig	Create a user identity store registration.
deleteUserIdentityStore	Delete a user identity store registration.
configRequestCacheType	Configure the SSO server request cache type.
displayRequestCacheType	Display the SSO server request cache type entry.
exportPolicy	Export Oracle Access Manager policy data from a test (source) to an intermediate Oracle Access Manager file.
importPolicy	Import Oracle Access Manager policy data from the Oracle Access Manager file specified.
importPolicyDelta	Import Oracle Access Manager policy changes from the Oracle Access Manager file specified.
migratePartnersToProd	Migrate partners from the source Oracle Access Manager Server to the specified target Oracle Access Manager Server.
exportPartners	Export the Oracle Access Manager partners from the source to the intermediate Oracle Access Manager file specified.
importPartners	Import the Oracle Access Manager partners from the intermediate Oracle Access Manager file specified.
disableCoexistMode	Disable the Coexist Mode.
editGITOValues	Edit GITO configuration parameters.
editWebgate11gAgent	Edit an 11g WebGate registration.
deleteWebgate11gAgent	Remove an 11g WebGate Agent registration.

Custom WLST command	Command description
displayWebgate11gAgent	Display an 11g WebGate Agent registration.
displayOAMMetrics	Display metrics of OAM Servers.
updateOIMHostPort	Update the Oracle Identity Manager configuration when integrated with Oracle Access Manager.
updateOSSOResponseCookieConfig	Updates OSSO Proxy response cookie settings.
deleteOSSOResponseCookieConfig	Deletes OSSO Proxy response cookie settings.

(Source: Oracle Corporation[45])

Table 19.2: Custom WLST Commands for OAM

To run WLST commands for OAM operations, you need to either start WLST from the OAM distribution or you need to extend your WLST configuration to recognize the OAM extensions.

Start the WLST environment from the OAM distribution:

```
Go to the OAM_HOME path: <Oracle_IDM>/common/bin.
Start wlst.sh  (wlst.bat or wlst.cmd on Windows)
```

WebCenter

Oracle WebCenter is the center of engagement for business powering exceptional experiences for customers, partners, and employees. It connects people, processes, and information with the most complete portfolio of portal, content management, Web experience management, and collaboration technologies.[46]

WebCenter consists of different major components. The most visible and best known component is the WebCenter portal, which allows users to create portal applications like internet/intranet sites. Please see the extensive Oracle documentation and web sites for detailed information.

Like the other tools from the Fusion Middleware family, Oracle has also enhanced WLST with WebCenter-specific custom commands.

Due to the fact that WebCenter is such a huge and complicated product, there are a large number of new WLST commands. They can be grouped in different categories like general commands, analytics, activity graph, mail, content repository, discussions, external applications, spaces, identity store, and many others.

---

[45] docs.oracle.com/cd/E14571_01/doc.1111/e15478/wlst.htm

[46] www.oracle.com/technetwork/middleware/webcenter/suite/overview/index.html

The following table describes a selection of these commands:

Custom WLST command	Command description
deleteConnection	Delete any WebCenter connection.
setWebCenterServiceFrameworkConfig	Set WebCenter Service Framework configuration properties.
getWebCenterServiceFrameworkConfig	Return WebCenter Service Framework configuration properties.
webcenterErrorOccurred	Return status information for the last WebCenter command executed.
getWebCenterConnectionTypes	List all the WebCenter connection types.
cloneWebCenterManagedServer	Clone a WebCenter Managed-Server.
createAnalyticsCollectorConnection	Online
setAnalyticsCollectorConnection	Online
listAnalyticsCollectorConnections	Online
listDefaultAnalyticsCollectorConnection	Online
createJCRContentServerConnection	Create an Oracle Content Server repository connection.
setJCRContentServerConnection	Edit an existing Oracle Content Server connection.
listJCRContentServerConnections	List individual or all Oracle Content Server connections that are configured for a WebCenter application.
createJCRPortalConnection	Create an Oracle Portal repository connection.
setJCRPortalConnection	Edit an existing Oracle Portal repository connection.
listJCRPortalConnections	List all Oracle Portal connections that are configured for a WebCenter application.
createJCRFileSystemConnection	Create a connection to a file system.
setJCRFileSystemConnection	Edit an existing file system repository connection.
listJCRFileSystemConnections	List individual or all file system connections configured for a WebCenter application.
createJCRSharePointConnection	Create a Microsoft SharePoint 2007 repository connection.
setJCRSharePointConnection	Edit a Microsoft SharePoint 2007 repository connection.
listJCRSharePointConnections	List all Microsoft SharePoint 2007 connections that are configured for a WebCenter application.
listDocumentsSpacesProperties	List properties for the back-end Oracle Content

Advanced WebLogic Server Automation

Custom WLST command	Command description
	Server repository that is being used by WebCenter Spaces.
setDocumentsSpacesProperties	Modify properties for the back-end Oracle Content Server repository used by WebCenter Spaces.

(Source: Oracle Corporation[47])

Table 19.3: Custom WLST Commands for WebCenter

A great example script for creating a WebCenter domain can be found at mgrundma.wordpress.com/2011/10/31/create-webcenter-portal-domain-using-wlst

Note that WebCenter is a complex environment with many different components hosted on different Managed-Servers. In addition, there are a number of dependencies between these Managed-Servers.

Summary

Automation is a process of developing a functionality to automate our daily tasks in order to save time. This requires a runtime/tool environment. There are many tools available such as JMX, WLST, Ant, MAVEN, etc. Based on the environment, choose a tool fits your needs.

This chapter provided an overview of different categories of tools, environments, and technologies. It is impossible within the scope of one chapter to describe all tools or to describe the tools mentioned in great detail. There are of course many other great tools and environments not mentioned here. The selection in this chapter simply provided some of the tools that have been most beneficial to the author based on project experience.

The goal of this chapter is to make the reader aware of these tools that really help in many different situations. Readers should also be aware that WebLogic should never be seen alone. Enterprise environments consist of many different tools and technologies that support development, testing, deployment, troubleshooting, and operation.

---

[47] docs.oracle.com/cd/E21764_01/web.1111/e13813/custom_webcenter_admin.htm

Part V

Summary and References

Summary and Comparison

Summary and Comparison

This book has discussed WebLogic automation based on the two major technologies provided by Oracle: WLST and JMX. Throughout the book, effort has been made to clearly state the benefits of the approach under discussion. WLST and JMX are two very different approaches but also have a lot in common. The final short discussion in this chapter tries to compare these two technologies and their implementations in WebLogic.

I have to emphasize here that all statements in this chapter only express the opinion of the author and none of these statements are Oracle or other official statements. The comparison here is only based on the lessons learned in many real projects of the author.

Technology and Implementation

In general, the technology of both approaches is quite similar. Both management environments (WLST and JMX) are based on JMX MBeans and the different MBean trees of WebLogic. The underlying communication layer talks to the same MBean trees and uses the same API and the same protocols. Both environments are able to speak T3, T3S, IIOP, IIOPS, and more.

WLST

WLST is a scripted environment based on Jython. As such, the programming of those scripts is simpler to more "shell like" than JMX. For experienced UNIX admins, this is a great benefit, especially since WLST simulates the MBean trees like a file system. WLST also offers file system-like commands such as *cd*, *pwd*, and more for navigation. Despite being a simplified approach, it is a powerful environment with a great level of functionality. Embedding WLST in other programs is usually a pain as it is necessary to call an interpreter from Java (i.e. use Java to code free lines of text with no test/debug abilities, then call an interpreter to translate these text lines back to Java and then execute the Java code).

JMX

JMX is pure Java and based on the standard Java JMX API. Therefore, this approach is much easier to understand and learn for Java developers who must write automation programs. Another big benefit is that JMX is native Java and does not need an interpreter. Therefore, embedding JMX automation code in other programs is natural and logical. As JMX is not interpreted, it is also faster, and reusing other Java libraries is also easier.

Domain Creation and Modification

In the domain life cycle, creating a domain is first. Domain creation can be divided into two phases. The first phase is the creation of a domain skeleton from template(s) and the creation of the file system structure and configuration files of the domain. In phase two the AdminServer will be started for the first time, and then it is possible to finish the initial configuration by talking to the running AdminServer. Note that not all tasks can be done in the offline mode.

WLST

For domain creation, WLST is the better environment as Oracle has extended WLST with the offline mode. The offline mode implements the ability to read templates, construct and create a domain, and in general work with the domain configuration files from disk (if running on the same machine). This is not available in JMX. Note that the communication with the NodeManager is much better in WLST and difficult or only partly available in JMX.

JMX

JMX does not have the offline functionality, therefore JMX is not well suited for domain creation. If you need to configure domain services, such as a network channel or a Managed-Server, then JMX is able to do it. As a rule of thumb: whatever you can do online with the AdminServer can be done with JMX. Whatever must be done offline can only be done with WLST.

Service Creation and Modification

After the basic domain has been created, it is necessary to configure the required services. The J2EE server environment relies on services like database access (WLS, datasources), messaging (JMS, WTC, web services), directory services (JNDI, LDAP), and others.

WLST

Service creation can be done online or offline. Creating a service and configuring it involves repeated subtasks, and the main task itself is usually not time critical. In all environments it is important that creating domains can be repeated as often as necessary. Due to the file system-like MBean navigation, service creation and configuration can be done easily with WLST as the navigation within the MBeans is much simpler than in JMX.

JMX

JMX offers similar functionality as WLST for the online mode configuration/creation of services. For integration with other tools, like management consoles, I recommend JMX as native Java API whereas for standalone scripts I would prefer WLST due to the better readability of the MBean navigation.

Security Aspects

A major aspect of all J2EE environments is security. Security is a very complex topic that affects every part of a J2EE server. WebLogic offers a wide range of security features. Most of them are combined into security realms.

WLST

Similar to service configuration, WLST is equally suited for all aspects of security configuration, including SSL/PKI, security store (RDBMS), security provider, policy management, and more. Unfortunately security is pretty complex and difficult to configure, and even the WLST recording feature does not record security actions. Note that for some security configurations like users/passwords, only the online mode can be used.

JMX

JMX offers similar functionality as WLST in the security area since security configurations are almost always performed in the online mode. Besides the different programming model, there are not many differences between WLST and JMX.

Administration

Administration involves working with the domains, controlling and changing the status of the server and services, deploying/undeploying/providing applications, and more.

WLST

Administration tasks can be done nicely with WLST. The only caveat is that for more complex scripts, it is often required to switch between the runtime and configuration MBean file system. The runtime MBeans in WLST do not always offer all information needed for scripts, so the user must be careful about which MBean references are collected and where these are used. Errors in this area very often have their root cause in mixing MBean trees in an inappropriate way.

JMX

JMX is very similar to WLST in this aspect. Usually administration tasks are done from the central management server, as these tasks are talking to the AdminServer and in most cases these management tasks need to be performed on many domains (e.g. start, stop). Talking to many domains in parallel is much better supported in JMX than in WLST. So for this category, JMX is a very interesting alternative to WLST, especially if these management activities must be integrated in other management tools/portals using Java.

Monitoring

Monitoring is a continuous process of getting important values, states, and information from the WebLogic Servers.

WLST

WLST supports everything needed to monitor all aspects of WebLogic. Based on project experience, I have found a number of disadvantages for WLST here. The biggest disadvantage is the fact that parallel invocations to different AdminServers are not supported. You need to create a Jython interpreter instance for each AdminServer connection. For dozens or even hundreds of AdminServers, this is hardly possible due to the huge resource consumption. Furthermore, switching between those AdminServers is too slow.

JMX

JMX is much better suited for monitoring due to its ability to connect to many different AdminServers at the same time and use multithreading efficiently to collect data in parallel from different servers/domains. Speed, parallel invocations, and easy integration in other monitoring tools are vital for monitoring, and in this area JMX has proven to be the better alternative.

Troubleshooting

Troubleshooting means analyzing problem situations. Keep in mind that troubleshooting usually involves many different tools like thread dump, heap dump, stack trace analyzer, and many more, therefore WLST as well as JMX are just additional tools to the zoo of troubleshooting tools.

WLST

WLST is a well suited solution for troubleshooting. For administrators who need to combine shell scripts and WLST scripts, WLST is a very good choice as both are scripting environments and therefore easier to understand for administrators.

JMX

All online actions, like forcing GC or thread dump, can be done via JMX. Note that virtual machine MBeans, which might not be part of the WebLogic MBean tree, can only be queried using JMX.

Summary

Both WLST and JMX have their strengths and weaknesses. Some of them are disjunct and some overlapping. It always depends on your requirements and goals. In general it can be said that WLST is better suited for creating and configuration and JMX is better for administration and monitoring, but this does not always need to be the case. For every requirement you should consider and compare both technologies. The experiences and guidelines above will hopefully help you for your comparison; however, the decision must be made based on your concrete requirements, which may lead to a different decision.

Additional References

Additional References

This Appendix provides a number of resources with information about the different topics covered in the book. As stated at the beginning, this book is neither a tutorial nor a beginner's guide, therefore most topics can only be briefly explained. Resources are mainly books, websites, or webpages.

References are provided for further reading and not as a list of resources used for this book.

Books

The following list of books are all about WebLogic administration and provide additional background information. All are very good for learning WebLogic. Most parts of the books listed below are using the WebConsole as a primary tool, therefore this book is considered complementary to the books below.

```
Title: Oracle WebLogic Server 11g Administration Handbook
Publisher: Mcgraw-Hill Professional
ISBN-10: 0071774254
ISBN-13: 978-0071774253

Title: Oracle Fusion Middleware 11g Architecture and Management
Publisher: Mcgraw-Hill Professional
ISBN-10: 0071754172
ISBN-13: 978-0071754170

Title: Oracle WebLogic Server 12c: Distinctive Recipes: Architecture,
Development and Administration
ISBN-10: 0980798019
ISBN-13: 978-0980798012
Publisher: munz & more

Title: WebLogic 12c Security Handbook
Publisher: Packt Publishing
ISBN-10: 1849687781
ISBN-13: 978-1849687782
```

```
Title: Oracle Fusion Middleware 11g Weblogic & Bi Server Architecture &
Installation
Publisher: Sideris Courseware Corp.
ISBN-10: 1936930234
ISBN-13: 978-1936930234
```

General Websites

Several websites exist that focus on WebLogic and also WLST. They provide a number of interesting examples. It is of course impossible to name all of them, therefore apologies for those I am missing here.

- http://www.oracle.com
- http://wlstbyexamples.blogspot.de
- http://www.middlewaremagic.com
- http://weblogic-wonders.com
- http://wlatricksntips.blogspot.de/

Web Links

The following list contains many links to blogs, documentation (mainly from Oracle), articles, and other information that provides more detailed background understanding of topics discussed in this book. As mentioned at the beginning of the book, this book will provide reduced theory and background information, so these links provide useful additional information.

A

ACLs (Access Control Lists)

- http://docs.oracle.com/middleware/1212/wls/WLACH/taskhelp/security_compat/DefineACLs.html

Ant

- http://ant.apache.org/

- http://en.wikipedia.org/wiki/Ant

- http://docs.oracle.com/middleware/1212/wls/WLPRG/wldeploy.htm

- http://docs.oracle.com/middleware/1212/wls/WLPRG/ant_tasks.htm

B

Bridge

- http://docs.oracle.com/middleware/1212/wls/BRDGE/basics.htm

- http://docs.oracle.com/middleware/1212/wls/JMSAD/wlst.htm

- http://middlewaremagic.com/weblogic/?p=7969

- http://docs.oracle.com/middleware/1212/wls/BRDGE/bridgefaq.htm

- http://middlewaremagic.com/weblogic/?p=4747

C

Creating domains using WLST offline and online:

- http://docs.oracle.com/middleware/1212/wls/DOMCF/understand_domains.htm

- http://docs.oracle.com/cd/E13179_01/common/docs102/tempref/tempref.html#wp1211028

- http://docs.oracle.com/middleware/1212/wls/WLDTB/tempbuild.htm

- http://docs.oracle.com/middleware/1212/wls/WLDTB/appbuild.htm

- http://docs.oracle.com/middleware/1212/wls/WLDTB/intro.htm

- http://docs.oracle.com/middleware/1212/wls/WLSTG/domains.htm#WLSTG156

- http://danielveselka.blogspot.de/2010/01/create-domain-using-wlst.html

- http://docs.oracle.com/middleware/1212/wls/WLSTG/domains.htm

Create your own template

- http://ananthkannan.blogspot.de/2009/10/how-to-create-domain-using-weblogic.html

- http://docs.oracle.com/middleware/1212/wls/WLDTB/appbuild.htm

- http://docs.oracle.com/middleware/1212/wls/WLDTB/tempbuild.htm

Cluster:

- http://docs.oracle.com/middleware/1212/wls/INTRO/clustering.htm

- http://www.informit.com/articles/article.aspx?p=101737&seqNum=4

- http://biemond.blogspot.de/2010/04/high-availability-load-balancer-for.html

- http://blog.c2b2.co.uk/2010/10/configuring-and-testing-weblogic.html

- http://www.javadev.org/files/cluster.pdf

- http://cybergav.in/2009/09/25/weblogic-ip-multicast-a-primer

Constants (interesting!)

- http://docs.oracle.com/cd/E16764_01/apirefs.1111/e13941/constant-values.html
- http://docs.oracle.com/middleware/1212/ums/UMSJD/constant-values.html

D

Domains:

- http://docs.oracle.com/middleware/1212/wls/DOMCF/understand_domains.htm

Durable subscribers

- http://docs.oracle.com/javaee/1.3/jms/tutorial/1_3_1-fcs/doc/basics.html
- http://docs.oracle.com/javaee/1.3/jms/tutorial/1_3_1-fcs/doc/advanced.html#1024758
- http://docs.oracle.com/middleware/1212/wls/WLACH/pagehelp/JMSjmssubscribersjmsdurablesubscriberruntimetitle.html
- http://docs.oracle.com/middleware/1212/wls/WLMDB/topic_sub_ids.htm

E

Extending domains

- http://docs.oracle.com/cd/E21764_01/web.1111/e14140/exten.htm
- http://docs.oracle.com/middleware/1212/wls/WLDCW/exten.htm

F

Filters (connection filters)

- http://docs.oracle.com/middleware/1212/wls/SCPRG/con_filtr.htm
- http://jagadesh4java.blogspot.de/2012/11/connection-filters-in-weblogic.html
- http://jvzoggel.wordpress.com/2011/07/12/using-weblogic-network-connection-filters/

G

GridLink datasources

- http://docs.oracle.com/middleware/1212/wls/JDBCA/gridlink_datasources.htm
- http://www.wikiconsole.com/wiki/?p=3155
- http://wlstbyexamples.blogspot.de/2011/02/unstoppable-datasources-from-weblogic.html
- http://www.oracle.com/technetwork/middleware/weblogic/gridlink-rac-wp-494900.pdf
- http://docs.oracle.com/cd/E29505_01/core.1111/e10106/dbac.htm

Oracle WebLogic Guardian

- http://docs.oracle.com/cd/E13152_01/user_guide/Overview.html
- http://docs.oracle.com/cd/E13152_01/install/deploy.html
- http://docs.oracle.com/cd/E15635_01/doc.1032/e15056.pdf

J

Jython and the Jython language

- http://www.jython.org
- http://wiki.python.org/jython
- http://www.javalobby.org/articles/jython/
- http://oreilly.com/catalog/jythoness/chapter/ch01.html
- http://www.apress.com/catalogsearch/result/?q=Jython&submit=Go
- http://www.amazon.com/Essentials-OReilly-Scripting-Samuele-Pedroni/dp/0596002475
- http://www.jython.org/jythonbook/en/1.0/LangSyntax.html

JMX:

- http://docs.oracle.com/javase/8/docs/technotes/guides/jmx/overview/intro.html
- http://docs.oracle.com/javase/8/docs/technotes/guides/jmx/overview/architecture.html#wp996882
- http://www.oracle.com/technetwork/java/javase/tech/javamanagement-140525.html
- http://ai2t.de/java/docs/technotes/guides/jmx/overview/intro.html
- http://www.informit.com/articles/article.aspx?p=31575

- http://www.jcp.org/en/jsr/detail?id=3

- http://www.oracle.com/technetwork/java/javase/tech/best-practices-jsp-136021.html

JMS

- http://jvzoggel.wordpress.com/tag/wlst/

- http://www.techpaste.com/tag/wlst/

- http://docs.oracle.com/middleware/1212/wls/JMXCU/subsystem.htm

- http://middlewaremagic.com/weblogic/?p=4931

- http://middlewaremagic.com/weblogic/?tag=messagescurrentcount

- http://middlewaremagic.com/weblogic/?p=6687

- http://wlstbyexamples.blogspot.de/2009/11/jms-monitoring-using-wlst.html#.UPWqERBwews

- http://www.techpaste.com/2012/11/wlst-script-create-queue-topic-distributedqueue-distributedtopic-connection-factory-cluster/

- http://weblogicserver.blogspot.de/2010/07/using-wlst-script-to-list-messages-from.html

L

Logs:

- http://docs.oracle.com/middleware/1212/core/ASADM/logs.htm

- http://biemond.blogspot.de/2011/07/change-log-files-location-of-weblogic.html

Logfilter

- http://middlewaremagic.com/weblogic/?p=4767

M

Managed-Server:

- http://docs.oracle.com/middleware/1212/wls/DOMCF/understand_domains.htm

Migration

- http://docs.oracle.com/middleware/1212/wls/TASKS/migratabletarget.htm

- http://docs.oracle.com/middleware/1212/wls/CLUST/service_migration.htm

- http://docs.oracle.com/cd/E16764_01/apirefs.1111/e13952/taskhelp/jms_servers/Con figureMigratableTargetsForJMSServers.html

MS overload protection

- http://docs.oracle.com/middleware/1212/wls/CNFGD/overload.htm

Migrating security Data

- http://docs.oracle.com/middleware/1212/wls/SECMG/security_data_migration.htm

Maven

- http://maven.apache.org/
- http://redstack.wordpress.com/2013/06/11/new-maven-support-in-fusion-middleware-12-1-2/

N

Network Channel:

- http://docs.oracle.com/middleware/1212/wls/CNFGD/network.htm

Nodemanager

- http://www.techpaste.com/tag/wlst/

O

Operating system access

- http://www.jython.org/docs/library/os.path.html
- http://www.jython.org/docs/library/shutil.html
- http://www.jython.org/docs/library/filecmp.html
- http://www.jython.org/docs/library/filesys.html

OPPS

- http://docs.oracle.com/cd/E23943_01/core.1111/e10043/wlstcmds.htm
- http://docs.oracle.com/cd/E12839_01/core.1111/e10043/apadvadmin.htm
- http://docs.oracle.com/cd/E17904_01/web.1111/e13813/custom_infra_security.htm

OWSM

- https://blogs.oracle.com/owsm/entry/owsm_concepts_11g

- https://blogs.oracle.com/owsm/entry/when_to_use_owsm

- http://www.oracle.com/technetwork/middleware/webservices-manager/index.html

- http://www.oracle.com/technetwork/middleware/webservices-manager/owsm-10gr3-fov-1-087696.html

- http://docs.oracle.com/cd/E21764_01/web.1111/b32511/attaching.htm

Overload

- http://docs.oracle.com/middleware/1212/wls/CNFGD/overload.htm

P

Password validation

- http://docs.oracle.com/cd/E15586_01/apirefs.1111/e13952/taskhelp/security/ConfigurePasswordValidationProviders.html

- http://docs.oracle.com/middleware/1212/wls/SECMG/atn.htm#i1213920

Q

WebLogic Queue

- http://weblogic-wonders.com/weblogic/2010/11/30/weblogic-jms-feature-using-a-queue/

- http://www.coderanch.com/t/497022/BEA-Weblogic/Weblogic-queue-connection-factory-queue

- https://forums.oracle.com/forums/thread.jspa?threadID=1014817

- http://docs.oracle.com/cd/E14571_01/apirefs.1111/e13952/pagehelp/JMSjmsdestinationsjmsqueuemonitortitle.html

- http://docs.oracle.com/middleware/1212/wls/JMSAD/basic_config.htm

- http://docs.oracle.com/middleware/1212/wls/JMSAD/manage_msg.htm#JMSAD265

R

Resource adapter (JCA connectors):

- http://docs.oracle.com/middleware/1212/wls/ADAPT/understanding.htm

S

SAF

- http://www.javamonamour.org/2011/09/wlst-to-create-saf-agent-with-imported.html
- http://weblogic-wonders.com/weblogic/2010/06/14/configuring-saf-store-and-forward-between-two-weblogic-server-domains/
- http://docs.oracle.com/middleware/1212/wls/SAFMG/overview.htm
- http://middlewaremagic.com/weblogic/?p=4854
- http://docs.oracle.com/middleware/1212/wls/SAFMG/monitor.htm
- http://docs.oracle.com/middleware/1212/wls/SAFMG/config_jms.htm

Security

- http://docs.oracle.com/middleware/1212/wls/SCOVR/archtect.htm
- http://docs.oracle.com/middleware/1212/wls/SCOVR/model.htm
- http://docs.oracle.com/middleware/1212/wls/SCOVR/concepts.htm
- http://docs.oracle.com/middleware/1212/wls/SCPRG/overview.htm
- http://weblogic-wonders.com/weblogic/security/
- http://weblogic-wonders.com/weblogic/2009/12/25/create-active-directory-authentication-provider-from-wlst/
- http://docs.oracle.com/middleware/1212/idm/IDMCR/custom_infra_security.htm

Security users/groups

- http://wlst101.blogspot.de/2011/07/wlst-list-user-groups-and-users-in.html
- http://biemond.blogspot.de/2010/01/creating-users-and-groups-in-weblogic.html
- http://www.techpaste.com/2012/06/managing-user-groups-wlst-scripts-weblogic/

Security Policies

- http://suhasonstuff.blogspot.de/2011/05/adding-weblogic-security-policies-using.html

Server states

- http://docs.oracle.com/middleware/1212/wls/START/server_life.htm

Starting/Stopping

- http://docs.oracle.com/middleware/1212/wls/START/overview.htm

- http://xmlandmore.blogspot.de/2012/04/how-to-force-shutdown-weblogic-managed.html

- http://docs.oracle.com/middleware/1212/wls/START/overview.htm#i1069181

- http://weblogicserveradministration.blogspot.de/2010/10/start-stop-weblogic-servers.html

- http://dirknachbar.blogspot.de/2012/08/startup-or-shutdown-of-multiple.html

SNMP

- http://middlewaremagic.com/weblogic/?tag=snmp

- http://weblogic-wonders.com/weblogic/2010/12/17/weblogic-snmp-for-string-monitor/

- http://docs.oracle.com/middleware/1212/wls/SNMPA/snmpagent.htm

Stuck Threads

- http://docs.oracle.com/cd/E24329_01/apirefs.1211/e24401/taskhelp/tuning/TuningExecuteThreads.html

- http://docs.oracle.com/middleware/1212/wls/PERFM/wls_tuning.htm

T

Timers

- https://blogs.oracle.com/jamesbayer/entry/a_simple_job_scheduler_example

- http://java.sys-con.com/node/43944

WebLogic Tuxedo Connector (WTC)

- http://docs.oracle.com/middleware/1212/wls/WTCCF/intro.htm

- http://docs.oracle.com/cd/E15523_01/web.1111/e13744/title.htm

- http://docs.oracle.com/cd/E15523_01/web.1111/e13744/bdconfig.htm

- http://docs.oracle.com/cd/E24329_01/web.1211/e24390/wtc.htm

- http://docs.huihoo.com/oracle/middleware/fusion/11g/web.1111/e14529/wtc.htm

- http://docs.oracle.com/cd/E24329_01/web.1211/e24978/troubleshooting.htm

- http://docs.oracle.com/cd/E12839_01/apirefs.1111/e14397/WTC.html

Tuning

- http://docs.oracle.com/middleware/1212/wls/PERFM/wls_tuning.htm

- http://docs.oracle.com/middleware/1212/wls/PERFM/topten.htm

U

Uniform distributed destinations

- http://weblogic-wonders.com/weblogic/2011/02/17/uniform-distributed-destinations-udd-feature-in-weblogic/

V

Virtual hosts

- http://middlewaremagic.com/weblogic/?p=2136

- http://docs.oracle.com/middleware/1212/wls/WLACH/taskhelp/virtual_hosts/VirtualHosts.html

- http://weblogic-wonders.com/weblogic/2010/11/19/virtual-hosts-configuration-with-weblogic-server/

W

WebLogic Diagnostics Framework

- http://docs.oracle.com/middleware/1212/wls/WLDFC/index.html

- http://www.oracle.com/pls/as111150/lookup?id=WLDFC365

WLST

- http://docs.oracle.com/middleware/1212/wls/WLSTC/reference.htm

WLST offline

- http://docs.oracle.com/middleware/1212/wls/WLSTG/domains.htm

WorkManager

- http://weblogic-wonders.com/weblogic/2010/11/21/understanding-the-work-managers/

- http://middlewaremagic.com/weblogic/?tag=workmanager
  (with good programming example)

- http://docs.oracle.com/middleware/1212/wls/CNFGD/self_tuned.htm

- http://docs.oracle.com/middleware/1212/wls/PERFM/wls_tuning.htm

X

XACML

- http://suhasonstuff.blogspot.de/2011/05/adding-weblogic-security-policies-using.html

- http://www.orastudy.com/oradoc/selfstu/fusion/web.1111/e13747/xacmlusing.htm

- http://xml.fido.gov/presentations/sun/xacml.pdf

- http://www.webfarmr.eu/2010/09/xacml-101-a-quick-intro-to-attribute-based-access-control-with-xacml/

- http://groupebiquity.umbc.edu/get/a/resource/259.ppt

- http://wso2.org/library/articles/2011/10/understanding-xacml-policy-language-xacml-extended-assertion-markup-langue-part-1

- https://www.oasis-open.org/committees/download.php/2713/Brief_Introduction_to_XACML.html

About the Author

Martin Heinzl is a senior/principal consultant in the areas of architecture, middleware and enterprise systems. Over the last 15 years, he has built up extensive experience in enterprise middleware technologies in distributed systems. His main areas of focus include architecture, integration, Java, J2EE, CORBA, distributed systems, integration approaches, and security. His project involvement has included analysis, design, architecture, SOA (like) systems, configuration, security, deployment, automation, management, and monitoring. This experience has given him a thorough knowledge of operations, automation, system architectures, development, and training.

Martin was also responsible for the automation of a complex web service security layer for an SOA infrastructure using single-sign on, SAML, and OWSM for a huge WebLogic farm (including Oracle service bus) with 500+ domains and 4000+ Managed-Servers. He was also responsible for the WebLogic infrastructure and monitoring concepts of in a high risk/high volume financial system. He is currently working in the middleware platform hosting team of a global bank.

In 2013, Martin joined the Oracle Customer Advisory Board for WebLogic and he always tries to be up to date on middleware technologies by attending conferences and taking part in beta programs. Martin is located in the Frankfurt/Main area in Germany, and you can reach him at wls_automation@mh-enterpriseconsulting.de.

Index

Made in the USA
Middletown, DE
25 September 2019